S0-CFH-865

The PRENTICE HALL American Nation

Civil War to the Present

Davidson ★ Castillo ★ Stoff

PRENTICE HALL

Upper Saddle River, New Jersey
Needham, Massachusetts
Glenview, Illinois

Authors

James West Davidson is coauthor of *After the Fact: The Art of Historical Detection* and *Nation of Nations: A Narrative History of the American Republic.* Dr. Davidson has taught at both the college and high school levels. He has also consulted on curriculum design for American history courses. Dr. Davidson is an avid canoeist and hiker. His published works on these subjects include *Great Heart,* the true story of a 1903 canoe trip in the Canadian wilderness.

Pedro Castillo teaches American history at the University of California, Santa Cruz, where he also co-directs the Chicano-Latino Research Center. He has earned a Rockefeller Foundation Research Fellowship and two Senior Fulbright-Hayes Lectureships in Latin America. Dr. Castillo's published works on American history and Chicano Latino history include *Mexico en Los Angeles* and *An Illustrated History of Mexican Los Angeles*.

Michael B. Stoff teaches history at the University of Texas at Austin, where he also directs the graduate program in history. He is the author of *Oil, War, and American Security: The Search for a National Policy on Foreign Oil, 1941–1947*, coauthor of *Nation of Nations: A Narrative History of the American Republic*, and co-editor of *The Manhattan Project: A Documentary Introduction to the Atomic Age*. Dr. Stoff has won numerous grants and fellowships.

AmericanHeritage® *American Heritage* magazine was founded in 1954, and it quickly rose to the position it occupies today: the country's preeminent magazine of history and culture. Dedicated to presenting the past in incisive, entertaining narratives underpinned by scrupulous scholarship, *American Heritage* today goes to more than 300,000 subscribers and counts the country's very best writers and historians among its contributors. Its innovative use of historical illustration and its wide variety of subject matter have gained the publication scores of honors across more than forty years, among them the National Magazine Awards.

Acknowledgments and Illustration Credits begin on page 936.

PRENTICE HALL

Printed in the United States of America.

ISBN 0-13-052270-8

2 3 4 5 6 7 8 9 10 04 03 02 01 00

Upper Saddle River, New Jersey Needham, Massachusetts Glenview, Illinois

Program Reviewers

Academic Consultants

David Beaulieu, Ph.D.
Director of Office of Indian Education
U.S. Department of Education
Washington, D.C.

Richard Beeman, Ph.D.
Professor of History
University of Pennsylvania
Philadelphia, Pennsylvania

William Childs, Ph.D.
Associate Professor of History
Ohio State University
Columbus, Ohio

Heidi Hayes Jacobs, Ed.D.
President, Curriculum Designs, Inc.
Rye, New York
Adjunct Professor of Curriculum and Teaching
Columbia University
New York, New York

Tetsuden Kashima, Ph.D.
Associate Professor of American Ethnic Studies
University of Washington
Seattle, Washington

Emma Lapsansky, Ph.D.
Professor of History and Curator of Special Collections
Haverford College
Haverford, Pennsylvania

Lyn Reese
Director, Women in World History Curriculum
Berkeley, California

Joel Silbey, Ph.D.
Professor of History
Cornell University
Ithaca, New York

Reading Specialist

Bonnie Armbruster, Ph.D.
Professor of Education
University of Illinois at Urbana–Champaign
Champaign, Illinois

Teacher Reviewers

Buckley Bangert
Social Studies Teacher
Ortega Middle School
Alamosa, Colorado

Clement R. Brown, III
Social Studies Teacher
Madison Junior High School
Naperville, Illinois

Lynn Castiaux
Social Studies Teacher/Mentor
Sylvan Middle School
Citrus Heights, California

Leslie Clark
Team Teacher
Lincoln Middle School
Hawthorne, New Jersey

Sandra Lee Eades, Ph.D.
Social Studies Content Leader
Ridgely Middle School
Lutherville, Maryland

Beverly Hooper
Social Studies Teacher
Dartmouth School
San Jose, California

Joseph Mancusi
Assistant Principal
Westhill School
Stamford, Connecticut

Bill McElree
Social Studies Teacher
Vista Compana Middle School
Apple Valley, California

Denis O'Rourke
Chairman, Dept. of Social Studies
Hommocks Middle School
Larchmont, New York

Sharon L. Pope
Secondary Social Studies Coordinator
Spring Branch Independent School District
Houston, Texas

Jill Schumacher
Social Studies Teacher
Brown Middle School
McAllen, Texas

Accuracy Panel

Esther Ratner
Greyherne Information Services
With Marvin Beckerman, Ph.D., University of Missouri–St. Louis; Muriel Beckerman, University of Missouri–St. Louis; Lynn D. Hoover, The Hoover Associates; Jane B. Malcolm, Professional Research Services; Bennet J. Parstek, Ed.D., St. John's University, NY; Alice Radosh, Ph.D., Academy of Educational Development; Lorraine Rosenberg, Baldwin School District, NY (Ret.); Cathy S. Zazueta, California State University, Los Angeles

Staff Credits

The people who made up ***The American Nation*** team—representing editorial, design services, market research, marketing, publishing processes, editorial services, production services, on-line services/multimedia development, electronic publishing technology, and marketing services—and their managers are listed below. Bold type denotes core team members.

Margaret Antonini, Tom Barber, Christopher Brown, Christina Burghard, **Sarah Carroll,** Lisa Charde, Lynda Cloud, Rhett Conklin, Martha Conway, Carlos Crespo, Kathy Dix, **Jim Doris,** Anne Falzone, Libby Forsyth, **Annemarie Franklin, Nancy Gilbert,** Holly Gordon, Linda Hardman, **Dorshia Johnson,** Carol Leslie, **Loretta Moe,** Gregory Myers, Rip Odell, Jim O'Shea, Kirsten Richert, **Emily Rose,** AnnMarie Roselli, Gerry Schrenk, Anne Shea, Annette Simmons, **Marilyn Stearns,** Frank Tangredi, Elizabeth Torjussen

PREVIEW
THE EMERGING NATION xiv

UNIT 5 Division and Reunion 420

▲ *Civil War army caps*

▲ *Emancipation Proclamation*

UNIT 6 Transforming the Nation 500

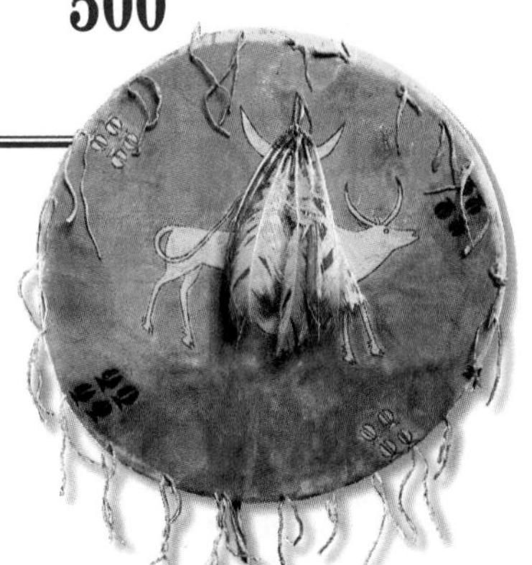

Cheyenne shield

Early light bulb

American Federation of Labor emblem

UNIT 7 A New Role for the Nation 584

Statue of a women's rights worker

Wilson campaign button

American soldiers wounded in World War I, in a painting by John Singer Sargent

Unit 8 Prosperity, Depression, and War 670

Magazine cover from the 1920s

General Douglas MacArthur

Battle of the Coral Sea

UNIT 9 The Nation Today and Tomorrow 760

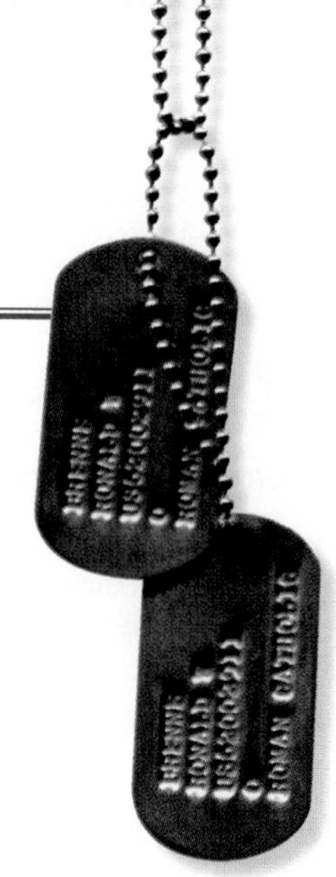

Dogtags of an American soldier in the Korean War

Poster honoring Martin Luther King Day

Reference Section

Special Features

American Heritage MAGAZINE

★ *With the editors of* American Heritage *magazine as your guides, you see and read about special sites where American history happened.*

HISTORY HAPPENED HERE

▲ *Yosemite National Park*

Linking ...

★ *The Linking features use engaging visuals to make historical connections.*

Linking Past and Present

Linking History and Technology

Linking United States and the World

Why Study History?

★ *These high-interest features show how history is relevant to American life today and to your life in particular.*

★ *Learn and practice valuable skills that you will be able to use throughout your life.*

Using the Internet

Maps and Geography Activities

Geography Activities

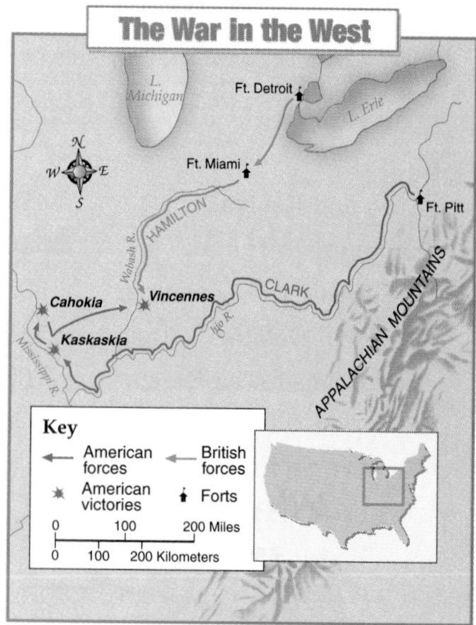

Geographic Atlas

Charts, Graphs, and Time Lines

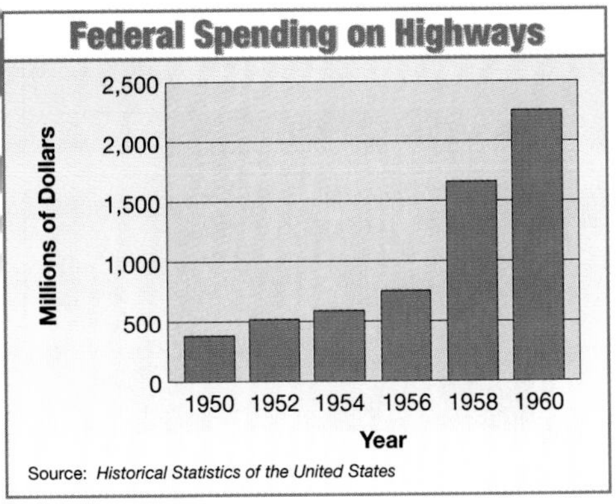

Federal Spending on Highways
Millions of Dollars
2,500
2,000
1,500
1,000
500
0
1950 1952 1954 1956 1958 1960
Year
Source: *Historical Statistics of the United States*

Graphic Organizers

Cause and Effect
Causes
Railroad boom spurs business
Businesses become corporations
Nation has rich supply of natural resources
New inventions make business more efficient
The Rise of Industry
Effects
Steel and oil become giant industries
Monopolies and trusts dominate important industries
Factory workers face harsh conditions
Membership in labor unions grows
Effects Today
United States is world's leading economic power
American corporations do business around the world
Government laws regulate monopolies

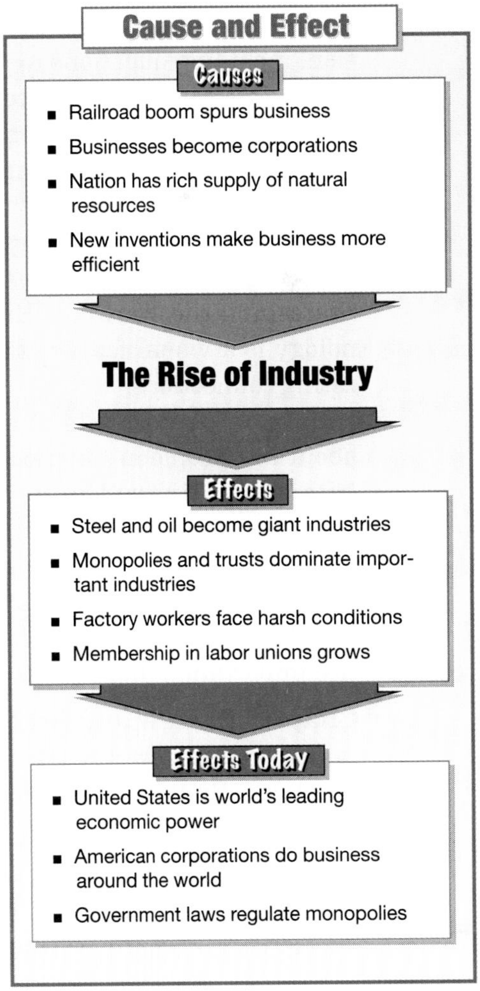

About This Book

The American Nation is organized into 5 units and 15 chapters. The Table of Contents lists units, chapters, sections, and special features.

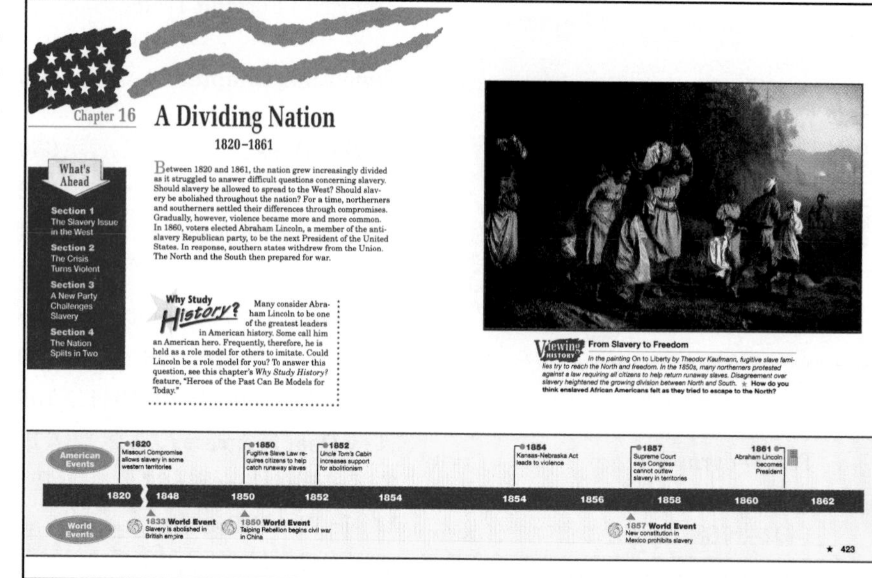

Chapter 16 A Dividing Nation

1820–1861

What's Ahead

Section 1 The Slavery Issue in the West

Section 2 The Crisis Turns Violent

Section 3 A New Party Challenges Slavery

Section 4 The Nation Splits in Two

Between 1820 and 1861, the nation grew increasingly divided as it struggled to answer difficult questions concerning slavery. Should slavery be allowed to spread to the West? Should slavery be abolished throughout the nation? For a time, northerners and southerners settled their differences through compromises. Gradually, however, violence became more and more common. In 1860, voters elected Abraham Lincoln, a member of the antislavery Republican party, to be the next President of the United States. In response, southern states withdrew from the Union. The North and the South then prepared for war.

Why Study History? Many consider Abraham Lincoln to be one of the greatest leaders in American history. Some call him an American hero. Frequently, therefore, he is held as a role model for others to imitate. Could Lincoln be a role model for you? To answer this question, see this chapter's *Why Study History?* feature, "Heroes of the Past Can Be Models for Today."

Viewing History **From Slavery to Freedom**

In the painting On to Liberty *by Theodor Kaufmann, fugitive slave families try to reach the North and freedom. In the 1850s, many northerners protested against a law requiring all citizens to help return runaway slaves. Disagreement over slavery heightened the growing division between North and South.* ★ **How do you think enslaved African Americans felt as they tried to escape to the North?**

American Events

1820 Missouri Compromise allows slavery in some western territories

1850 Fugitive Slave Law requires citizens to help catch runaway slaves

1852 *Uncle Tom's Cabin* increases support for abolitionism

1854 Kansas-Nebraska Act leads to violence

1857 Supreme Court says Congress cannot outlaw slavery in territories

1861 Abraham Lincoln becomes President

1820 1848 1850 1852 1854 1854 1856 1858 1860 1862

World Events

1833 World Event Slavery is abolished in British empire

1850 World Event Taiping Rebellion begins civil war in China

1857 World Event New constitution in Mexico prohibits slavery

★ 423

In Each Unit

- **Unit Opener** a two-page introduction to the contents and major theme of the unit.
- **History Through Literature** a two-page excerpt from a work of American literature.

In Each Chapter

- **Chapter Opener** a two-page introduction that includes a time line and chapter summary.
- **As You Read** an introduction to each section, including questions to guide your reading and lists of vocabulary terms and people.
- **Section Reviews** questions and activities that test your understanding of each section.
- **Skills for Life** a lesson that helps you to learn, practice, and apply a useful skill.
- **Linking...** Past and Present, or United States and the World, or History and Technology is a visual feature that shows interesting connections.
- **Biographies** portraits of and information about key people in American history.
- **Interdisciplinary Connections** footnotes that give connections to Geography, Economics, Civics, Arts, or Science.
- **Maps, Graphs, and Charts** visual tools that help you understand history and practice important skills.
- **Chapter Review and Activities** two pages to help you review key terms and ideas and practice valuable skills, with these special features:
    - *Using Primary Sources,* a primary source excerpt with questions that help you recognize different points of view.
    - *Activity Bank,* includes Interdisciplinary, Career Skills, Citizenship, and Internet activities.
    - *Eyewitness Journal,* writing activity that lets you take on different historical roles.
    - *Critical Thinking and Writing,* questions and exercises that go beyond simple recall.

Special Features

- **Why Study History?** This feature demonstrates the relevance of historical ideas and events to American life today and to your life in particular.
- **AmericanHeritage® Magazine History Happened Here** The editors of *American Heritage* magazine are your guides to interesting historic sites throughout the nation.

Reference Section

- Includes an Atlas, a Gazetteer, a Glossary, the Declaration of Independence, the Constitution of the United States, documents, information about the fifty states, information about the Presidents of the United States, and an Index.

Researching on the Internet

The Internet

The **Internet** includes millions of business, governmental, educational, and individual computers on the World Wide Web. Using programs called browsers, Internet users can find out what sites are available on the Web and then access those sites.

Searching the Internet

There are two basic ways to find information on the Internet. The first is to go directly to the Net site that contains the information you want. Each site has an address, called a **URL,** or Universal Resource Locator. (For example, http://www.phschool.com is the URL of the Prentice Hall Web site.) Of course, this method works only if you know the appropriate URL.

The second way is to use a **search engine,** such as Infoseek or Yahoo! Type the key words representing the topic you want to research. The search engine will then scan the Internet and list sites that pertain to your topic.

Whichever method you choose, you will encounter sites containing **hyperlinks.** These appear as colored or underlined text or as icons. Hyperlinks act as doorways to other documents at the same Web site or others. When you click your mouse on hyperlinked text or graphics, an entirely new document appears on your screen.

Pay careful attention to the source of the information you find. Is the source a government agency, or a university, or a private company, or an individual? Not all sources are equally accurate or reliable in what they present.

See us on the Internet

http://www.phschool.com

At Prentice Hall's Web site, you will find current event updates, social studies links, and other resources to help you learn about American history.

Tips for Successful Searches

Focus your search. Because the Internet contains so much, it is easy to "wander off" into other parts of the Internet and forget about the information that you are trying to locate. To avoid this problem, establish a specific research goal before you begin.

Make bookmarks for useful Web sites. A bookmark is a note to your computer to "remember" the location of a Web site. Later, you can reach any bookmarked site with a simple click of your mouse.

Use specific key words. If your key words are too general, your search might turn up thousands of Net sites. Make your key words specific. Many search engines have useful tips on searching with key words.

Seek guidance from teachers and parents. Ask a teacher, parent, or librarian for help in evaluating whether Web sites and information are reliable and appropriate to your research.

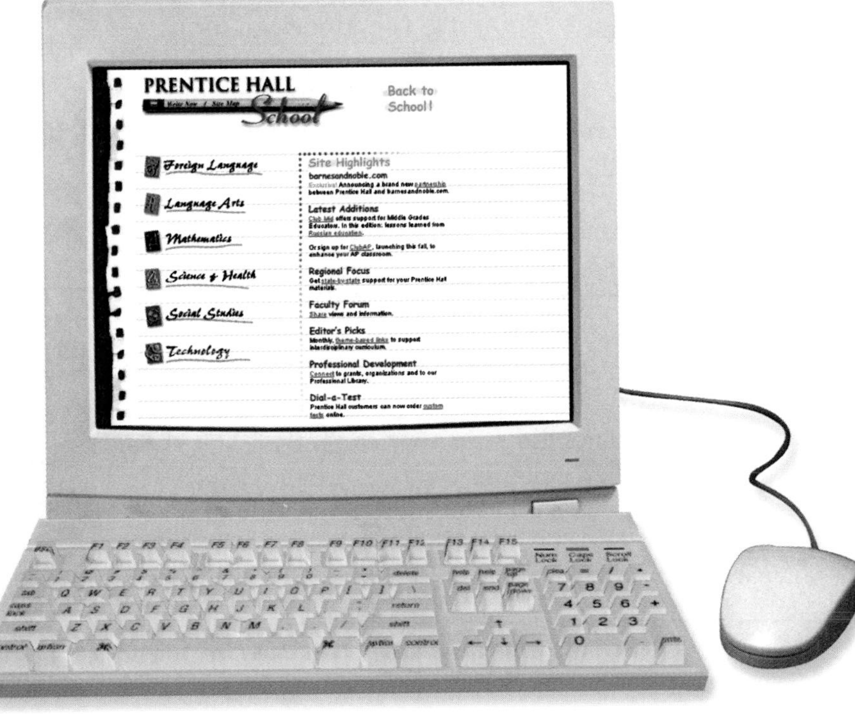

PREVIEW
THE EMERGING NATION

1. ONE LAND, MANY PEOPLES

Key Facts

- Over the centuries, different groups of people have settled in the Americas.
- Many European settlers came seeking religious and political freedom.
- Reform movements in the 1800s led to improved education, demands for women's rights, and a movement to end slavery.

"Here is not merely a nation, but a teeming nation of nations," wrote poet Walt Whitman. The people of the United States came from all over the world to form a "nation of nations." They brought with them different customs, religions, and languages. Yet today they form a single nation. The history of the United States is the story of how people from many nations and cultures formed one nation with its own heritage and traditions.

A Diverse Nation

From the beginning, the American land was open to not one, but many peoples. As early as 70,000 years ago, the first people came to North America from Asia by crossing the Bering Strait into Alaska. Over thousands of years, they spread throughout North and South America. When Christopher Columbus crossed the Atlantic Ocean from Europe in 1492, millions of Native Americans lived in the Americas.

Spain sent the first European settlers to the Americas in the 1500s. Other Europeans followed, as did many Africans. By 1775, the 13 English colonies on the Atlantic Coast were the most densely settled section of North America. Nearly 3 million people lived there. About half were English or had English ancestors. About a fifth were nonwhite.

These settlers came to North America for many reasons. Some were looking for rich farmland at low cost. Others came to escape fierce religious wars in Europe. Most Africans came against their will. They had been captured in Africa and shipped to the colonies as slaves.

During the 1800s, immigrants continued to arrive. A potato famine in Ireland in 1845 sparked a wave of newcomers. Others arrived after a failed revolution in Germany in 1848. In Texas, the Southwest, and California, hundreds of thousands of Mexicans and Native Americans became residents of the United States after the Mexican War of 1846–1848. Chinese immigrants arrived in increasing numbers after gold was discovered in California in 1848.

The Religious Tradition

Many European settlers fled to the colonies in search of religious freedom. The Pilgrims and the Puritans came to Massachusetts because the Church of England would not let them worship in their own way. Maryland was founded by Lord Baltimore to give Roman Catholics a place safe from persecution. At first, most colonies had their own **established churches,** or

Puritans settled in the Massachusetts Bay Colony in the early 1600s. They hoped to build a society based on the teachings of the Bible.

churches officially supported by the government. But there were many different religious groups in the colonies and established churches, in time, tolerated those with other beliefs.

After the Revolutionary War, most states did away with established churches. Freedom of religion became one of the fundamental rights in the Constitution of the United States.

The Reforming Spirit

In a democracy, people have the right to speak out to bring about change. During the mid-1800s, many reformers spoke out. They had different goals, but they all hoped to improve the quality of American life.

Religious reformers encouraged people to take personal responsibility for their faith and to lead holy lives. Many held **revivals,** meetings that stirred a religious spirit in those who attended.

Other reformers concentrated on changing the institutions of American society. Some, like Horace Mann, offered ideas for improving education. Through the efforts of Mann and others, many states had created free public elementary schools by the 1850s.

Reformers like Elizabeth Cady Stanton demanded more rights for women. In 1848, she and other feminists met in Seneca Falls, New York. Launching the women's rights movement, they declared, "All men and women are created equal."

The most intense crusade of the 1800s was the movement to abolish slavery. The **abolitionists** called for an immediate end to slavery. William Lloyd Garrison led the way, founding an antislavery newspaper in 1831. Free African Americans like Frederick Douglass were active in the cause.

An American Culture

As the young nation developed, American artists and writers began to celebrate the new American culture that was flowering around them.

Ralph Waldo Emerson reflected the optimism and individualism that were typical of the new nation. In his essay "Self-Reliance," Emerson advised his readers to depend on themselves rather than follow others. Henry David Thoreau revealed his own kind of individualism in *Walden,* the story of his solitary life by Walden Pond in Massachusetts.

American artists, such as Thomas Cole, developed their own style. They captured the optimism of the American people.

Perhaps more than anyone else, poet Walt Whitman captured the idealistic spirit of the republic. In *Leaves of Grass,* published in 1855, Whitman celebrated the many people of the new nation. "A southerner soon as a northerner," a Yankee "ready for trade," a Kentuckian in "deerskin leggins". . .

> "In all people I see myself, none
> more and not one barleycorn less,
>
> And the good or bad I say of myself
> I say of them."

2. BUILDING A REPUBLIC

Key Facts

- American democracy is rooted in English tradition.
- The United States Constitution provides the framework of American government.
- American democracy has developed over time.

Following the Revolutionary War, Americans began a dramatic political experiment. They decided to create a federal republic. Under this system, voters elect representatives to govern the country.

The plan was especially bold because the United States included many different peoples, spread out over a vast region. Few republics in history had survived for more than a few years. No republic so large had ever been created.

The English Heritage

Americans did have democratic traditions that they used to guide them. For hundreds of years, the power of English monarchs had been limited by **charters,** or documents that guaranteed certain rights and privileges to English citizens. The English Parliament, or legislature, wrote the charters. It also helped create the laws that governed England.

English settlers brought this tradition of representative government with them. In 1619, the Virginia colony received a charter that allowed eligible voters to elect a legislature. The Virginia House of Burgesses became the first representative assembly in the Americas.

The 13 colonies were founded at different times and under different conditions but all eventually set up elected legislatures. Representative government became a part of colonial life.

Independence

The colonies' break with England began in the 1760s. Britain had spent large sums of money to protect the colonies during a war with France. Afterward, Parliament decided to control the colonies more closely, particularly to collect taxes. The colonists protested that they did not elect representatives to Parliament. A free people, they argued, could be taxed only by its own legislature.

Parliament refused to back down. During ten years of colonial protests, it imposed harsh measures on the colonies. The colonists responded by sending representatives to a Continental Congress in Philadelphia. In 1776, Congress issued the Declaration of Independence.

Written by Thomas Jefferson, the Declaration became a landmark in American political thought. It proclaimed that all people

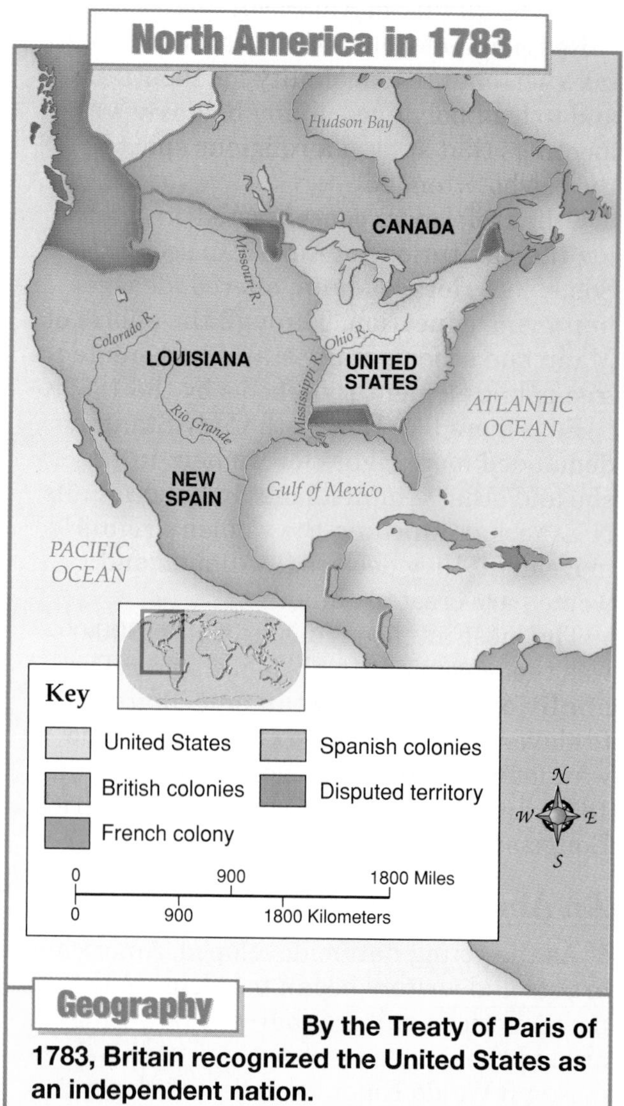

Geography By the Treaty of Paris of 1783, Britain recognized the United States as an independent nation.

were "endowed by their creator with certain unalienable rights," including "life, liberty, and the pursuit of happiness."

After independence, the new nation first governed itself under a set of rules that were called the **Articles of Confederation.** But the Articles gave most power to the states and little to the national government. Congress found it very difficult to solve crucial economic, political, and foreign policy questions. It could not collect taxes or enforce the laws that it passed.

In the hot summer of 1787, a special convention met in Philadelphia. Working behind closed doors, it drew up a new Constitution designed to replace the Articles of Confederation. In 1789, the new government went into effect.

The Federal System

Powers Delegated to the National Government	Shared Powers	Powers Reserved to the States
▪ Regulate interstate and foreign trade	▪ Provide for public welfare	▪ Create corporation laws
▪ Create and maintain armed forces	▪ Administer criminal justice	▪ Regulate trade within state
▪ Establish foreign policy	▪ Charter banks	▪ Establish and maintain schools
▪ Create federal courts	▪ Raise taxes	▪ Establish local governments
▪ Coin money	▪ Borrow money	▪ Make laws about marriage and divorce
▪ Declare war		▪ Conduct elections
▪ Admit new states		▪ Provide for public safety

Graphic Organizer **The system of federalism divides power between the national government and state governments.**

A Federal System

The Constitution set up a system of government called **federalism.** Under federalism, the states and the federal government share the power of governing. The Constitution gives certain powers entirely to the federal government. But all powers that the Constitution does not grant specifically to the federal government are reserved for the individual states.

The Constitution also put in place three separate branches of national government. The executive branch is headed by the President, whose job is to enforce the laws of the land. Congress forms the legislative branch, which makes the laws. The judicial branch, a system of federal courts, decides cases that involve federal law. It also settles disputes between the states.

To strengthen this basic principle of **separation of powers,** the Constitution also established a system of **checks and balances.** Under this system, each branch of government can check or limit the power of the other two.

A Growing Democracy

Even after the Constitution went into effect, many details of the political system remained to be worked out over time. The Constitution itself may be altered if enough people and enough states agree to a proposed **amendment,** or change. Over the past 200 years, 27 amendments have been adopted.

As the nation gained experience in governing itself, Americans developed new ideas about how a democracy should work. They came to believe that political parties were an effective way for people to organize in order to achieve change. Many states also dropped property requirements that had limited who was allowed to vote. They permitted **white male suffrage,** or voting by all adult white men.

During the presidency of Andrew Jackson (1829–1837), Americans could take pride in living in the most democratic country in the world at that time. Even so, that democracy had serious limits. Women, Native Americans, and most African Americans could not vote.

Even more disturbing was the institution of slavery in the South. Slaves had none of the basic liberties that other Americans cherished. As the nation expanded toward the Pacific Ocean, the debate increased over what a free society should do about slavery.

3. THE NATION EXPANDS

Key Facts

- The United States was rich in people and resources.
- The Industrial Revolution dramatically changed the American economy.
- The belief in Manifest Destiny drove American territorial expansion to the Pacific Ocean.

Alexis de Tocqueville, a French visitor to the United States in 1831, was amazed at the bustling activity he saw. "The Americans arrived but yesterday on the territory which they inhabit," he wrote, "and they have already changed the whole order of nature for their own advantage."

Tocqueville's observation was accurate. By the time of his travels, the United States was in the midst of a period of growth.

Colonial Economies

The booming economy of Toqueville's day was very different from the way Americans made their living during the colonial period. Before the 1800s, most trade involved sending raw materials from colonies to the parent countries in Europe.

In Spain's colonies, for example, silver was mined by Indian laborers and shipped to Europe. The English colonies along the Atlantic coast sent timber, tobacco, furs, and fish to England. There, manufacturers turned the raw materials into finished products like ships, hats, and cloth. English merchants then sold the products around the world.

This type of economic system was called **mercantilism.** It was meant to benefit the parent country more than it did the American colonies. Even after independence, most American products were sold abroad.

An Enterprising People

In the 1800s, that situation changed. American merchants and manufacturers began to sell more products to other Americans, not just to Europe. Encouraging its own industries, the young nation gradually built a strong, independent economy.

The economy grew for several reasons. Americans possessed a bountiful land. It had rich farmland, vast mineral deposits, fine forests, and good waterways for transportation. The population of the United States doubled about every 23 years in the 1800s, due to large families and immigration. Merchants and manufacturers had more customers to whom they could sell American goods.

The expanding economy also reflected the democratic character of the nation. In Europe, rigid social divisions made it difficult for anyone to rise out of poverty, but Americans wanted the opportunity to advance. Tocqueville noted, "in America most of the rich men were formerly poor," and "any man's son may become the equal of any other man's son."

An Industrial Revolution

The American economy also grew because of a revolution in the way goods were manufactured. By the late 1700s, steam engines had been developed in England. Such engines were used to run machines in English textile mills, spinning cotton thread and weaving it into cloth. Americans learned how to build similar machines in the early 1800s. New England became the center of a thriving textile industry.

The steam engine revolutionized American life in other ways. Two Americans, John Fitch and Robert Fulton, put steam engines on boats. Using these new steamboats, merchants could ship freight upstream even against strong currents. When the cost of shipping goods dropped, the American economy benefited. By the 1840s, engines were also put to work hauling cars along iron rails, or railroads.

Machines had far-reaching effects on farming, too. In 1793, Eli Whitney invented the cotton gin—short for "engine"—a machine that removed seeds from cotton. With a cotton gin, one person could clean as much

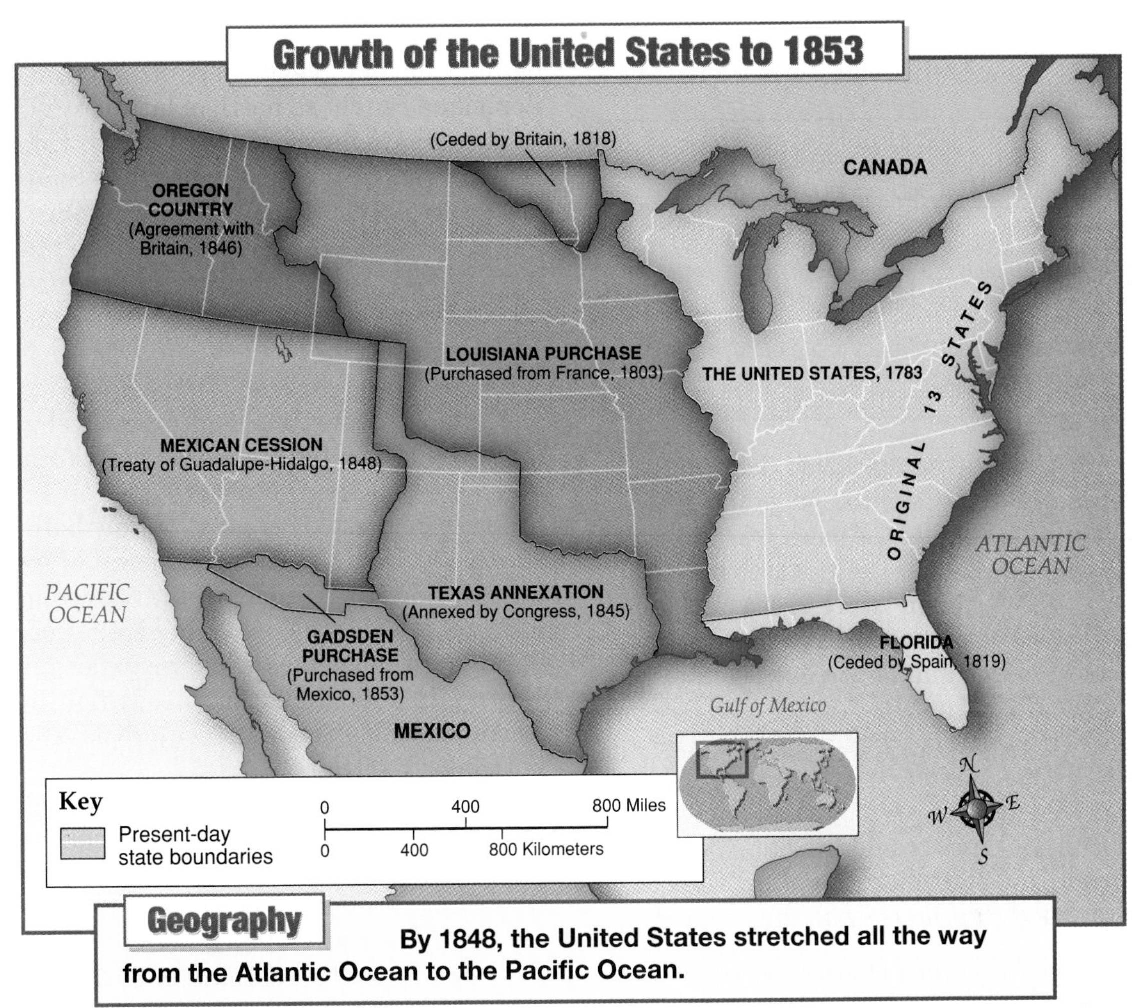

Geography By 1848, the United States stretched all the way from the Atlantic Ocean to the Pacific Ocean.

cotton as it had taken 50 people to clean before. Cotton production in the South spread rapidly. By the 1840s, the South was supplying 60 percent of the world's cotton.

From the Atlantic to the Pacific

As the economy grew, so did the nation itself. Between 1803 and 1853, the United States expanded westward from the Mississippi River to the Pacific Ocean.

In 1803, President Thomas Jefferson bought the Louisiana Territory from France for $15 million. Overnight, the Louisiana Purchase doubled the size of the nation.

The nation grew again when Texas joined the Union. Since 1821, groups of settlers from the United States had moved to Texas, which was then part of Mexico. As a result of disputes with the Mexican government, Texans declared their independence in 1836. The new Republic of Texas defeated the Mexican army in the war that followed. In 1845, Congress passed a joint resolution **annexing,** or adding, Texas to the United States.

In 1846, the United States and Britain agreed to divide the Oregon Country. That same year, the United States went to war with Mexico over the location of the Texas border. Victory in the war gave the United States control of a large new section of territory in the Southwest. The land included the present-day states of California, Nevada, and Utah as well as parts of Arizona, New Mexico, Colorado, and Wyoming.

By 1853, the United States had fulfilled what many believed was its clear mission, or **manifest destiny.** The nation spanned the continent, stretching from the Atlantic Ocean to the Pacific.

4. THE UNION SPLITS IN TWO

Key Facts

- The issue of slavery divided Americans in the 1800s.
- Congress passed compromises in an effort to avoid civil war.
- The war to return the South to the Union became a war to end slavery.

In 1850, an old and grizzled Senator John Calhoun of South Carolina gave his last speech in the Senate. Calhoun warned that "the cords which bind these states together in one common union" were breaking, one by one. He predicted that if disagreements between the North and South did not end, the Union would fall apart.

Calhoun's warning was prophetic. During the 1850s, a series of dramatic events brought the nation, step by step, to civil war. As Abraham Lincoln said in 1858, "A house divided against itself cannot stand." What most divided that house was the issue of slavery.

Half Slave, Half Free

The issue of slavery had long caused tension between the North and South. Even during the Constitutional Convention of 1787, the question stirred bitter debate.

As settlers moved west during the 1800s, the controversy over slavery continued. Each time a new territory was organized, Congress had to decide whether to allow slavery there and admit it as a slave state, or to ban slavery and admit it as a free state. Many northerners wanted Congress to ban slavery in all the territories. Many southerners argued that all territories should be open to slavery.

For a time, it seemed that the North and South could work out their differences. A crisis over how Missouri would enter the Union was settled by the **Missouri Compromise** of 1820. Congress decided that slavery would be permitted in Missouri. But it banned slavery everywhere else in the Louisiana Purchase north of latitude 36º30'.

The debate flared again after the United States conquered new lands in the Southwest during the Mexican War. But once more, members of Congress managed to work out their differences. They approved the **Compromise of 1850.**

The End of Compromise

These agreements began to unravel when Congress organized the territories of Kansas and Nebraska. At that time, Senator Stephen A. Douglas tried to satisfy both North and South with his proposal of "popular sovereignty." Under popular sovereignty, Kansas and Nebraska would be allowed to decide for themselves whether to permit slavery. In 1856, however, bloody fighting broke out in Kansas between proslavery and antislavery settlers.

A year later, the Supreme Court handed down the Dred Scott decision. To the surprise of most northerners, the Court ruled that Congress had no power to outlaw slavery in *any* territory. It seemed to support the extreme southern position that slavery could be permitted in all territories.

Tensions rose further in 1859 when a northerner named John Brown raided the federal arsenal in Harpers Ferry, Virginia. Brown hoped to lead slaves in an armed uprising. He was captured, tried, and hanged. Many outraged southerners considered Brown's raid a northern plot to destroy the South.

Secession

As these events divided the nation, a new political party formed in the North, called the Republican party. Its main goal was to oppose the spread of slavery. The Republican candidate for president, Abraham Lincoln of Illinois, won the election of 1860.

Lincoln's victory convinced southerners that only by **seceding,** or withdrawing, from the Union could they hope to save their way of life. In December 1860, South Carolina became the first of 11 southern states to secede. Banding together, they formed the Confederate States of America. In April 1861, Confederate forces bombarded federal troops at Fort Sumter in Charleston harbor. War had begun.

War and Emancipation

The Civil War continued for four terrible years. At first, it seemed that the Confederacy might be able to prevent a Union victory. White southerners, after all, were fighting to defend their homeland. The Confederacy's distinguished military leaders included Robert E. Lee and Thomas "Stonewall" Jackson.

It took the North took several years to find a general as skilled as Lee. In the end, the dogged Ulysees S. Grant wore down southern armies. Equally as important to the North were its greater resources: more soldiers, better weapons, many more factories, and a larger railroad network to transport soldiers and supplies.

As the war dragged on, calls for abolition grew stronger. On January 1, 1863, President Lincoln issued the **Emancipation Proclamation** freeing all slaves behind Confederate lines. The proclamation changed the character of the war. It became a fight for the freedom of slaves as well as for union.

During the war, over 200,000 African Americans fought for the Union. Furthermore, the war's end came sooner because hundreds of thousands of slaves fled southern plantations and crossed Union lines.

On April 9, 1865, Lee surrendered to Grant at Appomattox Court House, Virginia. The "House divided" by slavery had fallen in a ghastly war. The new house—the Union made whole and free—would face new storms.

For additional review of the major ideas of American history from its beginnings to the Civil War, see ***Guide to the Essentials of American History*** or ***The American Nation Interactive Student Tutorial CD-ROM***, which contains interactive review activities, graphic organizers, and practice tests.

▲ *The South depended on agriculture and slave labor.*

Events in American History, 1492–1788

1492–1606	**An Age of Exploration**
1492	Columbus reaches America
1513	Balboa sights Pacific Ocean
1517	Protestant Reformation begins in Europe
1587	English colonists settle at Roanoke
1607–1762	**The Early Colonial Period**
1607	Jamestown, first successful colony, founded
1619	First Africans arrive at Jamestown; Virginia House of Burgesses meets
1620	Puritans sign Mayflower Compact and establish Plymouth Colony
1630	Puritans establish Massachusetts Bay Colony
1673	Joliet and Marquette explore Mississippi River
1690s	Spanish missions established in Arizona and California
1754	French and Indian War begins
1763–1788	**The Revolutionary Era**
1763	Treaty of Paris ends French and Indian War
1765	Parliament passes Stamp Act; Stamp Act Congress meets
1773	Parliament passes Tea Act; Boston Tea Party takes place
1774	Parliament passes Intolerable Acts; First Continental Congress meets
1775	Shots fired at Lexington and Concord; Second Continental Congress meets; Battle of Breed's Hill and Bunker Hill fought
1776	Colonists declare independence from Britain
1781	British surrender at Yorktown; Articles of Confederation ratified
1783	Treaty of Paris ends Revolutionary War
1788	Constitution of the United States ratified

Events in American History, 1789–1865

George Washington	1789–1797	1789 Judiciary Act organizes Supreme Court 1791 Bill of Rights adopted 1793 Eli Whitney invents cotton gin
John Adams	1797–1801	1798 XYZ affair encourages war fever; Alien and Sedition Acts passed
Thomas Jefferson	1801–1809	1803 Louisiana Territory purchased from France 1804– 1806 Lewis and Clark explore Louisiana Purchase
James Madison	1809–1817	1811 Battle of Tippecanoe fought 1812 War of 1812 breaks out with Great Britain 1814 Treaty of Ghent ends war with England
James Monroe	1817–1825	1820 Missouri Compromise adopted 1823 Monroe Doctrine issued
James Quincy Adams	1825–1829	1825 Erie Canal Opens 1828 Tariff of Abominations passed
Andrew Jackson	1829–1837	1830 Congress passes Indian Removal Act 1835 1939 Indians forced west on Trail of Tears
Martin Van Buren	1837–1841	1837 Panic affects nation
William Henry Harrison	1841	1841 Harrison is first President to die in office
John Tyler	1841–1845	1842 Massachusetts court allows workers' strikes
James K. Polk	1845–1849	1845 Florida and Texas enter Union 1846 Mexican War begins 1847 Mexican War ends; United States receives California and New Mexico territories
Zachary Taylor	1849–1850	1849 California Gold Rush begins
Millard Fillmore	1850–1853	1850 Compromise of 1850 achieved 1851 *Uncle Tom's Cabin* published
Franklin Pierce	1853–1856	1854 Congress passes Kansas-Nebraska Act
James Buchanan	1857–1861	1857 Supreme Court issues Dred Scott decision 1858 John Brown raids Harpers Ferry 1859 South Carolina secedes from the Union
Abraham Lincoln	1861–1865	1861 Confederate States of America formed 1862 Homestead Act grants land to farmers 1863 Lincoln issues Emancipation Proclamation; construction of transcontinental railroad begins 1864 Civil War ends; Lincoln is assassinated

Unit 5

Division and Reunion

What's Ahead

Viewing UNIT THEMES

War Divides the Nation

In 1861, conflict between the North and the South erupted into war. Winslow Homer, one of the country's greatest artists, painted Prisoners From the Front. *It shows a northern officer (right) inspecting captured southern troops (left). The opposing soldiers look on each other with pride and hostility.* ★ **Based on what you have learned in earlier units, identify two differences between the North and South.**

Unit Theme Sectionalism

Sectionalism is loyalty to a state or region rather than to the country as a whole. From colonial days, Americans felt strong loyalties to the regions where they lived. By the mid-1800s, several issues increased sectional differences between the North and South. The most dramatic of these issues was slavery. Extreme sectionalism eventually led to war.

How did people of the time feel about sectional divisions? They can tell you in their own words.

Viewpoints on Sectional Divisions

"We have always been taught to look upon the people of New England as a selfish, cunning set of fellows."

Davy Crockett, Tennessee member of Congress (1835)

"I have heard something said about allegiance to the South. I know no South, no North, no East, no West, to which I owe any allegiance.... The Union, sir, is my country."

Henry Clay, senator from Kentucky (1848)

"Union! I can more easily conceive of the Lion and Lambs lying down together, than of a union of the North and South."

Sarah Chase, Massachusetts teacher in the South (1866)

Activity Writing to Learn Today, the United States is often divided into these geographic regions: the Northeast; the Midatlantic; the Southeast; the Midwest; the Rocky Mountain states; the Southwest; the Pacific Coast states. List three features, other than location, that make the region you live in special. Then, write a paragraph explaining whether you feel more loyal to your region or to the United States as a whole.

Chapter 16

A Dividing Nation

1820–1861

What's Ahead

Section 1
The Slavery Issue in the West

Section 2
The Crisis Turns Violent

Section 3
A New Party Challenges Slavery

Section 4
The Nation Splits in Two

Between 1820 and 1861, the nation grew increasingly divided as it struggled to answer difficult questions concerning slavery. Should slavery be allowed to spread to the West? Should slavery be abolished throughout the nation? For a time, northerners and southerners settled their differences through compromises. Gradually, however, violence became more and more common. In 1860, voters elected Abraham Lincoln, a member of the antislavery Republican party, to be the next President of the United States. In response, southern states withdrew from the Union. The North and the South then prepared for war.

Why Study History?

Many consider Abraham Lincoln to be one of the greatest leaders in American history. Some call him an American hero. Frequently, therefore, he is held as a role model for others to imitate. Could Lincoln be a role model for you? To answer this question, see this chapter's *Why Study History?* feature, "Heroes of the Past Can Be Models for Today."

American Events

1820 Missouri Compromise allows slavery in some western territories

1850 Fugitive Slave Law requires citizens to help catch runaway slaves

1852 *Uncle Tom's Cabin* increases support for abolitionism

1820 | 1848 | 1850 | 1852 | 1854

World Events

1833 World Event Slavery is abolished in British empire

1850 World Event Taiping Rebellion begins civil war in China

Viewing History: From Slavery to Freedom

In the painting On to Liberty *by Theodor Kaufmann, fugitive slave families try to reach the North and freedom. In the 1850s, many northerners protested against a law requiring all citizens to help return runaway slaves. Disagreement over slavery heightened the growing division between North and South.* ★ **How do you think enslaved African Americans felt as they tried to escape to the North?**

1854
Kansas-Nebraska Act leads to violence

1857
Supreme Court says Congress cannot outlaw slavery in territories

1861
Abraham Lincoln becomes President

1854 **1856** **1858** **1860** **1862**

1857 World Event
New constitution in Mexico prohibits slavery

The Slavery Issue in the West

Explore These Questions

- What were the various views on slavery in the West?
- What was the goal of the Free Soil party?
- What were the results of the Compromise of 1850?

Define

- sectionalism
- popular sovereignty
- secede
- fugitive
- civil war

Identify

- Missouri Compromise
- Wilmot Proviso
- Free Soil party
- Zachary Taylor
- Stephen Douglas
- Compromise of 1850
- Fugitive Slave Law of 1850

In 1820, Thomas Jefferson was in his seventies. The former President had vowed "never to write, talk, or even think of politics." Still, he voiced alarm when he heard about a fierce debate going on in Congress:

> "In the gloomiest moment of the revolutionary war, I never had any [fears] equal to what I feel from this source.... We have a wolf by the ears, and we can neither hold him nor safely let him go."

Jefferson feared that the "wolf," or the issue of slavery, would tear the North and South apart. He was correct. As settlers continued to move west, tension over slavery worsened. Again and again, Congress faced an agonizing decision. Should it prohibit slavery in the territories and later admit them to the Union as free states? Or should it permit slavery in the territories and later admit them as slave states?

The Missouri Compromise

When Missouri asked to join the Union as a slave state, a crisis erupted. The admission of Missouri would upset the balance of power in the Senate. In 1819, there were 11 free states and 11 slave states. (See the graph on page 427.) Missouri's admission would give the South a majority in the Senate. Determined not to lose power, northerners opposed letting Missouri enter as a slave state.

The argument over Missouri lasted many months. Finally, Senator Henry Clay proposed a compromise. During the long debate, Maine had also applied for statehood. Clay suggested admitting Missouri as a slave state and Maine as a free state. His plan, called the **Missouri Compromise,** kept the number of slave and free states equal.

As part of the Missouri Compromise, Congress drew an imaginary line across the southern border of Missouri at latitude 36° 30′N. Slavery was permitted in the part of the Louisiana Purchase south of that line. It was banned north of the line. The only exception to this was Missouri. (See the map on page 431.)

New Western Lands

The Missouri Compromise applied only to the Louisiana Purchase. In 1848, the Mexican War added a vast stretch of western land to the United States. (See the map on page 363.) Once again, the question of slavery in the territories arose.

The Wilmot Proviso

Many northerners feared that the South would extend slavery into the West. David Wilmot, a Congressman from Pennsylvania, called for a law to ban slavery in any lands won from Mexico. Southern leaders angrily opposed the **Wilmot Proviso.** They said that Congress had no right to ban slavery in the western territories.

Linking United States and the World

United States

Russia

Forced Labor

In the painting at left, enslaved African Americans await the results of a slave auction. At the same time in Russia, millions of workers were serfs. Serfs were bound to the land and had to work for wealthy nobles. One Russian observer sadly reported "of men and women torn from their families and their villages, and sold . . . of children taken from their parents and sold to cruel masters." ★ **How was slavery in the United States similar to serfdom in Russia?**

In 1846, the House passed the Wilmot Proviso, but the Senate defeated it. As a result, Americans continued to argue about slavery in the West even while their army fought in Mexico.

Opposing views

The Mexican War strengthened feelings of **sectionalism** in the North and South. Sectionalism is loyalty to a state or section, rather than to the country as a whole. Many southerners were united by their support for slavery. They saw the North as a growing threat to their way of life. Many northerners saw the South as a foreign country, where American rights and liberties did not exist.

As the debate over slavery heated up, people found it hard not to take sides. Northern abolitionists demanded that slavery be banned throughout the country. They insisted that slavery was morally wrong. By the late 1840s, many northerners agreed.

Southern slaveholders thought that slavery should be allowed in any territory. They also demanded that slaves who escaped to the North be returned to them. Even white southerners who did not own slaves generally agreed with these ideas.

Between these two extreme views were more moderate positions. Some moderates argued that the Missouri Compromise line should be extended across the Mexican Cession to the Pacific Ocean. Any new state north of the line would be a free state. Any new state south of the line could allow slavery.

$ Connections With Economics

In response to the Wilmot Proviso, some southern states proposed cutting off all trade with the North. Another economic threat was that southerners would stop payments on debts owed to northern banks and businesses.

Other moderates supported the idea of **popular sovereignty,** or control by the people. In other words, voters in a new territory would decide for themselves whether or not to allow slavery in the territory. Slaves, of course, could not vote.

The Free Soil Party

The debate over slavery led to the birth of a new political party. By 1848, many northerners in both the Democratic party and the Whig party opposed the spread of slavery. However, the leaders of both parties refused to take a stand on the question. They did not want to give up their chance of winning votes in the South. Some also feared that the slavery issue would split the nation.

In 1848, antislavery members of both parties met in Buffalo, New York. There, they founded the **Free Soil party.** Their slogan was "Free soil, free speech, free labor, and free men." The main goal of the Free Soil party was to keep slavery out of the western territories. Only a few Free Soilers were abolitionists who wanted to end slavery in the South.

In the 1848 presidential campaign, Free Soilers named former President Martin Van Buren as their candidate. Democrats chose Lewis Cass of Michigan. The Whigs selected **Zachary Taylor,** a hero of the Mexican War.

For the first time, slavery was an important election issue. Van Buren called for a ban on slavery in the Mexican Cession. Cass supported popular sovereignty. Because Taylor was a slave owner from Louisiana, many southern voters assumed that he supported slavery.

Zachary Taylor won the election, but Van Buren took 10 percent of the popular vote. Thirteen other Free Soil candidates won seats in Congress. The success of the new Free Soil party showed that slavery had become a national issue.

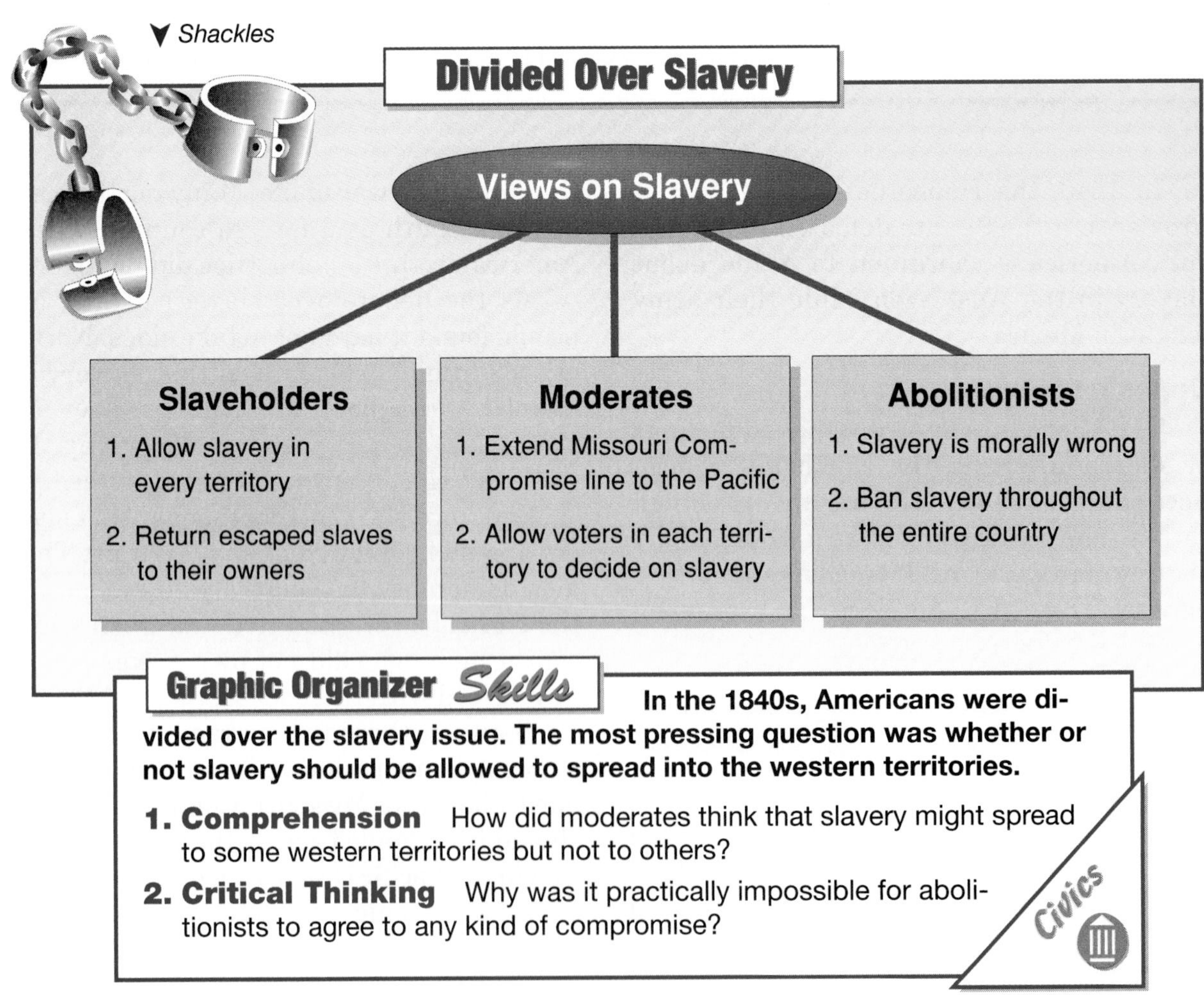

Graphic Organizer *Skills* **In the 1840s, Americans were divided over the slavery issue. The most pressing question was whether or not slavery should be allowed to spread into the western territories.**

1. **Comprehension** How did moderates think that slavery might spread to some western territories but not to others?
2. **Critical Thinking** Why was it practically impossible for abolitionists to agree to any kind of compromise?

Civics

Need for a New Compromise

For a time after the Missouri Compromise, both slave and free states entered the Union peacefully. However, when California requested admission to the Union as a free state in 1850, the balance of power in the Senate was once again threatened. (See the graph to the right.)

California's impact

In 1849, there were 15 slave states and 15 free states in the nation. If California entered the union as a free state, the balance of power would be broken. Furthermore, it seemed quite possible that Oregon, Utah, and New Mexico might also join the Union as free states.

Many Southerners feared that the South would be hopelessly outvoted in the Senate. Some even suggested that southern states might want to **secede,** or remove themselves, from the United States. Northern congressmen, meanwhile, argued that California should enter the Union as a free state because most of the territory lay north of the Missouri Compromise line.

As Congress tried to reach a new compromise, tempers raged. One frightening incident involved Senators Thomas Hart Benton of Missouri and Henry Foote of Mississippi. Benton supported California's entry as a free state even though he himself was a slave owner. He denounced Foote for opposing California's admission. In response, Foote rose angrily from his seat and aimed a pistol at Benton. As other senators watched in horror, Benton roared, "Let him fire. Stand out of the way and let the assassin fire!"

No blood was shed in the Senate that day. However, it was clear that the nation faced a crisis. Many in Congress looked to Senator Henry Clay for a solution.

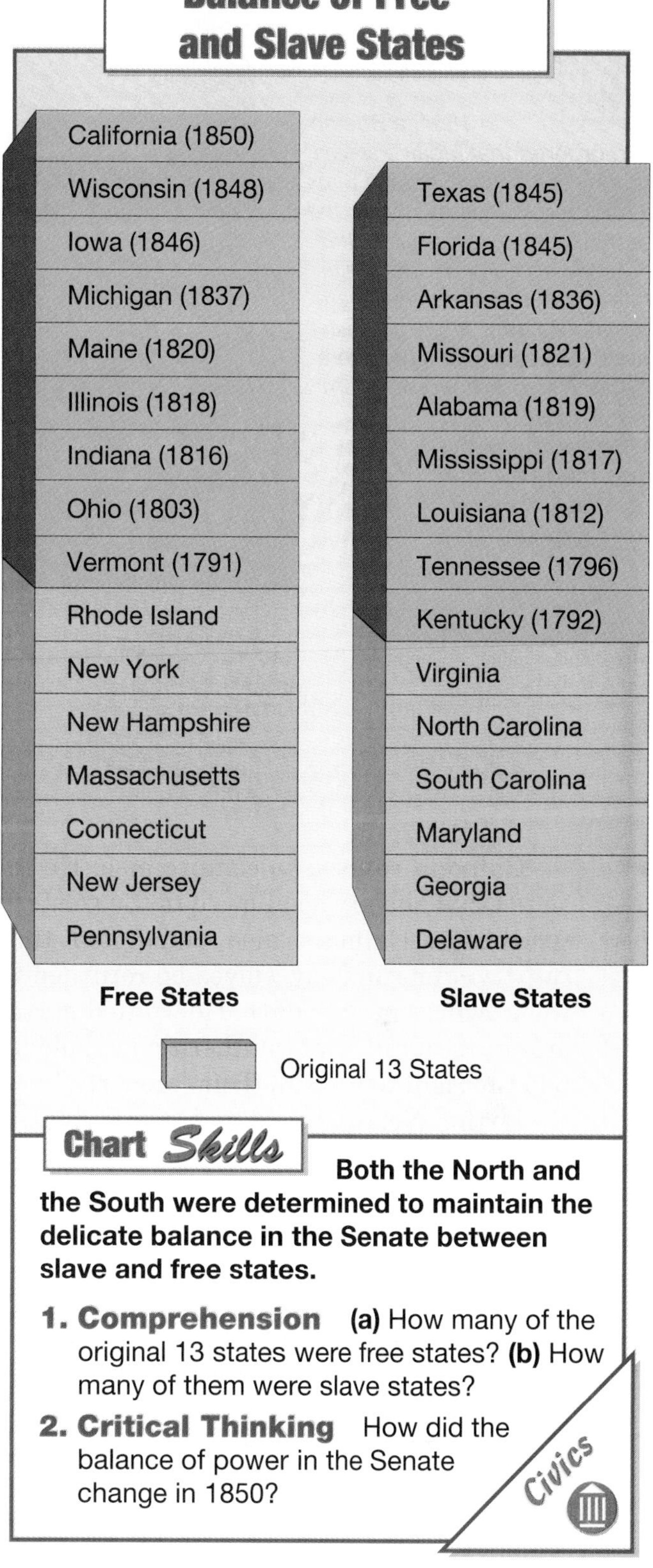

Chart Skills **Both the North and the South were determined to maintain the delicate balance in the Senate between slave and free states.**

1. **Comprehension** **(a)** How many of the original 13 states were free states? **(b)** How many of them were slave states?
2. **Critical Thinking** How did the balance of power in the Senate change in 1850?

Civics

Clay vs. Calhoun

Clay had won the nickname "the Great Compromiser" for working out the Missouri Compromise. Now, nearly 30 years later, the 73-year-old Clay was frail and ill. Still, he pleaded for the North and South to reach an agreement. If they failed to do so, Clay warned, the nation could break apart.

Senator John C. Calhoun of South Carolina prepared the South's reply to Clay. Calhoun was dying of tuberculosis and could not speak loudly enough to address the Senate. He stared defiantly at his northern foes while Senator James Mason of Virginia read his speech.

Viewing HISTORY **Protest!**

In 1854, a Boston court ordered that fugitive slaves Anthony Burns and Thomas Sims be returned to their owners in the South. Public outcry against the decision was so great that United States marines and artillery were sent into Boston. Angry protesters lined the streets as the two were led to the ship that would return them to slavery.

★ **Do you think the court made the right decision in this case? Explain.**

Calhoun refused to compromise. He insisted that slavery be allowed in the western territories. Calhoun also demanded that **fugitive,** or runaway, slaves be returned to their owners in the South. He wanted northerners to admit that southern slaveholders had the right to reclaim their "property."

If the North would not agree to the South's demands, Calhoun told the Senate, "let the states . . . agree to part in peace. If you are unwilling that we should part in peace, tell us so, and we shall know what to do." Everyone knew what Calhoun meant. If an agreement could not be reached, the South would secede from the Union.

Webster calls for unity

Daniel Webster of Massachusetts spoke next. He supported Clay's plea to save the Union. Webster stated his position clearly:

> "I speak today not as a Massachusetts man, nor as a northern man, but as an American. . . . I speak today for the preservation of the Union. . . . There can be no such thing as a peaceable secession. Peaceable secession is an utter impossibility."

Webster feared that the states could not separate without a **civil war.** A civil war is a war between people of the same country.

Like many northerners, Webster viewed slavery as evil. Disunion, however, he believed was worse. To save the Union, Webster was willing to compromise with the South. He would support its demand that northerners be required to return fugitive slaves.

Compromise of 1850

In 1850, as the debate raged, Calhoun died. His last words reportedly were "The South! The South! God knows what will become of her!" President Taylor also died in 1850. The new President was Millard Fillmore. Unlike Taylor, he supported Clay's compromise plan. An agreement finally seemed possible.

Henry Clay gave more than 70 speeches in favor of a compromise. At last, however, he became too sick to continue. **Stephen Douglas,** an energetic senator from Illinois, took up the fight for him. Douglas tirelessly guided each part of Clay's plan, called the **Compromise of 1850,** through Congress.

The Compromise of 1850 had five parts. First, it allowed California to enter the Union as a free state. Second, it divided the rest of the Mexican Cession into the territories of New Mexico and Utah. Voters in each would decide the slavery question according to popular sovereignty. Third, it ended the slave trade in Washington, D.C., the nation's capital. Congress, however, declared that it had no power to ban slave trade between slave states. Fourth, it included a strict fugitive slave law. Fifth, it settled a border dispute between Texas and New Mexico.

Fugitive Slave Law of 1850

Most northerners had ignored the Fugitive Slave Law of 1793. As a result, fugitive slaves often lived as free citizens in northern cities. The **Fugitive Slave Law of 1850** was harder to ignore. It required all citizens to help catch runaway slaves. People who let fugitives escape could be fined $1,000 and jailed for six months.

The new law also set up special courts to handle the cases of runaways. Judges received $10 for sending an accused runaway to the South. They received only $5 for setting someone free. Lured by the extra money, some judges sent African Americans to the South whether or not they were runaways.

The Fugitive Slave Law enraged antislavery northerners. By forcing them to catch runaways, the law made northerners feel they were part of the slave system. In several northern cities, crowds tried to rescue fugitive slaves from their captors.

Martin R. Delany, an African American newspaper editor, spoke for many northerners, black and white:

> "My house is my castle.... If any man approaches that house in search of a slave—I care not who he may be, whether constable or sheriff, magistrate or even judge of the Supreme Court... if he crosses the threshold of my door, and I do not lay him a lifeless corpse at my feet, I hope the grave may refuse my body a resting place."

The North and South had reached a compromise. Still, tensions remained because neither side got everything that it wanted. The new Fugitive Slave Law was especially hard for northerners to accept. Each time the law was enforced, it convinced more northerners that slavery was evil.

★ Section 1 Review ★

Recall

1. **Locate** **(a)** Missouri, **(b)** Maine, **(c)** Missouri Compromise Line, **(d)** California, **(e)** New Mexico Territory, **(f)** Utah Territory.
2. **Identify** **(a)** Missouri Compromise, **(b)** Wilmot Proviso, **(c)** Free Soil party, **(d)** Zachary Taylor, **(e)** Stephen Douglas, **(f)** Compromise of 1850, **(g)** Fugitive Slave Law of 1850.
3. **Define** **(a)** sectionalism, **(b)** popular sovereignty, **(c)** secede, **(d)** fugitive, **(e)** civil war.

Comprehension

4. Describe three different views on the issue of slavery in the West.
5. Why did some people leave the Whig and Democratic parties and create the Free Soil party?
6. Explain the five parts of the Compromise of 1850.

Critical Thinking and Writing

7. **Analyzing Ideas** Why might the goals of the Free Soil party have pleased some northerners but not others?
8. **Analyzing Visual Evidence** Based on your understanding of the painting on page 428, how did the Compromise of 1850 create new conflict over the slavery issue?

Activity **Making a Decision** You are a northerner of the 1850s. There is a knock at your door. It's a fugitive slave! Will you help the runaway or will you turn the person in to the authorities? Write a brief statement explaining the reasons for your decision.

The Crisis Turns Violent

Explore These Questions

- How did *Uncle Tom's Cabin* affect attitudes toward slavery?
- Why did a civil war break out in Kansas?
- How did the Dred Scott decision divide the nation?

Define

- repeal
- guerrilla warfare
- lawsuit

Identify

- Harriet Beecher Stowe
- *Uncle Tom's Cabin*
- Kansas-Nebraska Act
- Franklin Pierce
- Border Ruffians
- John Brown
- Bleeding Kansas
- Charles Sumner
- Dred Scott decision

In the mid-1850s, proslavery and antislavery forces battled for control of the territory of Kansas. An observer described election day in one Kansas district in 1855:

> "On the morning of the election, before the polls were opened, some 300 or 400 Missourians and others were collected in the yard... where the election was to be held, armed with bowie-knives, revolvers, and clubs. They said they came to vote, and whip the... Yankees, and would vote without being sworn. Some said they came to have a fight, and wanted one."

Hearing of events in Kansas, Abraham Lincoln, then a young lawyer in Illinois, predicted that "the contest will come to blows, and bloodshed." Once again, the issue of slavery in the territories divided the nation.

An Antislavery Bestseller

An event in 1852 added to the growing antislavery mood of the North. That year, **Harriet Beecher Stowe** published a novel called ***Uncle Tom's Cabin.*** Stowe wrote the novel to show the evils of slavery and the injustice of the Fugitive Slave Law. She had originally published the story as a serial in an abolitionist newspaper.

A powerful story

Stowe told the story of Uncle Tom, an enslaved African American noted for his kindness and his devotion to his religion. Tom is bought by Simon Legree, a cruel planter who treats his slaves brutally. In the end, Uncle Tom refuses to obey Legree's order to whip another slave. Legree then whips Uncle Tom to death.

Uncle Tom's Cabin had wide appeal in the North. The first 5,000 copies that were printed sold out in two days. In its first year, Stowe's novel sold 300,000 copies. The book was also published in many different languages. Soon, a play based on the novel appeared in cities not only in the North but around the world.

Nationwide reaction

Although *Uncle Tom's Cabin* was popular in the North, southerners objected to the book. They claimed that it did not give a true picture of slave life. Indeed, Stowe had seen little of slavery firsthand.

Even so, the book helped to change the way northerners felt about slavery. No longer could they ignore slavery as a political problem for Congress to settle. They now saw the slavery issue as a moral problem facing every American. For this reason, *Uncle Tom's Cabin* was one of the most important books in American history.

Kansas-Nebraska Act

Americans had hoped that the Compromise of 1850 would end debate over slavery in the West. In 1854, however, the issue of slavery in the territories surfaced yet again.

In January 1854, Senator Stephen Douglas introduced a bill to set up a government for the Nebraska Territory. This territory stretched from Texas north to Canada, and from Missouri west to the Rockies.

Douglas knew that white southerners did not want to add another free state to the Union. He proposed that the Nebraska Territory be divided into two territories, Kansas and Nebraska. (See the map below.) The settlers living in each territory would decide the issue of slavery by popular sovereignty. Douglas's bill was known as the **Kansas-Nebraska Act.**

Support for the act

The Kansas-Nebraska Act seemed fair to many people. After all, the Compromise of 1850 had applied popular sovereignty in New Mexico and Utah.

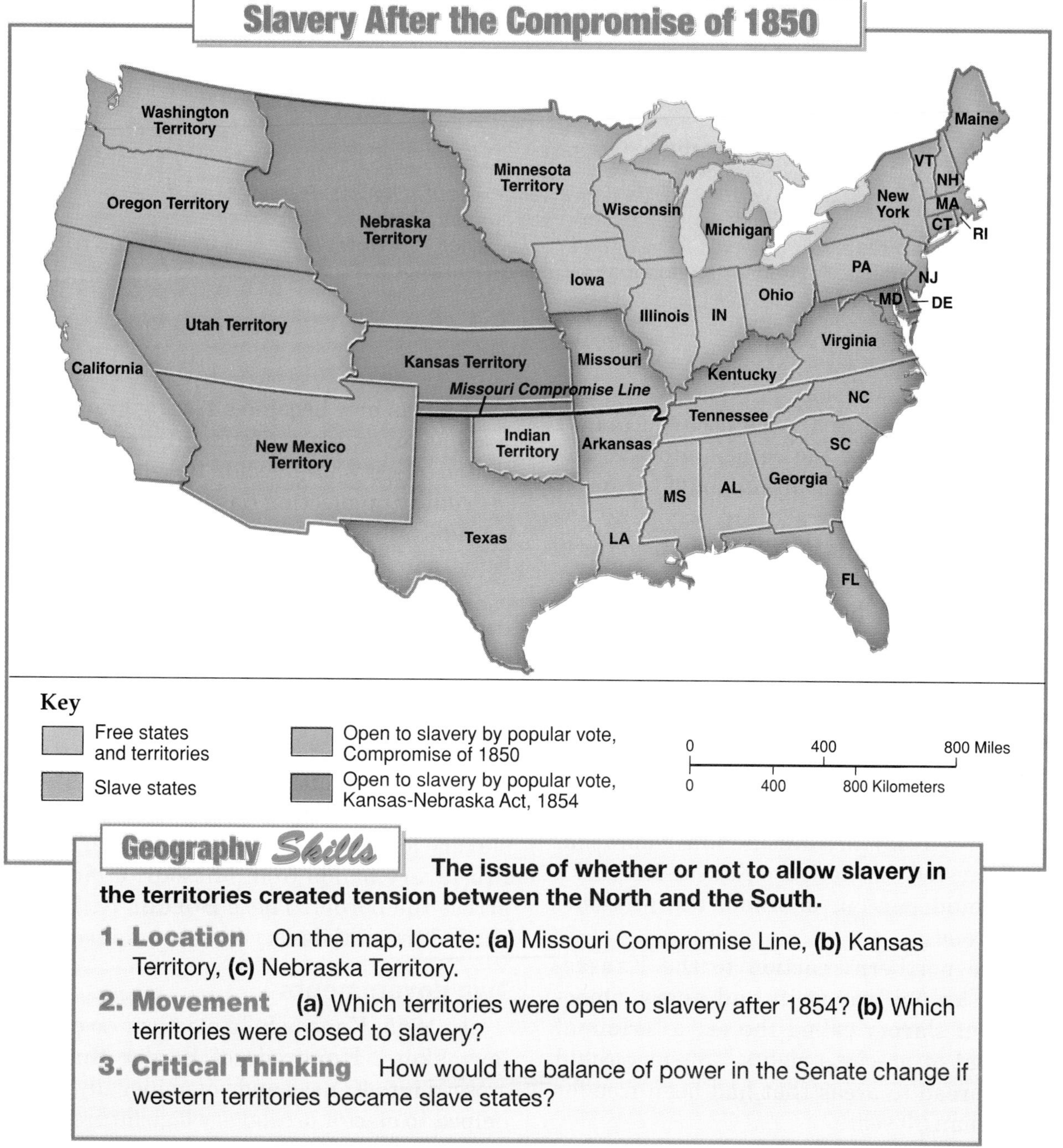

Geography Skills **The issue of whether or not to allow slavery in the territories created tension between the North and the South.**

1. **Location** On the map, locate: **(a)** Missouri Compromise Line, **(b)** Kansas Territory, **(c)** Nebraska Territory.
2. **Movement** **(a)** Which territories were open to slavery after 1854? **(b)** Which territories were closed to slavery?
3. **Critical Thinking** How would the balance of power in the Senate change if western territories became slave states?

Abolitionist's saber

Viewing HISTORY **Bleeding Kansas**

In 1856, a bloody civil war broke out in Kansas. Proslavery and antislavery forces fought for control of the territory. The battle depicted here took place at Hickory Point, 25 miles north of Lawrence. ★ **How was the violence in Kansas related to the Kansas-Nebraska Act?**

Southern leaders especially supported the Kansas-Nebraska Act. They were sure that slave owners from neighboring Missouri would move across the border into Kansas. In time, they hoped, Kansas would become a slave state.

President **Franklin Pierce,** a Democrat elected in 1852, also supported the bill. With the President's help, Douglas pushed the Kansas-Nebraska Act through Congress. He did not realize it at the time, but he had lit a fire under a powder keg.

Northern outrage

Other people were unhappy with the new law. The Missouri Compromise had already banned slavery in Kansas and Nebraska, they insisted. In effect, the Kansas-Nebraska Act would **repeal,** or undo, the Missouri Compromise.

The northern reaction to the Kansas-Nebraska Act was swift and angry. Opponents of slavery called the act a "criminal betrayal of precious rights." Slavery could now spread to areas that had been free for more than 30 years.

Bleeding Kansas

Kansas now became a testing ground for popular sovereignty. Stephen Douglas hoped that settlers would decide the slavery issue peacefully on election day. Instead, proslavery and antislavery forces sent settlers to Kansas to fight for control of the territory.

Most of the new arrivals were farmers from neighboring states. Their main interest in moving to Kansas was to acquire cheap land. Few of these settlers owned slaves. At the same time, abolitionists brought in more than 1,000 settlers from New England.

Proslavery settlers moved into Kansas as well. They wanted to make sure that antislavery forces did not overrun the territory. Proslavery bands from Missouri often rode across the border. These **Border Ruffians** battled the antislavery forces in Kansas.

Two governments

In 1855, Kansas held elections to choose lawmakers. Hundreds of Border Ruffians crossed into Kansas and voted illegally. They helped to elect a proslavery legislature.

The new legislature quickly passed laws to support slavery. One law said that people could be put to death for helping slaves escape. Another made speaking out against slavery a crime punishable by two years of hard labor.

Antislavery settlers refused to accept these laws. They elected their own governor and legislature. With two rival governments, Kansas was in chaos. Armed gangs roamed the land looking for trouble.

A bloody battleground

In 1856, a band of proslavery men raided the town of Lawrence, an antislavery stronghold. The attackers destroyed homes and smashed the press of a Free Soil newspaper.

John Brown, an abolitionist, decided to strike back. Brown had moved to Kansas to help make it a free state. He claimed that God had sent him to punish supporters of slavery.

Brown rode with his four sons and two other men to the town of Pottawatomie (paht uh WAHT uh mee) Creek. In the middle of the night, they dragged five proslavery settlers from their beds and murdered them.

The killings at Pottawatomie Creek led to more violence. Both sides fought fiercely and engaged in **guerrilla warfare,** or the use of hit-and-run tactics. By late 1856, more than 200 people had been killed. Newspapers called the territory **Bleeding Kansas.**

Violence in the Senate

Even before John Brown's attack, the battle over Kansas had spilled into the Senate. **Charles Sumner** of Massachusetts was the leading abolitionist senator. In one speech, the sharp-tongued Sumner denounced the proslavery legislature of Kansas. He then viciously criticized his southern foes, singling out Andrew Butler, an elderly senator from South Carolina.

Butler was not in the Senate on the day Sumner spoke. A few days later, however, Butler's nephew, Congressman Preston Brooks, marched into the Senate chamber. Using a heavy cane, Brooks beat Sumner until he fell down, bloody and unconscious, to the floor.

Many southerners felt that Sumner got what he deserved for his verbal abuse of another senator. Hundreds of people sent canes to Brooks to show their support. To northerners, however, the brutal act was just more evidence that slavery led to violence.

The Dred Scott Case

With Congress in an uproar, many Americans looked to the Supreme Court to settle the slavery issue and restore peace. In 1857, the Court ruled on a case involving a slave named Dred Scott. Instead of bringing harmony, however, the Court's decision further divided North and South.

Dred Scott had lived for many years in Missouri. Later, he moved with his owner to Illinois and then to the Wisconsin Territory,

Biography **Dred Scott**

Dred Scott filed a lawsuit for his freedom. He argued that he should be a free man because he had lived in a free territory. The Supreme Court, however, ruled that he had no right to sue because he was property and not a citizen. After the decision, Scott's new owner granted freedom to Scott and his family. Just one year later, Scott died of consumption. ★ **How did the Dred Scott decision overturn the Missouri Compromise?**

where slavery was not allowed. After they returned to Missouri, Scott's owner died. Antislavery lawyers helped Scott to file a **lawsuit,** a legal case brought by a person or group against another to settle a dispute between them. Scott's lawyers argued that since Scott had lived in a free territory, he was a free man.

The Supreme Court's decision

In time, the case reached the Supreme Court. The Court's decision startled Americans who opposed slavery. The Court ruled that Scott could not file a lawsuit because, as an enslaved person, he was not a citizen. Also, the Court clearly stated that slaves were property.

The Court's ruling did not stop there. Instead, the Justices went on to make a sweeping decision about the larger issue of slavery in the territories. According to the Court, Congress did not have the power to outlaw slavery in any territory. The Court's ruling meant that the Missouri Compromise was unconstitutional.

The nation reacts

White southerners rejoiced at the **Dred Scott decision.** It meant that slavery was legal in all the territories. This was just what white southerners had been demanding for years.

African Americans responded angrily to the Dred Scott decision. In the North, many held public meetings to condemn the ruling. At a meeting in Philadelphia, a speaker hoped that the Dred Scott decision would lead more whites to "join with us in our efforts to recover the long lost boon of freedom."

White northerners were also shocked by the ruling. Many had hoped that slavery would eventually die out if it were restricted to the South. Now, however, slavery could spread throughout the West. Even northerners who disliked abolitionists felt that the Dred Scott ruling was wrong. A newspaper in Cincinnati declared, "We are now one great... slaveholding community." In New England, another newspaper asked, "Where will it all end?"

★ Section 2 Review ★

Recall

1. **Locate** **(a)** Kansas Territory, **(b)** Nebraska Territory.
2. **Define** **(a)** repeal, **(b)** guerrilla warfare, **(c)** lawsuit.
3. **Identify** **(a)** Harriet Beecher Stowe, **(b)** *Uncle Tom's Cabin,* **(c)** Kansas-Nebraska Act, **(d)** Franklin Pierce, **(e)** Border Ruffians, **(f)** John Brown, **(g)** Bleeding Kansas, **(h)** Charles Sumner, **(i)** Dred Scott decision.

Comprehension

4. **(a)** How did *Uncle Tom's Cabin* portray slavery? **(b)** How did the book affect people's attitudes toward slavery?
5. How did the Kansas-Nebraska Act lead to violence in Kansas?
6. Explain how each of the following reacted to the Dred Scott decision: **(a)** white southerners, **(b)** African Americans, **(c)** white northerners.

Critical Thinking and Writing

7. **Analyzing Primary Sources** After the Kansas-Nebraska Act was passed, Stephen Douglas stated, "The struggle for freedom was forever banished from the halls of Congress to the western plains." **(a)** What did Douglas mean? **(b)** Do you agree or disagree with his statement? Explain.
8. **Comparing** Compare Harriet Beecher Stowe's and John Brown's contributions to the abolitionist movement.

Activity **Writing a Protest Letter** You are outraged by the Dred Scott decision! Write a protest letter to the justices of the Supreme Court explaining why you think their decision in this case was wrong.

A New Party Challenges Slavery

As You Read

Explore These Questions

- Why did the Republican party come into being in the mid-1850s?
- What were Abraham Lincoln's views on slavery?
- How did northerners and southerners respond differently to the raid on Harpers Ferry?

Define

- arsenal
- martyr

Identify

- Republican party
- John C. Frémont
- James Buchanan
- Abraham Lincoln

SETTING the Scene In the mid-1850s, people who opposed slavery in the territories needed a new political voice. Neither Whigs nor Democrats would take a strong stand against slavery. "We have submitted to slavery long enough," an Ohio Democrat declared.

Free Soilers, northern Democrats, and antislavery Whigs met in towns and cities across the North. In 1854, a group gathered in Michigan to form the **Republican party.** The new party grew quickly. By 1856, it was ready to challenge the older parties for power.

The Republican Party

In the 1850s, the main goal of the Republican party was to keep slavery out of the western territories. A few Republicans were abolitionists. They hoped to end slavery in the South as well. Most Republicans, however, wanted only to stop the spread of slavery.

In 1856, Republicans selected **John C. Frémont** to run for President. Frémont was a frontiersman who had fought for California's independence. (See page 362.) He had little political experience, but he opposed the spread of slavery.

John C. Frémont

Frémont's main opponent was Democrat **James Buchanan** of Pennsylvania. He had served as a senator and as Secretary of State. Many Democrats considered Buchanan to be a "compromise" candidate because he was a "northern man with southern principles." They hoped that he would attract voters in both the North and the South.

Buchanan won the election with support from a large majority of southerners and many northerners. Still, the Republicans made a strong showing in the election. Without the support of a single southern state, Frémont won one third of the popular vote. Southerners worried that their influence in the national government was fading.

Abe Lincoln of Illinois

The next test for the Republican party came in 1858 in the state of Illinois. **Abraham Lincoln,** a Republican, challenged Democrat Stephen Douglas for his seat in the Senate. The election captured the attention of the whole nation. The race was important because most Americans thought that Douglas would run for President in 1860.

Viewing HISTORY The Lincoln-Douglas Debates

In this painting, Stephen Douglas sits to Lincoln's right during a debate held at Charleston, Illinois, in September 1858. Thousands of people attended the Lincoln-Douglas debates. ★ **What was the most important issue discussed in the debates?**

A self-starter from Kentucky

Abraham Lincoln was born in the backcountry of Kentucky. Like many frontier people, his parents moved often to find better land. The family lived in Indiana and later in Illinois. As a child, Lincoln spent only a year in school. Still, he taught himself to read and spent many hours reading by firelight.

After Lincoln left home, he opened a store in Illinois. There, he studied law on his own and launched a career in politics. After spending eight years in the state legislature, Lincoln served one term in Congress. Bitterly opposed to the Kansas-Nebraska Act, he decided to run for the Senate in 1858.

"Just folks"

When the race began, Lincoln was not a national figure. Still, people in Illinois knew him well and liked him. To them, he was "just folks"—someone who enjoyed picnics, wrestling contests, and all their other favorite pastimes.

People also admired his honesty and wit. His plainspoken manner made him a good speaker. Even so, a listener once complained that he could not understand one of Lincoln's speeches. "There are always some fleas a dog can't reach" was Lincoln's reply.

Lincoln-Douglas Debates

During the Senate campaign, Lincoln challenged Douglas to a series of debates. Douglas was not eager to accept, but he did. During the campaign, the two debated seven times. Slavery was the important issue.

Views on slavery

Douglas wanted to settle the slavery question by popular sovereignty. He disliked slavery, but he thought that people in the territories should be able to vote "down or up" for it.

Lincoln, like nearly all whites of his day, did not believe in "perfect equality" between blacks and whites. He did, however, believe that slavery was a "moral, social, and political wrong." He believed that blacks were entitled to the rights named in the Declaration of Independence—"life, liberty, and the pursuit of happiness."

Since slavery was wrong, said Lincoln, Douglas and other Americans should not treat it as an unimportant question to be voted "down or up." Lincoln was totally opposed to slavery in the territories. Still, he was not an abolitionist. He had no wish to interfere with slavery in the states where it already existed.

Lincoln believed that the nation could not survive if it remained divided by slavery. On June 16, 1858, Lincoln spoke in a crowded hall in Springfield, Illinois:

> "A house divided against itself cannot stand. I believe this government cannot endure permanently half slave and half free. I do not expect the Union to be dissolved—I do not expect the house to fall—but I do expect it will cease to be divided. It will become all one thing, or all the other."

Why Study History?

Because Heroes of the Past Can Be Models for Today

Historical Background

Many consider Abraham Lincoln one of the truly heroic figures in American history. Through education and hard work, "Honest Abe" rose from humble beginnings to national leadership. As President, he would lead the nation through the horrors of a civil war and help bring an end to slavery.

Lincoln Memorial

Connections to Today

Today, we still honor Lincoln. Each year, we remember him on Presidents' Day. His image is on the money we use every day. In addition, thousands of people show their respect by visiting the Lincoln Memorial in Washington, D.C.

Admirers of Lincoln consider him a model for others to imitate. They point to his easygoing manner, keen wit, high sense of morality, and ability to make wise decisions in tough situations.

Connections to You

Do you think Lincoln is an American hero? Should you look to him as a role model? To help you decide, read the following excerpts from Lincoln's conversations, speeches, and writings.

"I have no other [ambition] so great as that of being truly esteemed of my fellow men, by rendering myself worthy of their esteem."—June 13, 1836

"The better part of one's life consists in his friendships." —May 19, 1849

"Let us have faith that Right makes Might, and in that faith, let us to the end, dare to do our duty." —February 27, 1860

"I want every man to have a chance—and I believe a black man is entitled to it—in which he can better his condition."—March 6, 1860

"The people's will, constitutionally expressed, is the ultimate law for all."—October 19, 1864

"Whenever I hear anyone arguing for slavery, I feel a strong impulse to see it tried on him personally." —March 17, 1865

1. Comprehension How do Americans show their respect for Abraham Lincoln today?

2. Critical Thinking **(a)** Which quotation deals most directly with the idea of racial equality? **(b)** What was Lincoln's position on equality?

Writing an Essay Do you consider Lincoln an American hero and role model? Develop your answer in a brief essay, using the quotations above to describe some of Lincoln's ideas and values.

A leader emerges

Week after week, both men spoke nearly every day to large crowds. Newspapers reprinted their campaign speeches. The more northerners read Lincoln's speeches, the more they thought about the injustice of slavery.

In the end, Douglas won the election by a slim margin. However, Lincoln was a winner, too. He was now known throughout the country. Two years later, the two rivals would again meet face to face—both seeking the office of President.

John Brown's Raid

In the meantime, more bloodshed pushed the North and South farther apart. In 1859, John Brown carried his antislavery campaign from Kansas to the East. He led a group of followers, including five African Americans, to Harpers Ferry, Virginia.

There, Brown planned to raid a federal **arsenal,** or gun warehouse. He thought that enslaved African Americans would flock to him at the arsenal. He would then give them weapons and lead them in a revolt.

Sentenced to death

Brown quickly gained control of the arsenal. No slave uprising took place, however. Instead, troops led by Robert E. Lee killed 10 of the raiders and captured Brown.

Most people, in both the North and the South, thought that Brown's plan to lead a slave revolt was insane. After all, there were not many enslaved African Americans in Harpers Ferry. At his trial, however, Brown seemed perfectly sane. He sat quietly as the court found him guilty of murder and treason and sentenced him to death.

Hero or villain?

Brown became a hero to many northerners. Some considered him a **martyr** because he was willing to give up his life for his beliefs. On the morning he was hanged, church bells rang solemnly throughout the North. In years to come, New Englanders would sing a popular song: "John Brown's body lies a mold'ring in the grave, but his soul is marching on."

To white southerners, the northern response to John Brown's death was outrageous. People were singing the praises of a man who had tried to lead a slave revolt! Many southerners became convinced that the North wanted to destroy slavery—and the South along with it. The nation was poised for a violent clash.

★ Section 3 Review ★

Recall

1. **Identify** **(a)** Republican party, **(b)** John C. Frémont, **(c)** James Buchanan, **(d)** Abraham Lincoln.
2. **Define** **(a)** arsenal, **(b)** martyr.

Comprehension

3. What was the main goal of the Republican party?
4. How did Abraham Lincoln's opinions on slavery differ from those of Stephen Douglas?
5. **(a)** How did Northerners respond to John Brown's execution? **(b)** How did Southerners respond?

Critical Thinking and Writing

6. **Identifying Main Ideas** Reread the subsection on page 436 called Just folks. State the main idea of this subsection.
7. **Analyzing Ideas** Lincoln said the nation could not "endure permanently half slave and half free." Do you agree that slavery was too great an issue to allow differences among the states? Explain.

Activity **Writing Headlines** You are a journalist in the 1850s. Choose three events discussed in Section 3. Write two headlines for each event—one for a northern newspaper, the other for a southern newspaper.

The Nation Splits in Two

As You Read

Explore These Questions

- Why was Abraham Lincoln able to win the election of 1860?
- How did the South react to Lincoln's election victory?
- What events led to the outbreak of the Civil War?

Identify

- John Breckinridge
- John Bell
- John Crittenden
- Confederate States of America
- Jefferson Davis
- Fort Sumter

In May 1860, thousands of people swarmed into Chicago for the Republican national convention. They filled the city's 42 hotels. When beds ran out, they slept on billiard tables. All were there to find out one thing. Who would win the Republican nomination for President—William Seward of New York or Abraham Lincoln of Illinois?

On the third day of the convention, a delegate rushed to the roof of the hall. There, a man stood waiting next to a cannon. "Fire the salute," ordered the delegate. "Old Abe is nominated!"

As the cannon fired, crowds surrounding the hall burst into cheers. Amid the celebration, a delegate from Kentucky struck a somber note. "Gentlemen, we are on the brink of a great civil war."

The Election of 1860

The Democrats held their convention in Charleston, South Carolina. Southerners wanted the party to support slavery in the territories. However, Northern Democrats refused to do so.

In the end, the party split in two. Northern Democrats chose Stephen Douglas to run for President. Southern Democrats picked **John Breckinridge** of Kentucky.

Some Americans tried to heal the split between North and South by forming a new party. The Constitutional Union party chose **John Bell** of Tennessee, a Whig, to run for President. Bell was a moderate who wanted to keep the Union together. He got support only in a few southern states that were still trying to find a compromise.

Republican campaign banner

Senator Douglas was sure that Lincoln would win the election. However, he believed that Democrats "must try to save the Union." He pleaded with southern voters to stay with the Union, no matter who was elected.

When the votes were counted, Lincoln had carried the North and won the election. Southern votes did not affect the outcome at all. Lincoln's name was not even on the ballot in 10 southern states. Northerners outnumbered southerners and outvoted them.

The Union Is Broken

Lincoln's election brought a strong reaction in the South. A South Carolina woman described how the news was received:

> "The excitement was very great. Everybody was talking at the same time. One... more moved than the others, stood up saying... 'The die is cast—No more vain regrets—Sad forebodings are useless. The stake is life or death—'... No doubt of it."

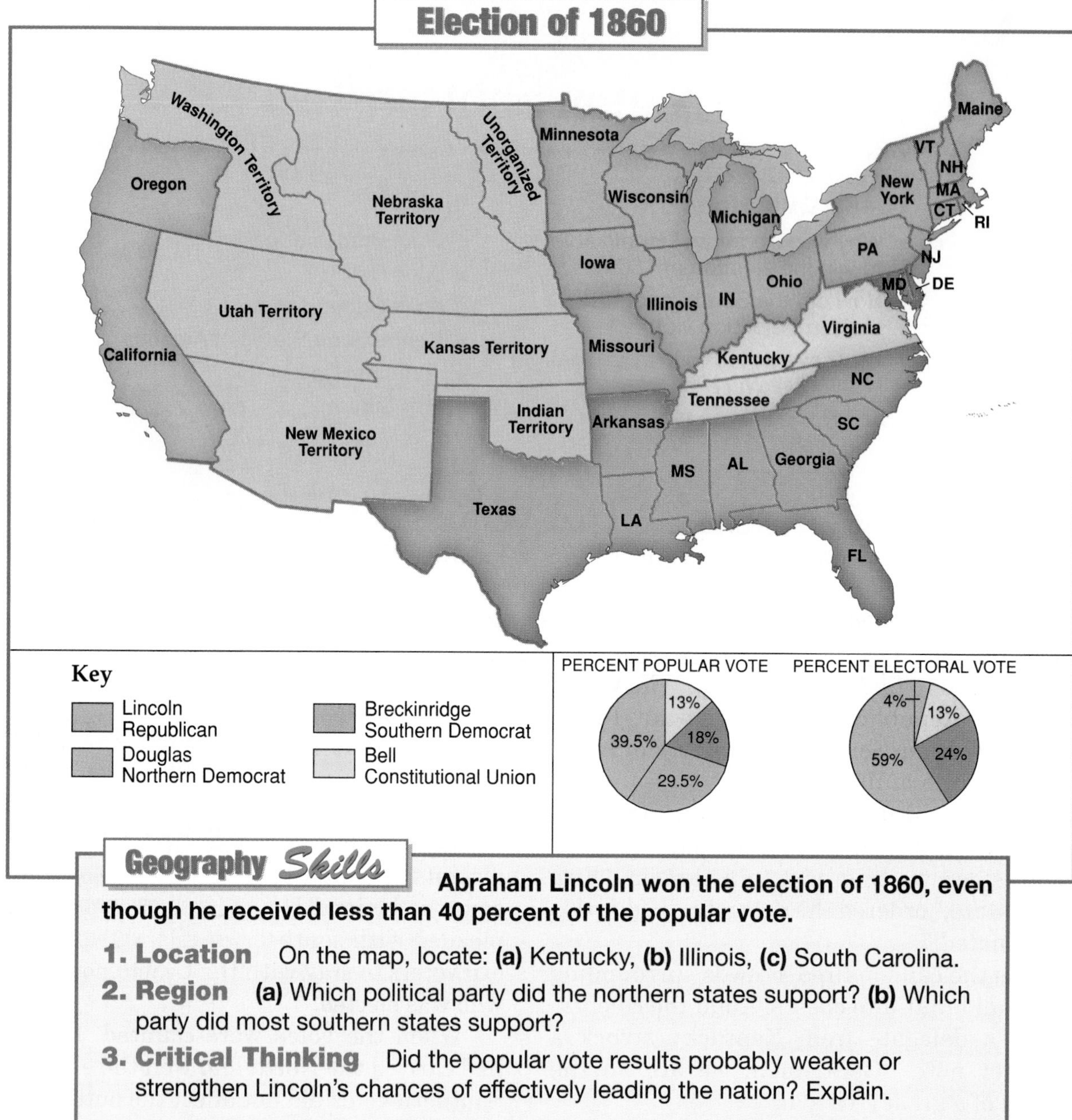

Geography Skills **Abraham Lincoln won the election of 1860, even though he received less than 40 percent of the popular vote.**

1. **Location** On the map, locate: **(a)** Kentucky, **(b)** Illinois, **(c)** South Carolina.
2. **Region** **(a)** Which political party did the northern states support? **(b)** Which party did most southern states support?
3. **Critical Thinking** Did the popular vote results probably weaken or strengthen Lincoln's chances of effectively leading the nation? Explain.

To many southerners, Lincoln's election meant that the South no longer had a voice in national government. They believed that the President and Congress were now set against their interests—especially slavery. Even before the election, South Carolina's governor had written to other southern governors. If Lincoln won, he wrote, it would be their duty to leave the Union.

Secession

Senator **John Crittenden** of Kentucky made a last effort to save the Union. In December 1860, he introduced a bill to extend the Missouri Compromise line to the Pacific. He also suggested adding an "unamendable" amendment to the Constitution to forever guarantee the right to hold slaves in states south of the compromise line.

The compromise bill received little support. Slavery in the West was no longer the issue. Many southerners believed that the North had put an abolitionist in the White House. They felt that secession was their only choice. Most Republicans also refused to compromise. They were unwilling to surrender what they had won in the national election.

Skills FOR LIFE

Critical Thinking | Managing Information | Communication | Maps, Charts, and Graphs

Comparing Points of View

How Will I Use This Skill?

When two or more people describe the same event, their descriptions of the event often differ. That is because each person's point of view is subjective, or influenced by personal experiences and feelings. By comparing different sources, you can learn objective information, or facts, as well as subjective points of view regarding those facts.

Bullying the Free States

November 19, 1860
The New York Tribune

Abraham Lincoln has been designated for next President of this Republic by the popular vote of nearly every Free State, and the ruling politicians of the Slave States are not pleased with the selection. We can fancy their feelings, as we felt much the same when they put a most undesired President upon us four years ago. Moreover, we. . .advise them to do as we did—Bear it with fortitude, and hope to do better next time.

Devotion to the Union Is Treason to the South

November 19, 1860
Oxford Mississippi Mercury

We have at last reached that point in our history when it is necessary for the South to withdraw from the Union. . . .

[A] powerful sectional majority are now about to seize upon the Government. . . to destroy the institution of Slavery. . . . We cannot stand still and quietly see the Government pass into the hands of such an infamous crew.

South Carolina, . . . Georgia, Mississippi, Alabama, Louisiana, Texas, and Arkansas, will soon be united as brothers to defend each other from the inroads of the fanatics of the North.

LEARN the Skill

You can compare points of view by following the steps below.

1. Identify the author of each source. Consider how each report might be affected by the author's point of view.
2. Find objective information common to two or more sources.
3. Identify subjective statements that reflect the author's point of view.
4. Draw conclusions about the historical event and different points of view on it.

PRACTICE the Skill

The newspaper articles above give different viewpoints on Abraham Lincoln's victory in the election of 1860. Compare the two viewpoints by answering the following questions.

1. (a) Which source is a southern newspaper? (b) Which source is a northern newspaper? (c) Why would you expect the two to have different opinions about Lincoln?
2. What factual information do you find in both articles?
3. How do the two articles describe the election result differently?
4. (a) Why did the election cause conflict between North and South? (b) What did the *Tribune* think the South should do? (c) What did the *Mercury* recommend?

APPLY the Skill

In two or more newspapers or news magazines, find different points of view on some issue or event. Use the steps you have learned to compare the various viewpoints.

American Heritage
M A G A Z I N E

HISTORY HAPPENED HERE

Fort Sumter

The Civil War began in 1861 when Confederate forces bombarded and captured Fort Sumter in Charleston Harbor, South Carolina. Later in the war, Union gunships reduced Sumter to rubble. The fort was rebuilt, and it remained part of the seacoast defenses until 1947. Today, Fort Sumter is a national monument. Tour boats to the fort leave regularly from downtown Charleston.

★ ***To learn more about this historic site, write:*** *Fort Sumter National Monument, Sullivan's Island, SC 29482.*

◀ *Union flag from Fort Sumter*

The first state to secede was South Carolina. On December 20, 1860, delegates to a convention in Charleston voted for secession. "The state of South Carolina has resumed her position among the nations of the world," the delegates proudly declared. By late February, 1861, Alabama, Florida, Georgia, Louisiana, Mississippi, and Texas had seceded.

The Confederacy

The seven states that had seceded held a convention in Montgomery, Alabama. There, the southern states formed a new nation, the **Confederate States of America.** To lead the new country, they named **Jefferson Davis** of Mississippi as the first president of the Confederacy.

Most southerners believed that they had every right to secede. After all, the Declaration of Independence said that "it is the right of the people to alter or to abolish" a government that denies the rights of its citizens. Lincoln, they believed, would deny white southerners their right to own slaves.

Lincoln Speaks to the Nation

When Abraham Lincoln took office on March 4, 1861, he faced a national crisis. Crowds gathered in Washington, D.C., to hear him take the presidential oath of office. In his Inaugural Address, the new President assured Americans of both the North and the South that he had two goals. He hoped to maintain the Union and avoid war.

On the first goal, preserving the Union, Lincoln would not compromise. Secession of states from the Union, he said, was unconstitutional. Lincoln believed that his duty as

Connections With Civics

Texas voters chose secession, but Governor Sam Houston refused to swear allegiance to the new Confederacy. He was replaced by a new governor. Houston sadly warned his fellow Texans that the North would "move with the steady momentum and perseverance of a mighty avalanche; and...overwhelm the South."

President was clear. He would take strong action to preserve national union.

> “In view of the Constitution and the law, the Union is unbroken; . . . I will take care . . . that the laws of the Union be faithfully executed in all the States.”

At the same time, however, Lincoln tried to reassure the South. He promised that there would not be war with the South unless southern states started it:

> “We are not enemies, but friends. We must not be enemies. Though passion may have strained, it must not break our bonds of affection.”

Civil War

The Confederacy, however, had already started seizing federal forts in the South. It felt that the forts were a threat because the United States was now a "foreign power."

Lincoln's difficult decision

President Lincoln faced a difficult decision. Should he let the Confederates take over federal property? If he did, he would seem to be admitting that states had the right to leave the Union. On the other hand, if he sent troops to hold the forts, he might start a civil war. He might also lose the support of the eight slave states that had not seceded from the Union.

In April, the Confederacy forced Lincoln to make up his mind. By then, Confederate troops controlled nearly all forts, post offices, and other federal buildings in the South. The Union held only three forts off the Florida coast and Fort Sumter in South Carolina. **Fort Sumter** was important to the Confederacy because it guarded Charleston Harbor.

Bombardment of Fort Sumter

President Lincoln learned that food supplies at Fort Sumter were running low. He notified the governor of South Carolina that he was going to ship food to the fort. Lincoln promised not to send troops or weapons.

The Confederates could not leave the fort in Union hands, however. On April 11, 1861, they asked for Fort Sumter's surrender.

Major Robert Anderson, the Union commander, refused to give in. Confederate guns then opened fire. Anderson and his troops quickly ran out of ammunition. On April 13, Anderson surrendered the fort.

When Confederate troops shelled Fort Sumter, people in Charleston had gathered on their rooftops to watch. To many, it was like a fireworks display. No one knew that the fireworks marked the beginning of a civil war that would last four terrible years.

★ Section 4 Review ★

Recall

1. **Identify** **(a)** John Breckinridge, **(b)** John Bell, **(c)** John Crittenden, **(d)** Confederate States of America, **(e)** Jefferson Davis, **(f)** Fort Sumter.

Comprehension

2. Why were there two Democratic candidates for President in 1860?
3. Why did many southerners feel that secession was necessary after Lincoln won the Presidency in 1860?
4. How did the Civil War begin at Fort Sumter in 1861?

Critical Thinking and Writing

5. **Making Inferences** How do you think the split in the Democratic party helped Lincoln win the election of 1860?
6. **Solving Problems** Write a compromise plan that tries to save the Union in 1861. Your plan should offer advantages to both the North and the South.

Activity **Writing Slogans** You are a famous political campaign manager of the mid-1800s. Write a campaign slogan for each of the four candidates in the presidential election of 1860.

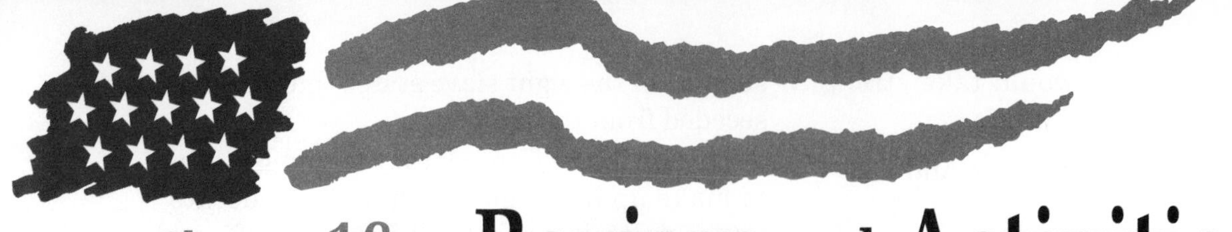

Chapter 16 Review and Activities

★ Sum It Up ★

Section 1 The Slavery Issue in the West

- Americans disagreed on whether slavery should be allowed in the western territories.
- The new Free Soil party wanted to limit the spread of slavery.
- The Compromise of 1850 settled the issue for a time, but the new Fugitive Slave Law angered many.

Section 2 The Crisis Turns Violent

- The novel *Uncle Tom's Cabin* turned many northerners against slavery.
- After the Kansas-Nebraska Act of 1854, proslavery and antislavery settlers battled for control of Kansas.
- In the Dred Scott case, the Supreme Court ruled that Congress could not outlaw slavery in any territory.

Section 3 A New Party Challenges Slavery

- The Republican party wanted to keep slavery out of the western territories.
- Abraham Lincoln emerged as a leader of the Republican party.
- John Brown's raid on Harpers Ferry brought the nation to the brink of war.

Section 4 The Nation Splits in Two

- Abraham Lincoln won the presidential election of 1860.
- Southern states seceded from the Union and formed a new nation.
- A civil war broke out between the North and the South.

For additional review of the major ideas of Chapter 16, see ***Guide to the Essentials of American History*** or ***Interactive Student Tutorial CD-ROM,*** which contains interactive review activities, graphic organizers, and practice tests.

Reviewing the Chapter

Define These Terms

Match each term with the correct definition.

Column 1

1. sectionalism
2. fugitive
3. civil war
4. arsenal
5. Wilmot Proviso

Column 2

a. a law to ban slavery in any lands won from Mexico
b. a runaway
c. a gun warehouse
d. a war between people of the same country
e. loyalty to a part of a nation rather than the whole

Explore the Main Ideas

1. What were the five parts of the Compromise of 1850?
2. Why was Kansas referred to as Bleeding Kansas in the 1850s?
3. What effect did the Dred Scott decision have on the Missouri Compromise?
4. What groups combined to form the new Republican party?
5. Why did South Carolina secede from the Union in 1860?

Geography Activity

Match the letters on the map with the following places: **1.** Missouri, **2.** Maine, **3.** California, **4.** Kansas Territory, **5.** Nebraska Territory, **6.** New Mexico Territory, **7.** Utah Territory. **Region** Which area listed above was admitted to the Union as a free state in 1850?

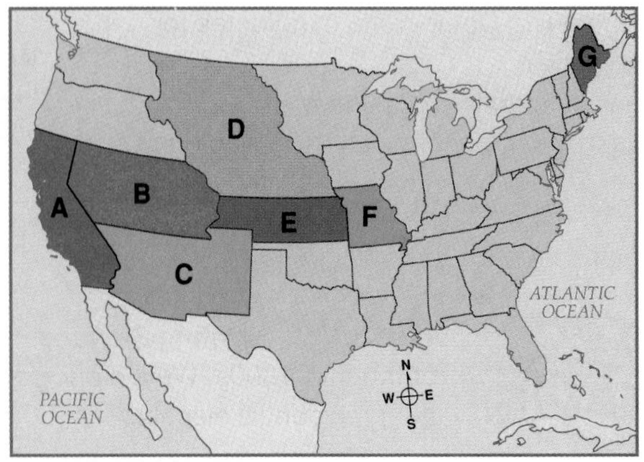

Critical Thinking and Writing

1. **Understanding Chronology** Place the following events in chronological order: **(a)** Kansas-Nebraska Act, **(b)** Compromise of 1850, **(c)** Lincoln becomes President, **(d)** Dred Scott decision.
2. **Understanding Cause and Effect** **(a)** What caused the Democratic party to split in 1860? **(b)** How did the split affect the election of 1860?
3. **Identifying Alternatives** Describe one alternative to secession that the slave states could have chosen.
4. Exploring Unit Themes **Sectionalism** The 1860 Republican convention was held in Illinois, then considered a western state. How did this help bring victory for Lincoln in the national election?

Using Primary Sources

In 1860, Abraham Lincoln was elected to succeed James Buchanan as President. As his term of office came to an end, President Buchanan offered his thoughts on the possibility of secession and civil war:

> "Our Union rests upon public opinion, and can never be cemented by the blood of its citizens shed in civil war. If it cannot live in the affections of the people, it must one day perish. Congress may possess many means of preserving it by [compromise], but the sword was not placed in their hand to preserve it by force."

Source: *The Rise and Fall of the Confederate Government* by Jefferson Davis, 1881.

Recognizing Points of View **(a)** Was Buchanan in favor of a war to prevent southern states from leaving the Union? Explain. **(b)** Do you agree or disagree with Buchanan? Defend your position.

Activity Bank

Interdisciplinary Activity

Exploring the Arts In a painting, drawing, collage, sculpture, or other form of art, express the reaction of the North or the South to one event described in this chapter. Display your work to the class. Ask other students to identify the event and point of view that your art work reflects.

Career Skills Activity

Lawyer Choose the role of prosecutor or defense lawyer at the trial of John Brown. Depending on the role you have chosen, write a speech declaring Brown to be either guilty or not guilty. Present your speech to the class and ask them to reach a verdict.

Citizenship Activity

Reaching a Compromise Find an issue in your community that is the subject of heated debate between two groups. Then brainstorm solutions to the problem that will offer something to both sides. Type up your suggestions and offer them to a neutral party who might be able to mediate between the two groups.

Internet Activity

Use the Internet to find sites dealing with Abraham Lincoln. Use your research to write a biography or a character sketch. Use as many quotations as possible. Make a bibliography by writing down the title, author, and address of each Web site that you use.

You are an African American or white American living in the North or the South between 1820 and 1861. In your EYEWITNESS JOURNAL, describe your reaction to the important events of these years: 1820, 1850, 1859, 1860, 1861.

Chapter 17

The Civil War

1861–1865

What's Ahead

Section 1
The Conflict Takes Shape

Section 2
A Long, Difficult Struggle

Section 3
A Promise of Freedom

Section 4
Hardships of War

Section 5
The War Ends

For more than four years, Americans fought Americans in the Civil War. The South wanted to exist as an independent nation. The North wanted to force the South back into the Union. The war was also linked closely to the question of slavery. President Lincoln made this clear when he issued the Emancipation Proclamation.

Throughout the North and the South, both soldiers and civilians experienced much suffering. The Union's armies struggled in the early years of the war. However, the North's superior resources wore heavily on the South. By the end of 1863, the South was in retreat. In 1865, the South surrendered and the Civil War came to an end.

Why Study *History?*

During the Civil War, millions of northerners and southerners served their nation well. Their efforts, as both soldiers and civilians, affected the course of the war. To see an example of how one person can affect the course of history, see this chapter's *Why Study History?* feature, "One Person Can Make a Difference." The feature focuses on the achievements of Clara Barton.

American Events

1861 Civil War begins with attack on Fort Sumter

1862 Union gunboats capture New Orleans and Memphis

1863 Abraham Lincoln issues Emancipation Proclamation

1861 — 1862 — 1863

World Events

1861 World Event Russian czar frees serfs

1862 World Event Britain refuses to recognize the Confederacy

Viewing History: The Soldiers of the Civil War

In A Rainy Day in Camp *by Winslow Homer, Civil War soldiers find time to gather around a campfire. It is estimated that more than 2,500,000 men served as soldiers in the Civil War. Over 600,000 of them died—more than in any other American war.* ★ **What emotions do you think soldiers felt on the eve of a battle? Explain.**

1863
Battle of Gettysburg ends Confederate drive into the North

1864
General Grant becomes commander of Union army

1865
General Lee surrenders at Appomattox Courthouse

1863 — 1864 — 1865

1863 World Event
First Red Cross societies established in Europe

The Conflict Takes Shape

As You Read

Explore These Questions
- What strengths and weaknesses did the Confederacy have?
- What strengths and weaknesses did the Union have?
- What special qualities did Presidents Abraham Lincoln and Jefferson Davis possess?

Define
- racism
- martial law

Identify
- border states
- Robert E. Lee

Confederate canteen

SETTING the Scene In April 1861, President Abraham Lincoln called for 75,000 volunteers to serve as soldiers for 90 days in a campaign against the South. The response was overwhelming. Throughout the North, crowds cheered the Stars and Stripes and booed the southern "traitors."

Southerners were just as enthusiastic for the war. They rallied to the Stars and Bars, as they called the new Confederate flag. Volunteers flooded into the Confederate army.

With flags held high, both northerners and southerners marched off to war. Most felt certain that a single, gallant battle would bring a quick end to the conflict. Few suspected that the Civil War would last four terrible years and be the most destructive war in the nation's history.

A Nation Divided

As the war began, each side was convinced that its cause was just. Southerners believed that they had the right to leave the Union. In fact, they called the conflict the War for Southern Independence. Southerners wanted independence so that they could keep their traditional way of life—including the institution of slavery.

Northerners, meanwhile, believed that they had to fight to save the Union. At the outset of the war, abolishing slavery was not an official goal of the North. In fact, many northerners, guided by feelings of racism, approved of slavery. **Racism** is the belief that one race is superior to another.

In April 1861, eight slave states were still in the Union. They had to make the difficult decision of which side to join. Virginia,* North Carolina, Tennessee, and Arkansas joined the Confederacy. The four **border states** of Delaware, Kentucky, Missouri, and Maryland remained in the Union. (See the map on page 449.)

Still, some citizens of the border states supported the South. For example, in April 1861, pro-Confederate mobs attacked Union troops in Baltimore, Maryland. In response, President Lincoln declared **martial law,** or rule by the army instead of the elected government. Many people who sided with the South were arrested.

Strengths and Weaknesses

Both sides in the conflict had strengths and weaknesses as the war began. The South had the strong advantage of fighting a defensive war. It was up to the North to go on the offensive, to attack and defeat the South. If the North did not move its forces into the South, the Confederacy would remain a separate country.

*Many people in western Virginia supported the Union. When Virginia seceded, westerners formed their own government. West Virginia became a state of the Union in 1863.

The South

Southerners believed that they were fighting a war for independence, similar to the American Revolution. Defending their homeland and their way of life gave them a strong reason to fight bravely. "Our men must prevail in combat," one Confederate said, "or they will lose their property, country, freedom—in short, everything."

Also, many southerners had skills that made them good soldiers. Hunting was an important part of southern life. From an early age, boys learned to ride horses and use guns. Wealthy young men often went to military school. Before the Civil War, many of the best officers in the United States Army were from the South.

The South, however, had serious economic weaknesses. (See the chart on page 450.) It had few factories to produce weapons and other vital supplies. It also had few railroads to move troops and supplies. The railroads that it did have often did not connect to one another. The South also had political problems. The Confederate constitution favored states' rights and limited the authority

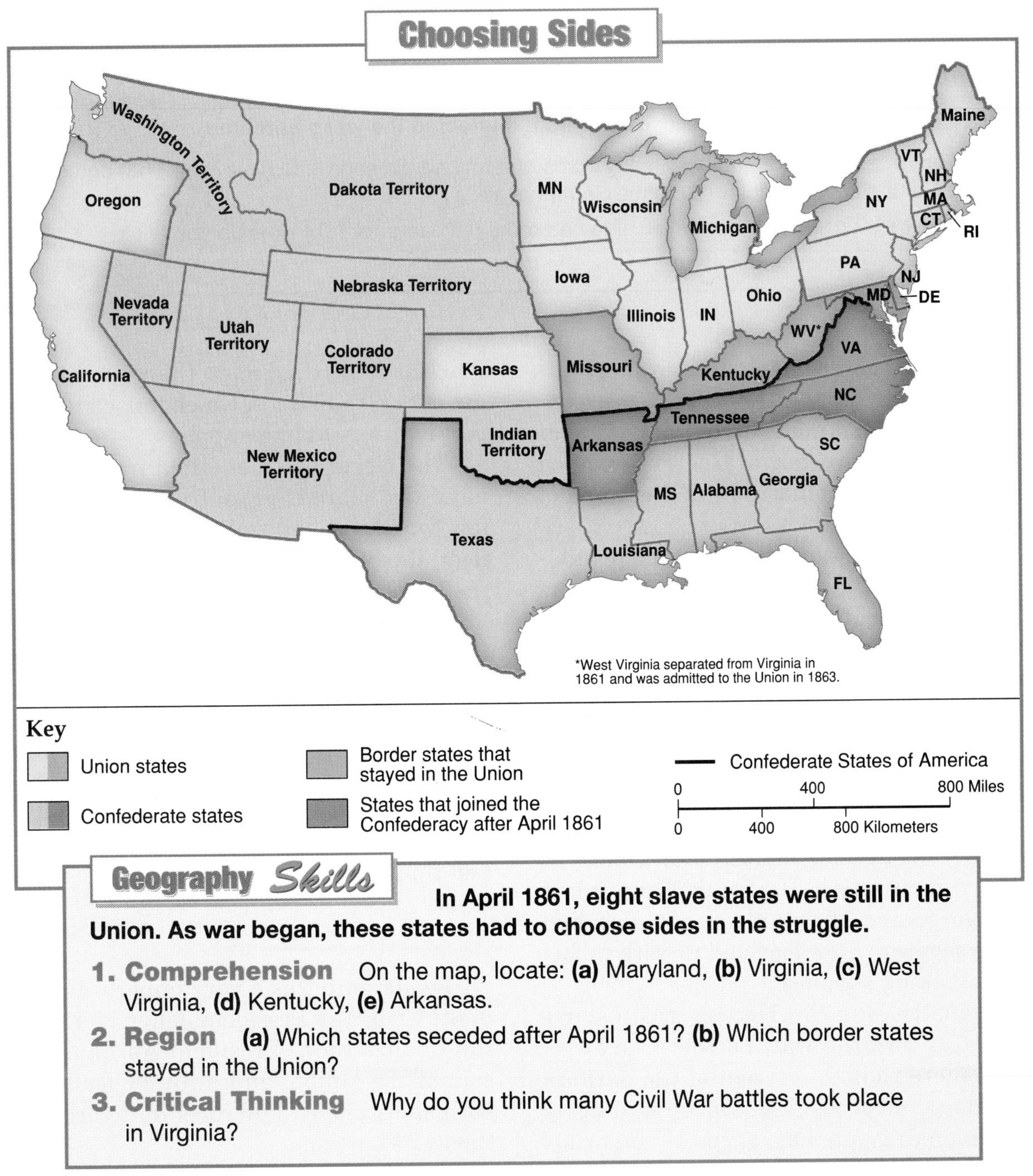

Geography Skills **In April 1861, eight slave states were still in the Union. As war began, these states had to choose sides in the struggle.**

1. **Comprehension** On the map, locate: **(a)** Maryland, **(b)** Virginia, **(c)** West Virginia, **(d)** Kentucky, **(e)** Arkansas.
2. **Region** **(a)** Which states seceded after April 1861? **(b)** Which border states stayed in the Union?
3. **Critical Thinking** Why do you think many Civil War battles took place in Virginia?

Resources of the North and South, 1861

Resources	North		South	
	Number	Percent of Total	Number	Percent of Total
Farmland	105,835 acres	65%	56,832 acres	35%
Railroad Track	21,847 miles	71%	8,947 miles	29%
Value of Manufactured Goods	$1,794,417,000	92%	$155,552,000	8%
Factories	119,500	85%	20,600	15%
Workers in Industry	1,198,000	92%	111,000	8%
Population	22,340,000	63%	9,103,000 (3,954,000 slaves)	37%

Source: *Historical Statistics of the United States*

Chart *Skills* **As the Civil War began, the North enjoyed a number of economic advantages over the South. These advantages affected the war's outcome.**

1. **Comprehension** **(a)** How many acres of farmland did each side have? **(b)** What percentage of the nation's factories did the South have?
2. **Critical Thinking** **(a)** Which side had more railroad track? **(b)** How do you think this advantage affected the war?

Economics $

of the central government. As a result, it was often difficult for the Confederate government to get things done. On one occasion, for example, the governor of Georgia insisted that only Georgia officers be in command of Georgia troops.

Finally, the South had a small population. Only about 9 million people lived in the Confederacy, compared with 22 million in the Union. More than one third of the southern population were enslaved African Americans. As a result, the South did not have enough people to serve as soldiers and to support the war effort.

The North

The North had almost four times as many free citizens as the South. Thus, it had a large source of volunteers. It also had many people to grow food and to work in factories making supplies.

Industry was the North's greatest resource. Before the war, northern factories made more than 90 percent of the nation's manufactured goods. These factories quickly began making supplies for the Union army. The North also had more than 70 percent of the nation's rail lines, which it used to transport both troops and supplies.

The North also benefited from a strong navy and a large fleet of trading ships. With few warships and only a small merchant fleet, the South was unable to compete with the North at sea.

Despite these advantages, the North faced a difficult military challenge. To bring the South back into the Union, northern soldiers had to conquer a huge area. Instead of defending their homes, they were invading unfamiliar land. As Union armies invaded the South, their lines of supply would be much longer than those of the Confederates and thus more open to attack.

Wartime Leaders

Leadership was a very important factor in the Civil War. President Jefferson Davis of the Confederacy, President Abraham Lincoln of the Union, and military leaders on both sides played key roles in determining the war's outcome.

Skills FOR LIFE

Critical Thinking | **Managing Information** | Communication | Maps, Charts, and Graphs

Keeping Files

How Will I Use This Skill ?

A file system is a method for organizing and storing information, usually in a cabinet or on a computer disk. By keeping files, you can save and retrieve information quickly and easily. In school, this skill is useful for research projects. At home, a file system can help organize recipes, coupons, or documents and bills. Finally, you will probably use a file system in your future job or career.

Recipe file

LEARN the Skill

1. Set up and name various file sections. For example, a recipe file would need separate sections for appetizers, entrees, and desserts.
2. Create and label file folders for each section of the file. For example, a dessert section of a recipe file might need one folder for pies and another for cakes.
3. Create or collect the information or material that will be filed.
4. File the informtion or material in the appropriate folders.

PRACTICE the Skill

Read the subsection titled Strengths and Weaknesses on pages 448–450. Use the following steps to file information on the North and South.

1. Create a file system with two sections. Label one section The South. What should you label the other section?
2. For each of the two sections, create a file folder labeled Economy. Create and name two other file folders for each section. (You will have a total of six folders.)
3. For each of the two sections, record two or three facts to go into the Economy file folders. Write each fact on a separate sheet of paper. Place each sheet of paper in the appropriate folder.
4. In the same way, record and file other facts about the North and South.

APPLY the Skill

Create a file system for discount grocery coupons. You might start by making a section for dairy products that includes a folder for yogurt, another for cheese, and a third for butter. Offer your completed file system to someone who uses discount coupons.

President Jefferson Davis

Many people thought Davis was a stronger leader than Lincoln. Davis had attended the United States Military Academy at West Point. He had served as an officer in the Mexican War. Later, he served as Secretary of War. He was widely respected for his honesty and courage.

Davis, however, did not like to turn over to others the details of military planning. When he made a decision, according to his wife, he "could not understand any other man coming to a different conclusion." As a result, Davis spent much time arguing with his advisers.

President Abraham Lincoln

At first, some northerners had doubts about Abraham Lincoln's ability to lead. He had little experience in national politics or military matters. In time, however, Lincoln proved to be a patient but strong leader and a fine war planner.

Day by day, Lincoln gained the respect of those around him. Many especially liked his sense of humor. They noted that Lincoln even accepted criticism with a smile. When Secretary of War Edwin Stanton called Lincoln a fool, Lincoln commented, "Did Stanton say I was a fool? Then I must be one, for Stanton is generally right and he always says what he means."

Military leaders

As the war began, army officers in the South had to make a choice. They could stay in the Union army and fight against their home states, or they could join the Confederate forces.

Robert E. Lee faced this dilemma when his home state of Virginia seceded. President Lincoln asked Lee to command the Union army. Lee refused. He explained in a letter to a friend:

> "I cannot raise my hand against my birthplace, my home, my children. I should like, above all things, that our difficulties might be peaceably arranged.... What ever may be the result of the contest, I foresee that the country will have to pass through a terrible ordeal."

Later, **Robert E. Lee** became commander of the Confederate army. In fact, many of the best officers served for the Confederacy. As a result, President Lincoln had trouble finding generals to match those of the South.

★ Section 1 Review ★

Recall

1. **Locate** **(a)** West Virginia, **(b)** Delaware, **(c)** Kentucky, **(d)** Missouri, **(e)** Maryland.
2. **Identify** **(a)** border states, **(b)** Robert E. Lee.
3. **Define** **(a)** racism, **(b)** martial law.

Comprehension

4. Describe two advantages that the South had over the North at the start of the Civil War.
5. Describe two advantages that the North had over the South at the start of the Civil War.
6. Explain one strength and one weakness of each of the following leaders: **(a)** President Abraham Lincoln, **(b)** President Jefferson Davis.

Critical Thinking and Writing

7. **Identifying Alternatives** List arguments for and against a border state's staying in the Union in 1861.
8. **Analyzing Ideas** Jefferson Davis said this of the Confederacy: "All we ask is to be left alone." **(a)** What do you think Davis meant? **(b)** Why was the Union unwilling to agree to Davis's wish?

Activity **Making a Decision** You are the captain of your hometown school basketball team. A rival school's coach has offered you a scholarship if you will play for them. Write the coach a letter informing him of your decision and the reasons for your decision. As you write your letter, keep in mind Robert E. Lee's difficult choice at the start of the Civil War.

A Long, Difficult Struggle

Explore These Questions

- What were the military plans of each side?
- Which of its military goals did the Union achieve?
- Why did the Union fail to win major battles in the East?

Identify

- Stonewall Jackson
- Battle of Bull Run
- George McClellan
- *Merrimack*
- *Monitor*
- Battle of Antietam
- Battle of Fredericksburg
- Battle of Chancellorsville
- Ulysses S. Grant
- Battle of Shiloh

Union infantry drum

SETTING the Scene In the summer of 1861, the armies of the North and the South marched off to war with flags flying and crowds cheering. Each side expected a quick victory. However, the reality of war soon shattered this dream. Abner Small, a volunteer from Maine, described a scene that would be repeated again and again:

> "I saw...the dead and hurt men lying limp on the ground. From somewhere across the field a battery [heavy guns] pounded us. We wavered, and rallied, and fired blindly; and men fell writhing."

It soon became clear that there would be no quick, easy end to the war. Leaders on both sides began to plan for a long, difficult struggle.

Strategies for Victory

The North and South had different strategies for victory. The Union planned to use its naval power to cripple the South's economy. At the same time, Union armies would invade southern territory. The South, meanwhile, planned to defend itself until the North lost the will to fight.

Union plans

First, the Union planned to use its navy to blockade southern ports. This would cut off the South's supply of manufactured goods by halting its trade with Europe.

In the East, Union generals wanted to seize Richmond, Virginia, the Confederate capital. They thought that they might end the war quickly by capturing the Confederate government.

In the West, the Union planned to seize control of the Mississippi River. This would prevent the South from using the river to supply its troops. It would also separate Arkansas, Texas, and Louisiana from the rest of the Confederacy.

Confederate plans

The South's strategy was simpler: The Confederate army would fight a defensive war until northerners tired of the fighting. If the war became unpopular in the North, President Lincoln would have to stop the war and recognize the South's independence.

The Confederacy counted on European money and supplies to help fight the war. Southern cotton was important to the textile mills of England and other countries. Southerners were confident that Europeans would quickly recognize the Confederacy as an

The Civil War in the East, 1861–1863

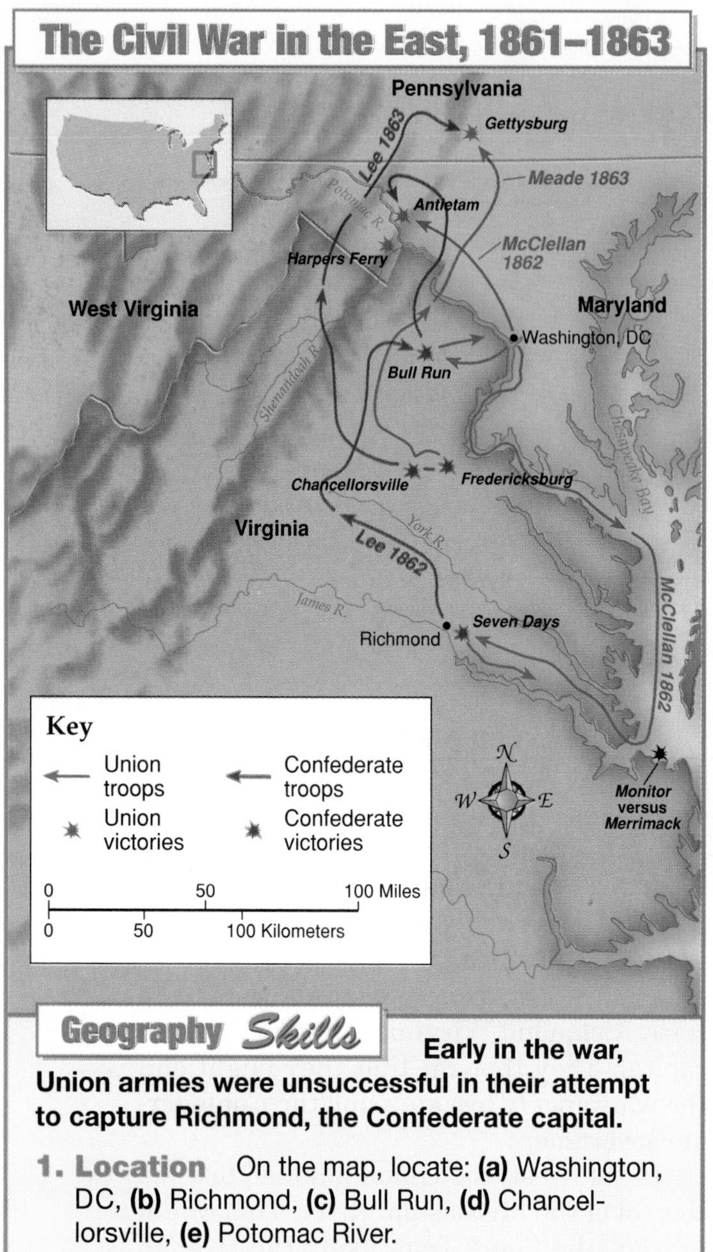

Geography *Skills* **Early in the war, Union armies were unsuccessful in their attempt to capture Richmond, the Confederate capital.**

1. **Location** On the map, locate: **(a)** Washington, DC, **(b)** Richmond, **(c)** Bull Run, **(d)** Chancellorsville, **(e)** Potomac River.
2. **Movement** Describe the route that General McClellan took when he tried to capture Richmond in 1862.
3. **Critical Thinking** Do you think the Confederacy made a wise decision in locating its capital at Richmond? Explain.

independent nation and continue to buy southern cotton for their factories.

Forward to Richmond!

"Forward to Richmond! Forward to Richmond!" Every day for more than a month, the influential *New York Tribune* blazed this "Nation's War Cry" across its front page. Responding to popular pressure for a quick victory, President Lincoln ordered the attack.

Battle of Bull Run

In July 1861, Union troops set out from Washington, D.C., for Richmond, about 100 miles (160 km) away. They met with Confederate soldiers soon after they left. The battle that followed took place near a small stream called Bull Run, in Virginia.

July 21, 1861, was a lovely summer day. Hundreds of Washingtonians rode out to watch their army crush the Confederates. Many carried picnic baskets. In a holiday mood, they spread out on a grassy hilltop overlooking Bull Run and awaited the battle.

The spectators, however, were shocked. Southern troops did not turn and run as expected. Inspired by the example of General Thomas Jackson, they held their ground. A Confederate officer remarked that Jackson stood his ground "like a stone wall." From that day on, the general was known as **"Stonewall" Jackson.**

In the end, it was Union troops who panicked and ran. A congressman who witnessed the retreat reported,

> ❝ Off they went . . . across fields, toward the woods, anywhere, everywhere, to escape. . . . To enable them better to run, they threw away their blankets, knapsacks, canteens, and finally muskets, cartridge-boxes, and everything else. ❞

The Confederates did not pursue the fleeing Union army. Had they done so, they might even have captured Washington, D.C. Instead, they remained behind to gather the gear thrown away by the Union troops.

The **Battle of Bull Run** showed both the Union and the Confederacy that their soldiers needed training. It also showed that the war would be long and bloody.

Caution, delay, and retreat

After the shocking disaster at Bull Run, President Lincoln appointed General **George McClellan** as commander of the Union army of the East, known as the Army of the Potomac. McClellan, a superb

Biography

Robert E. Lee and Stonewall Jackson

Robert E. Lee (left) was perhaps the greatest general of the Civil War. Earlier, he had served admirably in the Mexican War and as superintendent of the United States Military Academy. Stonewall Jackson (right) was one of Lee's most skillful generals. Jackson's clever tactics and swift troop movements contributed to many victories.
★ **How did Jackson earn the nickname of "Stonewall" Jackson?**

organizer, transformed inexperienced recruits into an army of trained soldiers prepared for battle.

McClellan, however, was very cautious. He delayed leading his troops into battle. Newspapers reported "all quiet along the Potomac" so often that the phrase became a national joke. Finally, President Lincoln lost patience. "If McClellan is not using the army," the President snapped, "I should like to borrow it."

Finally, in March 1862, McClellan was ready to move. He and most of his troops left Washington by steamboat and sailed down the Potomac River for Richmond. The rest of the army stayed in Washington.

Landing south of Richmond, McClellan began inching slowly toward the Confederate capital. General Robert E. Lee launched a series of brilliant counterattacks. Lee also sent General Stonewall Jackson north to threaten Washington. Lincoln was thus prevented from sending the rest of the Union army to help McClellan. Cautious as usual, McClellan abandoned the attack and retreated. Once again, there was a lull in the war in the East.

Naval Action

Early in the war, Union ships blockaded southern ports. At first, some small, fast ships slipped through the blockade. These "blockade runners" brought everything from matches to guns into the Confederacy.

In time, however, the blockade became more effective. Trade through southern ports dropped by more than 90 percent. The South desperately needed a way to break the Union blockade. One method it tried was the ironclad ship.

At the start of the war, the Union abandoned a warship named the ***Merrimack*** near Portsmouth, Virginia. Confederates covered the ship with iron plates 4 inches (10.2 cm) thick and sent it into battle against the Union navy. On March 8, 1862, the *Merrimack* sank one Union ship, drove another aground, and forced a third to surrender. The Union vessels' cannonballs bounced harmlessly off the *Merrimack's* metal skin.

The Union countered with its own ironclads. One of these, the ***Monitor,*** battled the *Merrimack* in the waters off Hampton Roads, Virginia. The Confederate ship had more firepower, but the *Monitor* maneuvered more easily. In the end, neither ship seriously damaged the other, and both withdrew.

Ironclad ships changed naval warfare. Both sides rushed to build more of them. However, the South never mounted a serious attack against the Union navy. The Union blockade held throughout the war.

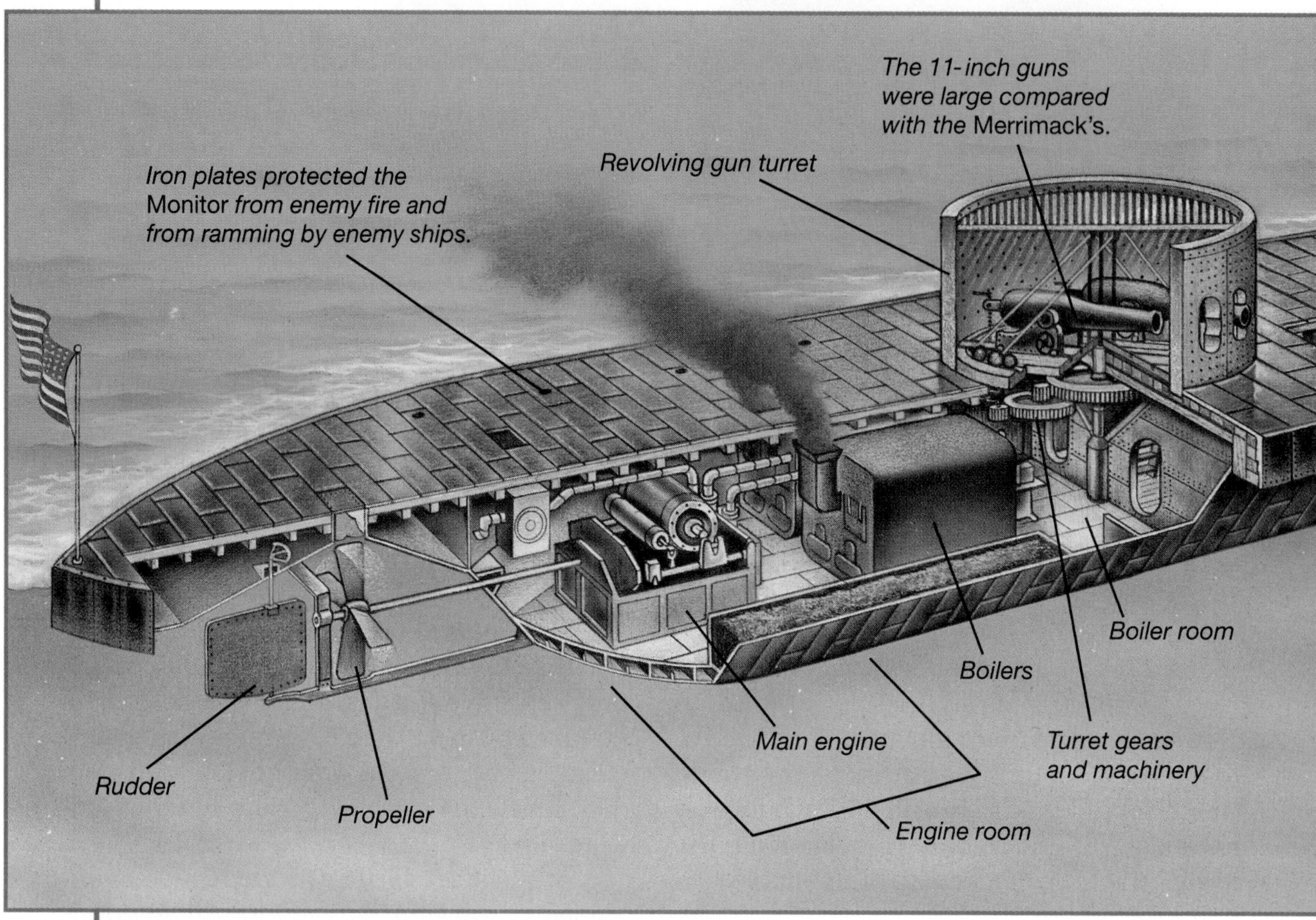

Antietam

In September 1862, General Lee took the offensive and marched his troops north into Maryland. He believed that a southern victory on northern soil would be a great blow to northern morale.

Luck was against Lee, however. A Confederate messenger lost Lee's battle plans. Two Union soldiers found them and turned them over to General McClellan.

Even with Lee's battle plan before him, however, McClellan was slow to act. After waiting a few days, he finally attacked Lee's main force at Antietam (an TEE tuhm) on September 17. In the day-long battle that followed, more than 23,000 Union and Confederate soldiers were killed or wounded.

On the night of September 18, Lee ordered his troops to slip back into Virginia. The Confederates breathed a sigh of relief when they saw that McClellan was not pursuing them.

Neither side was a clear winner at the **Battle of Antietam.** The North was able to claim victory, though, because Lee had ordered his forces to withdraw. As a result, northern morale increased. Still, President Lincoln was keenly disappointed. The Union army had suffered huge numbers of dead and wounded. Furthermore, General McClellan had failed to follow up his victory by pursuing

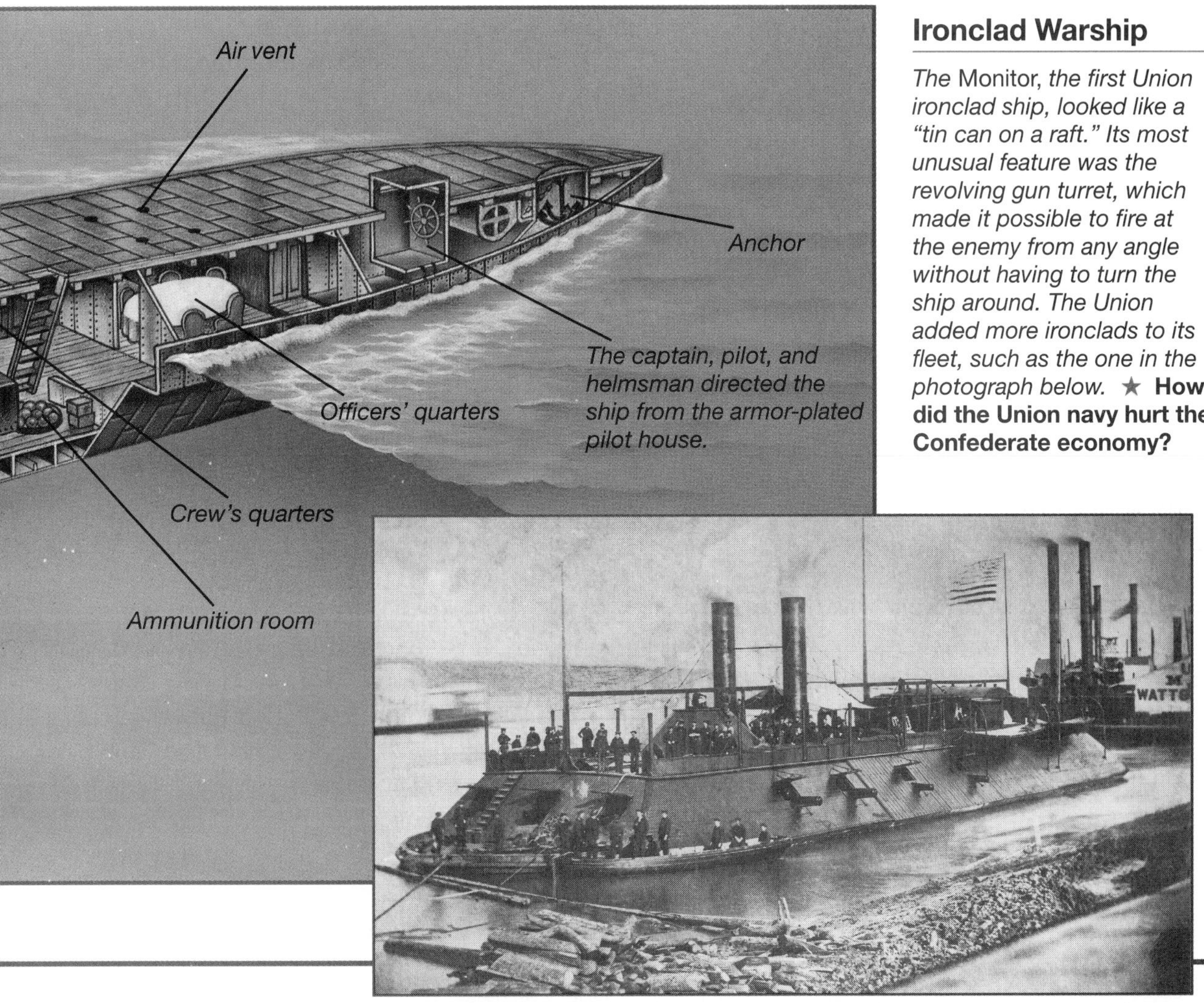

Ironclad Warship

The Monitor, *the first Union ironclad ship, looked like a "tin can on a raft." Its most unusual feature was the revolving gun turret, which made it possible to fire at the enemy from any angle without having to turn the ship around. The Union added more ironclads to its fleet, such as the one in the photograph below.* ★ **How did the Union navy hurt the Confederate economy?**

the Confederates. In November, Lincoln appointed General Ambrose Burnside to replace McClellan as commander of the Army of the Potomac.

Confederate Victories

Two stunning victories for the Confederacy came in late 1862 and 1863. (See the map on page 454.) General Robert E. Lee won by outsmarting the Union generals who fought against him.

Fredericksburg

In December 1862, Union forces set out once again toward Richmond. This time, they were led by General Ambrose Burnside.

Meeting Lee's army outside Fredericksburg, Virginia, Burnside ordered his troops to attack. Lee pulled back and left the town to Burnside. The Confederates dug in at the crest of a treeless hill above Fredericksburg. There, in a strong defensive position, they waited for the Union attack.

As the Union soldiers advanced, Confederate guns mowed them down by the thousands. Six times Burnside ordered his men to charge. Six times the rebels drove them back. "We forgot they were fighting us," one southerner wrote, "and cheer after cheer at their fearlessness went up along our lines." The **Battle of Fredericksburg** was one of the Union's worst defeats.

Chancellorsville

In May 1863, Lee, aided by Stonewall Jackson, again outwitted the Union army. This time, the battle took place on thickly wooded ground near Chancellorsville, Virginia. Lee and Jackson defeated the Union troops in three days.

Although the South won the **Battle of Chancellorsville,** it paid a high price for the victory. At the end of one day, nervous Confederate sentries fired at what they thought was an approaching Union soldier. The "Union soldier" was General Stonewall Jackson. Jackson died as a result of his injuries several days later.

The War in the West

While Union forces struggled in the East, those in the West met with success. As you have read, the Union strategy was to seize control of the Mississippi River. General **Ulysses S. Grant** began moving toward that goal. (See the map on page 470.) In February 1862, Grant attacked and captured Fort Henry and Fort Donelson in Tennessee. These Confederate forts guarded two important tributaries of the Mississippi.

Grant now pushed south to Shiloh, a village on the Tennessee River. At Shiloh, on April 6, he was surprised by Confederate forces. The Confederates won the first day of the **Battle of Shiloh.** They drove the Union troops back toward the river.

Grant now showed the toughness and determination that would enable him to win many battles in the future. "Retreat?" he replied to his doubting officers after that first day. "No. I propose to attack at daylight and whip them."

With the aid of reinforcements, Grant was able to win his victory and beat back the Confederates. However, the Battle of Shiloh was one of the bloodiest encounters of the Civil War. More Americans were killed or wounded at Shiloh than in the American Revolution, the War of 1812, and the Mexican War combined.

While Grant was fighting at Shiloh, the Union navy moved to gain control of the Mississippi River. In April 1862, Union gunboats captured New Orleans. Other ships seized Memphis, Tennessee. By capturing these two cities, the Union controlled both ends of the Mississippi. No longer could the South use the river as a supply line.

★ Section 2 Review ★

Recall

1. **Locate** **(a)** Richmond, **(b)** Washington, D.C., **(c)** Potomac River, **(d)** Fort Henry, **(e)** Fort Donelson, **(f)** New Orleans, **(g)** Memphis.
2. **Identify** **(a)** Stonewall Jackson, **(b)** Battle of Bull Run, **(c)** George McClellan, **(d)** *Merrimack,* **(e)** *Monitor,* **(f)** Battle of Antietam, **(g)** Battle of Fredericksburg, **(h)** Battle of Chancellorsville, **(i)** Ulysses S. Grant, **(j)** Battle of Shiloh.

Comprehension

3. **(a)** Describe the North's three-part plan for defeating the South. **(b)** Which part of the plan did the North achieve first?
4. Why was President Lincoln unhappy with General McClellan's performance as commander of the Union armies?
5. How did the loss of New Orleans and Memphis affect the South?

Critical Thinking and Writing

6. **Analyzing Primary Sources** In response to Stonewall Jackson's death, General Lee said, "I have lost my right arm." What did Lee mean by this statement?
7. **Analyzing Visual Evidence** Study the ironclad ships on pages 456-457. Explain how such ships were superior to wooden sailing ships.

Activity **Making a Map** You are the chief cartographer for the Union army. Your assignment is to make a map illustrating the Union's three-part plan for defeating the South.

A Promise of Freedom

As You Read

Explore These Questions
- Why did Lincoln issue the Emancipation Proclamation?
- What were the effects of the Proclamation?
- How did African Americans contribute to the Union war effort?

Define
- emancipate
- discrimination

Identify
- Emancipation Proclamation
- 54th Massachusetts Regiment
- Fort Wagner

Antislavery potholders

At first, the Civil War was not a war against slavery. Yet wherever Union troops went, enslaved African Americans eagerly rushed to them, expecting to be freed. Most were sorely disappointed. Union officers often held these runaways until their masters arrived to take them back to slavery.

Some northerners began to raise questions. Was slavery not the root of the conflict between North and South? Were tens of thousands of men dying so that a slaveholding South would come back into the Union? Questions like these led Northerners to wonder what the real aim of the war should be.

Lincoln Was Cautious

The Civil War began as a war to restore the Union, not to end the institution of slavery. President Lincoln made this clear in the following statement.

> "If I could save the Union without freeing any slave, I would do it; and if I could save it by freeing all the slaves, I would do it; and if I could do it by freeing some and leaving others alone, I would also do that."

Lincoln had a reason for handling the slavery issue cautiously. As you have read, four slave states remained in the Union. The President did not want to do anything that might cause these states to shift their loyalty to the Confederacy. The resources of the border states might allow the South to turn the tide of the war.

The Emancipation Proclamation

By mid-1862, however, Lincoln came to believe that he could save the Union only by broadening the goals of the war. He decided to **emancipate,** or free, enslaved African Americans living in the Confederacy. In the four loyal slave states, however, slaves would not be freed. Nor would slaves be freed in Confederate lands that had already been captured by the Union, such as the city of New Orleans.

Motives and timing

Lincoln had practical reasons for his emancipation plan. At the start of the Civil War, more than 3 million enslaved people labored for the Confederacy. They helped grow the food that fed Confederate soldiers. They also worked in iron and lead mines that were vital to the South's war effort. Some served as nurses and cooks for the army. Lincoln knew that emancipation would weaken the Confederacy's ability to carry on the war.

However, Lincoln did not want to anger slave owners in the Union. Also, he knew that many northerners opposed freedom for

Viewing History **The Emancipation Proclamation**

The Emancipation Proclamation meant that Union troops were now fighting to end slavery. Lincoln's action, however, did not please all northerners. Opposition to the preliminary proclamation contributed to Republican party losses in the Congressional elections of 1862.

★ **How does this poster make use of symbolism?**

enslaved African Americans. Lincoln therefore hoped to introduce the idea of emancipation slowly, by limiting it to territory controlled by the Confederacy.

The President had another very important motive, too. As you read in Chapter 16, Lincoln believed that slavery was wrong. When he felt that he could act to free slaves without threatening the Union, he did so.

Lincoln was concerned about the timing of his announcement. The war was not going well for the Union. He did not want Americans to think he was freeing slaves as a desperate effort to save a losing cause. He waited for a victory to announce his plan.

Freedom proclaimed

On September 22, 1862, five days after the Union victory at Antietam, Lincoln issued a preliminary proclamation. It warned that on January 1, 1863, anyone held as a slave in a state still in rebellion against the United States would be emancipated.

Then, on January 1, 1863, Lincoln issued the formal Emancipation Proclamation. The **Emancipation Proclamation** declared:

> "On the 1st day of January, in the year of our Lord 1863, all persons held as slaves within any state or... part of a state [whose] people... shall then be in rebellion against the United States, shall be then, thenceforward, and forever free."

Impact of the Proclamation

Because the rebelling states were not under Union control, no slaves actually gained their freedom on January 1, 1863. Nevertheless, as a result of the Emancipation Proclamation, the purpose of the war changed. Now, Union troops were fighting to end slavery as well as to save the Union.

The opponents of slavery greeted the proclamation with joy. In Boston, African American abolitionist Frederick Douglass witnessed one of the many emotional celebrations that took place:

> "The effect of this announcement was startling... and the scene was wild and grand.... My old friend Rue, a Negro preacher,... expressed the heartfelt emotion of the hour, when he led all voices in the anthem, 'Sound the loud timbrel o'er Egypt's dark sea, Jehovah hath triumphed, his people are free!'"

Connections With Arts

Many northerners greeted the Emancipation Proclamation with music and song. At Boston's Music Hall, people celebrated with performances of Mendelssohn's *Hymn of Praise*, and Handel's *Hallelujah Chorus*.

The Proclamation won the Union the sympathy of people in Europe, especially workers. As a result, it became less likely that Britain or any other European country would come to the aid of the South.

African Americans Help

When the war began, thousands of free blacks volunteered to fight for the Union. At first, federal law forbade African Americans to serve as soldiers. When Congress repealed that law in 1862, however, both free African Americans and escaped slaves enlisted in the Union army.

In the Union army

The army assigned these volunteers to all-black units, commanded by white officers. At first, the black troops served only as laborers. They performed noncombat duties such as building roads and guarding supplies. Black troops received only half the pay of white soldiers.

African American soldiers protested against this policy of **discrimination** that denied them the same rights and treatment as other soldiers. Gradually, conditions changed. By 1863, African American troops were fighting in major battles against the Confederates. In 1864, the United States War Department announced that all soldiers would receive equal pay. By the end of the war, about 200,000 African Americans had fought for the Union. Nearly 40,000 lost their lives.

Acts of bravery

One of the most famous African American units in the Union army was the **54th Massachusetts Regiment.** The 54th accepted African Americans from all across the

Viewing History **Assault on Fort Wagner**

In this painting by Tom Lovell, African American soldiers of the 54th Massachussetts Regiment charge against Confederate troops at Fort Wagner. Nearly half the regiment died in the failed attack, including the regiment's commander, Colonel Robert Gould Shaw. ★ **Why do you think the Union army was reluctant to appoint African American officers?**

North. Frederick Douglass helped recruit troops for the regiment, and two of his sons served in it.

On July 18, 1863, the 54th Massachusetts Regiment led an attack on **Fort Wagner** near Charleston. Under heavy fire, troops fought their way into the fort before being forced to withdraw. In the desperate fighting, almost half the regiment, including its young commander, Robert Shaw, were killed.

The courage of the 54th Massachusetts and other regiments helped to win respect for African American soldiers. Sergeant William Carney of the 54th Massachusetts was awarded the Congressional Medal of Honor for acts of bravery. He was the first of 16 African American soldiers to be so honored during the Civil War. In a letter to President Lincoln, Secretary of War Stanton praised African American soldiers.

> "[They] have proved themselves among the bravest of the brave, performing deeds of daring and shedding their blood with a heroism unsurpassed by soldiers of any race."

Behind Confederate lines

In the South, despite the Emancipation Proclamation, African Americans still had to work as slaves on plantations. However, many enslaved African Americans slowed down their work. Others refused to work at all or to submit to punishment. In so doing, they knew they were helping to weaken the South's war effort. They knew that when victorious Union troops arrived in their area, they would be free.

Throughout the South, thousands of enslaved African Americans also took direct action to free themselves. Whenever a Union army appeared in an area, the slaves from all around would flee their former masters. They crossed over to the Union lines and to freedom. By the end of the war, about one fourth of the enslaved population in the South had escaped to freedom.

The former slaves helped Union armies achieve victory in a variety of ways. They used their knowledge of the local terrain to serve as guides and spies. Many more enlisted in African American regiments of the Union army.

★ Section 3 Review ★

Recall

1. **Identify** **(a)** Emancipation Proclamation, **(b)** 54th Massachusetts Regiment, **(c)** Fort Wagner.
2. **Define** **(a)** emancipate, **(b)** discrimination.

Comprehension

3. **(a)** Why was President Lincoln cautious about making emancipation a goal of the war? **(b)** Why did he finally decide to issue the Emancipation Proclamation?
4. Why were no slaves actually freed when the Proclamation was issued?
5. **(a)** How did the 54th Massachussetts Regiment's attack on Fort Wagner affect public opinion about enslaved African American soldiers? **(b)** How did African Americans help to weaken the Confederacy?

Critical Thinking and Writing

6. **Drawing Conclusions** What did the Union army's policy toward all-black regiments reveal about northern attitudes toward African Americans? Explain.
7. **Analyzing Primary Sources** In 1861, Frederick Douglass said, "This is no time to fight with one hand when both hands are needed. This is no time to fight with only your white hand, and allow your black hand to remain tied!" **(a)** What did Douglass mean by this statement? **(b)** Did the United States Congress agree with Douglass? Explain.

Activity **Writing a Poem** A monument is being built to honor the courageous African American soldiers of the Civil War. Write a poem to be engraved on the monument, mentioning some of the facts you have learned in this section.

Hardships of War

Explore These Questions

- What was life like for soldiers in the Civil War?
- How did women contribute to the war effort?
- What problems did each side face during the war?

Define

- civilians
- draft
- habeas corpus
- income tax
- inflation
- profiteer

Identify

- Copperheads
- Loreta Janeta Velazquez
- Rose Greenhow
- Dorothea Dix
- Clara Barton
- Sojourner Truth
- Sally Tompkins

The Civil War caused hardships not only for soldiers but for people at home as well. Southerners, especially, suffered from the war, because most of the fighting took place in the South.

On both sides, **civilians,** or people who were not in the army, worked on farms and labored in factories to support the war effort. They used their mules to move troops and supplies. They tended the wounded. As their hardships increased, so did opposition to the war.

The Hard Life of Soldiers

On both sides, most soldiers were under age 21. However, war quickly turned gentle boys into tough men. Soldiers drilled and marched for long hours. They slept on the ground even in rain and snow. In combat, boys of 18 learned to stand firm as cannon blasts shook the earth and bullets whizzed past their ears.

New technology added to the horror of war. Cone-shaped bullets, which made rifles twice as accurate, replaced round musket balls. New cannons could hurl exploding shells several miles. The new weapons had deadly results. In most battles, one fourth or more of the soldiers were killed or wounded.

Sick and wounded soldiers faced other horrors. Medical care on the battlefield was crude. Surgeons routinely cut off injured arms and legs. Minor wounds often became infected. With no medicines to fight infection, thousands of wounded died. Diseases like pneumonia and malaria killed more men than guns or cannons did.

▲ *Confederate cap*

▲ *Union cap*

On both sides, prisoners of war faced horrifying conditions. At Andersonville, a prison camp in Georgia, more than one Union prisoner out of three died of disease or starvation. One prisoner wrote:

> "There is no such thing as delicacy here.... In the middle of last night I was awakened by being kicked by a dying man. He was soon dead. I got up and moved the body off a few feet, and went to sleep to dream of the hideous sights."

Discontent in the North

Some northerners opposed using force to keep the South in the Union. Supporters of the war called these people **Copperheads,** after the poisonous snake. Other northerners supported the war but opposed the way Lincoln was conducting it. In some northern cities, this opposition led to riots.

Viewing HISTORY **The Faces of War**

Confederate soldiers wore gray uniforms and were sometimes called Johnny Rebs. Union soldiers wore blue and were called Billy Yanks. During the Civil War, about 1 of every 10 soldiers deserted from service. ★ **Why do you think desertion rates were high in both armies?**

The draft law

As the war dragged on, public support dwindled. Soon, not enough men were volunteering to serve in the Union army. The government took action.

In 1863, Congress passed a **draft** law. It required all able-bodied males between the ages of 20 and 45 to serve in the military if they were called.

Under the law, a man could avoid the draft by paying the government $300 or by hiring someone to serve in his place. This angered many people. They began to see the Civil War as "a rich man's war and a poor man's fight."

Riots in the cities

Opposition to the draft law led to riots in several northern cities. The draft law had gone into effect soon after Lincoln issued the Emancipation Proclamation. As a result, some northerners believed that they were being forced to fight to end slavery. This idea angered some white workers, especially recent immigrants in the cities. Like many other northerners, some of these immigrants held racist beliefs. They also feared that free African Americans would be employed at jobs that they needed, too.

The worst riot took place in New York City during July 1863. For four days, white workers attacked free blacks. Rioters also attacked rich New Yorkers who had paid to avoid serving in the army. At least 74 people were killed during the riot.

President Lincoln moved to stop the riots and other "disloyal practices." Several times, he denied **habeas corpus** (HAY bee uhs KOR puhs), the right to have charges filed or a hearing before being jailed. Lincoln defended his actions by saying that the Constitution gave him the right to deny people their rights "when in the cases of rebellion or invasion, the public safety may require it."

Problems in the South

President Davis, meanwhile, struggled to create a strong federal government for the Confederacy. Many southerners were strong supporters of states' rights. They resisted paying taxes to a central government. At one point, Georgia threatened to secede from the Confederacy!

Like the North, the South had to pass a draft law to fill its army. However, men who owned or supervised more than 20 slaves did not have to serve in the army. Southern farmers who owned few or no slaves resented this law.

Near war's end, the South no longer had enough white men to fill the ranks. Robert E. Lee urged that enslaved African Americans be allowed to serve as soldiers. Desperate, the Confederate congress finally agreed. However, the war ended before any enslaved people put on Confederate uniforms.

Why Study History?

Because One Person Can Make a Difference

Historical Background

In the early days of the Civil War, Clara Barton and other women provided medical care to wounded soldiers. However, the government required women to stay far from battle. As a result, many soldiers received treatment too late and died of their wounds. Barton therefore sought permission to work directly on the fields of battle.

After some initial refusals, the government gave in. Through the remainder of the war, Clara Barton served as a battlefield nurse. Because of her courageous efforts, she became known as the "Angel of the Battlefield."

Connections to Today

After the Civil War, Barton continued to make a difference. In Europe, she worked with the International Red Cross, an organization that aided victims of war. In 1881, after returning to the United States, she founded the American Red Cross. This new organization served both victims of war and victims of natural disaster.

Today, disaster relief remains a primary service of the Red Cross. The Red Cross helps people recover from natural disasters such as fires, floods, and hurricanes. It provides victims with medical assistance, food, clothing, and shelter.

The American Red Cross provides other services as well. It helps homeless people and seniors in need. It supervises donations of blood and other organs. It also provides instruction in a variety of safety programs.

Connections to You

Like Clara Barton, you too can make a difference. You can learn about first aid and safety procedures in a Red Cross educational course. Courses include first aid, water safety, fire prevention, and even babysitting. Some local Red Cross chapters invite teens to serve as volunteers. You might also organize or participate in a drive to help raise funds for the Red Cross. Red Cross disaster relief services are provided free of charge because of contributions made by caring Americans.

▲ *Clara Barton*

▲ *Red Cross book*

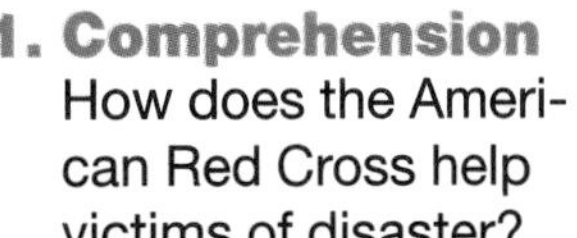

1. **Comprehension** How does the American Red Cross help victims of disaster?
2. **Critical Thinking** At the start of the Civil War, why do you think government officials allowed men, but not women, to aid wounded soldiers on the field of battle?

★Activity **Making an Advertisement** Create an advertisement that seeks public support for the Red Cross by informing people about the many services the Red Cross provides.

Viewing History **Nursing the Wounded**

In this Civil War scene, painted by Allyn Cox, women are nursing the wounded in the rotunda of the Capitol building. During the war, many public buildings served as temporary hospitals. The painting decorates a corridor of the Capitol today. ★ **How else did women help in the war effort?**

The Northern Economy

The Civil War cost far more than any earlier war. The Union had to use several strategies to raise money. In some ways, though, war helped the North's economy.

Taxation and inflation

In 1861, to pay for the war, Congress established the nation's first **income tax** on people's earnings. In addition, the Union issued bonds worth millions of dollars. Still, taxes and bonds did not raise enough money. To get the funds it needed, the North printed more than $400 million in paper money.

As the money supply increased, each dollar was worth less. In response, businesses charged more for their goods. The North was experiencing **inflation,** a rise in prices and a decrease in the value of money. During the war, prices for goods nearly doubled in the North.

Economic benefits

In some ways, the war helped the North's economy. Because many farmers went off to fight, more machines were used to plant and harvest crops. As a result, farm production actually went up during the war.

The wartime demand for clothing, shoes, guns, and other goods helped many northern industries. Some manufacturers made fortunes by profiteering. **Profiteers** charged excessive prices for goods the government desperately needed for the war.

The Southern Economy

For the South, war brought economic ruin. The South had to struggle with the cost of the war, the loss of the cotton trade, and severe shortages brought on by the Union blockade.

The economy suffers

To raise money, the Confederacy imposed an income tax and a tax-in-kind. The tax-in-kind required farmers to turn over one tenth of their crops to the government. The government took crops because it knew that southern farmers had little money.

Like the North, the South printed paper money. It printed so much, in fact, that wild inflation set in. By 1865, one Confederate dollar was worth only two cents in gold.

The war did serious damage to the cotton trade, the South's main source of income. Early in the war, President Davis halted cotton shipments to Britain. He hoped that Britain would side with the South in order to get cotton. The tactic backfired. Britain simply bought more cotton from Egypt and

$ Connections With Economics

As inflation in the South worsened, it became more and more difficult to feed and clothe a family. Near the end of the war, a barrel of flour cost $1,000 and a pair of shoes cost $400.

India. Davis succeeded only in cutting the South's income.

Effects of the blockade

The Union blockade created severe shortages in the South. Confederate armies sometimes had to wait weeks for supplies of food and clothing. Guns and ammunition were also in short supply. With few factories of its own, the South bought many of its weapons in Europe. However, the blockade cut off most deliveries from Europe.

For civilians, the blockade brought food shortages. Even the wealthy went hungry. "I had a little piece of bread and a little molasses today for my dinner," wrote plantation mistress Mary Chesnut in her diary. By 1865, there was widespread famine in the Confederacy.

Women at War

Women of both the North and South played vital roles during the war. As men left for the battlefields, women took jobs in industry, in teaching, and on farms.

Women and the military

Women's aid societies helped supply the troops with food, bedding, clothing, and medicine. Throughout the North, women held fairs and other fund-raising events to pay for the supplies. They succeeded in raising millions of dollars.

A few women disguised themselves so they could serve as soldiers. **Loreta Janeta Velazquez,** for example, fought for the South at Bull Run and Shiloh. Other women worked as spies. **Rose Greenhow** gathered information for the South while entertaining Union leaders in her Washington, D.C., home. She was caught, convicted of treason, and exiled.

Nursing the wounded

Women on both sides worked as nurses. Doctors were unwilling at first to permit even trained nurses to work in military hospitals. When wounded men began to swamp army hospitals, however, this attitude soon changed.

Dorothea Dix, famous for her work reforming prisons and mental hospitals, became superintendent of nurses for the Union army. **Clara Barton** earned fame as a Civil War nurse. She later founded the American Red Cross. **Sojourner Truth,** the African American antislavery leader, worked in Union hospitals and in camps for freed slaves. In the South, **Sally Tompkins** set up a hospital in Richmond, Virginia.

★ Section 4 Review ★

Recall

1. **Identify** **(a)** Copperheads, **(b)** Loreta Janeta Velazquez, **(c)** Rose Greenhow, **(d)** Dorothea Dix, **(e)** Clara Barton, **(f)** Sojourner Truth, **(g)** Sally Tompkins.
2. **Define** **(a)** civilians, **(b)** draft, **(c)** habeas corpus, **(d)** income tax, **(e)** inflation, **(f)** profiteer.

Comprehension

3. Describe three hardships faced by soldiers during the Civil War.
4. Describe three ways women contributed to the war effort.
5. How did the Union blockade affect the South?

Critical Thinking and Writing

6. **Linking Past and Present** **(a)** What advances in technology made Civil War battles deadly? **(b)** In what ways would a war today be even more deadly?
7. **Defending a Position** What facts support the charge that the Civil War was "a rich man's war and a poor man's fight"?

Activity **Making a Chart** You are the graphic illustrator for an economics magazine. Create a flowchart or cause-and-effect chart to illustrate how the high cost of the Civil War led to high inflation.

The War Ends

As You Read

Explore These Questions

- What was the significance of the Union victories at Vicksburg and Gettysburg?
- What ideals did Lincoln express in the Gettysburg Address?
- How did Union generals use a new type of war to defeat the Confederacy?

Define

- siege
- total war

Identify

- Battle of Gettysburg
- Gettysburg Address
- Ulysses S. Grant
- Philip Sheridan
- William Tecumseh Sherman

As you have read, Confederate armies won major battles at Fredericksburg in December 1862 and at Chancellorsville in May 1863. These were gloomy days for the North.

Then, in July 1863, the tide of war turned against the South. In the West, the Union extended its control of the Mississippi River and cut the South in two. At the Battle of Gettysburg, in Pennsylvania, both Union and Confederate forces suffered terrible losses. However, as President Davis later explained, "Theirs could be repaired, ours could not."

The following year, President Lincoln would appoint Ulysses S. Grant commander in chief of the Union army. In Grant, Lincoln had found the general who could lead the Union to victory.

The Fall of Vicksburg

After capturing New Orleans and Memphis, the Union controlled both ends of the Mississippi River. Still, the North could not safely use the river because Confederates held Vicksburg, Mississippi. Vicksburg sat on a cliff high above the river. Cannons there could shell boats traveling between New Orleans and Memphis.

Early in 1863, Grant's forces tried again and again to seize Vicksburg. The Confederates held out bravely. At last, Grant devised a brilliant plan. Marching his troops inland, he launched a surprise attack on Jackson, Mississippi. Then, he turned west and attacked Vicksburg from the rear. (See the map on page 470.)

For over six weeks, Grant's forces lay siege to Vicksburg. A **siege** is a military blockade of an enemy town or position in order to force it to surrender. Day after day, the Union soldiers pushed their lines closer to the town. Union artillery and gunboats on the Mississippi bombarded the besieged soldiers and inhabitants. As their food supplies ran out, the southerners began to use mules and rats as food. Finally, on July 4, 1863, the Confederates surrendered Vicksburg.

On July 9, Union forces also captured Port Hudson, Louisiana. The entire Mississippi was now under Union control. The Confederacy was split into two parts. Texas, Arkansas, and Louisiana were cut off from the rest of the Confederacy.

Union Victory at Gettysburg

In the East, after his victory at Chancellorsville, General Lee moved his army north into Pennsylvania. He hoped to take the Yankees by surprise. If he was successful, Lee planned to then swing south and capture Washington, D.C.

American Heritage
M A G A Z I N E

HISTORY HAPPENED HERE

Ohio regiment monument

Vicksburg National Military Park

You can learn about the siege of Vicksburg, Mississippi, by touring the actual battle site. The park includes a museum, miles of defensive earthworks, and more than 125 cannons. You can even walk the deck of a Union ironclad gunboat, raised from the Mississippi River in the 1960s. Throughout the park, numerous monuments honor the soldiers who fought and died for control of this small Mississippi River town.

★ ***To learn more about this historic site, write:*** *Vicksburg National Military Park, 3201 Clay Street, Vicksburg, MS 39180.*

On June 30, 1863, a Union force under General George C. Meade met part of Lee's army at the small town of Gettysburg, Pennsylvania. Both sides quickly sent in reinforcements. The three-day Battle of Gettysburg that followed was one of the most important battles of the Civil War.

At the start of the battle, the Confederates drove the Union forces out of Gettysburg. The Yankees took up strong positions on Cemetery Ridge, overlooking the town. On July 2, a Confederate attack failed with heavy casualties. Nevertheless, Lee decided to launch another attack. On July 3, he ordered General George Pickett to lead 15,000 men in a daring charge against the center of the Union line. To reach the Yankees, Pickett's men had to cross an open field and run up a steep slope.

Pickett gave the order to charge and the Union guns opened fire. Row after row of soldiers fell to the ground, bleeding. Still, the Confederate troops continued to rush forward against a rain of bullets and shells. Few were able to reach the Union lines. A Union soldier described the fighting at the crest of the ridge:

> "Men fire into each other's faces not five feet apart. There are bayonet thrusts, saber strokes, pistol shots, men going down on their hands and knees... gulping blood, falling, legless, armless, headless."

Pickett's charge failed. As the survivors limped back, Lee rode among them. "It's all my fault," he admitted humbly. Lee had no choice but to retreat. After their defeat at the **Battle of Gettysburg,** the Confederates would never again invade the North.

The Union victories at Vicksburg and Gettysburg marked the turning point of the Civil War. On July 4, 1863, northerners had good reason to celebrate.

The Gettysburg Address

The Battle of Gettysburg left more than 40,000 dead or wounded. When the soldiers who died there were buried, their graves stretched as far as the eye could see. On November 19, 1863, northerners held a ceremony to dedicate this cemetery.

President Lincoln attended the ceremony, but he was not the main speaker. At the time, his popularity was quite low. Lincoln sat with his hands folded as another speaker talked for two hours. When it was his turn, the President rose and spoke for about three minutes.

In his **Gettysburg Address,** Lincoln said that the Civil War was a test of whether or not a democratic nation could survive. He reminded Americans that their nation was founded on the belief that "all men are created equal." Looking out at the thousands of graves, Lincoln told the audience:

> "We here highly resolve that these dead shall not have died in vain—that this nation, under God, shall have a new birth of freedom—and that government of the people, by the people, for the people, shall not perish from the earth."

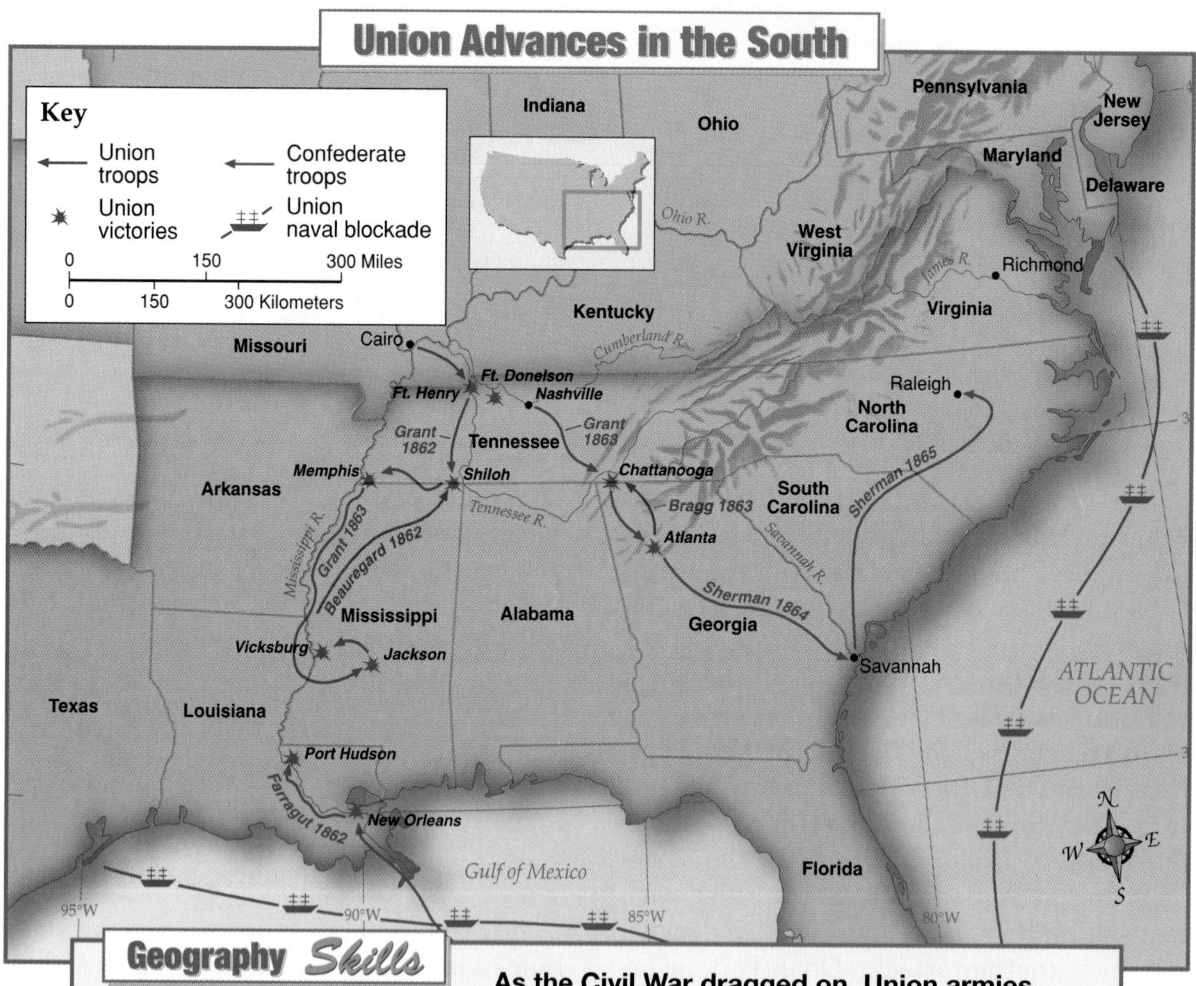

Geography Skills **As the Civil War dragged on, Union armies advanced deeper and deeper into the South. General Sherman marched his troops through Georgia and the Carolinas.**

1. **Location** On the map, locate: **(a)** Vicksburg, **(b)** Atlanta, **(c)** Savannah.
2. **Place** What three Confederate states were cut off from the rest of the Confederacy after Union forces gained control of the Mississippi River?
3. **Critical Thinking** Based on the map, why would the South be hurt more than the North—no matter who won the war?

Few people listened to Lincoln that day. Newspapers gave his speech little attention. Later generations, however, have honored Lincoln's brief address as a profound statement of American ideals.

The Union Wages Total War

For three years, Lincoln had searched for a general who could lead the Union to victory. More and more, he thought of **Ulysses S. Grant.** After capturing Vicksburg, Grant continued to win battles in the West. In 1864, Lincoln appointed him commander of the Union forces.

Some questioned the choice, but President Lincoln felt that "Unconditional Surrender" Grant was the general who would lead the Union to victory. "I can't spare this man," Lincoln said. "He fights."

Grant and other Union generals began to wage **total war** against the South. In total war, civilians as well as soldiers are affected. The Union army waged total war by destroying food and equipment that might be useful to the enemy. Civilians in the South suffered the same hardships as soldiers.

Sheridan in the Shenandoah

Grant had a plan for ending the war. He wanted to destroy the South's ability to fight. Grant sent General **Philip Sheridan** and his cavalry into the rich farmland of Virginia's Shenandoah Valley. He instructed Sheridan:

> "Leave nothing to invite the enemy to return. Destroy whatever cannot be consumed. Let the valley be left so that crows flying over it will have to carry their rations along with them."

Sheridan obeyed. In the summer and fall of 1864, he marched through the valley, destroying farms and livestock.

Sherman's march to the sea

Grant also ordered General **William Tecumseh Sherman** to capture Atlanta, Georgia, and then march to the Atlantic coast. Like Sheridan, Sherman had orders to destroy everything useful to the South.

Cause and Effect

Causes

- Issue of slavery in the territories divides the North and South
- Abolitionists want slavery to end
- South fears it will lose power in the national government
- Southern states secede after Lincoln's election
- Confederates bombard Fort Sumter

The Civil War

Effects

- Lincoln issues the Emancipation Proclamation
- Northern economy booms
- South loses its cotton trade with Britain
- Total war destroys the South's economy
- Hundreds of thousands of Americans killed

Effects Today

- Sectionalism is less of a force in American life and politics
- African Americans have equal protection under the Constitution
- Millions of Americans visit Civil War battlefields each year

Graphic Organizer *Skills*

The Civil War was a major turning point in the history of the United States.

1. **Comprehension** How did the war affect the northern and southern economies differently?
2. **Critical Thinking** Describe another cause or effect that could be added to this chart.

Sherman's troops captured Atlanta in September 1864. They burned the city in November. Then Sherman began his "march to the sea."

Sherman's troops ripped up railroad tracks, built bonfires from the ties, then heated and twisted the rails. They killed livestock and tore up fields. They burned barns, homes, and factories.

Lincoln Is Reelected

In 1864, Lincoln ran for reelection. At first, his defeat seemed, in his own words, "extremely probable." Before the capture of Atlanta, Union chances for victory looked bleak. Lincoln knew that many northerners were unhappy with his handling of the war. He thought that this might cost him the election.

The Democrats nominated General George McClellan to oppose Lincoln. Although he had commanded the Union army, McClellan was more willing than Lincoln to compromise with the South. If peace could be achieved, he was ready to restore slavery.

When Sherman took Atlanta in September, the North rallied around Lincoln. Sheridan's smashing victories in the Shenandoah Valley in October further increased Lincoln's popular support. In the election in November, the vote was close, but Lincoln remained President.

In his second Inaugural Address, Lincoln looked forward to the coming of peace:

> "With malice toward none, with charity for all... let us strive... to bind up the nation's wounds... to do all which may achieve a just and a lasting peace among ourselves and with all nations."

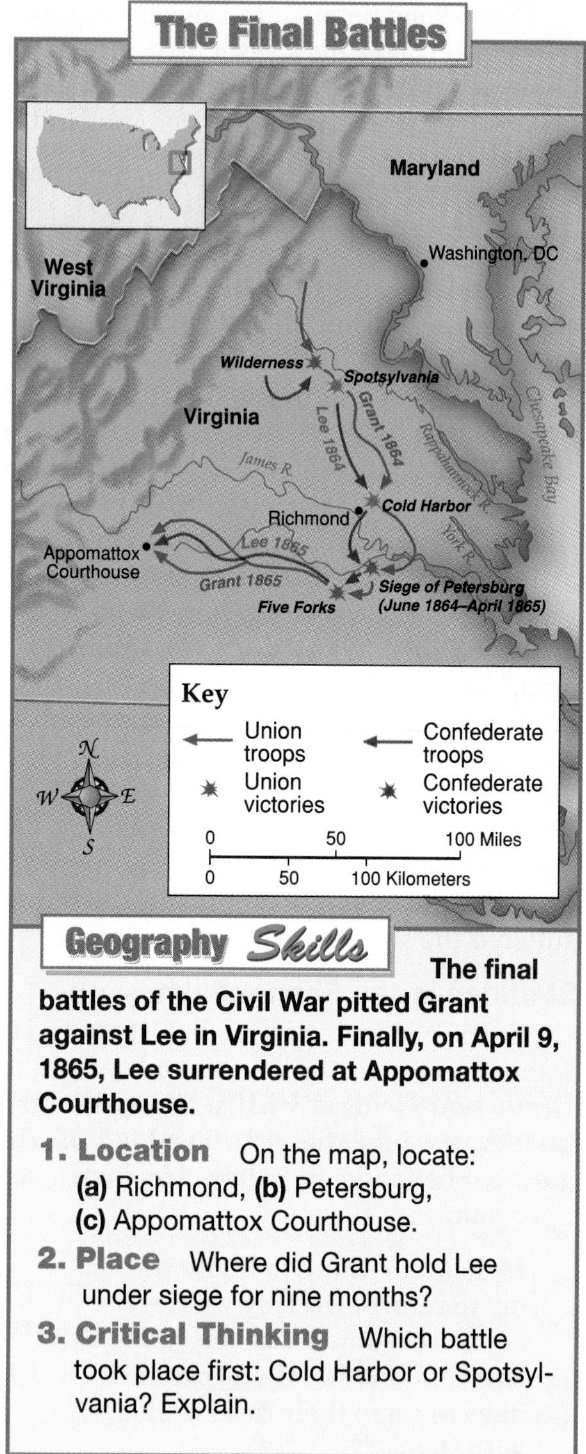

Geography Skills **The final battles of the Civil War pitted Grant against Lee in Virginia. Finally, on April 9, 1865, Lee surrendered at Appomattox Courthouse.**

1. **Location** On the map, locate: **(a)** Richmond, **(b)** Petersburg, **(c)** Appomattox Courthouse.
2. **Place** Where did Grant hold Lee under siege for nine months?
3. **Critical Thinking** Which battle took place first: Cold Harbor or Spotsylvania? Explain.

The War Ends

Grant had begun a drive to capture Richmond in May 1864. Throughout the spring and summer, he and Lee fought a series of costly battles.

Northerners read with horror that Grant had lost 60,000 dead and wounded in a single month at the battles of the Wilderness, Spotsylvania, and Cold Harbor. Still, Grant pressed on. He knew that the Union could replace men and supplies. The South could not.

Lee dug in at Petersburg, near Richmond. Here, Grant kept Lee under siege for nine months. At last, with a fresh supply of troops, Grant took Petersburg on April 2, 1865. The same day, Richmond fell.

General Lee surrenders to General Grant at Appomattox Courthouse.

Lee and his army withdrew to a small Virginia town called Appomattox Courthouse. There, a week later, they were trapped by Union troops. Lee knew that his men would be slaughtered if he kept fighting. On April 9, 1865, Lee surrendered.

At Appomattox Courthouse, Grant offered generous terms of surrender to the defeated Confederate army. Soldiers were required to turn over their rifles, but officers were allowed to keep their pistols. Soldiers who had horses could keep them. Grant knew that southerners would need the animals for spring plowing.

As the Confederates surrendered, Union soldiers began to cheer. Grant ordered them to be silent. "The war is over," he said. "The rebels are our countrymen again."

Effects of the War

More than 360,000 Union soldiers and 250,000 Confederate soldiers lost their lives in the Civil War. No war has ever resulted in more American deaths. As a result, feelings of bitterness remained among both northerners and southerners.

Southerners had special reasons to view the North with resentment. They had lost their struggle for independence. Their way of life had been forcibly changed. Union armies had destroyed much of their land. In addition, many southerners feared that the North would seek revenge against the South after the war.

Finally, the Civil War was a major turning point in American history. The Union was secure. States' rights had suffered a terrible blow. As a result, the power of the federal government grew. The war also brought freedom to millions of African Americans. Still, a long and difficult struggle for equality lay ahead.

★ Section 5 Review ★

Recall

1. **Locate** **(a)** Vicksburg, **(b)** Port Hudson, **(c)** Gettysburg, **(d)** Atlanta, **(e)** Petersburg, **(f)** Appomattox Courthouse.
2. **Identify** **(a)** Battle of Gettysburg, **(b)** Gettysburg Address, **(c)** Ulysses S. Grant, **(d)** Philip Sheridan, **(e)** William Tecumseh Sherman.
3. **Define** **(a)** siege, **(b)** total war.

Comprehension

4. Why did the Union victories at Vicksburg and Gettysburg mark a turning point in the war?
5. What ideals did Lincoln express in his Gettysburg Address and Second Inaugural Address?
6. How did Sheridan and Sherman use total war to destroy the South's ability to fight?

Critical Thinking and Writing

7. **Predicting Consequences** If Sherman and Sheridan had not won victories just before the election of 1864, how might the election and the war have turned out differently?
8. **Defending a Position** Some people have condemned Grant's decision to wage total war. Do you agree or disagree with this position? Explain.

Activity **Writing a Speech** It is a sad day for the South. You are a member of the Confederate Congress and you have just heard of Lee's surrender. Write a speech in which you reflect on the hardships of the war and offer hope for the future.

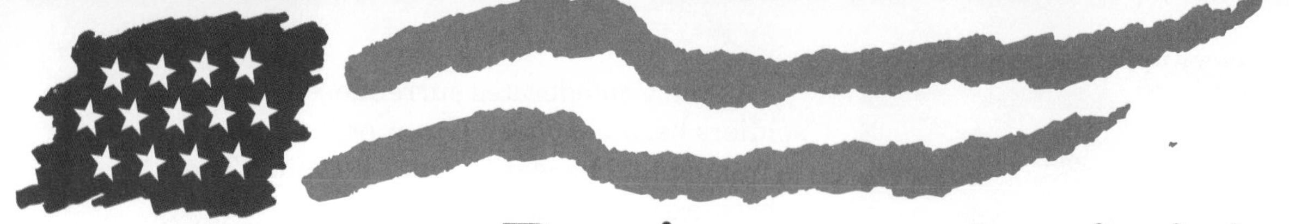

Chapter 17 Review and Activities

★ Sum It Up ★

Section 1 The Conflict Takes Shape

- The Union's advantages included a greater population and superior industrial resources.
- The Confederacy's advantages included better military leaders and its position of defending the homeland.

Section 2 A Long, Difficult Struggle

- The Union navy blockaded southern ports. Union armies tried to take Richmond and the Mississippi Valley.
- The Confederates won major battles in the East. Union armies were more successful in the West.

Section 3 A Promise of Freedom

- The Emancipation Proclamation made the end of slavery a goal of the war.
- African Americans worked, fought, and died in the effort to preserve the Union and end slavery.

Section 4 Hardships of War

- Both men and women suffered hardships in their efforts to win the war.
- During the war, the Union and Confederacy both struggled with political and economic problems.

Section 5 The War Ends

- The North waged total war deep into the South, disrupting civilian lives and inflicting great losses.
- Lee surrendered his army at Appomattox Courthouse, Virginia, on April 9, 1865.

For additional review of the major ideas of Chapter 17, see ***Guide to the Essentials of American History*** or ***Interactive Student Tutorial CD-ROM,*** which contains interactive review activities, graphic organizers, and practice tests.

Reviewing the Chapter

Define These Terms

Match each term with the correct definition.

Column 1

1. emancipate
2. martial law
3. draft
4. profiteers
5. inflation

Column 2

a. rule by the army
b. set free
c. people who overcharge for desperately needed goods
d. a rise in prices
e. a law requiring people to serve in the military

Explore the Main Ideas

1. What advantages did the United States have over the Confederate States?
2. Why were Confederate armies in the East often victorious in the early years of the war?
3. What were the results of the Emancipation Proclamation?
4. How did women support the war effort?
5. Explain how total war affected the South.

Chart Activity

Use the chart below to answer the following questions: **1.** How many members of Company D were captured and imprisoned by the Union? **2.** How many soldiers were in Company D at the start of the war? **Critical Thinking** Why do you think so many soldiers died from disease?

Seventh Virginia Infantry, Company D

Original members	122
Killed in battle or died of wounds	17
Died of disease	14
Discharged	29
Transferred	6
Prisoners of war	27
On leave, hospitalized, or at home	8
Deserted	12
Surrendered at Appomattox	9

Source: David E. Johnston, *The Story of a Confederate Boy in the Civil War*

Critical Thinking and Writing

1. **Understanding Chronology** For each pair of events that follow, select the event that happened first: **(a)** Battle of Bull Run, Battle of Gettysburg; **(b)** fall of Richmond, Emancipation Proclamation; **(c)** Sherman's march to the sea, fall of Vicksburg.
2. **Linking Past and Present** How do you think Americans would react today if a general lost 60,000 soldiers in one month as General Grant once did? Explain your answer.
3. **Identifying Alternatives** Should African American men have volunteered to serve in the Union army in 1862? Explain two reasons for volunteering and two reasons for not volunteering.
4. Exploring Unit Themes **Sectionalism** Do you think sectional differences and conflicts continued even after the end of the Civil War? Explain the reasons for your answer.

Using Primary Sources

Confederate General John B. Gordon described how his troops felt at Appomattox Courthouse as General Lee was about to surrender:

> "The men cried like children. Worn, starved, and bleeding as they were, they had rather have died than have surrendered.... But I could not permit it.... That these men should have wept at surrendering so unequal a fight, at being taken out of this constant [bloodshed] and storm, at being sent back to their families ... was [proof of bravery] and patriotism that might set an example."

Source: *Reminiscences of the Civil War* by John B. Gordon, 1903.

Recognizing Points of View **(a)** Why did General Gordon's troops cry? **(b)** How did Gordon feel about the behavior of the soldiers? **(c)** How do you think Confederate veterans felt about northern soldiers occupying southern lands after the war?

Activity Bank

Interdisciplinary Activity

Exploring Science Research and prepare a report on medical care during the Civil War. Include information on battlefield hospitals, common diseases, and people who cared for the sick and wounded.

Career Skills Activity

Cartographer Choose a Civil War battle and make a map showing the positions and movements of troops in the battle. Do research to find the information you need.

Citizenship Activity

Writing a Speech In the late 1860s, Memorial Day emerged as a day to honor soldiers who had died in the Civil War. Today, the holiday honors those whose lives were sacrificed in all American wars. Write a brief speech explaining why it is important to honor those who have died in American wars.

Internet Activity

On the Internet, find sites dealing with the Civil War. Choose a specific Civil War topic and prepare a five-minute presentation to give to the class. Possible topics include: a specific battle, a particular military or political leader, or the poetry and music of the Civil War.

Eyewitness Journal

Assume the role of an enslaved African American living in the Confederacy or an enslaved African American living in the Union. In your EYEWITNESS JOURNAL, describe your thoughts and feelings on January 1, 1863, the day the Emancipation Proclamation took effect.

Chapter 18

The Reconstruction Era

1864–1877

What's Ahead

After the Civil War, rebuilding the ruined South was a tremendous job. Just as troubling was the task of bringing the former Confederate states back into the Union. Should southerners who had fought against the United States government be welcomed back or treated harshly? How could the nation protect the newly won rights of freed African Americans?

During a period called Reconstruction, North and South slowly reunited. At the same time, the economy of the South slowly recovered, and African Americans in the South gained several important rights and freedoms. However, in the years following Reconstruction, many of these rights were lost.

Why Study *History?* During Reconstruction and after, many African Americans became victims of violence. Groups like the Ku Klux Klan used terror to prevent black citizens from voting. Today, Americans continue to battle "hate crimes" and encourage tolerance, or acceptance of all people. To focus on this connection, see the *Why Study History?* feature in this chapter, "Tolerance Begins With You."

American Events

- **1865** Abraham Lincoln is assassinated
- **1867** Reconstruction Act imposes strict measures on southern states
- **1868** House of Representatives votes to impeach President Johnson

1864 | 1866 | 1868 | 1870

World Events

1864 World Event Maximillian becomes Emperor of Mexico

1867 World Event Dominion of Canada is formed

Viewing History: Reunion Begins

This painting by Dennis Malone Carter shows Abraham Lincoln arriving in Richmond, Virginia. The President visited the captured Confederate capital during the final days of the Civil War. The painting shows Lincoln receiving a hero's welcome. In fact, though, many Richmond residents resented the visit by the leader of the victorious North. The reunion of the nation would not be easy. ★ **Predict two problems that the nation would face as the North and South reunited.**

1870
Fifteenth Amendment guarantees voting rights for African American men

1872
Congress pardons former Confederate officials

1877
Rutherford B. Hayes becomes President; Reconstruction ends

1870 | **1872** | **1874** | **1876**

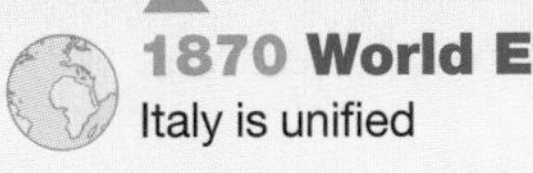

1870 World Event
Italy is unified

1873 World Event
Abolition of slave markets in Zanzibar

First Steps to Reunion

As You Read

Explore These Questions

- What hardships did the South face after the Civil War?
- What was President Lincoln's plan for reuniting the nation?
- Why did Congress oppose President Johnson's Reconstruction plan?

Define

- freedmen
- amnesty

Identify

- Reconstruction
- Ten Percent Plan
- Wade-Davis Bill
- Freedmen's Bureau
- John Wilkes Booth
- Andrew Johnson
- Thirteenth Amendment

SETTING the Scene At the end of the Civil War, the future looked bleak to many southerners. Susan Dabney Smedes described how her father, once a wealthy planter, coped with life after the war:

> "My father had come home to a house stripped of nearly every article of furniture and to a plantation stripped of the means of cultivating any but a small proportion of it. A few mules and one cow were all that were left of the stock.... When he was 70 years of age, he decided to grow a garden. He had never performed manual labor, but he now applied himself to learn to hoe as a way of supplying his family with vegetables."

The South faced staggering problems after the war. Southern cities and farmlands lay in ruins, and a whole way of life had ended. All southerners—rich and poor, black and white—faced a long, uphill struggle to rebuild their lives.

Postwar Problems

After four years of war, both northerners and southerners had to adjust to a changed world. The adjustment was far more difficult in the South.

The victorious North

Despite their victory, the North faced some economic problems after the Civil War. Some 800,000 returning Union soldiers needed jobs. Yet the government was canceling its war orders. Factories were laying off workers, not hiring them. Still, the North's economic disruption was only temporary. Boom times quickly returned.

The North lost more soldiers in the war than the South did. However, except for the battles of Gettysburg and Antietam, no fighting had taken place on northern soil. Northern farms and cities were hardly touched. One returning Union soldier remarked, "It seemed... as if I had been away only a day or two, and had just taken up... where I had left off."

The defeated South

Confederate soldiers had little chance of taking up where they left off. In some areas, every house, barn, and bridge had been destroyed. "The fine houses have fallen to decay or been burnt down," reported one witness, "the grounds neglected and grown over with weeds." Two thirds of the South's railroad tracks had been turned into twisted heaps of scrap. The cities of Columbia, Richmond, and Atlanta had been leveled.

The war wrecked the South's financial system. After the war, Confederate money was worthless. People who lent money to the Confederacy were never repaid. Many southern banks closed, and depositors lost their savings.

Southern society was changed forever by the war. No longer were there white owners and black slaves. Now, almost four million **freedmen**—men and women who had been slaves—lived in the South. Most had no land, no jobs, and no education. Under slavery, they had been forbidden to own property and to learn to read and write. What would become of them?

Early Plans for Reconstruction

Even before the war ended, President Lincoln worried about rebuilding the South. He wanted to make it fairly easy for southerners to rejoin the Union. The sooner the nation was reunited, Lincoln believed, the faster the South would be able to rebuild.

As early as 1863, Lincoln outlined a Reconstruction plan. **Reconstruction** refers to the rebuilding of the South after the Civil War. Under Lincoln's **Ten Percent Plan,** a southern state could form a new government after 10 percent of its voters swore an oath of loyalty to the United States. Once it was formed, the new government had to abolish slavery. Voters could then elect members of Congress and take part in the national government once again.

Lincoln's plan also offered **amnesty,** or a government pardon, to Confederates who swore loyalty to the Union. Amnesty would not apply to former leaders of the Confederacy, however.

Many Republicans in Congress felt that Lincoln's plan was too generous toward the South. In 1864, they passed the **Wade-Davis Bill,** a rival plan for Reconstruction. It required a majority of white men in each southern state to swear loyalty to the Union. It also denied the right to vote or hold office to anyone who had volunteered to fight for the Confederacy.

The Freedmen's Bureau

Lincoln refused to sign the Wade-Davis Bill because he felt it was too harsh. Congress and the President did agree on one proposal, however. One month before Lee

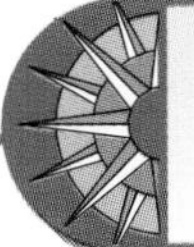
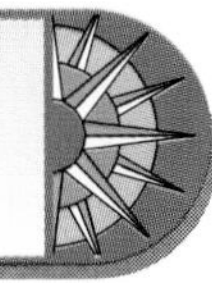

Linking Past and Present

Past

Present

Ruin and Revival

If you visit the city of Richmond, Virginia, today, you will see an attractive, modern city. You would not guess that, at one time, the city was largely in ruins. Rebuilding its cities and farms was one of the first tasks facing the South after the Civil War. ★ **Why was Richmond so badly damaged in the Civil War?**

Biography **Charlotte Forten**

Charlotte Forten came from a wealthy Philadelphia family. A strong abolitionist, she devoted her life to helping other African Americans improve their lives through education. When she was 25, she helped set up a school on the Sea Islands off South Carolina. Later, she helped recruit other teachers for the Freedmen's Bureau. ★ **Why do you think education was so important to freedmen?**

surrendered, Congress passed a bill creating the **Freedmen's Bureau.** Lincoln signed it.

The Freedmen's Bureau gave food and clothing to former slaves. It also tried to find jobs for freedmen. The bureau helped poor whites as well. It provided medical care for more than one million people. One former Confederate was amazed to see "a Government which was lately fighting us with fire, and sword, and shell, now generously feeding our poor and distressed."

One of the bureau's most important tasks was to set up schools for freed slaves in the South. By 1869, about 300,000 African Americans attended bureau schools. Most of the teachers were volunteers, often women, from the North.

Both old and young were eager to learn. Grandparents and grandchildren sat side by side in the classroom. One bureau agent in South Carolina observed that freedmen "will starve themselves, and go without clothes, in order to send their children to school." Charlotte Forten, an African American woman from Philadelphia, came south as a volunteer teacher. She wrote of her students:

> "I never before saw children so eager to learn.... It is wonderful how a people who have been so long crushed to the earth... can have so great a desire for knowledge, and such a capacity for attaining it."

The Freedmen's Bureau laid the foundation for the South's public school system. It set up more than 4,300 grade schools. It also created colleges for African American students, including Howard, Morehouse, and Fisk. Many graduates of these schools became teachers themselves. By the 1870s, African Americans were teaching in grade schools throughout the South.

Lincoln Is Assassinated

President Lincoln hoped to persuade Congress to accept his Reconstruction plan. However, he never got the chance.

On April 14, 1865, just five days after Lee's surrender, the President attended a play at Ford's Theater in Washington, D.C. As Lincoln watched the play, **John Wilkes Booth,** a popular actor from the South, crept into the President's box and shot Lincoln in the head. Within a few hours, the President was dead. Booth was later caught and killed in a barn outside the city.

Connections With Arts

Walt Whitman's famous poem "O Captain! My Captain!" expresses his grief at the death of Lincoln. It begins, "O Captain! my Captain! our fearful trip is done, / The ship has weather'd every rack, the prize we sought is won." You can find this and other Civil War poems in Whitman's collection *Leaves of Grass.*

The nation plunged into grief. Millions who had been celebrating the war's end now mourned Lincoln's death. "Now he belongs to the ages," commented Secretary of War Edwin Stanton.

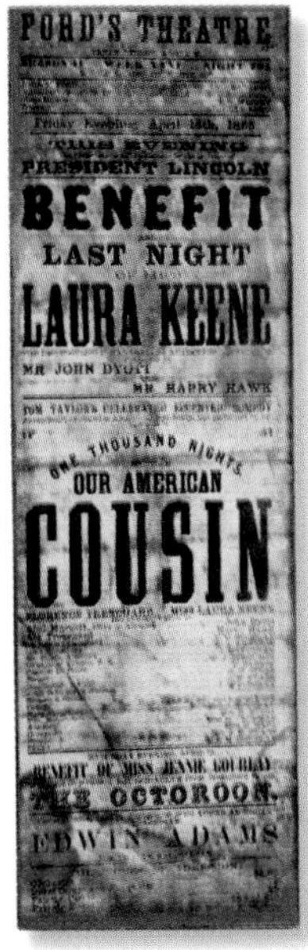

Playbill from Ford's Theater on the night Lincoln was shot

A New President

Vice President **Andrew Johnson** became President when Lincoln died. Johnson had served as governor of Tennessee and had represented that state in Congress. When Tennessee seceded, Johnson had remained loyal to the Union.

At first, many Republicans in Congress were pleased when Johnson became President. They believed that he would support a strict Reconstruction plan. As it turned out, Johnson's plan was much milder than expected.

Johnson called for a majority of voters in each southern state to pledge loyalty to the United States. He also demanded that each state ratify the **Thirteenth Amendment,** which banned slavery throughout the nation. (As you have read, Lincoln's Emancipation Proclamation did not free slaves in states that remained loyal to the Union.) Congress had approved the Thirteenth Amendment in January 1865.

Rebellion in Congress

The southern states quickly met Johnson's conditions. As a result, the President approved their new state governments in late 1865. Voters in the South then elected representatives to Congress. Many of those elected had held office in the Confederacy. For example, Alexander Stephens, the former vice president of the Confederacy, was elected senator from Georgia.

Republicans in Congress were outraged. The men who had led the South out of the Union were being elected to the House and Senate. Also, no southern state allowed African Americans to vote.

When Congress met in December 1865, Republicans refused to let southern representatives take their seats. Instead, they set up a Joint Committee on Reconstruction to draw up a new plan for the South. The stage was set for a showdown between Congress and the President.

★ Section 1 Review ★

Recall

1. **Identify** **(a)** Reconstruction, **(b)** Ten Percent Plan, **(c)** Wade-Davis Bill, **(d)** Freedmen's Bureau, **(e)** John Wilkes Booth, **(f)** Andrew Johnson, **(g)** Thirteenth Amendment.
2. **Define** **(a)** freedmen, **(b)** amnesty.

Comprehension

3. Describe two problems the South faced after the Civil War.
4. **(a)** What was President Lincoln's Reconstruction plan? **(b)** How did it differ from the Wade-Davis Bill?
5. **(a)** What was President Johnson's plan for readmitting the former Confederate states to the Union? **(b)** How did Republicans in Congress react to Johnson's plan?

Critical Thinking and Writing

6. **Analyzing Information** The North lost more soldiers in the Civil War than the South did. Why was it easier for the North to recover from the war?
7. **Ranking** **(a)** What services did the Freedmen's Bureau provide? **(b)** Which do you think was most important? Explain.

Activity **Writing a Poem** President Lincoln has been shot! Taking the viewpoint of a northerner or southerner, write a poem about the death of Lincoln. If you like, you may set your poem to music.

Radical Reconstruction

Explore These Questions

- What were the goals of the Radical Republicans?
- Why did Congress try to remove President Johnson from office?
- What were the Fourteenth and Fifteenth Amendments?

Define

- black codes
- radical
- impeach

Identify

- Radical Republicans
- Thaddeus Stevens
- Charles Sumner
- Fourteenth Amendment
- Radical Reconstruction
- Reconstruction Act
- Fifteenth Amendment

In the spring of 1866, disturbing reports trickled into Congress. In some southern cities, peddlers were openly selling Confederate flags. Throughout the South, people sang a new song, "I'm a good old rebel / And I don't want no pardon for anything I done."

These reports confirmed what many Republicans had suspected. "The rebellion has not ended," declared one angry Republican. "It has only changed its weapons!"

Black Codes

After the war, most southern states had promptly ratified the Thirteenth Amendment, which banned slavery. At the same time, however, Southern legislatures passed **black codes,** laws that severely limited the rights of freedmen.

Black codes forbade African Americans to vote, own guns, or serve on juries. In some states, African Americans were permitted to work only as servants or farm laborers. In others, the codes required freedmen to sign contracts for a year's work. Those without contracts could be arrested and sentenced to work on a plantation.

Black codes did give African Americans some rights they did not have before the Civil War. For example, the codes permitted African Americans to marry legally and to own some kinds of property. Still, the codes were clearly meant to keep freedmen from gaining political or economic power.

The North Reacts

Republicans were angered by the black codes, as well as by the election of former Confederate leaders to Congress. The Joint Committee on Reconstruction sent the President a report accusing the South of trying to "preserve slavery in its original form as much and as long as possible." When Johnson ignored the report, members of Congress vowed to take Reconstruction out of the President's hands.

Those who led the opposition to President Johnson were called **Radical Republicans,** or Radicals. A **radical** wants to make drastic changes in society. **Thaddeus Stevens** of Pennsylvania led the Radicals in the House. **Charles Sumner** of Massachusetts was the chief Radical Republican in the Senate.

Radicals had two main goals. First, they wanted to break the power of wealthy planters who had long ruled the South. Radicals blamed these "aristocrats" for the Civil War. Second, Radicals wanted to ensure that freedmen received the right to vote.

Radical Republicans did not control Congress. To accomplish their goals, they needed the support of moderate Republicans, the largest group in Congress. Moderates and Radicals disagreed on many issues. However, they shared a strong political motive for endorsing strict treatment of the South. Most southerners were Democrats. With southerners barred from Congress, Republicans easily controlled both houses.

The President vs. Congress

The conflict between the President and Congress came to a head in 1866. In April, Congress passed the Civil Rights Act, giving citizenship to African Americans. Congress hoped to combat the black codes and secure basic rights for African Americans. When Johnson vetoed the bill, Congress overrode the veto.

The Fourteenth Amendment

Congressional Republicans worried that the Supreme Court might declare the Civil Rights Act unconstitutional. In the Dred Scott decision of 1857, the Court had ruled that African Americans were not citizens. Hoping to avoid a similar ruling, Republicans proposed the Fourteenth Amendment.

The **Fourteenth Amendment** granted citizenship to all persons born in the United States. This included nearly all African Americans. It also guaranteed all citizens "equal protection of the laws" and declared that no state could "deprive any person of life, liberty, or property without due process of law." This provision made it illegal for states to discriminate against an individual on unreasonable grounds, such as skin color.

The Fourteenth Amendment also provided that any state that denied African Americans the right to vote would have its representation in Congress reduced. Republicans believed that freedmen would be able to defend their rights if they could vote.

With the Fourteenth Amendment, Republicans hoped to secure basic political rights for African Americans in the South. In fact, the nation had far to go before all Americans achieved equality. Over the next 100 years, citizens would seek to obtain their rights by asking the courts to enforce the Fourteenth Amendment.

Election of 1866

President Johnson urged the former Confederate states to reject the Fourteenth Amendment. He also decided to make the amendment an issue in the November 1866 congressional elections. Traveling through the North, the President called on voters to reject the Radical Republicans.

Viewing History **New Rights for Freedmen**

Under the black codes, former slaves gained some new rights, such as the right to marry legally. Forms like this one helped freedmen keep their marriage and family records. ★ **Why were family records so valuable to freedmen?**

In many towns, audiences heckled the President. One heckler shouted that Johnson should hang Jefferson Davis. Losing his temper, Johnson yelled back, "Why not hang Thad Stevens?" Many northerners criticized Johnson for acting in an undignified manner.

In July, white mobs in New Orleans, Louisiana, killed 34 African Americans. This convinced many northerners that stronger measures were needed to protect freedmen.

In the end, the election results were a disaster for Johnson. Republicans won majorities in both houses of Congress. They also won every northern governorship and majorities in every northern state legislature.

The Radical Program

In 1867, Republicans in Congress prepared to take charge of Reconstruction. The period that followed is often called **Radical Reconstruction.** With huge majorities in

Rival Plans for Reconstruction

Plan	Ten Percent Plan	Wade-Davis Bill	Johnson Plan	Reconstruction Act
Proposed by	President Abraham Lincoln (1863)	Republicans in Congress (1864)	President Andrew Johnson (1865)	Radical Republicans (1867)
Conditions for former Confederate states to rejoin Union	▪ 10 percent of voters must swear loyalty to Union ▪ Must abolish slavery	▪ Majority of white men must swear loyalty ▪ Former Confederate volunteers cannot vote or hold office	▪ Majority of white men must swear loyalty ▪ Must ratify Thirteenth Amendment ▪ Former Confederate officials may vote and hold office	▪ Must disband state governments ▪ Must write new constitutions ▪ Must ratify Fourteenth Amendment ▪ African American men must be allowed to vote

Graphic Organizer *Skills* **In the early years of Reconstruction, federal leaders debated several plans for readmitting southern states.**

1. **Comprehension** **(a)** Identify one similarity between the Wade-Davis Bill and President Johnson's plan. **(b)** Identify one difference.
2. **Critical Thinking** If Lincoln had lived, do you think he would have supported the 1867 Reconstruction Act? Explain.

Civics

both the House and the Senate, Congress could easily override a presidential veto.

First Reconstruction Act

In March 1867, Congress passed the first **Reconstruction Act** over Johnson's veto. The Reconstruction Act threw out the southern state governments that had refused to ratify the Fourteenth Amendment—all the former Confederate states except Tennessee. The act also divided the South into five military districts under army control.

The Reconstruction Act required the former Confederate states to write new constitutions and to ratify the Fourteenth Amendment before rejoining the Union. Most important, the act stated that African Americans must be allowed to vote in all southern states.

Further Republican victories

Once the new constitutions were in place, the reconstructed states held elections to set up new state governments. To show their disgust with Radical Reconstruction policies, many white southerners stayed away from the polls. Freedmen, on the other hand, proudly turned out to exercise their new right to vote. As a result, Republicans gained control of all of the new southern state governments.

Congress passed several more Reconstruction acts. Each time, the Republicans easily overrode Johnson's veto.

Johnson Is Impeached

It was Johnson's duty, as President, to enforce the new Reconstruction laws. However, many Republicans feared he would not do so. Republicans in Congress decided to remove the President from office.

On February 24, 1868, the House of Representatives voted to impeach President Johnson. To **impeach** means to bring formal charges of wrongdoing against an elected official. According to the Constitution, the House can impeach the President only for "high crimes and misdemeanors." The Senate tries the case. The President is removed from office only if found guilty by two thirds of the senators.

During Johnson's trial, it became clear that he was not guilty of high crimes and misdemeanors. Even Charles Sumner, the President's bitter foe, admitted that the charges were "political in character."

Despite intense pressure, seven Republican senators refused to vote for conviction. The Constitution, they believed, did not allow a President to be removed from office simply because he disagreed with Congress. In the end, the Senate vote was 35 for and 19 against impeachment—one vote short of the two-thirds majority needed to remove the President from office. Johnson served out the few remaining months of his term.

A New President

In 1868, Republicans nominated General Ulysses S. Grant as their candidate for President. Grant was the Union's greatest hero in the Civil War.

By election day, most of the southern states had rejoined the Union. As Congress demanded, the new southern governments allowed African Americans to vote. About 500,000 blacks went to the polls in the 1868 election. Nearly all cast their votes for Grant. He easily defeated his opponent, Horatio Seymour.

The Fifteenth Amendment

In 1869, Republicans in Congress proposed another amendment to the Constitution. The **Fifteenth Amendment** forbade any state to deny African Americans the right to vote because of their race.

Many Republicans had moral reasons for supporting the Fifteenth Amendment. They remembered the great sacrifices that were made by African American soldiers in the Civil War. They also felt it was wrong to let African Americans vote in the South but not in the North.

Some Republicans also supported the Fifteenth Amendment for political reasons. African American votes had brought Republicans victory in the South. If African Americans could also vote in the North, they would help Republicans to win elections there, too.

The Fifteenth Amendment was ratified in 1870. At last, all African American men over age 21 had the right to vote.

★ Section 2 Review ★

Recall

1. **Identify** **(a)** Radical Republicans, **(b)** Thaddeus Stevens, **(c)** Charles Sumner, **(d)** Fourteenth Amendment, **(e)** Radical Reconstruction, **(f)** Reconstruction Act, **(g)** Fifteenth Amendment.
2. **Define** **(a)** black codes, **(b)** radical, **(c)** impeach.

Comprehension

3. Describe the Reconstruction plan enacted by Congress in 1867.
4. **(a)** Why did Congress impeach President Johnson? **(b)** What was the result?
5. Describe the goals of: **(a)** the Fourteenth Amendment; **(b)** the Fifteenth Amendment.

Critical Thinking and Writing

6. **Defending a Position** **(a)** Compare Johnson's plan for Reconstruction with the Radical Reconstruction plan. **(b)** Which plan would you have supported? Defend your position.
7. **Analyzing Ideas** A senator who voted against the removal of President Johnson later said that he did not vote in favor of Johnson but in favor of the presidency. What do you think he meant?

Activity **Writing a Speech** Write a speech from the point of view of a radical or moderate Republican. Present your position on Reconstruction and give reasons for your opinion.

Changes in the South

As You Read

Explore These Questions
- What groups dominated southern politics during Reconstruction?
- What did Reconstruction governments do to rebuild the South?
- Why did many southerners sink into a cycle of poverty?

Define
- scalawag
- carpetbagger
- sharecropper

Identify
- Hiram Revels
- Blanche K. Bruce
- Conservatives
- Ku Klux Klan

SETTING the Scene By 1867, life in the South had changed dramatically. African Americans were free to work for themselves, to vote, and to run for office. In Alabama, a political convention of freedmen drew up this ringing declaration:

> "We claim exactly the same rights, privileges and immunities as are enjoyed by white men. We ask nothing more and will be content with nothing less."

Before the Civil War, a small group of rich planters controlled southern politics. During Reconstruction, however, new groups dominated state governments in the South. They tried to reshape southern politics. At the same time, others were taking strong action to reverse the gains made by African Americans.

New Forces in Southern Politics

The state governments created during Radical Reconstruction were different from any governments the South had known before. The old leaders had lost much of their influence. Three groups stepped in to replace them. These new groups were white southerners who supported the Republicans, northerners who moved south after the war, and African Americans.

Scalawags

Some white southerners supported the new Republican governments. Many were business people who had opposed secession in 1860. They wanted to forget the war and get on with rebuilding the South.

Many whites in the South felt that any southerner who helped the Republicans was a traitor. They called white southern Republicans **scalawags,** a word used for small, scruffy horses.

Carpetbaggers

Northerners who came south after the war were another important force. To white southerners, the new arrivals from the North were **carpetbaggers**—fortune hunters hoping to profit from the South's misery. Southerners claimed that these northerners were in such a hurry they had time only to fling a few clothes into cheap suitcases, or carpetbags.

In fact, northerners went south for a number of reasons. A few were fortune hunters who hoped to profit as the South was being rebuilt. Many more, however, were Union soldiers who had grown to love the South's rich land. Others, both white and

To many southerners, the carpetbag became a hated symbol of Reconstruction.

Viewing History **African Americans in Congress**

During Reconstruction, several African Americans won election to Congress. Here, Robert Brown Elliott of South Carolina stands in the House of Representatives to argue for a civil rights bill. Words from his speech appear on the banner above. "What you give to one class, you must give to all. What you deny to one class, you shall deny to all." ★ **Summarize Elliott's main point in your own words.**

black, were teachers, ministers, and reformers who sincerely wanted to improve the lives of the freedmen.

African Americans

Freedmen and other African Americans were the third major new group in southern politics. Before the war, African Americans had no voice in southern government. During Reconstruction, they not only voted in large numbers, but they also ran for and were elected to public office in the South.

African Americans became sheriffs, mayors, and legislators in the new state and local governments. Between 1869 and 1880, 16 African Americans were elected to Congress.

Two African Americans, both representing Mississippi, served in the Senate. **Hiram Revels,** a clergyman and teacher, became the nation's first black senator in 1870. He completed the unfinished term of former Confederate president Jefferson Davis. In 1874, **Blanche K. Bruce** became the first African American to serve a full term in the Senate. Born into slavery, Bruce escaped to freedom when the Civil War began and later served as a country sheriff.

Freedmen had less political influence than many whites claimed, however. Only in South Carolina did African Americans win a majority in one house of the state legislature. No state elected a black governor.

Conservatives Resist

From the start, most prominent white southerners resisted Reconstruction. These **Conservatives** wanted the South to change as little as possible. They were willing to let African Americans vote and hold a few offices. Still, they were determined that real power would remain in the hands of whites.

A few wealthy planters tried to force African Americans back onto plantations. Many small farmers and laborers wanted the government to take action against the millions of freedmen who now competed with them for land and power.

Most of these white southerners were Democrats. They declared war on anyone who cooperated with the Republicans. "This is a white man's country," they cried, "and white men must govern it."

Spreading terror

White southerners formed secret societies to help them regain power. The most dangerous was the **Ku Klux Klan,** or KKK. The Klan worked to keep blacks and white Republicans out of office.

Viewing HISTORY **Spreading Terror**

Wearing white hoods, the Ku Klux Klan used terror and violence to keep African Americans from voting. Famous cartoonist Thomas Nast attacked the Klan and other secret societies.

★ **Identify two Klan actions shown in the cartoon. Why do you think Nast labeled his cartoon "WORSE THAN SLAVERY"?**

Ku Klux Klan hood ➤

Dressed in white robes and hoods to hide their identity, Klansmen rode at night to the homes of African American voters, shouting threats and burning wooden crosses. When threats did not work, the Klan turned to violence. Klan members murdered hundreds of African Americans and their white allies.

Congress responds

Many moderate southerners condemned the violence of the Klan. Yet they could do little to stop the Klan's reign of terror. Freedmen turned to the federal government for help. In Kentucky, African American voters wrote to Congress:

> "We believe you are not familiar with the Ku Klux Klan's riding nightly over the country spreading terror wherever they go by robbing, whipping, and killing our people without provocation."

Congress tried to end Klan violence. In 1870, Congress made it a crime to use force to keep people from voting. As a result, Klan activities decreased. Yet the threat of violence lingered. Some African Americans continued to vote and hold office despite the risk. Many others were frightened away from the ballot box.

The Task of Rebuilding

Despite political problems, Reconstruction governments tried to rebuild the South. They built public schools for both black and white children. Many states gave women the right to own property. In addition, Reconstruction governments rebuilt railroads, telegraph lines, bridges, and roads. Between 1865 and 1879, the South put down 7,000 miles of railroad track.

Rebuilding cost money. Before the war, southerners paid very low taxes. Reconstruction governments raised taxes sharply. This created discontent among many southern whites.

Southerners were further angered by widespread corruption in the Reconstruction governments. One state legislature, for example, voted $1,000 to cover a member's bet on a horse race. Other items billed to the state included hams, perfume, and a coffin.

Corruption was not limited to the South. After the Civil War, dishonesty plagued northern governments as well. In fact, most southern officeholders served their states honestly.

A Cycle of Poverty

In the first months after the war, freedmen left the plantations on which they had

$ Connections With Economics

While the Ku Klux Klan carried out its program of violence, others used economic weapons to intimidate African Americans. Planters refused to rent land to blacks. Employers refused to hire them, and storekeepers denied them credit. What effect do you think such pressures had?

Skills FOR LIFE

Critical Thinking | Managing Information | Communication | Maps, Charts, and Graphs

Interpreting a Political Cartoon

How Will I Use This Skill?

Almost every newspaper today includes political cartoons. Cartoonists comment on current events through both visual imagery and words. Their pictures often use symbols and exaggeration to make their point. Learning to analyze cartoons can help you better understand views on current issues.

LEARN the Skill

1. Identify the characters and symbols used in the cartoon. Remember that a symbol is an object that represents something beyond itself. The eagle, for example, is often used as a symbol for the United States.
2. Note details in the drawing. Are some details larger or smaller than normal? Are any facial features or actions in the cartoon exaggerated?
3. Analyze the relationship between the pictures and any words in the cartoon.
4. Identify the cartoonist's point of view. Try to identify policies or actions that the cartoonist wants readers to support.

PRACTICE the Skill

The cartoon on the right appeared in a northern newspaper in the 1870s. Use the steps above to analyze the cartoon.

1. The figure at the top of the cartoon is President Grant. Explain what these other symbols represent: (a) the woman; (b) the soldiers; (c) the carpetbag.
2. (a) Note the size of the details in this drawing. Are any larger than normal? Why? (b) What do Grant's facial expression and the position of his arms suggest about his attitude toward the South?
3. (a) What words are written on the paper sticking out of the carpetbag? What do they mean? (b) What is the woman doing? (c) Is her task easy or difficult?
4. (a) How do you think this cartoonist felt about Radical Reconstruction? Explain. (b) What policy do you think the cartoonist would want his readers to support?

APPLY the Skill

Find a current political cartoon in the editorial section of a newspaper. Using the skills you have learned in this section, write a paragraph explaining the cartoon.

lived and worked. They found few opportunities, however.

"Nothing but freedom"

Some Radical Republicans talked about giving each freedman "40 acres and a mule." Thaddeus Stevens suggested breaking up big plantations and distributing the land. Most Americans opposed the plan, however. In the end, former slaves received—in the words of a freedman—"nothing but freedom."

Through hard work or good luck, some freedmen were able to become landowners. Most, however, had little choice but to return to where they had lived in slavery.

Sharecropping

Some large planters had held onto their land and wealth through the war. Now, they had land but no slaves to work it. During Reconstruction, many freedmen and poor whites went to work on the large plantations. These **sharecroppers** farmed the land, using seed, fertilizer, and tools provided by the planters. In return, the planters got a share of the crop at harvest time. Sharecroppers hoped to have their own land one day. Meanwhile, they were lucky to have enough food for themselves and their families.

Even farmers who owned land faced hard times. Each spring, the farmers received supplies on credit. In the fall, they had to repay what they had borrowed. Often, the harvest did not cover the debt. Unable to pay, many farmers lost their land and became sharecroppers themselves. Many southerners became locked in a cycle of poverty.

Sharecroppers growing cotton behind their cabin

★ Section 3 Review ★

Recall

1. **Identify** **(a)** Hiram Revels, **(b)** Blanche K. Bruce, **(c)** Conservatives, **(d)** Ku Klux Klan.
2. **Define** **(a)** scalawag, **(b)** carpetbagger, **(c)** sharecropper.

Comprehension

3. **(a)** What role did freedmen play in Reconstruction governments? **(b)** How was this different from the role of African Americans before the Civil War?
4. **(a)** What were two accomplishments of Reconstruction governments? **(b)** What were two problems?
5. Why did many freedmen and poor whites become sharecroppers?

Critical Thinking and Writing

6. **Understanding Causes and Effects** During Reconstruction, freedmen proved that, given the chance, they could do the same jobs as whites. Do you think this made southern Conservatives more willing or less willing to accept African Americans as equals? Explain.
7. **Linking Past and Present** Many southerners were angered by high taxes imposed by Reconstruction governments. **(a)** How do voters today feel about paying high taxes? **(b)** Do you think some services should be provided even if they require high taxes? Explain.

Activity **Drawing a Political Cartoon** Draw a political cartoon expressing your opinion about scalawags, carpetbaggers, the Ku Klux Klan, or another aspect of Reconstruction in the South.

Reconstruction Ends

Explore These Questions
- Why did Reconstruction end?
- How did the southern economy expand after Reconstruction?
- How did African Americans in the South lose rights?

Define
- poll tax
- literacy test
- grandfather clause
- segregation
- lynching

Identify
- Rutherford B. Hayes
- Henry Grady
- James Duke
- Jim Crow laws
- *Plessy* v. *Ferguson*

SETTING the Scene In 1876, millions of Americans visited a great Centennial Exposition held in Philadelphia. The fair celebrated the first hundred years of the United States. Visitors gazed at the latest wonders of modern industry—the elevator, the telephone, a giant steam engine.

As Americans looked to the future, they lost interest in Reconstruction. By the late 1870s, white Conservatives had regained control of the South.

Radicals in Decline

By the 1870s, Radical Republicans were losing power in Congress. Many northerners grew weary of trying to reform the South. It was time to forget the Civil War, they believed, and let southerners run their own governments—even if that meant African Americans might lose their rights.

Republicans were also hurt by disclosure of widespread corruption in the government of President Grant. The President had appointed many friends to office. Some used their position to steal large sums of money from the government. Grant won reelection in 1872, but many northerners had lost faith in Republican leaders and their policies.

Congress reflected the new mood of the North. In May 1872, it passed the Amnesty Act, which restored the right to vote to nearly all white southerners. As expected, they voted solidly Democratic. At the same time, southern whites terrorized African Americans who tried to vote.

White Conservatives were firmly in control once more. One by one, the Republican governments in the South fell. By 1876, only three southern states—Louisiana, South Carolina, and Florida—were still controlled by Republicans.

Election of 1876

The end of Reconstruction came with the election of 1876. The Democrats nominated Samuel Tilden, governor of New York, for President. Tilden was known for fighting corruption. The Republican candidate was **Rutherford B. Hayes,** governor of Ohio. Like Tilden, Hayes vowed to fight dishonesty in government.

Tilden won 250,000 more popular votes than Hayes. However, Tilden had only 184 electoral votes—one vote short of the number needed to win. Twenty other votes were in dispute. The outcome of the election hung on these votes. All but one of the disputed votes came from Florida, Louisiana, and South Carolina—the three southern states still controlled by Republicans.

As inauguration day drew near, the nation still had no one to swear in as President. Congress set up a special commission to settle the crisis. A majority of the commission members were Republicans. The commission decided to give all the disputed electoral votes to Hayes.

Southern Democrats could have fought the election of Hayes. Hayes, however, had privately agreed to end Reconstruction. Once in office, he removed all remaining federal troops from South Carolina, Louisiana, and Florida. Reconstruction was over.

Industry and the "New South"

During Reconstruction, the South made some progress toward rebuilding its economy. Cotton production, long the basis of the South's economy, slowly recovered. By 1880, planters were growing as much cotton as they had in 1860.

After Reconstruction, a new generation of southern leaders worked to expand the economy. **Henry Grady,** editor of the *Atlanta Constitution,* made stirring speeches calling for the growth of a "New South." Grady argued that the South should use its vast natural resources to build up its own industry, instead of depending on the North.

Agricultural industries

Southerners agreed that the best way to begin industrializing was to process the region's agricultural goods. Investors built textile mills to turn cotton into cloth. By 1880, the entire South was still producing fewer textiles than Massachusetts. In the next decade, though, more and more communities started building textile mills.

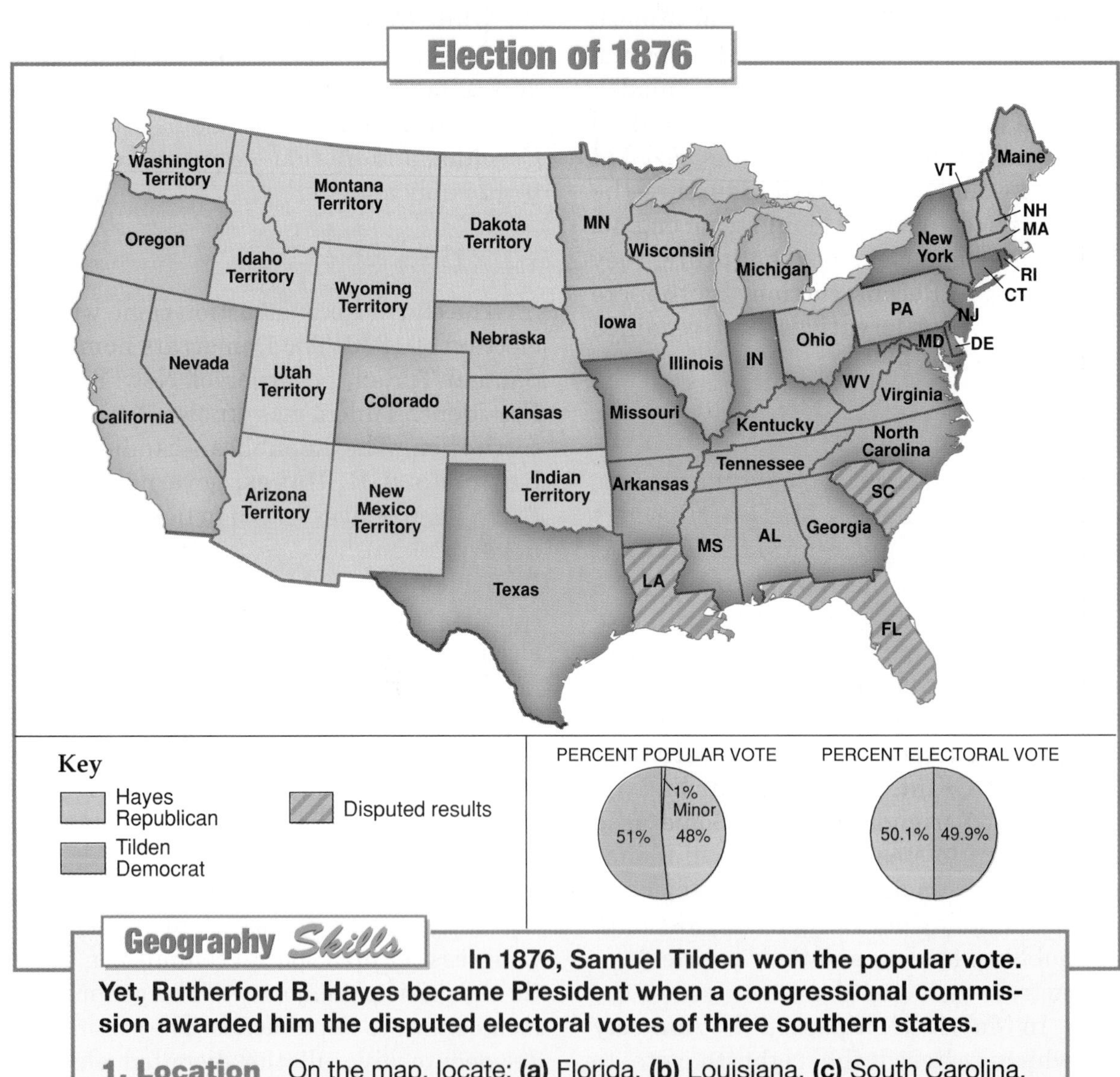

Geography *Skills* **In 1876, Samuel Tilden won the popular vote. Yet, Rutherford B. Hayes became President when a congressional commission awarded him the disputed electoral votes of three southern states.**

1. **Location** On the map, locate: **(a)** Florida, **(b)** Louisiana, **(c)** South Carolina.
2. **Movement** Which candidate carried the undisputed southern vote?
3. **Critical Thinking** Based on the map, do you think the Civil War ended sectionalism in the United States? Explain.

The tobacco industry also grew rapidly. In North Carolina, **James Duke** used new machinery to revolutionize production of tobacco products. In 1890, he bought out several competitors to form the American Tobacco Company. Duke eventually controlled 90 percent of the nation's tobacco industry.

New industries

The South also tapped its mineral resources. Local deposits of iron ore and coal, as well as low wages for workers, made steel production cheaper in Alabama than in Pennsylvania. Oil refineries developed in Louisiana and Texas. Other states became leading producers of coal, copper, granite, and marble.

By the 1890s, many northern forests had been cut down. The southern yellow pine was competing with the northwestern white pine as a lumber source. Some southern factories began to make cypress shingles and hardwood furniture.

A visitor from New England described what he found on a visit to the South in 1887:

> "We find a South wide awake with business, excited and even astonished at the development of its own immense resources in metals, marbles, coal, timber, fertilizers, eagerly laying lines of communication, rapidly opening mines, building furnaces, foundries, and all sorts of shops for utilizing the native riches."

By 1900, the South had developed a more balanced economy. Still, it failed to keep up with even more rapid growth in the North and the West.

Viewing HISTORY **Rise of the New South**

From Darkness to Light *by Grant Hamilton shows the New South rising from the ruins of war. Hamilton created this picture for one of several industrial expositions held in Atlanta, Georgia, in the late 1800s.* ★ **According to this picture, what products helped the southern economy grow?**

Restricting the Rights of African Americans

The years after Reconstruction brought prosperity to some southerners. For African Americans, though, the end of Reconstruction had tragic effects.

With the North out of southern affairs, white Conservatives tightened their grip on southern governments. Some groups continued to use violence to keep African Americans from voting. Southern states also found new ways to keep African Americans from exercising their rights.

Voting restrictions

In the 1880s, many southern states began passing new laws that restricted the right to vote. **Poll taxes** required voters to pay a fee each time they voted. As a result, poor freedmen could rarely afford to vote. **Literacy tests** required voters to read and explain a section of the Constitution. Since most freedmen had little education, such tests kept them away from the polls.

Many poor southern whites also could not pass the literacy test. To increase the number of eligible white voters, states passed **grandfather clauses.** If a voter's father or grandfather had been eligible to vote on January 1, 1867, the voter did not have to take

Why Study History?

Because Tolerance Begins With You

Historical Background

During and after Reconstruction, hate groups like the Ku Klux Klan used violence and terror to keep African Americans from voting or holding any political office. Angry mobs set fire to African American homes, churches, and schools. They even lynched people. Often, these tactics worked. Yet many whites and African Americans continued to speak out against injustice.

Artist Jim Osborn created this painting to encourage respect and tolerance.

Connections to Today

Discrimination and hate crimes have not been limited to African Americans in the South in the 1800s. Almost every group in this nation has suffered the pain of senseless hatred. People feel the sting of prejudice for many reasons: religion, race, economic status, age, or physical or mental abilities.

Acts of prejudice continue today. In recent years, Jewish cemeteries have been vandalized. African American churches have been burned. Asian American stores have been covered in racist graffiti. Mexican American or Arab American businesses have been attacked. In some areas, police have set up special "hate crime" units to investigate actions such as these.

Connections to You

Tolerance begins with you. You can fight prejudice by respecting and appreciating people's differences. Everyone in your class has different talents and experiences. You can get to know your classmates for who they are, rather than on the basis of what you think you know about them. You will find that you have much in common with students who seem different.

Many schools provide opportunities for you to increase your ability to get along with others. Human relations clubs promote understanding of diverse groups. Peer-mediation programs can teach you how to deal with anger and conflict. By keeping an open mind and educating yourself, you can help end discrimination and prejudice.

1. **Comprehension** **(a)** What tactics did hate groups use against African Americans in the South? **(b)** Identify two kinds of discrimination some people face today.
2. **Critical Thinking** How do prejudice and discrimination begin?

Making a Poster Make a list of three things that you could do to promote tolerance. Create a poster illustrating one of them.

a literacy test. Since no African Americans in the South could vote before 1868, grandfather clauses were a way to ensure that only white men could vote.

Racial segregation

Southern blacks lost more than the right to vote. After 1877, segregation became the law of the South. **Segregation** means separating people of different races in public places. Southern states passed laws that separated blacks and whites in schools, restaurants, theaters, trains, streetcars, playgrounds, hospitals, and even cemeteries. **Jim Crow laws,** as they were known, trapped southern blacks in a hopeless situation. In 1885, the Louisiana novelist George Washington Cable described segregation as:

> "... a system of oppression so rank that nothing could make it seem small except the fact that [African Americans] had already been ground under it for a century and a half."

African Americans brought lawsuits to challenge segregation. In 1896, in the case of **Plessy v. Ferguson,** the Supreme Court ruled that segregation was legal so long as facilities for blacks and whites were equal. In fact, facilities were rarely equal. For example, southern states spent much less on schools for blacks than for whites.

Violence

When Reconstruction ended, groups like the Ku Klux Klan declined. However, violent acts against African Americans continued. During the 1890s, almost 200 Americans were lynched each year. **Lynching** is the illegal seizure and execution of someone by a mob. Four out of five lynchings took place in the South, and the majority of the victims were African American.

Some lynching victims were accused of crimes. Others were simply considered troublemakers. Victims—including some women and children—were hanged, shot, or burned to death, often after painful torture. Members of lynch mobs rarely faced punishment. By the late 1800s, some reformers began to speak out against lynching.

Results of Reconstruction

Reconstruction was a time of both success and failure. Southerners faced hard times. Still, the South gained a public education system and expanded its rail lines.

As a result of Reconstruction, all African Americans became citizens for the first time. These rights eroded after Reconstruction ended. However, the laws passed during Reconstruction, such as the Fourteenth Amendment, became the basis of the civil rights movement almost 100 years later.

★ Section 4 Review ★

Recall

1. **Identify** **(a)** Rutherford B. Hayes, **(b)** Henry Grady, **(c)** James Duke, **(d)** Jim Crow laws, **(e)** *Plessy* v. *Ferguson*.
2. **Define** **(a)** poll tax, **(b)** literacy test, **(c)** grandfather clause, **(d)** segregation, **(e)** lynching.

Comprehension

3. Why did Radical Republicans' power decline?
4. How did the economy of the South change?
5. Describe two ways that African Americans lost their rights after Reconstruction ended.

Critical Thinking and Writing

6. **Evaluating Information** Do you think that Reconstruction was successful? Explain.
7. **Predicting Consequences** How do you think *Plessy* v. *Ferguson* affected later efforts to achieve equality for African Americans?

Activity **Acting a Scene** With a partner, act out a scene of an African American man trying to vote in the South in the late 1880s. Begin by considering how you might feel if you knew that you had the right to vote, yet someone was able to prevent you from voting.

Chapter 18 Review and Activities

★ Sum It Up ★

Section 1 First Steps to Reunion

- After the Civil War, the South faced the task of repairing tremendous destruction.
- The Freedmen's Bureau helped newly freed African Americans learn to read, and provided food and clothing to the needy.
- Presidents Lincoln and Johnson recommended mild plans for Reconstruction, but Congress refused to accept either one.

Section 2 Radical Reconstruction

- Radical Republicans wanted to break the power of rich planters in the South and make sure that freedmen could vote.
- Congress tried and failed to remove President Johnson from office.
- Republicans proposed the Fourteenth and Fifteenth amendments to ensure the civil rights of African Americans.

Section 3 Changes in the South

- Southern Republicans, whites from the North, and freed African Americans played important roles in southern governments.
- Landless black and white sharecroppers became locked in a cycle of poverty.

Section 4 Reconstruction Ends

- Reconstruction ended after presidential candidate Rutherford B. Hayes made a private deal with southern politicians.
- After Reconstruction, a new industrial economy began to emerge in the South.
- Southern whites passed new laws to deny African Americans equal rights.

For additional review of the major ideas of Chapter 18, see ***Guide to the Essentials of American History*** or ***Interactive Student Tutorial CD-ROM,*** which contains interactive review activities, graphic organizers, and practice tests.

Reviewing the Chapter

Define These Terms

Match each term with the correct definition.

Column 1

1. freedman
2. black codes
3. scalawag
4. poll tax
5. segregation

Column 2

a. laws that severely limited the rights of freedmen
b. tax required before someone could vote
c. white southern Republican
d. former slave
e. separating people of different races in public places

Explore the Main Ideas

1. Describe the condition of the South after the war.
2. How did Republicans in Congress gain control of Reconstruction?
3. Give two reasons why Republicans supported the Fifteenth Amendment.
4. Describe the economic recovery of the South after the Civil War.
5. Why did most Americans lose interest in Reconstruction in the 1870s?
6. What was the purpose of Jim Crow laws?

Geography Activity

Match the letters on the map with the following places: **1.** South Carolina, **2.** Florida, **3.** Louisiana, **4.** Ohio, **5.** New York. **Region** Which southern states were under Republican control in 1876?

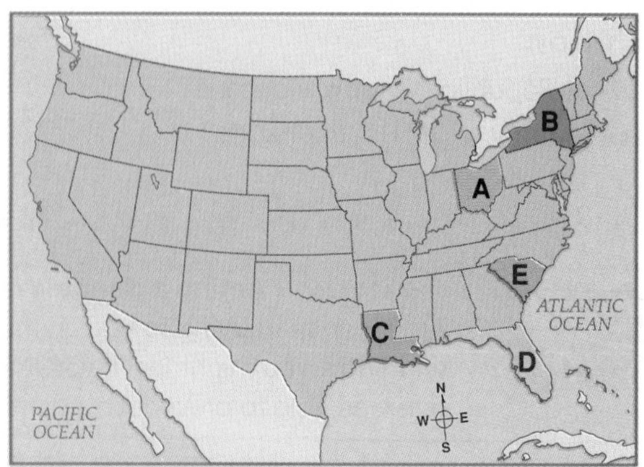

Critical Thinking and Writing

1. **Understanding Chronology** **(a)** Put the following in the order in which they were first proposed: the Reconstruction Acts; the Wade-Davis Bill; the Ten Percent Plan; Jim Crow laws. **(b)** Why did Lincoln have so little influence on Reconstruction?
2. Exploring Unit Themes **Sectionalism** Briefly state your own plan for repairing the bitter feelings between North and South.
3. **Analyzing Ideas** Most people call groups such as the Ku Klux Klan "un-American." Explain the reasons for this belief.
4. **Predicting Consequences** After the Civil War, the United States entered a period of industrial growth that made it the richest nation in the world. How do you think the South's experiences during Reconstruction affected its share in this industrial boom?

Using Primary Sources

Born into slavery, Booker T. Washington became a leading educator. Here, he describes one of the problems that came with emancipation:

> "Was it any wonder that within a few hours the wild rejoicing ceased and a feeling of deep gloom seemed to pervade the slave quarters? To some it seemed that, now that they were in actual possession of it, freedom was a more serious thing than they expected to find it. Some of the slaves were seventy or eighty years old; their best days were gone. They had no strength with which to earn a living in a strange place and among strange people, even if they had been sure where to find a new place of abode."

Source: *Up From Slavery,* Booker T. Washington, 1901.

Recognizing Points of View **(a)** What caused the "wild rejoicing" Washington mentions? **(b)** Why did the rejoicing end so quickly? **(c)** Why do you think many African Americans were unprepared for the realities of freedom?

Activity Bank

Interdisciplinary Activity

Connections With Arts Review the goals of the Freedmen's Bureau. Then create a poster advertising the Bureau's work and encouraging volunteers to participate.

Career Skills Activity

Playwrights and Actors Find out more about the events and issues leading up to the trial of President Andrew Johnson. Then prepare a skit in which you act out Johnson's trial in the United States Senate.

Citizenship Activity

Understanding the Constitution Study the text of the Fourteenth and Fifteenth amendments printed in the Reference Section. Create a graphic organizer for each amendment. Include the main ideas of each amendment and show how it affects the daily lives of Americans today. You may illustrate your work with original drawings or clippings.

Internet Activity

Use the Internet to find primary sources on Reconstruction. Then use the primary source to create a newspaper interview with the person who wrote the material you have found. Create questions that are answered by quotations taken from the primary source.

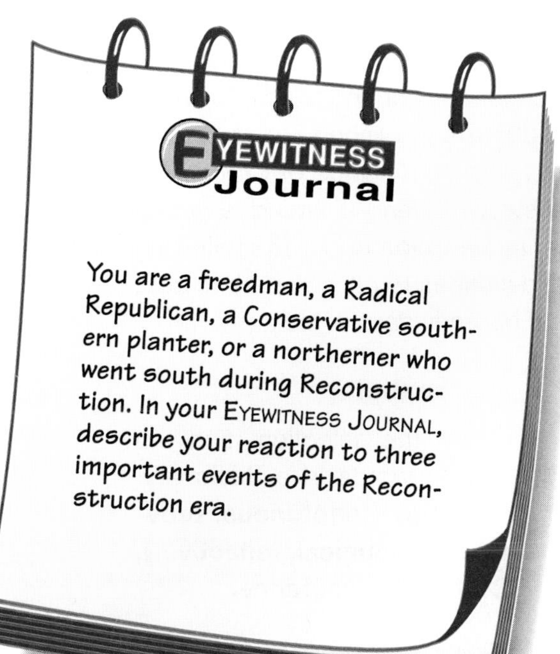

The Red Badge of Courage

Stephen Crane

Introduction

Stephen Crane was born six years after the Civil War ended. He spent many hours reading about the war and talking to veterans. In 1895, he published his great Civil War novel, *The Red Badge of Courage.* It tells the story of Henry Fleming, a young volunteer in the Union Army. The following passage describes Henry's departure from home and his early days in the army.

Vocabulary

Before you read the selection, find the meaning of these words in a dictionary: **doggedly, shirking, monotonous, province, pickets, philosophical, reflectively, reproached, infantile, assurance.**

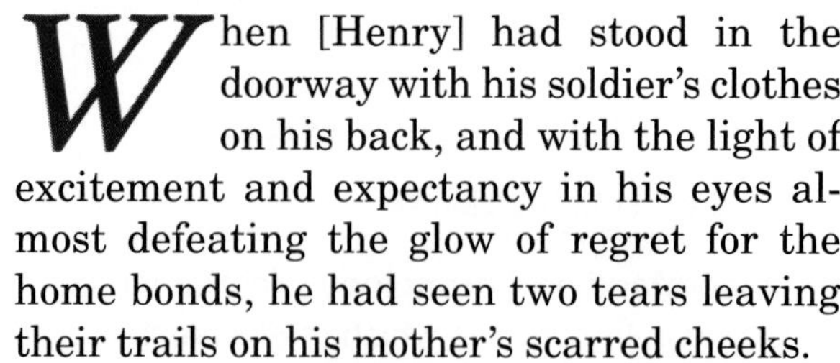

When [Henry] had stood in the doorway with his soldier's clothes on his back, and with the light of excitement and expectancy in his eyes almost defeating the glow of regret for the home bonds, he had seen two tears leaving their trails on his mother's scarred cheeks.

Still, she had disappointed him by saying nothing whatever about returning with his shield or on it.* He had privately primed himself for a beautiful scene. He had prepared certain sentences which he thought could be used with touching effect. But her words destroyed his plans. She had doggedly peeled potatoes and addressed him as follows: "You watch out, Henry, an' take good care of yerself in this here fighting business —you watch out, an' take good care of yerself. Don't go a-thinkin' you can lick the hull rebel army at the start, because yeh can't. Yer jest one little feller amongst a hull lot of others, and yeh've got to keep quiet an' do what they tell yeh. I know how you are, Henry.

"I've knet yeh eight pair of socks, Henry, and I've put in all yer best shirts, because I want my boy to be jest as warm and comf'able as anybody in the army. Whenever they get holes in 'em, I want yeh to send 'em rightaway back to me, so's I kin dern 'em.

"An' allus be careful an' choose yer comp'ny. There's lots of bad men in the army, Henry. The army makes 'em wild, and they like nothing better than the job of leading off a young feller like you, as ain't never been away from home much and has allus had a mother, an' a-learning 'em to drink and swear. Keep clear of them folks, Henry. . . .

"I don't know what else to tell yeh, Henry, excepting that yeh must never do no shirking, child, on my account. If so be a time comes when yeh have to be kilt or do a mean thing, why, Henry, don't think of anything 'cept what's right, because there's many a woman has to bear up 'ginst sech things these times, and the Lord'll take keer of us all.

"Don' forget about the socks and the shirts, child; and I've put a cup of blackberry jam with yer bundle, because I know yeh like it

---

* The Spartan people of ancient Greece carried home their dead warriors on their shields.

Viewing HISTORY A Soldier Says Goodbye

This anonymous painting, Off to the Front, 1861, *is owned by the museum of the United States Military Academy at West Point, New York. It shows a young soldier saying goodbye to his family in the first year of the Civil War. Scenes like this were common in homes throughout the North and South.* ★ **Choose one of the people in this painting. What do you think are that person's thoughts and feelings?**

above all things. Good-by, Henry. Watch out, and be a good boy."

He had, of course, been impatient under the ordeal of this speech. It had not been quite what he expected, and he had borne it with an air of irritation. He departed feeling vague relief.

Still, when he had looked back from the gate, he had seen his mother kneeling among the potato parings. Her brown face, upraised, was stained with tears, and her spare form was quivering. He bowed his head and went on, feeling suddenly ashamed....

After complicated journeyings with many pauses, there had come months of monotonous life in a camp. He had had the belief that real war was a series of death struggles with small time in between for sleep and meals; but since his regiment had come to the field the army had done little but sit still and try to keep warm....

He had grown to regard himself merely as a part of a vast blue demonstration. His province was to look out, as far as he could, for his personal comfort. For recreation he could twiddle his thumbs and speculate on the thoughts which must agitate the minds of the generals. Also, he was drilled and drilled and reviewed, and drilled and drilled and reviewed.

The only foes he had seen were some pickets along the river bank. They were a suntanned, philosophical lot, who sometimes shot reflectively at the blue pickets. When reproached for this afterward, they usually expressed sorrow, and swore by their gods that the guns had exploded without their permission. The youth, on guard duty one night, conversed across the stream with one of them. He was a slightly ragged man, who spat skillfully between his shoes and possessed a great fund of bland and infantile assurance. The youth liked him personally.

"Yank," the other had informed him, "yer a right dum good feller." This sentiment, floating to him upon the still air, had made him temporarily regret war.

Analyzing Literature

1. What advice did Henry's mother give him?
2. How was a soldier's life different than what Henry expected?
3. **Making Generalizations** What does Henry's experience with the enemy picket suggest about the special problems of fighting a civil war?

Unit 6

Transforming the Nation

What's Ahead

Viewing UNIT THEMES **A Triumph of Technology**

On May 24, 1883, New Yorkers celebrated the opening of the Brooklyn Bridge with fireworks and a boat parade. The bridge was one of the greatest feats of American engineering. At first, the Brooklyn Bridge carried pedestrians and horse-drawn carriages. Soon after, a new invention—the automobile—would appear.

★ **Name two earlier inventions that improved transportation in the United States.**

Unit Theme Industrialization

After the Civil War, the United States underwent a great transformation. Industrialists opened thousands of new factories. Shrewd business leaders made fortunes building railroads, manufacturing steel, or drilling for oil. New inventions, from the light bulb to the automobile, changed daily life. Industrialization fueled the rapid growth of cities.

How did people of the time feel about industrialization? They can tell you in their own words.

Viewpoints on Industrialization

" In factories where labor-saving machinery has reached its most wonderful development, little children are at work. "

Henry George, economist and journalist (1879)

" Better morals, better sanitary conditions, better health, better wages, these are the practical results of the factory system. "

Carroll D. Wright, United States labor commissioner (1882)

" Law, I reckon I was born to work in a mill. I started when I was ten years old and I aim to keep right on just as long as I'm able. I'd a-heap rather do it than housework. "

Alice Caudle, textile worker, recalling her childhood (1938)

Activity Writing to Learn Industrialization transformed the way people worked. You are a young American of the late 1800s. You grew up in the country, working on the family farm. You have just moved to a big city where you are about to begin your new job in a factory making lawnmowers. Make a list of the ways in which your new job differs from your old one.

Chapter 19

An Era of Change in the West 1865–1914

What's Ahead

Section 1
The Plains Indians

Section 2
Miners and Railroaders

Section 3
Ranchers and Cowhands

Section 4
A Way of Life Ends

Section 5
The Farmers

After the Civil War, settlers flooded the West. Miners sought gold and silver. Railroad builders spanned the continent with rail lines. Ranchers raised great herds of cattle. Farmers changed grasslands into fields of wheat and corn. As these westerners gained political influence, they urged government leaders to address their needs and concerns.

Native Americans, meanwhile, were driven from their homelands. The Indians struggled to keep their way of life. In the end, however, they were defeated. On reservations, they were forced to learn new ways. Native Americans suffered greatly from the changes that swept the West.

Why Study *History?*

According to most historians, the cowhand was an important figure in the American West for only a short time. Nevertheless, the cowboy entered American culture as an enduring mythic hero. The image of the cowboy still speaks to people today. To learn more about this topic, see this chapter's *Why Study History?* feature, "The Cowboy Is Part of Our Culture."

American Events

- **1869** Nation's first transcontinental railroad is completed
- **1876** Sitting Bull defeats Custer during the Sioux War
- **1887** Dawes Act encourages Native Americans to change their lifestyle

1865 | 1870 | 1875 | 1880 | 1885 | 1890

World Events

1869 World Event
Suez canal opens in Egypt

1879 World Event
British and Zulus go to war in southern Africa

Viewing History: Cold Morning on the Range

In the late 1800s, the West and its wide-open spaces captured the imagination of adventurers, settlers, business people, writers, and artists. They all saw the frontiers of the West as places of opportunity. Sadly, few people were concerned with the Native Americans who already lived there. In this colorful painting by Frederic Remington, a cowhand tries to ride a bucking bronco. ★ **How do you think this and similar paintings affected people's ideas about the West? Explain.**

1891
Farmers and labor unions join to form Populist Party

1897
William McKinley becomes President

1913
States ratify income tax amendment to the Constitution

1890 | 1895 | 1900 | 1905 | 1910 | 1915

1891 World Event
Work begins on Trans-Siberian railroad to connect Moscow to Pacific coast

1910 World Event
China abolishes slavery

The Plains Indians

As You Read

Explore These Questions

- How did Plains Indians rely on the horse and the buffalo?
- What traditions were important to the Plains Indians?
- How did the roles of women and men differ?

Define

- tepee
- travois
- corral
- jerky

Identify

- Sun Dance

SETTING the Scene Standing Bear, a Lakota, or Sioux* Indian, recalled the buffalo-rib sled his father made for him when he was a boy living on the Plains:

> "After all the meat had been cleaned from the bones, my father took six of the ribs and placed them together. He then split a piece of cherry wood and put the ends of the bones between the pieces of wood. The whole affair was then laced together with rawhide rope."

Standing Bear's rib sled is only one example of the many uses that Plains Indians had for the buffalo that roamed their homeland. Indians had been living for centuries on the Great Plains. They developed ways of life that were well suited to the region.

Way of Life

Many different Native American nations lived on the Great Plains. (See the map on page 31.) A number of nations, such as the Arikaras, had lived on the Plains for hundreds of years. Others, like the Lakotas, did not move to the Plains until the 1700s.

Plains Indians had rich and varied cultures. They had well-organized religions, made fine handicrafts, and created much poetry. Each nation had its own language. People from different nations used sign language to talk to one another.

At one time, most Plains Indians were farmers who lived in semipermanent villages. From there, they sent out hunting parties that pursued herds of buffalo and other animals on foot. Agriculture, however, was their main source of food.

During the 1600s, the Plains Indians' way of life changed as they captured and tamed wild horses. These horses were descended from animals that the Spanish had brought to the Americas. On horseback, the Indians could travel farther and faster. As a result, buffalo hunting replaced farming as the basis of life for many Plains people.

Following the buffalo

Plains Indians followed the huge herds of buffalo that roamed the Plains. They began to live in **tepees** (TEE pees), or tents made by stretching buffalo skins on tall poles. The tepees could easily be carried on a **travois** (trə VOI), or sled pulled by a dog or horse.

Connections With Science

Plains Indians rubbed buffalo fat on their skin to protect themselves from the weather and from insects. They used paints made from clay, charred wood, and copper ore to decorate their faces.

*Sioux was the French name for these Indians. In fact, the Sioux included many different groups who had their own names for themselves, including Lakota, Dakota, and Nakota.

Viewing History: Following the Buffalo Run

During buffalo hunts, Plains women packed, moved, and unpacked the group's possessions. In this painting by Charles M. Russell, women have loaded their belongings on a travois. They are following the buffalo to a new location, where they will set up camp. ★ **Do you think Plains Indians had many personal possessions? Why or why not?**

▲ *Kiowa baby carrier*

The migration of the Plains Indians mirrored the movement of the buffalo. In winter, small groups of buffalo moved off the Plains to protected valleys and forests. In summer, huge buffalo herds gathered on the Plains where the grass was growing high. In the same way, Plains Indians spent the winter in small bands and gathered in large groups during the summers. The people worked together and owned many things in common.

These groups often staged buffalo drives. Shouting and waving colored robes, hunters drove a herd of buffalo into a **corral,** or enclosure. There, they killed the trapped buffalo. After a kill, the band celebrated with a feast of roasted buffalo meat.

Uses of the buffalo

Plains Indians depended on the buffalo for food, clothing, and shelter. Buffalo meat, rich in protein, was a main item in the Indians' diet. Women cut up and dried the meat on racks. The dried meat was called **jerky.**

Women also tanned buffalo hides to make leather. They wove buffalo fur into coarse, warm cloth. Buffalo horns and bones were carved into tools and toys. The sinews of the buffalo could be used as thread or bowstrings.

Traditions

In summer, many Native American groups met on the Plains. They hunted together, played games, and staged foot and horse races.

Summer gatherings were also the time for councils. At the councils, leaders consulted with elders about problems that affected the whole nation. Indian doctors treated the sick.

One of the most important events was a religious ceremony known as the **Sun Dance.** Thousands of people attended the four-day ceremony to thank the Great Spirit for help in times of trouble.

The Sun Dance took place in a lodge made of tree branches. A sacred tree stood in the middle, and people hung their offerings from it. Dancers circled the tree and asked the Great Spirit for good fortune in the coming year.

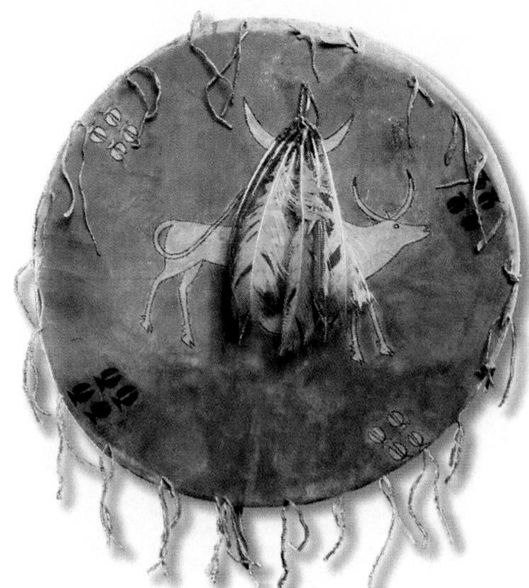
Cheyenne war shield

A Well-Ordered Society

Women oversaw life in the home. They gathered foods and prepared meals for their families. They also performed such heavy work as raising and taking down tepees. Women cared for the children and taught them the traditions of their people.

Women also engaged in many crafts. They sewed animal hides to make clothing and tepees. They made the baskets, pottery, and blankets that were essential to the community. Their work often displayed great artistic skill and design. In fact, a woman's ability in crafts established her rank in society. The woman who made the most beautiful clothing or prepared the greatest number of baskets gained much the same honor as a man who performed bravely in battle.

In some of the tribes, women helped men with the duties of hunting and governing. A Blackfoot woman, Running Eagle, led many hunting parties herself. In other bands, a woman respected for her wisdom made the final decisions about important matters.

The men of the Plains Indians had important responsibilities too. They hunted and traded. They passed on their valuable skills and knowledge to the boys. They supervised the spiritual life of the community by leading religious ceremonies. Men with special skills provided medical care for the sick and injured.

Another important responsibility of the men was to provide military leadership. They waged war to defend or extend territory, to gain horses and other riches, or to seek revenge. More than anything else, however, men waged war to protect their people and to prove their bravery and ability. The most successful warriors gained great respect and status among their nation.

★ Section 1 Review ★

Recall

1. **Identify** Sun Dance.
2. **Define** **(a)** tepee, **(b)** travois, **(c)** corral, **(d)** jerky.

Comprehension

3. **(a)** How did the use of horses change the way Plains Indians lived? **(b)** Why did Plains Indians live in different places at different times of the year?
4. Describe three ways in which Native Americans made use of buffalo.
5. What activities took place at the summer gatherings of Plains Indians?

Critical Thinking and Writing

6. **Making Inferences** How did the dependence on hunting buffalo affect the roles of Indian women and men on the Plains?
7. **Making Generalizations** Based on what you know about the Sun Dance ceremony, what were some religious beliefs of the Plains Indians?

Activity **Making a Graphic Organizer** Based on what you have learned in this section, make a graphic organizer to show the different ways in which the Plains Indians relied on the buffalo.

Miners and Railroaders

As You Read

Explore These Questions

- How did mining change the West?
- What was life like for miners and railroad workers?
- How did railroads help the West develop?

Define

- vigilante
- subsidy
- transcontinental railroad

Identify

- Comstock Lode
- Union Pacific Railroad
- Central Pacific Railroad
- Leland Stanford

Setting the Scene Many Americans were lured west by the chance to strike it rich mining gold and silver. "What a clover-field is to a steer, the sky to the lark, a mudhole to a hog, such are new diggings to a miner," wrote one observer in 1862.

Miners reversed the traditional pattern of expansion. Instead of moving from east to west as the earlier pioneers had done, many journeyed from west to east. From the California coast, they fanned out eastward, ever in search of new ways to make their fortune.

The Mining Boom

The western mining boom had begun with the California Gold Rush of 1849. When the Gold Rush ended, miners looked for new opportunities. The merest rumor sent them racing east in search of new strikes.

Gold and silver strikes

In 1859, two young prospectors struck gold in the Sierra Nevada. Suddenly, another miner, Henry Comstock, appeared. "The land is mine," he cried, and demanded to be made a partner. From then on, Comstock boasted about "his" mine. The strike became known as the **Comstock Lode.** A lode is a rich vein of gold or silver.

Comstock and his partners often complained about the heavy blue sand that was mixed in with the gold. It clogged the devices used for separating the gold and made the gold hard to reach. When Mexican miners took the "danged blue stuff" to an expert in California, tests showed it was loaded with silver. Comstock had stumbled onto one of the richest silver mines in the world.

Miners moved into many other areas of the West. Some found valuable ore in Montana and Idaho. Others struck it rich in Colorado. In the 1870s, miners discovered gold in the Black Hills of South Dakota. (See the map on page 510.) In the late 1890s, thousands rushed north to Alaska after major gold strikes were made there.

Boom towns and ghost towns

Gold and silver strikes attracted thousands of prospectors. Miners came from across the United States, as well as from Germany, Ireland, Mexico, and China. Towns sprang up near all the major mining sites.

First, miners built a tent city near the diggings. Then, thousands of people came to supply the miners' needs. Traders brought mule teams loaded with tools, food, and clothing. Merchants hauled in wagonloads of supplies and set up stores.

Connections With Arts

After failing as a prospector, Samuel Clemens became a writer for a Nevada newspaper. His amusing articles appeared in papers throughout the West. In 1863, Clemens signed one of his articles with a new name, one well-known to readers today—Mark Twain.

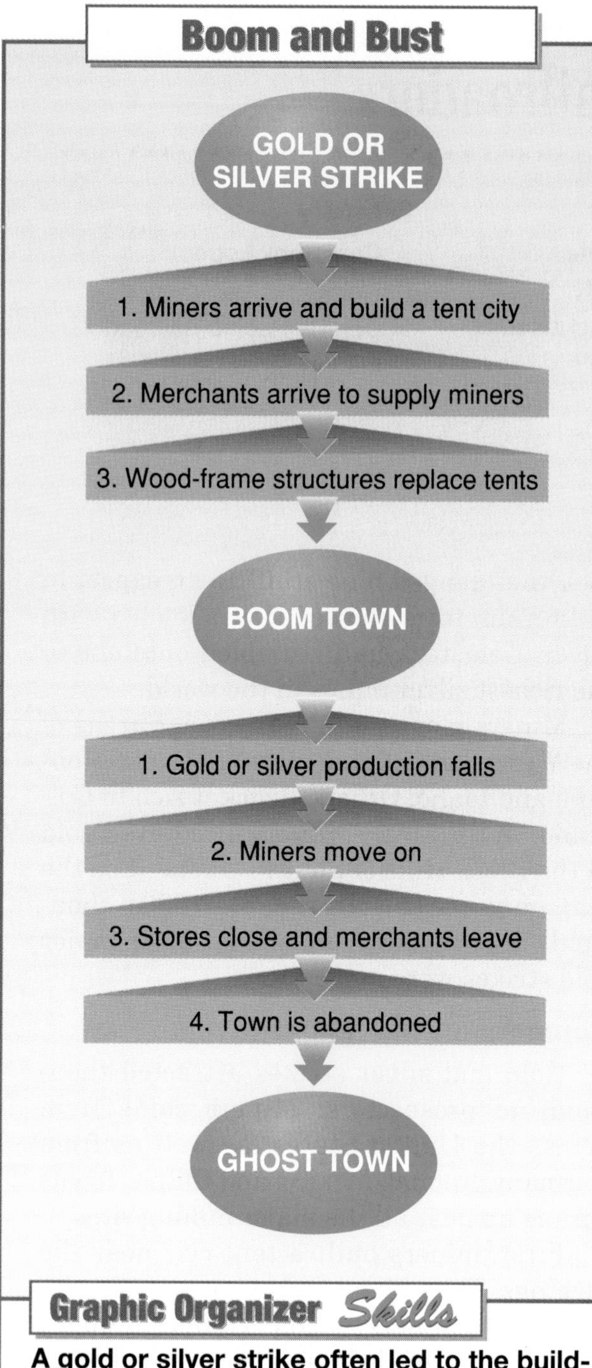

Graphic Organizer Skills

A gold or silver strike often led to the building of a boom town. However, many boom towns quickly became ghost towns.

1. **Comprehension** **(a)** Why did merchants often follow miners? **(b)** What caused large numbers of miners to suddenly leave a boom town?
2. **Critical Thinking** Based on this chart and on the map on page 510, why do you think there are more ghost towns today in Colorado than there are in Texas?

Economics $

Soon, wood frame houses, hotels, restaurants, and stores replaced the tents. For example, it took less than a year for the mining camp at the Comstock Lode to become the boom town of Virginia City, Nevada.

Most settlers in the boom towns of the mining frontier were men. However, enterprising women also found ways to profit. Some women ran boarding houses and laundries. Others opened restaurants, where miners gladly paid high prices for a home-cooked meal.

Many boom towns lasted for only a few years. When the gold or silver ore was gone, miners moved away. Without miners for customers, businesses often had to close. In this way, a boom town could quickly go bust and turn into a ghost town.

Still, some boom towns survived and prospered even after the mines shut down. In these towns, miners stayed and found new ways to make a living.

Impact of the boom

The surge of miners into the West created problems. Mines and towns polluted clear mountain streams. Miners cut down forests to get wood for buildings. As you will read, they also forced Native Americans from the land.

Foreign miners were often treated unfairly. In many camps, mobs drove Mexicans from their claims. Chinese miners were heavily taxed or forced to work claims abandoned by others.

Few miners got rich quickly. Much of the gold and silver lay deep underground. It could be reached only with costly machinery. Eventually, most mining in the West was taken over by large companies that could afford to buy this equipment.

Governing the mining frontier

Lawlessness and disorder often accompanied the rapid growth of a town. In response, miners sometimes resorted to organizing groups of **vigilantes.** These self-appointed law enforcers tracked down outlaws and punished them, usually without a trial. A common punishment used by vigilantes was lynching.

American Heritage
M A G A Z I N E

HISTORY HAPPENED HERE

Bannack State Park

In 1862, gold was found along Grasshopper Creek in Montana. The boom town of Bannack grew up at the site and became Montana's first territorial capital. Bannack was a wild frontier town, complete with saloons, gambling, and gunfights. But, when the gold disappeared, so did the people. Today, the ghost town is Bannack State Park. Visitors can walk among the remains of more than 50 buildings, including the Montana Territorial Capitol, the Hotel Meade, and the town jail.

★ ***To learn more about this historic site, write:*** *Bannack State Park, 4200 Bannack Road, Dillon, MT 59725.*

Informal methods of government gradually gave way to more formal arrangements. In 1861, Colorado, Dakota, and Nevada were organized into territories. Idaho and Arizona followed in 1863 and Montana in 1864. The process of more permanent settlement and government had begun.

The Railroads

The people of the mining towns needed large amounts of supplies. They also needed to transport their gold and silver. As a result, railroad companies raced to lay track to the mines and boom towns.

Spanning the continent

The federal government helped the railroad companies because it felt that rail lines in the West would benefit the entire nation. The government's aid came in the form of subsidies. A **subsidy** is financial aid or a land grant from the government. Congress lent money to the railroad companies and gave them land. Often, both business and government ignored the fact that Native Americans lived on the land.

In 1863, two companies began a race to build the first transcontinental railroad. A **transcontinental railroad** is one that stretches across a continent from coast to coast. The **Union Pacific** started building a rail line from Omaha, Nebraska, westward. The **Central Pacific** began in Sacramento, California, and built eastward. The *Sacramento Union* of January 8, 1863, reported:

> "With rites appropriate to the occasion . . . ground was formally broken at noon for the commencement of the Central Pacific Railroad—the California link of the continental chain that is to unite American communities now divided by thousands of miles of trackless wilderness."

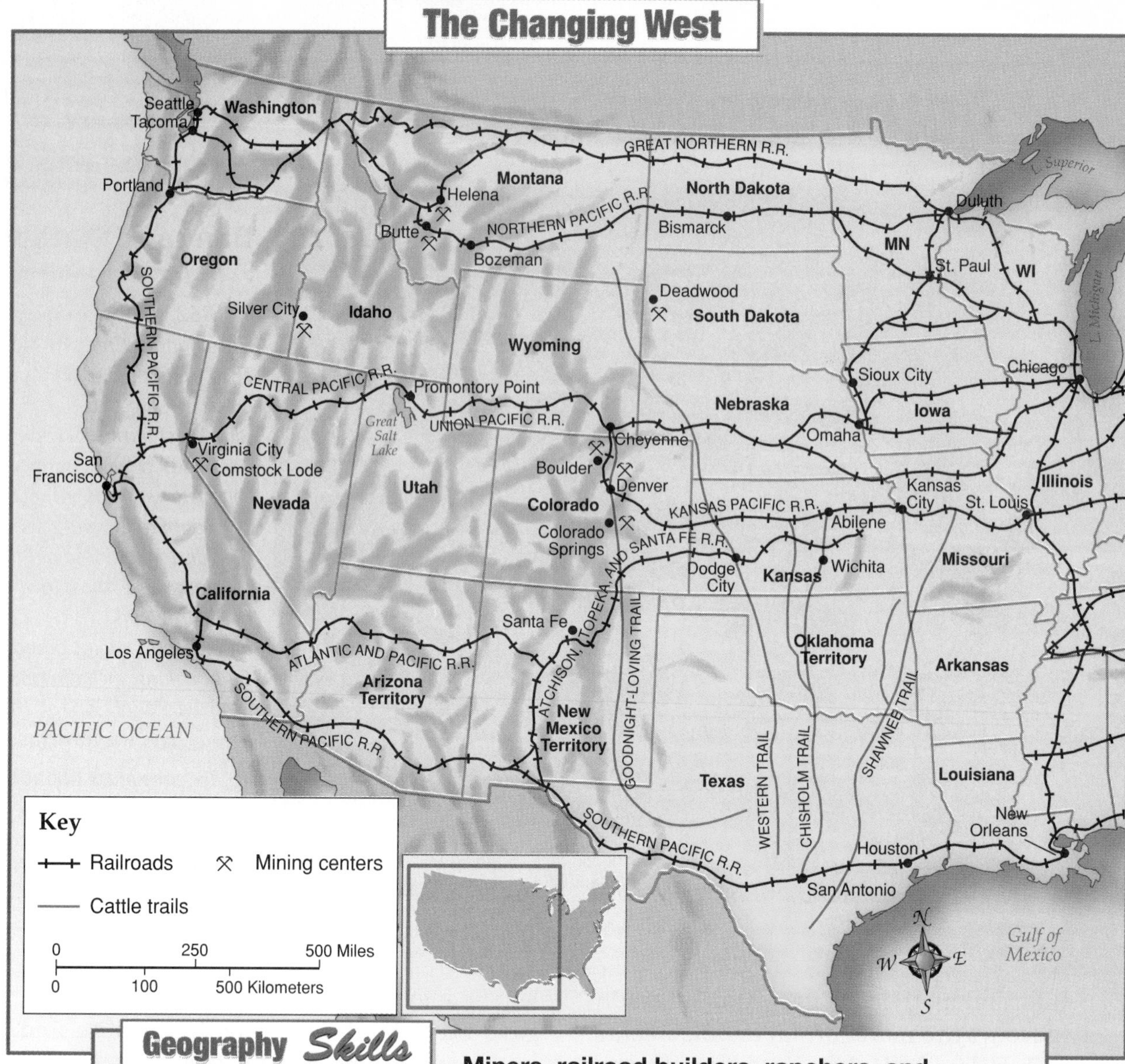

Geography Skills **Miners, railroad builders, ranchers, and cowhands all played a major role in changing the West.**

1. **Location** On the map, locate: **(a)** Comstock Lode, **(b)** Central Pacific Railroad, **(c)** Promontory Point, **(d)** Chisholm Trail.
2. **Interaction** How did mining affect nearby soil, water, and other natural resources?
3. **Critical Thinking** Why did most railroad lines in the West run east-west rather than north-south?

Immigrant workers

Both companies had trouble getting workers. Labor was scarce during the Civil War. Also, the work was backbreaking and dangerous and the pay low.

The railroad companies hired immigrant workers, who accepted the low wages. The Central Pacific brought in thousands of workers from China. The Union Pacific hired newcomers from Ireland. African Americans and Mexican Americans also worked for each line.

The workers faced a tough task. The Central Pacific had to carve a path through the rugged Sierra Nevada. The Union Pacific had to cut through the towering Rockies. Snowstorms and avalanches killed workers and slowed progress. At times, crews advanced only a few inches a day.

Viewing HISTORY Working on the Railroad

Chinese and European immigrants worked together to complete the transcontinental railroad. ★ **What dangers and hardships did the workers face?**

Impact of the railroads

The Central Pacific and Union Pacific met at Promontory Point, Utah, on May 10, 1869. **Leland Stanford,** president of the Central Pacific, hammered a golden spike into the rail that joined the two tracks and united the country. The nation's first transcontinental railroad was completed.

With the Civil War fresh in their minds, people cheered this new symbol of unity. The words that were engraved on the golden spike expressed their feelings:

> "May God continue the unity of our Country as the Railroad unites the two great Oceans of the world."

Before long, other major rail lines linked the West and the East. The railroads brought growth and new settlement all across the West. They enabled people, supplies, and mail to move quickly and cheaply across the plains and mountains. Wherever rail lines went, settlements sprang up along the tracks. The largest towns and cities developed where major railroad lines met.

Because of their rapid growth, western territories began to apply for statehood. Nevada became a state in 1864, Colorado in 1876, North Dakota, South Dakota, Montana, and Washington in 1889. Idaho and Wyoming entered the Union in 1890.

★ Section 2 Review ★

Recall

1. **Locate** **(a)** Virginia City, **(b)** Idaho, **(c)** Montana, **(d)** Colorado, **(e)** South Dakota, **(f)** Promontory Point.
2. **Identify** **(a)** Comstock Lode, **(b)** Union Pacific Railroad, **(c)** Central Pacific Railroad, **(d)** Leland Stanford.
3. **Define** **(a)** vigilantes, **(b)** subsidy, **(c)** transcontinental railroad.

Comprehension

4. How did mining encourage the growth of towns?
5. Describe two problems that immigrants faced as miners or railroad workers.
6. How did transcontinental railroads help to bring more states into the Union?

Critical Thinking and Writing

7. **Understanding Causes and Effects** Why did railroad companies hire immigrants to build the first transcontinental railroad?
8. **Linking Past and Present** Are railroads as important today as they were in the late 1800s? Explain.

Activity **Writing a Speech** You are a railroad official in 1869. Write a short speech to celebrate the completion of the first transcontinental railroad. In your speech, explain how you think the railroad will benefit the entire nation.

Ranchers and Cowhands

As You Read

Explore These Questions

- Why were there cattle drives?
- What was the life of a cowhand like?
- Why did the Cattle Kingdom end?

Define

- cattle drive
- cowhand
- vaquero
- cow town

Identify

- Chisholm Trail
- Cattle Kingdom

SETTING the Scene In the 1860s, a new group of Americans arrived in the West. These riders on horseback came from Texas, leading dusty lines of bellowing cattle. As they rode along, these cattle herders passed the time by singing songs like this one:

> "Well, come along, boys, and listen
> to my tale;
> I'll tell you of my troubles on the old
> Chisholm Trail.
> With a ten dollar horse and a forty
> dollar saddle,
> I started in herding these Texas
> cattle."

The Cattle Drives

Before the arrival of settlers from the United States, the Spanish and then the Mexicans set up cattle ranches in the Southwest. Over the years, strays from these ranches grew into large herds of wild cattle, known as longhorns. They roamed freely across the grassy plains of Texas.

After the Civil War, the demand for beef increased. Growing cities in the East needed more meat. Miners, railroad crews, and soldiers in the West added to the demand.

In response, Texas ranchers began rounding up herds of longhorns. They drove the animals hundreds of miles north to railroad lines in Kansas and Missouri. The long trips were called **cattle drives.**

Jesse Chisholm blazed one of the most famous cattle trails. Chisholm was half Scottish and half Cherokee. In the late 1860s, he began hauling goods by wagon between Texas and the Kansas Pacific Railroad. His route crossed rivers at the best places and passed by water holes. Ranchers began using the **Chisholm Trail** in 1867. Within five years, more than one million head of cattle had walked the road. (See the map on page 510.)

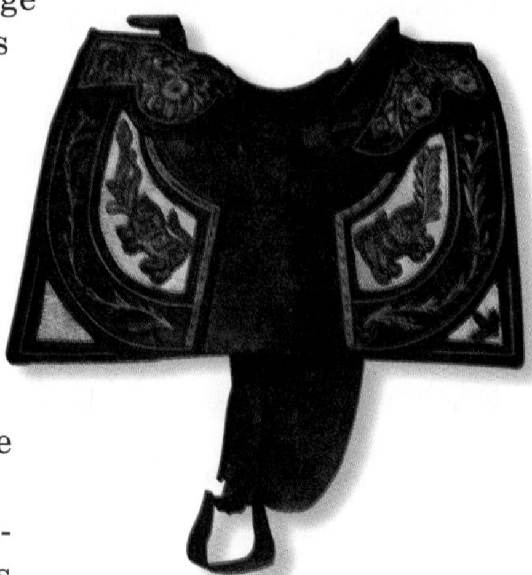

Saddle used by a Mexican vaquero

The Cowhands

Ranchers employed **cowhands** to tend their cattle and drive herds to market. These hard workers rode alongside the huge herds in good and bad weather. They kept the cattle moving and rounded up strays. It is estimated that nearly one in three cowhands was either Mexican American or African American.

Spanish heritage

American cowhands learned much about riding, roping, and branding from Spanish and Mexican **vaqueros** (vah KEHR ohs). Vaqueros were skilled riders who herded cattle on ranches in Mexico, California, and the Southwest.

California Vaqueros

Mexican American vaqueros were very important to the cattle industry of California, Texas, and the entire Southwest. The American artist James Walker painted this scene in the 1870s. ★ **Why did vaqueros and cowhands wear wide-brimmed hats?**

The gear used by American cowhands was modeled on the tools of the vaquero. Cowhands used the lariat—a leather rope—to catch runaway cattle. *Lariat* comes from the Spanish word for rope. Cowhands wore wide-brimmed hats like the Spanish sombrero. Their leather leggings, called chaps, were modeled on Spanish chaparreras (chap ah RAY rahs). Chaps protected a rider's legs from the thorny plants that grow in the Southwest.

On the trail

A cattle drive was hot, dirty, tiring work. Cowhands worked in all kinds of weather and faced many dangers. They had to prevent nervous cattle from drowning while crossing a fast-flowing river. They had to fight raging grass fires. They also faced attacks from cattle thieves who roamed the countryside.

One of the cowhand's worst fears on a cattle drive was a stampede. A clap of thunder or a gunshot could set thousands of longhorns off at a run. Cowhands had to ride into the crush of hoofs and horns. They slowed the stampeding herd by turning the cattle in a wide circle.

Most cowhands did not work for themselves. Instead, they were hired hands for the owners of large ranches. For all their hard work, cowhands were lucky to earn $1 a day! Even in the 1870s, this was low pay.

The Cow Towns

Cattle drives ended in **cow towns** that had sprung up along the railroad lines. The Chisholm Trail, for example, ended in Abilene, Kansas. (See the map on page 510.) In cow towns, cattle were held in great pens until they could be loaded on railroad cars and shipped to markets in the East.

In Abilene and other busy cow towns, dance halls, saloons, hotels, and restaurants catered to the cowhands. Sheriffs often had a hard time keeping the peace. Some cowhands spent wild nights drinking, dancing, and gambling.

Cow towns also attracted settlers who wanted to build stable communities where families could thrive. Doctors, barbers, artisans, bankers, and merchants helped to establish the cow towns.

The main street of a town was where people conducted business. Almost every town

Why Study History?

Because the Cowboy Is Part of Our Culture

Historical Background

In the late 1800s, writers and artists created the popular image of the American cowboy. The mythic and heroic cowboy was a hard worker—brave, dependable, and self-reliant. He helped the weak, fought for justice, and punished wrongdoers. He was a man of action.

People throughout the nation were captivated by the exciting adventures of this new American folk hero. They read about him in dime novels and magazines. They admired him in paintings and sculptures. They saw him in Wild West shows entertaining audiences with trick riding, fancy roping, and mock gunfights. In the early 1900s, people began watching their favorite cowboy stars in the motion pictures.

Pawnee Bill, shown here, is the popular cowboy star of a Wild West Show.

Connections to Today

Today, the cowboy remains an important part of American culture. Wild West shows are still popular, and rodeos are enjoying increasing attention. Some men and women try to take part in the action by vacationing on a dude ranch. Also, the heroic cowboy still rides the range in film and television. Sometimes, though, the cowboy is an "intergalactic starfighter," the West is outer space, and the outlaws are aliens bent on destroying the Earth.

Connections to You

The heroic cowboy image seems to capture the imagination of each new generation. Many young people enjoy listening to country-western music. Others like to wear western jeans and boots. Cowboys and western scenes often appear in commercial advertisements for a variety of products.

The heroic cowboy remains a popular figure in American culture today because of the ideals that are often associated with him. These ideals include independence, courage, hard work, and justice. The cowboy will probably remain an enduring American symbol as long as Americans cherish those values.

1. **Comprehension** **(a)** How was the heroic cowboy image created? **(b)** What were the key characteristics of the heroic cowboy?
2. **Critical Thinking** How are science-fiction films such as those of the *Star Wars* and *Star Trek* series similar to traditional movie westerns?

Interviewing Interview several people of different generations. Ask them to describe some ideals that they associate with the cowboy heroes of literature, film, and television. Share your findings in a report to the class.

had a general store that sold groceries, tools, clothing, and all sorts of goods. The general store also served as a social center where people could talk and exchange the latest news. As a town grew, more and more specialty shops lined its main street. These included drug stores, hardware stores, and even ice cream parlors.

Religion also played an important role for the townspeople. Throughout the West, places of worship grew in number and membership. They served as spiritual and social centers, and as symbols of progress and stability. "A church does as much to build up a town as a school, a railroad, or a fair," noted one New Mexico newspaper.

The Cattle Boom

In the 1870s, ranching spread north from Texas across the grassy Plains. Soon, cattle grazed from Kansas to present-day Montana. Ranchers had built a **Cattle Kingdom** in the West.

The open range

Ranchers let their cattle run wild on the open range. To identify cattle, each ranch had its own brand that was burned into the cattle's hide. Twice a year, young calves were rounded up and branded.

Sometimes, there were conflicts on the range. Since water was scarce, ranchers battled over rights to water holes and streams. When sheepherders moved onto the Plains, ranchers tried to drive them out. The ranchers complained that sheep nibbled the grass so low that cattle could not eat it.

End of an era

In the 1870s, farmers began moving onto the range. They fenced their fields with barbed wire. Sharp barbs kept cattle and sheep from pushing over fences and trampling plowed fields. As more farmers bought land and strung barbed wire, the open range began to disappear.

Bad weather on the Great Plains speeded the end of the Cattle Kingdom. The bitterly cold winters of 1886 and 1887 killed millions of cattle. By the spring of 1887, nine out of ten head of cattle on the northern Plains had frozen to death.

Cattle owners began to buy land and fence it in. Soon, farmers and ranchers divided the open range into a patchwork of large fenced plots. The days of the Cattle Kingdom were over.

★ Section 3 Review ★

Recall

1. **Locate** **(a)** Texas, **(b)** Kansas, **(c)** Abilene, **(d)** Dodge City, **(e)** Montana.
2. **Identify** **(a)** Chisholm Trail, **(b)** Cattle Kingdom.
3. **Define** **(a)** cattle drive, **(b)** cowhand, **(c)** vaquero, **(d)** cow town.

Comprehension

4. After the Civil War, why did Texas ranchers drive cattle herds to Kansas?
5. Describe some of the dangers that cowhands faced.
6. Explain two reasons why the Cattle Kingdom came to an end.

Critical Thinking and Writing

7. **Analyzing Visual Evidence** Study the painting of California vaqueros on p. 513. Then, identify and describe some of the equipment used by both vaqueros and cowhands.
8. **Predicting Consequences** How do you think the growth of the Cattle Kingdom affected the Plains Indians? Explain.

Activity **Writing a Song** Round 'em up! Move 'em out! You are driving cattle along the old Chisholm Trail. Review the song verse at the start of this section. Then, based on what you have learned about a cowhand's life, write a second verse to the song.

A Way of Life Ends

As You Read

Explore These Questions

- Why did Native Americans and settlers come into conflict?
- How did Native Americans try to preserve their way of life?
- How did government policies affect Native American culture?

Define

- reservation

Identify

- Sitting Bull
- Fort Laramie Treaty
- Chivington Massacre
- Battle of Little Bighorn
- Chief Joseph
- Geronimo
- Ghost Dance
- Susette La Flesche
- Helen Hunt Jackson
- Dawes Act

In 1876, **Sitting Bull,** a Lakota chief, wrote to the commander of United States Army troops, who had been sent to force him off his land:

> "I want to know what you are doing on this road. You scare all the buffalo away. I want to hunt in this place. I want you to turn back from here. If you don't, I will fight you."

After the Civil War, many Americans moved west. At first, the United States government promised to protect Indian hunting grounds. However, as settlers pushed westward, the government broke its promises. When Indians resisted the arrival of settlers, wars spread across the West. For Native Americans, tragedy was the result.

Broken Promises

Conflict began as early as the 1840s when settlers and miners began to cross Indian hunting grounds. The settlers and miners asked for government protection from the Indians.

Fort Laramie Treaty

In 1851, federal government officials met with Indian nations near Fort Laramie in Wyoming. The officials asked each nation to keep to a limited area. In return, they promised money, domestic animals, agricultural tools, and other goods. Officials told the Native Americans that the lands that were reserved for them would be theirs forever.

Native American leaders agreed to the terms in the **Fort Laramie Treaty.** However, in 1858, gold was discovered at Pikes Peak in Colorado. A wave of miners rushed to land that the government had promised to the Cheyennes and Arapahos.

Federal officials forced Indian leaders to sign a new treaty giving up the land around Pikes Peak. Some Native Americans refused to accept the agreement. They attacked white settlers.

The Chivington Massacre

The settlers struck back. In 1864, Colonel John Chivington led his militia against a peaceful Cheyenne village that the government had promised to protect. When Chivington attacked, the Indians raised a white flag of surrender. Chivington ignored the flag. He ordered his men to destroy the village and take no prisoners. In the **Chivington Massacre,** the militia slaughtered more than 100 men, women, and children.

People throughout the United States were outraged. "When the white man comes in my country he leaves a trail of blood behind him," said Lakota War Chief Red Cloud. Across the Plains, soldiers and Indians went to war.

Learning "American" ways

In 1867, federal officials established a peace commission. The commission wanted to end the wars on the Plains so that railroad builders and miners would be safe. The commission urged Native Americans to settle down and live as white farmers did. It also urged them to send their children to white schools to learn "American" ways.

At one white school in Indiana, Lakota children were horrified to hear that their hair would be cut short. Among the Lakotas, only cowards had short hair. One girl described her distress:

> "I cried aloud... I felt the cold blades of the scissors against my neck, and heard them gnaw off one of my thick braids. Then I lost my spirit."

Forced onto reservations

In 1867, the Kiowas, Comanches, and other southern Plains Indians signed a new treaty with the government. They promised to move to Indian Territory in present-day Oklahoma. The soil there was poor. Also, most Plains Indians were hunters, not farmers. The Indians did not like the treaty but knew they had no choice.

The Lakotas and Arapahos of the northern Plains also signed a treaty. They agreed to live on reservations in present-day South Dakota. A **reservation** is a limited area set aside for Native Americans.

End of the Buffalo

The Plains Indians suffered from lost battles and broken treaties. Even worse for them, however, was the destruction of the buffalo.

As the railroads moved west, buffalo hunting became a fashionable sport. Trainloads of easterners shot the animals from the comfort of railroad cars. Then, in the 1870s, buffalo hide blankets became popular in the East. Commercial hunters began shooting

Linking United States and the World

United States

Surrendering Their Land

In 1868, Sioux leaders met with United States government officials at Fort Laramie. The Indians signed a treaty agreeing to live on a reservation. In 1840, on the other side of the world, the Maori people of New Zealand signed the Treaty of Waitangi. By this treaty, the Maori leaders gave Great Britain control over New Zealand. ★ **Why do you think the United States and Britain both wanted more land?**

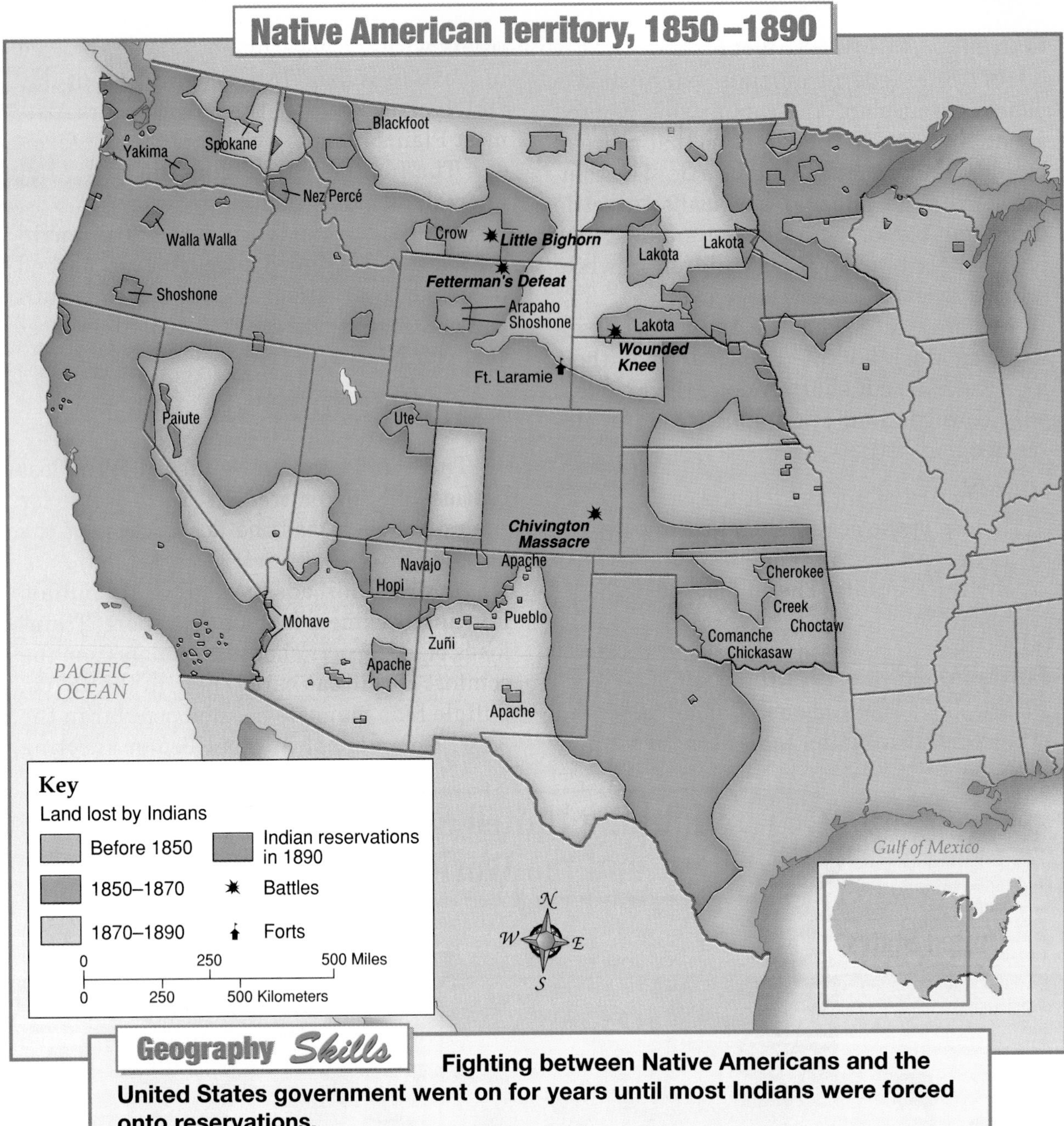

Geography Skills **Fighting between Native Americans and the United States government went on for years until most Indians were forced onto reservations.**

1. **Location** On the map, locate: **(a)** Fort Laramie, **(b)** Little Bighorn, **(c)** Apache reservations, **(d)** Wounded Knee.
2. **Region** In which areas of the country did Native Americans still retain much of their land in 1870?
3. **Critical Thinking** Why do you think the Apaches of the desert Southwest were one of the last Indian nations to lose their land?

2 to 3 million buffalo every year. The number of buffalo fell from 13 million in 1860 to a few hundred in 1900.

Facing starvation, the Plains Indians had to struggle simply to survive. As the buffalo disappeared, so did the Plains Indians' way of life. Years later, Pretty Shield, a woman of the Crow nation, sadly recalled the tragedy. "When the buffalo went away the hearts of my people fell to the ground, and they could not lift them up again.... I [saw] dead buffalo scattered all over our beautiful country."

The Final Battles

Settlers and miners continued to move into the West. They wanted more and more land for themselves. Even on reservations, the Indians were not left in peace.

Sioux War of 1876

In 1874, prospectors found gold in the Black Hills region of the Lakota, or Sioux, reservation. Thousands of miners rushed to the area. Led by Sitting Bull and Crazy Horse, another Lakota chief, the Indians fought back in what became known as the Sioux War of 1876.

In June 1876, Colonel George A. Custer led a column of soldiers into the Little Bighorn Valley. Indian scouts warned Custer that there were many Lakotas and Cheyennes camped ahead. Custer did not wait for more soldiers. Instead, he attacked with only 225 men. Custer and all his men died in the **Battle of Little Bighorn.**

The Indian victory at the Little Bighorn was shortlived. The army soon defeated the Lakotas and Cheyennes. Then, Congress ordered that no food rations be distributed to the Indians until they agreed to the government's demands. To avoid starvation, the Lakotas gave up all claims to the Black Hills and other territory. In this way, they surrendered about one third of the lands that the United States government had guaranteed them by the Fort Laramie Treaty.

Chief Joseph

The Nez Percés lived in the Snake River valley, at a place where Oregon, Washington, and Idaho meet. In the 1860s, gold strikes brought miners onto Nez Percé land. The government ordered the Nez Percés to move to a reservation in Idaho.

At first, **Chief Joseph,** a Nez Percé leader, refused to leave. Then, in 1877, he and his people, including women and children, fled north toward Canada. Army troops followed close behind.

In the months that followed, Chief Joseph earned the respect and admiration of many. Again and again, he fought off or eluded pursuing army units. He set high standards for his soldiers, warning them not to injure women or children as the white soldiers did. He also made sure that his soldiers paid settlers for any supplies that they took.

Finally, after a tragic journey of more than 1,000 miles, Chief Joseph decided that he must surrender. Of the approximately 700 Nez Percés who had set out with him, fewer than 450 remained. As he lay down his weapons, he sadly said:

> "It is cold, and we have no blankets. The little children are freezing to death.... Hear me, my chiefs! I am tired. My heart is sick and sad. From where the sun now stands, I will fight no more forever."

The Apache wars

In the arid lands of the Southwest, the Apaches fiercely resisted the loss of their lands. One leader, **Geronimo,** continued fighting the longest. In 1876, he assumed leadership of a band of Apache warriors when the government tried to force his people onto a reservation.

Geronimo waged war off and on for the next ten years. From Mexico, he led frequent raids into Arizona and New Mexico. In the end, 5,000 United States soldiers were trying to capture Geronimo, who, by this time, had fewer than forty followers. Geronimo finally surrendered in 1886. His capture marked the end of formal warfare between Indians and whites.

A Way of Life Lost

Many Indians longed for their lost way of life. On the reservations, the Lakotas and other Plains Indians turned to a religious ceremony called the **Ghost Dance.** It celebrated the time when Native Americans lived freely on the Plains.

The Ghost Dance

In 1889, word spread that a prophet named Wovoka had appeared among the Paiute people of the southern Plains. Wovoka said that the Great Spirit would make a new world for his people, free from whites and filled with plenty. To bring about this new

Biography **Geronimo**

For many years, Geronimo (on horseback) fought against both Mexico and the United States. He paid a high price for his fierce resistance. At a peace conference in the 1850s, Mexican soldiers murdered his mother, wife, and three children. After he surrendered to the United States Army, he was imprisoned for two years. ★ **Why do you think Geronimo refused to surrender for so long?**

world, all the Indians had to do was to dance the Ghost Dance.

Across the Plains, many Indians began preparing for the new world. Ghost Dancers painted their faces red and put on the sacred Ghost Dance shirt. Some believed that the shirt protected them from harm, even from the bullets of soldiers' guns.

In their ceremonies, Ghost Dancers joined hands in a large, spinning circle. As they danced, they all cried and laughed. A "growing happiness" filled them, said one. They saw a glowing vision of a new and perfect world.

Settlers react

Many settlers grew alarmed. The Ghost Dancers, they said, were preparing for war. The settlers persuaded the government to outlaw the Ghost Dance.

In December 1890, police officers entered a Lakota reservation to arrest Sitting Bull, who had returned from Canada and was living on the reservation. They claimed that he was spreading the Ghost Dance among the Lakotas. In the struggle that followed, Sitting Bull was accidentally shot and killed.

Wounded Knee

Upset by Sitting Bull's death, groups of Lakotas fled the reservations. Army troops pursued them to Wounded Knee Creek, in present-day South Dakota. On December 29, the Indians were preparing to surrender. As nervous troops watched, they began to give up their guns.

Suddenly, a shot rang out. The army opened fire with rifles and artillery. By the time the shooting stopped, nearly 300 Native American men, women, and children lay dead. About 25 soldiers also died.

The fighting at Wounded Knee marked the end of the Ghost Dance religion. Years later, Black Elk, a former Ghost Dancer, remembered the events at Wounded Knee:

> “When I look back now from this high hill of my old age, I can still see the . . . women and children lying [on the ground there]. . . . And I can see that something else died there. . . . A people's dream died there.”

Failed Reforms

The Native Americans were no longer able to resist the government. During the late 1800s, the army forced more Indians onto reservations every year.

Reformers speak out

Many people—Indian and white—spoke out against the tragedy that was occurring. **Susette La Flesche,** daughter of an Omaha chief, wrote and lectured about the destruction of the Native American way of life. Her work led others to take up the Indian cause.

One reformer influenced by La Flesche was **Helen Hunt Jackson.** In 1881, Jackson published *A Century of Dishonor.* The book vividly recounted the long history of broken treaties between the United States and the Native Americans. In her book, Jackson urged the United States government to end its policy of "cheating, robbing, [and] breaking promises."

Alice Fletcher was another reformer who worked for the Indians. She became an agent of the Indian Bureau, the government department that handled Indian affairs. To better understand Native American culture, Fletcher lived for a time with various Indian nations, including the Omahas and Winnebagos of Nebraska.

Ghost Dance shirt

The Dawes Act

Calls for reform led Congress to pass the **Dawes Act** in 1887. The act encouraged Native Americans to become farmers. Some tribal lands were divided up and given to individual Native American families.

The Dawes Act worked poorly. To Native Americans, land was an open place for riding and hunting—not something to divide into small parcels. As a result, Indians often sold their parcels to whites for low prices. In the end, Native Americans lost more than one half of the land that they had owned before the passage of the Dawes Act.

Life on the reservations changed Native American culture. The federal government took away the power of Indian leaders. In their place, it appointed government agents to make most decisions. These agents believed that Native Americans should give up their old ways, including their language, religion, and traditional customs.

Because Native Americans could no longer hunt buffalo, many had to depend on food and supplies guaranteed by treaties. Few Indians were content with life on the reservations.

★ Section 4 Review ★

Recall

1. **Locate** (a) Wyoming, (b) Colorado, (c) Oklahoma, (d) South Dakota, (e) Little Bighorn, (f) Wounded Knee.
2. **Identify** (a) Sitting Bull, (b) Fort Laramie Treaty, (c) Chivington Massacre, (d) Battle of Little Bighorn, (e) Chief Joseph, (f) Geronimo, (g) Ghost Dance, (h) Susette La Flesche, (i) Helen Hunt Jackson, (j) Dawes Act.
3. **Define** reservation.

Comprehension

4. Why did treaties between Native Americans and the United States fail to bring peace to the Plains?
5. Why were many Plains Indians attracted to Wovoka's teachings about the Ghost Dance?
6. How did each of the following affect Native Americans: (a) peace commission of 1867, (b) destruction of the buffalo, (c) establishment of reservations?

Critical Thinking and Writing

7. **Recognizing Points of View** Why do you think the government wanted Plains Indians to settle down and become farmers?
8. **Solving Problems** What do you think the federal government could have done to avoid wars with Native Americans in the West?

Activity **Writing a Poem** You are a Native American looking back at the changes that have occurred between 1865 and 1890. Write a poem describing your thoughts and feelings about those changes.

5 The Farmers

As You Read

Explore These Questions
- What were the different origins of western farmers?
- Why was life hard for Plains farmers?
- Why did farmers unite in the late 1800s?

Define
- sod house
- sodbuster
- cooperative
- wholesale

Identify
- Mary Elizabeth Lease
- Homestead Act
- Exodusters
- Hispanic-American Alliance
- National Grange
- Farmers' Alliance
- Populist party
- William Jennings Bryan
- William McKinley

Like miners and ranchers who arrived before them, farmers dreamed of a new life in the West. Mary Zimmerman and her family were among the first farmers on the Great Plains. She recalled their early struggle:

> "The soil was [new]. It had to be broken, turned, stirred, and taught to produce. With the simple means of the time, the process was slow, but . . . I helped my father on the farm and learned to do the work pretty well."

Later, western farmers would face other challenges. In the 1890s, **Mary Elizabeth Lease,** a fiery Kansas reformer, spoke bitterly of a struggle against low prices:

> "We raised the big crop . . . and what came of it? Eight-cent corn, ten-cent oats, two-cent beef. . . . Then the politicians told us we suffered from overproduction."

Farmers Settle in the West

Congress passed the **Homestead Act** in 1862. The law promised 160 acres of land to anyone who farmed it for five years. The government was encouraging farmers to settle the West. It also wanted to give poor easterners a chance to own a farm.

Homesteaders

Many easterners rushed to accept the offer of free land. They planted their 160 acres with wheat and corn. By 1900, half a million Americans had set up farms under the Homestead Act.

The Homestead Act had its problems. The land was free, but poor people did not have the money to move west and start a farm. Also, only about 20 percent of the homestead land went directly to small farmers. Land-owning companies took large areas of land illegally. They divided the land and resold it to farmers at a high price.

Exodusters

African Americans joined the rush for homestead land. The largest group moved west at the end of Reconstruction. At this time in the South, blacks were seeing many of their hard-won freedoms slip away.

In 1879, a group of African Americans moved to Kansas. They called themselves **Exodusters.** They took the name from Exodus, the book of the Bible that tells about the Jews escaping slavery in Egypt.

Some white southerners did not want to lose the cheap labor supplied by African Americans. They used force to stop boats from carrying Exodusters up the Mississippi. Nevertheless, between 40,000 and 70,000 African Americans moved to Kansas by 1881.

Mexicanos

Easterners who moved to the Southwest met a large Spanish-speaking population there. As you recall, the United States had gained the Southwest through the Mexican War. Spanish-speaking southwesterners called themselves Mexicanos. White Americans who lived in the region were known as Anglos.

Most Mexicanos lived in small villages. They farmed and raised sheep for themselves and their families. A few wealthy Mexicanos were large landowners and merchants.

As growing numbers of Anglos settled in the Southwest, they acquired the best jobs and land. Often, Mexicanos found themselves working as low-paid laborers on Anglo farms. Many Mexicanos ended up living in poverty.

Some Mexicanos fought back. In New Mexico, in the 1880s, angry farmers known as "Las Gorras Blancas," or "White Caps," demanded fair treatment. They protested the fencing of their grazing lands by cutting the barbed wire fences of Anglo cattle ranchers.

Other Mexicanos united in political organizations. In 1894, Mexicanos in Arizona founded the **Hispanic-American Alliance.** It vowed "to protect and fight for the rights of Spanish Americans" through political action.

A Final Rush for Land

As settlers spread across the West, free land began to disappear. The last major land rush took place in Oklahoma. Several Indian nations lived there, but the government forced them to sell their land. The government then announced that farmers could claim free homesteads in Oklahoma. They could not stake their claims, however, until noon on April 22, 1889.

On the appointed day, as many as 100,000 land seekers lined up at the Oklahoma border. At noon, a gunshot rang out. The "boomers" charged into Oklahoma, but they found that others were already there.

Viewing History **Exodusters**

In this photograph, Exodusters await the arrival of a steamboat to take them up the Mississippi River. Most Exodusters settled in Kansas. African American homesteaders also settled in Nebraska, Oklahoma, and other western states. ★ **Why did some white southerners try to prevent African Americans from moving west?**

Viewing History **On the Homestead**

These homesteaders posed for a family picture in front of their sod house. ★ **Why did people on the Plains build sod houses rather than wood houses?**

"Sooners" had sneaked into Oklahoma before the official opening and had staked out much of the best land.

Hard Life on the Plains

Farmers on the western plains faced many hardships. The first problem was shelter. Since wood was scarce on the Great Plains, many farmers built houses of sod—soil held together by grass roots. Rain was a serious problem for **sod houses.** One pioneer woman complained that her sod roof "leaked two days before a rain and for three days after."

Sodbusting

The fertile soil of the Great Plains was covered with a layer of thick sod that could crack wood or iron plows. A new sodbusting plow made of steel reached the market by 1877. It enabled **sodbusters,** as Plains farmers were called, to cut through the sod to the soil below.

Technology helped farmers in other ways. On the Great Plains, water often lay hundreds of feet underground. Farmers built windmills to pump the water to the surface. New reapers, threshing machines, and binders helped farmers to harvest crops.

Battling the climate

The dry climate was a constant threat. When too little rain fell, the crops shriveled and died. Dry weather also brought the threat of fire. In the strong winds that whipped across the land, a grass fire traveled "as fast as a horse could run."

The summers often brought swarms of grasshoppers that darkened the sky like a storm. Grasshoppers ate everything in their path—crops, food, tree bark, even clothing.

Pioneers dreaded the winters most. With few trees or hills to block the wind, icy gusts built huge snowdrifts. The deep snow buried farm animals and trapped families inside their homes. Wise sodbusters kept enough food on hand to help them survive during a long blizzard.

Women on the Plains

Women had to be strong to survive the hardships of life on the Great Plains. Since there were few stores, women made clothing, soap, candles, and other goods by hand. They also cooked and preserved food needed through the long winter.

Women served their families and their communities in many ways. They often helped with planting and harvesting. Most schoolteachers were women. When there were no doctors nearby, women treated the sick and injured.

Pioneer families usually lived miles apart. They relaxed by visiting with neighbors and gathering for church services. Picnics, dances, and weddings were eagerly awaited events. "Don't think that all of our time and thoughts were taken up with the problems of living," one woman wrote. "We were a social people."

Skills FOR LIFE

Critical Thinking | **Managing Information** | Communication | Maps, Charts, and Graphs

Working in Teams

How Will I Use This Skill ?

By forming a team, you bring together the skills, knowledge, and experience of a number of people. A team can often produce better results in less time than an individual. In the classroom, on the playing field, or in the workplace, people often work together on a team to achieve some common goal.

LEARN the Skill

You can work as a member of a team by following these four steps:

1. Organize a team and identify your goal.
2. Identify the tasks needed to complete the goal. Sometimes, team members work together for the entire project. Other times, they divide the tasks, work separately, and then come together to share their results.
3. The team members complete their tasks by working together, individually, or in smaller groups or committees.
4. The team develops a presentation to share their work with others.

A marching band relies on teamwork.

PRACTICE the Skill

Using the information on pages 526–527, work in teams to learn about efforts to help farmers in the late 1800s.

1. Organize three teams. One team will focus on the Grange, a second team will learn about the Farmers' Alliance, and a third team will study the Populist Party.
2. The members of each team should read and take notes on their assigned topic.
3. Each team should come together to discuss their findings and to make sure that everyone understands the material.
4. Each team should prepare a presentation that includes a poster and a speech. Some members should prepare the poster, while others prepare the speech. Finally, one member will present and explain the poster to the class. Another team member will make the speech.

APPLY the Skill

Organize a team to research and present information on a current issue. Use newspapers, magazines, or the Internet as sources.

Biography **Mary Elizabeth Lease**

Kansas lawyer Mary Elizabeth Lease won fame as an activist for the Farmers' Alliance and Populist party. She was a stirring, dynamic speaker. The way to fight falling grain prices, she told Kansan farmers, was to "raise less corn and more hell."

★ **Why were grain prices falling in the late 1800s?**

Crisis for farmers

Despite the harsh conditions, farmers began to thrive in the West. Before long, they were selling huge amounts of wheat and corn in the nation's growing cities and even in Europe.

Then, however, farmers faced a strange problem. The more they harvested, the less they earned. In 1881, a bushel of wheat sold for $1.19. By 1894, the price had plunged to 49 cents.

Western farmers were hurt most by low grain prices. They had borrowed money during good times to buy land and machinery. When wheat prices fell, they could not repay their debts. In the South, cotton farmers faced the same problem when the price of cotton dropped.

Farmers Take Action

As early as the 1860s, farmers began to work together. They learned that they could improve their condition through economic cooperation and political action.

The Grange

In 1867, farmers formed the **National Grange.** Grangers wanted to boost farm profits. They also wanted to reduce the rates that railroads charged for shipping grain.

Grangers helped farmers set up cooperatives. In a **cooperative,** a group of farmers pooled their money to buy seeds and tools wholesale. **Wholesale** means buying or selling something in large quantities at lower prices. Grangers built cooperative warehouses so that farmers could store grain cheaply while waiting for better selling prices.

Leaders of the Grange urged farmers to use their vote. In 1873, western and southern Grangers pledged to vote only for candidates who supported their aims. They elected officials who understood the farmers' problems.

As a result, several states passed laws limiting what could be charged for grain shipment and storage. Nevertheless, crop prices continued to drop. Farmers sank deeper and deeper into debt.

Farmers' Alliance

Another group, the **Farmers' Alliance,** joined the struggle in the 1870s. Like the Grange, the Alliance set up cooperatives and warehouses. The Farmers' Alliance spread from Texas through the South and into the Plains states. In the South, the Alliance tried to bring black and white farmers together. Alliance leaders also tried to join with factory workers and miners who were angry about their treatment by employers.

The Populist Party

In 1891, farmers and labor unions joined together to form the **Populist party.** At their first national convention, the Populists demanded government help with falling farm prices and regulation of railroad rates. They also called for an income tax, an eight-hour workday, and limits on immigration.

Another Populist party demand was "free silver." Populists wanted all silver mined in the West to be coined into money. They said that farm prices dropped because there was not enough money in circulation. Free silver would increase the money supply and make it easier for farmers to repay their debts.

Eastern bankers and factory owners disagreed. They argued that increasing the money supply would cause inflation, or runaway prices. Business people feared that inflation would wreck the economy.

Rise and Fall of the Populists

The Populist candidate for President in 1892 won one million votes. The next year, a severe depression brought the Populists new support. In 1894, they elected six senators and seven representatives to Congress.

Election of 1896

The Populists looked toward the election of 1896 with high hopes. Their program had been endorsed by one of the great orators of the age—**William Jennings Bryan.**

Bryan was a young Democratic congressman from Nebraska. He was called the "Great Commoner," because he championed the cause of common people. Like the Populists, he believed that the nation needed to increase the supply of money. He often spoke out on behalf of the farmers.

At the Democratic convention in 1896, Bryan made a powerful speech. Delegates cheered wildly as he thundered against the rich and powerful and for free silver.

Both Democrats and Populists supported Bryan for President. However, bankers and business people feared that Bryan would ruin the economy. They supported **William McKinley,** the Republican candidate.

Bryan narrowly lost the election of 1896. He carried the South and West, but McKinley won the heavily populated states of the East.

Populist Party Fades

The Populist party broke up after 1896. One reason was that the Democrats adopted several Populist causes. Also, prosperity returned in the late 1890s. People worried less about railroad rates and free silver.

Still, the influence of the Populists lived on. In the years ahead, the eight-hour workday became standard for American workers. In 1913, the states ratified an income tax amendment. Perhaps most important, the Populists had helped to tie the West more tightly to the politics of the nation.

★ Section 5 Review ★

Recall

1. **Identify** **(a)** Mary Elizabeth Lease, **(b)** Homestead Act, **(c)** Exodusters, **(d)** Hispanic-American Alliance, **(e)** National Grange, **(f)** Farmers' Alliance, **(g)** Populist party, **(h)** William Jennings Bryan, **(i)** William McKinley.
2. **Define** **(a)** sod house, **(b)** sodbuster, **(c)** cooperative, **(d)** wholesale.

Comprehension

3. **(a)** Why did Exodusters move to the Plains? **(b)** How did the arrival of white settlers affect Mexicano farmers in the Southwest?
4. Describe three hardships that farmers faced on the Great Plains.
5. Identify and explain two goals that the National Grange and Populist party shared.

Critical Thinking and Writing

6. **Analyzing Primary Sources** An army general wrote to President Hayes, "Every river landing is blockaded by white enemies of the colored exodus." Explain in fuller detail the event to which the general was referring.
7. **Understanding Causes and Effects** How did the amount of grain that farmers produced affect the price of that grain? Explain.

Activity **Drawing a Political Cartoon** You are a political commentator of the late 1800s. Draw a political cartoon to illustrate one of the problems that farmers faced during this period.

Chapter 19 Review and Activities

★ Sum It Up ★

Section 1 The Plains Indians

- On the Great Plains, Native American nations depended on the buffalo for survival.
- Plains Indians had a rich religious life and a well-ordered society.

Section 2 Miners and Railroaders

- With gold and silver strikes came a rush of miners and the building of boom towns.
- Transcontinental railroads brought rapid growth to the West.

Section 3 Ranchers and Cowhands

- In the 1860s and 1870s, cattle ranching spread across the Great Plains.
- The life of the cowhand was difficult and dangerous.

Section 4 A Way of Life Ends

- Native Americans struggled to keep their lands and their way of life.
- The United States government forced Indians to move onto reservations and to adopt new ways of life.

Section 5 The Farmers

- By 1900, despite many hardships, half a million farmers had settled on the Great Plains.
- To improve their condition, farmers united to form several economic and political organizations.

For additional review of the major ideas of Chapter 19, see ***Guide to the Essentials of American History*** or ***Interactive Student Tutorial CD-ROM,*** which contains interactive review activities, graphic organizers, and practice tests.

Reviewing the Chapter

Define These Terms

Match each term with the correct definition.

Column 1	Column 2
1. travois	**a.** a limited area set aside for a group of people
2. corral	**b.** an enclosure for livestock
3. reservation	**c.** early farmers on the Great Plains
4. sodbusters	**d.** sled pulled by a dog or horse
5. cooperative	**e.** an organization in which people pool their resources for more buying power

Explore the Main Ideas

1. Why was the buffalo very important to the Plains Indians?
2. How did the mining boom lead to the growth of western towns?
3. **(a)** What caused the cattle boom of the 1870s? **(b)** Why did the Cattle Kingdom decline in the 1880s?
4. How did life change for the Plains Indians between the 1860s and 1880s?
5. **(a)** What problems did sodbusters and other farmers face? **(b)** How did the Grange help farmers?

Geography Activity

Match the letters on the map with the following places: **1.** Texas, **2.** Colorado, **3.** Nevada, **4.** Promontory Point, **5.** Omaha, **6.** San Francisco. **Interaction** What natural obstacles slowed the building of the first transcontinental railroad?

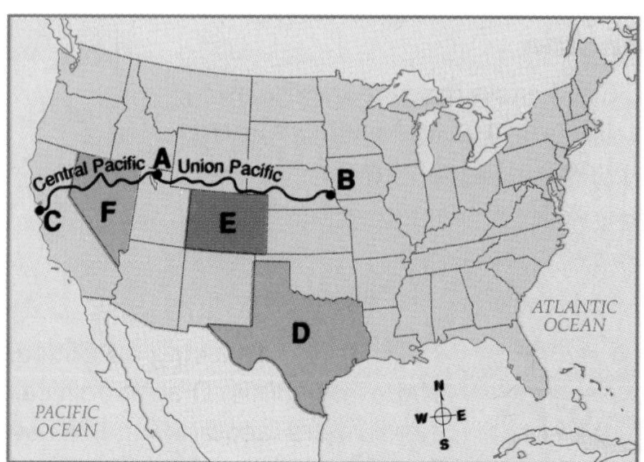

Critical Thinking and Writing

1. Understanding Chronology Place the following events in chronological order: **(a)** Dawes Act, **(b)** Fort Laramie Treaty, **(c)** Battle of Little Bighorn, **(d)** discovery of gold on Lakota land, **(e)** death of Sitting Bull, **(f)** fighting at Wounded Knee.

2. Linking Past and Present **(a)** What places are considered frontiers today? **(b)** How do these frontiers compare with the American frontiers of the 1800s?

3. Evaluating Information **(a)** What is inaccurate in the way movie westerns depict the life of the American cowhand? **(b)** Why do you think these inaccuracies exist?

4. Exploring Unit Themes **Industrialization** Why were easterners and westerners both eager to build transcontinental railroads?

Using Primary Sources

Hamilton Wicks was a "boomer" who staked a land claim during the Oklahoma land rush of April 1889. Years later, Wicks recalled the early days of Guthrie, Oklahoma—the town where he settled:

> "All that there was of Guthrie . . . on April 22, at 1:30 P.M., . . . was a water tank, a small station house, a shanty for the Wells Fargo Express, and a Government Land Office. . . . [By day's end] ten thousand people had [settled] upon a square mile of virgin prairie . . . and . . . [thousands] of white tents [had] suddenly appeared upon the face of the country. . . . Here indeed was a city laid out and populated in half a day."

Source: "The Opening of Oklahoma" by Hamilton Wicks, 1889, in *Voices of America,* 1963.

Recognizing Points of View **(a)** What happened to Guthrie, Oklahoma, on April 22, 1889? **(b)** Why did the town change so suddenly?

Activity Bank

Interdisciplinary Activity

Exploring the Arts Working with other students, prepare a skit about the hopes and dreams of the Exodusters. Perform the skit for the class.

Career Skills Activity

Farmer Do research to find out about the challenges facing farmers today. In a written report, compare conditions that exist today with those of the 1890s.

Citizenship Activity

Writing a Petition Citizens can bring about change by submitting petitions with many signatures to government leaders. Write a petition that Helen Hunt Jackson might have composed in the 1880s. In your petition, list the actions that you would like the government to take to improve conditions for Native Americans.

Internet Activity

Use the Internet to find sites dealing with one of the Native American nations discussed in this chapter. Gather information related to these questions: **(a)** How do Native Americans work to preserve their culture today? **(b)** What special problems still face Native Americans? Present your findings in a written or oral presentation.

Eyewitness Journal

Write three different eyewitness reports of what happened at Wounded Knee on December 29, 1890. Write one description as a United States soldier, a second description as a Lakota Ghost Dancer, and a third description as a white settler in South Dakota. You may wish to do additional research before completing this assignment.

Chapter 20

The Rise of Industry and Unions 1865–1914

What's Ahead

After the Civil War, American industry boomed. One reason for this tremendous growth was the rapid increase in the number of railways in the nation. Shrewd, energetic (and sometimes ruthless) business leaders created vast companies. A constant stream of new inventions also helped industry grow.

In the new economy, workers often faced long hours, unsafe conditions, and low pay. They soon banded together to win improvements in their lives. Slowly, organized labor became a powerful new force in American society.

Why Study History?

In 1859, Americans discovered a valuable new natural resource—oil! This "black gold" became a major source of fuel, and a major source of wealth for those individuals who controlled it. Today, we use oil and oil products every day. Limits on the world's oil supply make it an even more valuable resource. To focus on this connection, see the *Why Study History?* feature, "The Need for Oil Affects You," in this chapter.

American Events

- **1876** Alexander Graham Bell develops first telephone
- **1882** Standard Oil trust controls oil industry
- **1886** American Federation of Labor is formed

1865 | 1870 | 1875 | 1880 | 1885 | 1890

World Events

1871 World Event Britain makes labor unions legal

1886 World Event Electricity is introduced to Japan

Viewing HISTORY

Business Was Booming!

In the 1880s, William Henry Jackson used a secret chemical process to create early colored photographs like this one. It shows a glass-roofed shopping arcade in Cleveland, Ohio. There, shoppers could buy anything from the latest fashions to new products such as the phonograph. In the late 1800s, new inventions, new industries, and new business practices helped the American economy to boom.

★ **Based on this picture, how was this arcade similar to a modern shopping mall? How was it different?**

1894
Federal court rules Pullman strike illegal

1911
Triangle Shirtwaist fire shows need for safety measures

1913
Henry Ford uses assembly line to mass produce automobiles

1890 | 1895 | 1900 | 1905 | 1910 | 1915

1901 World Event
FIrst transatlantic wireless message is sent

1909 World Event
French aviator makes first flight across English Channel

Railroads and Industry

Explore These Questions

- How did railroads expand after the Civil War?
- What effects did competition have on the railroad industry?
- How did railroads spur the growth of industry?

Define

- network
- consolidate
- rebate
- pool

Identify

- George Westinghouse
- George Pullman
- Cornelius Vanderbilt
- James Hill

In 1873, Americans began singing a new folk song. "John Henry" tells the story of a legendary African American railroad worker who drives steel spikes into rock with a hammer. When the boss introduces a steam-powered drill, John Henry vows:

> "Before I'll let that steam drill
> beat me down
> I'll die with my hammer in my hand."

True to his word, John Henry dies after beating the steam drill in a contest.

Railroad workers loved singing of John Henry's victory over the machine. Still, nothing could slow down the nation's amazing industrial growth. Of the many factors spurring this growth, none was more important than the railroad.

A Railroad Network

The Civil War showed the importance of railroads. Railroads carried troops and supplies to the battlefields. They also moved raw materials to factories. After the war, railroad companies began to build new lines all over the country. (See page 509.)

Connecting lines

Early railroads were short lines that served local communities. Many lines ran for no more than 50 miles (80 km). When passengers and freight reached the end of one line, they had to move to a train on a different line to continue their journey.

Even if the lines had been connected, the problem would not have been solved. Different lines used rails of different gauges, or widths. As a result, the trains from one line could not run on the tracks of another line. In general, the tracks of northern and southern rail lines used different gauges .

In 1886, railroads in the South decided to adopt the northern gauge. On May 30, southern railroads stopped running so that work could begin. Using crowbars and sledgehammers, crews worked from dawn to dusk to move the rails a few inches farther apart. When they had finished, some 13,000 miles (20,800 km) of track had been changed.

Once the track was standardized, American railroads formed a **network,** or system of connected lines. The creation of a rail network brought benefits to shippers. Often, rail companies arranged for freight cars on one line to use the tracks of another. For example, goods loaded in Chicago could stay on the same car all the way to New York, instead of being transferred from one car to another. As a result, the shipper had to pay only one fare for the whole distance.

New rails knit the sprawling nation together. By 1900, there were more miles of tracks in the United States than in Europe and Russia combined.

Other improvements

To simplify train schedules, the railroad companies set up a system of standard time zones in 1883. Before that, each town kept its own time, based on the position of the sun. Towns in Illinois, for example, had 27 different local times! The new system divided the nation into four time zones: Eastern, Central, Mountain, and Pacific. Every place within the same time zone observed the same time.

New inventions helped make railway travel safer and faster. In 1869, **George Westinghouse** began selling his new air brake. On early trains, each railroad car had its own brakes and its own brake operator. If different cars stopped at different times, serious accidents could result. Westinghouse's air brake allowed a locomotive engineer to stop all the railroad cars at once.

The air brake increased safety and allowed for longer, faster trains. By 1900, a passenger could travel from New York to San Francisco in only six days, rather than months.

Long distance travel also became more comfortable. In 1864, **George Pullman** designed a railroad sleeping car. Pullman cars had convertible berths as well as lavatories. Rail lines also added dining cars. Porters, conductors, and waiters attended to the needs of passengers. A national magazine described the comforts of a rail trip in 1872:

> "From Chicago to Omaha your train will carry a dining car.... You sit at little tables which comfortably accommodate four persons; you order your breakfast, dinner, or supper from a bill of fare which contains a surprising number of dishes; you eat from snow-white linen . . . admirable cooked food, and pay a modest price."

Consolidation

As railroads grew, they looked for ways to operate more efficiently. Many companies began to **consolidate,** or combine. Larger

Viewing History **A Nation Linked by Rail**

By the late 1800s, a complex network of rail lines linked the nation. Freight trains, like the one below, hauled tons of coal and other resources needed by industry. Passenger lines advertised a new level of elegance and comfort (right).

★ **How were the nation's local rail lines transformed into a network?**

Viewing History **Farmers *vs.* Railroads**

In this 1873 cartoon, Thomas Nast portrayed railroads as a monster snaking through American farmland. A bearded farmer bravely opposes the monster. ★ **The building shown in the background is the Capitol building. Why do you think Nast showed the Capitol in the monster's coils?**

companies bought up smaller ones or forced them out of business. The Pennsylvania Railroad, for example, consolidated 73 companies into its system.

Tough-minded business people led the drive for consolidation. The most powerful of these "railroad barons" was **Cornelius Vanderbilt.** The son of a poor farmer, Vanderbilt earned his fortune in steamship lines. He then began to buy up railroad lines in New York State.

Vanderbilt sometimes used ruthless tactics to force smaller owners to sell to him. In the early 1860s, he decided to buy the New York Central Railroad. The owners refused to sell. Vanderbilt then announced that New York Central passengers would not be allowed to transfer to his trains. With their passengers stranded and business dropping sharply, the New York Central owners gave in and sold their line to Vanderbilt.

Vanderbilt then bought up most of the lines between Chicago and Buffalo. By the time of his death in 1877, his companies controlled 4,500 miles (7,200 km) of track and linked New York City to the Great Lakes region.

Other consolidations were soon underway. Before long, the major railroads of the nation were organized into systems directed by a handful of powerful men.

Building New Lines

Railroad builders raced to create thousands of miles of new tracks. In the years after Leland Stanford hammered in the golden spike in 1869, Americans built three more transcontinental railroads. **James Hill,** a Canadian-born railroad baron, finished the last major cross-country line in 1893. (See the map on page 510.) His Great Northern Railway wound from Duluth, Minnesota, to Everett, Washington.

Unlike other rail lines, the Great Northern was built without financial aid from Congress. To make his railroad succeed, Hill had to turn a profit from the start. He encouraged farmers and ranchers to settle near his railroad. He gave seed to farmers and helped them buy equipment. He even imported special bulls to breed hardier cattle. Not only was Hill's policy generous, it made good business sense.

Abuses

With builders rushing to share in the profits of the railroad boom, overbuilding occurred. Soon, there were too many rail lines in some parts of the country. Between Atlanta and St. Louis, for example, 20 different lines competed for business. There was not nearly enough rail traffic to keep all these lines busy.

Reducing competition

In the West, especially, there were too few people for the railroads to make a profit. Competition was fierce. Rate wars broke out as rival railroads slashed their fares to win customers. Usually, all the companies lost money as a result.

To win new business or keep old business, big railroads secretly offered **rebates,** or discounts, to their biggest customers. This practice forced many small companies out of business. It also hurt small shippers, such as farmers, who still had to pay the full price.

Railroad barons soon realized that cutthroat competition was hurting even their large lines. They looked for ways to end the competition. One method was pooling. In a **pool,** several railroad companies agreed to divide up business in an area. They then fixed their prices at a high level.

High prices for farmers

Railroad rebates and pools angered small farmers in the South and the West. Both practices kept shipping prices high for them. Indeed, rates were so high that at times farmers burned their crop for fuel rather than ship it to market.

As you read in Chapter 19, many farmers joined the Populist party. Populists called for government regulation of rail rates. Congress and several states passed laws regulating railroad companies. However, the laws did not end abuses. Railroad barons bribed officials to keep the laws from being enforced.

Spurring Economic Growth

Despite their problems, railroads made possible the rapid growth of industry after 1865. As railroads expanded, they stimulated the whole economy.

Building rail lines created thousands of jobs. Steelworkers turned millions of tons of iron into steel for tracks and engines. Lumberjacks cut down whole forests to supply wood for railroad ties. Miners sweated in dusty mine shafts digging coal to fuel railroad engines. The railroad companies themselves employed thousands of workers. They laid tracks, built trestles across rivers, and carved tunnels through mountains.

Because they were so large, railroads also pioneered new ways of managing business. Rail companies created special departments for shipping and accounting and for servicing equipment. Expert managers headed each department, while chains of command ensured that the organization ran smoothly. Other big businesses soon copied these management techniques.

Railroads opened every corner of the country to settlement and growth. They brought people together, especially in the West. New businesses sprang up, and towns sprouted where rail lines crossed. With rail lines in place, the United States was ready to become the greatest industrial nation the world had ever seen.

★ Section 1 Review ★

Recall

1. **Identify** **(a)** George Westinghouse, **(b)** George Pullman, **(c)** Cornelius Vanderbilt, **(d)** James Hill.
2. **Define** **(a)** network, **(b)** consolidate, **(c)** rebate, **(d)** pool.

Comprehension

3. Describe three changes that took place in the railroad industry after the Civil War.
4. **(a)** What methods did big railroads use to win and keep business? **(b)** How did these practices affect small businesses and farmers?
5. List three ways that railroads spurred the growth of industry.

Critical Thinking and Writing

6. **Synthesizing Information** After the Civil War, railroads consolidated as large railroad companies took over smaller ones. **(a)** What were the advantages of consolidation? **(b)** What were the disadvantages?
7. **Linking Past and Present** Are railroads as important today as they were in the 1800s? Why or why not?

Activity **Asking Questions** "Tonight's special guest: railroad baron Cornelius Vanderbilt. The phone lines are now open." Jot down three or four questions you would ask Vanderbilt if he appeared on a talk show. The questions may concern his goals, his business practices, and his achievements.

Big Business

As You Read

Explore These Questions

- Why did the steel industry become important after the Civil War?
- What new ways of doing business did Americans develop?
- What were the arguments for and against the growth of giant corporations?

Define

- vertical integration
- corporation
- stock
- dividend
- trust
- monopoly
- free enterprise system

Identify

- John D. Rockefeller
- Bessemer process
- Andrew Carnegie
- J. Pierpont Morgan
- Standard Oil Company
- Sherman Antitrust Act

On a February day in 1865, an unusual auction was held. The owners of an Ohio oil refinery stood toe to toe, the only two people in the room. Each was bidding to buy the other's share in the company.

Bidding opened at $500. The price swiftly jumped higher and higher. Finally, the bid reached $72,500. "I'll go no higher, John," said one of the men. "The business is yours." John paid the $72,500 and became sole owner of the company. It was a smart buy. When he died more than 70 years later, **John D. Rockefeller** was a multimillionaire who dominated the entire American oil industry.

Rockefeller was one of a new breed of American business leaders in the late 1800s. They were bold, imaginative—and sometimes ruthless. During the next 50 years, these leaders shaped the nation's emerging businesses and industries.

Growth of the American Steel Industry

The growth of railroads after the Civil War fueled the growth of the steel industry. Early trains ran on iron rails that wore out quickly. Railroad owners knew that steel rails were much stronger and not as likely to rust as iron. Steel, however, was costly and difficult to make.

A new way to make steel

In the 1850s, William Kelly in the United States and Henry Bessemer in England each discovered a new way to make steel. The **Bessemer process,** as it came to be called, enabled steelmakers to produce strong steel at a lower cost. As a result, railroads began to lay steel rails.

Other industries also took advantage of the cheaper steel. Manufacturers made steel nails, screws, needles, and other items. Steel girders supported the great weight of the new "skyscrapers."

Steel mills spring up

Steel mills sprang up in cities throughout the Midwest. Pittsburgh became the steelmaking capital of the nation. Nearby coal mines and good transportation helped Pittsburgh's steel mills to thrive.

The thriving steel mills brought jobs and prosperity to Pittsburgh and other steeltowns. They also caused problems. The mills belched thick black smoke that turned the air gray. Soot blanketed houses, trees, and streets. Waste polluted local rivers.

Andrew Carnegie

Many Americans made fortunes in the steel industry. Richest of all was a Scottish immigrant, **Andrew Carnegie.** Carnegie's ideas on how to make money—and how to spend it—had a wide influence.

Carnegie's career reads like a history of American industry. As a child, he went to work in a textile mill. Later, he became a telegraph operator. When the railroad boom started, Carnegie got a job with the Pennsylvania Railroad.

Traveling in England in the 1870s, Carnegie visited a factory and saw the Bessemer process at work. When he returned to the United States, he built a steel mill at Homestead, Pennsylvania, south of Pittsburgh. His friendships with railroad owners helped him win contracts for the steel he manufactured.

Controlling the steel industry

Within a short time, Carnegie was earning huge profits from his steel mill. He used the money to buy out rivals. He also bought iron mines, railroad and steamship lines, and warehouses.

Soon, Carnegie controlled all phases of the steel industry—from mining iron ore to shipping finished steel. Acquiring control of all the steps required to change raw materials into finished products is called **vertical integration.** Vertical integration gave Carnegie a great advantage over other steel companies.

In 1892, Carnegie combined all of his businesses into the Carnegie Steel Company. By 1900, it was turning out more steel than all of Great Britain.

The "gospel of wealth"

Like other business owners, Carnegie drove his workers hard, Still, he believed that the rich had a duty to help the poor and improve society. He called this idea the "gospel of wealth." He wrote:

> "Wealth, passing through the hands of the few, can be made a much more powerful force for the elevation of our race than if it had been distributed in small sums to the people themselves."

Carnegie himself gave millions to charities. He donated $60 million to build public libraries in towns all over the country. After selling Carnegie Steel in 1901, he spent his time and money helping people.

Rise of Corporations

Before the railroad boom, nearly every American town had its own small factories. They produced goods for people in the area. By the late 1800s, however, big factories were producing goods more cheaply than small factories could. Railroads distributed these goods to nationwide markets. As demand for local goods fell, many small factories closed. Big factories then increased their output.

Expanding factories needed capital, or money, for investment. Factory owners used the capital to buy raw materials, pay workers, and cover shipping and advertising costs. To raise capital, Americans adopted new ways of organizing their businesses.

Biography **Andrew Carnegie**

As a teenager, Andrew Carnegie worked in a textile mill for $1.20 a week. By the age of 50, he was the nation's "Steel King." Carnegie believed that the rich had a right to make money, and a duty to spend it for the public good. He gave away millions to schools, libraries, and the cause of world peace.

★ **What business methods did Carnegie use to build his steel company?**

Many expanding businesses became corporations. A **corporation** is a business that is owned by investors. A corporation sells **stock,** or shares in the business, to investors, who are known as stockholders. The corporation can use the money invested by stockholders to build a new factory or buy new machines.

In return for their investment, stockholders hope to receive **dividends,** or shares of a corporation's profit. To protect their investment, stockholders elect a board of directors to run the corporation.

Thousands of people bought stock in corporations. Stockholders faced fewer risks than owners of private businesses. If a private business goes bankrupt, the owner must pay all the debts of the business. By law, stockholders cannot be held responsible for a corporation's debts.

Banks and Industry

In the years after the Civil War, corporations attracted large amounts of capital from American investors. Corporations also borrowed millions of dollars from banks. These loans helped American industry grow at a rapid pace. At the same time, the banks made huge profits.

The most powerful banker of the late 1800s was **J. Pierpont Morgan.** Morgan's influence was not limited to banking. He used his banking profits to gain control of major corporations.

During economic hard times in the 1890s, Morgan and other bankers invested in the stock of troubled corporations. As large stockholders, they easily won seats on the boards of directors. They then adopted policies that reduced competition and ensured big profits. "I like a little competition, but I like combination more," Morgan used to say.

Between 1894 and 1898, Morgan gained control of most of the nation's major rail lines. He then began to buy up steel companies, including Carnegie Steel, and merge them into a single large corporation. By 1901, Morgan had become head of United States Steel Company. It was the first American business worth more than $1 billion.

Connections With Arts

J. Pierpont Morgan used much of his wealth to collect manuscripts and rare books—some of them more than 400 years old. By 1906, his collection could no longer fit into his private library. Morgan then had a separate building constructed. After Morgan's death, the Pierpont Morgan Library in New York City was opened to the public.

The Oil Industry

Industry could not have expanded so quickly in the United States without the nation's rich supply of natural resources. Iron ore was plentiful, especially in the Mesabi Range of Minnesota. Pennsylvania, West Virginia, and the Rocky Mountains had large deposits of coal. The Rockies also contained minerals such as gold, silver, and copper. Vast forests provided lumber for building.

In 1859, Americans discovered a valuable new resource—oil. Drillers near Titusville, Pennsylvania, made the nation's first oil strike. An oil boom quickly followed. Hundreds of prospectors rushed to western Pennsylvania ready to drill wells in search of a "gusher."

Rockefeller and Standard Oil

Among those who came to the Pennsylvania oil fields was young John D. Rockefeller. Rockefeller, however, did not rush to drill for oil. He knew that oil had little value until it was refined, or purified, to make kerosene. Kerosene was used as a fuel in stoves and lamps.

The son of a humble New York peddler, Rockefeller moved with his family to Ohio when he was 14. At 23, he invested in his first oil refinery.

Rockefeller believed that competition was wasteful. He used the profits from his refinery to buy up other refineries. He then combined the companies into the **Standard Oil Company** of Ohio.

Rockefeller was a shrewd businessman. He was always trying to improve the quality of his oil. He also did whatever he could to get rid of competition. Standard Oil slashed

Why Study History?

Because the Need for Oil Affects You

Historical Background

In 1859, drillers struck oil in Pennsylvania. At the time, most refined oil ended up as kerosene for lamps. Factories also used oil to lubricate machines.

By the early 1900s, new inventions like the automobile created a demand for gasoline—another oil product. Before long, filling stations sprang up in cities and towns. Oil was fueling a growing nation.

Connections to Today

You know that we use oil as fuel for cars, buses, airplanes, lawn mowers, and heaters. Did you also know that manufacturers use petroleum to make plastics, cloth, paints, and medicines? Oil also fuels generators that supply electricity.

This valuable resource is also limited. The world's supply of petroleum could eventually run out. Scientists are working to develop alternate sources of energy.

Connections to You

How would your future change if the use of oil was restricted? High fuel costs might limit your ability to travel. Expensive heating oil might force you to live in a colder home. Prices for other items would rise, too, as factories paid higher prices for oil.

Such extreme shortages are not likely to happen soon. However, saving energy in small ways can help stretch our precious oil resources. Here are some things you can do:

- Recycle plastics and other products.
- Turn off lights when you leave a room.
- Avoid wasting hot water.
- Whenever possible, take the bus or train.

1. **Comprehension** **(a)** How was oil used in the late 1800s? **(b)** List three ways you use oil and petroleum products.
2. **Critical Thinking** Today, the United States imports much of its oil supply from other countries. Why do you think many Americans worry about dependence on foreign oil?

★Activity **Writing an Advertisement** List the qualities that you would want a new fuel source to have. Then, create a name and write an advertisement for your new fuel.

Petroleum is used to make hundreds of products, from plastic combs to pool floats.

Linking Past and Present

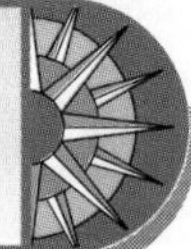

Past

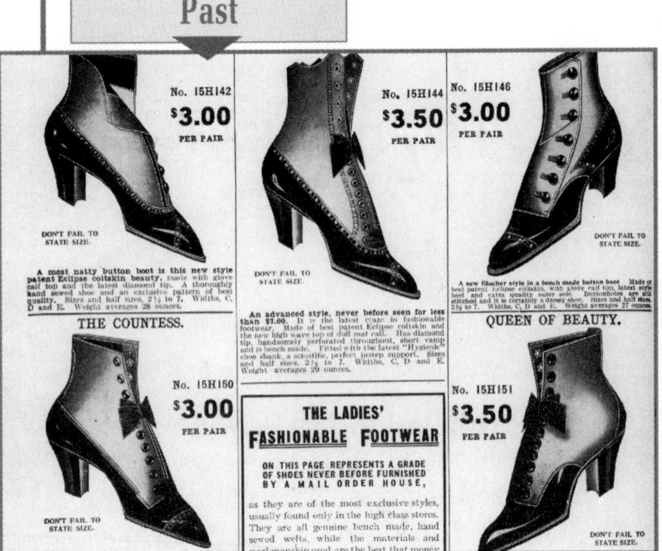

Present

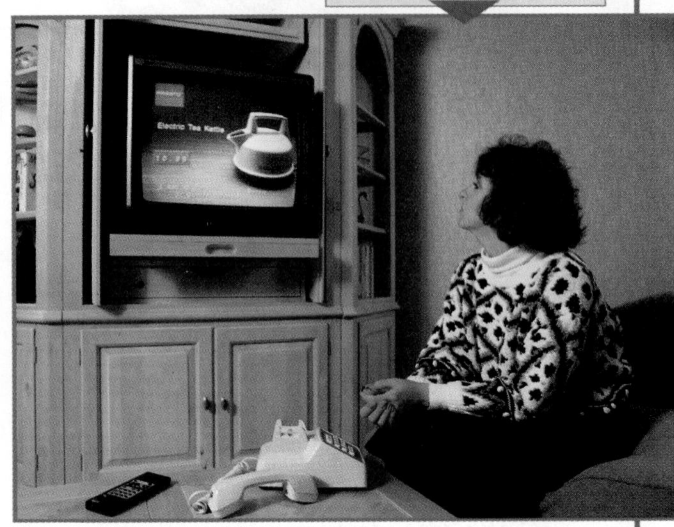

Shopping at Home

In the late 1800s, manufacturers pioneered new ways to sell their products nationwide. Companies like Sears, Roebuck used mail order catalogs (left) to sell goods to isolated western farmers. Today, Americans can turn on their televisions and instantly order anything from jewelry to cookware (right). ★ **What are the advantages and disadvantages of shopping at home?**

its prices to drive rivals out of business. It pressured its customers not to deal with other oil companies. Rockefeller even persuaded railroad companies eager for his business to grant rebates to Standard Oil. Lower shipping costs gave Rockefeller an important edge over his competitors.

Creating a trust

To tighten his hold over the oil industry, Rockefeller formed the Standard Oil trust in 1882. A **trust** is a group of corporations run by a single board of directors.

Stockholders in dozens of smaller oil companies turned over their stock to Standard Oil. In return, they got stock in the newly created trust. The trust stock paid the stockholders high dividends. However, the stockholders gave up their right to choose the board of directors. The board of Standard Oil, headed by Rockefeller, managed all the companies, which before had been rivals.

The Standard Oil trust created a monopoly in the oil industry. A **monopoly** controls all or nearly all the business of an industry. The Standard Oil trust controlled 95 percent of all oil refining in the United States.

Other businesses followed Rockefeller's lead. They set up trusts and tried to build monopolies. By the late 1890s, monopolies and trusts controlled some of the nation's most important industries.

Big Business: Two Viewpoints

Some Americans charged that the leaders of giant corporations were abusing the free enterprise system. In a **free enterprise system,** businesses are owned by private citizens. Owners decide what products to make, how much to produce, where to sell products, and what prices to charge. Companies compete to win customers by making the best product at the lowest price.

Opposition to trusts

Critics argued that trusts and monopolies reduced competition. Without competition, there was no reason for companies to keep prices low or to improve their products. It was also hard for new companies to start up and compete against powerful trusts. Workers, moreover, often felt that large corporations treated them badly.

Critics were also upset about the political influence of trusts. Leaders of big business were richer than Americans had ever been before. Some people worried that millionaires were using their wealth to buy favors from elected officials. The *Chicago Tribune* warned that "liberty and monopoly cannot live together." John Reagan, a member of Congress from Texas, said:

> "There were no beggars till Vanderbilts and . . . Morgans . . . shaped the actions of Congress and molded the purposes of government. Then the few became fabulously wealthy, the many wretchedly poor."

Under pressure from the public, the government slowly moved toward controlling giant corporations. Congress approved the **Sherman Antitrust Act** in 1890. The act banned the formation of trusts and monopolies. However, it was too weak to be effective. Some state governments passed laws to regulate business, but the corporations usually sidestepped them. Later reformers began to demand even stronger measures.

Support for trusts

Naturally, business leaders defended trusts. Andrew Carnegie published articles arguing that too much competition ruined businesses and put people out of work. In an article titled "Wealth and Its Uses," he wrote:

> "It will be a great mistake for the community to shoot the millionaires, for they are the bees that make the most honey, and contribute most to the hive even after they have gorged themselves full."

Defenders of big business argued that the growth of giant corporations brought lower production costs, lower prices, higher wages, and a better quality of life for millions of Americans. By 1900, Americans enjoyed the highest standard of living in the world. Innovative business leaders also helped usher in a new age of technology and invention that revolutionized American life.

★ Section 2 Review ★

Recall

1. **Identify** **(a)** John D. Rockefeller, **(b)** Bessemer process, **(c)** Andrew Carnegie, **(d)** J. Pierpont Morgan, **(e)** Standard Oil Company, **(f)** Sherman Antitrust Act.
2. **Define** **(a)** vertical integration, **(b)** corporation, **(c)** stock, **(d)** dividend, **(e)** trust, **(f)** monopoly, **(g)** free enterprise system.

Comprehension

3. Name three uses for cheap steel in the 1800s.
4. Why did many American businesses become corporations?
5. Why did some Americans think that big business threatened the free enterprise system?

Critical Thinking and Writing

6. **Understanding Causes and Effects** **(a)** What were two causes of the growth of the steel industry? **(b)** What were two effects?
7. **Applying Information** Andrew Carnegie once said of people who held onto their fortunes, "The man who dies thus rich, dies disgraced." **(a)** Restate Carnegie's meaning in your own words. **(b)** Did Carnegie carry out this philosophy in his own life? Explain.

Activity **Creating a Business Plan** You are a clever business owner in the late 1800s. Describe the business you would choose to build. Then, outline a plan showing how you would go about doing it.

A Flood of Inventions

As You Read

Explore These Questions

- What inventions improved communication in the 1800s?
- Why was Menlo Park called an "invention factory"?
- How did Henry Ford revolutionize the automobile industry?

Define

- assembly line
- mass production

Identify

- Cyrus Field
- Alexander Graham Bell
- Thomas Edison
- Jan Matzeliger
- Gustavus Swift
- George Eastman
- Henry Ford
- Orville and Wilbur Wright

Josephine Cochrane was annoyed. The wife of an Illinois politician, she hosted many elegant dinners. Her fine china, though, often broke when being washed.

Cochrane took a hose, some wire, a motor, and a large copper boiler to the woodshed. There, she built the first automatic dishwasher. Soon, Cochrane was selling her machine to restaurants. She patented her invention in 1886.

A flood of invention swept the United States in the late 1800s. By the 1890s, Americans were patenting 21,000 new inventions a year. These inventions helped industry to grow and become more efficient. New devices also made daily life easier in many American homes.

Advanced Communication

Some remarkable new devices filled the need for faster communication. The telegraph had been in use since 1844. (See Chapter 14.) It helped people around the nation stay in touch. It also helped business. For example, a steelmaker in Pittsburgh could instantly order iron ore from a mine in Minnesota.

Transatlantic cable

The telegraph speeded communication within the United States. It still took weeks, however, for news from Europe to arrive by boat.

In 1866, **Cyrus Field** ran an underwater telegraph cable across the Atlantic Ocean. Field marveled at his success:

> "In five months . . . the cable had been manufactured, shipped . . . stretched across the Atlantic, and was sending messages . . . swift as lightning from continent to continent."

Field's transatlantic cable brought the United States and Europe closer together.

The telephone

Morse and Field used a dot and dash code to send messages over telegraph wires. Meanwhile, **Alexander Graham Bell,** a Scottish-born teacher of the deaf, was trying to transmit sound.

In March 1876, Bell was ready to test his "talking machine." Before the test, Bell accidentally spilled battery acid on himself. His assistant, Thomas Watson, was in another

Alexander Graham Bell's telephone

room. Bell spoke into the machine, "Watson, come here, I want you!" Watson rushed to Bell's side. "Mr. Bell," he cried, "I heard every word you said, distinctly!" The telephone worked.

Bell's telephone aroused little interest at first. Scientists praised the invention. Most people, however, saw it as a toy. Bell offered to sell the telephone to the Western Union Telegraph Company for $100,000. The company refused—a costly mistake. In the end, the telephone earned Bell millions.

Bell formed the Bell Telephone Company in 1877. By 1885, he had sold more than 300,000 phones, mostly to businesses. The telephone speeded up the pace of business even more. Instead of having to go to a telegraph office, people could find out about prices or supplies simply by talking on the telephone.

Thomas Edison

In an age of invention, **Thomas Edison** was right at home. In 1876, he opened a research laboratory in Menlo Park, New Jersey. There, Edison boasted that he and his 15 co-workers set out to create "minor" inventions every 10 days and "a big thing every 6 months or so."

The "invention factory"

The key to Edison's success lay in his approach. He turned inventing into a system. Teams of experts refined Edison's ideas and translated them into practical inventions. Menlo Park became an "invention factory."

The results were amazing. Edison became known as the "Wizard of Menlo Park" for inventing the light bulb, the phonograph, and hundreds of other devices.

One invention from Edison's laboratory launched a new industry—the movies. In 1893, Edison introduced his first machine for showing moving pictures. Viewers watched short films by looking through a peephole in a cabinet. Later, Edison developed a motion picture projector, making it possible for many people to watch a film at the same time. By 1905, thousands of silent movie houses called nickelodeons were opening in cities across the United States.

▲ *Electric light bulb* ▲ *Phonograph*

Biography **Thomas Alva Edison**

A poor student, Thomas Edison grew up to invent the light bulb, the phonograph and dozens of other devices. The photo above was taken after Edison went without sleep for three days working on his phonograph. At last, he heard his own voice reciting "Mary Had a Little Lamb." ★ **Edison said, "Genius is one percent inspiration and ninety-nine percent perspiration." What do you think he meant?**

Electric power

One of Edison's most important creations was the electric power plant. Edison built the first power plant in New York City in 1882. He wired the business district first in hopes of attracting investors. With the flip of a switch, Edison set the district ablaze in light.

Within a year, Edison's power plant was supplying electricity to homes as well as businesses. Soon, more power plants were built. Factories replaced steam-powered engines with safer, quieter electric engines. Electric energy powered streetcars in cities and lighted countless homes. The modern age of electricity had begun.

Skills FOR LIFE

Critical Thinking | **Managing Information** | Communication | Maps, Charts, and Graphs

Using a Computerized Card Catalog

How Will I Use This Skill?

Whether you are hunting for information on the development of the automobile, or the newest bestseller, you may find yourself searching in a library. Today, most libraries are equipped with computerized catalogs to assist you during your search.

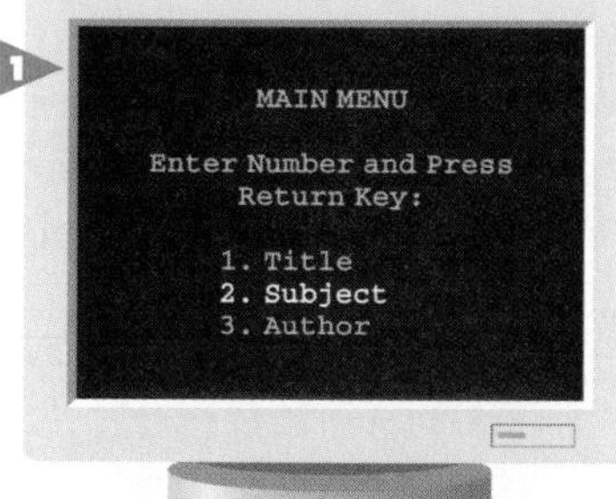

LEARN the Skill

1. Decide whether your search should start with a specific author, a title of a publication, or a subject.
2. Use the main menu to start your search. The main menu presents you with a list of options. From this list, choose the path to begin your search: Author, Title, or Subject.
3. Narrow your search. Follow the instructions on the computer screen to locate the books you need.
4. Select books that might be helpful. Write down the call numbers, titles, and authors of the books. The call numbers will allow you to find the books on the library shelves.

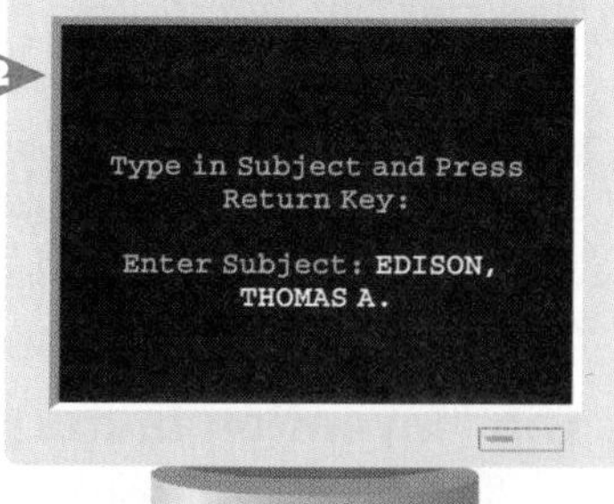

PRACTICE the Skill

Using the sample screens to the right, practice searching a typical library computer catalog.

1. Review screens 1 and 2. Which option has been chosen to begin the library search: Author, Title, or Subject?
2. Look at Screen 1, Main Menu. Which number would you type to begin the search documented on these diagrams?
3. Look at Screens 2 and 3. Identify the topic chosen for research. On Screen 3, note the books available on this topic.
4. Look at Screen 4. What are the title and call number of the chosen book?

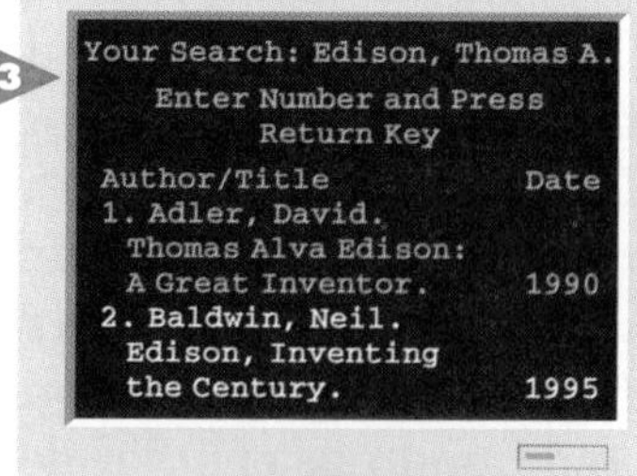

APPLY the Skill

Use the computerized catalog in your school or community library to research the history of any invention discussed in this chapter.

A Rush of Technology

Almost every day, it seemed, American inventors were creating new devices that made business more efficient and life more pleasant. The United States became known as the land of invention.

Inventions by African Americans

African Americans contributed to the flood of inventions. In 1872, Elijah McCoy created a special device that oiled engines automatically. It was widely used on railroad engines and in factories. Granville T. Woods found a way to send telegraph messages between moving railroad trains.

Jan Matzeliger invented a machine that could perform almost all the steps in shoemaking that had been done before by hand. Patented in 1883, Matzeliger's machine was eventually used in shoe factories everywhere.

Many African American inventors had trouble getting patents for their inventions. Even so, in 1900, an assistant in the patent office compiled a list of patents issued to African American inventors. The list, together with drawings and plans of all the inventions, filled four huge volumes.

Refrigeration

In the 1880s, **Gustavus Swift** came up with an idea that transformed the American diet. Swift introduced refrigeration to the meatpacking industry. In the past, cattle, pigs, and chickens had been raised and sold

A Time of Invention

Inventor	Date	Invention
Elisha Otis	1852	passenger elevator brake
George Pullman	1864	sleeping car
George Westinghouse	1869	air brake
Elijah McCoy	1872	automatic engine-oiling machine
Andrew S. Hallidie	1873	cable streetcar
Stephen Dudley Field	1874	electric streetcar
Alexander Graham Bell	1876	telephone
Thomas Alva Edison	1877	phonograph
Anna Baldwin	1878	milking machine
Thomas Alva Edison	1879	first practical incandescent light bulb
James Ritty	1879	cash register
Jan E. Matzeliger	1883	shoemaking machine
Lewis E. Waterman	1884	fountain pen
Granville T. Woods	1887	automatic air brake
Charles and J. Frank Duryea	1893	gasoline-powered car
King C. Gillette	1895	safety razor with throwaway blades
John Thurman	1899	motor-driven vacuum cleaner
Leo H. Baekeland	1909	improved plastic

Chart *Skills* **New inventions transformed daily life in the United States. They also helped the American economy grow.**

1. **Comprehension** **(a)** What did George Westinghouse invent? In what year? **(b)** Who improved on Westinghouse's invention? In what year?
2. **Critical Thinking** **(a)** Which of these inventions made transportation easier? **(b)** Which of these inventions might be found in a home today?

AmericanHeritage
MAGAZINE

HISTORY HAPPENED HERE

The Henry Ford Museum

Not far from his Detroit auto plant, Henry Ford built a place to display "every household article, every kind of vehicle, every sort of tool." Today at the Henry Ford Museum, you can explore the world's largest transportation collection, from canoes to giant locomotives to classic cars. You can also see devices you might have had in your home 100 years ago.

★ ***To learn more about this historic site, write:*** *Henry Ford Museum, P.O. Box 1970, Dearborn, MI 48121.*

Early American washing machine ➤

locally. Meat spoiled quickly, so it could not be shipped over distances.

Swift set up a meatpacking plant in Chicago, a railroad hub midway between the cattle ranches of the West and the cities of the East. Cattle were shipped by train to Chicago. At Swift's plant, the animals were slaughtered and carved up into sides of beef. The fresh beef was quickly loaded onto refrigerated railroad cars and carried to market. Even in summer, Swift sent fresh meat to eastern cities. As a result, Americans began to eat more meat.

Inventions for home and office

New inventions also affected life at home and in the office. Christopher Sholes perfected the typewriter in 1868. This invention made office work easier.

In 1888, **George Eastman** introduced the lightweight Kodak camera. No longer did photography require bulky equipment and chemicals. The cost was only $25, including a roll of film. After 100 snaps of the shutter, the owner returned the camera to Kodak. The company developed the pictures and sent them back, along with a reloaded camera. Taking pictures became a popular pastime.

The Automobile

No single person invented the automobile. Europeans had produced motorized vehicles as early as the 1860s. Several Americans began building cars in the 1890s. Still, only the wealthy could afford them.

Ford and mass production

It was **Henry Ford,** with his "motor car for the multitude," who made the auto a part of everyday American life. In 1913, Ford introduced the **assembly line.** In this method of production, workers are stationed in one place as products edge along on a moving belt. At Ford's auto plant, one group of workers would bolt seats onto a passing car frame, the next would add the roof, and so on. The assembly line greatly reduced the time needed to build a car. Other industries soon adopted it.

Ford's assembly line allowed mass production of cars. **Mass production** means making large quantities of a product quickly and cheaply. Because of mass production, Ford could sell his cars at a lower price than other auto makers.

Cars become popular

At first, most people laughed at the "horseless carriage." Some thought automobiles were dangerous. A backfiring auto engine could scare a horse right off the road. Towns and villages across the nation posted signs: "No horseless carriages allowed."

Slowly, attitudes toward the automobile changed. No other means of travel offered such freedom. As prices dropped, more people could afford to buy cars. In 1900, only 8,000 Americans owned cars. By 1917, more than 4.5 million autos were chugging along American roads.

Automobiles were at first regarded as machines for men only. Auto makers soon realized, however, that women could drive—and buy—cars. Companies began to direct advertisements to women, stressing the comfort and usefulness of automobiles. Driving gave women greater independence.

A hit song from 1905 shows the growing popularity of the automobile. "In My Merry Oldsmobile" is a love story about a boy, a girl, and a car:

> "Johnnie Steel has an Oldsmobile;
> He loves a dear little girl:
> She is the queen of his gas machine;
> She has his heart in a whirl.
> Now when they go for a spin, you know,
> She tries to learn the auto, so
> He lets her steer while he gets her ear
> And whispers soft and low:
>
> 'Come away with me Lucile,
> In my merry Oldsmobile....'"

The Airplane

Meanwhile, two Ohio bicycle mechanics, **Orville and Wilbur Wright,** were experimenting with another new method of transportation—flying. After trying out hundreds of designs, the Wright brothers tested their first "flying machine" on December 17, 1903. At Kitty Hawk, North Carolina, Orville took off. The plane, powered by a small gasoline engine, stayed in the air for 12 seconds and flew a distance of 120 feet (37m).

The Wrights' flight did not attract much attention. Most people saw little use for flying machines. Slowly, however, air pioneers built better planes and made longer flights. In time, the airplane changed the world.

★ Section 3 Review ★

Recall

1. **Identify** **(a)** Cyrus Field, **(b)** Alexander Graham Bell, **(c)** Thomas Edison, **(d)** Jan Matzeliger, **(e)** Gustavus Swift, **(f)** George Eastman, **(g)** Henry Ford, **(h)** Orville and Wilbur Wright.
2. **Define** **(a)** assembly line, **(b)** mass production.

Comprehension

3. Describe two inventions that transformed communication in the 1800s.
4. Why was Edison's electric power plant important?
5. How did the assembly line change auto making?

Critical Thinking and Writing

6. **Drawing Conclusions** Why might inventors be more creative working in an "invention factory" than working on their own?
7. **Ranking** Which invention discussed in this section had the greatest impact on American life? Explain your answer.

Activity **Playing a Role** Which invention mentioned in this section would have amazed you the most if you lived at that time? In a brief skit, play the role of a person seeing that invention for the first time.

Labor in the Age of Industry

As You Read

Explore These Questions

- How did the role of the worker change in the new industrial age?
- What were the goals of early unions?
- Why was progress slow for labor?

Define

- sweatshop
- strikebreaker
- anarchist
- collective bargaining
- injunction

Identify

- Knights of Labor
- Terence Powderly
- Haymarket Riot
- Samuel Gompers
- American Federation of Labor
- Mother Jones
- International Ladies' Garment Workers Union
- Triangle Fire
- Western Federation of Miners

In 1896, Frederick Taylor observed workers at a steel plant. He wrote down the number of times a worker picked up a shovel and the amount of time he took to swing it. Taylor then redesigned the shovels and work pattern in order to make the workers more productive.

Many factory owners adopted Taylor's system of "scientific management." Workers, however, often complained that they were being treated as parts of the machinery.

The rise of industry changed the workplace. By the late 1800s, harsh new conditions led workers to organize.

The American Federation of Labor and other unions fought to win workers an eight-hour day.

A Changing Workplace

Factories drew workers from many different backgrounds. Most workers were native-born white men. Many had left farms to take jobs in large cities.

Some northern factory workers were African Americans who had migrated from the South. Large numbers of immigrants from Europe, Asia, and Mexico also found jobs in factories. Women and children worked in factories, too. All of these groups earned lower wages than native-born white men.

Workers and employers

Workers had to adjust to the new kinds of factories of the late 1800s. Before the Civil War, most factories were small and family-run. Bosses knew their workers by name and chatted with them about their families. Because most workers had skills that the factory needed, they could bargain with the boss for wages.

By the 1880s, the relationship between worker and boss declined. Workers stood all day tending machines in a large, crowded, noisy room. Their skills were no longer needed, and they worked for wages fixed by their bosses. In the garment trade and other industries, sweatshops became common. A **sweatshop** is a workplace where people labor long hours in poor conditions for low pay. Most sweatshop workers were immigrants, young women, or children.

Child labor

The 1900 census reported nearly 2 million children under age 15 at work through-

Viewing HISTORY **Children at Work**

Children—many of them from immigrant families—labored in the nation's industries. "Breaker boys" hand-sorted slate from coal in grimy mines (right). Young girls operated heavy machinery in textile mills (left). ★ **How do you think the lives of these children were affected by having to go to work at an early age?**

out the country. Boys and girls labored in hazardous textile mills, tobacco factories, and garment sweatshops. In coal mines, they picked stones out of the coal for 12 hours a day, 6 days a week.

Working children had little time for schooling. Lack of education reduced their chance to build a better life as adults.

Many Americans believed that child labor was wrong. However, as long as factory owners could hire children at low pay, and as long as their families needed the money, child labor continued.

Dangerous conditions

Factories brimmed with hazards. Lung-damaging dust filled the air of textile mills. Cave-ins and gas explosions plagued mines. In steel mills, vats of red-hot metal spilled without warning.

Owners were more concerned with profits than with worker safety. They spent little to improve working conditions. Some workers had their health destroyed. Others were severely injured or killed in industrial accidents. In one year, 195 workers died in the steel mills of Pittsburgh.

Workers Organize

Low pay, long hours, and unhealthful conditions threatened the well-being of workers. Many found ways to fight back. Some workers took days off or slowed their work pace. Others went on strike. Strikes were usually informal, organized by workers in individual factories.

Sometimes, workers banded together to win better conditions. Most early efforts to form unions failed, however. (See page 379.)

Knights of Labor

In 1869, workers formed the **Knights of Labor.** At first, the union was open to skilled workers only. Members held meetings in secret because employers fired workers who joined unions.

In 1879, the Knights of Labor selected **Terence Powderly** as their president. Powderly worked to strengthen the union by opening membership to immigrants, blacks, women, and unskilled workers.

Powderly wanted the Knights to make the world a better place for both workers and employers. He did not believe in strikes.

Rather, he relied on rallies and meetings to win public support. Goals of the Knights included a shorter workday, an end to child labor, and equal pay for men and women.

In 1885, some Knights of Labor launched a strike that forced the Missouri Pacific Railroad to restore wage cuts. The Knights did not officially support the strike. Still, workers everywhere saw the strike as a victory for the union. Membership soared to 700,000, including 60,000 African Americans.

Haymarket Riot

The following year, the Knights of Labor ran into serious trouble. Workers at the McCormick Harvester Company in Chicago went on strike. Again, the Knights did not endorse the strike.

Like many companies at the time, the McCormick company hired **strikebreakers,** or replacements for striking workers. On May 3, 1886, workers clashed with strikebreakers outside the factory. Police opened fire. Four workers were killed.

The next day, thousands of workers gathered in Haymarket Square to protest the killings. The rally was led by **anarchists,** people who oppose all forms of organized government. Suddenly, a bomb exploded, killing one police officer and wounding others. Police peppered the crowd with bullets, killing or wounding many more people.

Eight anarchists were arrested for their part in the **Haymarket Riot,** as the incident was called. No real evidence linked these men to the bombing, but four were tried, convicted, and hanged. A wave of anti-labor feeling swept the nation. Membership in the Knights of Labor dropped sharply.

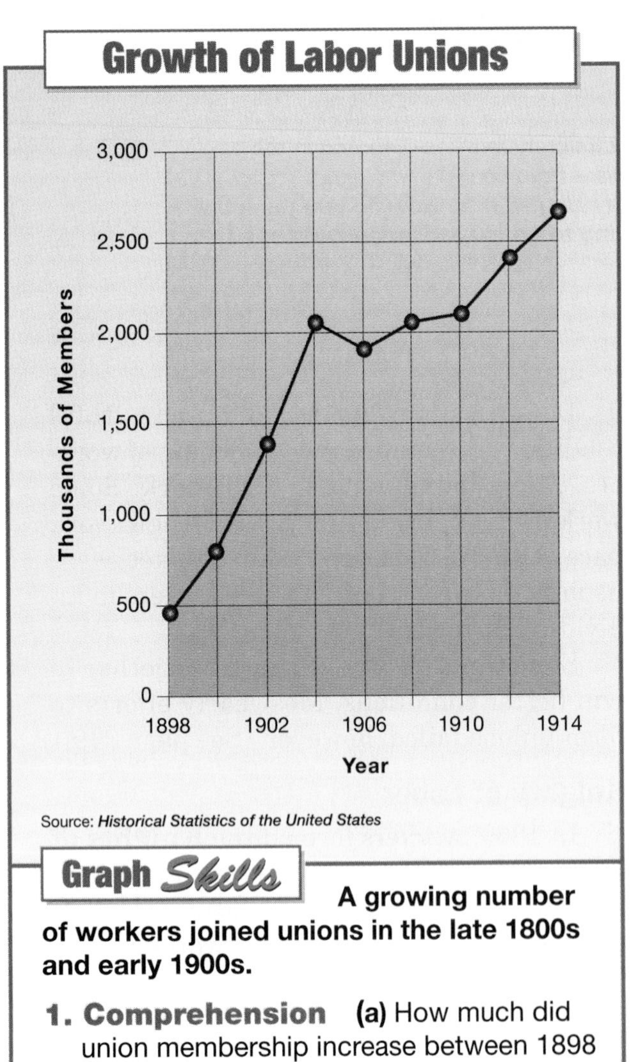

Graph Skills A growing number of workers joined unions in the late 1800s and early 1900s.

1. **Comprehension** **(a)** How much did union membership increase between 1898 and 1914? **(b)** What years showed a decrease in membership?
2. **Critical Thinking** Why did membership in unions grow so much?

Economics

American Federation of Labor

Despite the failure of the Knights of Labor, the labor movement continued to grow. In 1886, a British-born cigarmaker named **Samuel Gompers** organized a new union in Columbus, Ohio. The **American Federation of Labor,** or AFL, was open to skilled workers only.

Workers did not join the AFL directly. Rather, they joined a trade union, a union of persons working at the same trade. For example, a typesetter would join a typesetter's union. The union then joined the AFL. In effect, the AFL was a union made up of other unions.

Limited goals

Unlike the Knights of Labor, the AFL did not set out to change the world. It stressed practical goals. As one AFL leader said:

> "Our organization does not consist of idealists. We are going on from day to day. We are fighting only for immediate objects—objects that can be realized in a few years."

The AFL stressed higher wages, shorter hours, and improved working conditions. It led the fight for **collective bargaining,** the right of unions to negotiate with management for workers as a group.

A powerful union

Unlike the Knights of Labor, the AFL supported the use of strikes to achieve its goals. The AFL collected money from its member unions. Some of it went into a strike fund. When AFL members went on strike, they were paid from the fund so that they could still feed their families.

Its practical approach helped the AFL become the most powerful union in the nation. Between 1886 and 1910, membership in the AFL swelled from 150,000 to more than one and a half million. However, because African Americans, immigrants, and unskilled workers were barred from most trade unions, they could not join the AFL.

Biography Mother Jones

"Join the union, boys!" urged Mary Jones. Traveling from strike to strike, she moved in with miners' families, organized marches, and cared for the sick. She always urged strikers to avoid violence. When she died in 1930—at the age of 100—Mother Jones had become a legend. ★ **Jones was jailed many times. Why do you think this was so?**

Women in the Labor Movement

By 1890, one million women worked in American factories. In the textile mills of New England and the tobacco factories of the South, women formed the majority of workers. In New York City, women outnumbered men in the garment industry.

During the 1800s, women formed their own unions. A few, like the all-black Washerwomen's Association of Atlanta, struck for higher wages. None of these unions succeeded, however.

Mother Jones

The best-known woman in the labor movement was Irish-born Mary Harris Jones, known as **Mother Jones.** Jones worked as a dressmaker in Chicago until the Chicago fire of 1871 destroyed her business. Faced with the need to start all over again, she devoted the rest of her life to the cause of workers.

In 1877, Jones supported striking railroad workers in Pittsburgh. Later, she traveled around the country, organizing coal miners and campaigning for improved working conditions.

Jones spoke out about the hard lives of children in textile mills, "barefoot . . . reaching thin little hands into the machinery." By calling attention to such abuses, Mother Jones helped pave the way for reform.

Organizing garment workers

In 1900, garment workers organized the **International Ladies' Garment Workers Union,** or ILGWU. More than 20,000 women and men in the ILGWU walked off their jobs

$ Connections With Economics

Some immigrant workers banded together to demand higher wages. In 1903, Mexican and Japanese farm workers in Oxnard, California, organized the Japanese-Mexican Labor Association. Their strike forced farmers to pay them $5 per acre for thinning beets.

Cause and Effect

Causes

- Railroad boom spurs business
- Businesses become corporations
- Nation has rich supply of natural resources
- New inventions make business more efficient

The Rise of Industry

Effects

- Steel and oil become giant industries
- Monopolies and trusts dominate important industries
- Factory workers face harsh conditions
- Membership in labor unions grows

Effects Today

- United States is world's leading economic power
- American corporations do business around the world
- Government laws regulate monopolies

Graphic Organizer Skills

American industry boomed after the Civil War. The effects of industrial growth are still being felt today.

1. **Comprehension** List two causes for the rise of industry.
2. **Critical Thinking** Why do you think the government now tries to regulate monopolies?

Economics $

in 1910. After a few weeks, employers met union demands for better pay and shorter hours. The ILGWU became a key member of the AFL.

Despite the efforts of the ILGWU and other labor groups, most women with factory jobs did not join unions. They continued to work long hours for low pay. Many labored under unsafe conditions. Then, a tragic event focused attention on the dangers faced by women workers.

The Triangle Fire

In 1911, a fire broke out in the Triangle Shirtwaist Factory, a sweatshop in New York City. Within minutes, the upper stories were ablaze. Hundreds of workers raced for the exits, only to find them locked. The company had locked the doors to keep workers at their jobs. In their panic, workers ran headlong into the doors, blocking them with their bodies.

Fire trucks arrived almost immediately, but their ladders could not reach the upper floors. One after another, workers trying to escape the flames leaped to their deaths. One reporter wrote:

> "As I looked up . . . there, at a window, a young man was helping girls to leap out. Suddenly one of them put her arms around him and kiss[ed] him. Then he held her into space and dropped her. He jumped next. Thud . . . dead. Thud . . . dead."

Nearly 150 people, mostly young women, lost their lives in the **Triangle Fire.** The deaths shocked the public. As a result, New York and other states approved new safety laws to help protect factory workers.

Slow Progress for Labor

The new era of industry led to vast economic growth. At the same time, it created economic strain. In the rush for profits, many industries overexpanded. As goods flooded the market, prices dropped. To cover their losses, factory owners often fired workers. In time, factories geared up again, and the cycle was repeated.

The economy swung wildly between good times and bad. Between 1870 and 1900, two major depressions and three smaller recessions rocked the country. Workers lost their jobs or faced pay cuts. Often, they had no money to pay rent or buy food.

Violent strikes

During a severe depression in the 1870s, railroad workers were forced to take several cuts in pay. In July 1877, workers went on strike, shutting down rail lines across the country. Riots erupted in many cities as workers burned rail yards and ripped track from the ground. In Pittsburgh, a battle between strikebreakers and strikers left more than 20 people dead.

Violent strikes also broke out in the West. In the 1870s, miners in Idaho tried to shut down two large mines. Violence flared until the territorial governor threatened to bring in troops. In 1893, after another bitter strike, miners formed the **Western Federation of Miners.** This militant union gained great strength in the Rocky Mountain states. Between 1894 and 1904, it organized strike after strike when owners refused to negotiate.

A major setback

The federal government usually sided with factory owners. Several Presidents sent in troops to end strikes. Courts ruled against strikers, too.

In 1894, a Chicago court dealt a serious blow to unions. A year earlier, George Pullman had cut the pay of workers at his railroad car factory. Yet, he did not reduce the rents he charged them for company-owned houses. Workers walked off the job in protest.

A federal judge issued an injunction against the strikers. An **injunction** is a court order to do or not to do something. The judge ordered the Pullman workers to stop their strike. Leaders of the strike were jailed for violating the Sherman Antitrust Act. This act had been meant to keep trusts from limiting free trade. The courts, however, said that the strikers were limiting free trade. This decision was a major setback for unions.

Small gains

Union workers staged thousands of strikes during the late 1800s. Strikers won little sympathy at first. Few Americans supported unions. They believed that individuals who worked hard would be rewarded. Many were afraid that unions were run by foreign-born radicals. Because unions were unpopular, owners felt free to crush them.

Workers did make some gains. Skilled workers in the AFL won better conditions and higher pay. Overall, wages for workers rose slightly between 1870 and 1900. Still, progress was slow. In 1910, only one worker in 20 belonged to a union. Some 30 years would pass before large numbers of unskilled workers were able to join unions.

★ Section 4 Review ★

Recall

1. **Identify** **(a)** Knights of Labor, **(b)** Terence Powderly, **(c)** Haymarket Riot, **(d)** Samuel Gompers, **(e)** American Federation of Labor, **(f)** Mother Jones, **(g)** International Ladies' Garment Workers Union, **(h)** Triangle Fire, **(i)** Western Federation of Miners.
2. **Define** **(a)** sweatshop, **(b)** strikebreaker, **(c)** anarchist, **(d)** collective bargaining, **(e)** injunction.

Comprehension

3. How did factory work change in the late 1800s?
4. What were the goals of **(a)** the Knights of Labor? **(b)** the AFL?
5. How did the public view labor unions in the late 1800s?

Critical Thinking and Writing

6. **Making Inferences** Why did machines make some workers' skills useless?
7. **Drawing Conclusions** Why do you think workers gained so little from strikes in the late 1800s and early 1900s?

Activity **Drawing a Cartoon** Choose one of the events or issues you have read about in this section. Draw a political cartoon illustrating the topic you have chosen.

Chapter 20 Review and Activities

★ Sum It Up ★

Section 1 Railroads and Industry

- ▶ After the Civil War, thousands of miles of new railway lines were built, creating a nationwide rail network.
- ▶ Despite many abuses by large railroads, the growth of railroads stimulated the nation's economy.

Section 2 Big Business

- ▶ In the late 1800s, steelmaking became a huge source of wealth and power for American companies.
- ▶ Large corporations formed trusts and monopolies to control competition and maximize profit.

Section 3 A Flood of Inventions

- ▶ Advances in communication in the late 1800s included the laying of the first transatlantic telegraph cable and the invention of the telephone.
- ▶ At his research laboratory, Thomas Edison invented the light bulb, the phonograph, and hundreds of other useful devices.
- ▶ Through his use of the assembly line, Henry Ford made it possible for millions of Americans to afford automobiles.

Section 4 Labor in the Age of Industry

- ▶ Though various labor unions had differing ideals and methods, they all worked to improve conditions and pay for workers.
- ▶ Labor unions made slow progress at first because few Americans supported their goals.

For additional review of the major ideas of Chapter 20, see ***Guide to the Essentials of American History*** or ***Interactive Student Tutorial CD-ROM,*** which contains interactive review activities, graphic organizers, and practice tests.

Reviewing the Chapter

Define These Terms

Match each term in Column 1 with the correct definition in Column 2.

Column 1	Column 2
1. trust	**a.** discount
2. rebate	**b.** business owned by investors
3. corporation	**c.** court order
4. stock	**d.** share in a business
5. injunction	**e.** group of corporations run by a single board of directors

Explore the Main Ideas

1. What tactics did railroads use to fight competition?
2. What methods did American businesses use to raise capital in the late 1800s?
3. Summarize the arguments for and against monopolies.
4. Why was Edison's research laboratory an important development?
5. How did the Triangle Fire influence public opinion?

Chart Activity

Look at the table below and answer the following questions: **1.** During what five-year period did the government issue the most patents? **2.** How many patents were issued between 1881 and 1890? **Critical Thinking** Make two generalizations about American technology in the late 1800s.

United States Patents, 1861–1900

Five-Year Periods	Number of Patents
1861–1865	20,725
1866–1870	58,734
1871–1875	60,976
1876–1880	64,462
1881–1885	97,156
1886–1890	110,358
1891–1895	108,420
1896–1900	112,188

Source: *Historical Statistics of the United States*

Critical Thinking and Writing

1. **Understanding Chronology** Suppose you were asked to create a graphic organizer in the shape of a pyramid showing the growth of American industry. At the bottom you plan to place three items that began that growth. What three items would you choose?
2. **Linking Past and Present** Today, airlines often have "price wars" to attract customers. Judging from what you know about railroad competition, what do you think might be the long-term result of these "wars"?
3. **Exploring Unit Themes Industrialization** Describe one way each of the following transformed the nation: **(a)** steel, **(b)** new sources of power, **(c)** advances in communication, **(d)** new forms of transportation.
4. **Analyzing a Quotation** Jay Gould, a railroad owner, once said, "I can hire one half of the working class to kill the other half." **(a)** What do you think he meant? **(b)** Based on the statement, what do you think was Gould's opinion of unions? Explain.

Using Primary Sources

James J. Davis began working in the iron mills of Pittsburgh when he was twelve. He later described his job:

> "I had iron biscuits to bake; my forge fire must be hot as a volcano. There were five bakings every day and this meant the shoveling in of nearly two tons of coal. In summer I was stripped to the waist and panting while sweat poured down across my heaving muscles. My palms and fingers, scorched by the heat, became hardened like goat hoofs. . . . Do [weight-lifting exercises] ten hours in a room so hot it melts your eyebrows and you will know what it is like to be [an ironworker]."

Source: *The Life of an Iron Puddler*, James W. Davis, 1922.

Recognizing Points of View **(a)** To what did Davis compare the work of an ironworker? **(b)** How do you think Mother Jones would have reacted to this description? Explain.

Activity Bank

Interdisciplinary Activity

Exploring Economics Review the material on railroads and the growth of industry. Then make a concept map to show the industries that resulted from or were related to the growth of a railroad network in the United States.

Career Skills Activity

Advertising Writers Create advertisements for a mail-order catalog selling the new inventions discussed in the chapter. Write text and use pictures in your ads. Then organize your ads into a catalog.

Citizenship Activity

Learning About Corporate Citizenship Many corporations today make an effort to be good citizens in their communities. Interview the public relations officer at a large local corporation to find out what that company has done to help your community. Write up your interview and prepare a report.

Internet Activity

Use the Internet to find sites dealing with the Carnegie Foundation. After learning about the work of the foundation, write a proposal for a project that you would like to see the foundation support.

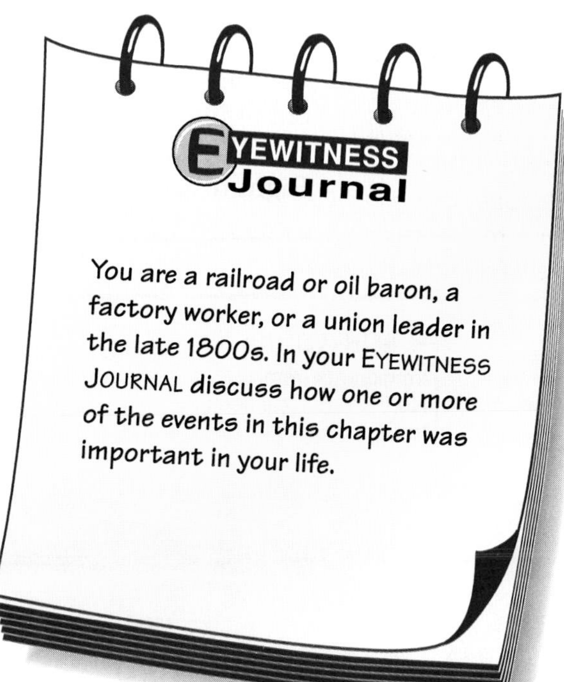

Chapter 21

Immigration and the Growth of Cities

1865–1914

What's Ahead

In the 50 years after the Civil War, 25 million immigrants poured into the United States. Most were driven by hunger and poverty and drawn by hope of a better life. They came from places such as Italy, Eastern Europe, Armenia, China, and Mexico. During this time, American cities grew rapidly.

Population growth brought problems including poor housing and strained city services. At the same time, it led to a rich mix of cultures. Cities fostered new leisure-time activities, such as sports. As education improved, newspapers, magazines, and new American fiction gained a larger audience.

Why Study History?

In the late 1800s, educators made vast improvements in public education. Today, Americans continue to stress the role of education in producing good citizens and preparing them for a changing future. To focus on this connection, see the *Why Study History?* feature, "You Have a Right to an Education," in this chapter.

American Events

Mid-1800s Immigrants from Northern Europe flock to United States

1882 Chinese Exclusion Act bars Chinese immigrants

1886 Statue of Liberty is dedicated

1865 | 1870 | 1875 | 1880 | 1885 | 1890

World Events

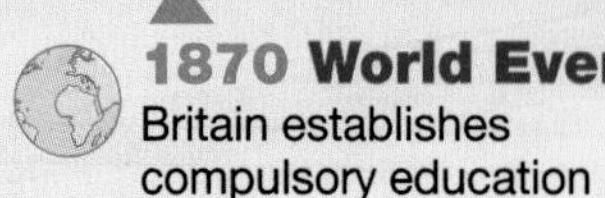

1870 World Event Britain establishes compulsory education

1881 World Event Russia increases violent pogroms against Jews

A Busy City Street

In his painting Houston Street, *George Benjamin Luks captured the bustle of a crowded New York City street. Many of these pushcart vendors, shopping housewives, or playing children probably spoke Italian, Russian, or other foreign languages. In the late 1800s and early 1900s, a boom in immigration fed the rapid growth of American cities.* ★ **Why do you think many immigrants wanted to come to the United States at this time?**

1889
Jane Addams founds Hull House to help poor immigrants

1902
Macy's department store opens nine-story building

1904
New York opens its subway system

1890 1895 1900 1905 1910 1915

1891 World Event
Arthur Conan Doyle publishes *Adventures of Sherlock Holmes*

1905 World Event
Chinese in Shanghai boycott American goods to protest exclusion laws

The New Immigrants

As You Read

Explore These Questions

- Why did immigration boom in the late 1800s?
- How did immigrants adjust to life in their new land?
- Why did anti-immigrant feeling grow?

Define

- push factor
- pull factor
- pogrom
- steerage
- ethnic group
- assimilation
- nativist

Identify

- Statue of Liberty
- Emma Lazarus
- Ellis Island
- Angel Island
- Chinese Exclusion Act

Setting the Scene In 1884, Rosa Cristoforo left her village in Italy to join her husband in "l'America." After two weeks on a cramped steamship, she finally caught sight of land:

> "America! The country where everyone could find work! Where wages were so high no one had to go hungry! Where all men were free and equal and where even the poor could own land! But now we were so near it seemed too much to believe."

Millions of immigrants flooded into the United States after the Civil War. Most came from eastern and southern Europe. Latin Americans and Asians came, too. All left homelands that offered them little hope for a better future. The United States, they heard, was a land of opportunity.

Reasons for Immigration

Between 1866 and 1915, more than 25 million immigrants poured into the United States. Both push and pull factors played a part in this vast migration. **Push factors** are conditions that drive people from their homes. **Pull factors** are conditions that attract immigrants to a new area.

Push factors

Many immigrants were small farmers or landless farm workers. As European populations grew, land became scarce. Small farms could barely support the families who worked them. In some areas, new farm machines replaced farm workers.

Political and religious persecution pushed many people to leave their homes. In the late 1800s, the Russian government supported **pogroms** (poh GRAHMZ), or organized attacks on Jewish villages. "Every night," recalled a Jewish girl who fled Russia, "they were chasing after us, to kill everyone." Millions of Jews fled Russia and Eastern Europe to settle in American cities.

Persecution was also a push factor for Armenian immigrants. The Armenians lived in the Ottoman Empire (present-day Turkey). Between the 1890s and the 1920s, the Ottoman government killed a million or more Armenians. Many fled, eventually settling in California and elsewhere.

After 1910, a revolution led thousands of Mexicans to cross the border into the Southwest. For the Chinese, poverty and hardship at home acted as push factors, driving them to make new homes across the Pacific.

Pull factors

The promise of freedom and hopes for a better life attracted poor and oppressed people from Europe, Asia, and Latin America. Often, one bold family member—usually a young single male—set off for the United States. Before long, he would write home with news of the rich land across the ocean or across the border. Once settled, he would send for family members to join him.

Once settled, the newcomers helped pull neighbors from the "old country" to the United States. In the late 1800s, one out of every ten Greeks left their homes for the United States. Thousands of Italians, Poles, and Eastern European Jews also sailed to the Americas.

Jobs were another pull factor. American factories needed workers. Factory owners sent agents to Europe and Asia to hire workers at low wages. Steamship companies competed to offer low fares for the ocean crossing. Railroads posted notices in Europe advertising cheap land in the American West.

The Long Voyage

Leaving home required great courage. The voyage across the Atlantic or Pacific was often miserable. Most immigrants could afford only the cheapest berths. Ship owners jammed up to 2,000 people in **steerage,** as the airless rooms below deck were called. On the return voyage, cattle and cargo filled those same spaces.

In such close quarters, diseases spread rapidly. An outbreak of measles infected every child on a German immigrant ship. The dead were thrown into the water "like cattle," reported a horrified passenger.

A "golden door" in New York

For most European immigrants, the voyage ended in New York City. There, after 1886, they saw the giant **Statue of Liberty** in the harbor. The statue was a gift from France to the United States.

The Statue of Liberty became a symbol of the hope and freedom offered by the United States. **Emma Lazarus** wrote a poem, "The New Colossus," that was carved at the base of the statue. It welcomes all newcomers and ends with these lines:

> "Give me your tired, your poor,
> Your huddled masses yearning to
> breathe free,
> The wretched refuse of your teeming
> shore.
> Send these, the homeless, tempest-
> tossed to me:
> I lift my lamp beside the golden
> door!"

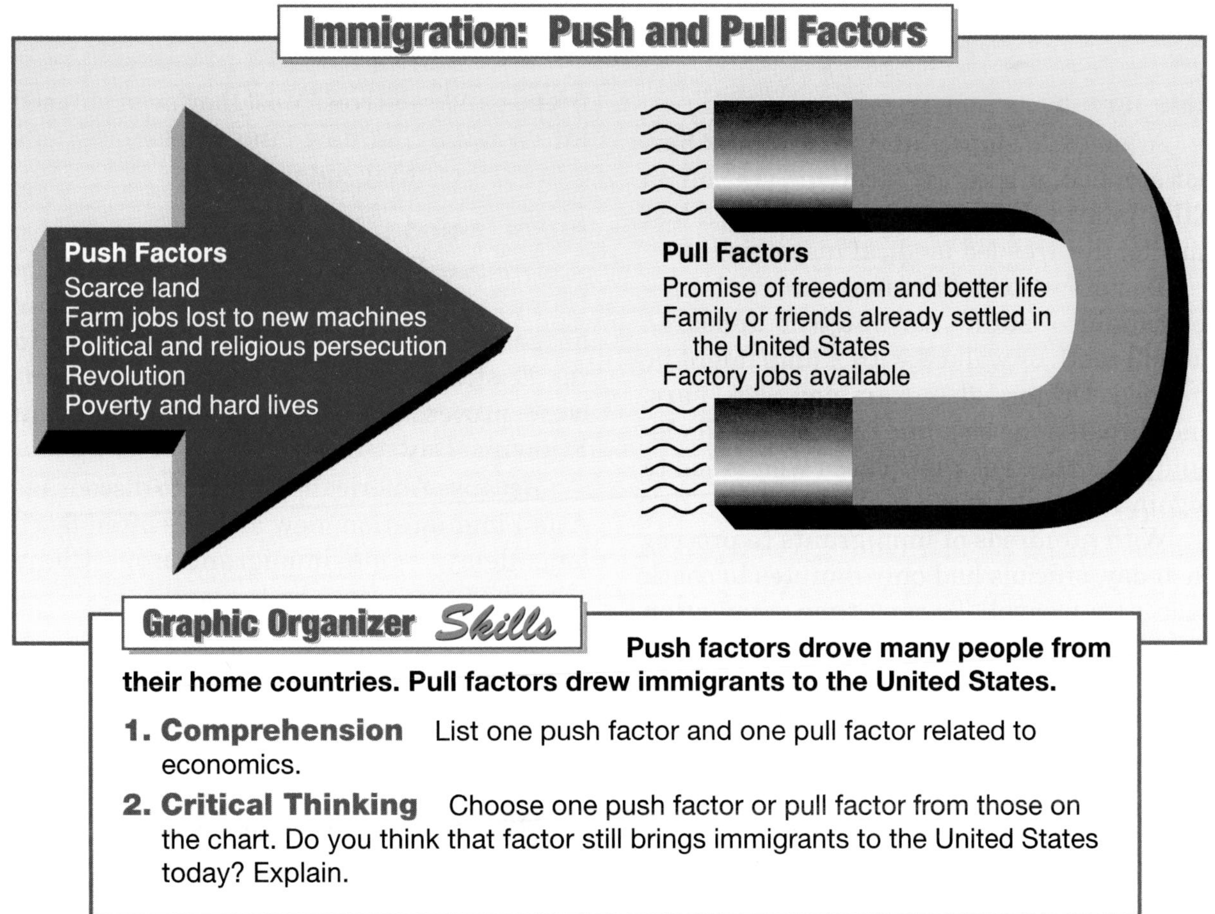

Graphic Organizer *Skills* **Push factors drove many people from their home countries. Pull factors drew immigrants to the United States.**

1. **Comprehension** List one push factor and one pull factor related to economics.
2. **Critical Thinking** Choose one push factor or pull factor from those on the chart. Do you think that factor still brings immigrants to the United States today? Explain.

American Heritage
MAGAZINE

HISTORY HAPPENED HERE

Ellis Island

In the harbor between New York and New Jersey, Ellis Island was the gateway for millions of European immigrants. Hopeful newcomers were crowded into pens in the main hall (left), nervously awaiting interviews with immigration officials. For years, Ellis Island fell into disrepair. In the 1980s, it was restored and is now a museum devoted to the immigrant experience. You can see hundreds of items carried by immigrants, like the ones shown here.

★ ***To learn more about this historic site, write:*** *Ellis Island National Monument, New York, NY 10004.*

▲ Czechoslovakian vest

Italian pasta pot ▲

Ellis Island

After 1892, ships entering New York harbor stopped at the new receiving station on **Ellis Island.** Here, immigrants faced a last hurdle, the dreaded medical inspection.

Doctors watched the newcomers climb a long flight of stairs. Anyone who appeared out of breath or walked with a limp might be stopped. Doctors also examined eyes, ears, and throats. The sick had to stay on Ellis Island until they got well. Those who failed to regain full health were sent home.

With hundreds of immigrants to process each day, officials had only minutes to check each new arrival. To save time, they often changed names that they found difficult to spell. Krzeznewski became Kramer. Smargiaso ended up as Smarga. One Italian immigrant found that even his first name had been changed—from Bartolomeo to Bill.

A few lucky immigrants went directly from Ellis Island into the welcoming arms of friends and relatives. Most, however, stepped into a terrifying new land whose language and customs they did not know.

Angel Island

On the West Coast, immigrants from China, and later from Japan, faced even harsher experiences than the Europeans in the East. By the early 1900s, many Asians were processed on **Angel Island** in San Francisco Bay.

Because Americans wanted to discourage Asian immigration, new arrivals often faced long delays. One immigrant from China scratched these lines on the wall:

> “Why do I have to languish in this jail?
> It is because my country is weak and my family poor.
> My parents wait in vain for news;
> My wife and child, wrapped in their quilt, sigh with loneliness.”

Changing Patterns of Immigration

Before 1885, most new immigrants to the United States were Protestants from Northern and Western Europe. Those from England and Ireland already spoke English. The Irish, English, Germans, and Scandinavians became known as "old immigrants." At first, the old immigrants faced some discrimination. As the nation grew, though, they were drawn into American life.

In the late 1800s, the patterns of immigration changed. Large numbers of people arrived from Southern and Eastern Europe. Millions of Italians, Poles, Greeks, Russians, and Hungarians landed in the eastern United States. On the West Coast, a smaller but growing number of Asian immigrants arrived, first from China, then from Japan. There were also a few immigrants from Korea, India, and the Philippines.

Few of these "new immigrants" spoke English. Many of the Europeans were Catholic, Eastern Orthodox, or Jewish. Immigrants from Asia might be Buddhist or Daoist. Their languages and religions set the new immigrants apart. As a result, they found it harder to adapt to a new life.

Adjusting to a New Land

Many immigrants had heard stories that the streets in the United States were paved with gold. Once in the United States, the newcomers had to adjust their dreams to reality. They immediately set out to find work. European peasants living on the land had little need for money, but it took cash to survive in the United States. Through friends, relatives, labor contractors, and employment agencies, the new arrivals found jobs.

Most immigrants stayed in the cities where they landed. The slums of cities soon became packed with poor immigrants. By 1900, one such neighborhood on the lower east side of New York City had become the most crowded place in the world.

Ethnic neighborhoods

Immigrants adjusted to their new lives by settling in neighborhoods with their own ethnic group. An **ethnic group** is a group of people who share a common culture. Across the United States, cities were patchworks of Italian, Irish, Polish, Hungarian, German, Jewish, and Chinese neighborhoods.

Within these ethnic neighborhoods, newcomers spoke their own language and celebrated special holidays with foods prepared as in the old country. Italians joined ethnic clubs such as the Sons of Italy. Hungarians bought and read Hungarian newspapers.

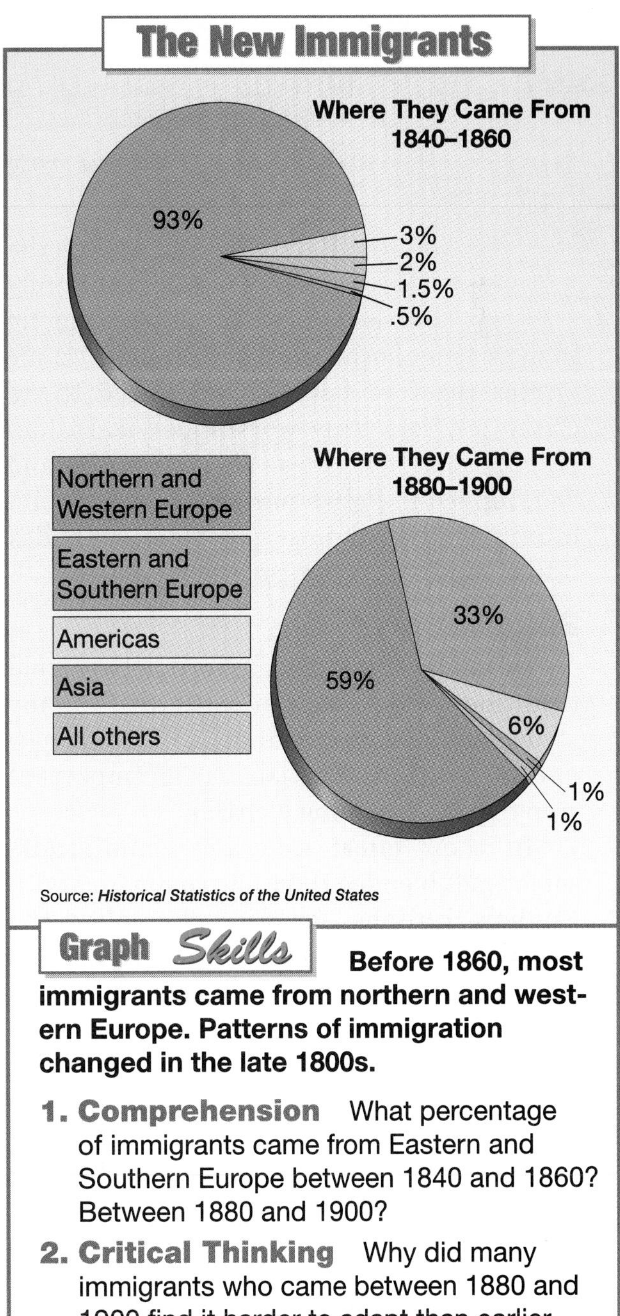

Source: *Historical Statistics of the United States*

Graph Skills **Before 1860, most immigrants came from northern and western Europe. Patterns of immigration changed in the late 1800s.**

1. **Comprehension** What percentage of immigrants came from Eastern and Southern Europe between 1840 and 1860? Between 1880 and 1900?
2. **Critical Thinking** Why did many immigrants who came between 1880 and 1900 find it harder to adapt than earlier immigrants?

ENGLISH-CHINESE PHRASEOLOGY.

汝有乜貨物出賣
What goods have you for sale?

樣樣都有
I have all kinds.

我想買条好褲
I want to get a pair of your best pants.

汝愛乜價銀
What do you ask for them?

汝能減少[illegible]
Can you take less for them?

不能先生
I can not, sir.

◀ *Phrase book for Chinese immigrants*

Viewing HISTORY **Chinese Americans**

This photograph shows Chinese children sitting on a stoop in San Francisco's Chinatown. For many immigrants like these, learning English was important. Books of useful phrases helped immigrants get through shopping and other activities of day-to-day life. ★ **Do you think these children had already assimilated into American culture when this picture was taken? How can you tell?**

Religion stood at the center of immigrant family life. Houses of worship sprang up in most neighborhoods. They brought ethnic groups together but also separated them. Catholics from Italy worshipped in Italian neighborhood parishes. Those from Poland worshipped in Polish parishes. Jewish communities divided into the older orthodox branch and the newer conservative wing.

Becoming Americans

Often, newcomers were torn between old traditions and American ways. Still, many struggled to learn the language of their new nation. Learning English was an important step toward becoming a citizen.

In their effort to adapt, immigrants sometimes blended their native tongues with English. Italians, for example, called the Fourth of July *"Il Forte Gelato,"* an Italian phrase that sounds like the holiday name but means "the great freeze." In El Paso, Texas, Mexican immigrants developed *Chuco,* a language that blended English and Spanish.

The process of becoming part of another culture is called **assimilation.** Children assimilated more quickly than their parents. They learned English in school and then helped their families learn to speak it. Because children wanted to be seen as Americans, they often gave up customs their parents honored. They played American games and dressed in American-style clothes.

Connections With Arts

One Russian Jewish immigrant became the nation's most popular songwriter. Israel Baline came to New York in 1893, when he was five years old. Under the name Irving Berlin, he went on to write such familiar tunes as "Easter Parade," "White Christmas," and "God Bless America."

A New Surge of Nativism

Many Americans opposed the increase in immigration. They felt the newcomers would not assimilate because their languages, religions, and customs were too different.

Even before the Civil War, **nativists** had wanted to limit immigration and preserve the country for native-born white Protestants. In the late 1800s, nativist feelings reached a new peak. Many workers resented the new immigrants because they took jobs for low pay. One newspaper complained:

> "The Poles, Slavs, Huns, and Italians come over without any ambition to live as Americans live and... accept work at any wages at all, thereby lowering the tone of American labor as a whole."

Nativist pressure grew wherever new immigrants settled. Nativists targeted Jews and Italians in the Northeast and Mexicans in the Southwest. On the West Coast, nativists worked to end immigration from China.

Chinese exclusion

Since the California Gold Rush and the building of the railroads, Chinese immigrants had helped build the West. Most lived in cities, in tight-knit communities called "Chinatowns." Others made their living as farmers.

Most Americans did not understand Chinese customs. Also, some Chinese did not try to learn American ways. Like many other immigrants, they planned to stay only until they made a lot of money. They then hoped to return home, to live out their lives as rich and respected members of Chinese society. When that dream failed, many Chinese settled in the United States permanently.

As the numbers of Chinese grew, so did the prejudice and violence against them. Gangs attacked and sometimes killed Chinese people, especially during hard times.

Congress responded to this anti-Chinese feeling by passing the **Chinese Exclusion Act** in 1882. Under it, no Chinese laborer could enter the United States. In addition, no Chinese living in the United States could return once they left the country.

The Chinese Exclusion Act was the first law to exclude a specific national group from immigrating to the United States. Congress renewed the original 10-year ban several times. It was finally repealed in 1943.

Other limits

In 1887, nativists formed the American Protective Association. It soon had a million members. The group campaigned for laws to restrict immigration. Congress responded by passing a bill that denied entry to people who could not read their own language.

President Grover Cleveland vetoed the bill. It was wrong, he said, to keep out peasants just because they had never gone to school. Congress passed the bill again and again. Three more presidents vetoed it. In 1917, Congress overrode President Woodrow Wilson's veto, and the bill became law.

★ Section 1 Review ★

Recall

1. **Locate** **(a)** Italy, **(b)** Russia, **(c)** Armenia, **(d)** Greece, **(e)** China.
2. **Identify** **(a)** Statue of Liberty, **(b)** Emma Lazarus, **(c)** Ellis Island, **(d)** Angel Island, **(e)** Chinese Exclusion Act.
3. **Define** **(a)** push factor, **(b)** pull factor, **(c)** pogrom, **(d)** steerage, **(e)** ethnic group, **(f)** assimilation, **(g)** nativist.

Comprehension

4. Identify one push factor and one pull factor that caused people to come to the United States.
5. Why did children adjust more easily to the United States than their parents?
6. **(a)** Why did many Americans resent the new immigrants? **(b)** What steps did they take to limit immigration?

Critical Thinking and Writing

7. **Making Inferences** **(a)** How did the "old immigrants" differ from the "new immigrants"? **(b)** Why do you think the new immigrants faced greater problems when they first arrived in the United States than the old immigrants had?
8. **Distinguishing Facts From Opinions** Read the following statement: "Immigrants work for almost nothing and seem to be able to live on wind." **(a)** Is this a fact or an opinion? How do you know? **(b)** Who would most likely have made a statement like this? Explain.

Activity **Writing a Handbook** You are an immigrant to the United States in the 1880s. Write at least one page for a handbook for future immigrants from your country. Tell them what problems they should expect to have and how they can overcome those problems.

Booming Cities

As You Read

Explore These Questions
- Why did cities grow in the late 1800s?
- What hazards did city dwellers face?
- How did reformers help to improve city life?

Define
- urbanization
- tenement
- building code
- settlement house

Identify
- Jane Addams
- Hull House
- Mother Cabrini
- Social Gospel
- Salvation Army
- Young Men's Hebrew Association

SETTING the Scene A small fire started in the barn behind the O'Leary cottage. Within hours, dry winds had whipped the blaze into an inferno that raged across Chicago. A survivor described how panicked residents fled their homes:

> "Everybody was running north. People were carrying all kinds of crazy things. A woman was carrying a pot of soup, which was spilling all over her dress. People were carrying cats, dogs, and goats. In the great excitement, people saved worthless things and left behind good things."

Fire was a constant danger in cities. However, Americans agreed they had never seen anything like the great Chicago Fire of 1871. The blaze killed nearly 300 people, left almost 100,000 homeless, and destroyed the entire downtown.

Yet from the ashes, a new city rose. By the end of the century, Chicago was the fastest growing city in the world, with a population of over one million. Other American cities, too, underwent a population explosion. For new and old Americans alike, the golden door of opportunity opened into the city.

City Populations Grow

"We cannot all live in cities," declared the newspaper publisher Horace Greeley, "yet nearly all seem determined to do so." **Urbanization,** the movement of population from farms to cities, began slowly in the early 1800s. As the nation industrialized after the Civil War, urbanization became much more rapid. In 1860, only one American in five lived in a city. By 1890, one in three did.

Chicago street in the late 1800s

Jobs drew people to cities. As industries grew, so did the need for workers. New city dwellers took jobs in steel mills, meatpacking plants, and garment factories. They worked as sales clerks, waiters, barbers, bank tellers, and secretaries.

Immigrants and farmers

The flood of immigrants swelled city populations. Also, by the 1890s, most land in the West had been divided into farms and ranches. As a result, fewer pioneers went there to homestead. In fact, many Americans left farms to find a better life in the city. A young man in a story by western writer Hamlin Garland summed up the feelings of many farmers:

> "I'm sick of farm life... it's nothing but fret, fret, and work the whole time, never going any place, never seeing *anybody.*"

African Americans migrate

African Americans, too, moved to cities to improve their lives. Most African Americans lived in the rural South. When hard times hit or prejudice led to violence, some blacks headed to northern cities. By the 1890s, the south side of Chicago had a thriving African American community. Detroit, New York, Philadelphia, and other northern cities also had growing African American neighborhoods. The migration to the north began gradually, but increased rapidly after 1915.

As with immigrants from overseas, black migration usually began with one family member moving north. Later, relatives and friends joined the bold pioneer. Like immigrants from rural areas in Europe, many African Americans faced the challenge of adjusting to urban life.

City Life

Cities grew outward from their old downtown sections. Before long, many took on a similar shape.

Poor families crowded into the city's center, the oldest section. Middle-class people lived farther out in row houses or new apartment buildings. Beyond them, the rich built fine homes with green lawns and trees.

The poor

Poor families struggled to survive in crowded slums. The streets were jammed with people, horses, pushcarts, and garbage.

Because space was so limited, builders devised a new kind of house to hold more people. They put up buildings six or seven stories high. They divided the buildings into small apartments, called **tenements.** Many tenements had no windows, heat, or indoor bathrooms. Often, 10 people shared a single room.

Typhoid and cholera raged through the tenements. Tuberculosis, a lung disease, was the biggest killer, accounting for thousands of deaths each year. Babies, especially, fell victim to disease. In one Chicago slum, more than half of all babies died before they were one year old.

Despite the poor conditions, the population of slums grew rapidly. Factory owners moved in to take advantage of low rents and cheap labor. They took over buildings for use as factories, thus forcing more and more people into fewer and fewer apartments.

The middle class

Beyond the slums stood the homes of the new middle class, including doctors, lawyers, business managers, skilled machinists, and office workers. Rows of neat houses lined tree-shaded streets. Here, disease broke out less frequently than in the crowded slums.

The Growth of Cities

Population Growth in Ten Selected Cities

City	Population in 1870	Population in 1900
New York	1,478,103	3,437,202
Chicago	298,977	1,698,575
Philadelphia	674,022	1,293,697
St. Louis	351,189	575,238
Boston	250,526	560,892
San Francisco	149,473	342,782
New Orleans	191,418	287,104
Denver	4,759	133,859
Los Angeles	5,728	102,479
Memphis	40,226	102,320

Rural and Urban Population in the United States, 1860–1920

Year	Rural Population	Urban Population
1860	80%	20%
1870	74%	26%
1880	72%	28%
1890	65%	35%
1900	60%	40%
1910	54%	46%
1920	49%	51%

Source: *United States Census Bureau*

Graph Skills **City populations grew rapidly in the United States in the decades following the Civil War.**

1. **Comprehension** Between 1870 and 1900, which cities on the chart above more than doubled in population?
2. **Critical Thinking** Study the bar graphs above. Make one generalization about the population of the United States after 1870.

Viewing HISTORY **Lives of the Wealthy**

The Brown Family, a painting by Eastman Johnson, suggests the elegance and fine manners of a wealthy American family. Many of the furnishings in this home, such as the crystal chandelier, were probably imported from Europe. Later, American manufacturers like Louis Tiffany produced fine glassware and other items for the rich. ★ **In a typical American city, where did the rich live?**

Middle-class people joined singing societies, bowling leagues, and charitable organizations. Such activities gave them a sense of community and purpose. As one writer said, the clubs "bring together many people who are striving upward, trying to uplift themselves."

The wealthy

On the outskirts of the city, behind brick walls or iron gates, lay the mansions of the very rich. In New York, huge homes dotted Fifth Avenue, which was still on the city's outskirts. In Chicago, by the 1880s, 200 millionaires lived along the exclusive lake front. In San Francisco, wealthy residents lived nearer the center of the city, but they built their mansions in the exclusive Nob Hill area. ("Nob" is British slang for a person of wealth and position.)

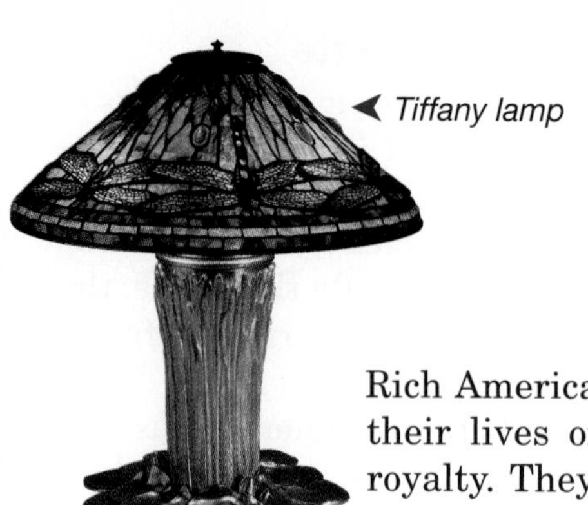

Tiffany lamp

Rich Americans modeled their lives on European royalty. They filled their mansions with priceless artworks and gave lavish parties. At one banquet, the host handed out cigarettes rolled in hundred-dollar bills.

Cleaning Up the Cities

As more and more people crowded into cities, problems grew. Tenement buildings were deathtraps if fires broke out. One magazine reporter in 1888 wrote:

> "It would be impossible for the occupants of the crowded rooms to escape by the narrow stairways, and the flimsy fire-escapes . . . are so laden with broken furniture, bales, and boxes that they would be worse than useless."

Garbage rotted in the streets. Factories polluted the air. Crime flourished. Thieves and pickpockets haunted lonely alleys, especially at night.

By the 1880s, reformers were demanding change. They forced city governments to pass **building codes**—laws that set standards for how structures should be built. The codes required new buildings to have fire escapes and decent plumbing. Cities also hired workers to collect garbage and sweep the streets. To reduce pollution, zoning laws kept factories out of neighborhoods where people lived.

Safety improved when cities set up professional fire companies and trained police forces. Gas—and later electric—lights made streets less dangerous at night. As you will read, many cities built new systems of public transportation as well.

Pushed by reformers, city governments hired engineers and architects to design new water systems. New York City, for example,

Skills FOR LIFE

Critical Thinking | Managing Information | Communication | Maps, Charts, and Graphs

Synthesizing Information

How Will I Use This Skill ?

Most of the things we learn about in life do not come to us from just one source. When something happens in your community, you may see a report on local television, read an account in a newspaper, and hear what friends say about it. Then, you put together and analyze the different pieces of information to form a complete picture. This process is called synthesizing.

LEARN the Skill

1. Identify the different sources of information and the facts and ideas in each.
2. Compare the evidence from each source. Do the pieces support one another? Is there any contradictory evidence?
3. Synthesize the evidence so that you can draw conclusions.

PRACTICE the Skill

To practice the skill, use the following pieces of information: the photograph on this page; the painting on page 566; the quotation to the right; the information in your textbook.

1. (a) What is the subject of the photograph? (b) What does the painting show? (c) What topic is Riis talking about?
2. (a) How does the family in the painting differ from that in the photograph? List three details that show the differences. (b) Does the quotation describe the photograph or the painting? (c) What information in the text is supported by the painting? The photograph?
3. Based on the evidence, make two generalizations about city life in the late 1800s.

Tenement family in New York City

> "In this house, where a case of smallpox was reported, there were fifty-eight babies and thirty-eight children...over five years of age."
>
> —Journalist Jacob Riis, describing a Jewish community in New York City

APPLY the Skill

Research a current topic in a newsmagazine or newspaper. Synthesize the written information with evidence from a photograph.

Singing class at Hull House ➤

Biography Jane Addams

A wealthy woman, Jane Addams dedicated her life to serving the poor. She founded Hull House in Chicago, which provided many services to immigrants and others. Above, neighbors enjoy a singing class at Hull House. Addams also worked for world peace. In 1931, she became the first American woman to win the Nobel Peace Prize.

★ **Addams insisted on living at Hull House herself. What does this tell you about her?**

dug underground tunnels to the Catskill Mountains—100 miles to the north. The tunnels brought a clean water supply to the city every day.

The Settlement House Movement

Some people looked for ways to help the poor. By the late 1800s, individuals began to organize settlement houses. A **settlement house** is a community center that offers services to the poor. The leading figure of the settlement house movement was a Chicago woman named **Jane Addams.**

Connections With Civics

Most settlement houses did not admit African Americans, so some black women opened their own settlement houses. In New York City, Victoria Earle Matthews started the White Rose Mission and Verna Morton-Jones opened Lincoln House. They offered shelter, child care, and classes to their communities.

Hull House

Addams came from a well-to-do family but had strong convictions about helping the poor. After college, she moved into one of the poorest slums in Chicago. There, in an old mansion, she opened a settlement house in 1889. She called it **Hull House.**

Other idealistic young women soon joined Addams. They took up residence in Hull House so that they could experience firsthand some of the hardships of the slum community in which they worked. These women dedicated their lives to service and to sacrifice—"like the early Christians," in the words of one volunteer.

The Hull House volunteers provided day nurseries for children whose mothers worked outside the home. They organized sports and a theater for young people. They taught English to immigrants and gave classes in health care. They also launched investigations into social and economic conditions in the city.

Over the years, the settlement house movement spread. By 1900, about 100 such centers had opened in cities across the United States.

Working for reform

Jane Addams and her Hull House staff were an important influence in bringing about reform legislation to improve the living and working conditions of the poor. They studied the slum neighborhoods where they worked and lived. They realized that the problems were too big for any one person or group, and they urged the government to act.

Alice Hamilton, a Hull House doctor, campaigned for better health laws. Florence Kelley worked to ban child labor. Jane Addams herself believed that reform legislation would be speeded if women could vote. She campaigned tirelessly for women's suffrage.

Religious Organizations Help the Poor

Religious groups also provided services to the poor. The Catholic Church ministered to the needs of Irish, Polish, and Italian immigrants. An Italian nun, **Mother Cabrini,** helped found more than 70 hospitals in North and South America. These hospitals treated people who could not afford doctors.

In cities, Protestant ministers began preaching a new **Social Gospel.** They called on their well-to-do members to do their duty as Christians by helping society's poor. One minister urged merchants and industrialists to pay their workers enough to enable them to marry and have families. He also proposed that they grant their workers a half day off on Saturdays.

Protestant groups set up programs for needy slum dwellers. In 1865, a Methodist minister named William Booth created the **Salvation Army** in London. By 1880, it expanded to the United States. In addition to spreading Christian teachings, the Salvation Army offered food and shelter to the poor.

In Jewish neighborhoods, too, religious organizations provided community services. The first **Young Men's Hebrew Association** (YMHA) began in Baltimore in 1854. The YMHA provided social activities, encouraged good citizenship, and helped Jewish families preserve their culture. In the 1880s, the Young Women's Hebrew Association (YWHA) grew out of the YMHA.

Other groups—like the YMCA (Young Men's Christian Association) and the YWCA (Young Women's Christian Association)—taught classes, organized team sports, and held dances. Such activities offered young people a brief escape from the problems of slum life.

★ Section 2 Review ★

Recall

1. **Identify** **(a)** Jane Addams, **(b)** Hull House, **(c)** Mother Cabrini, **(d)** Social Gospel, **(e)** Salvation Army, **(f)** Young Men's Hebrew Association
2. **Define** **(a)** urbanization, **(b)** tenement, **(c)** building code, **(d)** settlement house.

Comprehension

3. Name three causes for the growth of city populations in the late 1800s.
4. What problems did cities face as their populations grew?
5. What reforms did cities make?

Critical Thinking and Writing

6. **Comparing** Compare and contrast the lives of the rich, the middle class, and the poor in American cities in the late 1800s.
7. **Linking Past and Present** How do the problems of city dwellers today compare to those of city dwellers in the late 1800s?

Activity **Writing a Grant Proposal** You are a modern-day reformer who wants to start a settlement house somewhere in a nearby city or town. Choose a good location. Then write a proposal in which you ask a charitable foundation for funds to start your settlement house. Explain why the settlement is needed and what kind of services you plan to offer.

3 City Life Transformed

As You Read

Explore These Questions

- How did cities change in the late 1800s?
- Why did newspapers grow in number and importance?
- How did Americans spend their leisure time?

Define

- yellow journalism
- vaudeville
- ragtime

Identify

- Joseph Pulitzer
- William Randolph Hearst
- Nellie Bly
- Will Rogers
- Scott Joplin
- John Philip Sousa
- James Naismith

SETTING the Scene Bells rang. Cannons thundered. Fireworks crackled in the afternoon sky. New Yorkers were celebrating the opening of the Brooklyn Bridge. In 1883, its soaring arches were a triumph of modern engineering. Linking Manhattan Island and Brooklyn, the bridge was soon carrying 33 million people each year across New York City's East River.

The Brooklyn Bridge was only one sign of the changing face of New York. Other American cities, too, underwent vast changes that transformed their appearance and their way of life.

A New Look for Cities

A building boom changed the face of American cities in the late 1800s. Cities like Chicago and New York ran out of space in their downtown areas. Resourceful city planners and architects decided to build up instead of out.

Skyscrapers

After fire leveled downtown Chicago, planners tried out many new building ideas. Using new technology, they designed tall buildings with many floors. Called skyscrapers, these high-rise buildings had frames of lightweight steel to hold the weight of the structure.

Newly invented electric elevators carried workers to upper floors. Elevators moved so quickly, according to one rider, that "the passenger seems to feel his stomach pass into his shoes."

Public transportation

As skyscrapers crowded more people into smaller spaces, cities began to face a new problem: the traffic jam. Downtown streets were choked with horse-drawn buses, carriages, and carts.

Electricity offered one solution. In 1887, Frank Sprague, an engineer from Richmond, Virginia, designed the first electric streetcar system. Streetcars, or trolleys, were fast, clean, and quiet. Many trolley lines ran out from the center of a city to the outlying countryside.

Other cities, such as New York, built steam-driven passenger trains on overhead tracks. In 1897, Boston led the way in building the first American subway, or underground electric railway. In 1904, New York opened the first section of its subway system. These trains carried workers rapidly to and from their jobs.

Open spaces

While cities grew up and out, some planners wanted to preserve open spaces. They believed that open land would calm busy city dwellers.

In the 1850s, architect Frederick Law Olmsted planned Central Park in New York City. Other cities followed this model. They

Linking History and Technology

The Reliance Building in Chicago

Bay windows let in light and air. This was important at a time when few buildings had electric lights and no one had even heard of air conditioning.

The steel frame carried the weight of the building.

Clay tile walls protected the building from fire.

Elevators made it practical for buildings to have more than five or six stories.

The upper floors were used for offices. The ground floor held stores.

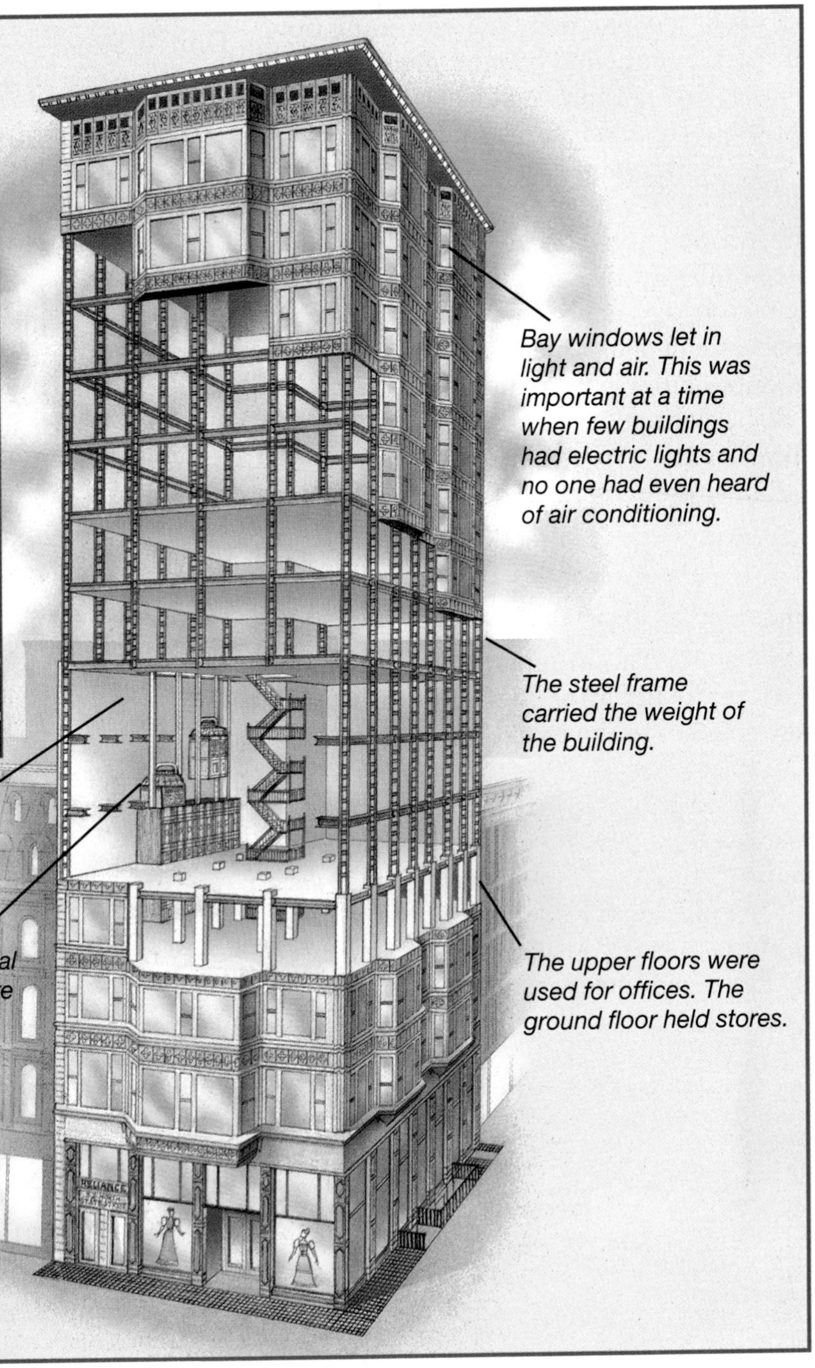

Skyscraper

As people crowded into American cities, architects began building up instead of out. Today, the Reliance Building in Chicago, shown here, does not look very tall. When it was built in the 1890s, however, its 16 stories made it a "skyscraper." ★ **Based on this drawing, what new kinds of technology made skyscrapers possible?**

set aside land for zoos and gardens so that city people could enjoy green grass and trees during their leisure time.

Department stores

Shopping areas also got a new look. In the late 1800s, department stores sprang up. In the past, people had bought shoes in one store, socks in another, and dishes in a third. The new department stores sold all kinds of goods in one building.

In 1902, R. H. Macy opened a nine-story building in New York. It had 33 elevators and a motto that became famous: "We sell goods cheaper than any house in the world." Soon, other cities had department stores. Shopping became a popular pastime. People browsed each floor, looking at clothes, furniture, and jewelry. On the street, "window shoppers" paused to enjoy elaborate window displays.

The Daily Newspaper

"Read all about it!" cried newsboys on city street corners. The number of newspapers grew dramatically after 1880. By 1900, half the newspapers in the world were printed in the United States.

The rapid growth in the number of newspapers was linked to the growth of cities. In towns and villages, neighbors shared news when they met. In the city, people had thousands of "neighbors." Also, there was so much news that people needed newspapers to be informed.

Newspapers reported on major events of the day. Most featured stories about local government, business, fashion, and sports. Many immigrants learned to read English by spelling their way through a daily paper. At the same time, they learned about life in the United States.

Two newspaper giants

Joseph Pulitzer created the first modern, mass-circulation newspaper. Pulitzer was a Hungarian immigrant. In 1883, he bought the New York *World.* He set out to make it lively and "truly democratic."

To win readers, Pulitzer slashed prices and added comic strips. He introduced bold "scare" headlines to attract reader attention and used pictures to illustrate stories. The *World* splashed crimes and political scandals across its front page. The paper's circulation jumped from 20,000 to one million.

William Randolph Hearst, who came to New York City from San Francisco, challenged Pulitzer. Hearst's New York *Journal* began to outdo the *World* in presenting scandals, crime stories, and gossip. Critics coined the term **yellow journalism** for the sensational reporting style of the *World* and the *Journal.* They complained that the papers offered less news and more scandal every day.

Women journalists

Newspapers competed for women readers. They added special sections on fashion, social events, health, homemaking, and family mat-

Viewing HISTORY **A Popular Newspaper**

This 1880 advertisement for the New York Sun *shows the growing popularity of newspapers. The ad suggests that* The Sun *covered everything from politics and shipping news to horse races and weddings. Readers could buy from a corner newsboy or get home delivery.* ★ **Why did newspapers become more important as cities grew?**

ters. Newspapers rarely pushed for women's rights, however. Most were afraid to take bold positions that might anger some readers.

A few women worked as reporters, like **Nellie Bly** of the *World.* Once, Bly pretended to be insane in order to find out about treatment of the mentally ill. Her articles about cruelty in mental hospitals led to reforms.

Biography **Scott Joplin**

Fingers flying swiftly over the piano keys, Scott Joplin was the "King of Ragtime." By the age of 14, he was already making a living as a piano player. He went on to compose more than 60 pieces of music, including his popular "Maple Leaf Rag." Joplin also wrote an opera, Treemonisha, *which was not performed until more than 60 years after his death.*★ **How did popular music styles like ragtime spread across the country?**

A World of Entertainment

By the late 1800s, American cities supported a wide variety of cultural activities. Talented Italian, German, Jewish, and other immigrants contributed to a new world of music and theater.

Music and other kinds of entertainment brought Americans together. People from different cultures sang the same songs and enjoyed the same shows. As railroads grew, circuses, acting companies, and "Wild West" shows toured the country. These traveling groups helped spread American culture beyond the cities to small towns throughout the United States.

Vaudeville

Many large cities organized symphony orchestras and opera companies. Generally, only the wealthy attended the symphony or the opera. For other city dwellers, an evening out often meant a trip to a vaudeville house. **Vaudeville** (VAWD vihl) was a variety show that included comedians, song-and-dance routines, and acrobats.

Vaudeville provided opportunities for people from many ethnic backgrounds, such as Irish American dancer-singer George M. Cohan and Jewish comedians like the Marx Brothers. **Will Rogers,** a performer of Cherokee descent, was one of the best-loved performers in the nation. Wearing a cowboy hat and twirling a rope, Rogers used gentle wit to comment about American life.

Popular music

Songwriters produced many popular tunes, such as "Shine On, Harvest Moon." Later, Thomas Edison's phonograph sparked a new industry. By 1900, millions of phonograph records had been sold.

Ragtime was a new kind of music with a lively, rhythmic sound. **Scott Joplin,** an African American composer, helped make ragtime popular. His "Maple Leaf Rag" was a nationwide hit.

In towns and cities, marching bands played the military music of **John Philip Sousa.** Sousa wrote more than 100 marches, including "The Stars and Stripes Forever." His marches became favorites at Fourth of July celebrations.

Sports and Leisure

The rise of the factory split the worlds of work and play more sharply than ever. With less chance to socialize on the job, there was more interest in leisure. In sports, Americans found a great escape from factories, stores, and offices.

Baseball: the national pastime

Baseball was the most popular sport in the nation. The game was first played in New York in the 1840s. During the Civil War, New York soldiers showed other Union troops how to play the game. By the 1870s, the country had several professional teams and its first league.

Early baseball was very different from today's game. Pitchers threw underhanded. Catchers caught the ball after one bounce. Fielders did not wear gloves. As a result, high scores were common. One championship game ended with a score of 103 to 8!

At first, African Americans played professional baseball. In the 1880s, however, the major leagues barred black players. In 1885, Frank Thompson organized a group of waiters into one of the first African American professional teams, the Cuban Giants of Long Island.

Football

Football grew out of soccer, which Americans had played since colonial times. Early football called for lots of muscle and little skill. On every play, the opposing teams crashed into each other like fighting rams. The quarterback ran or jumped over the tangle of bodies.

This toy bank shows three unhelmeted football players. If you drop in a coin, the players turn and collide.

Players did not wear helmets and were often hurt. In one brutal season, 44 college football players died from injuries. Some colleges banned the sport or drew up stricter rules of play for the game.

Basketball

In 1891, **James Naismith** invented a new sport: basketball. Naismith was teaching physical education at a YMCA in Springfield, Massachusetts. He wanted to find a sport that could be played indoors in winter. Naismith had two bushel baskets nailed to the gym walls. Players tried to throw a soccer ball into the baskets.

Basketball caught on quickly. It spread to other YMCAs and then to schools and colleges around the country.

★ Section 3 Review ★

Recall

1. **Identify** **(a)** Joseph Pulitzer, **(b)** William Randolph Hearst, **(c)** Nellie Bly, **(d)** Will Rogers, **(e)** Scott Joplin, **(f)** John Philip Sousa, **(g)** James Naismith.
2. **Define** **(a)** yellow journalism, **(b)** vaudeville, **(c)** ragtime.

Comprehension

3. How did new technology change the face of American cities?
4. Describe newspapers of the late 1800s.
5. **(a)** How did entertainment unite Americans? **(b)** What sports were popular in the late 1800s?

Critical Thinking and Writing

6. **Understanding Cause and Effect** Describe the cause-and-effect relationship between population growth and development of the skyscraper.
7. **Identifying Alternatives** Some journalists defend sensational stories by saying they are giving the public what it wants. What types of stories do you think newspapers and other media should provide? Explain your answer.

Activity **Creating a Poster** You are a printer in the early 1900s. Create an illustrated poster advertising one of the following: a new department store; a sporting event; a vaudeville show.

4 Education and Culture

As You Read

Explore These Questions

- How did public education improve in the late 1800s?
- How did American reading habits change?
- What themes did American writers and painters explore?

Define

- dime novel
- realist
- local color

Identify

- Chautauqua Society
- Horatio Alger
- Stephen Crane
- Paul Laurence Dunbar
- Mark Twain
- Winslow Homer
- Henry Tanner
- Mary Cassatt

SETTING the Scene The writer Mark Twain felt sure that the new mechanical typesetter would revolutionize publishing. The machine could do the work of four people. He invested $5,000 in it—a huge sum in 1880. "Very much the best investment I have ever made," he concluded.

In fact, Twain lost his investment. The company that he backed was a failure. The mechanical typesetter, however, did change publishing. It made printing easier and cheaper. Mass-produced, affordable books helped spread American culture.

Public Education

Before 1870, fewer than half of American children went to school. Many who did attended one-room schoolhouses, with only one teacher. Often, several students shared a single book.

Growth of schools

As industry grew after the Civil War, the nation needed an educated work force. As a result, states improved public schools at all levels. St. Louis created the first kindergarten in the United States in 1873. By 1900, there were 4,000 such programs serving children from ages 3 through 7 across the nation.

In the North, most states passed laws that required children to attend school, usually through sixth grade. In the South, the Freedmen's Bureau built grade schools for both African American and white students. However, most schools in the South were segregated.

In cities such as Boston and New York, public schools taught English to young immigrants. Native-born and immigrant children also learned about the duties and rights of citizens. In the 1880s, Catholic immigrants became worried that public schools stressed Protestant teachings. They opened their own, church-sponsored schools.

The school day

The typical school day lasted from 8:00 A.M. to 4:00 P.M. Pupils learned the "three Rs": reading, 'riting, and 'rithmetic. The most widely used textbook was *McGuffey's Eclectic Reader*. Students memorized and recited passages from *McGuffey's Reader*. With titles like "Waste Not, Want Not," the poems and stories taught not only reading but religion, ethics, and values.

Schools emphasized discipline and obedience. A 13-year-old boy complained:

> "They hits ye if yer don't learn and they hits ye if ye whisper, . . . and they hits ye if yer seat squeaks, and they hits ye if ye don't stan' up in time, and they hits ye if yer late, and they hits ye if ye ferget the page."

High schools and colleges

After 1870, many cities and towns built public high schools. By 1900, the United States had 6,000 high schools.

Why Study History?

Because You Have a Right to an Education

Historical Background

Today, it is easy to take education for granted. This was not true 150 years ago. Many states did not require children to go to school. If you were from a poor family, your chances of getting an education were slim. Then, reformers expanded American public education. They insisted that every child had a right to an education.

Schooling was especially valuable to young immigrants. Most had little opportunity for schooling in their homelands. Few could speak English. However, free public schools gave immigrant children the opportunity to succeed in their new homeland. They learned not only English, but American customs, laws, and history.

Graduation day

Connections to Today

In today's information age, education is more important than ever before. The modern world depends on advanced electronics, rapid communication, and computer technology. There are fewer and fewer good-paying, steady jobs for people who do not have at least a high school education.

Schools develop skills employers seek, such as creative thinking, organization, and public speaking. Schools also stress values like responsibility, self-discipline, and teamwork. Perhaps most important, schools prepare Americans for the duties of citizenship. Today, as in the past, democracy depends on an informed public.

Connections to You

It is your responsibility to get the most out of your education. The variety of classes you take give you an opportunity to explore your talents. A subject or activity may interest you enough for you to pursue a career in that field.

In addition, school gives you the opportunity to know and work with people who have different backgrounds and viewpoints. By taking advantage of what your school has to offer, you will prepare yourself for whatever your future brings.

1. **Comprehension** **(a)** How did immigrant children benefit from public schools? **(b)** List three skills that employers look for today.
2. **Critical Thinking** List three qualities that you need to do well in your classes. Write a sentence explaining how each quality can be important outside of school.

Making a Poster With a partner, create a poster that encourages students to stay in school. Use a catchy slogan as well as images.

To help meet the need for trained workers, the Chicago Manual Training School opened in 1884. It offered courses in "shop work" as well as a few academic subjects. Within a decade, almost every public school in the nation had programs aimed at educating students for jobs in business and industry.

Higher education also expanded. New private colleges for both women and men opened. Many states built universities that offered free or low-cost education. However, for women, African Americans and others, opportunities for a college education were often limited.

Adult education

A new form of family education grew up along Lake Chautauqua in New York State. There, in 1874, a Methodist minister opened a summer school for Bible teachers. So many people enrolled that the next year the camp was opened to the general public and nonreligious subjects were introduced.

By the 1880s, some 75,000 thousand people gathered at Lake Chautauqua each summer not only for spiritual guidance but for lectures about art, politics, philosophy, and other subjects. Reformers, religious leaders, and seven American presidents spoke there. The mostly middle-class audiences discovered that education could be fun as well as uplifting.

In 1903, the **Chautauqua Society** began to send out traveling companies. Before long, Chautauquas were reaching as many as 5 million people in 10,000 American towns every year.

New Reading Habits

As more Americans learned to read in the late 1880s, they read not only newspapers but also more books and magazines. New printing methods lowered the cost of magazines. Magazines also added eye-catching pictures to attract readers.

Each magazine had its special audience. The *Ladies' Home Journal* appealed mostly to middle-class women with articles about famous people and stories by well-known authors. By 1900, it had one million readers. Other magazines, such as *Harper's Monthly* and *The Nation,* specialized in politics and current events.

Dime novels

In the late 1800s, paperback books became popular. Bestsellers were often **dime novels.** These low-priced paperbacks offered thrilling adventure stories. Many told about the "Wild West." Young people loved dime novels, but parents often disapproved of the stories. One critic complained:

> "Stories for children used to begin, 'Once upon a time there lived—.' Now they begin, 'Vengeance, blood, death,' shouted Rattlesnake Jim."

Horatio Alger, a popular writer, produced more than 100 dime novels for children. Most told the story of a poor boy who became rich and respected through hard work, luck, and honesty. Americans snapped up these rags-to-riches stories. They offered

Biography **Horatio Alger, Jr.**

In the novels of Horatio Alger, virtue and hard work were always rewarded. Alger published more than 130 "rags-to-riches" tales, with titles such as Tattered Tom, Phil the Fiddler, *and* Paul the Peddler. *Alger devoted many of the profits from his books to a New York home for orphans and runaways.*

★ **How did Alger's books reflect an optimistic view of the United States?**

Viewing HISTORY **A Painting by Mary Cassatt**

Mothers and children were a favorite theme of Mary Cassatt. This 1880 painting is titled Mother About to Wash Her Sleepy Child. *Cassatt was influenced by new French styles as well as by Japanese prints, which were becoming popular in Europe.*
★ **Describe the work of one other American painter of the late 1800s.**

the hope that even the poorest person could become rich and successful in the United States.

New American writers

In the 1880s, a new crop of writers appeared. For the first time, Americans read more books by American authors than by British authors. One group of writers, known as **realists,** tried to show the harsh side of life as it was. Many realists had worked as newspaper reporters. They had seen the poverty and the growth of cities created by the Industrial Revolution.

Stephen Crane was best known for his Civil War novel *The Red Badge of Courage.* (See page 498.) Crane also wrote about the hard lives of young city slum dwellers in novels like *Maggie: A Girl of the Streets.* Hamlin Garland described the harsh lives of farmers in the 1890s. Jack London, born in California, wrote about the hardships of miners and sailors on the West Coast.

Kate Chopin found an audience for short stories about New Orleans life in women's magazines. Chopin's stories showed women breaking out of traditional roles.

Paul Laurence Dunbar was the first African American to make a living as a writer. He wrote poems, such as "We Wear the Mask," in a serious, elegant style. In other poems, short stories, and novels, he used everyday language to express the feelings of African Americans of the time.

Mark Twain

The most famous and popular author of this period was Samuel Clemens, better known by his pen name, **Mark Twain.** As a young man, Clemens worked on a Mississippi River steamboat. There, he heard the boatman's cry "Mark twain," meaning that the river was two "marks," or 12 feet, deep. He took it as his name when he sent out his first story.

Popular stories

Like many other American writers, Twain used local color to make his stories more realistic. **Local color** refers to the speech and habits of a particular region. Twain's novels captured the speech patterns of Southerners who lived and worked along the Mississippi. Twain used homespun, nononsense characters to poke fun at serious issues. Novels like *The Adventures of Tom Sawyer* and short stories like "The Celebrated Jumping Frog of Calaveras County" became so well known that people often quoted them to win arguments.

Huckleberry Finn

Twain's greatest work was probably *The Adventures of Huckleberry Finn.* The novel takes place along the Mississippi River before the Civil War. Huck is a country boy who helps an escaped slave named Jim. The two become good friends as they raft down the river together.

Twain filled his novel with humor and adventure to entertain his readers. At the same time, he made a serious point. In the beginning, Huck Finn accepts slavery. During the novel, Huck comes to respect Jim and decides that their friendship is more important than the unjust laws that enslaved Jim. In the following passage, Huck tells of Jim's longing to be reunited with his family:

> "He was saying how the first thing he would do when he got to a free state he would go to saving up money, . . . and when he got enough he would buy his wife, which was owned on a farm close to where Miss Watson lived; and then they would both work to buy the two children, and if their master wouldn't sell them, they'd get an Ab'litionist to go and steal them."

Although *Huckleberry Finn* became a classic American novel, some schools and libraries refused to buy the book. They claimed that Huck was a crude character who would have a bad influence on "our pure-minded lads and lasses."

Realism in Art

Like writers of the period, many artists sought to capture local color and the gritty side of modern life. In the late 1800s, leading artists painted realistic everyday scenes.

As a young man during the Civil War, **Winslow Homer** drew scenes of brutal battles for magazines. Later, he gained fame for realistic scenes of the New England coast. Painter Thomas Eakins learned anatomy and dissected dead bodies to be able to portray the human form accurately. Many of his paintings depicted sports scenes or medical operations. **Henry Tanner,** an African American student of Eakins, won fame for pictures of black sharecroppers. Later, Tanner moved to Paris to enjoy greater freedom.

Other American artists preferred to work in Europe, too. James Whistler left Massachusetts for Paris and London, where his use of color and light influenced young European artists. John Singer Sargent made money painting portraits of wealthy Europeans.

The painter **Mary Cassatt** (kuh SAT) was born in Pennsylvania but settled in Paris. She carved out a place for herself in the French art world. Cassatt painted bright, colorful scenes of people in everyday situations, especially mothers with their children.

★ Section 4 Review ★

Recall

1. **Identify** **(a)** Chautauqua Society, **(b)** Horatio Alger, **(c)** Stephen Crane, **(d)** Paul Laurence Dunbar, **(e)** Mark Twain, **(f)** Winslow Homer, **(g)** Henry Tanner, **(h)** Mary Cassatt.
2. **Define** **(a)** dime novel, **(b)** realist, **(c)** local color.

Comprehension

3. How did public education change after the Civil War?
4. Describe two new kinds of reading matter that became popular in the late 1800s.
5. What was Mark Twain's goal in *Huckleberry Finn?*

Critical Thinking and Writing

6. **Understanding Causes and Effects** How do you think the growth of public education was related to the popularity of newspapers, magazines, and books in the late 1800s?
7. **Drawing Conclusions** Why do you think many American artists and writers turned to realism in the late 1800s?

Activity **Writing a Short Story** Horatio Alger lives! Write the outline and first page for a "rags-to-riches" dime novel. Make your story begin with a thrilling "hook" that captures the attention of the reader.

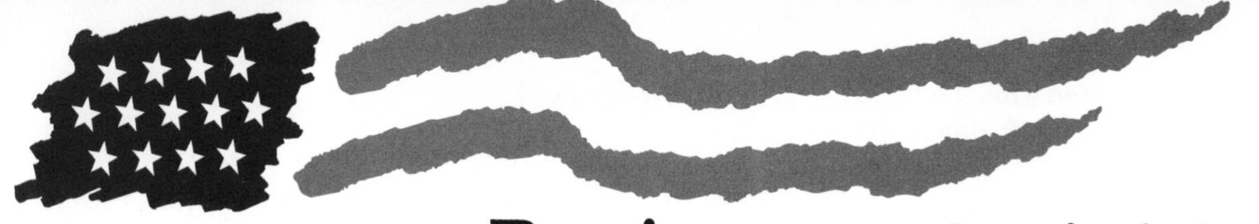

Chapter 21 Review and Activities

★ Sum It Up ★

Section 1 The New Immigrants

- Immigrants from southern and eastern Europe, Asia, and Latin America poured into the United States after the Civil War.
- Most immigrants settled in ethnic neighborhoods in cities while they assimilated into American culture.
- A new surge of nativism arose in response to the so-called new immigrants.

Section 2 Booming Cities

- Cities grew rapidly in the late 1800s, and many poor people lived in crowded slums.
- Under pressure from reformers, cities passed building codes and improved city services.
- Church groups, along with idealistic reformers like Jane Addams, worked to improve the life of poor city residents.

Section 3 City Life Transformed

- Skyscrapers, public transportation, and public parks became a part of the city scene in the late 1800s.
- Newspaper circulation grew as publishers introduced new features, comics, and sensational "yellow journalism."
- Leisure activities such as sports and entertainment helped unite Americans.

Section 4 Education and Culture

- In the late 1800s, education improved in the United States.
- American literature and art ranged from dime novels to new works of realism.

For additional review of the major ideas of Chapter 21, see ***Guide to the Essentials of American History*** or ***Interactive Student Tutorial CD-ROM,*** which contains interactive review activities, graphic organizers, and practice tests.

Reviewing the Chapter

Define These Terms

Match each term with the correct definition.

Column 1	Column 2
1. ethnic group	**a.** process of becoming part of another culture
2. assimilation	**b.** apartment in a slum building
3. tenement	**c.** variety show
4. vaudeville	**d.** group of people who share a common culture
5. dime novel	**e.** low-priced paperback, usually offering thrilling adventure stories

Explore the Main Ideas

1. Why did many Armenians and Russian Jews immigrate to the United States in the late 1800s?
2. How did nativist reaction to immigration vary by region?
3. Describe the three sections of cities in the late 1800s.
4. How did church programs help the poor?
5. How did cities cope with traffic problems?

Chart Activity

Look at the graph below and answer the following questions: **1.** About how many daily newspapers were printed in the United States in 1860? in 1900? **2.** During what 10-year period did the number of newspapers increase the most? **Critical Thinking** List two causes for the rapid increase in the number of newspapers.

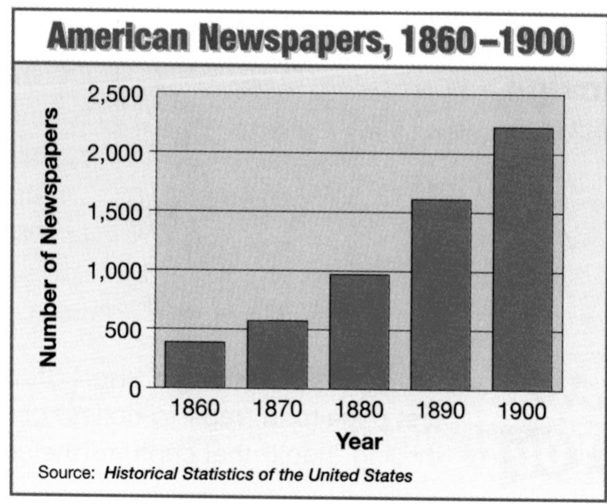

Critical Thinking and Writing

1. Exploring Unit Themes **Industrialization** What effect do you think the increased supply of immigrant workers in industry had on American industrial output?
2. **Understanding Chronology** Place the following events in their proper order: American cities boomed; city governments did not adequately serve their citizens; immigrants moved to the United States; reforms helped cities work better; Europeans and Asians were looking for economic opportunities.
3. **Linking Past and Present (a)** What did city dwellers in the 1800s do to escape the pressures of city life? **(b)** How do people in cities today relax?
4. **Making Decisions** If you had been alive in the late 1800s, would you have preferred to live in a large city like New York or Chicago, or on a ranch or farm in the West? Explain.

Using Primary Sources

A New York journalist reporting on Chicago in 1893 told his readers:

> “I do not know how many very tall buildings Chicago contains, but they must number nearly two dozen.... The best of them are very elegantly and completely [decorated], and the communities of men inside them might almost live their lives within their walls, so [varied] are the occupations and services of the tenants.... It is a great mistake to think that we in New York possess all the elegant, rich, and ornamental [products] of taste.”

Source: *Harper's Chicago and the World's Fair,* Julian Ralph, 1893.

Recognizing Points of View (a) Does the reporter approve or disapprove of Chicago's buildings? **(b)** How does the writer think Chicago's buildings compare with those of New York?

Activity Bank

Interdisciplinary Activity

Exploring Geography Research population figures for San Francisco, Chicago, and New York between 1865 and 1910. Create a line graph that shows how the population of these cities grew during this period.

Career Skills Activity

Architects Find out more about the layout and the buildings of a city in the late 1800s. Then create a model of a city. Include skyscrapers, tenements, stores, theaters, parks, and other features.

Citizenship Activity

Understanding Reform Look for a problem in your community that is similar to the problems faced by reformers like Jane Addams. Consult with officials and action groups in your area. Then, work out a proposal for reform of the problem.

Internet Activity

Use the Internet to find sites dealing with Angel Island. Use the information you find to write a poem like the one on page 560. In your poem, refer to specific conditions described by sites you visited.

You are an immigrant living in an American city in the 1880s or 1890s. In your EYEWITNESS JOURNAL, *describe a typical day in your life. You might describe work, education, the importance of family and religion, neighborhood life, and leisure activities.*

My Ántonia

Willa Cather

Introduction

Willa Cather was one of the greatest American novelists. When she was nine, her family moved to Nebraska. Cather's experiences on the frontier inspired her 1918 novel *My Ántonia.* It tells the story of two young people growing up in Nebraska: the narrator, Jim, and his immigrant friend, Ántonia. In this passage, Jim describes a Nebraska winter on his family's farm.

Vocabulary

Before you read the selection, find the meaning of these words in a dictionary: **boisterously, bile, mottled.**

We had three weeks of this mild, open weather. The cattle in the corral ate corn almost as fast as the men could shell it for them, and we hoped they would be ready for an early market. One morning the two big bulls, Gladstone and Brigham Young, thought spring had come, and they began to tease and butt at each other across the barbed wire that separated them. Soon they got angry. They bellowed and pawed up the soft earth with their hoofs, rolling their eyes and tossing their heads. Each withdrew to a far corner of his own corral, and then they made for each other at a gallop. Thud, thud, we could hear the impact of their great heads, and their bellowing shook the pans of the kitchen shelves. Had they not been dehorned, they would have torn each other to pieces. Pretty soon the fat steers took it up and began butting and horning each other. Clearly, the affair had to be stopped. We all stood by and watched admiringly while Fuchs rode into the corral with a pitchfork and prodded the bulls again and again, finally driving them apart.

The big storm of the winter began on my eleventh birthday, the twentieth of January. When I went down to breakfast that morning, Jake and Otto came in white as snowmen, beating their hands and stamping their feet. They began to laugh boisterously when they saw me, calling:

"You've got a birthday present this time, Jim, and no mistake. They was a full-grown blizzard ordered for you."

All day the storm went on. The snow did not fall this time, it simply spilled out of heaven, like thousands of feather-beds being emptied. That afternoon the kitchen was a carpenter-shop; the men brought in their tools and made two great wooden shovels with long handles. Neither grandmother nor I could go out in the storm, so Jake fed the chickens and brought in a pitiful contribution of eggs.

Next day our men had to shovel until noon to reach the barn—and the snow was still falling! There had not been such a storm in the ten years my grandfather had lived in Nebraska. He said at dinner that we would

A Homestead in Nebraska

Like Willa Cather, Sallie Cover grew up in rural Nebraska. In her painting Homestead of Ellsworth L. Ball, *Cover shows a neighboring farm in the 1880s. Mrs. Ball tends to her baby in the doorway of the house. Her husband works with a team of horses in the field.*

★ **Compare this painting to the photograph on page 524. What differences can you see between the two homesteads?**

not try to reach the cattle—they were fat enough to go without their corn for a day or two; but to-morrow we must feed them and thaw out their water-tap so that they could drink. We could not so much as see the corrals, but we knew the steers were over there, huddled together under the north bank. Our ferocious bulls, subdued enough by this time, were probably warming each other's backs. "This'll take the bile out of 'em!" Fuchs remarked gleefully.

At noon that day the hens had not been heard from. After dinner Jake and Otto, their damp clothes now dried on them, stretched their stiff arms and plunged again into the drifts. They made a tunnel through the snow to the hen-house, with walls so solid that grandmother and I could walk back and forth in it. We found the chickens asleep; perhaps they thought night had come to stay. One old rooster was stirring about, pecking at the solid lump of ice in their water-tin. When we flashed the lantern in their eyes, the hens set up a great cackling and flew about clumsily, scattering down-feathers. The mottled, pin-headed guinea-hens, always resentful of captivity, ran screeching out into the tunnel and tried to poke their ugly, painted faces through the snow walls. By five o'clock the chores were done—just when it was time to begin them all over again! That was a strange, unnatural sort of day.

Analyzing Literature

1. How does Cather show that the blizzard was unusually harsh? Give two examples.
2. **(a)** Identify two extra chores that had to be done because of the blizzard. **(b)** What chore is Jim unable to do?
3. **Making Inferences** **(a)** What attitude do the men seem to have toward the storm? **(b)** What does this suggest about the people who settled the Plains?

Unit 7 A New Role for the Nation

What's Ahead

Viewing UNIT THEMES **Becoming a World Power**

J.R. Campbell created this poster to celebrate a giant industrial fair in Chicago. At left are Uncle Sam and Columbia, two symbols of the United States. They welcome representatives of many lands—from Britain and Turkey to Mexico and China. By the late 1800s, the United States was becoming a major force in world trade and politics. ★ **How does this poster express national pride?**

Unit Theme Global Interaction

George Washington had advised the United States to limit its involvement with other nations. By the late 1800s, however, many Americans wanted the country to become more involved in world affairs. American industry, they said, needed new markets for its products. National pride also led some Americans to push for overseas colonies and a stronger military.

How did Americans of the time feel about global interaction? They can tell you in their own words.

VIEWPOINTS ON GLOBAL INTERACTION

"Whether they will or no, Americans must begin to look outward. The growing production of the country demands it."

Alfred Thayer Mahan, naval officer (1897)

"You cannot govern a foreign territory, a foreign people, another people than your own . . . you cannot [conquer] them and govern them against their will, because you think it is for their good."

George Hoar, representative from Massachusetts (1899)

"This is the divine mission of America. . . . American law, American order, American civilization, and the American flag will plant themselves on shores hitherto bloody and [ignorant]."

Albert Beveridge, senator from Indiana (1900)

Activity Writing to Learn Americans still disagree about how involved our country should be in global affairs. Conduct a survey of ten adults you know outside of school. Ask: "Do you think the United States should be more involved or less involved in foreign affairs?" Tally the responses in writing and share them with the class.

Chapter 22

Progressives and Reformers

1876–1914

What's Ahead

Section 1
Early Reforms

Section 2
The Progressives and Their Goals

Section 3
Presidents Support Reforms

Section 4
Progress for Women

Section 5
Fighting for Equality

A period of reform known as the Progressive Era took shape in the late 1800s. During this time, Americans worked to fight corruption in government, reduce the power of big business, and improve society. Government became more democratic as people in many states gained the power to pass laws directly. After years of effort, American women finally won the right to vote. From 1901 to 1921, three Presidents played a leading role in reform efforts.

African Americans and other minorities also took action against discrimination during the Progressive Era. Despite many setbacks, they laid the groundwork for future progress in civil rights.

Why Study History? During the Progressive Era, journalists helped expose a variety of social ills, from child labor to lynching. Today, investigative reporters still play an important role in society. Yet their methods are often subject to criticism. To explore this connection, see the *Why Study History?* feature, "Journalists Keep Us Informed," in this chapter.

American Events

1881 Booker T. Washington founds Tuskegee Institute

1887 Interstate Commerce Act bans some railroad practices

1890 Wyoming is first state with women's suffrage admitted to union

1875 | 1880 | 1885 | 1890 | 1895

World Events

1875 World Event Japan reforms its courts of law

1893 World Event New Zealand gives vote to women

Viewing History: Fighting the Power of Trusts

Horace Taylor created this cartoon, The Trust Giant's Point of View, *in 1900. Taylor was one of several cartoonists who used his art to protest against the power of giant corporations. Here, oil tycoon John D. Rockefeller holds the White House in his hand.* ★ **What do the buildings in the background represent? Why do you think Taylor put smokestacks on top of them?**

1901 Theodore Roosevelt becomes President

1906 Pure Food and Drug Act bans use of impure ingredients

1913 Federal Reserve Act regulates banks

1895 | 1900 | 1905 | 1910 | 1915

1900 World Event Chinese rebels seek to expel foreigners

1910 World Event Revolution begins in Mexico

1 Early Reforms

As You Read

Explore These Questions

- What was American politics like in the 1870s and 1880s?
- Why did many Americans oppose the spoils system?
- How did the government try to regulate business?

Define

- patronage
- civil service

Identify

- Gilded Age
- James Garfield
- Chester Arthur
- Grover Cleveland
- Interstate Commerce Commission
- Benjamin Harrison
- Sherman Antitrust Act

SETTING the Scene In the 1870s, Mark Twain and Charles Dudley Warner wrote *The Gilded Age.* ("Gilded" means coated with a thin layer of gold paint.) The novel poked fun at greed and political corruption. In one scene, a land speculator describes how he gets funds from Congress:

> "A majority of the House committee, say, $10,000 apiece—$40,000; a majority of the Senate committee, the same each—say $40,000; . . . a lot of dinners to members—say $10,000 altogether; lot of [gifts] for Congressmen's wives and children—those go a long way. . . ."

Of course, Twain and Warner were exaggerating. Still, for many Americans, the novel captured the spirit of the time. Before long, the decades between the 1870s and 1890s became known as the **Gilded Age.** During this period, reformers began to take steps to combat political corruption.

The Gilded Age
by Twain and Warner

Gilded Age Politics

During the Gilded Age, political power was split between the two major parties. By and large, the North and Far West voted Republican, the South Democrat. In national elections, margins of victory were often paper-thin. Neither party could win control of Congress for more than a term or two. The Republican party did hold on to the White House for nearly 25 years. However, Presidents during the Gilded Age generally had less power than Congress.

For Americans of the Gilded Age, politics was mass entertainment. Campaigns featured brass bands, torchlight parades, free picnics, and three-hour speeches. Millions turned out to march, eat, drink, and listen. Voter turnout in presidential elections was higher than at any other time before or since: almost 80 percent.

Two concerns shaped the politics of the Gilded Age. Many Americans worried over the growing power of "special interests." Americans feared that bankers, industrialists, and other men of wealth were gaining control of politics and overpowering the interests of the public. A second worry was political corruption. Bribery and voter fraud angered voters. Reformers especially targeted the corrupt spoils system, the practice of rewarding supporters with government jobs.

Taming the Spoils System

Since the days of Andrew Jackson, the spoils system had grown. When a new President entered the White House, thousands of job seekers swarmed into Washington. They sought government jobs as rewards for their political support. Giving jobs to loyal supporters is called **patronage.** By handing out jobs, politicians cemented ties with their supporters and increased their control of government.

Patronage often led to corruption. Some officeholders helped themselves to public money. Many people appointed to government jobs had no skills for those jobs. For example, one man appointed as a court reporter in New York could not read or write.

Early reform efforts

Calls for reform slowly brought change. In 1877, President Rutherford Hayes took steps toward ending the spoils system. He refused to appoint his own supporters to office unless they were qualified for the job. Hayes also launched an investigation of the New York customs house. Investigators found that more than 200 appointed officials received high salaries for doing no work. Despite the protests of leading Republicans, Hayes dismissed two senior customs house officials.

James Garfield entered the White House in 1881. He thought that people should get government jobs on the basis of merit, or ability, rather than as a political reward. However, like other Presidents, Garfield found himself swamped by people seeking patronage.

One disappointed office seeker, Charles Guiteau, blamed Garfield for his failure. In July 1881, Guiteau shot the President in a train station. Two months later, Garfield died. The assassination outraged Americans and sparked new efforts to end the spoils system.

Exams for federal jobs

Upon Garfield's death, Vice President **Chester Arthur** became President. As a New York politician, Arthur had used the spoils system. In fact, he was one of the customs house officials dismissed by President Hayes only a few years earlier! "Elegant Arthur" was better known for his fine wardrobe than his political ideals. Yet, as President, he prosecuted corrupt politicians and worked with Congress to reform the spoils system.

In 1883, Congress passed the Pendleton Act. It created a Civil Service Commission to conduct exams for federal jobs. The **civil service** includes all federal jobs except elected positions and the armed forces. The aim of the civil service was to fill jobs on the basis of merit. People who scored highest on the civil service exams earned the posts.

At first, the Civil Service Commission controlled only a few federal jobs. Under pressure from reformers, however, later Presidents added more jobs to the civil service list. By 1900, the commission controlled about 40 percent of all federal jobs.

Wealthy Americans in a Gilded Age

This painting by William T. Smedley shows a golf tournament at a country club near Washington, D.C. The Gilded Age was a time of great luxury for wealthy Americans like these. They built great mansions, dressed in the latest fashions, and enjoyed leisure activities like tennis and polo. Some also used their fortunes to buy political influence. ★ **Why were many Americans concerned about the power of the rich?**

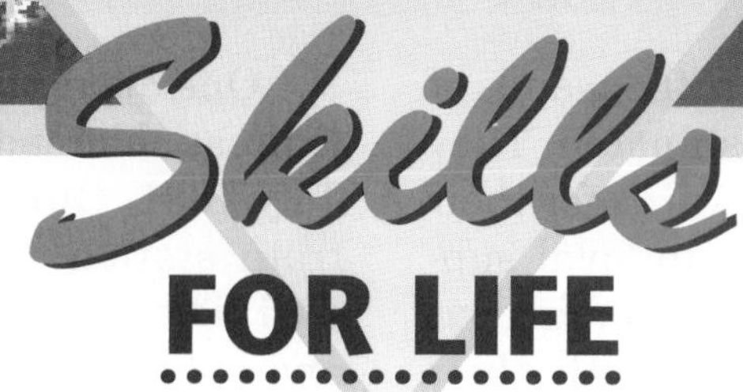

Skills FOR LIFE

Critical Thinking | Managing Information | Communication | Maps, Charts, and Graphs

Solving Problems

How Will I Use This Skill?

Every day, you face problems and make decisions about how to solve them. Sometimes, the problem is so simple the solution is automatic. When the issue is more complex, you have to put more effort into considering possible solutions and the consequences of each alternative. In the community, leaders and citizens try to come up with practical solutions that not only solve problems but eliminate their causes as well.

LEARN the Skill

To solve a problem, you first have to define what the problem is. Use the following steps to help you in this process:

1. Identify the problem.
2. Determine the impact of the problem.
3. Identify alternate solutions to the problem.
4. Determine the effectiveness of the solution.

PRACTICE the Skill

Reread what you have learned about the spoils system. Then, answer the following questions:

1. Reformers during the Gilded Age considered the spoils system to be a problem. Describe how the spoils system worked.
2. (a) How did the spoils system lead to corruption? (b) Do you think the spoils system made government more or less efficient? Explain.
3. (a) What actions did Congress take to tame the spoils system? (b) Jot down two or three other alternatives you might have considered if you had been in Congress at the time.
4. How effective was Congressional action in solving the negative effects of the spoils system? Explain.

APPLY the Skill

Think about some problem that you or your classmates faced in school recently. Describe the problem. Give as many alternatives as you can to resolve the issue. Which do you think is the best solution? Explain your answer.

President Grover Cleveland supported reforms to expand the civil service.

Regulating Big Business

In 1877, Collis Huntington, builder of the Central Pacific Railroad, faced a problem. A bill before Congress aimed at breaking his control of rail routes to southern California. To Huntington, the solution was simple—bribe members of Congress to kill the bill. "It costs money to fix things," he explained.

The behavior of men like Huntington convinced many Americans that big businesses controlled the government. Public outcry against monopolies grew.

Interstate Commerce Act

The government responded by taking steps to regulate railroads and other large businesses. In 1887, President **Grover Cleveland** signed the Interstate Commerce Act. The new law forbade practices such as pools and rebates. (See pages 534–535.) It also set up the **Interstate Commerce Commission,** or ICC, to oversee the railroads.

At first, the ICC was weak. Richard Olney, an attorney for one of the railroad owners, explained:

> "The Commission... satisfies the popular clamor for a government supervision of the railroads, at the same time that supervision is almost entirely [ineffective]."

In court challenges, most judges ruled in favor of the railroads. Still, Congress had shown that it was ready to regulate big business. Later laws made the Interstate Commerce Commission more effective.

Sherman Antitrust Act

In 1888, President Cleveland lost his bid for reelection. **Benjamin Harrison** became President. In 1890, Harrison signed the **Sherman Antitrust Act.** The act prohibited trusts or other businesses from limiting competition.

The Sherman Antitrust Act sounded strong, but in practice trusts used the courts to block enforcement. Judges ruled that the law was an illegal attempt by government to control private property.

Instead of regulating trusts, the Sherman Antitrust Act was first used to stop labor unions. The courts said union strikes blocked free trade and thereby threatened competition. As the reform spirit spread, however, courts began to use the Sherman Act against monopolies.

★ Section 1 Review ★

Recall

1. **Identify** **(a)** Gilded Age, **(b)** James Garfield, **(c)** Chester Arthur, **(d)** Grover Cleveland, **(e)** Interstate Commerce Commission, **(f)** Benjamin Harrison, **(g)** Sherman Antitrust Act.
2. **Define** **(a)** patronage, **(b)** civil service.

Comprehension

3. What two concerns dominated Gilded Age politics?
4. Why did many Americans favor creation of a civil service?
5. **(a)** Why did Congress create the ICC? **(b)** Was the ICC effective? Explain.

Critical Thinking and Writing

6. **Making Inferences** The term "golden age" is used to describe a period of great progress and achievement. What point do you think Twain and Warner were making by calling the 1870s the Gilded Age?
7. **Synthesizing Information** Why do you think early efforts to regulate big business had little success?

Activity **Writing an Editorial** You are a newspaper editor in 1881. Write an editorial on President James Garfield's death. Explain the circumstances and tell why the assassination shows the need to reform the spoils system.

The Progressives and Their Goals

Explore These Questions

- Why did reformers attack city governments?
- How did the press contribute to reform efforts?
- What new practices gave more power to voters?

Define

- muckraker
- public interest
- primary
- initiative
- referendum
- recall
- graduated income tax

Identify

- William Tweed
- Ida Tarbell
- Upton Sinclair
- Progressives
- John Dewey
- Robert La Follette
- Wisconsin Idea
- Sixteenth Amendment

Joseph Folk, city prosecutor of St. Louis, was furious. Local politicians had just ordered him to hire men he felt were dishonest.

"I and my office, the criminal law, was to be run by—criminals!" he complained to reporter Lincoln Steffens. Instead, Folk led a crusade against dishonest politicians and businessmen. Elsewhere, other reformers fought to oust corrupt politicians and to give voters greater power.

Reforming City Government

How had city governments become so corrupt? Growing cities needed many improvements, such as new sewers, better garbage collection, and more roads. In many cities, politicians traded these jobs for money. In some places, bribes and corruption became a way of life.

Boss rule

Powerful politicians, known as bosses, came to rule many cities. They controlled all work done in the city and demanded payoffs from businesses. Often, bosses did not hold office. Instead, they worked behind the scenes to influence officeholders. In California, for example, Abraham Ruef was the Republican boss for northern San Francisco. At one time, Boss Ruef controlled enough delegates to choose his party's nominee for governor.

City bosses were popular with the poor, especially with immigrants. Bosses provided jobs and made loans to the needy. They handed out extra coal in winter and turkeys at Thanksgiving. In exchange, the poor voted for the boss or his candidate.

Boss Tweed

In New York City, Boss **William Tweed** carried corruption to new heights. During the 1860s and 1870s, Tweed cheated New York out of more than $100 million. Reformers tried to have him jailed.

Journalists exposed Tweed's wrongdoings. Cartoonist Thomas Nast showed Boss Tweed as a vulture destroying the city. Nast's attacks upset Tweed. He complained that his supporters might be unable to read, but they could understand pictures.

Faced with prison, Tweed fled to Spain. There, local police arrested him when they recognized him from a Nast cartoon. Tweed died in jail in 1878. Thousands of poor New Yorkers mourned his death.

Good government leagues

Reformers in many cities formed good government leagues. Their goal was to replace corrupt officials with honest leaders.

The leagues met with some success. The good government league in Minneapolis sent a corrupt mayor to jail. In Cleveland, reformers elected Tom Johnson as mayor. Johnson improved garbage collection and sewage systems in the city. He also set up services to help the poor of Cleveland.

Muckrakers Rouse Public Opinion

To bring about change, reformers first had to ignite public anger. A major weapon was the press. Newspaper reporters visited the slums. They described burned-out tenements and exposed how corruption led to inadequate fire protection. They talked to mothers whose babies were dying of tuberculosis, a lung disease. Photographer Jacob Riis provided shocking images of slum life.

Crusading journalists like Riis became known as **muckrakers.** People said they raked the dirt, or muck, and exposed it to public view. One muckraker, **Ida Tarbell,** targeted the unfair practices of big business. Her articles about the Standard Oil Company led to demands for tighter controls on trusts.

In 1906, **Upton Sinclair** shocked the nation when he published *The Jungle.* This novel revealed gruesome details about the meatpacking industry in Chicago. Although the book was fiction, it was based on things Sinclair had seen. One passage described the rats in a meatpacking house:

> "These rats were nuisances, and the packers would put poisoned bread out for them: they would die, and then rats, bread, and meat would go into the hoppers together."

Muckrakers helped change public opinion. For years, middle-class people had ignored the need for reform. When they saw how corruption menaced the nation, they joined with muckrakers to demand change.

Viewing History **Rousing Public Anger**

Danish-born muckraker Jacob Riis used a powerful weapon—the camera—to influence public opinion. In books like How the Other Half Lives, *he showed middle-class readers what poverty really looked like. This Riis photograph shows an Italian ragpicker and her baby in a New York City tenement.*

★ **How do you think photographs like this encouraged reform?**

Camera of the 1890s

Connections With Civics

Mayor Tom Johnson of Cleveland fought to make public parks more open to the public. Upper-class people protested, especially when Johnson ordered the removal of "Keep Off the Grass" signs. Eventually, Johnson created a citywide system of parks with hundreds of playgrounds and baseball fields.

The Progressives

By 1900, reformers were calling themselves **Progressives.** By that, they meant they were forward-thinking people who wanted to improve American life. They won many changes from 1898 to 1917. This period is often called the Progressive Era.

Progressives were never a single group with a single aim. They backed various causes. What united them was their faith that the problems of society could be solved.

Progressive beliefs

Progressives drew inspiration from two sources. One was religion. In the late 1800s, Protestant ministers had begun preaching a social gospel. (See page 569.) It stressed the duty of Christians to improve society.

Why Study History?

Because Journalists Keep Us Informed

Historical Background

During the Progressive Era, Josiah Flynt wrote about crime in American cities. His reports were accurate because Flynt had gone undercover. He had assumed the role of an urban thug and joined criminal gangs. To blend in, he committed crimes himself.

Some people found Flynt's methods inexcusable. Nevertheless, Flynt's muckraking articles exposed illegal gang activities and corruption among police and political officials. His work helped spark needed reforms.

Connections to Today

Today, investigative journalists are everywhere, from your local paper to national news programs such as *60 Minutes*. Like muckrakers of the past, today's reporters continue to provide information that can benefit the public. Some critics, though, say that reporters go too far.

In 1992, a television station used undercover reporters with hidden cameras to show unsanitary conditions at a supermarket. The reporters lied in order to be hired. They also took pictures without the store's permission. After the report aired, the supermarket sued. A jury found that reporters had trespassed and engaged in fraud to get their story. The court ordered the network to pay the supermarket $5.5 million.

Connections to You

We may disagree about the methods investigative journalists use. Yet these muckrakers of today often provide useful information that can have a direct effect on your community. Some journalists have exposed illegal dumping of toxic wastes. Others have uncovered facts about overcrowded classrooms or child labor in sweatshops. Such reports may bring about needed reforms.

Television news teams have exposed many public health violations, such as illegal dumping of dangerous chemicals.

1. **Comprehension** How did Josiah Flynt get the information to write his stories?
2. **Critical Thinking** Do you think journalists should be allowed to break some laws to expose wrongdoing? Explain.

Exploring Local News Read a local newspaper or watch a local television news program to find an example of investigative journalism. Write a brief summary of the story.

Advances in science also inspired Progressives. Like scientists, Progressives made use of careful analysis and statistics.

Progressive reformers believed that the **public interest,** or the good of the people, should guide government actions. The public interest, they said, must not be sacrificed to the greed of a few trusts and city bosses.

Progressives stressed the importance of education. **John Dewey,** a Progressive educator, wanted schools to promote reform. They must not only teach democratic values, he argued, but reflect them. Dewey encouraged students to ask questions and work together to solve problems. On college campuses, Progressive educators stressed the need to teach skills to help society. Colleges offered new courses in areas such as social work.

Women played leading roles in the Progressive Era. In the mid-1800s, a new view of women emerged. Many Americans believed that women were morally superior to men. In a world of corruption, they said, women had the moral force to bring about change. This view encouraged many women to work for reform. To increase their social influence, they also sought the right to vote.

The Wisconsin Idea

Progressivism got its start in the states of the Midwest. Among the leading Progressives was **Robert La Follette** of Wisconsin. "The will of the people shall be the law of the land," was his motto. His fighting spirit won him the nickname "Battling Bob."

In 1900, La Follette was elected governor. He introduced a statewide program of Progressive reforms, called the **Wisconsin Idea.** For example, he lowered railroad rates. The result was increased rail traffic, which helped both railroad owners and customers.

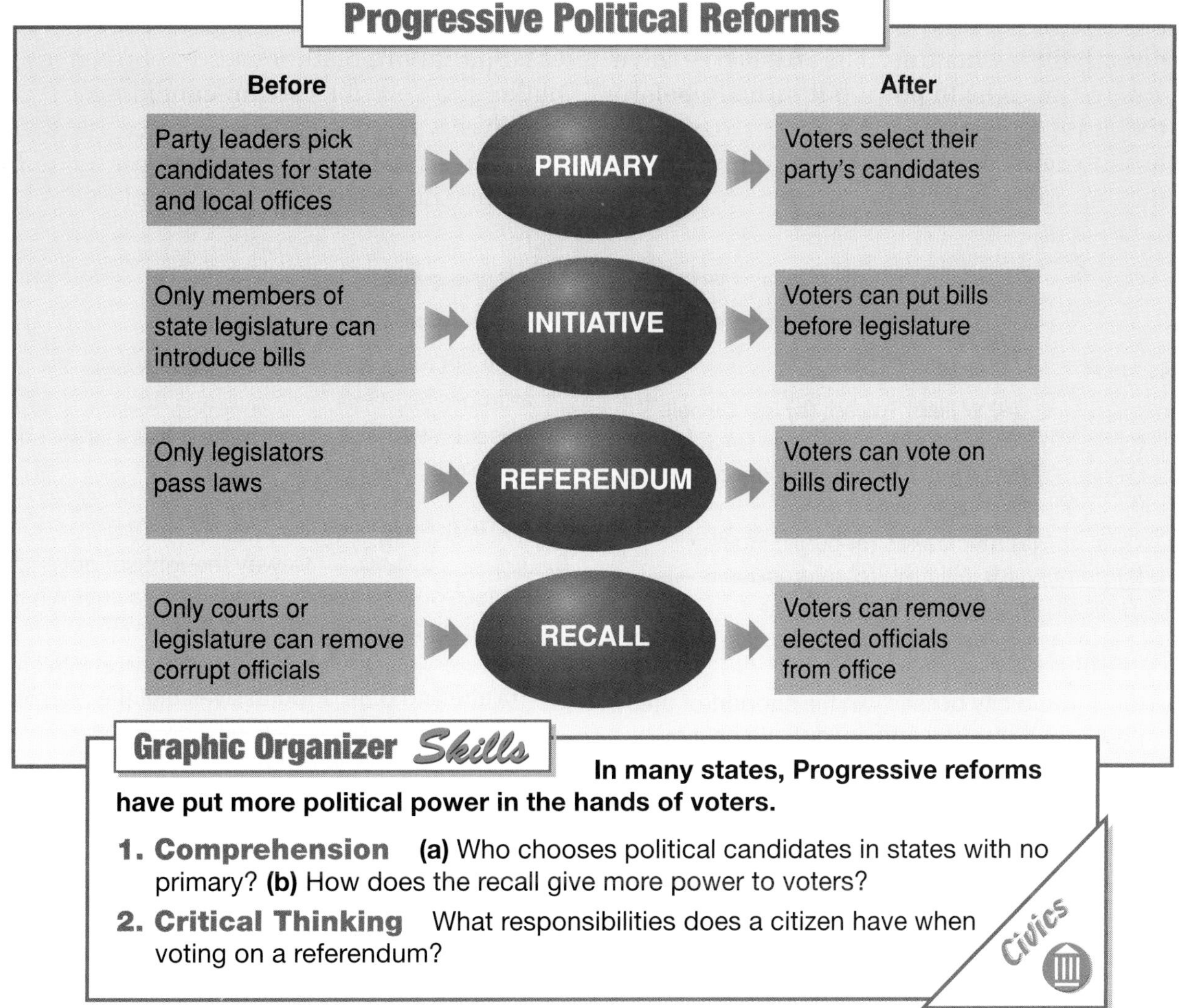

Graphic Organizer *Skills* **In many states, Progressive reforms have put more political power in the hands of voters.**

1. **Comprehension** **(a)** Who chooses political candidates in states with no primary? **(b)** How does the recall give more power to voters?
2. **Critical Thinking** What responsibilities does a citizen have when voting on a referendum?

Progressives from other states visited Wisconsin to study La Follette's system. Before long, voters in California, Indiana, Arkansas, Oregon, and New York were talking about the Wisconsin Idea. They, too, elected Progressive governors who introduced far-reaching changes.

The will of the people

LaFollette and other Progressives believed that the people would make the right decisions if given the chance. As a result, they pressed for reforms to give voters more power.

Since Andrew Jackson's time, party leaders had picked candidates for local and state offices. Instead, Progressives pressed for **primaries,** in which voters choose their party's candidate for the general election. In 1903, Wisconsin was the first state to adopt the primary. By 1917, all but four states had done so.

Progressives also urged states to adopt measures that allowed voters to participate directly in lawmaking. The **initiative** gave voters the right to put a bill directly before the state legislature. The **referendum** allowed them to vote the bill into law at the next election.

Another Progressive measure was the **recall.** The recall allowed voters to remove an elected official in the middle of his or her term. This gave ordinary people a chance to get rid of corrupt officials.

Other Reforms

Other Progressive reforms required federal action. Most Progressives supported a **graduated income tax,** which taxes people from different income levels at different rates. The wealthy pay taxes at a higher rate than the poor or the middle class.

In 1895, the Supreme Court had ruled that a federal income tax was unconstitutional. In response, Progressives campaigned to amend the Constitution. In 1913, the states ratified the **Sixteenth Amendment.** It gave Congress the power to impose an income tax.

Progressives backed another amendment. Since 1789, senators had been elected by state legislatures, rather than directly by voters. Special interests sometimes bribed lawmakers to vote for certain candidates. Progressives wanted to end such abuses. In 1913, the states ratified the Seventeenth Amendment for the direct election of senators.

★ Section 2 Review ★

Recall

1. **Identify:** **(a)** William Tweed, **(b)** Ida Tarbell, **(c)** Upton Sinclair, **(d)** Progressives, **(e)** John Dewey, **(f)** Robert La Follette, **(g)** Wisconsin Idea, **(h)** Sixteenth Amendment.
2. **Define** **(a)** muckraker, **(b)** public interest, **(c)** primary, **(d)** initiative, **(e)** referendum, **(f)** recall, **(g)** graduated income tax.

Comprehension

3. **(a)** How did city bosses win the support of the poor? **(b)** Why did reformers oppose bosses?
4. How did muckrakers help change public attitudes?
5. Describe two ways the Progressives increased the power of voters.

Critical Thinking and Writing

6. **Analyzing Ideas** Dewey thought school classes should reflect democratic values. What did he mean?
7. **Defending a Position** Do you agree with La Follette and other Progressives that the people will make the right decisions if given the chance? Why or why not?

Activity **Drawing a Political Cartoon** You are Thomas Nast. Boss Tweed and his pals are stealing millions from the city you love. Draw a political cartoon commenting on Tweed's corruption.

Presidents Support Reforms

As You Read

Explore These Questions

- How did Theodore Roosevelt try to control trusts?
- What other reforms did Roosevelt support?
- What were Woodrow Wilson's goals as President?

Define

- trustbuster
- conservation
- national park

Identify

- Theodore Roosevelt
- Square Deal
- Pure Food and Drug Act
- William Howard Taft
- Bull Moose party
- Woodrow Wilson
- New Freedom
- Federal Reserve Act
- Federal Trade Commission

In 1900, Republicans needed a reform-minded candidate to run with President William McKinley. They offered the job to **Theodore Roosevelt,** a New York politician. However, Roosevelt was not interested in serving as Vice President. "I will not accept under any circumstances," he replied.

As a loyal Republican, Roosevelt finally did accept the nomination. A year later, McKinley was shot and Roosevelt became President.

By 1901, Progressives were having success in many states. With Roosevelt in the White House, they hoped to push national reforms and turn the federal government into a protector of the people.

Teddy Roosevelt

Teddy Roosevelt—or "TR," as he was called—belonged to an old, wealthy New York family. As a child, he suffered from asthma and was often sick. To build his strength, he lifted weights, ran, and boxed.

Early career

The children of wealthy, old families were expected to live lives of ease and privilege. Instead, TR entered politics after college, determined to end corruption and protect the public interest.

Roosevelt's friends mocked his political ambitions. He later recalled:

> "They assured me that the men I met would be rough and brutal and unpleasant to deal with. I answered that I certainly would not quit until I... found out whether I was really too weak to hold my own in the rough and tumble."

By age 26, Roosevelt was serving in the New York state legislature. Then tragedy almost ended his political career. In 1884, his mother and his young wife died on the same day. Overcome by grief, Roosevelt quit the legislature. He went west to work on a cattle ranch in present-day North Dakota.

After two years, Roosevelt returned to the East and to politics. He served on the Civil Service Commission. Later on, he held posts as head of the New York City police department and as assistant secretary of the navy.

In 1898, when the United States went to war against Spain, Roosevelt fought in Cuba. He returned home to a hero's welcome. That same year, he was elected governor of New York.

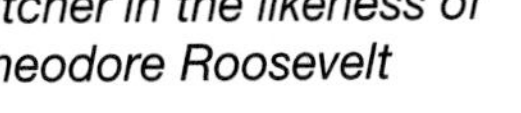

Pitcher in the likeness of Theodore Roosevelt

Teddy bear of the early 1900s

Viewing History **TR on the Campaign Trail**

This photograph shows Theodore Roosevelt campaigning in Wyoming in 1903. TR put tremendous energy into his speeches, pounding his fists into the air as he spoke. Roosevelt's activities as an outdoorsman also helped his public image. After he refused to shoot a small captured bear, a toy company named a new product after the President: the Teddy bear. ★ **How did Roosevelt's actions as President support his image as an energetic fighter?**

A progressive governor

Since his days in the legislature, Roosevelt had pushed for reform. Other legislators called him a "goo goo," a mocking name for someone who wanted good government. As governor, Roosevelt worked for Progressive reforms.

New York Republican bosses were relieved when Roosevelt became Vice President. Then, in September 1901, an assassin shot President McKinley. At age 42, Roosevelt became the nation's youngest President.

TR and Big Business

Roosevelt promised to continue McKinley's pro-business policies. Still, many business people worried about the new President's Progressive ideas.

Roosevelt believed that giant corporations were here to stay. He thought, however, that there were good trusts and bad trusts. Good trusts were efficient and fair and should be left alone, TR said. Bad trusts took advantage of their workers and cheated the public. The government should either control them or break them up.

Taking on the trusts

Roosevelt wanted to test the power of the government to break up bad trusts. In 1902, he ordered the Attorney General, the government's chief lawyer, to bring a lawsuit against the Northern Securities Company. Roosevelt argued that Northern Securities used unfair business practices in violation of the Sherman Act.

Stock prices on Wall Street, the New York center of business and finance, fell at news of the lawsuit. One newspaper editor noted:

> "Wall Street is paralyzed at the thought that a President of the United States would sink so low as to try to enforce the law."

While business leaders worried, ordinary people supported the President.

In 1904, the Supreme Court ruled that Northern Securities had violated the Sherman Antitrust Act by limiting trade. It ordered the trust to be broken up. The decision showed the effects of Progressive reform. In the 1890s, the Sherman Antitrust Act had been used to break up unions, not trusts.

President Roosevelt hailed the case as a victory. He then ordered the Attorney General to file suit against other trusts, including Standard Oil and the American Tobacco Company. The courts later ordered both trusts to be broken up on the grounds that they blocked free trade.

Some business leaders called Roosevelt a **trustbuster** who wanted to destroy all trusts. "Certainly not," replied Roosevelt, only those that "have done something we regard as wrong." He preferred to control or regulate trusts, not "bust" them.

Support for labor

Roosevelt also clashed with the nation's mine owners. In 1902, Pennsylvania coal miners went on strike. They wanted better pay and a shorter workday. Mine owners refused to talk to the miners' union.

As winter approached, schools and hospitals around the country ran out of coal. Furious at the stubbornness of mine owners, Roosevelt threatened to send in troops to run the mines. In response, owners sat down with the union and reached an agreement.

Working men and women around the country cheered. Earlier Presidents had used federal troops to break strikes. Roosevelt was the first to side with labor.

The Square Deal

In 1904, Roosevelt ran for President in his own right. During the campaign, he promised Americans a **Square Deal.** By this, he meant that many different groups—farmers and consumers, workers and owners—should have an equal opportunity to succeed. The promise of a Square Deal helped Roosevelt win a landslide victory.

Railroads were a key target of the Square Deal. Roosevelt knew that the Interstate Commerce Act of 1887 had done little to end rebates and other abuses. He urged Congress to pass the Elkins Act in 1903. It outlawed rebates. In 1906, Congress gave the ICC the power to set railroad rates.

Protecting consumers

Roosevelt had read Upton Sinclair's shocking novel, *The Jungle.* In response, he sent more government inspectors to meatpacking houses. The owners refused to let the inspectors in.

Roosevelt fought back. He gave the newspapers copies of a government report that supported Sinclair's picture of the meatpacking industry. As public rage mounted, Congress passed the Meat Inspection Act of 1906. It forced packers to open their doors to more inspectors.

Roosevelt supported other reforms to protect consumers. Muckrakers had revealed that the drug companies made false claims about their medicines. They also found that

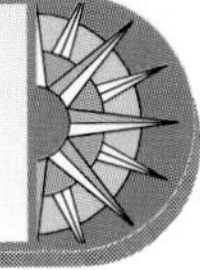

Linking Past and Present

Past

Present

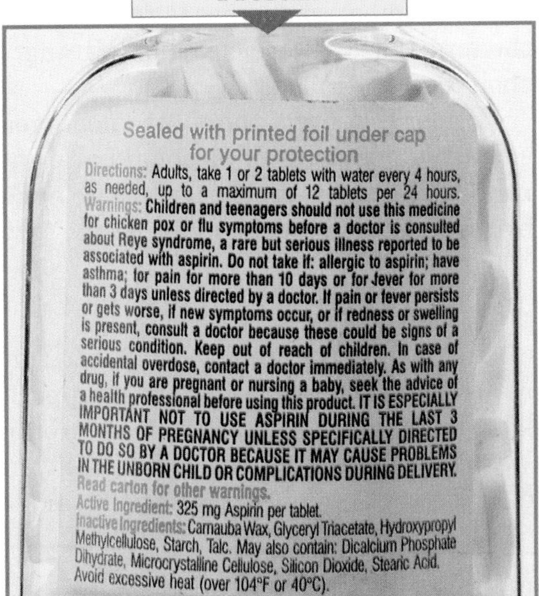

Protecting the Consumer

Before the Progressive Era, drug manufacturers were not controlled by the law. Advertisers often made wild, exotic claims for medicines that actually did nothing. Today, every medicine label must include a list of ingredients, exact directions for use, and warnings about possible side effects. ★ **How is the advertisement at the top different from a medicine ad you might see in a magazine today?**

the food industry added dangerous chemicals to canned foods. In 1906, Congress passed the **Pure Food and Drug Act.** It required food and drug makers to list ingredients on their packages. It also tried to end false advertising and the use of impure ingredients.

Protecting resources

Roosevelt grew alarmed about the destruction of the American wilderness. To fuel the nation's industrial growth, lumber companies were cutting down whole forests. Miners were taking iron and coal from the earth at a frantic pace and leaving gaping holes.

Roosevelt loved the outdoors and objected to this destruction of the land. He believed in **conservation,** the protection of natural resources. "The rights of the public to natural resources outweigh private rights," he said.

Roosevelt thought that natural resources could serve both the public interest and private companies. Some forest and mountain areas, he said, should be left as wilderness. Others could supply wood for lumber. He wanted lumber companies to replant trees in the forests they were clearing. Mining, too, should be controlled.

Under Roosevelt, the government created some 170,000 acres of national parkland. A **national park** is an area set aside and run by the federal government for people to visit.

Taft and the Reformers

In 1908, Roosevelt decided not to run for reelection. Instead, he threw his support behind **William Howard Taft,** his Secretary of War. With Roosevelt's backing, Taft won an easy victory. A confident Roosevelt said:

> "Taft will carry on the work... as I have. His policies, principles, purposes, and ideals are the same as mine. The Roosevelt policies will not go out with Roosevelt."

Roosevelt then set off for Africa to hunt big game for a year. He left behind an impressive record as a reformer. He also left the presidency more powerful than it had been at any time since the Civil War.

Taft was different from Roosevelt. Unlike the hard-driving, energetic Roosevelt, Taft was quiet and careful. Roosevelt loved power. Taft feared it.

Nevertheless, Taft supported many Progressive causes. He broke up even more trusts than TR. He supported the graduated income tax, approved new safety regulations for mines, and signed laws setting an eight-hour day for government employees. Under Taft, the Department of Labor set up a bureau to deal with the problems of working children.

Despite such successes, Taft lost Progressive support. In 1909, Taft signed a bill that raised most tariffs. Progressives opposed high tariffs because they felt tariffs raised prices for consumers. Also, Taft fired the chief of the United States Forest Service during a dispute over the sale of wilderness areas in Alaska. Progressives accused Taft of blocking conservation efforts.

Election of 1912

When Roosevelt returned from Africa, he found that reformers felt Taft had betrayed them. Roosevelt declared that Taft was "a flub-dub with a streak of the second-rate." TR decided to run against Taft for the Republican nomination in 1912.

The Bull Moose party

Roosevelt won wide public support. He won almost every state primary he entered. Still, many Republican business leaders distrusted Roosevelt. Also, Taft still controlled the party leadership. At the Republican convention, the party nominated Taft.

Right in the middle of Taft's nomination, angry Progressive Republicans stormed out

Connections With Geography

Theodore Roosevelt's conservation efforts encouraged Mexican immigration. In 1902, Congress passed the Newlands Act to finance construction of irrigation projects in arid states. The law created millions of acres of new farmland in California, Texas, and Arizona. As a result, many Mexicans entered the United States in search of work.

AmericanHeritage
M A G A Z I N E

HISTORY HAPPENED HERE

Yosemite National Park

Almost 100 years ago, President Theodore Roosevelt camped out in the Yosemite Valley in California. He viewed its majestic mountains and walked beneath its towering sequoia trees—the oldest living things on Earth. Today, thanks to the work of conservationists like Roosevelt, you can still enjoy Yosemite and other natural beauties. In fact, you can even see the very same redwoods Roosevelt saw!

★ ***To learn more about this historic site, write:*** *Yosemite National Park, PO Box 577, Yosemite, CA 95389.*

This sign welcomes you to Yosemite's sequoia forest.

of the convention. They set up a new Progressive party and chose Roosevelt as their candidate. He eagerly accepted. "I feel as strong as a bull moose," he boasted. Roosevelt and his supporters became known as the **Bull Moose party.**

A Democratic victory

Democrats picked **Woodrow Wilson,** a Progressive, as their candidate. Born in Virginia, Wilson was the son of a Presbyterian minister. His father taught him that the world was strictly divided between good and evil. As a boy, Wilson made up his mind always to fight for what he thought was right. Wilson had served as president of Princeton University and as governor of New Jersey. He was known as a brilliant scholar and a cautious reformer.

Together, Taft and Roosevelt won more votes than Wilson. However, they split the Republican vote. Their quarrel helped Wilson win the election of 1912.

President Wilson

Wilson took the oath of office in March 1913. His inaugural address reflected his strong, unbending sense of morality:

> "The nation has been deeply stirred, stirred by a solemn passion, stirred by the knowledge of wrong, of ideals lost, of government too often... made an instrument of evil. The feelings with which we face this new age of right and opportunity sweep across our heart-strings like some air out of God's own presence."

Wilson asked honest, forward-looking Americans to stand at his side. "God helping me," he pledged, "I will not fail them."

The New Freedom

At first, Wilson's goal was to break up trusts into smaller companies. By doing so, he hoped to restore the competition that had once existed in the American economy. "If America is not to have free enterprise, then she can have freedom of no sort whatever," he said. Wilson called his program the **New Freedom.**

Campaign song for Woodrow Wilson

Wilson worked with Congress for laws to spur competition. He pushed first for a lower tariff to create more competition from imports. After a struggle, Congress lowered the tariff. It also imposed a graduated income tax to make up for lost revenues.

To regulate banking, Congress passed the **Federal Reserve Act** in 1913. The act set up a nationwide system of federal banks. The system gave the government the power to raise or lower interest rates and control the money supply.

Regulating competition

To ensure fair competition, President Wilson persuaded Congress to create the **Federal Trade Commission** (FTC) in 1914. The FTC had power to investigate companies and order them to stop using business practices that destroyed all competitors.

That same year, Wilson signed the Clayton Antitrust Act. The law was weaker than he wanted. However, it did ban some business practices that limited free enterprise. It also barred antitrust laws from being used against unions—a major victory for labor.

Despite Wilson's successes, the Progressive movement slowed after 1914. By then, the Progressives had achieved many of their goals. In addition, the outbreak of war in Europe seized public attention. Americans became concerned that the fighting in Europe might soon involve the United States.

★ Section 3 Review ★

Recall

1. **Identify** **(a)** Theodore Roosevelt, **(b)** Square Deal, **(c)** Pure Food and Drug Act, **(d)** William Howard Taft, **(e)** Bull Moose party, **(f)** Woodrow Wilson, **(g)** New Freedom, **(h)** Federal Reserve Act, **(i)** Federal Trade Commission.
2. **Define** **(a)** trustbuster, **(b)** conservation, **(c)** national park.

Comprehension

3. **(a)** How did Roosevelt feel about trusts? **(b)** What action did he take in the Northern Securities case?
4. Describe one action Roosevelt took to achieve each of the following goals: **(a)** consumer protection, **(b)** protection of natural resources.
5. Describe two actions Wilson took to ensure competition.

Critical Thinking and Writing

6. **Analyzing Ideas** Reread the comment of the newspaper editor on page 598. **(a)** Why were many business leaders surprised by Roosevelt's actions in the Northern Securities case? **(b)** What point was the editor making about the role of the President?
7. **Making Inferences** "I'm glad to be going," commented William Howard Taft as he left the White House in 1913. "This is the lonesomest place in the world." Why do you think Taft might have felt this way?

Activity **Expressing an Opinion** You are the owner of a large area of wilderness. Theodore Roosevelt wants to use your land for a park. Write him a letter in which you explain your reaction to his proposal.

Progress for Women

As You Read

Explore These Questions

- How did women work for suffrage in the Progressive Era?
- What new opportunities did women earn?
- How did the temperance movement gain strength?

Define

- suffragist
- temperance movement

Identify

- Carrie Chapman Catt
- Alice Paul
- Nineteenth Amendment
- Florence Kelley
- Frances Willard
- Carry Nation
- Eighteenth Amendment

SETTING the Scene Susan B. Anthony had broken the law. Her crime was voting. Along with 15 other women, Anthony registered to vote in her home town of Rochester, New York, in 1872. When she cast her ballot, she was arrested.

At her trial, the judge directed that Anthony be found guilty. The judge then asked if she had anything to say. Anthony responded defiantly:

> "Yes, your honor, I have many things to say; for in your ordered verdict of guilty, you have trampled underfoot every vital principle of our government. My natural rights, my civil rights, my political rights, are all alike ignored. Robbed of the fundamental privilege of citizenship, I am degraded from the status of a citizen to that of a subject; and not only myself individually, but all of my sex, are . . . doomed to political subjection."

Anthony refused to quiet down or to ask for mercy. The judge then ordered her to pay a fine of $100. "May it please your honor," Anthony replied, "I shall never pay a dollar of your unjust penalty." Anthony never did pay the fine. Her courageous stand won her many new followers.

Porcelain figure of a women's suffrage campaigner

During the Progressive Era, women continued their long battle to win the right to vote. They also worked for many other reforms. Women spoke out against trusts, supported pure food laws, and called for an end to child labor. They also led a renewed effort to ban the sale of alcohol.

Working for the Vote

The struggle to grant women the vote, or suffrage, went back many years. As you read in Chapter 15, the Seneca Falls Convention in 1848 was the start of an organized women's rights movement in the United States. Delegates at the convention called for many reforms, including women's suffrage.

After the Civil War, Elizabeth Cady Stanton and Susan B. Anthony led a renewed drive to win the vote. In 1869, they formed the National Woman Suffrage Association. This group worked to amend the Constitution to give women the vote. Stanton and Anthony opposed the Fifteenth Amendment because it gave the vote to African American men but not to women.

Women vote in the West

Few politicians favored women's suffrage. Still, in the late 1800s, women gained the right to vote in four western states: Wyoming, Utah, Colorado, and Idaho. Pioneer women had worked alongside men

Biography Carrie Chapman Catt

Carrie Chapman Catt was the only woman in Iowa State College's Class of 1880. She became a tireless lecturer and fighter for women's suffrage. In 1919, she visited 13 states in 8 weeks, urging listeners to ratify the Nineteenth Amendment. After ratification, she declared that women were finally "free and equal citizens." ★ **What strategy did Catt use to win the vote?**

to build the farms and cities of the West. By giving women the vote, these states recognized women's contributions.

When Wyoming applied for statehood in 1890, many members of Congress wanted the state to change its voting law. During the debate, Wyoming lawmakers wired Congress: "We may stay out of the Union for 100 years, but we will come in with our women." Wyoming barely won admission.

Suffragists

In the early 1900s, the women's suffrage movement gained strength. More than 5 million women were earning wages outside the home. Although women were paid less than men, wages gave women a sense of power. Many demanded a say in making the laws that governed them.

By 1906, Elizabeth Cady Stanton and Susan B. Anthony had died. A new generation of leaders took up their cause. **Carrie Chapman Catt** spoke powerfully in favor of suffrage. Catt had worked as a school principal and a reporter. Later, she became head of the National American Woman Suffrage Association.

Catt was an inspired speaker and a brilliant organizer. She devised a detailed battle plan for fighting the war for suffrage, state by state. Around the country, **suffragists,** or people who campaigned for women's right to vote, followed her strategy.

Slowly, the efforts of Catt and other suffragists succeeded. Year by year, more states in the West and Midwest gave women the vote. For the most part, women in these states were allowed to vote only in state elections. In time, more and more women called for an amendment to the Constitution to give them a voice in national elections.

Amending the Constitution

Some suffragists took strong measures to achieve their goal. **Alice Paul** was one of them. In 1907, Paul had gone to England. There, she had marched with suffragists in London. She had been jailed and gone on hunger strikes—all to help British women win the vote. Later, Paul returned home to support the cause of suffrage for American women.

Protest at the White House

Paul and other suffragists met with President Wilson soon after he took office in 1913. Wilson was not opposed to women's suffrage. He did not, however, support a constitutional amendment. Paul told the President what suffragists wanted:

> "We said we're going to try and get [a constitutional amendment] through Congress, that we would like to have his help and needed his support very much. And then we sent him another delegation and another and another and another and another and another and another—every type of women's group we could get."

In January 1917, Paul and other women stopped sending delegations and began to picket at the White House. After several months of these silent demonstrations, police began arresting the protesters. Paul received a seven-month jail sentence for obstructing the sidewalk. To protest their arrest, Paul and others went on a hunger strike. Prison officials force fed the women in an attempt to end the strike. Upon release, Paul and the other women resumed their picketing.

Victory at last

By early 1918, the tide began to turn in favor of the suffrage cause. The tireless work of Catt, Paul, and others began to pay off. President Wilson agreed to support the suffrage amendment.

Finally, in 1919, Congress passed the **Nineteenth Amendment** guaranteeing women the right to vote. By August 1920, three fourths of the states had ratified the Nineteenth Amendment. The amendment doubled the number of eligible voters in the United States.

Women Win New Opportunities

For years, women struggled to open doors to jobs and education. Most states refused to grant women licenses to practice in professions such as law, medicine, or college teaching. Myra Bradwell taught herself law, just as Abraham Lincoln had done. Still, Illinois denied her a license in 1869 because she was a woman. In 1890, Illinois at last let Bradwell practice law.

Higher education

Despite obstacles, a few women managed to get the higher education needed to enter the professions. In 1877, Boston University granted the first Ph.D. to a woman. In the next decades, women made important advances. By 1900, about 1,000 women lawyers and 7,000 women doctors were in practice.

Women entered the sciences, too. Mary Engle Pennington earned a degree in chemistry. She became the nation's top expert on preserving foods.

Viewing History **Suffragists on the March**

Suffragists parading for the right to vote were a common sight in many cities and towns. These women, along with their children, are marching down a New York City street in 1912. ★ **Why do you think these suffragists carried American flags as they marched?**

▲ *Window banner from 1915*

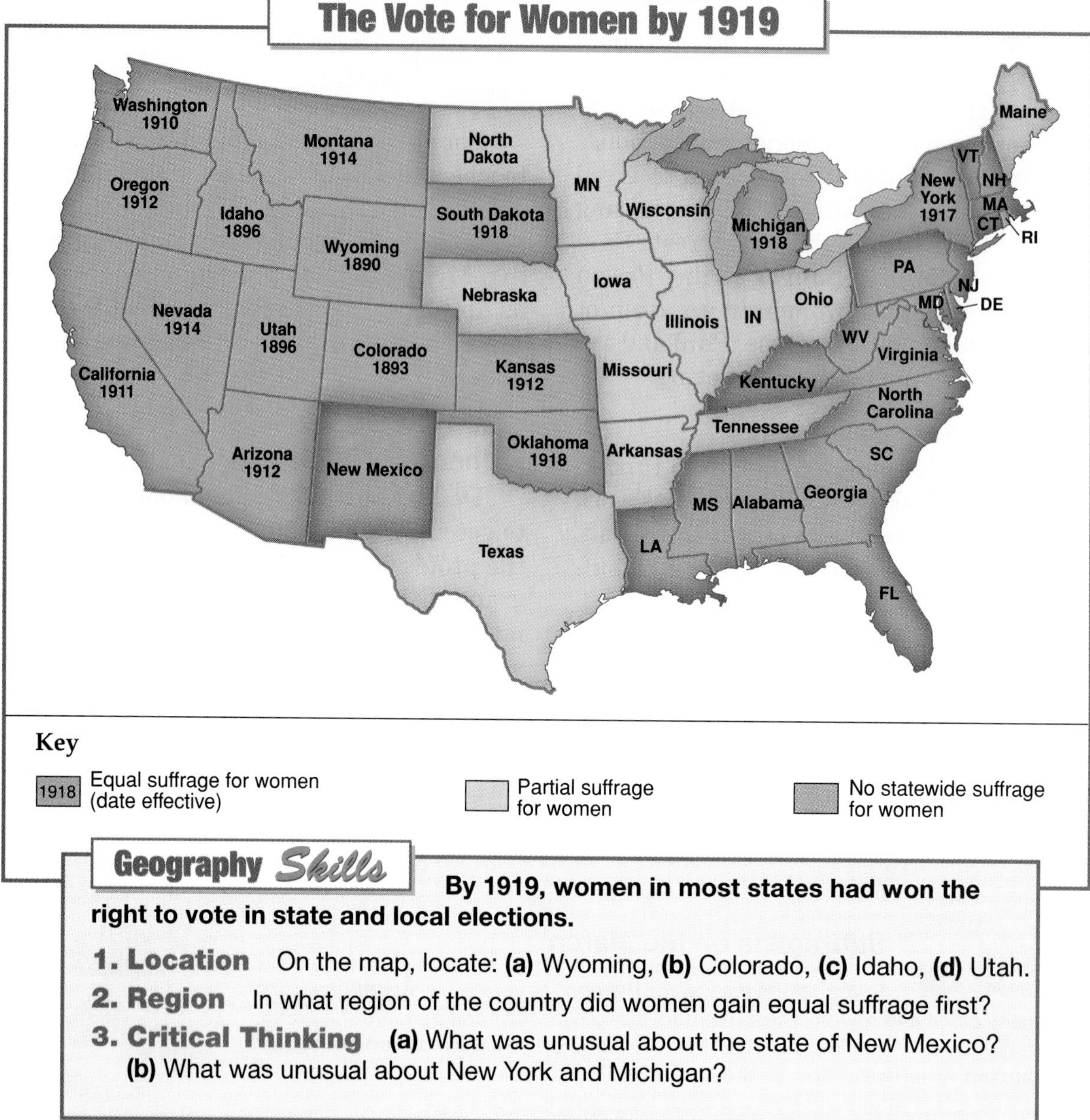

Geography Skills **By 1919, women in most states had won the right to vote in state and local elections.**

1. **Location** On the map, locate: **(a)** Wyoming, **(b)** Colorado, **(c)** Idaho, **(d)** Utah.
2. **Region** In what region of the country did women gain equal suffrage first?
3. **Critical Thinking** **(a)** What was unusual about the state of New Mexico? **(b)** What was unusual about New York and Michigan?

Commitment to reform

Women in the Progressive Era were committed to reform. Some entered the new profession of social work. Others worked to call attention to social ills. **Florence Kelley** investigated conditions in sweatshops. She became the first chief factory inspector for the state of Illinois.

Kelley's chief concern was child labor. As secretary of the National Consumer's League (NCL), she organized a boycott of products made with child labor. The NCL published a list of manufacturers whose factories met their approval. By 1907, many businesses vied to get the NCL "white label" of approval on their products.

Many women joined the women's clubs that had sprung up in the late 1800s. At first, clubwomen read books, went to plays, and sought other ways to improve their minds. By the early 1900s, they were caught up in the reform spirit. Clubwomen raised money for libraries, schools, and parks. They fought for laws to protect women and children, for pure food and drug laws, and for the right to vote.

Faced with racial barriers, African American women formed their own clubs, such as the National Association of Colored Women. These members crusaded against lynching and racial separation, as well as for suffrage and other causes.

The Temperance Crusade

The **temperance movement** against the use of alcoholic beverages began in the early 1800s. By the end of the century, the temperance movement was gaining strength.

Women reformers were the major force in the crusade against alcohol. Many wives and mothers recognized alcohol as a threat to their families. Drinking was a frequent cause of violence and economic hardship in the home. Other women campaigned against the saloon for political reasons. In saloons, male political bosses often decided matters of politics far from the reach of women. Most saloons refused entry to women.

Willard and Nation

In 1874, a group of women founded the Women's Christian Temperance Union, or WCTU. **Frances Willard** became a leader of the WCTU. Willard recalled joining temperance leaders as they entered a saloon in Pittsburgh:

> "The tall, stately lady who led us placed her Bible on the bar and read a psalm.... Then we sang "Rock of Ages" as I thought I had never sung it before.... This was my Crusade baptism. The next day I went on to the West."

In 1880, Willard became president of the WCTU. She worked to educate people about the evils of alcohol. She urged states to pass laws banning the sale of liquor. She also worked to outlaw saloons as a step toward strengthening democracy. Later, Willard joined the suffrage movement, bringing many WCTU members along with her.

A more radical temperance crusader was **Carry Nation.** After her husband died from heavy drinking, Nation dedicated her life to fighting "demon rum." Swinging a hatchet, she stormed into saloons where she smashed beer kegs and liquor bottles. Nation won publicity, but her actions embarrassed many WCTU members.

The Eighteenth Amendment

Temperance crusaders wanted to amend the Constitution to prohibit the sale of liquor. After 1917, support for such an amendment grew. In that year the United States entered World War I. Temperance forces argued that grain used to make liquor should go to feed American soldiers instead.

Temperance leaders finally persuaded Congress to pass the **Eighteenth Amendment** in 1917. By 1919, three fourths of the states had ratified the amendment. The amendment made it illegal to sell alcoholic drinks anywhere in the United States.

★ Section 4 Review ★

Recall

1. **Identify** **(a)** Carrie Chapman Catt, **(b)** Alice Paul, **(c)** Nineteenth Amendment, **(d)** Florence Kelley, **(e)** Frances Willard, **(f)** Carry Nation, **(g)** Eighteenth Amendment.
2. **Define** **(a)** suffragist, **(b)** temperance movement.

Comprehension

3. Describe two methods suffragists used to achieve their goal.
4. Describe two opportunities women gained during the Progressive Era.
5. Why did many women support temperance?

Critical Thinking and Writing

6. **Defending a Position** Do you think Alice Paul's tactics to win suffrage for women were necessary? Explain your position.
7. **Linking Past and Present** Frances Willard considered alcohol a threat to society. What threats does alcohol abuse pose today?

Activity **Writing a Song** You have worked for passage of the Nineteenth Amendment, and finally it has become law. Using a tune you know, write a song celebrating your success.

5 Fighting for Equality

As You Read

Explore These Questions

- What problems did African Americans face during the Progressive Era?
- How did African American leaders try to fight discrimination?
- What challenges faced other minorities?

Define

- barrio
- mutualista

Identify

- Ida B. Wells
- Booker T. Washington
- W.E.B. Du Bois
- NAACP
- George Washington Carver
- Society of American Indians
- Gentlemen's Agreement

SETTING the Scene The Thirteenth Amendment abolished slavery in 1865. Yet, 50 years later, life for many African Americans had not changed for the better. One woman declared:

> "Whether in the cook kitchen, at the washtub, over the sewing machine, behind the baby carriage, or at the ironing board, we are but little more than pack horses, beasts of burden, slaves!"

In general, white Progressives did little for the needs of nonwhites. It was up to African Americans to help themselves. Mexican Americans, Native Americans, and Asian Americans, too, had to fight for justice.

African Americans

After the end of Reconstruction, African Americans in the South lost their hard-won political rights. Jim Crow laws led to segregation in schools, trains, and other public places. (See Chapter 18.)

Northern blacks also faced prejudice. Landlords in white neighborhoods refused to rent homes to African Americans. Many hotels and restaurants would not serve blacks. In the North and the South, African Americans were hired only for low-paying jobs.

In the 1890s, life grew worse for African Americans. The depression of 1893 threw many people out of work. In some areas, mainly in the South, unemployed whites took out their anger on blacks. In the 1890s, lynch mobs murdered more than 1,000 blacks.

Such violence outraged the African American journalist **Ida B. Wells.** In her newspaper, *Free Speech,* Wells published shocking statistics about lynching. She urged African Americans to protest by refusing to ride the streetcars or shop in white-owned stores. Wells spoke out despite threats to her life.

Washington's solution

Booker T. Washington offered one answer to the question of how to fight discrimination. In his autobiography, *Up From Slavery,* Washington told how he had succeeded. Born into slavery, he taught himself to read. In 1881, he founded Tuskegee Institute in Alabama. It became a center for black higher education.

Washington stressed living in harmony with whites. He urged African Americans to work patiently and move upward slowly. First, learn trades and earn money, advised Washington. Only then would African Americans have the power to insist on political and social equality.

In the meantime, Washington accepted segregation. "In all things that are purely social," he said, "we can be as separate as the fingers, yet one as the hand in all things essential to mutual progress."

Viewing History: Du Bois Fights for Equality

W.E.B. Du Bois refused to accept discrimination. As editor of The Crisis, *the journal of the NAACP, he spoke out against injustice and demanded equal rights for African Americans. Here, Du Bois is shown standing at right in the offices of* The Crisis. ★ **How did the view of Du Bois differ from those of Booker T. Washington?**

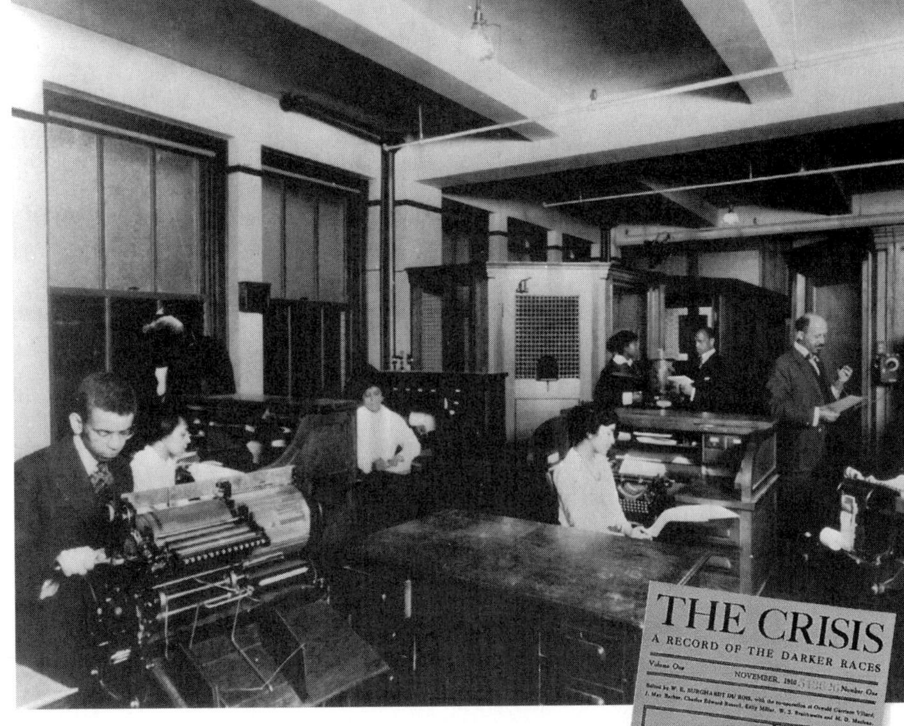

Journal of the NAACP ➤

Booker T. Washington was a spokesman for many African Americans. Business tycoons such as Andrew Carnegie and John D. Rockefeller gave him money to build trade schools for African Americans. Several Presidents sought his advice on racial issues.

Du Bois disagrees

Other African Americans disagreed with Washington. How could blacks move ahead, they asked, when whites denied them advanced education and jobs? Racial harmony was impossible when whites were lynching blacks and denying them the right to vote.

W.E.B. Du Bois (doo BOYS) was one leader who took this view. Du Bois was a professor, author, and public speaker. In 1895, he became the first African American to earn a Ph.D. from Harvard University.

Du Bois agreed with Booker T. Washington on the need for "thrift, patience, and industrial training." However, he added, "So far as Mr. Washington apologizes for injustice, we must firmly oppose him." Instead, Du Bois urged blacks to fight discrimination actively.

In 1909, Du Bois joined with Jane Addams, Lincoln Steffens, and other reformers to form the National Association for the Advancement of Colored People, or **NAACP.** Blacks and whites in the NAACP worked to gain equal rights for African Americans.

Obstacles and successes

Still, most Progressives thought little about the problems of African Americans. When black soldiers were accused of rioting in Brownsville, Texas, President Roosevelt ordered their whole regiment to be dishonorably discharged. Later, President Wilson ordered the segregation of black and white government workers. When black leaders protested, Wilson replied that "segregation is not humiliating, but a benefit." His action led hotels, restaurants, and stores in the nation's capital to enforce segregation.

Some African Americans succeeded despite huge obstacles. **George Washington Carver** discovered hundreds of new uses for peanuts and other crops grown in the South.

Connections With Science

George Washington Carver established a "school on wheels." In this traveling classroom, he taught Alabama farmers how intensive cultivation of cotton and tobacco depleted the soil, while growing peanuts and sweet potatoes helped to enrich it.

Biography **Octaviano Larrazolo**

Born in Mexico, Octaviano Larrazolo later settled in New Mexico. He studied law and then entered politics. Larrazolo was shocked by living conditions of Mexican Americans in the Southwest. When New Mexico became a state in 1910, he demanded that the state constitution spell out the right of nuevomexicanos *to vote, hold office, and serve on juries. Later, he became the state's third governor.*
★ **Why do you think Larrazolo wanted the New Mexico constitution to specify basic rights?**

His writings about crop rotation changed southern farming practices. Sarah Walker, better known as Madame C. J. Walker, created a line of hair care products for African American women. She became the first American woman to earn over $1 million.

Ordinary African Americans felt a sense of pride in their communities. Churches like the African Methodist Episcopal Church offered a strong foundation for religious and family life. They were also training grounds for African American leaders. Black colleges and universities trained young people to enter the professions. Black-owned insurance companies, banks, and other businesses served community needs.

Mexican Americans

In 1910, revolution and famine swept Mexico. To escape the disorder, thousands of Mexicans crossed the border into the American Southwest. Many were poor farmers forced off their land. Others were soldiers or political leaders who had supported the losing side. Although many later returned to Mexico, some remained.

Living in the Southwest

Many of the poor Mexican immigrants worked in the fields, harvesting crops. They built highways and dug irrigation ditches. Some lived in shacks alongside the railroads they had helped to construct. Others moved to cities.

Like other immigrant groups, Mexicans created ethnic neighborhoods, or **barrios.** There, they preserved their language and much of their culture. Los Angeles had the largest barrio in the United States. From 1910 to 1920, the Mexican population of Los Angeles almost tripled.

Need for mutual aid

Some Americans in the Southwest responded with violence to the flood of immigrants from Mexico. Nativists often attacked citizens as well as newcomers.

In defense, Mexican Americans formed **mutualistas,** or mutual aid groups. The constitution of one mutualista defined its goals:

> "To bring closer together... the relations of the Mexicanos... in order that they extend to each other the hand of brotherly love for their protection [and] mutual benefits."

Members of mutualistas pooled money to buy insurance and pay for legal advice. They also collected money for the sick.

Native Americans

The Dawes Act had granted Native Americans plots on reservation lands. With these lands, Indians were supposed to become farmers and enter the mainstream of American life. Instead, Indians were swindled out of millions of acres of land.

In the early 1900s, a new generation of Native American leaders emerged. One group set up the **Society of American Indians.** It included artists, writers, Christian ministers, lawyers, and doctors from many Native American groups. The Society worked for social justice and tried to educate other Americans about Indian life.

Japanese farmers in California

Asian Americans

As you have read, anti-Chinese feelings led Congress to pass the Chinese Exclusion Act of 1882. With new immigration cut off, the Chinese population slowly declined.

Japanese immigration increases

Americans on the West Coast then turned to other Asian lands for cheap labor. They hired Filipino and Japanese workers, mostly young men. More than 100,000 Japanese entered the United States in the early 1900s.

Many Japanese were farmers. They settled on dry, barren land that other western farmers thought was useless. Through hard work and careful management, the Japanese made their farms profitable. Other Japanese immigrants went to work in canneries, lumber mills, and mines.

San Francisco school crisis

Many Americans mistrusted the Asian newcomers because they competed for jobs and had an unfamiliar culture. In 1906, the San Francisco Board of Education placed the city's 93 Asian pupils, including some adults, in a separate school. Japan protested the insult.

Eager to soothe Japanese feelings, President Roosevelt denounced the school board's action. He persuaded the school board to accept a compromise. If the board would return Asian children of proper age to regular schools, he would take steps to restrict further Japanese immigration.

President Roosevelt reached a **Gentlemen's Agreement** with Japan in 1907. Japan agreed to curb the number of workers coming to the United States. In exchange, Roosevelt agreed to allow the wives of Japanese men already living in the United States to join them.

★ Section 5 Review ★

Recall

1. **Identify** **(a)** Ida B. Wells, **(b)** Booker T. Washington, **(c)** W.E.B. Du Bois, **(d)** NAACP, **(e)** George Washington Carver, **(f)** Society of American Indians, **(g)** Gentlemen's Agreement.
2. **Define** **(a)** barrio, **(b)** mutualista.

Comprehension

3. **(a)** How did Booker T. Washington and W.E.B. Du Bois agree in their views? **(b)** How did they disagree?
4. How did Mexican Americans protect their rights?
5. **(a)** How did the Chinese Exclusion Act affect Japanese immigration to the United States? **(b)** How were Japanese immigrants greeted?

Critical Thinking and Writing

6. **Applying Information** Would you consider Ida B. Wells a muckraker? Why or why not?
7. **Comparing** How were the situations of African Americans and Mexican Americans similar during the Progressive Era?

Activity **Listing Pros and Cons** It is 1912. You are a Mexican American who escaped from revolution and famine in Mexico and made a life in the United States. Make two lists—one of the good qualities of your new life, and one of the problems you face in your new country.

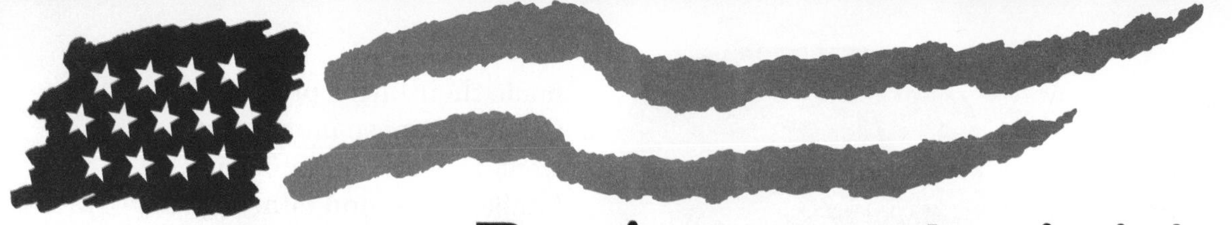

Chapter 22 Review and Activities

★ Sum It Up ★

Section 1 Early Reforms

- During the Gilded Age, reformers worked to end the spoils system.
- Early laws intended to break up monopolies were weak and had little effect.

Section 2 The Progressives and Their Goals

- Journalists brought the problems of society to the attention of the middle class.
- In the early 1900s, Progressives pushed to limit trusts, reform city governments, and give more power to voters.

Section 3 Presidents Support Reforms

- President Theodore Roosevelt supported programs to break up some trusts, conserve resources, and protect consumers.
- Under President Woodrow Wilson, Congress pushed to preserve competition in American businesses.

Section 4 Progress for Women

- The long campaign for women's suffrage finally succeeded with the passage of the Nineteenth Amendment.
- During the Progressive Era, women took a leading role in promoting social reforms including temperance.

Section 5 Fighting for Equality

- African American leaders pursued different paths to improve their lives.
- Faced with discrimination, Asian Americans and Mexican Americans carved a place in society.

For additional review of the major ideas of Chapter 22, see ***Guide to the Essentials of American History*** or ***Interactive Student Tutorial CD-ROM,*** which contains interactive review activities, graphic organizers, and practice tests.

Reviewing the Chapter

Define These Terms

Match each term with the correct definition.

Column 1	Column 2
1. patronage	**a.** vote to make a bill a law
2. referendum	**b.** crusading journalist
3. muckraker	**c.** Mexican American neighborhood
4. public interest	**d.** giving of jobs to loyal supporters
5. barrio	**e.** good of the people

Explore the Main Ideas

1. How did Congress try to regulate railroads and big business in the late 1800s?
2. What was the goal of good government leagues?
3. Explain the goal of the following: **(a)** Elkins Act, **(b)** Meat Inspection Act, **(c)** Federal Reserve Act.
4. Why did the women's suffrage movement gain strength?
5. What were the goals of the NAACP?

Graph Activity

Look at the graph and answer the following questions:
1. How many women were enrolled in higher education in 1880? **2.** How much did enrollment increase from 1910 to 1920? **Critical Thinking** Do you think education helped the suffragist movement? Explain.

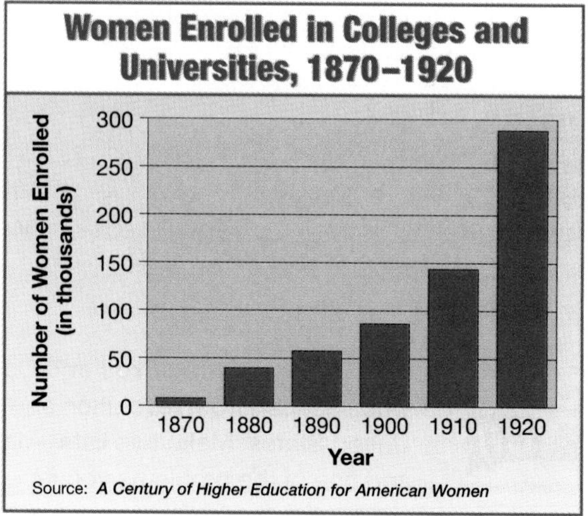

Critical Thinking and Writing

1. **Understanding Chronology** **(a)** List one event that resulted from each of the following: Nast publishes cartoons attacking Boss Tweed; Sinclair publishes *The Jungle;* Tarbell reveals business practices of Standard Oil. **(b)** Make one generalization about the role of the press in bringing about reform.
2. **Linking Past and Present** Congress passed the Pure Food and Drug Act in 1906. **(a)** What does the law provide? **(b)** How does the government protect consumers today?
3. **Recognizing Points of View** "The way for people to gain their reasonable rights is not by voluntarily throwing them away." Who do you think made this statement: Booker T. Washington or W.E.B. Du Bois? Explain your reasoning.
4. **Exploring Unit Themes** **Global Interaction** **(a)** What was the purpose of the Gentlemen's Agreement between the United States and Japan? **(b)** Why do you think Roosevelt wanted the cooperation of the Japanese government?

Using Primary Sources

A 1905 book explained the work of a "district leader" in the corrupt political organization of New York City:

> "Nearly everybody goes to him for assistance of one sort or another, especially the poor of the tenements. He is always obliging. He will go to the police courts to put in a good word for the 'drunks and disorderlies' or pay their fines, if a good word is not effective. He will attend christenings, weddings, and funerals. He will feed the hungry and help bury the dead. A philanthropist? Not at all. He is playing politics all the time."

Source: *Plunkitt of Tammany Hall,* William L. Riordon, 1905.

Recognizing Points of View **(a)** What kind of work does the district leader do? **(b)** A philanthropist is someone who helps others out of sheer kindness. Why does the writer insist that the district leader is not a philanthropist?

Activity Bank

Interdisciplinary Activity

Exploring Geography Research and prepare a report on methods used to preserve land and water resources in Theodore Roosevelt's day. You may wish to focus on the work of an important conservationist such as John Muir or Gifford Pinchot.

Career Skills Activity

Political Strategist Review the steps necessary to pass an amendment to the Constitution. Prepare a flowchart for display in the class, using the Eighteenth or Nineteenth Amendment as an example.

Citizenship Activity

Learning About Democracy Does your state allow initiatives or referendums? If so, find out about some recent examples. Working with other class members, prepare for a debate or panel discussion of one of these issues.

Internet Activity

Use the Internet to find sites dealing with George Washington Carver. When you locate the sites, use them to find the titles of books about Carver. Then find the books in a library and do research for a biography about Carver. Your biography should include a list of some of Carver's many inventions.

Eyewitness Journal

It is the Progressive Era. You are a Progressive President, a muckraker, a city boss, a suffragist, the president of a railroad, or a member of a minority group. Choose the one event during the Progressive Era that was most important to you and describe it and your reaction to it in your Eyewitness Journal.

Chapter 23

Becoming a World Power

1865–1916

What's Ahead

The United States increased its role in world affairs throughout the second half of the nineteenth century. As the nation became an industrial and commercial power, American leaders sought new trade opportunities in Asia. Alaska, Hawaii, and other overseas territories came under United States control.

As a result of the Spanish-American War of 1898, the United States acquired an overseas empire. After the war, the United States played an increasing role in the affairs of Latin America. As a result, many Latin Americans began to view the United States with distrust and anger.

Why Study History? In 1898, the United States sent soldiers to Cuba to help Cubans gain independence from Spain. Today, the United States continues to send American soldiers to troubled spots around the world. To study some of the reasons for these actions, see this chapter's *Why Study History?* feature, "Americans Are Involved in World Affairs."

American Events

- **1867** United States buys Alaska from Russia
- **1898** United States defeats Spain in Spanish-American War
- **1899** Open Door Policy keeps trade with China open to all nations

1865 | 1890 | 1895 | 1900

World Events

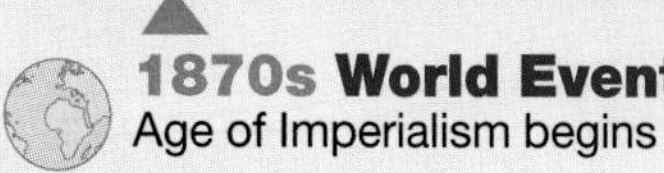

1870s World Event Age of Imperialism begins

1895 World Event Cubans rebel against Spain

Viewing HISTORY

The Great White Fleet

In this painting by Henry Reuterdahl, the "Great White Fleet" of the United States steams into the harbor of San Francisco. The fleet, named for the fact that its ships were painted white, proclaimed the new role of the United States in the world. In his autobiography, President Theodore Roosevelt referred to the fleet as "the most important service that I rendered to peace." ★ **What do you think Roosevelt meant by his statement?**

1900
Hawaii becomes territory of United States

1904
President Roosevelt declares right of United States to intervene in Latin America

1914
Panama Canal opens

1900 **1905** **1910** **1915**

1904 World Event
Russo-Japanese war begins

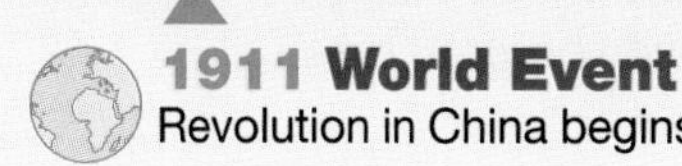
1911 World Event
Revolution in China begins

Across the Pacific

As You Read

Explore These Questions

- How did treaties with Japan and Russia benefit the United States?
- Why did some Americans favor imperialism in the late 1800s?
- How did United States policy concerning Hawaii differ from American policy in China?

Define

- isolationism
- expansionism
- annex
- imperialism
- sphere of influence

Identify

- Matthew Perry
- Treaty of Kanagawa
- William Seward
- Alfred Mahan
- Great White Fleet
- Liliuokalani
- John Hay
- Open Door Policy
- Boxer Rebellion

Setting the Scene In 1880, the ruler of the Turkish empire thought of a way to save his country money. He would shut down his nation's embassies in "minor" countries. One of these minor countries was the United States, a nation known to play only a small role in world affairs.

Turkey's plan was badly timed. By 1880, the United States was making moves to increase its diplomatic contacts with the rest of the world. In fact, it was on the verge of becoming a world power.

Isolationism and Expansionism

In his Farewell Address, as you recall, George Washington had advised the nation to "steer clear of permanent alliances." He urged Americans to have "as little political connection as possible" with foreign nations. Later Presidents continued this policy of **isolationism,** or having little to do with the political affairs of other nations. Americans had no wish to be dragged into Europe's frequent wars.

Earlier in his career, however, Washington had also called the United States a "rising empire." Indeed, from its earliest existence, the American republic followed a policy of **expansionism,** or extending its national boundaries. The people of the United States were constantly pressing westward across the continent.

At the same time, Americans conducted a lively foreign trade. From the early 1700s, sailing ships carried American goods to Europe. American traders also traveled to Asia, including China and the Philippines. The Asian nation of Japan, however, refused to open its doors to American trade.

Opening Trade With Japan

Japan was a small island nation. Fearing outsiders, the Japanese had cut themselves off from the world in the 1600s. They expelled all Westerners* and allowed only one ship a year—from the Dutch East India Company—to trade at the port of Nagasaki. Foreign sailors wrecked on the shores of Japan were not allowed to leave.

Perry's mission

American merchants wanted to open Japan to trade. They also wanted the Japanese to help shipwrecked sailors who washed up on their shores. To achieve these goals, President Millard Fillmore sent Commodore **Matthew Perry** to Japan in the early 1850s.

With four warships, Perry entered Tokyo Bay in July 1853. The Japanese had never seen steam-powered ships. They denounced the Americans as "barbarians in floating volcanoes" and ordered them to leave.

* To the Japanese, Westerners were white people from Europe and North America.

Before departing, Perry presented Japanese officials with a letter from President Fillmore. In it, the President asked the Japanese to open trading relations with the United States. Perry said he would return the following year for an answer.

A new treaty

Perry returned in February 1854, this time with seven warships. Impressed by this show of strength, the Japanese emperor signed the **Treaty of Kanagawa.** The treaty accepted American demands to help shipwrecked sailors. It also opened two Japanese ports to trade.

Perry's visit had important effects. First, it launched trade between Japan and the West. Second, it made the Japanese aware of the power of the Western industrial nations. As a result, Japan soon set out to become a modern, industrial nation itself, with the United States as one of its models.

The Purchase of Alaska

American interest in Asia and the Pacific continued. In the 1860s, Secretary of State **William Seward** wanted the United States to dominate trade in the Pacific. In 1867, he persuaded Congress to **annex** Midway Island, in the middle of the Pacific Ocean. In this way, the island became part of the United States. In that same year, Seward made a deal to buy the vast territory of Alaska.

An amazing land deal

In the 1800s, Alaska belonged to Russia. The Russians, however, were eager to get rid of the territory, which was too far away to govern effectively. Seward saw Alaska as an important stepping stone for increasing United States commerce in Asia and the Pacific.

One night in 1867, Seward was playing cards in Washington, D.C. He was interrupted by a message from the Russian ambassador. The czar of Russia, said the ambassador, was willing to sell Alaska to the United States for $7.2 million. Seward did not hesitate. He agreed to buy the land then and there.

Viewing History **Opening Trade With Japan**

Perry's mission to Japan in 1853 is portrayed in the painting Perry's First Landing in Japan at Kurihama *by Gessan Ogata. Perry gave the Japanese many gifts, including several clocks, a telescope, and a toy train.* ★ **Why did the United States government send Perry to Japan?**

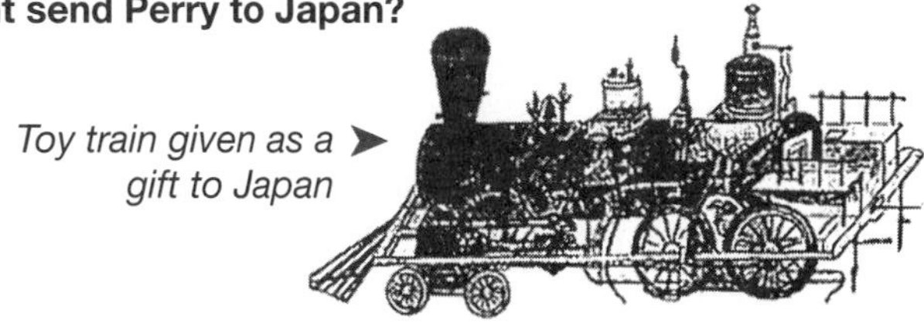

Toy train given as a gift to Japan

"But your Department is closed," said the ambassador. "Never mind that," Seward replied. "Before midnight you will find me at the Department, which will be open and ready for business."

Next morning, Seward completed the deal. The cost came to 2 cents an acre. The purchase of Alaska increased the area of the United States by almost one fifth.

"Seward's Folly"

To most Americans, the purchase of Alaska—which they thought of as a barren land of icy mountains and frozen fish—seemed foolish. They mockingly called Alaska "Seward's Ice Box" and referred to the purchase as "Seward's Folly."

American Heritage
MAGAZINE

HISTORY HAPPENED HERE

White Pass and Yukon Railroad

This rail line was built during the mad gold rush of 1898. It carried miners and supplies from Skagway, Alaska, to the rich Klondike goldfields in Canada. Today, tourists can ride the train along the very trail that the miners used in 1898. As you view the spectacular natural beauty of Alaska's mountains, you pass Bridal Veil Falls, Inspiration Point, and Dead Horse Gulch.

★ ***To learn more about this historic site, write:*** *White Pass and Yukon Railroad, P.O. Box 435, Skagway, AK 99840.*

In fact, Seward was correct in considering Alaska a very valuable territory. The lowlands of southern Alaska are well suited to farming. The land is also rich in timber, copper, and other natural resources. In the 1890s, miners rushed to the territory after prospectors found gold in Alaska and nearby Canada. In 1959, Alaska was admitted as the forty-ninth state. Today, the state is a very important source of petroleum and natural gas.

Age of Imperialism

The period between 1870 and 1914 has often been called the Age of Imperialism. **Imperialism** is the policy of powerful countries seeking to control the economic and political affairs of weaker countries or regions. Between 1870 and 1914, European nations seized control of almost the entire continent of Africa and much of southern Asia. During this period, the United States and Japan also became imperial powers.

Reasons for imperialism

One reason for the growth of imperialism in the 1800s was economic. The industrial nations of Europe wanted raw materials from Africa and Asia. European factories would use the raw materials to manufacture goods. Some of these goods would then be sold to people in Africa and Asia.

Imperialism had other causes. Many Europeans believed that they had a duty to spread their religion and culture to people whom they considered to be less civilized. British writer Rudyard Kipling called this responsibility "the white man's burden." Such thinking ignored the fact that Africans and Asians already had rich cultures of their own.

A third cause was competition. When a European country colonized an area, it often closed the area's markets to other countries. A European nation might take over an area just to keep a rival nation from gaining control of it.

American interests in empire

Americans could not ignore Europe's race for colonies. By the 1890s, the United States was a world leader in both industry and agriculture. American factories turned out huge amounts of steel and other goods. American farms grew bumper crops of corn, wheat, and cotton. The nation was growing rapidly, and arguments in favor of expansion held great appeal.

Many people believed that the American economy would collapse unless the United States gained new foreign markets for its products. Albert Beveridge, campaigning for the Senate from Indiana in 1898, summed up the arguments for commercial expansion:

> "Today we are raising more than we can consume. Today we are making more than we can use. Today our industrial society is congested; there are more workers than there is work.... Therefore we must find new markets for our produce, new occupations for our capital, new work for our labor."

Expansionists also argued that Americans had a right and a duty to bring Western culture to the "uncivilized" peoples of the world. Josiah Strong, a Congregational minister, declared that Americans were "divinely commissioned" to spread democracy and Christianity "down upon Mexico, down upon Central and South America, out upon the islands of the sea."

Other expansionists stressed the need to offset the vanishing frontier. For 100 years, the economy had boomed as Americans settled the western frontier. The 1890 census said, however, that the frontier was gone. People in crowded eastern cities had no new land to settle. The solution, said some, was to take new land overseas.

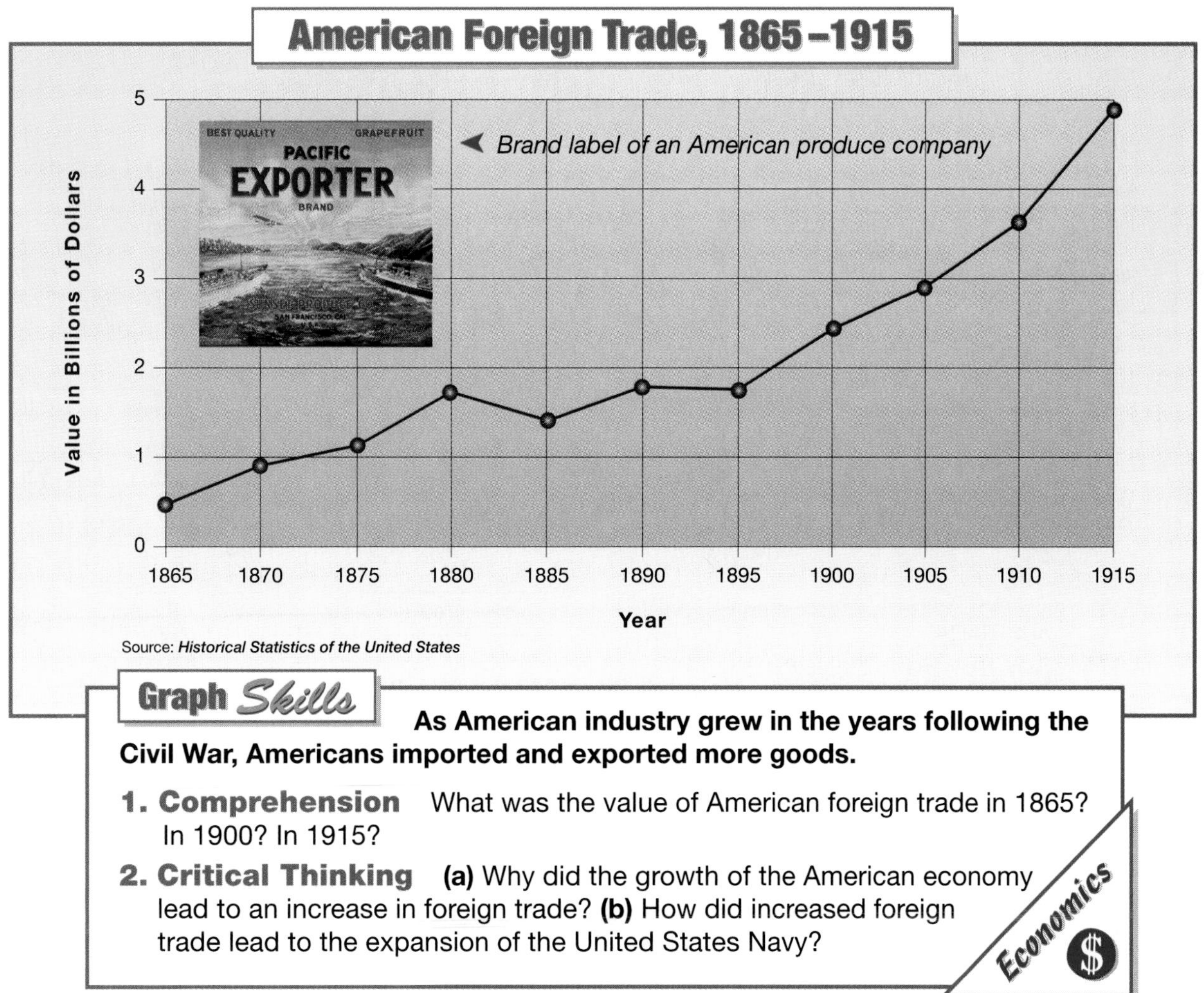

◄ Brand label of an American produce company

Source: *Historical Statistics of the United States*

Graph Skills **As American industry grew in the years following the Civil War, Americans imported and exported more goods.**

1. **Comprehension** What was the value of American foreign trade in 1865? In 1900? In 1915?
2. **Critical Thinking** **(a)** Why did the growth of the American economy lead to an increase in foreign trade? **(b)** How did increased foreign trade lead to the expansion of the United States Navy?

American naval power

One leading supporter of American imperialism was Captain **Alfred Mahan** of the United States Navy. He argued that the prosperity of the United States depended on foreign trade. Furthermore, he said a bigger navy was needed to protect American merchant ships. "When a question arises of control over distant regions," Mahan wrote, "it must ultimately be decided by naval power."

In Mahan's view, the United States could not expand its navy unless it acquired overseas territories A bigger navy would need bases throughout the world. Mahan was especially interested in acquiring harbors in the Caribbean and the Pacific as stepping stones to Latin America and Asia.

Even before Mahan's appeal, Congress had begun to enlarge and modernize the navy. New steam-powered warships with steel hulls were already being built in the 1880s. By the late 1890s, a large and powerful American navy was ready for action. Its ships were called the **Great White Fleet** because they were all painted white.

A Naval Base in Samoa

As naval power grew, the United States showed increasing interest in Samoa, a chain

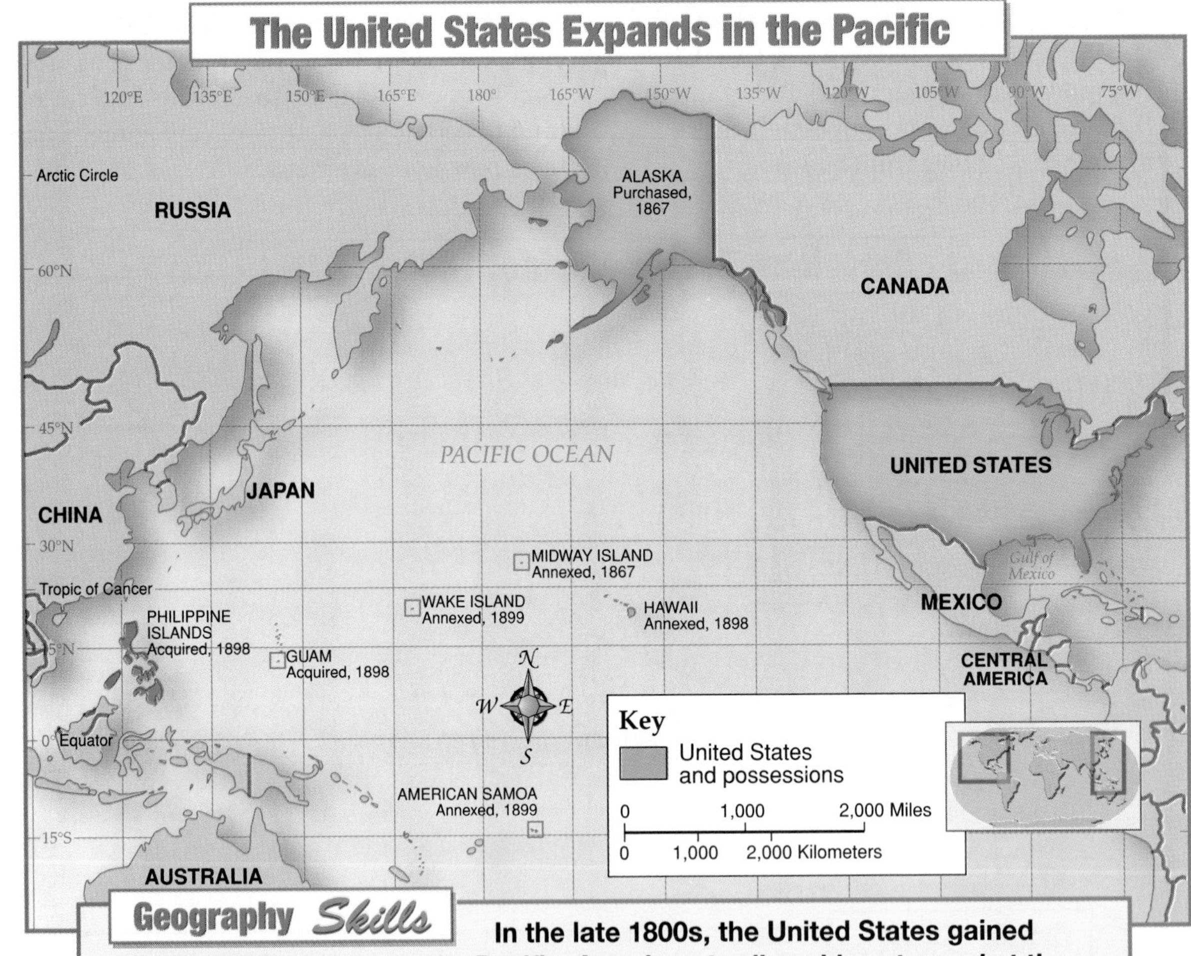

Geography Skills **In the late 1800s, the United States gained control of islands across the Pacific. American trading ships stopped at these islands on their way to China and Japan.**

1. **Location** On the map, locate: **(a)** Japan, **(b)** China, **(c)** Alaska, **(d)** Hawaii, **(e)** American Samoa.
2. **Region** **(a)** Which Pacific island did the United States acquire first? **(b)** Which territory was farthest from the United States mainland?
3. **Critical Thinking** Compare this map to the world map on pages 898–899. Which United States Pacific possession is now an independent country?

of islands in the South Pacific. Samoa had a fine harbor that could serve as a naval base and commercial port. Germany and Great Britain also realized the value of the harbor. As a result, the three nations competed for control of the islands.

In 1889, a military clash seemed very likely. German ships had fired upon Samoan villages that were friendly to the Americans. For months, German and American sailors eyed each other nervously from their warships. Then, just as tensions were at their highest, a powerful storm struck and sank ships of both countries.

Later, the three nations arranged a peaceful settlement. The United States and Germany divided Samoa, while Britain received territories elsewhere in the Pacific. The people of Samoa, meanwhile, had little say in the matter. The United States had demonstrated that it would assert its power in the Pacific Ocean.

Annexing Hawaii

Another territory that had long interested the United States was Hawaii. Hawaii is a chain of eight large islands and more than 100 smaller islands. They are located in the Pacific Ocean, about 2,400 miles (3,800 km) southwest of California. The islands have rich soil, a warm climate, and plenty of rainfall. These conditions make it possible to grow crops all year round.

About 2,000 years ago, people from Polynesia—islands in the Central and South Pacific—first settled Hawaii. Europeans and Americans first learned about Hawaii in 1778. That year, a British sea captain, James Cook, stopped at the islands for water on his way to China. In the early 1800s, American ships bound for China began stopping in Hawaii, and a few American sailors and traders settled there.

Missionaries and planters

In 1820, the first American missionaries arrived. Their goal was to convert the Hawaiians to Christianity. The missionaries and other Americans advised the rulers of Hawaii from the 1830s on. Americans also helped write Hawaii's first constitution in 1840.

Biography **Liliuokalani**

In her youth, Liliuokalani was educated by an American missionary. She also toured the United States and Europe. As queen of Hawaii, however, she worked to reduce foreign influence in her country. ★ **How did Liliuokalani oppose American influence in Hawaii?**

Hawaiian royal crown ➤

By the mid-1800s, Americans had set up large sugar plantations in Hawaii. The planters wanted cheap labor. They brought thousands of workers from China, Korea, the Philippines, and Japan. By 1900, one fourth of Hawaii's population had been born in Japan.

As the sugar industry grew, so did the power of American planters. In 1887, they forced the Hawaiian king, Kalakaua, to accept a new constitution. It reduced the king's power and increased the planters' influence.

Planters stage a revolt

In 1891, Kalakaua died, and his sister **Liliuokalani** (lih lee oo oh kah LAH nee) came to the throne. The new queen cherished Hawaiian independence and deeply resented the growing power of American planters. She

Viewing HISTORY **Rivalry in China**

In this cartoon, titled "Putting His Foot Down," Uncle Sam holds a copy of the treaty that put the Open Door Policy into effect. The figures holding scissors represent (left to right) Germany, Italy, Britain, Austria (background), Russia, and France.
★ **Why are the figures holding scissors?**

therefore rejected the new constitution. She hoped to reduce the influence and privileges of foreign merchants.

In early 1893, the American planters rebelled against the queen's attempt to limit their power. The American ambassador called for United States marines to land on Hawaii and protect American lives. In fact, the marines helped topple the queen.

Faced with American guns, Liliuokalani gave up her throne. However, she wrote a protest to the United States government:

> "I, Liliuokalani, . . . do hereby solemnly protest against any and all acts done against myself and the constitutional Government of the Hawaiian Kingdom. . . .
>
> I yield to the superior force of the United States of America, whose [ambassador] . . . has caused United States troops to be landed [on Hawaii]. . . .
>
> Now, to avoid any collision of armed forces and perhaps the loss of life, I do this under protest, and impelled by said force, yield my authority."

Liliuokalani later sued the United States government for losses totaling $450,000. The lawsuit was unsuccessful. However, the Hawaiian territorial government granted her a pension of $4,000 per year and allowed her some income from a sugar plantation.

A United States territory

With Liliuokalani gone, the planters quickly set up a republic and asked the United States to annex Hawaii. A debate raged in Congress for months. President Grover Cleveland blocked moves to take over the islands. "Our interference in the Hawaiian Revolution of 1893 was disgraceful," he later said. "I am ashamed of the whole affair."

Congress finally annexed Hawaii in 1898, after Cleveland left office. Two years later, Hawaii became a United States territory. In 1959, Hawaii became the fiftieth state.

Rivalry in China

By acquiring Hawaii and Samoa, the United States gained important footholds in the Pacific. Still, the United States was a latecomer in the race for Pacific and Asian territory. Britain, Germany, Japan, and other nations were already competing for colonies in Asia. Rivalry among the industrial nations was especially fierce in China.

China had once been the most advanced empire in the world. However, years of civil war had weakened the empire. In addition, China had failed to industrialize as other nations had in the 1800s. As a result, it was unable to fight off industrial nations that wanted to reap profits from its vast resources and markets.

The Open Door Policy

In the late 1800s, Britain, France, Germany, Russia, and Japan carved spheres of influence in China. A **sphere of influence** was an area, usually around a seaport, where a nation had special trading privileges. Each nation made laws for its own citizens in its own sphere.

American leaders feared that the Europeans and Japanese would try to bar the United States from trading in China. In 1899, therefore, Secretary of State **John Hay** sent a letter to all the nations that had spheres of influence in China. He urged them to follow an **Open Door Policy** in China. Under the policy, any nation could trade in the spheres of others.

Reluctantly, the imperialist powers accepted the Open Door Policy. The agreement allowed the United States to trade freely with the Chinese without interference from the foreign powers in China.

The Boxer Rebellion

Many Chinese opposed foreign influence in their country. Some belonged to a secret society called the Righteous Fists of Harmony, or Boxers. The Boxers wanted to rid China of "foreign devils."

In 1900, the Boxers rebelled. They attacked foreigners all over China, killing more than 200. The Boxers trapped hundreds of foreigners in Beijing, the Chinese capital. Foreign governments quickly organized an international army that included 2,500 Americans. Armed with modern weapons, the international army fought its way into Beijing. They freed the trapped foreigners and crushed the rebellion.

Several nations saw the **Boxer Rebellion** as an excuse to seize more land in China. Secretary of State Hay sent another Open Door letter, urging all nations to respect China's independence. Britain, France, and Germany accepted Hay's letter. Japan and Russia, fearing that any attempt to divide China might lead to war, quietly observed Hay's policy. Hay's Open Door letters showed that the United States was playing a new role in world affairs.

★ Section 1 Review ★

Recall

1. **Locate** **(a)** Japan, **(b)** Alaska, **(c)** Samoa, **(d)** Hawaii, **(e)** China.
2. **Identify** **(a)** Matthew Perry, **(b)** Treaty of Kanagawa, **(c)** William Seward, **(d)** Alfred Mahan, **(e)** Great White Fleet, **(f)** Liliuokalani, **(g)** John Hay, **(h)** Open Door Policy, **(i)** Boxer Rebellion.
3. **Define** **(a)** isolationism, **(b)** expansionism, **(c)** annex, **(d)** imperialism, **(e)** sphere of influence.

Comprehension

4. How did the United States benefit from: **(a)** the Treaty of Kanagawa; **(b)** the purchase of Alaska?
5. In the late 1800s, why did some Americans favor a policy of imperialism?
6. **(a)** How did United States policy concerning Hawaii differ from the policy concerning China? **(b)** Why did the United States pursue these different policies?

Critical Thinking and Writing

7. **Understanding Causes and Effects** What were the causes and effects of the 1893 rebellion against Hawaii's Queen Liliuokalani?
8. **Linking Past and Present** Do you think that the United States could follow a policy of isolationism today? Explain.

★ ★

Activity **Summarizing Ideas** You are Secretary of State William Seward. Write a brief telegram to Congress and the President summarizing your reasons for buying Alaska and annexing Midway Island.

The Spanish-American War

Explore These Questions
- What were the causes of the Spanish-American War?
- What were the major events of the war?
- What were the results of the war?

Define
- yellow journalism
- armistice
- protectorate

Identify
- Lola Rodríguez de Tió
- José Martí
- George Dewey
- Emilio Aguinaldo
- Rough Riders
- Battle of San Juan Hill
- Platt Amendment
- Foraker Act

Replica of 1890s United States Army hat

In the late 1890s, Americans opened their daily newspapers to find shocking tales of violence. The reports told about a revolution in Cuba, a Spanish-owned island just 90 miles off the Florida coast. A typical story cried out against Spanish actions toward the Cuban people:

> "Blood on the roadsides, blood in the fields, blood on the doorsteps, blood, blood, blood!"

Such sensational reports were often inaccurate or one-sided. Yet they succeeded in stirring American anger against Spain. In 1898, the United States put aside its long policy of neutrality to intervene in the Cuban revolution. In the process, American power grew in the Caribbean and across the Pacific.

Trouble in Cuba

For many years, Americans had looked longingly at Cuba. In 1823, Secretary of State John Quincy Adams compared Cuba to a ripe apple. A storm, he said, might tear that apple "from its native tree"—the Spanish empire—and drop it into American hands.

By the 1890s, Spain's once-vast empire in the Western Hemisphere had shrunk to two islands in the Caribbean, Cuba and Puerto Rico. Then, Cuban rebels created the storm that Adams had hoped for.

Revolts against Spain

In 1868, the Cuban people had rebelled against Spanish rule. The revolution was finally crushed after 10 years of fighting. Some of the revolutionaries fled to New York where they kept up the battle for freedom. **Lola Rodríguez de Tió** wrote patriotic poems in support of Cuban independence. **José Martí** told of the Cuban struggle for freedom in his newspaper, *Patria*.

In 1895, Martí returned to Cuba. With cries of *Cuba Libre!*—Free Cuba!—rebels launched a new fight against Spain. Martí died early in the fighting, but the rebels won control of much of the island.

The rebels burned sugar cane fields and sugar mills all over Cuba. They hoped that this would make the island unprofitable for Spain, and convince the Spanish to leave. The rebels killed workers who opposed them. They even blew up some passenger trains.

In response, Spain sent a new governor to Cuba, General Valeriano Weyler (WAY ee lair). Weyler used brutal tactics to crush the revolt.

Connections With Economics

An American tariff helped cause the Cuban Revolution. The Wilson-Gorman Tariff of 1894 placed a high tariff on imported sugar. As Americans bought less Cuban sugar, the island's economy declined. Increasing poverty contributed to popular discontent.

His men moved about half a million Cubans into detention camps so they could not aid the rebels. At least 100,000 died from starvation and disease.

Americans react

In the United States, people watched the revolt in nearby Cuba with growing concern. Americans had invested about $50 million in the island. The money was invested in sugar and rice plantations, railroads, tobacco, and iron mines. American trade with Cuba was worth about $100 million a year.

Opinion split over whether the United States should intervene in Cuba. Many business leaders opposed American involvement. They thought that it might hurt trade. Other Americans sympathized with Cuban desires for freedom and wanted the government to take action.

War Fever

The press whipped up American sympathies for Cuba. Two New York newspapers—Joseph Pulitzer's *World* and William Randolph Hearst's *Journal*—competed to print the most grisly stories about Spanish cruelty. The publishers knew that war with Spain would boost sales of their newspapers.

Yellow journalism

To attract readers, Hearst and Pulitzer used **yellow journalism,** or sensational stories that were often biased or untrue. "You supply the pictures," Hearst supposedly told a photographer bound for Cuba. "I'll supply the war." News stories described events in Cuba in graphic and horrifying detail.

President Cleveland wanted to avoid war with Spain. He called the war fever in the United States an "epidemic of insanity." Stories in the press, he grumbled, were nonsense. When William McKinley became President in 1897, he also tried to keep the country neutral.

Sinking of the *Maine*

In 1898, fighting broke out in Havana, the Cuban capital. Acting promptly, President McKinley sent the battleship *Maine* to Havana to protect American citizens and property there.

On the night of February 15, the *Maine* lay at anchor. Just after the bugler played taps, a huge explosion ripped through the ship. The explosion killed at least 260 of the 350 sailors and officers on board.

The yellow press quickly pounced on the tragedy. "DESTRUCTION OF THE WARSHIP *MAINE* WAS THE WORK OF AN ENEMY," screamed one New York newspaper. "THE WARSHIP *MAINE* SPLIT IN TWO BY AN ENEMY'S SECRET INFERNAL MACHINE?" suggested another.

The real cause of the explosion remains a mystery. Most historians believe it was an accident. But Americans, urged on by Pulitzer and Hearst, clamored for war with Spain. "Remember the *Maine*!" they cried.

Viewing HISTORY **Yellow Journalism**

The front page of the New York Journal and Advertiser *shouted that an enemy had sunk the* Maine. *To the reading public, that enemy was Spain. Today, most historians believe that the explosion was accidental.* ★ **Why did newspaper publishers favor sensationalist headlines such as this?**

$50,000 REWARD.—WHO DESTROYED THE MAINE?—$50,000 REWAR

EDITION FOR GREATER NEW YORK

NEW YORK JOURNAL

AND ADVERTISER.

NO. 5,572. NEW YORK, THURSDAY, FEBRUARY 17, 1898.—16 PAGES. PRICE ONE CENT

DESTRUCTION OF THE WAR SHIP MAINE WAS THE WORK OF AN ENEM

$50,000!

$50,000 REWARD! For the Detection of the Perpetrator of the Maine Outrage!

Assistant Secretary Roosevelt Convinced the Explosion of the War Ship Was Not an Accident.

The Journal Offers $50,000 Reward for the Conviction of the Criminals Who Sent 258 American Sailors to Their Death. Naval Officers Unanimous That the Ship Was Destroyed on Purpose.

$50,000!

$50,000 REWARD For the Detection of the Perpetrator of the Maine Outrage!

NAVAL OFFICERS THINK THE MAINE WAS DESTROYED BY A SPANISH MINE.

Hidden Mine or a Sunken Torpedo Believed to Have Been the Weapon Used Against the American Man-of-War---Of and Men Tell Thrilling Stories of Being Blown Into the Air Amid a Mass of Shattered Steel and Exploding Shells---Survivors Brought to Key West Scout the Idea of Accident---Spanish Officials Protest Too Much---Our Cabinet Orders a Searching Inquiry---Journal Sends Divers to Havana to Report Upon the Condition of the Wreck. Was the Vessel Anchored Over a Mine?

Still hoping to avoid war, McKinley tried to get Spain to talk with the Cuban rebels. In the end, however, he gave in to war fever. On April 25, 1898, Congress declared war on Spain.

The Spanish-American War

The Spanish-American War lasted only four months. The battlefront stretched from the nearby Caribbean to the distant Philippine Islands.

Fighting in the Philippines

Two months earlier, Assistant Secretary of the Navy Theodore Roosevelt had begun making preparations for a possible war with Spain. Roosevelt realized that a conflict with Spain would be fought, not only in the Caribbean, but wherever Spanish sea power lay. The Philippine Islands, a Spanish colony and Spain's main naval base in the Pacific, would be a major objective.

Roosevelt believed it was important to attack the Spanish in the Philippines as soon as war began. He wired secret orders to Commodore **George Dewey,** commander of the Pacific fleet:

> “Order the squadron . . . to Hong Kong. . . . [I]n the event of declaration of war [with] Spain, your duty will be to see that the Spanish squadron does not leave the Asiatic coast. And then [begin] offensive operations in Philippine Islands.”

Dewey followed Roosevelt's instructions. Immediately after war was declared, the Commodore sailed his fleet swiftly to Manila, the main city of the Philippines. On April 30, 1898, Dewey's ships slipped into Manila

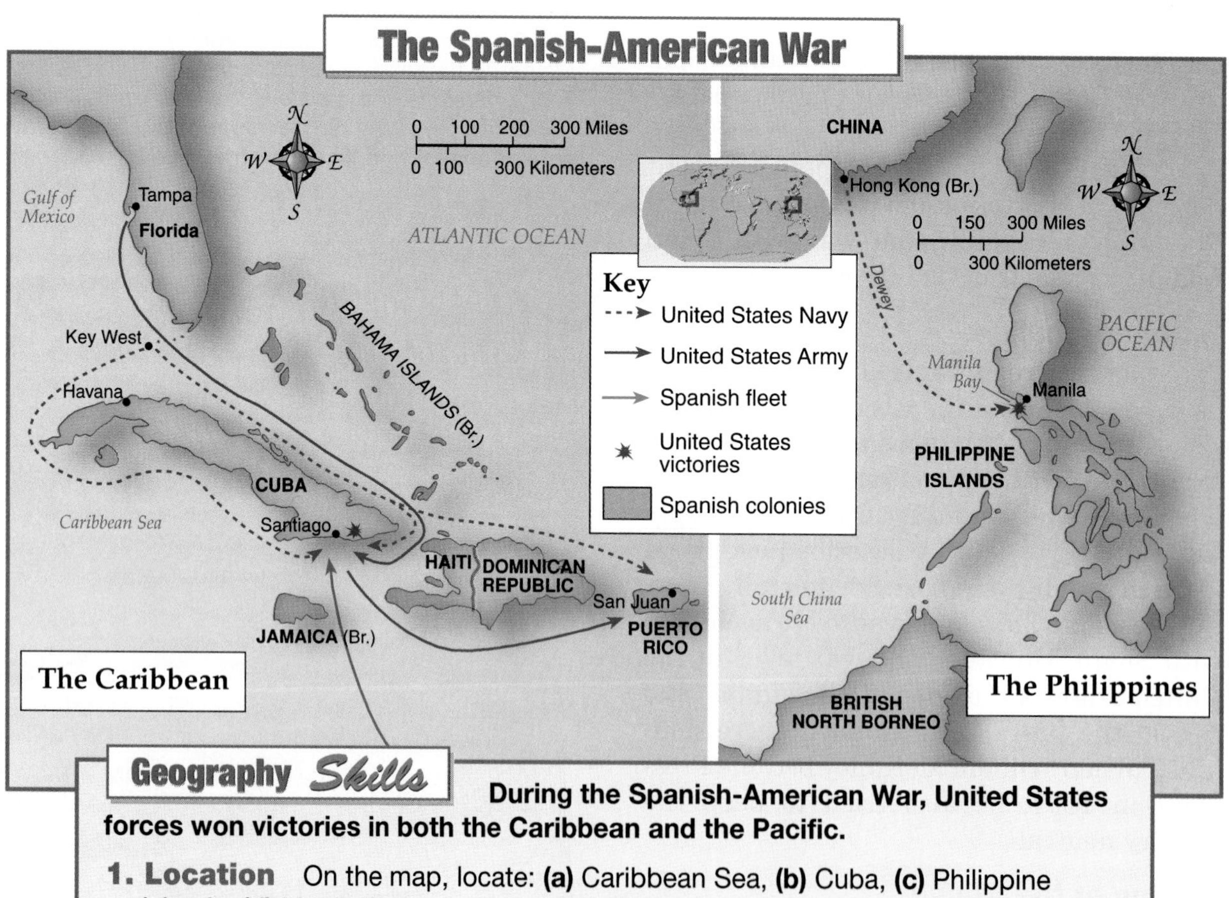

Geography Skills **During the Spanish-American War, United States forces won victories in both the Caribbean and the Pacific.**

1. **Location** On the map, locate: **(a)** Caribbean Sea, **(b)** Cuba, **(c)** Philippine Islands, **(d)** Manila Bay.
2. **Movement** **(a)** Describe the route Dewey took to reach the Philippines. **(b)** On what Caribbean islands did American forces land?
3. **Critical Thinking** Why do you think Dewey was able to trap the Spanish fleet in Manila Bay?

harbor under cover of darkness. There lay the Spanish fleet.

At dawn, Dewey told his flagship commander, Charles Gridley, "You may fire when you are ready, Gridley." Taking their cue, the Americans bombarded the surprised Spanish ships. By noon, the Spanish fleet had been destroyed.

By July, American troops had landed in the Philippines. As in Cuba, local people had been fighting for independence from Spain for years. With the help of the rebels, led by **Emilio Aguinaldo** (ah gwee NAHL doh), the Americans captured Manila.

Fighting in the Caribbean

Meanwhile, American troops had also landed in Cuba. The expedition was badly organized. Soldiers wore heavy woolen uniforms in the tropical heat, and they often had to eat spoiled food. Yet, most were eager for battle.

None was more eager than Theodore Roosevelt. When the war broke out, Roosevelt resigned his position as Assistant Secretary of the Navy. He then organized the First Volunteer Cavalry Regiment, later called the **Rough Riders.** The Rough Riders were a mixed crew—ranging from cowboys to college students and adventurers.

During the battle for the key Cuban city of Santiago, Roosevelt led the Rough Riders in a charge up San Juan Hill. They were joined by African American soldiers of the 9th and 10th Cavalries. Under withering fire, American troops took the hill. John J. Pershing, commander of the 10th Cavalry, described how the troops united in the **Battle of San Juan Hill:**

> "White regiments, black regiments, regulars and Rough Riders, representing the young manhood of the North and South, fought shoulder to shoulder... mindful of their common duty as Americans."

Two days later, the Americans destroyed the Spanish fleet in Santiago Bay. The Spanish army in Cuba surrendered. American troops then landed on Puerto Rico and claimed the island.

Biography **Emilio Aguinaldo**

"Filipino citizens! Now is the occasion for shedding our blood for the last time, that we may achieve our beloved freedom." With these words, Aguinaldo urged Filipinos to throw off Spanish rule. Later, he led an unsuccessful revolt against United States rule. The Philippines did not become an independent nation until 1946. ★ **Was Aguinaldo an imperialist or an anti-imperialist? Explain.**

Spain was defeated. On August 12, Spain and the United States agreed to sign an **armistice,** thus ending the fighting. American losses in battle were fairly light—379 killed. However, more than 5,000 Americans died of other causes, such as yellow fever, typhoid, and malaria.

John Hay, who was soon to become Secretary of State, summed up American enthusiasm for the war. "It's been a splendid little war," he wrote. A malaria-ridden veteran of the war had a different view: "I was lucky—I survived."

Viewing HISTORY **American Soldiers in Cuba**

This United States Army cavalry unit served in Cuba during the Spanish-American War. A number of African American cavalry units also fought against Native Americans in the American West.
★ **How do you think these soldiers felt about fighting in Cuba?**

Army bugle

The Fruits of Victory

In a peace treaty signed in Paris in December 1898, Spain agreed to grant Cuba its freedom. Spain also gave the United States two islands: Puerto Rico in the Caribbean and Guam in the Pacific. Finally, in return for $20 million, Spain handed over the Philippines to the United States.

Before the Senate approved the treaty, a great debate occurred. Many Americans objected to the treaty. They said it violated American principles of democracy by turning the United States into a colonial power.

Expansionists favored the treaty. They said that the navy needed bases in the Caribbean and the Pacific. They pointed out that the Philippines and Puerto Rico offered new territory for American businesses. Also, many Americans agreed with President McKinley, who said that the United States would "uplift and civilize and Christianize [the Filipinos]." In fact, most Filipinos already were Christians.

Urged on by McKinley, the Senate narrowly approved the treaty in early 1899. At last, the United States had an empire.

Ruling Cuba and Puerto Rico

Americans had to decide how to rule their new territories. When the war with Spain began, the United States had pledged to "leave the government and control of [Cuba] to its people." That promise was not kept.

After the war, American soldiers remained in Cuba while the nation debated. Many in Congress believed that Cuba was not ready for independence. American business leaders feared that an independent Cuba might threaten their investments there.

In the end, the United States let the Cuban people write their own constitution. However, Cuba had to accept the **Platt Amendment.** The amendment allowed the United States to intervene in Cuba and gave the United States control of the naval base at Guantanamo Bay.

Why Study History?

Because Americans Are Involved in World Affairs

Historical Background

In 1897, American observer William Calhoun described the terrible situation in Cuba. "Every house had been burned... and everything in the shape of food destroyed. ... The country was wrapped in the stillness of death."

Both Cuban rebels and Spanish soldiers were responsible for the destruction. All over the island, rebels had burned sugar fields so that Cuba would not yield a profit for Spain. To prevent people from aiding the rebels, the Spanish moved 500,000 Cubans into detention camps. One hundred thousand people, including women and children, died from lack of food, shelter, and medicine.

An American soldier in Somalia

Economic and humanitarian concerns fueled the drive for the United States to get involved. On April 19, 1898, the United States Congress recognized Cuban independence and authorized President McKinley to use military force to end the fighting in Cuba. On April 24, Spain declared war on the United States.

Connections to Today

When should the United States intervene in conflicts within or between other nations? Some say only when vital American interests are at stake. Such was the case when Iraq invaded Kuwait and threatened the United States oil supply. In the Persian Gulf War that followed, American and United Nations military forces defeated Iraq.

Other people think that the United States should also intervene for humanitarian reasons. American peacekeeping forces were sent to Somalia in Africa to help the innocent victims of a civil war. The war itself did not provide a direct threat to the United States in this case.

Connections to You

What do you think? Under what circumstances should the United States commit American soldiers to foreign military conflicts? The question is one that each generation of Americans must answer for themselves by weighing the benefits of a policy against its costs. The answer is not always easy.

1. **Comprehension** Why did the United States get involved in the war in Cuba?
2. **Critical Thinking** How can American voters influence United States foreign policy decisions?

Writing an Editorial Do research to learn about a current or recent military intervention by the United States. Then write an editorial in which you agree or disagree with the use of American military power in this case.

In effect, the amendment made Cuba an American **protectorate,** a nation whose independence is limited by the control of a more powerful country. The United States pulled its army out of Cuba in 1902. However, American soldiers would return to Cuba in 1906 and again in 1917.

In Puerto Rico, the United States set up a new government under the **Foraker Act** of 1900. The act gave Puerto Ricans only a limited say in their own affairs. In 1917, Puerto Ricans were made citizens of the United States. Americans set up schools, improved health care, and built roads on the island. Even so, many Puerto Ricans wanted to be free of foreign rule.

Filipino War for Independence

Filipino nationalists had begun fighting for independence long before the Spanish-American War. When the United States took over their land after the war, Filipinos felt betrayed. Led by Emilio Aguinaldo, they now fought for freedom against a new imperial power—the United States.

Aguinaldo, who had fought beside the Americans against Spain, accused the United States of forgetting its beginnings. The United States, he said, was using military force to keep the Filipinos from attaining "the same rights that the American people proclaimed more than a century ago."

The war in the Philippines dragged on for years. At one point, about 60,000 American troops were fighting there. Aguinaldo was captured in 1901, and the war finally came to an end.

The war against Aguinaldo's nationalists was longer and more costly than the original war against Spain in 1898. More than 4,000 Americans died in the Philippines. Nearly 20,000 Filipino soldiers were killed. Another 200,000 civilians died from shelling, famine, and disease.

In 1902, the United States set up a government in the Philippines similar to the one in Puerto Rico. Filipinos, however, were not made American citizens because the United States planned to give them independence in the future. It was not until 1946, however, that the United States allowed Filipinos to govern themselves.

★ Section 2 Review ★

Recall

1. **Locate** **(a)** Cuba, **(b)** Philippine Islands, **(c)** Puerto Rico.
2. **Identify** **(a)** Lola Rodríguez de Tió **(b)** José Martí, **(c)** George Dewey, **(d)** Emilio Aguinaldo, **(e)** Rough Riders, **(f)** Battle of San Juan Hill, **(g)** Platt Amendment, **(h)** Foraker Act.
3. **Define** **(a)** yellow journalism, **(b)** armistice, **(c)** protectorate.

Comprehension

4. Explain one long-term cause and one immediate cause of the Spanish-American War.
5. **(a)** How did the United States Navy help win the war? **(b)** How did Theodore Roosevelt contribute to American victory? **(c)** What role did African American soldiers play in the war?
6. How did the war affect the relationship between the United States and each of the following? **(a)** Cuba, **(b)** Puerto Rico, **(c)** Philippines

Critical Thinking and Writing

7. **Analyzing Primary Sources** Review the newspaper headlines that reported the sinking of the *Maine.* How are they examples of yellow journalism?
8. **Analyzing Ideas** Why did Emilio Aguinaldo fight alongside American soldiers as an ally, but later fight against them?

Activity **Drawing a Political Cartoon** You are a journalist covering international affairs after the Spanish-American War. Draw a cartoon about some topic related to the results of the war.

3 Relations With Latin America

As You Read

Explore These Questions

- Why did the United States build the Panama Canal?
- What policies did the United States adopt toward Latin America?
- Why did the United States invade Mexico in 1916?

Define

- isthmus
- dollar diplomacy
- moral diplomacy

Identify

- William Gorgas
- George Goethals
- Roosevelt Corollary
- Francisco "Pancho" Villa
- John J. Pershing

SETTING the Scene In 1889, Secretary of State James G. Blaine invited Latin American nations to a conference in Washington, D.C. He wanted to remove trade barriers between the United States and Latin America. He also wanted to ease concerns that the United States might extend its growing power across the Western Hemisphere.

The conference failed to remove the fears. The Latin American states refused to open their borders to trade with the United States for fear that a flood of American imports would ruin their own industries. Cuban patriot and writer José Martí charged that the real purpose of the conference was to achieve "an era of United States dominion over the nations of America."

U.S. postage stamp honoring the Panama Canal

Roosevelt and the Panama Canal

When Theodore Roosevelt became President in 1901, he was determined to build a canal through the Isthmus of Panama. (See the map on page 632.) An **isthmus** is a narrow strip of land connecting two larger bodies of land. Panama was a perfect place for a canal because of its location between the Caribbean Sea and the Pacific Ocean. Also, the isthmus was narrow—only about 50 miles (80 km) wide.

Roosevelt knew that a canal through the isthmus would greatly benefit American commerce and military capability. By avoiding the long trip around South America, ships could shorten the journey from New York City to San Francisco by nearly 8,000 miles (12,800 km). Thus, a canal would reduce the cost of shipping goods. In addition, in the event of a war, naval ships could move back and forth between the Pacific Ocean and Atlantic Ocean more quickly than ever before.

A failed deal

In order to build the canal, Roosevelt had to deal with Colombia, the Latin American country to which Panama belonged. Roosevelt asked Secretary of State John Hay to approach Colombia. Hay offered $10 million cash plus $250,000 a year to rent a strip of land across Panama. Colombian officials turned down the offer.

President Roosevelt was furious. He exclaimed to Secretary of State Hay:

> "I do not think the [Colombian] lot of obstructionists should be allowed permanently to bar one of the future highways of civilization."

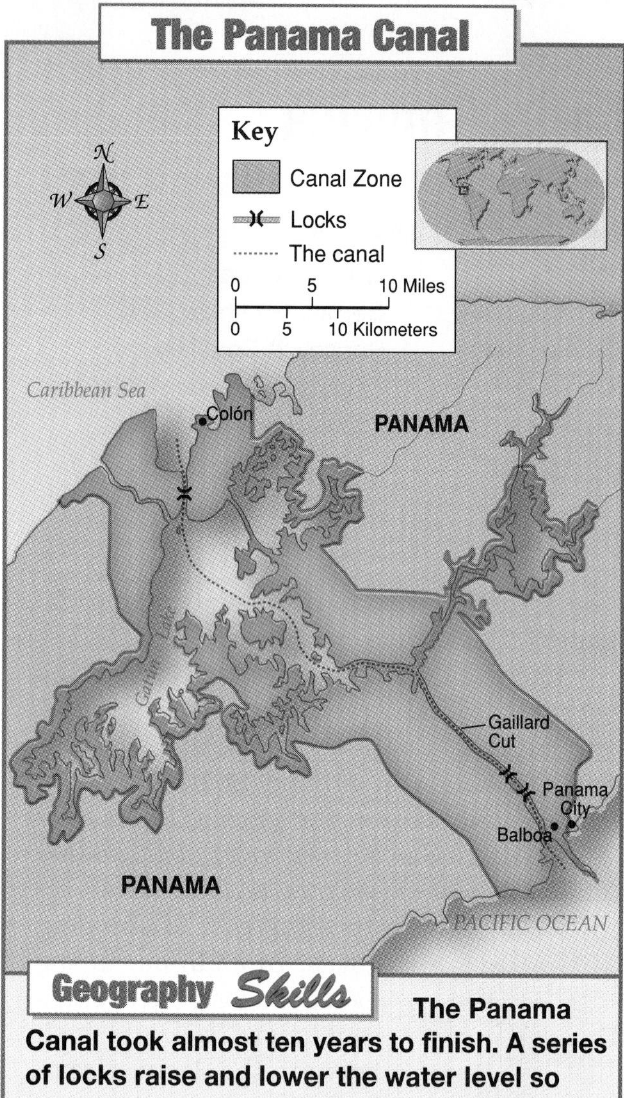

Geography *Skills* **The Panama Canal took almost ten years to finish. A series of locks raise and lower the water level so that ships can move through the canal.**

1. **Location** On the map, locate: **(a)** Panama, **(b)** Canal Zone, **(c)** Panama City.
2. **Movement** In what direction do ships travel to get from the Caribbean Sea to the Pacific Ocean?
3. **Critical Thinking** **(a)** Describe the location of the Canal Zone in relation to the country of Panama. **(b)** How do you think Panamanians felt about United States control of the zone?

At times like this, Roosevelt often quoted an African proverb: "Speak softly and carry a big stick, and you will go far." He meant that words should be supported by strong action.

Revolution in Panama

Roosevelt knew that some Panamanians wanted to rebel and break away from Colombia. He made it known that he would not help Colombia suppress the rebels. In fact, he might even support the rebellion.

On November 2, 1903, the American warship *Nashville* dropped anchor in the port of Colón, Panama. The next day, the people of Panama rebelled against Colombia. American forces stopped Colombian troops from crushing the revolt. On November 3, Panama declared itself an independent republic.

The United States recognized the new nation at once. Panama then agreed to let the United States build a canal on terms similar to those it had offered to Colombia.

Roosevelt's high-handed action in Panama angered many Latin Americans. It also upset some members of the United States Congress. The President, however, was proud of his action. "I took the Canal Zone," he said later, "and let Congress debate."

Battling disease

With its tropical heat, heavy rainfall, and plentiful swamps, Panama was a "mosquito paradise." This presented serious difficulties for the canal builders. Mosquitoes carry two of the deadliest tropical diseases: malaria and yellow fever.

Dr. **William Gorgas,** an army physician who had helped wipe out yellow fever in Cuba, arrived in Panama to help control the mosquitoes and the spread of disease. He ordered workers to locate all pools of water, where mosquitoes laid their eggs. Day after day, the workers drained swamps, sprayed tons of insecticide, and spread oil on stagnant water to kill mosquito eggs.

By 1906, Gorgas had won his battle. Yellow fever had disappeared from Panama. Malaria cases dropped dramatically. Work on the Panama Canal could proceed.

Digging the canal

Under the supervision of army engineer Colonel **George Goethals,** more than 40,000 workers struggled to dig the canal. Most were blacks from the West Indies. They blasted a path through mountains and carved out the largest artificial lake in the world up to that time. In all, they removed more than 200 million cubic yards of earth. Then, they built gigantic locks to raise and lower ships as they

Skills FOR LIFE

Critical Thinking | Managing Information | **Communication** | Maps, Charts, and Graphs

Using the Internet

How Will I Use This Skill?

The Internet is a global computer network. By "surfing the Net," you can link to millions of computer sites sponsored by businesses, governments, educational groups, and individuals all over the world. The Internet provides many services, including information, electronic mail, and on-line shopping.

Students using the Internet ➤

LEARN the Skill

You can search the Internet by using an on-line search engine such as Yahoo, Lycos, or Excite, and by following these steps:

1. Choose a search engine and type in key words to describe your research topic.
2. Scan the site descriptions that the search engine provides and click on one that seems to apply best to your topic.
3. At each Internet site, you can take notes on the on-screen information. Usually, you can also print the information or copy and import it to your own computer. You can also click on highlighted hyperlinks to take you to other related Internet sites.
4. Return to the search engine. Continue your search by scanning more site descriptions, or start a new search by typing in new key words.

PRACTICE the Skill

Use these steps to learn about the economic importance of the Panama Canal today.

1. Choose a search engine. What key words should you type?
2. Based on the site descriptions you see, which site seems most pertinent to your topic? Go to the site by clicking on the description.
3. Look for information on the volume of goods and ships that travel through the canal. When you find the information, take notes, print, or import the data. What hyperlinks does the site provide to other sites?
4. Return to the search engine and continue scanning site descriptions. How could you start a new search on the history of the canal?

APPLY the Skill

Use a search engine to see if your state's department of education provides an Internet site. If it does, visit and explore the site. What kinds of useful information and hyperlinks do you find there? Do you have any ideas for improving the site? Perhaps, you could E-mail your suggestions directly to the department of education.

Linking United States and the World

Colombia

United States

Trading Partners

During the early 1900s, trade increased between the United States and Latin America. At left, young Colombian farm workers display a harvest of coffee beans. At right, an American coffee company advertises the finished product: packaged, ground coffee.

★ **Does Colombia import coffee or export coffee?**

passed through the canal. Finally, in 1914, the first ocean-going steamship traveled through the Panama Canal.

The new waterway helped the trade of many nations. American merchants and manufacturers benefited most. They could now ship goods cheaply to South America and Asia. However, many Latin American nations remained bitter about the way in which the United States had gained control of the canal.

Policing Latin America

The Panama Canal involved the United States more than ever in Latin America. Gradually, President Roosevelt and succeeding Presidents established a policy of intervening in Latin America to settle disputes and disturbances. The United States was especially concerned when disturbances threatened American lives, property, and interests in Latin America.

The Roosevelt Corollary

In 1902, several European countries sent warships to force Venezuela to repay its debts. The United States did not want Europeans to interfere in Latin America. President Roosevelt decided that the United States must step in to keep Europeans out. Roosevelt declared that it was the responsibility of the United States to prevent disorder and lawlessness in Latin America:

> “If we intend to say hands off to the powers of Europe, then sooner or later we must keep order ourselves.”

In 1904, Roosevelt announced an important addition to the Monroe Doctrine. In the **Roosevelt Corollary,** he claimed the right of the United States to intervene in Latin America to preserve law and order. By using this “international police power,” the United States could force Latin Americans to pay their debts to foreign nations. It would also keep those nations from meddling in Latin American affairs.

Over the next 20 years, several Presidents, including Roosevelt, used this police power. Most Latin Americans strongly resented this interference in their affairs.

Dollar diplomacy

Roosevelt's successor, William Howard Taft, also favored a strong American role in Latin America. Taft, however, wanted to "substitute dollars for bullets." He urged American bankers to invest in Latin America. It was better to use trade than warships to expand American influence in Latin America, he said. This policy of building strong economic ties to Latin America became known as **dollar diplomacy.**

American investors responded eagerly. They helped build roads, railroads, and harbors in Latin America. These improvements increased trade, benefiting both Americans and local governments. The new railroads, for example, brought minerals and other resources to Latin American ports. From there, they were shipped all over the world.

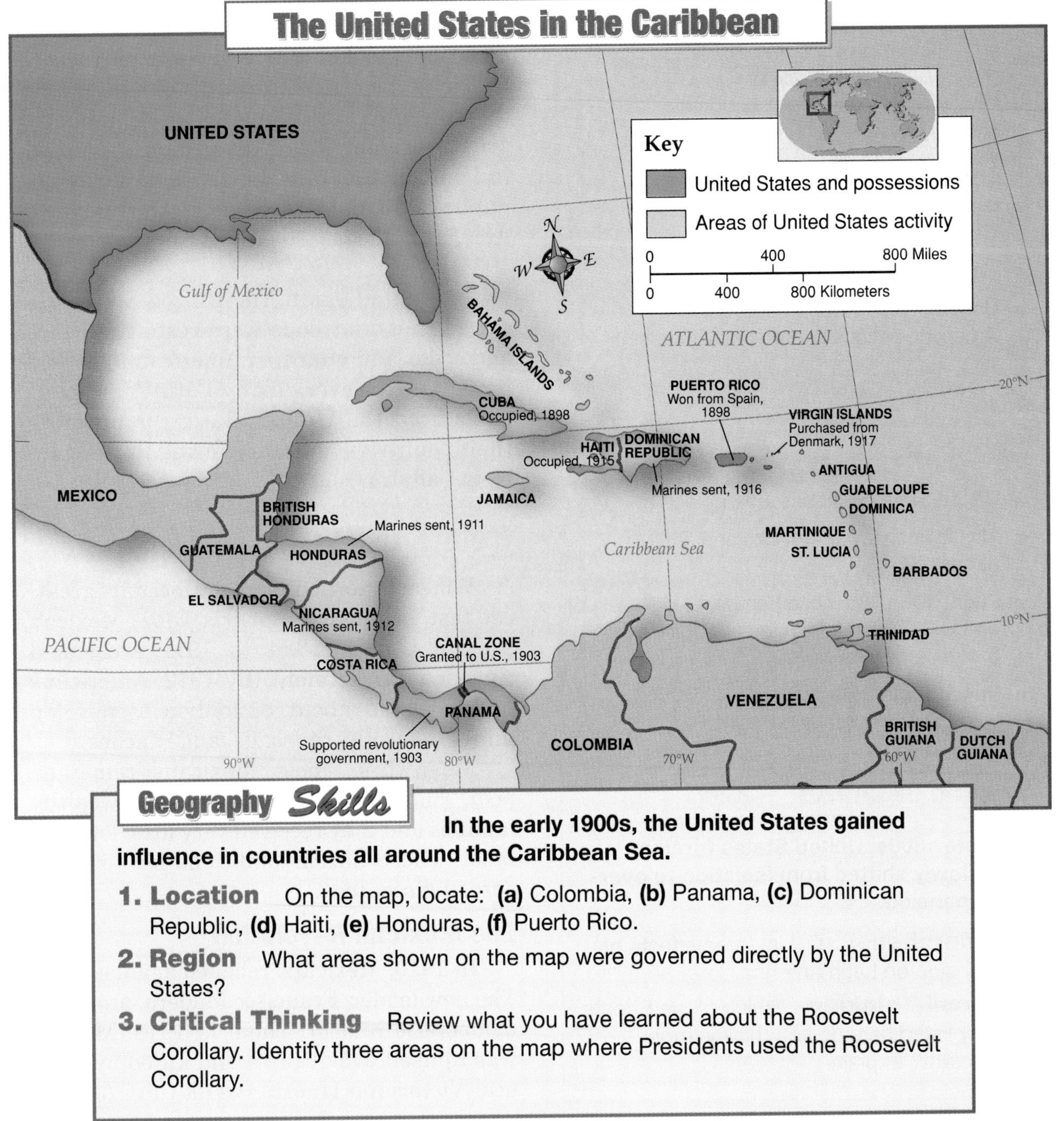

Geography *Skills* **In the early 1900s, the United States gained influence in countries all around the Caribbean Sea.**

1. **Location** On the map, locate: **(a)** Colombia, **(b)** Panama, **(c)** Dominican Republic, **(d)** Haiti, **(e)** Honduras, **(f)** Puerto Rico.
2. **Region** What areas shown on the map were governed directly by the United States?
3. **Critical Thinking** Review what you have learned about the Roosevelt Corollary. Identify three areas on the map where Presidents used the Roosevelt Corollary.

Cause and Effect

Causes

- Western frontier closes
- Businesses seek raw materials and new markets
- European nations compete for resources and markets

Overseas Expansion

Effects

- United States develops strong navy
- Open Door Policy protects trade with China
- United States governs lands in Caribbean and Pacific
- United States builds Panama Canal
- United States sends troops to Latin American nations to protect its interests

Effects Today

- United States is global superpower
- Alaska and Hawaii are 49th and 50th states
- Puerto Rico, American Samoa, Guam, and U.S. Virgin Islands remain United States territories
- United States has close economic ties with Latin America and Pacific Rim

Graphic Organizer *Skills*

In the late 1800s, United States foreign policy slowly shifted from isolation to overseas expansion.

1. **Comprehension** List three effects of expansion on Latin America.
2. **Critical Thinking** Which of the Effects Today listed here do you think is most important? Explain.

Dollar diplomacy created problems, too. American businesses, such as the United Fruit Company, often meddled in the political affairs of host countries. Sometimes, the United States used military force to keep order. In 1912, when a revolution erupted in Nicaragua, the United States sent in marines to protect American investments.

Wilson and moral diplomacy

Woodrow Wilson, elected President in 1912, disliked the heavy-handed foreign policy of his predecessors. He proposed instead a policy of **moral diplomacy.** "The force of America is the force of moral principle," he said. Wilson's goals were to condemn imperialism, spread democracy, and promote peace.

Nevertheless, Wilson ordered military intervention in Latin America more than any prior President. When disturbances erupted in Haiti in 1915 and in the Dominican Republic in 1916, Wilson sent in the marines. American troops remained in Haiti until 1934.

Again and again, the United States declared that its troops were restoring peace and order and guarding American lives and property. However, many Latin Americans denounced the United States for invading their countries and interfering in their internal affairs.

Relations With Mexico

Wilson's moral diplomacy faced its greatest test in Mexico. Porfirio Díaz, Mexico's president from 1884 to 1911, welcomed American investment. By 1912, Americans had invested about $1 billion to develop mines, oil wells, railroads, and ranches.

Meanwhile, most Mexicans remained poor. They worked the land of a few wealthy families and they received very little for their labor. These harsh conditions led to widespread discontent.

The Mexican Revolution

In 1910, Mexicans rebelled against Díaz. The new leader, Francisco Madero, promised democratic reform. Then, in 1913, Madero was himself overthrown and killed by General Victoriano Huerta (WEHR tuh). As civil war raged in Mexico, Wilson vowed that he would never recognize this "government of butchers."

Wilson tried to stay neutral. He hoped that Mexico would develop a democratic government without American interference. However, Huerta's dictatorship grew more brutal. In response, Wilson authorized the sale of arms to Huerta's rival, Venustiano Carranza.

Finally, a minor incident led to American intervention. In 1914, Huerta's troops arrested several American sailors. The sailors were quickly released and an apology issued. Still, Wilson ordered the United States Navy to occupy the Mexican port of Veracruz. Rallied by the American show of strength, Carranza's forces drove Huerta from power. The United States troops withdrew.

American soldiers in Mexico

Still, civil war continued in Mexico. Now, General **Francisco "Pancho" Villa** hoped to overthrow Carranza. The United States, meanwhile, supported Carranza.

In January 1916, Villa's soldiers removed 17 American citizens from a train in Mexico and shot them. In March, Villa raided the town of Columbus, New Mexico, killing 19 Americans. He hoped that his actions would weaken relations between the United States and the Carranza government. Villa's plan backfired.

To capture Villa, President Wilson sent General **John J. Pershing** with an army of several thousand soldiers into Mexico. When Mexico demanded that the "invasion" be halted, the United States refused. There were some calls for war, but both Wilson and Carranza opposed the idea. In 1917, after failing to capture Villa, Wilson ordered Pershing's army to withdraw.

Once again, the United States had demonstrated its willingness to use force to protect its interests. However, there was a cost. Like many other Latin Americans, Mexicans became more resentful of their powerful neighbor to the North.

As United States troops headed home from Mexico, many Americans realized that their nation's role in world affairs had dramatically changed over the years. Now the United States kept troops and ships in both Asia and Latin America. American business interests spanned the globe. It would be very difficult for the United States to ignore the war that had been raging in Europe since 1914.

★ Section 3 Review ★

Recall

1. **Locate** **(a)** Colombia, **(b)** Panama, **(c)** Panama Canal, **(d)** Venezuela, **(e)** Mexico.
2. **Identify** **(a)** William Gorgas, **(b)** George Goethals, **(c)** Roosevelt Corollary, **(d)** Francisco "Pancho" Villa, **(e)** John J. Pershing.
3. **Define** **(a)** isthmus, **(b)** dollar diplomacy, **(c)** moral diplomacy.

Comprehension

4. Why did President Roosevelt think it was important for the United States to build the Panama Canal?
5. How were the foreign policies of Roosevelt, Taft, and Wilson similar?
6. **(a)** Why did Mexicans rebel against their government in 1910? **(b)** Why did President Wilson send General Pershing into Mexico?

Critical Thinking and Writing

7. **Understanding Causes and Effects** How did geographic conditions in Panama make it difficult to build a canal there?
8. **Thinking Creatively** What do you think President Wilson could have done to help bring the Mexican Revolution to a peaceful end?

Activity **Preparing for an Interview** You are a historian about to interview President Theodore Roosevelt concerning his policy in Latin American countries. Write three questions you would ask him.

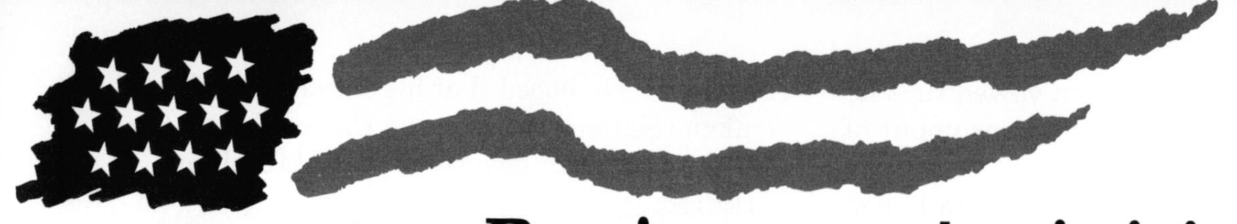

Chapter 23 Review and Activities

★ Sum It Up ★

Section 1 Across the Pacific

- In the mid-1800s, the United States increased its influence in the Pacific by opening trade with Japan and by buying Alaska from Russia.
- Americans began to favor imperialism because they wanted raw materials and markets in other regions.
- After American planters rebelled against the Hawaiian government, the United States annexed Hawaii.
- To protect American trading rights in China, the United States established the Open Door Policy.

Section 2 The Spanish-American War

- The Cuban revolt against Spain led to war between the United States and Spain.
- United States forces defeated the Spanish in Cuba, Puerto Rico, and the Philippines.
- After the war, the United States took control of Spain's former colonies in the Caribbean Sea and the Pacific Ocean.
- Filipino nationalists fought unsuccessfully against the United States Army.

Section 3 Relations With Latin America

- The United States built the Panama Canal through Central America.
- Roosevelt and succeeding Presidents intervened repeatedly in Latin American affairs.
- In response to events of the Mexican Revolution, President Wilson sent United States troops into Mexico.

For additional review of the major ideas of Chapter 23, see ***Guide to the Essentials of American History*** or ***Interactive Student Tutorial CD-ROM,*** which contains interactive review activities, graphic organizers, and practice tests.

Reviewing the Chapter

Define These Terms

Match each term with the correct definition.

Column 1	Column 2
1. isolationism	**a.** policy of having little to do with foreign nations
2. sphere of influence	**b.** agreement to end fighting
3. isthmus	**c.** part of a nation where another nation has special trading privileges
4. yellow journalism	**d.** sensational news reporting
5. armistice	**e.** narrow strip of land connecting two larger areas of land

Explore the Main Ideas

1. Why did many Americans favor imperialism in the late 1800s?
2. How did the United States extend its interests in Asia and the Pacific?
3. **(a)** What was one cause of the Spanish-American War? **(b)** What was one effect of the war?
4. How did the United States acquire the rights to build a canal in Panama?
5. Explain each of the following: **(a)** Roosevelt Corollary, **(b)** dollar diplomacy, **(c)** moral diplomacy.

Geography Activity

Match the letters on the map with the following places: **1.** United States, **2.** Puerto Rico, **3.** Panama Canal, **4.** Cuba, **5.** Nicaragua, **6.** Dominican Republic. **Place** Why was the Isthmus of Panama a good place to build a canal?

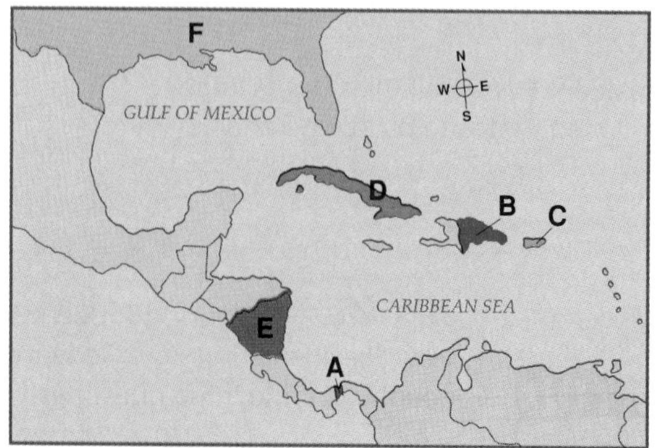

Critical Thinking and Writing

1. **Understanding Chronology** List the following events in chronological order: **(a)** Filipino War for Independence, **(b)** Spanish-American War, **(c)** Cuban rebellion against Spain, **(d)** the sinking of the battleship *Maine.*
2. **Linking Past and Present** What national projects today present challenges similar to those overcome in building the Panama Canal? Explain.
3. **Making Inferences** In the quotation on page 555, Pershing described the American forces at San Juan as being made up of men "of North and South." Why did he choose this way of describing the military?
4. **Exploring Unit Themes** **Global Interaction** Captain Mahan insisted that the navy was the decisive power that would control events in distant regions. **(a)** Give evidence to prove or disprove that his view was correct in his time. **(b)** Does his view hold true today?

Using Primary Sources

Naval Lieutenant John Blandin was on the *Maine* when it exploded. He later made this statement about the event:

> "I have no theories as to the cause of the explosion. I cannot form any. I, with others, had heard that the Havana harbor was full of [explosive mines], but the officers whose duty it was to examine into that reported that they found no signs of any. Personally, I do not believe that the Spanish had anything to do with the disaster. Time may tell. I hope so."

Source: *Memories of Two Wars: Cuban and Philippine Experiences,* Frederick Funston, 1911.

Recognizing Points of View **(a)** According to Blandin, what evidence was there that the Spanish were to blame for the sinking of the *Maine*? **(b)** Why did the views of Blandin and other witnesses have little effect on American public opinion about the explosion?

Activity Bank

Interdisciplinary Activity

Exploring Geography Choose one of the lands the United States acquired during its period of foreign expansion. Prepare a geographic fact sheet on its geography. Then, write a short essay explaining why the geography of the place you have chosen made it a target for American imperialists.

Career Skills Activity

Cartographers On a large sheet of paper, draw a map of the world. Indicate the following on the map: **(a)** the territory of the United States in 1850, **(b)** the territory gained by the United States between 1850 and 1914.

Citizenship Activity

Writing an Editorial The question of whether the United States should act as the police officer of the world arose many times during the early 1900s. Write an editorial in which you either support or oppose the use of United States military forces to settle disputes and disturbances in other parts of the world.

Internet Activity

Use the Internet to find sites dealing with the Spanish-American War. Gather information on a single event of the war. Then, write a newspaper story as it might have appeared in the yellow press of the time. How do the facts and your story differ?

You are an American farmer, industrialist, missionary, or naval officer during the Age of Imperialism. In your EYEWITNESS JOURNAL, describe your thoughts on the increasing role of the United States in world affairs.

Chapter 24

World War I

1914–1919

What's Ahead

Section 1
War Erupts in Europe

Section 2
The United States Enters the War

Section 3
Winning the War

Section 4
Wilson and the Peace

In 1914, long-standing rivalries among European nations exploded into war. At first, President Woodrow Wilson tried to keep the United States neutral. However, after several of Germany's actions affected American citizens, the United States entered the war against Germany in 1917.

World War I, as the war is now called, cost millions of lives. After the war ended, Wilson worked hard to build a lasting peace. However, because of conflicts at the peace conference and at home, he was unable to achieve all of his goals.

Why Study History? World War I ended on November 11, 1918. Today, Americans celebrate November 11 as Veterans Day. On this day, we remember and honor all the men and women who have served the nation in the armed services. To focus on this connection, see the *Why Study History?* feature, "We Honor Our Veterans," in this chapter.

American Events

1915 Americans die when Germany sinks the *Lusitania*

1916 Avoiding war helps President Wilson win reelection

1917 United States enters World War I

1914 — 1915 — 1916 — 1917

World Events

1914 World Event World War I begins in Europe

1916 World Event Hundreds of thousands die in Battle of Verdun

Viewing HISTORY Americans Fight in Europe

During World War I, the government sent artists to the battleground in Europe. This painting, 18 on the Trail of the San Mihiel, *is by W. J. Aylward. It shows American troops in 1918 moving equipment to the front.* ★ **Why do you think the government sent artists to the front lines?**

1918 Armistice ends World War I fighting

1919 Senate rejects Treaty of Versailles

1921 United States signs peace treaty with Germany

1917 **1918** **1919** **1920**

1917 World Event
Russian Revolution begins

1918 World Event
Influenza epidemic kills millions

War Erupts in Europe

As You Read

Explore These Questions

- Why were tensions high in Europe in 1914?
- What event triggered World War I?
- How did Americans react to the outbreak of war in Europe?

Define

- nationalism
- militarism
- mobilize
- kaiser
- stalemate
- trench warfare
- propaganda
- U-boat

Identify

- Triple Alliance
- Triple Entente
- Franz Ferdinand
- World War I
- Central Powers
- Allied Powers
- *Lusitania*

President Woodrow Wilson's friend and adviser Colonel Edward House visited Europe in May 1914. He quickly saw that tensions among the continent's nations threatened the peace. "The situation is extraordinary," he noted. "There is too much hatred, too many jealousies."

It was not long before events proved House correct. Three months after the colonel returned home, Europe exploded into war.

Tensions in Europe

The fact that war erupted in August 1914 did not surprise many Europeans. After all, tensions had torn Europe for years.

Extreme nationalism

Extreme feelings of **nationalism,** or pride in one's nation, fueled the tension. In the 1870s, European nationalists demanded freedom and self-government. They believed that people with a common language and culture should throw off foreign rule and form their own countries.

While nationalism encouraged unity, it also created mistrust and bitter rivalry between nations. For example, France and Germany had gone to war in 1870. As a result of that war, France had to give Germany the iron-rich territory of Alsace-Lorraine. The French never forgot this blow to their national pride. They hoped for an opportunity to regain their lost territory.

In Eastern Europe, nationalism deepened hostility between Austria-Hungary and Russia. Russia encouraged Serbs and other minorities in Austria-Hungary to rise up against their rulers.

Imperialism and militarism

Imperialism fueled rivalries between powerful nations. Between 1870 and 1914, Britain, France, Germany, Italy, and Russia scrambled for colonies in Africa, Asia, and the Pacific. Often, several nations competed for power in the same region. This competition sometimes led to wars in places far from Europe.

Militarism was a third source of tension. **Militarism** is the policy of building up strong armed forces to prepare for war. European nations expanded their armies and navies, creating new stresses. For example, Germany built up its navy. Britain responded by adding more ships to its fleet. This race for naval dominance strained relations between the two nations.

Rival alliances

To protect themselves, European powers formed rival alliances. Germany organized the **Triple Alliance** with Austria-Hungary and Italy. France responded by linking itself to Russia and Britain in the **Triple Entente** (ahn TAHNT).

The alliance system posed a new danger. Allies agreed to support one another in case of an attack. Thus, a crisis involving one member of an alliance affected that nation's allies. This meant that a minor incident could spark a major war. On June 28, 1914, that incident finally took place.

War Breaks Out

For years, nationalism had caused turmoil in the Balkan peninsula in southeastern Europe. (See the map on page 646.) There, the rival nations of Albania, Bulgaria, Greece, Montenegro, Romania, and Serbia battled for territory. At the same time, Balkan nationalists called on related people in Austria-Hungary to free themselves of Austrian rule.

Assassination in Serbia

In June 1914, a new crisis struck the region. Archduke **Franz Ferdinand,** heir to the throne of Austria-Hungary, was visiting Sarajevo, the capital of Bosnia. At the time, Bosnia was part of the Eastern European empire ruled by Austria-Hungary. Franz Ferdinand's visit angered members of the Black Hand, a Serbian terrorist group. The Black Hand wanted Bosnia to break away from Austria-Hungary and join Serbia.

On June 28, the archduke and his wife, Sophie, rode through Sarajevo in an open car. Suddenly, a young terrorist named Gavrilo Princip stepped from the curb, waving a pistol. Taking aim, he fatally shot Franz Ferdinand and Sophie.

Alliances lead to war

In the days that followed, Austria-Hungary accused the Serbian government of organizing the archduke's assassination. When Austria-Hungary threatened war, Russia moved to protect Serbia. Diplomats rushed to ease tensions, but they could not stop the system of alliances from running its fateful course.

On July 28, Austria-Hungary declared war on Serbia. The next day, Russia ordered its forces to **mobilize,** or prepare for war. Austria-Hungary's ally, Germany, called on Russia to cancel the order to mobilize. When it received no reply, Germany declared war on Russia on August 1.

On August 2, the American ambassador to Britain, Walter Page, wrote:

> "The Grand Smash is come.... I walked out in the night a while ago. The stars are bright, the night is silent, the country quiet—as quiet as peace itself. Millions of men are in camp and on warships. Will they all have to fight and many of them die—to untangle this network of treaties and alliances... so that the world may start again?"

The answer came the next day. On August 3, Germany declared war on Russia's ally France. When German armies sliced through neutral Belgium on their march to

Alliances Lead to War

Distressed Americans looked on as World War I unfolded in Europe. This cartoon appeared in an American newspaper in the summer of 1914.

★ **What does the woman in the background represent? What are the nations of Europe doing in the cartoon?**

France, Britain declared war on Germany. Long before, Britain had promised to defend Belgium if it were attacked.

In this way, what began as a local crisis in Bosnia exploded into a major war. For years, Europeans had expected war. When it came, many welcomed the chance to show their power and strength. Others, however, feared what war might bring.

On the Battlefront

"You will be home before the leaves have fallen from the trees," the kaiser, or German emperor, promised his troops as they marched to war. Europeans on both sides of the conflict thought the war would end soon. Sadly, they were mistaken. The war dragged on for four blood-soaked years, from 1914 to 1918. At the time, the conflict was called the Great War. Later, it became known as **World War I.**

The war pitted the **Central Powers**—Germany, Austria-Hungary, and the Ottoman or Turkish Empire—against the **Allied Powers**—France, Britain, and Russia. In time, 21 other nations, including Italy, joined the Allies.

By November 1914, a German advance and an Allied counterattack had produced nothing but a deadly stalemate. A stalemate is a deadlock in which neither side is strong enough to defeat the other. For three years, the two armies fought huge battles, but with little to show for it. While thousands of young Europeans lost their lives, neither side gained much territory.

Both sides dug in, creating a maze of trenches protected by mines and barbed wire. Soldiers spent weeks in these muddy, rat-infested holes in the ground. One soldier later recalled: "The men slept in mud, washed in mud, ate mud, and dreamed mud." Some trenches were shallow ditches. Others were elaborate tunnels that served as headquarters and first-aid stations. Between the front-line trenches of each side lay a "no man's land" of barbed wire and deadly land mines.

In trench warfare, soldiers spent day after day shelling the enemy. Then, on orders from an officer, the troops charged bravely "over the top" of the trenches. Soldiers raced across "no man's land" to attack the enemy.

Most offensives were long and deadly. The Battle of Verdun in 1916 lasted 10 months. The Germans lost some 400,000 men trying to overrun French lines. The French lost even more lives defending their position.

In the meanwhile, in the east, the vast armies of Germany and Austria-Hungary faced off against those of Russia and Serbia. Stalemate and trench warfare brought mounting tolls there as well. By mid-1916, the Russians had lost more than one million soldiers. Yet, neither side could win a decisive victory.

The United States Remains Neutral

When war broke out in Europe, the United States was determined to avoid being dragged into the conflict. The government adopted an official position of neutrality. President Woodrow Wilson called on Americans to "be neutral in fact as well as in name."

Public opinion, however, was divided, often along ethnic lines. Most Americans favored the Allies because of long-standing ties of language, history, and culture to Britain. The United States and France had been allies in the American Revolution.

On the other hand, many of the 8 million Americans of German or Austrian descent favored the Central Powers. Millions of Irish Americans also sympathized with the Central Powers. They hated Britain, which had ruled Ireland for centuries. Many American Jews favored Germany against Russia. Some of them had fled persecution in Russia only a few years earlier.

Impact of the war

The war had several immediate effects on the United States. First, the economy boomed. American farmers and manufacturers rushed to fill orders for war goods. By 1917, trade with the Allies had grown seven times in value and by a smaller amount with

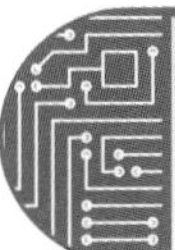

Linking History and Technology

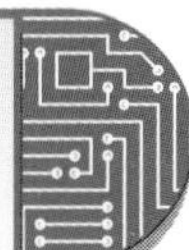

Trench Warfare

During World War I, soldiers on both sides dug networks of trenches. The typical trench was about 6 to 8 feet (1.8 to 2.4 m) deep and just wide enough for two men to pass. "No man's land," a stretch of barren ground protected by barbed wire and land mines, lay between enemy trenches. ★ **How do you think trench warfare affected the land and resources of the surrounding environment?**

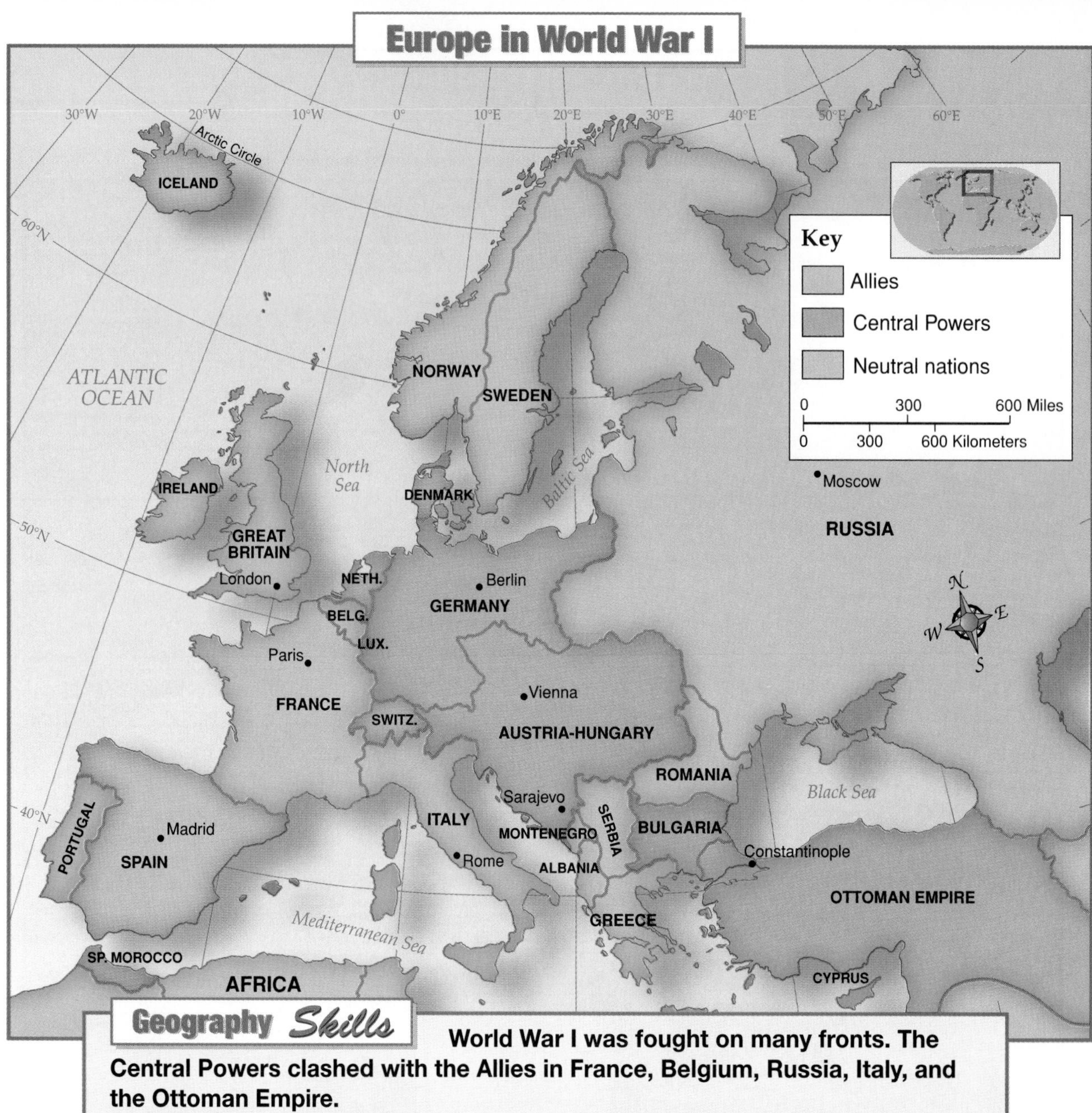

Geography Skills **World War I was fought on many fronts. The Central Powers clashed with the Allies in France, Belgium, Russia, Italy, and the Ottoman Empire.**

1. **Location** On the map, locate: **(a)** Sarajevo, **(b)** Serbia, **(c)** Austria-Hungary, **(d)** Germany, **(e)** Russia, **(f)** France, **(g)** Great Britain.
2. **Movement** Through which country did German troops march on their way to France?
3. **Critical Thinking** Judging from the map, why was the alliance between France and Russia a threat to Germany?

the Central Powers. This trade imbalance meant that the United States was not strictly neutral.

Both sides waged a propaganda war in the United States. **Propaganda** is the spreading of ideas that help a cause or hurt an opposing cause. Each side pictured the other as savage beasts who killed innocent civilians. Anti-German propaganda often referred to the Germans as "Huns," the name of a tribe of ancient barbarians.

Submarine warfare

In the end, it was not propaganda that brought the United States into the war against Germany. Rather, anti-German feeling hardened when Germany interfered with what Americans saw as their freedom of the seas.

As a neutral nation, the United States claimed the right to trade with either side in the conflict. Early in the war, however, Britain blockaded German ports, hoping to starve Germany into surrender. In response, Germany set up a blockade around Britain. To enforce the blockade, Germany used a powerful new weapon—a fleet of submarines known as **U-boats.** German U-boats attacked any ship that entered or left British ports.

U-boat attacks on neutral shipping raised a storm of protest. Under international law, a country at war could stop and search a neutral ship suspected of carrying war goods. But German submarines were not equipped to conduct a search. After surfacing, they simply torpedoed enemy and neutral ships, often killing scores of civilians.

Germany warned the United States and other neutral nations to keep their ships out of the blockade zone. President Wilson rejected this limit on neutral shipping. He vowed to hold Germany responsible if its U-boats caused any loss of American life or property.

"All the News That's Fit to Print."

The New York Times. EXTRA 5:30 A.M.

LUSITANIA SUNK BY A SUBMARINE, PROBABLY 1,260 DEAD; TWICE TORPEDOED OFF IRISH COAST; SINKS IN 15 MINUTES; CAPT. TURNER SAVED, FROHMAN AND VANDERBILT MISSING; WASHINGTON BELIEVES THAT A GRAVE CRISIS IS AT HAND

The New York Times headline of May 8, 1915

Sinking of the *Lusitania*

Germany ignored Wilson's threat. On May 7, 1915, a German submarine torpedoed the ***Lusitania,*** a British passenger ship, off the coast of Ireland. Nearly 1,200 people died, including 128 Americans.

An outraged Wilson called the sinking of the *Lusitania* "murder on the high seas." He threatened to break off diplomatic relations if Germany did not stop sinking passenger ships. Germany was not ready to risk war with the United States. It agreed to stop attacking neutral ships without warning.

★ Section 1 Review ★

Recall

1. **Locate** **(a)** France, **(b)** Germany, **(c)** Austria-Hungary, **(d)** Russia, **(e)** Britain, **(f)** Italy, **(g)** Serbia.
2. **Identify** **(a)** Triple Alliance, **(b)** Triple Entente, **(c)** Franz Ferdinand, **(d)** World War I, **(e)** Central Powers, **(f)** Allied Powers, **(g)** *Lusitania.*
3. **Define** **(a)** nationalism, **(b)** militarism, **(c)** mobilize, **(d)** kaiser, **(e)** stalemate, **(f)** trench warfare, **(g)** propaganda, **(h)** U-boat.

Comprehension

4. List three causes for tension in Europe in 1914.
5. What was the immediate cause of World War I?
6. **(a)** How did war in Europe affect the American economy? **(b)** Why did anti-German feeling grow in the United States?

Critical Thinking and Writing

7. **Analyzing Ideas** How did the alliance system help bring about war?
8. **Predicting Consequences** Based on what you have read in Section 1, do you think that the United States stayed out of World War I? Explain.

Activity **Writing a Letter** You are a soldier in one of the European armies. Write a letter home describing your feelings about the conflict. Be sure to date your letter. Your feelings in 1914 might be different than your feelings two years later.

The United States Enters the War

As You Read

Explore These Questions

- Why did the United States enter the war in 1917?
- How did the nation organize its war effort?
- How did the government respond to critics of the war?

Define

- warmonger
- czar
- draft
- illiterate
- bureaucracy
- pacifist
- socialist

Identify

- Zimmermann telegram
- Jeannette Rankin
- Selective Service Act
- Herbert Hoover
- Liberty Bonds

SETTING the Scene The outbreak of war in Europe horrified American automaker Henry Ford. In December of 1915, Ford sailed on a mission to Europe. His goal was to bring the warring powers to the peace table. "We're going to have the boys out of the trenches by Christmas," Ford confidently announced.

Christmas passed, yet the war went on. Ford's mission had failed. Still, his efforts for a negotiated peace reflected the American belief that an end to the fighting could be achieved with words instead of guns.

Wilson Tries to Bring Peace

President Wilson, too, tried to bring both sides to peace talks. He believed that the United States, as a neutral, could lead warring nations to a fair peace, a "peace without victory." But Wilson's peace efforts, like Ford's, failed.

Even as he was trying to make peace, Wilson knew that the United States might be drawn into the war. Thus, the President began to lobby for a stronger army and navy.

In 1916, Wilson ran for reelection against Republican Charles Evans Hughes, a Supreme Court Justice. Although Hughes also favored neutrality, Democrats were able to portray him as a **warmonger,** or person who tries to stir up war. At the same time, they boosted Wilson's image with the slogan "He kept us out of war!"

This Wilson campaign button stressed military readiness.

The race was close. On election night, Hughes went to bed believing he had won. Just after midnight, his telephone rang. "The President cannot be disturbed," a friend told the caller. "Well, when he wakes up," the caller replied, "just tell him he isn't President." Late returns from California had given Wilson the election.

Moving Toward War

In January 1917, Wilson issued what proved to be his final plea for peace. It was too late. In a desperate effort to break the Allied blockade, Germany had already decided to renew submarine warfare. Germany warned neutral nations that after February 1, 1917, its U-boats would have orders to sink any ship nearing Britain.

German leaders knew that renewed U-boat attacks would probably bring the United States into the war. They gambled that they would defeat the Allies before American troops could reach Europe. To protest Germany's action, Wilson broke off diplo-

Should the United States Declare War on Germany?

NO	United States in 1917	YES
United States has tradition of neutrality		Americans outraged by German submarine warfare
Some Americans sympathize with Central Powers		Many Americans favor Britain and France
Wilson opposes alliance with Russian czar		Zimmermann telegram angers Americans
Pacifists oppose war		American trade with Allies grows

Graphic Organizer *Skills* **As World War I progressed, the United States found it harder and harder to maintain neutrality.**

1. **Comprehension** **(a)** List two factors that led the United States government to try to remain neutral. **(b)** List two factors that pushed the nation toward war.
2. **Critical Thinking** Review what you have learned about President George Washington's Farewell Address. (See page 252.) What policy do you think Washington would have favored during World War I? Explain.

matic relations with Germany. Even so, the President still hoped to maintain neutrality.

The Zimmermann telegram

A few weeks later, a startling discovery moved the United States closer to war. In February, Wilson learned that Arthur Zimmermann, Germany's foreign secretary, had sent a secret note to the German minister in Mexico. The **Zimmermann telegram** instructed the minister to urge Mexico to attack the United States if the United States declared war on Germany. In return, Germany would help Mexico win back its "lost provinces" in the American Southwest.*

When Americans heard about the Zimmermann telegram, anti-German feeling soared. They were furious that the alliance system that had plunged Europe into war was spreading to the Americas.

The Russian Revolution

Two other events in early 1917 pushed the country still closer to war. First, German submarines sank several American merchant ships. Second, a revolution in Russia drove Czar Nicholas II from power.

For hundreds of years, **czars,** or Russian emperors, had ruled with absolute power. Several times in the 1800s and early 1900s, Russians had revolted against czarist rule. Their efforts all ended in failure.

When the war in Europe began in 1914, Russians united behind the czar. However, as the war brought heavy losses at the front and economic hardship at home, discontent resurfaced. In March 1917, riots protesting the shortage of food turned into a revolution. The czar was forced to step down. Revolutionaries then set up the Provisional Government and called for democratic reforms.

President Wilson welcomed the Russian Revolution. He was a firm believer in democracy, and it was against his principles to be

*The "lost provinces" referred to land that the United States gained as a result of the Mexican War. See Chapter 13.

▲ Sheet music for "Over There"

Biography **George M. Cohan**

A popular singer and dancer, George M. Cohan was also famous for his patriotism. He wrote such songs as "You're a Grand Old Flag" and "I'm a Yankee Doodle Dandy." During World War I, "Over There" boosted soldiers' morale and earned money for the war effort. In appreciation, Congress awarded Cohan a special medal. ★ **Why are patriotic songs important to a nation?**

an ally of an absolute ruler. Without the czar, it would be easier for Wilson to support the Allied cause.

Declaration of war

On April 2, President Wilson went before Congress to ask for a declaration of war. "The world must be made safe for democracy," he declared. His war message assured the American people that entering the war was not only just, it was noble. He concluded:

> ❝ It is a fearful thing to lead this great peaceful people into war, into the most terrible and disastrous of all wars, civilization itself seeming to be in the balance. But the right is more precious than peace, and we shall fight for the thing which we have always carried nearest our hearts—for democracy. ❞

Congress voted for war 455 to 56. Among those who voted against the declaration was **Jeannette Rankin** of Montana, the first woman elected to Congress. She hated war as much as she loved her country. "I want to stand by my country, but I cannot vote for war. I vote no!" she said.

On April 6, the President signed the declaration of war. It thrust Americans into the deadliest war the world had yet seen.

The Nation at War

The day after Congress declared war, George M. Cohan wrote a new song, "Over There." The patriotic tune swept the nation. Its opening lines expressed the confidence that Americans felt :

> ❝ Over there, over there,
> Send the word, send the word, over there,
> That the Yanks are coming... ❞

Its closing message promised, "We'll be over, we're coming over, And we won't come back till it's over over there."

Americans had to do more than sing patriotic tunes, however. They had to prepare to fight—and quickly. The Allies needed everything from food to arms. Britain and France were on the verge of collapse. In Russia, soldiers at the front were deserting to join the revolution.

Building an army

Before it could fight, the United States needed an army. On May 18, Congress passed the **Selective Service Act.** It required all young men from age 21 to 30 to register for the military draft. A **draft** is a law requiring people of a certain age to serve in the military.

In the next 18 months, 4 million men and women joined the armed forces. People from every ethnic group enlisted. About 20,000 Puerto Ricans served in the armed forces, as did many Filipinos. Scores of soldiers were immigrants who had recently arrived in the United States.

Many Native Americans were not citizens, so they could not be drafted. Large numbers of Native Americans enlisted anyway. One family of Winnebago Indians provided 35 volunteers! They served together in the same unit.

At first, the armed forces did not allow African Americans in combat. When the government abandoned this policy, more than 2 million African Americans registered for the draft. Nearly 400,000 were accepted for duty. They were forced into segregated "black-only" units that were commanded mostly by white officers.

Still, African Americans rallied behind the war effort. Blacks like W.E.B. Du Bois voiced strong support for the war's goals:

> "Let us, while the war lasts, forget our special grievances and close ranks ... with our fellow citizens and the allied nations that are fighting for democracy."

In training

While men drilled for combat, women served as radio operators, clerks, and stenographers. At training camps, there were not always enough weapons for everyone. Until supplies increased, some recruits trained using broomsticks for guns.

Despite long hours of drill, soldiers got caught up in the war spirit. A young recruit wrote, "We don't know where we are going, but the band plays 'Over There' every day, and they can't send us any too soon." To many, the war seemed like a great adventure. "Here was our one great chance for excitement and risk," wrote a volunteer. "We could not afford to pass it up."

Educating the recruits

For many recruits, especially African Americans, southerners, and immigrants, the Army offered several firsts. It was their first exposure to military authority and discipline. It was the first time most had ventured outside their farms and villages, let alone outside their country. Some had never taken regular baths or eaten regular meals before. Others had never used indoor plumbing. About 25 percent were **illiterate,** that is, unable to read or write.

The Army became a great educator. It taught millions of young Americans not only how to fight but also how to read, how to eat nutritious meals, and how to care for their daily health needs.

Shocking rates of illiteracy and other low test scores among recruits fueled a drive to reform public education. State and local school boards lengthened the school day and

Building an Army

The Selective Service Act required young men between the ages of 21 and 30 to register for the draft. In this photograph, a blindfolded woman selects the numbers of men to be called for duty. ★ **Do you think a draft is a fair way to raise an army? Explain.**

required students to spend more years in school. They raised teacher training standards. More truancy officers patrolled the streets. By 1920, 75 percent of all school-age children were enrolled in school.

Organizing the War Effort

The United States reorganized its economy to produce food, arms, and other goods needed to fight the war. President Wilson set up government agencies to oversee the effort. A huge bureaucracy (byoo ROK ruh see) emerged to manage the war effort. A **bureaucracy** is a system of managing government through departments run by appointed officials.

"Food will win the war"

Wilson chose **Herbert Hoover** to head the Food Administration. Hoover's job was to boost food production. The nation had to feed its troops and help the Allies.

In keeping with the nation's democratic traditions, Hoover relied on cooperation rather than force. He tried to win support for his programs with publicity campaigns that encouraged Americans to act voluntarily. "Food Will Win the War," proclaimed one Food Administration poster. A magazine urged:

> "Do not permit your child to take a bite or two from an apple and throw the rest away; nowadays even children must be taught to be patriotic to the core."

Encouraged by rising food prices, farmers grew more crops. Families planted "victory gardens." People went without wheat on "wheatless Mondays," and without meat on "meatless Tuesdays." The food they saved helped the men in the trenches.

$ Connections With Economics

President Wilson also did his part for the war effort. He kept a herd of sheep to trim the White House lawn. The sheep replaced gardeners who had been drafted. In addition, Wilson raised $100,000 for the Red Cross by selling the wool of the White House sheep.

Wartime industry

War caught the nation short of supplies. The military had on hand only around 600,000 rifles, 2,000 machine guns, and fewer than 1,000 pieces of artillery. Disorder threatened as the military competed with private industry to buy scarce materials.

To meet this crisis, President Wilson set up a new government agency, the War Industries Board. It told factories what they had to produce. It also divided up limited resources.

Without the support of workers, industry could not mobilize. In 1918, Wilson created the War Labor Board. It settled disputes over working hours and wages and tried to prevent strikes. With workers in short supply, unions were able to win better pay and working conditions. With the President supporting workers, union membership rose sharply.

The Home Front

Americans on the home front united behind the war effort. Movie stars, such as Charlie Chaplin and Mary Pickford, helped sell **Liberty Bonds.** By buying bonds, American citizens were lending money to the government to pay for the war. The sale of Liberty Bonds raised $21 billion, just over half of what the United States spent on the war.

To rally public support for the war, the government sent out 75,000 speakers known as "Four-Minute Men." Their name reminded people of the heroic Minutemen of 1776. It also referred to the four-minute speeches the men gave at public events, movies, and theaters. The speakers urged Americans to make sacrifices for the goals of freedom and democracy.

Women at work

As men joined the armed forces, women stepped into their jobs. Women received better pay in war industries than they had in peacetime. Still, they earned less than the men they replaced.

In factories, women assembled weapons and airplane parts. Some women drove trol-

Viewing History **Women Support the War Effort**

Whether in uniform or on the job, American women rallied behind the war effort. The poster at right urged support for women serving in the military. The shipyard workers above hold the tongs and buckets they used to work with red-hot steel rivets. ★ **How do you think wartime work helped women win the right to vote?**

ley cars and delivered the mail. Others served as police officers. By performing well in jobs once reserved for men, women helped change the view that they were fit only for "women's work." Unfortunately, most of the gains made by women disappeared when the men returned to the work force at the end of the war.

Anti-German feelings

German Americans endured suspicion and intolerance during the war. Newspapers questioned their loyalty. Mobs attacked them on the streets. In 1918, a mob lynched Robert Prager, whose only crime was that he had been born in Germany. A jury later refused to convict the mob leaders.

Anti-German prejudice led some families to change their names. Schools stopped teaching the German language. Concert halls banned works by German composers. Americans began referring to German measles as "liberty measles" and sauerkraut as "liberty cabbage."

Other ethnic tensions

During the war, almost a half million African Americans and thousands of Mexican Americans embarked on a great migration. They left the South and Southwest for cities in the North, hoping to escape poverty and discrimination.

In northern cities, many blacks found better-paying jobs in war industries. At the

Skills FOR LIFE

Critical Thinking | Managing Information | Communication | Maps, Charts, and Graphs

Recognizing Propaganda

How Will I Use This Skill?

Propaganda is an attempt to spread ideas that support a particular cause or hurt an opposing cause. In our everyday lives, propaganda can be found in advertisements, in political posters and speeches, even in movies and television shows. Being aware of propaganda techniques can help us evaluate the messages we receive and make reasoned judgments.

LEARN the Skill

Propaganda often stresses emotional appeals. It may use half-truths, stressing some truths but ignoring others. In extreme cases, propaganda may even use outright lies. Other common propaganda techniques include name-calling and using symbols and words that show the opposition in the worst light. To recognize propaganda, look for these points:

1. Identify factual information, exaggerations, or misinformation.
2. Analyze the type of emotion the propaganda wants the reader to feel. Look for name-calling and the use of emotional symbols and words.
3. Try to determine the source of the propaganda. Identify the action or opinion the propaganda is trying to support or oppose.
4. Judge whether the propaganda is effective.

PRACTICE the Skill

The propaganda poster above appeared after the United States declared war on Germany in 1917. Look at the poster and answer the following questions.

1. Is any factual information about the war included in this poster? Explain.
2. (a) What image of the enemy do the words and picture convey? (b) What emotions is the poster trying to stir?
3. (a) Who do you think produced this poster? (b) What action do they want to encourage?
4. Do you think this poster was effective propaganda at the time? Why or why not?

APPLY the Skill

Advertisements, like propaganda, use emotions and facts to persuade us to perform certain actions. Choose an advertisement from a newspaper or magazine. Using the steps given above, analyze the advertisement as propaganda.

same time, they ran into prejudice and even violence. Competition for housing and jobs sometimes led to race riots. In 1917, 39 African Americans were killed during a riot in East St. Louis, Illinois. A New York parade protested the deaths. Marchers carried signs demanding, "Mr. President, Why Not Make AMERICA Safe for Democracy?"

In the Southwest, ranchers pressed the government to let more Mexicans cross the border. Almost 100,000 Mexicans entered the United States to work on farms, mostly in California and Texas. By 1920, Mexicans were the leading foreign-born group in California. Some Mexicans moved on to northern cities, where they worked in factories.

Throughout the war, Mexicans worked in cotton and beet fields, in copper mines, and in steel mills. All these jobs were important to the war effort. Yet after the war, when veterans returned and unemployment grew, the United States tried to force Mexican workers to return to Mexico.

Silencing protest

Some Americans opposed the war. Among them were Progressives such as Jane Addams. Many of these critics were **pacifists,** people who refuse to fight in any war because they believe war is evil.

Antiwar feeling also ran high among socialists and radical labor groups. A **socialist** believes that the people as a whole rather than private individuals should own all property and share the profits from all businesses. Socialists argued that the war benefited factory owners but not workers.

To encourage unity, Congress passed laws making it a crime to criticize the government or to interfere with the war. Nearly 1,600 men and women were arrested for breaking these laws. Eugene V. Debs, Socialist candidate for President five times, was jailed for protesting the draft. The government also jailed "Big Bill" Haywood, head of the Industrial Workers of the World (IWW), a radical union. Using special powers granted under the wartime laws, government authorities ransacked the IWW's offices.

A few people questioned these laws. They argued that silencing critics violated the Constitution's guarantee of freedom of speech. Most Americans, however, felt that the laws were necessary in wartime.

★ Section 2 Review ★

Recall

1. **Identify** **(a)** Zimmermann telegram, **(b)** Jeannette Rankin, **(c)** Selective Service Act, **(d)** Herbert Hoover, **(e)** Liberty Bonds.
2. **Define** **(a)** warmonger, **(b)** czar, **(c)** draft, **(d)** illiterate, **(e)** bureaucracy, **(f)** pacifist, **(g)** socialist.

Comprehension

3. Identify three events that moved the United States toward war.
4. **(a)** List three government agencies that were set up to organize the war effort. **(b)** What did each agency do?
5. What steps did the government take to silence critics of the war?

Critical Thinking and Writing

6. **Synthesizing Information** Review the account of the East St. Louis race riot on page 655. Why did the marchers carry signs demanding: "Mr. President, Why Not Make AMERICA Safe for Democracy?"
7. **Defending a Position** Do you think that the government should have the right to silence critics during wartime? Defend your position.

★ ★

Activity **Preparing a Speech** You have only four minutes. *GO!* As one of Wilson's "Four-Minute Men," you must give a speech urging Americans to make sacrifices for the war effort. Be sure to think about what kind of arguments would most appeal to your listeners.

Winning the War

As You Read

Explore These Questions

- Why did the Allies face hard times in 1917?
- How did Americans help defeat Germany?
- What were the human costs of the war?

Define

- armistice
- abdicate
- epidemic

Identify

- Bolsheviks
- V. I. Lenin
- Treaty of Brest-Litovsk
- John J. Pershing
- Harlem Hell Fighters
- Battle of Belleau Wood
- Ferdinand Foch
- Alvin York
- Battle of the Argonne Forest

Soon after war was declared, an official at the War Department asked the Senate for $3 billion for arms and other supplies. "And we may have to have an army in France," he added. "Good grief!" sputtered one senator. "You're not going to send soldiers over there, are you?"

American soldiers carried shaving kits like this one to the trenches in France.

The United States would send more than 2 million soldiers to France. The buildup took time. First, troops had to be trained and armed. By March 1918, fewer than 300,000 American troops had reached France. Then they poured in. Fresh and eager to fight, they gave the Allies a much-needed boost.

Hard Times for the Allies

The first American troops reached France in June 1917. They quickly saw the desperate situation of the Allies. The Allies had lost millions of soldiers. Troops in the trenches were exhausted and ill. Many civilians in Britain and France were near starvation.

Russia withdraws from the war

To make matters worse, Russia withdrew from the war. In November 1917, a group known as the **Bolsheviks** seized power from the Provisional Government. Under the leadership of **V. I. Lenin,** the Bolsheviks wanted to bring a communist revolution to Russia.

Lenin embraced the ideas of Karl Marx, a German thinker of the 1800s. Marx had predicted that workers around the world would unite to overthrow the ruling class. After the workers revolted, they would end private property and set up a classless society. Lenin was determined to lead such a revolution in Russia.

Once in power, Lenin opened talks with Germany. He had opposed the war, arguing that it benefited only the ruling class. In March 1918, Russia and Germany signed the **Treaty of Brest-Litovsk.** Although Russia had to give up land to Germany, Lenin welcomed peace. With war ended, he could focus on the communist revolution.

The Allies saw the treaty as a betrayal. It gave Germany coal mines and other resources in Russia. More important, with Russia out of the way, Germany could move its armies away from the Russian front and into France. In early 1918, Germany used these troops in an all-out attack on the Allies.

A new German offensive

By March 21, German forces had massed near the French town of Amiens. (See the map at right.) The Germans called this move a "peace offensive." They hoped that a final push would end the war.

Dozens of German divisions massed up against a small British force. Late at night, 6,000 German cannons began pounding the British troops camped at Amiens. Despite the heavy fire, the British held on. The battle lasted for two weeks. At last, on April 4, the Germans gave up their attack.

The Germans continued their offensive elsewhere. By late May, they had smashed through Allied lines along the Aisne (EHN) River. On May 30, they reached the Marne River, just east of Château-Thierry (sha TOH tee ER ee). Paris lay only 50 miles (80 km) away. At this point, American troops entered the war in force.

Americans in France

By June 1918, American troops were reaching France in record numbers. Commanding the American Expeditionary Force (AEF) was General **John J. Pershing.** Pershing was already well known at home for leading American troops into Mexico in 1916 to hunt for Mexican rebel leader Francisco "Pancho" Villa. (See page 637.)

Allied generals wanted the fresh troops to reinforce their own war-weary soldiers. Pershing refused. He insisted that American troops operate as separate units. The United States wanted to have an independent role in shaping the peace. Only by playing "a definite and distinct part" in the war would it win power at the peace table.

In the end, Pershing agreed to let some Americans fight with the British and French. At the same time, he set up an American operation to fight on its own.

Harlem Hell Fighters

Among the first American units attached to the French Army was the 369th United States Infantry. This African American unit became known as the **Harlem Hell Fighters.** Although the United States allowed few African Americans to train for combat, the French respected the bravery of African American soldiers and were glad to fight side by side with them.

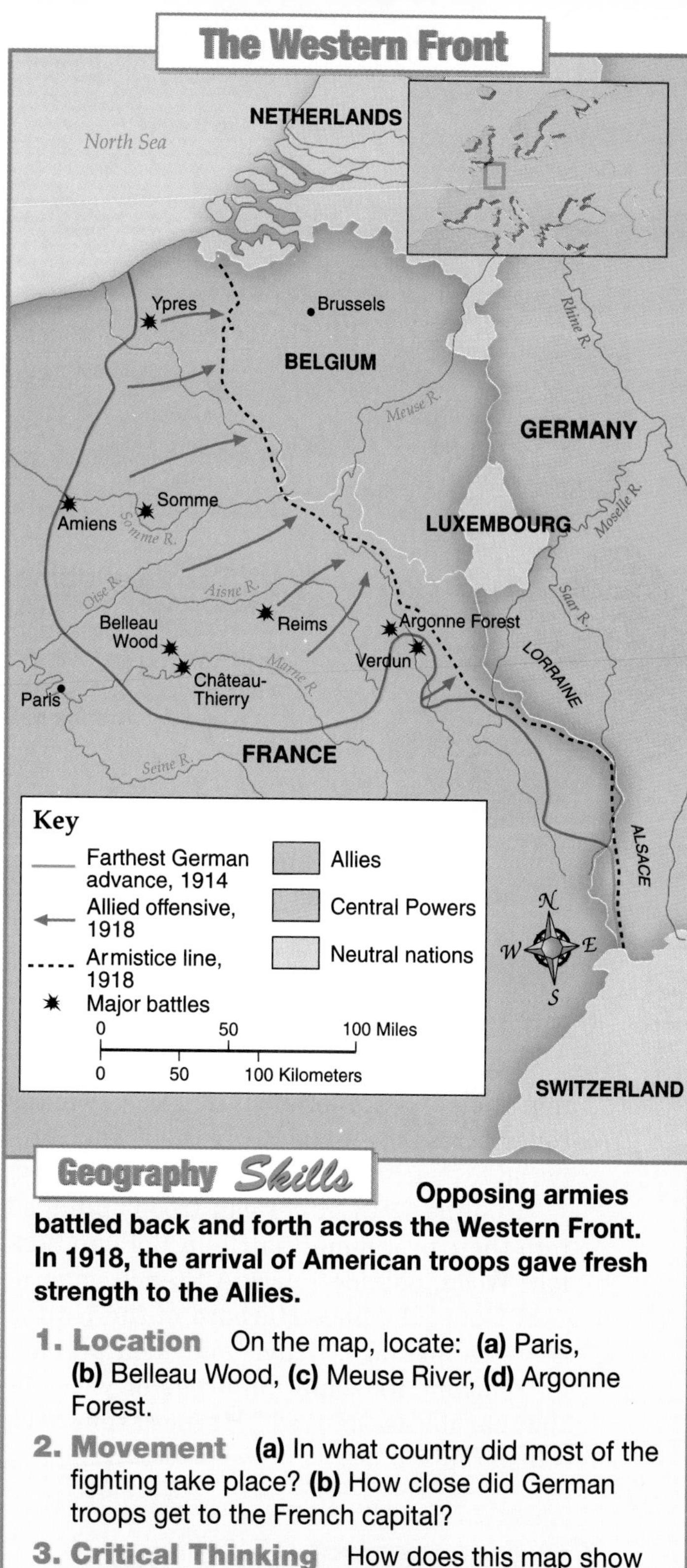

Geography Skills **Opposing armies battled back and forth across the Western Front. In 1918, the arrival of American troops gave fresh strength to the Allies.**

1. **Location** On the map, locate: **(a)** Paris, **(b)** Belleau Wood, **(c)** Meuse River, **(d)** Argonne Forest.
2. **Movement** **(a)** In what country did most of the fighting take place? **(b)** How close did German troops get to the French capital?
3. **Critical Thinking** How does this map show the effect of the arrival of American troops in 1918?

In the end, the Harlem Hell Fighters spent more time under fire than any other American unit. For their bravery, the French awarded them the Croix de Guerre, or Cross

Viewing History **Victims of Poison Gas**

Gassed, by John Singer Sargent, shows troops disabled by poison gas in 1918. Gas was one of the most feared weapons of World War I. Various gases caused choking, blindness, or severe skin blisters.
★ **Why do you think nations later agreed to ban the use of poison gas?**

◄ *World War I gas mask*

of War, and numerous other decorations. After the war, New Yorkers greeted them with a huge parade.

Belleau Wood

Meanwhile, the Germans were continuing their "peace offensive." As Germans rolled across the Aisne River, the French prepared to evacuate Paris.

In June 1918, American troops plunged into their first major battle in Belleau (BEH loh) Wood, outside Paris. A French general sent General James Harbord of the United States a message: "Have your men prepare entrenchments some hundreds of yards to the rear in case of need." Harbord sent back a firm reply:

John Singer Sargent, who painted *Gassed* (above), was one of the leading American artists of his time. Sargent gained fame for his portraits of elegant society women. Wealthy American and European women flocked to his Paris studio. Sargent was over 60 years old when he volunteered to serve as a war artist.

> "We dig no trenches to fall back on. The marines will hold where they stand."

The **Battle of Belleau Wood** raged for three weeks. At last, on June 25, General Harbord passed along the good news: "Wood now exclusively U.S. Marine Corps."

Final Battles

In mid-July, the Germans launched another drive to take Paris. They pushed the Allies back until they came up against American troops. Within three days, the Allies had forced the Germans to retreat.

The Allies now took the offensive. French Marshal **Ferdinand Foch** (FOHSH), commander of the Allied forces, ordered attacks along a line from Verdun to the North Sea. American forces stormed the area between the Meuse (MYOOZ) River and the Argonne Forest. (See the map on page 657.)

Into the Argonne Forest

On September 26, 1918, more than one million American soldiers pushed into the Argonne Forest. Years of fierce fighting had left the land scarred with trenches and shell

Why Study History?

Because We Honor Our Veterans

Historical Background

In 1919, on the first anniversary of the end of World War I, President Wilson proclaimed a new holiday. November 11 would be celebrated as Armistice Day. In 1954, the holiday was renamed Veterans Day—the day we honor all men and women who have served in the nation's armed forces.

To honor the dead of World War I, the United States also dedicated the Tomb of the Unknown Soldier. In 1921, the body of an unidentified American soldier was brought from an unmarked grave in France to a military cemetery in Arlington, Virginia. Above his grave, a marble monument bears the inscription: "Here rests in honored glory an American soldier known but to God." Since then, unknown soldiers from three later wars have joined him.

VFW members salute as a Veterans Day parade passes.

Connections to Today

Today, the government and private organizations continue to honor and serve veterans. The Department for Veterans Affairs oversees veterans' pensions and benefits and runs veterans' hospitals. The Veterans of Foreign Wars (VFW), a nonprofit organization, offers support to veterans, as well as sponsoring community projects.

Each year, tourists visit the Tomb of the Unknown Soldier, the Vietnam War Memorial, and other monuments. Many families fly the flag on Veterans Day and Memorial Day.

Connections to You

How can you honor veterans? You might attend a parade or put flowers on a war memorial. Your local VFW post can supply a list of monuments in your area. You can enter the VFW's annual essay contest for seventh, eighth, and ninth graders. As you get older, you may do volunteer work in a veterans' hospital.

Mostly, you can honor veterans by remembering the past. As the Secretary of the Army said on Veterans Day 1996:

> "American veterans all . . . your nation and your Army honor you for your sacrifice and continuing selfless service."

1. **Comprehension** List three ways that Americans honor veterans.
2. **Critical Thinking** Why do you think groups like the VFW urge young people to learn more about American history?

Creating a Memory Book With your classmates, interview veterans in your community. Some students can write questions, while others set up the interviews. Write up your interviews and compile them in an illustrated binder. Ask your school or library to display your memory book on Veterans Day.

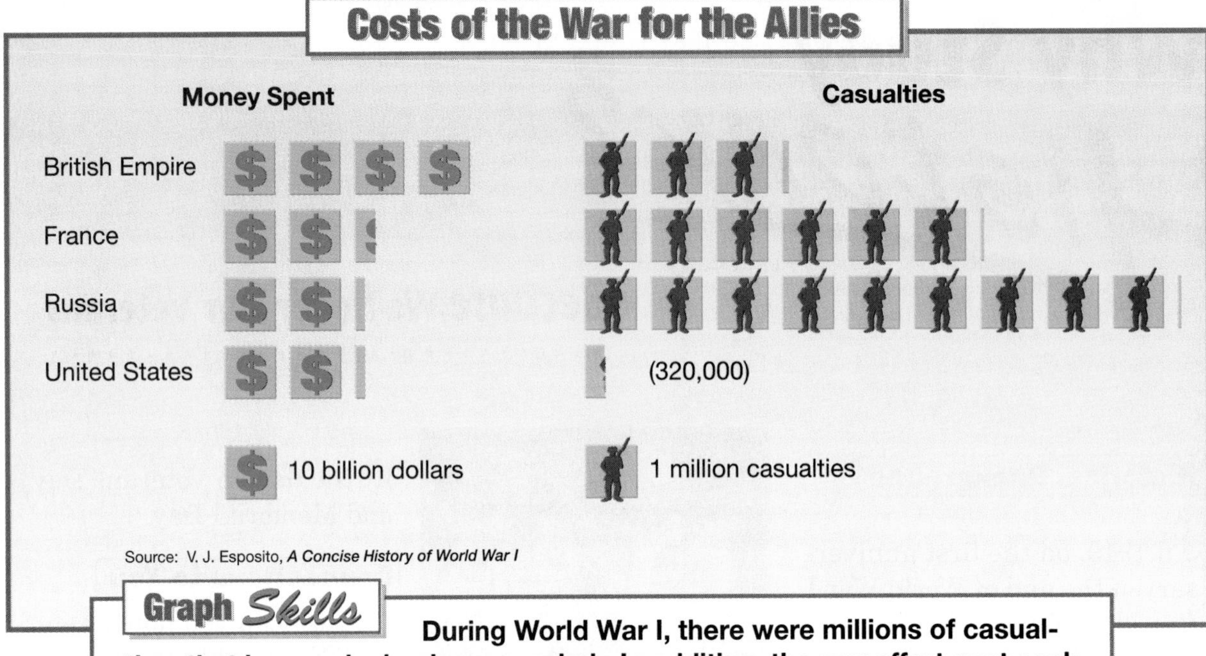

Graph *Skills* **During World War I, there were millions of casualties, that is, people dead or wounded. In addition, the war effort cost each side billions of dollars.**

1. **Comprehension** **(a)** Which Allied nation had the greatest number of casualties in World War I? **(b)** How much money did the United States spend on the war effort?
2. **Critical Thinking** **(a)** Which nation shown here had the fewest casualties? **(b)** Why was this so?

holes. The air still smelled of poison gas from earlier battles.

At first, the Americans advanced despite heavy German fire. Then, rains and the thick woods slowed their movement. Small units drove forward to capture deadly German positions. Armed with a single rifle, Sergeant **Alvin York** of Tennessee wiped out a nest of German machine gunners. His bravery helped clear the way for advancing American troops. York became the most decorated American soldier of the war.

Finally, after 47 days, the Americans broke through the German defense. They had won the **Battle of the Argonne Forest.** The cost was high on both sides. Americans and Germans each suffered more than 100,000 casualties in the battle.

British, French, and Belgian forces also smashed through the German lines in their areas. By November, German forces were in retreat. After more than four years of fighting, the Great War was finally nearing its end.

The war ends

In September, German generals told the kaiser that the war could not be won. On October 4, Prince Max of Baden, head of the German cabinet, secretly cabled President Wilson:

> “To avoid further bloodshed, the German government requests the President to arrange the immediate conclusion of an armistice on land, by sea, and in the air.”

An **armistice** is an agreement to stop fighting. Wilson set two conditions for an armistice. First, Germany must accept his plan for peace. Second, the German emperor must **abdicate,** that is, give up power.

While German leaders debated a response, rebellion simmered in the ranks. Daily, the German army lost ground. Morale plunged among the troops. German sailors mutinied. Several German cities threatened to revolt.

On November 9, the German emperor was forced to resign. He and his son fled to Holland, and Germany became a republic. The new German leaders agreed to the armistice terms. At 11 A.M. on November 11, 1918—the eleventh hour of the eleventh day of the eleventh month—World War I ended at last.

The costs of war

The costs of the war were staggering. A generation of young Europeans lost their lives. Between 8 million and 9 million people died in battle. Germany, alone, lost close to 2 million men. Almost 4 million Russian, French, and British soldiers were killed. The United States lost over 50,000 men. Many more died of diseases. More than 20 million soldiers on both sides were wounded.

Much of northern France lay in ruins. Millions of Germans were near starvation. In France and other nations, many children were left orphaned and homeless.

In 1918, a new disaster struck. A terrible influenza epidemic spread around the world. An **epidemic** is the rapid spread of a contagious disease among large numbers of people. Between 1918 and 1919, more than half a million Americans died in the flu epidemic. The death toll in other countries was even higher. All told, the epidemic killed more than 20 million people—twice as many as the war itself!

A wounded veteran and his family

★ Section 3 Review ★

Recall

1. **Locate** **(a)** Amiens, **(b)** Marne River, **(c)** Château Thierry, **(d)** Belleau Wood, **(e)** Argonne Forest.
2. **Identify** **(a)** Bolsheviks, **(b)** V. I. Lenin, **(c)** Treaty of Brest-Litovsk, **(d)** John J. Pershing, **(e)** Harlem Hell Fighters, **(f)** Battle of Belleau Wood, **(g)** Ferdinand Foch, **(h)** Alvin York, **(i)** Battle of the Argonne Forest.
3. **Define** **(a)** armistice, **(b)** abdicate, **(c)** epidemic.

Comprehension

4. Describe the situation of the Allies when the Americans arrived in June 1917.
5. What role did the Americans play in ending the war?
6. What conditions did Europeans face at the end of the war?

Critical Thinking and Writing

7. **Making Inferences** Why do you think General Pershing wanted American troops to fight as independent units rather than alongside the British and French?
8. **Analyzing Visual Evidence** Study the paintings on pages 641 and 658. **(a)** Describe what each painting shows. **(b)** How is the mood of the first picture different from that of the second picture?

Activity **Planning a Celebration** It is November 11, 1918. The armistice has just been signed. You have been asked to plan a community celebration in honor of the event. Prepare a schedule for the celebration, including at least four meaningful events.

Wilson and the Peace

As You Read

Explore These Questions

- What was Wilson's plan for peace?
- How did Wilson's goals for peace differ from those of the other Allies?
- Why did the Senate reject the Versailles Treaty?

Define

- self-determination
- reparation
- isolationist

Identify

- Fourteen Points
- League of Nations
- Big Four
- Treaty of Versailles
- Henry Cabot Lodge

Huge crowds cheered Woodrow Wilson when he arrived in France in December 1918. Some people cried with joy to see the American leader. After years of suffering, Europeans saw Wilson as a symbol of hope. He was the man who had promised to make the world "safe for democracy."

Wilson went to France determined to achieve a just and lasting peace. He believed that most Europeans shared his views. He soon learned, however, that his goals were often at odds with those of the other Allies.

Wilson's Peace Plan

In Europe, Wilson visited Paris, London, Milan, and Rome. Everywhere, cheering crowds welcomed him. To Wilson, this was a sign that Europeans supported his goal of "peace without victory." In fact, he was wrong. The people who greeted Wilson so warmly scoffed at his high-minded proposals. They and their leaders were determined to punish the Germans for the war.

In January 1918, even before the war ended, Wilson outlined his peace plan. Known as the **Fourteen Points,** it was meant to prevent international problems from causing another war.

President Woodrow Wilson

The first point in Wilson's plan called for an end to secret agreements. Secrecy, Wilson felt, had created the rival alliances that had helped lead to war. Next, he called for freedom of the seas, free trade, and a limit on arms. He urged peaceful settlement of disputes over colonies. He also supported the principle of national **self-determination,** that is, the right of national groups to their own territory and forms of government.

For Wilson, however, the fourteenth point was the most important. It called for a "general association of nations," or **League of Nations.** Its job would be to protect the independence of all countries—large or small. The goal was simple, he noted:

> "...justice to all peoples and nationalities, and their right to live on equal terms of liberty and safety with one another, whether weak or strong."

Wilson persuaded the Allies to accept the Fourteen Points as the basis for making peace. However, the plan soon ran into trouble. Some goals were too vague. Others conflicted with reality. In Paris,

Wilson faced a constant battle to save his Fourteen Points. He discovered that the Allies were more concerned with protecting their own interests.

The Peace Treaty

Diplomats from more than 30 nations met in Paris and Versailles (vuhr SI), hoping to make a lasting peace. Key issues were decided by the **Big Four**—Woodrow Wilson of the United States, David Lloyd George of Britain, Georges Clemenceau (kleh mahn SOH) of France, and Vittorio Orlando of Italy.

Conflicting goals

Each leader had his own aims. Wilson had called for "peace without victory." He opposed punishing the defeated powers.

The other Allies, however, ached for revenge. Germany must pay, they said. They insisted on large **reparations,** or cash payments, for the losses they had suffered during the war. Further, they wanted Germany to accept responsibility for the war.

The Allies were also determined to prevent Germany from rebuilding its military strength. In particular, Clemenceau wanted to weaken Germany so that it could never again threaten France. During the months of haggling, Wilson had to compromise on his Fourteen Points in order to save his key goals, especially the League of Nations.

Viewing History: Wilson at the Peace Conference

British artist William Orpen painted this scene at the 1919 Paris peace conference. The Big Four, including Woodrow Wilson, are seated center. Facing them, two German representatives read the treaty.
★ **How do you think the Germans responded to the Treaty of Versailles?**

The final treaty

By June 1919, the **Treaty of Versailles** was ready. None of the Allies was satisfied with it. Germany, which had not even been allowed to send delegates to the peace talks, was horrified by the terms of the treaty. Still, it had no choice but to sign.

Under the treaty, Germany had to take full blame for the war. It had to pay the Allies huge reparations, including the cost of pensions for Allied soldiers or their widows and children. The total cost of German reparations would come to over $300 billion.

Other provisions of the Treaty of Versailles were aimed at weakening Germany. The treaty severely limited the size of the German military. It returned Alsace-Lorraine to France. In addition, the treaty stripped Germany of its overseas colonies. However, instead of gaining independence, the colonies were put under the control of Britain or France.

Wilson's successes

Wilson had his way on a few issues, however. In Eastern Europe, the Allies provided for several new nations to be formed on the principle of national self-determination. They included Poland, Czechoslovakia, and Yugoslavia. They were created out of lands once ruled by Germany, Russia, and Austria-Hungary. (See the map on page 664.)

Still, some people were dissatisfied with the new boundaries. Many Germans, for example, had settled in Poland and Czechoslovakia. Before long, Germany would seek to

Geography *Skills* **A series of treaties ended World War I. The treaties created several new nations in Eastern Europe.**

1. **Location** On the map, locate: **(a)** Poland, **(b)** Czechoslovakia, **(c)** Yugoslavia.
2. **Region** **(a)** In what region of Europe were most of the new nations created? **(b)** Which new nations bordered Russia?
3. **Critical Thinking** Compare this map to the map on page 646. **(a)** What happened to Austria-Hungary? **(b)** What happened to Serbia? **(c)** What happened to the city of Sarajevo?

regain control of German-speaking peoples in Eastern Europe.

To Wilson, however, his greatest achievement was persuading the Allies to include the League of Nations in the treaty. Wilson was certain that the League would prevent future wars by allowing nations to talk over their problems. If talk failed, members would join together to fight aggressors. "A living thing is born," he declared. The League "is definitely a guarantee of peace."

Battle Over the Treaty

When President Wilson returned home, he faced a new battle. He had to persuade the Senate to approve the Versailles Treaty.

Opposition to the League

Most Americans favored the treaty. A vocal minority opposed it, however. Some said that it was too soft on the defeated powers. Many German Americans felt that it was too harsh. Some Republicans hoped to embarrass

President Wilson, a Democrat, by rewriting or defeating the treaty. **Isolationists,** people who wanted the United States to stay out of world affairs, opposed the League of Nations.

Critics of the treaty found a leader in **Henry Cabot Lodge** of Massachusetts. Lodge, a Republican, was chairman of the powerful Senate Foreign Relations Committee. Lodge accepted the idea of the League of Nations. However, he wanted changes in some provisions relating to the League.

Specifically, Lodge objected to Article 10 of the treaty. It called for the League to protect any member whose independence or territory was threatened. Lodge argued that Article 10 could involve the United States in future European wars. He wanted changes in the treaty that would ensure that the United States remained independent of the League. He also wanted Congress to have the power to decide whether the United States would follow League policy.

Wilson believed that Lodge's changes would weaken the League. Advisers urged the President to compromise, giving up some of his demands in order to save the League. Wilson replied, "Let Lodge compromise." He refused to make any changes.

A defeat for Wilson

As the battle grew hotter, the President took his case to the people. In early September 1919, Wilson set out across the country, making 37 speeches in 29 cities. He urged Americans to let their senators know that they supported the treaty.

Wilson kept up a killing pace. On September 25, the exhausted President complained of a headache. His doctors canceled the rest of the trip. Wilson returned to Washington. A week later, his wife found him unconscious. He had suffered a stroke that left him bedridden for weeks.

In November 1919, the Senate rejected the Versailles Treaty. "It is dead," Wilson mourned, "[and] every morning I put flowers on its grave." Gone, too, was Wilson's cherished goal—American membership in the League of Nations.

The United States did not sign a peace treaty with Germany until 1921. Many nations had already joined the League of Nations. Without the United States, though, the League failed to live up to its goals of protecting members against aggression. Wilson's dream of a world "safe for democracy" would have to wait.

★ Section 4 Review ★

Recall

1. **Identify** **(a)** Fourteen Points, **(b)** League of Nations, **(c)** Big Four, **(d)** Treaty of Versailles, **(e)** Henry Cabot Lodge.
2. **Define** **(a)** self-determination, **(b)** reparation, **(c)** isolationist.

Comprehension

3. **(a)** Describe the major points of Wilson's peace plan. **(b)** Which point did Wilson consider most important? Why?
4. Why did Wilson's peace plan run into trouble at Versailles?
5. **(a)** What changes did critics want to make in the peace treaty? **(b)** How did the President respond to their demands?

Critical Thinking and Writing

6. **Predicting Consequences** **(a)** List three ways that the Treaty of Versailles punished Germany. **(b)** What do you think the effects of this harsh treatment might be?
7. **Defending a Position** Many historians blame Wilson for the defeat of the Versailles Treaty in Congress. What reasons can you give to support this position?

Activity **Drawing a Political Cartoon** Draw a political cartoon expressing your feelings about the conflict over the League of Nations. If possible, include figures representing Henry Cabot Lodge and Woodrow Wilson.

Chapter 24 Review and Activities

★ Sum It Up ★

Section 1 War Erupts in Europe

- Nationalism, imperialism, and militarism increased tensions in Europe in the early years of the 1900s.
- After Austria-Hungary declared war on Serbia in 1914, the alliance system drew other nations into the conflict.
- While the United States remained neutral, German submarine warfare outraged Americans.

Section 2 The United States Enters the War

- After declaring war on Germany in 1917, the United States set up a military draft.
- A huge government bureaucracy built support for the war effort.
- The government silenced protests against the war by arresting people who criticized the government.

Section 3 Winning the War

- In the final battles of the war, American troops helped defeat German forces at Belleau Wood and the Argonne Forest.
- World War I was a costly war, with some 30 million people killed or wounded.

Section 4 Wilson and the Peace

- Wilson's plan for peace included a call for a League of Nations to settle disputes between nations.
- The Senate rejected the peace treaty because critics believed that the League of Nations might draw the United States into future wars.

For additional review of the major ideas of Chapter 24, see ***Guide to the Essentials of American History*** or ***Interactive Student Tutorial CD-ROM,*** which contains interactive review activities, graphic organizers, and practice tests.

Reviewing the Chapter

Define These Terms

Match each term with the correct definition.

Column 1

1. nationalism
2. militarism
3. bureaucracy
4. armistice
5. self-determination

Column 2

a. system of managing government though departments
b. pride in one's country
c. right of a national group to its own territory and own form of government
d. policy of building up armed forces to prepare for war
e. agreement to stop fighting

Explore the Main Ideas

1. How did the alliance system help lead to World War I?
2. **(a)** What nations formed the Central Powers? **(b)** What nations formed the Allied powers?
3. How did the Russian Revolution affect the war?
4. **(a)** Describe the German "peace offensive" of 1918. **(b)** What were the results?
5. How did Britain and France feel about Germany during the Paris peace conference?

Geography Activity

Match the letters on the map with the following places: **1.** Allied Powers, **2.** Central Powers, **3.** Sarajevo, **4.** Great Britain, **5.** France, **6.** Russia, **7.** Germany, **8.** Austria-Hungary. **Movement** Why did European nations seek colonies in Asia and Africa?

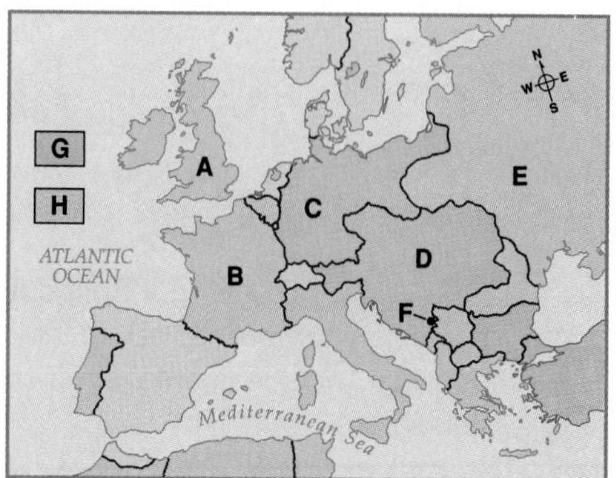

Critical Thinking and Writing

1. **Understanding Chronology (a)** List the following events in chronological order: Zimmermann telegram is discovered; U-boats sink the *Lusitania;* Archduke Franz Ferdinand is assassinated; United States declares war on Germany; armistice is signed. **(b)** Describe the relationship between any two events on the list.
2. **Linking Past and Present** During World War I, inventions such as submarines and machine guns changed the nature of the fighting. List two kinds of technology that are important in warfare today.
3. **Analyzing Ideas** Why do you think Americans accepted government controls on the economy during World War I?
4. Exploring Unit Themes **Global Interaction** Based on what you have learned, make two generalizations about American isolationism and global interaction before, during, and after World War I.

Using Primary Sources

President Wilson toured the nation in 1919, hoping to gain support for the Versailles Treaty. In one speech, he talked about how the sight of American soldiers impressed him:

> “I saw many fine sights in Paris, many gallant sights, many sights that quickened the pulse; but my pulse never beat so fast as when I saw groups of our boys [marching] along the street. They looked as if they owned something, and they did. They owned the finest thing in the world. . . . They owned the ideals . . . that will govern the world.”

Source: “The Destiny of America,” Woodrow Wilson, *Senate Document 120,* 1919–1920.

Recognizing Points of View (a) Why was Wilson thrilled to see American soldiers in Paris? **(b)** What did Wilson mean by his statement that American ideals would “govern the world”? **(c)** Do you think Georges Clemenceau would have agreed with Wilson’s statement?

Activity Bank

Interdisciplinary Activity

Exploring the Arts Learn the song “Over There” by George M. Cohan. Write an additional stanza for the song or write a new song of your own. Perform the song for the class.

Career Skills Activity

Economists Find out more about the effects that the war had on the nation’s economy. Then make a concept map showing these effects.

Citizenship Activity

Organizing a Debate Organize a classroom debate about freedom of speech during wartime. One team of students will argue that the government should be allowed to silence protests during wartime. The other team will argue that the government does not have the right to silence protests. Assign one student to act as moderator. After the debate, write a paragraph explaining your position.

Internet Activity

Use the Internet to find sites dealing with the causes of World War I. Then, use the results of your research to write a short essay on whether you think the war could have been avoided.

You are one of the following: an American isolationist in 1914; a Mexican immigrant working in America for the war effort; a German American; a woman working in a factory; an American soldier in Europe; President Wilson. In your EYEWITNESS JOURNAL, describe the events of the war years that had the greatest impact on you.

Picture Bride

Yoshiko Uchida

Introduction

In the early 1900s, many Japanese women who came to the United States were "picture brides." The marriages were arranged by relatives, with the bride and bridegroom seeing each other only through pictures. Yoshiko Uchida tells the story of one of these immigrants in her novel *Picture Bride.* Here, young Hana Omiya looks back on her decision to go to the United States.

Vocabulary

Before you read the selection, find the meaning of these words in a dictionary: **samurai, conscientious, affluence, latitude, tuberculosis.**

It was she who had first planted in her uncle's mind the thought that she would make a good wife for Taro Takeda, the lonely man who had gone to America to make his fortune in Oakland, California.

It all began one day when her uncle had come to visit her mother.

"I must find a nice young bride," he had said, startling Hana with this blunt talk of marriage in her presence. She blushed and was ready to leave the room when her uncle quickly added, "My good friend Takeda has a son in America. I must find someone willing to travel to that far land."

This last remark was intended to indicate to Hana and her mother that he didn't consider this a suitable prospect for Hana who was the youngest daughter of what once had been a fine family. Her father, until his death fifteen years ago, had been the largest landholder of the village and one its last *samurai.* They had once had many servants and field hands, but now all that was changed. Their money was gone. . . .

Her uncle spoke freely of Taro Takeda only because he was so sure Hana would never consider him. "He is a conscientious, hardworking man who has been in the United States for almost ten years. He is thirty-one, operates a small shop and rents some rooms above the shop where he lives." Her uncle rubbed his chin thoughtfully. "He could provide well for a wife," he added.

"Ah," Hana's mother said softly.

"You say he is successful in this business?" Hana's sister inquired.

"His father tells me he sells many things in his shop—clothing, stockings, needles, thread and buttons—such things as that. He also sells bean paste, pickled radish, bean cake and soy sauce. A wife of his would not go cold or hungry."

They all nodded, each of them picturing this merchant in varying degrees of success and affluence. There were many Japanese emigrating to America these days, and Hana had heard of the picture brides who went with nothing more than an exchange of photographs to bind them to a strange man.

Viewing HISTORY **A Workshop in Japan**

This 1897 woodblock print shows young women working in a Japanese clothing factory. The machinery and the clothing worn by the workers show the influence of American ways. ★ **Why were many young Japanese women permitted to come to the United States after 1907?**

Almost before she realized what she was doing, Hana spoke to her uncle. "Oji San, perhaps I should go to America to make this lonely man a good wife."

"You, Hana Chan?" Her uncle observed her with startled curiosity. "You would go all alone to a foreign land so far away from your mother and family?"

"I would not allow it." Her mother spoke fiercely. Hana was her youngest and she had lavished upon her the attention and latitude that often befall the last child. How could she permit her to travel so far, even to marry the son of Takeda who was known to her brother.

But now, a notion that had seemed quite impossible a moment before was lodged in his receptive mind, and Hana's uncle grasped it with pleasure that comes from an unexpected discovery....

"You know," he said looking at Hana, "it might be a very good life in America."

Hana felt a faint fluttering in her heart. Perhaps this lonely man in America was her means of escaping. . . .

Her uncle spoke with increasing enthusiasm of sending Hana to become Taro's wife. And the husband of Hana's sister, who was head of their household, spoke with equal eagerness. Although he never said so, Hana guessed he would be pleased to be rid of her, the spirited younger sister who stirred up his placid life with what he considered radical ideas about life and the role of women. He often claimed that Hana had too much schooling for a girl.

A man's word carried much weight for Hana's mother.... Finally, she agreed to an exchange of family histories and an investigation was begun into Taro Takeda's family, his education and his health, so they would be assured there was no insanity or tuberculosis or police records concealed in his family's past.

Analyzing Literature

1. What did Hana know about Taro Takeda before she left Japan?
2. Why did Hana's mother agree to let her go?
3. **Making Inferences** Give two reasons why Hana might have wanted to go to the United States.

Unit 8 Prosperity, Depression, and War

What's Ahead

Chapter 25
The Roaring Twenties (1919–1929)

Chapter 26
The Great Depression (1929–1941)

Chapter 27
World War II (1935–1945)

Viewing UNIT THEMES

A Growing Role for the Federal Government

In the 1930s, the nation was in the midst of an economic depression. President Franklin Roosevelt used the power of government to help the needy. This mural shows Roosevelt signing a bill to build dams in the Tennessee Valley. However, critics argued the federal government was growing too large and costly. ★ **According to this mural, who would benefit from the bill Roosevelt is signing?**

Unit Theme Role of Government

In 1849, author Henry David Thoreau wrote, "that government is best which governs least." Most early American leaders would have agreed. In the 1920s, Presidents like Calvin Coolidge and Herbert Hoover were especially opposed to government regulation of the economy. Soon after, though, the nation faced two major crises: a massive economic depression, followed by the largest war the world had ever seen. As a result, the federal government began to take on a vast new role.

How did Americans of the time feel about the role of government? They can tell you in their own words.

Viewpoints on the Role of Government

"You cannot extend the mastery of the government over the daily working life of a people without at the same time making it master of the people's souls and thoughts."

President Herbert Hoover (1932)

"A government that could not care for its old and sick, that could not provide work for the strong... was not a government that could endure...."

Franklin Roosevelt, Candidate for President (1932)

"In a country as vast as the United States, with its range of physical and economic variations, power cannot be administered entirely from the national capital."

David E. Lilienthal, government official (1940)

Activity **Writing to Learn** Make a chart with two columns. Label one column Advantages and the other column Disadvantages. Then, list as many as you can of the advantages and disadvantages associated with having a big federal government that gets involved in many areas of people's lives.

Chapter 25

The Roaring Twenties

1919–1929

What's Ahead

Section 1
Politics and Prosperity

Section 2
New Ways of Life

Section 3
The Jazz Age

Section 4
Trouble Below the Surface

In the decade after World War I, Presidents Harding and Coolidge encouraged business growth. The economy grew rapidly as factories churned out new consumer goods, and stock prices soared. American society also changed dramatically. Inexpensive cars and a wide variety of new products for the home became available for the first time. Manners became freer. Young people danced to a wild, new music called jazz.

Not all Americans shared in the good times of the boom years. Even for those Americans who seemed fortunate, trouble loomed ahead.

Why Study History? In the 1920s, going to the movies was one of the most popular American pastimes. Silent films united audiences all over the nation. Still, some people worried about the effects of movies on young audiences. Today, movies are just as popular—and as controversial. To explore this connection, see this chapter's *Why Study History?* feature, "Movies Have a Powerful Effect on Us."

American Events

1919 Eighteenth Amendment bans making or selling of alcohol

1921 Emergency Quota Act limits immigration to the United States

1923 Teapot Dome scandal reveals government corruption

1918 | 1920 | 1922 | 1924

World Events

1919 World Event Treaty of Versailles is signed

1922 World Event Union of Soviet Socialist Republics is formed

Life

FEBRUARY 18, 1926 Teaching old Dogs new tricks PRICE 15 CENTS

Viewing History

An Image of the Roaring Twenties

In magazine covers like this one, artist John Held, Jr., poked fun at the new fashions, dances, and attitudes of the 1920s. American life was not always as carefree as Held showed it to be. Still, his drawings helped create a popular image of the "Roaring Twenties." ★ **Do you think most Americans of the time dressed and danced like the people in Held's illustration? Explain.**

1926 Langston Hughes publishes his first volume of poetry

1927 Charles Lindbergh flies alone across the Atlantic Ocean

1929 Great Depression begins

1924 | 1926 | 1928 | 1930

1926 World Event United States intervenes in Nicaragua

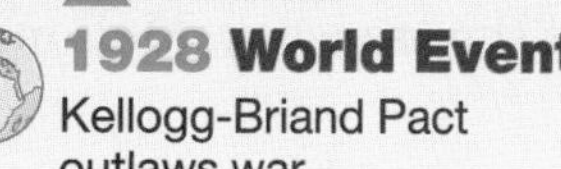

1928 World Event Kellogg-Briand Pact outlaws war

Politics and Prosperity

As You Read

Explore These Questions

- What problems faced the Harding administration?
- How did the economy grow in the 1920s?
- What role did the United States play in world affairs?

Define

- recession
- installment buying
- stock
- bull market
- on margin
- communism
- disarmament

Identify

- Warren G. Harding
- Teapot Dome Scandal
- Calvin Coolidge
- Kellogg-Briand Pact

Setting the Scene The word on the page was plain as day: "normality." Yet **Warren G. Harding,** an Ohio Republican who was running for President in 1920, got it wrong. What the country needs is "normalcy," he declared.

Still, the crowd knew what Harding meant. Normalcy suggested a welcome return to calm after years of war and reform. Harding's slip of the tongue soon became his campaign slogan: "Back to Normalcy."

Returning to Normalcy

World War I had helped the economy. Europeans ordered vast amounts of supplies from American factories. After the United States entered the war in 1917, American factories expanded rapidly to meet the demand for military supplies.

When the war ended, more than 2 million soldiers came home and began to look for jobs. At the same time, factories stopped turning out war materials. The result was a sharp **recession,** or economic slump.

Harding takes office

The recession fed voter discontent with the Democrats, who had held power for eight years. In the 1920 election, Warren Harding swamped his Democratic opponent.

For the top Cabinet posts, Harding chose able men who followed strongly pro-business policies. Andrew Mellon, a wealthy financier, became secretary of the treasury. Mellon balanced the budget and lowered taxes.

Harding campaign button

Herbert Hoover became the new secretary of commerce. During World War I, Hoover had earned the world's admiration by organizing efforts to supply food to millions of starving Belgians. As secretary of commerce, he worked to help American businesses expand overseas.

Political scandals

To fill most other Cabinet posts, however, Harding brought in his old friends. They became known as the "Ohio Gang." Harding himself was honest and hard-working, but the Ohio Gang saw government service as a way to enrich themselves. A series of scandals resulted. For example, Harding made Charles Forbes head of the Veterans Bureau. Forbes was later convicted of stealing millions of dollars from the bureau.

Harding looked on Forbes's crime as a betrayal. When rumors of new scandals surfaced, he grew even more distressed. "I can take care of my enemies all right," he said, "but my... friends, they're the ones that keep me walking the floors nights!" In August 1923, Harding died of a heart attack. Many believed that the scandals contributed to his sudden death.

Viewing History: Scandals Rock Washington

The scandals in the Harding administration were a popular subject for political cartoons. Here, the Democratic donkey laughs merrily at the problems of the Republican elephant. ★ **What is tied to the elephant's tail? What point is the cartoonist making?**

The First Good Laugh They've Had in Years.

After Harding died, new scandals came to light. The most serious involved Secretary of the Interior Albert Fall. Two oil executives had bribed Fall. In return, he secretly leased them government land in California and at Teapot Dome, Wyoming. As a result of the **Teapot Dome Scandal,** Fall became the first Cabinet official ever sent to prison.

Coolidge takes office

On the day Harding died, Vice President **Calvin Coolidge** was visiting his father's farm in Vermont. Coolidge recalled, "I was awakened by my father. . . . I noticed that his voice trembled." Coolidge's father, a justice of the peace, used the family Bible to swear his son in as President. The simple ceremony reassured Americans.

"Silent Cal" Coolidge was very different from Harding. Harding loved throwing parties and making long speeches. Coolidge was tight with both money and words. A woman reportedly told Coolidge she had bet that she could get him to say more than three words. "You lose," Coolidge replied.

Coolidge set out to repair the damage caused by the scandals. He forced the officials involved in scandals to resign. In 1924, Coolidge ran against Democrat John Davis and Progressive Robert La Follette. Voters chose to "Keep Cool With Coolidge" and returned the cautious New Englander to office.

Coolidge Prosperity

Like Harding, Coolidge believed that prosperity for all Americans depended on business prosperity. He told reporters:

> "The business of America is business. The man who builds a factory builds a temple. The man who works there worships there."

True to this philosophy, Coolidge cut regulations on business. He also named business leaders to head government agencies.

Industry booms

Coolidge's pro-business policies contributed to a period of rapid economic growth. People referred to this boom as "Coolidge prosperity." As factories switched to consumer goods, the postwar recession ended. From 1923 to 1929, the quantity of goods made by industry almost doubled.

For most Americans, incomes rose. As a result, they were able to buy a flood of new consumer products. Electric refrigerators, radios, phonographs, vacuum cleaners, and many other appliances took their place in American homes.

Businesses used advertising to boost sales of consumer goods. Advertisements encouraged people to think that their happiness depended on owning a wealth of shiny, new products.

Faced with so many goods, people often wanted to buy things they could not afford. In response, businesses allowed **installment buying,** or buying on credit. For example, buyers could take home a new refrigerator by paying down just a few dollars. Each month, they paid an installment until they had paid the full price, plus interest.

The new policy of "buy now, pay later" increased the demand for goods. At the same time, however, consumer debt jumped. By the end of the decade, consumers owed more than the amount of the federal budget. The comedian Will Rogers joked:

> ❝ If we want anything, all we have to do is go and buy it on credit. So that leaves us without any economic problems whatsoever, except perhaps some day to have to pay for them. ❞

A soaring stock market

The economic boom of the 1920s gave the stock market a giant boost. As you read in Chapter 20, corporations sold **stocks,** or shares of ownership, to investors. Investors made or lost money depending upon whether the price of the shares went up or down.

By the later 1920s, more people were investing in the stock market than ever before. Stock prices rose so fast that some people made fortunes almost overnight. Stories of ordinary people becoming rich drew others into the stock market. Such a period of increased stock trading and rising stock prices is known as a **bull market.**

Many people bought stocks **on margin.** Under this system, an investor bought a stock for just a 10 percent down payment. The buyer held the stock until the price rose and then sold it at a profit. Margin buying worked as long as stock prices kept going up.

In 1928 and 1929, however, the prices of many stocks rose faster than the value of the companies themselves. A few experts warned that the bull market could not last forever. Still, most investors ignored the warnings.

Foreign Affairs

After World War I, the United States was the world's leading economic power. Europeans expected the United States to take a major role in world affairs.

Presidents Harding and Coolidge wanted to keep the hard-won peace in Europe. However, they did not want to commit the United States to the job of keeping world peace. The United States sent observers to the League of Nations but refused to join. Most Americans supported this return to prewar isolationism. However, one American diplomat warned:

> ❝ We feel that we can stand outside all international organizations and that our prosperity is such that it cannot be touched by external events. We are profoundly mistaken. ❞

Latin America

During the war, Latin American nations had been cut off from Europe. As a result, United States trade and investment in the region increased. This trend continued after the war.

At times, the United States intervened to protect its economic interests in Latin America. In 1926, for example, a revolution broke

Viewing HISTORY **Advertising New Products**

Advertising fed the business boom of the 1920s. This ad from a 1921 magazine encourages women to buy an amazing new product—an electric vacuum cleaner. ★ **What message does this advertisement try to give to homemakers?**

Skills FOR LIFE

Critical Thinking | Managing Information | Communication | Maps, Charts, and Graphs

Decision Making

How Will I Use This Skill?

You make dozens of decisions each day. Some are as simple as deciding what to wear. Others might be very important, such as choosing what career you want to follow. Decision making involves reviewing many possible choices and picking the best one.

LEARN the Skill

To make a decision, you have to recognize your goal and evaluate the many possible ways of reaching it. Use the following steps to make a decision:

1. Identify the goal or purpose.
2. Review possible options to achieve the goal.
3. Predict the probable results of each alternative.
4. Select the choice whose probable results best meet your needs with the fewest negative consequences.

PRACTICE the Skill

Review the subsection Foreign Affairs. Answer the following questions:

1. What was the goal of the United States in Latin America after World War I?
2. (a) What option did the United States choose to achieve its goal in Nicaragua? (b) What option did the United States choose to achieve its goal in Mexico?
3. Predict the possible positive and negative effects of (a) military intervention and (b) diplomacy.
4. Which of these two options do you think was better? Explain your answer.

APPLY the Skill

Think about what you would like to do for summer vacation. List the possibilities for young people. Review the positive and negative aspects for each choice. Then, write a paragraph explaining your decision.

When revolution broke out in Nicaragua in 1926, President Coolidge sent in the marines.

out in Nicaragua, where Americans owned plantations and railroads. Coolidge sent marines to oversee new elections.

In 1927, Mexico announced plans to take over foreign-owned oil and mining companies. American investors called on President Coolidge to send in troops. Instead, Coolidge sent a diplomat, Dwight Morrow, to Mexico. After much hard bargaining, Morrow was able to work out a compromise with the Mexican government.

The Soviet Union

Meanwhile, in the Soviet Union, V. I. Lenin was creating the world's first communist state.* **Communism** is an economic system in which all wealth and property is owned by the community as a whole.

The United States refused to recognize Lenin's government. Most Americans disliked communism. It shocked them when the Soviet government did away with private property and attacked religion.

Despite disapproval of the Soviet government, Congress voted $20 million in aid when famine threatened Russia in 1921. American aid may have saved as many as 10 million Russians from starvation.

* In 1922, Russia was renamed the Union of Soviet Socialist Republics (USSR), or Soviet Union.

Disarmament

An arms race in Europe had helped cause World War I. For this reason, many people in the 1920s favored **disarmament,** or the reduction of armed forces and weapons of war. Pacifist groups such as the Woman's International League for Peace and Freedom, founded by Jane Addams, led the call for disarmament in the United States and Europe.

Presidents Harding and Coolidge also backed peace efforts. At the Washington Conference of 1921, the United States, Britain, and Japan agreed to limit the size of their navies. Seven years later, the United States and 61 other nations signed the **Kellogg-Briand Pact.** This treaty outlawed war. Secretary of State Frank Kellogg signed the treaty with a foot-long pen made of gold. "Peace is proclaimed," he said.

The treaty had a fatal flaw. It did not set up any means for keeping the peace. One nation could still use force against another without fear of punishment. Still, many hailed the Kellogg-Briand pact as the beginning of a new age of peace.

★ Section 1 Review ★

Recall

1. **Identify** **(a)** Warren G. Harding, **(b)** Teapot Dome Scandal, **(c)** Calvin Coolidge, **(d)** Kellogg-Briand Pact.
2. **Define** **(a)** recession, **(b)** installment buying, **(c)** stock, **(d)** bull market, **(e)** on margin, **(f)** communism, **(g)** disarmament.

Comprehension

3. What problems did the Ohio Gang cause?
4. **(a)** What policies did Harding and Coolidge adopt toward business? **(b)** Give two examples of how the economy grew in the 1920s.
5. How did most Americans in the 1920s view the nation's role in world affairs?

Critical Thinking and Writing

6. **Analyzing Ideas** President Harding once complained: "I listen to one side and they seem right. . . . I talk to the other side and they seem just as right, and here I am where I started." What does this statement tell you about the problems faced by a President?
7. **Predicting Consequences** The Kellogg-Briand Pact outlawed war. Do you think it could succeed in achieving its goal? Why or why not?

Activity **Writing Persuasively** Buy now, pay later! You are a teenager in the 1920s. Write a list of arguments you might use to persuade your parents to purchase your family's first electric refrigerator on installment.

New Ways of Life

As You Read

Explore These Questions

- What was Prohibition?
- How did women's lives change in the 1920s?
- How did a mass culture begin to emerge in the 1920s?

Define

- bootlegger
- speakeasy
- repeal
- suburb

Identify

- Prohibition
- League of Women Voters
- Ana Roqué de Duprey
- Equal Rights Amendment
- Henry Ford
- Charlie Chaplin

At the stroke of midnight on the morning of January 16, 1920, church bells rang all across the United States. What some people called the "noble experiment" had begun. The experiment was **Prohibition,** a ban on the manufacture, sale, and transportation of liquor anywhere in the United States.

Button supporting the Eighteenth Amendment

Supporters of Prohibition were overjoyed. Popular preacher Billy Sunday predicted that the ban on alcohol would cure a wide variety of social ills:

> "The slums will soon be only a memory. We will turn our prisons into factories and our jails into storehouses and corncribs. Men will walk upright now. Women will smile and children will laugh."

Only time would tell if the "noble experiment" would succeed or fail.

Prohibition was one of many developments that had a dramatic impact on society in the 1920s. New ideas, new products, and new forms of entertainment were rapidly changing the American way of life.

A Ban on Alcohol

For nearly a century, reformers like the Women's Christian Temperance Union had worked to ban alcoholic beverages. They achieved their triumph when the states ratified the Eighteenth Amendment in January 1919. (See page 607.) One year later, Prohibition went into effect.

In 1920, as today, alcohol abuse was a serious problem. Many Americans hoped the ban on liquor would improve American life. In fact, the ban did have some positive effects. Alcoholism declined during Prohibition. So did liver diseases caused by liquor. In the end, however, the ban did not work.

Getting around the law

One reason Prohibition failed was that many Americans found ways to get around the law. Some people manufactured their own alcohol in homemade stills. Others smuggled in liquor from Canada and the Caribbean. Because these smugglers sometimes hid bottles of liquor in their boots, they became known as **bootleggers.**

Illegal bars, called **speakeasies,** opened in nearly every city and town. A visitor to Pittsburgh reported that it took him only 11 minutes to find a speakeasy. In some ways, speakeasies made drinking liquor even more popular than ever. Before Prohibition, it was not considered proper for a woman to go into a saloon. Speakeasies, however, welcomed women as well as men.

Viewing HISTORY **Enforcing the Ban on Alcohol**

During Prohibition, federal agents like these destroyed hundreds of barrels of illegal liquor. Still, both bootleggers and "respectable" citizens kept finding ways around the law. ★ **What effect did Prohibition have on crime?**

To enforce the ban, the government sent out federal prohibition agents. These "g-men" traveled across the United States, shutting down speakeasies, breaking up illegal stills, and stopping smugglers. Still, the lawbreaking was too widespread for just 1,500 federal agents to control.

Rise of organized crime

Prohibition gave a huge boost to organized crime. Every speakeasy needed a steady supply of liquor. Professional criminals, or gangsters, took over the job of meeting this need. As bootleggers earned big profits, crime became a big business. "Ours is a business nation," said one official. "Our criminals apply business methods."

Prohibition laws allowed manufacturers to produce alcohol for industrial uses. Some bootleggers took advantage of this loophole by converting industrial alcohol to liquor. Unfortunately, most bootleggers lacked knowledge of chemistry. Their illegal product often caused blindness, paralysis, or even death.

Gangsters divided up cities and forced speakeasy owners in their "territories" to buy liquor from them. Sometimes, gangsters gunned down their rivals in battles for control. Newspapers played up alarming tales of gangland violence. Journalists also showed the public how gangsters broke the law and got away with it. Gangsters used some of their profits to bribe police officers, public officials, and judges.

Repeal of Prohibition

Gradually, more and more Americans came to think that Prohibition was a mistake. The ban reduced drinking but never stopped it. Even worse, argued critics, Prohibition was undermining respect for the law. Every day, millions of Americans were buying liquor in speakeasies. By the mid-1920s, almost half of all federal arrests were for Prohibition crimes.

By the end of the decade, many Americans were calling for the **repeal,** or cancellation, of Prohibition. In 1933, the states ratified the Twenty-first Amendment, which repealed the Eighteenth Amendment.* The noble experiment was over.

New Rights for Women

Another constitutional amendment also changed American life, but in a very different way. The Nineteenth Amendment, ratified in 1920, gave women the right to vote. (See page 605.)

Women voters

Women went to the polls nationwide for the first time in November 1920. Their votes helped elect Warren Harding as President.

* To date, the Eighteenth Amendment is the only constitutional amendment that has ever been repealed.

Women did not vote as a group, however, as some people had predicted. Like men, some women voted for Republicans, some for Democrats, and many did not vote at all.

In 1920, Carrie Chapman Catt, head of the National Woman Suffrage Association, set up the **League of Women Voters.** The organization worked to educate voters, as it still does today. It also worked to guarantee other rights, such as the right of women to serve on juries.

As women in the United States voted for the first time, women in Puerto Rico asked if the new law applied to them. They were told that it did not. Led by **Ana Roqué de Duprey,** an educator and writer, Puerto Rican women crusaded for the vote. In 1929, their crusade finally succeeded.

Fighting for equal rights

Leaders in the suffrage movement also worked for other goals. Alice Paul, who had been a leading suffragist, pointed out that women still lacked many legal rights. For example, many professional schools still barred women, and many states gave husbands legal control over their wives' earnings. Paul called for a new constitutional amendment in 1923. Paul's proposed **Equal Rights Amendment** (ERA) stated that "equality of rights under the law shall not be denied or abridged by the United States or by any State on account of sex."

Many people feared that the ERA went too far. Some even argued that women would *lose* some legal safeguards, such as laws that protected women in factories. Paul worked vigorously for the ERA until her death in 1977, but the amendment never passed.

Women's work

Women's lives changed in other ways in the 1920s. During World War I, thousands of women had worked outside the home for the first time. They filled the jobs of men who had gone off to war. When the troops came home, many women were forced to give up their jobs. Still, some remained in the work force.

For some women, working outside the home was nothing new. Poor women and working-class women had been cooks, servants, and seamstresses for many years. In the 1920s, they were joined by middle-class women who worked as teachers, typists, secretaries, and store clerks. A few women even managed to become doctors and lawyers, despite discrimination.

Life at home also changed for women. More of them bought ready-made clothes instead of sewing for the whole family as in the past. Electric appliances such as refrigerators, washers, irons, and vacuum cleaners made housework easier. On the other hand, such conveniences also encouraged some women to spend even more time on housework. Even women who worked outside the home found they had to work a second shift when they came home. Most husbands expected their wives to cook, clean, and care for children even if they held full-time jobs.

Biography Nellie Tayloe Ross

The first state to allow women to vote, Wyoming was also the first to have a woman as governor. In 1924, Nellie Tayloe Ross was elected to succeed her late husband. In office, Governor Ross supported tax relief for farmers and better funding for schools. She later served for 20 years as director of the United States Mint. ★ **Why do you think no state elected a woman governor before the 1920s?**

Impact of the Automobile

"Why on earth do you need to study what's changing this country?" one man asked the experts. "I can tell you what's happening in just four letters: A-U-T-O." In the 1920s, Americans traveled to more places and moved more quickly than ever before—all because of the automobile.

The auto industry played a central role in the business boom of the 1920s. Car sales grew rapidly during the decade. The auto boom spurred growth in related fields such as steel and rubber.

Affordable cars

Lower prices sparked the auto boom. By 1924, the cost of a Model T had dropped from $850 to $290. As a result, an American did not have to be rich to buy a car.

Car prices fell because factories became more efficient. As you have read, **Henry Ford** introduced the assembly line in his automobile factory in 1913. (See page 546.) The goal, Ford said, was to make the cars identical, "just like one pin is like another pin." Before the assembly line, it took 14 hours to put together a Model T. In Ford's new factory, workers could assemble a Model T in 93 minutes!

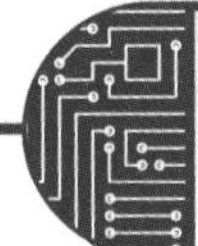

Linking History and Technology

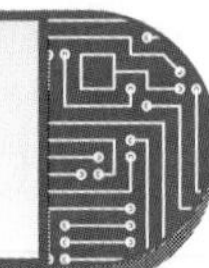

Ford Assembly Line

Henry Ford transformed manufacturing and daily life with the automobile assembly line. Workers stood at their stations while unfinished cars moved past them on a conveyor belt. Each worker performed one task on each car as it passed by. ★ **What disadvantages might there be to working on an assembly line?**

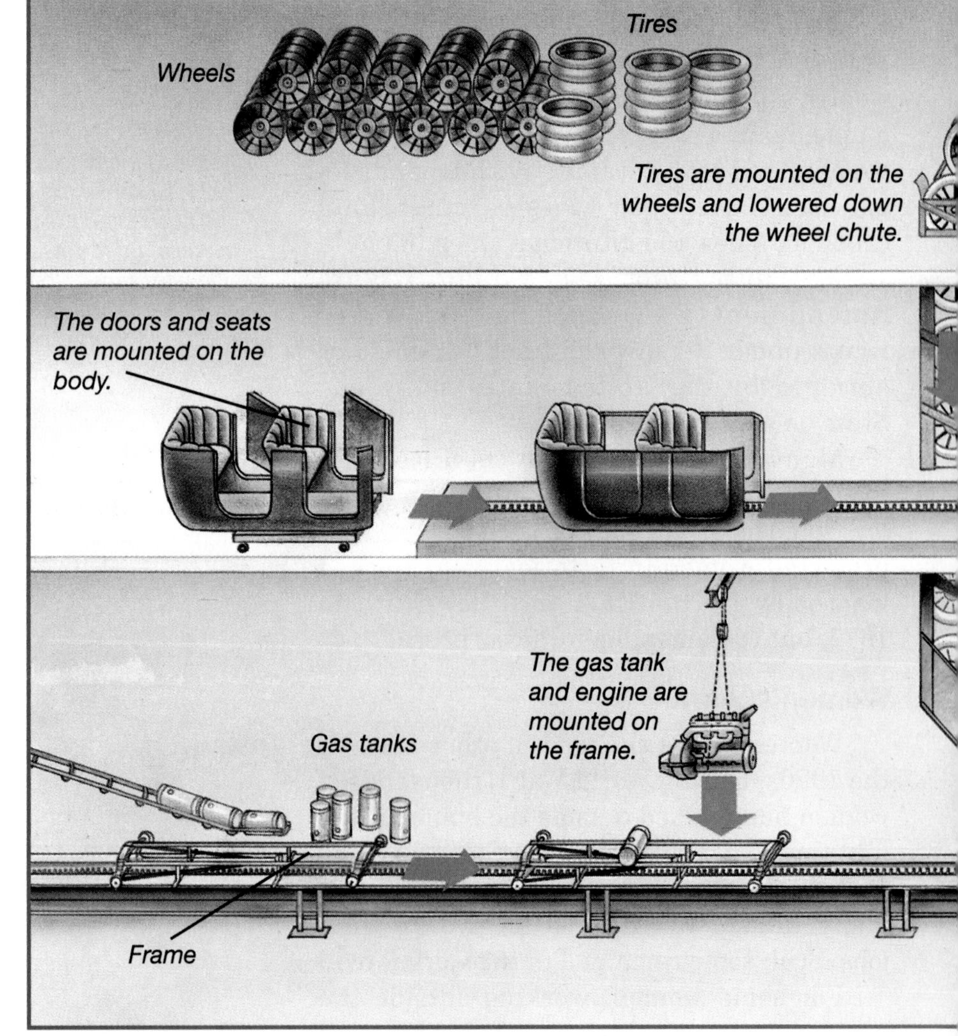

Other companies copied Ford's methods. In 1927, General Motors passed Ford as the top auto maker. Unlike Ford, General Motors sold cars in a variety of models and colors. Henry Ford had once boasted that people could have his cars in "any color so long as it's black." Faced with the success of General Motors, he changed his mind. His next car, the Model A, came in different colors. Before long, car companies were offering new makes and models every year.

Economic effects

Car sales spurred growth in other parts of the economy. By 1929, some four million Americans owed their jobs to the automobile, directly or indirectly. Tens of thousands of people worked in steel mills, producing metal parts for cars. Others made tires, paint, and glass for cars. Some drilled for oil in the Southwest or worked in the oil refineries where crude petroleum was converted into usable gasoline.

The car boom had other effects. States and towns paved more roads and built new highways. In 1925, the Bronx River Parkway in New York was the first of many highways in parklike settings.

Gas stations, tourist camps, and roadside restaurants sprang up across the country to

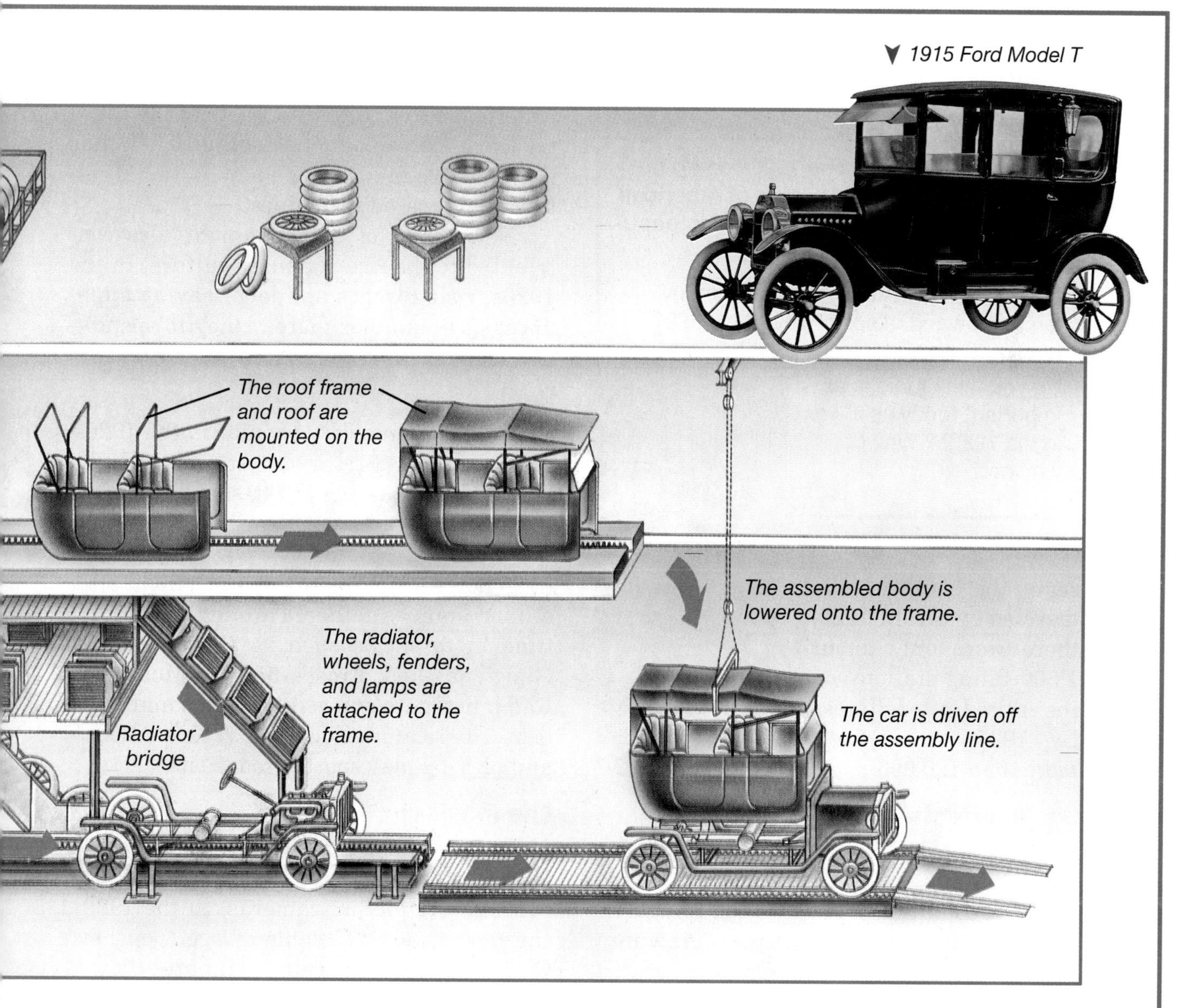

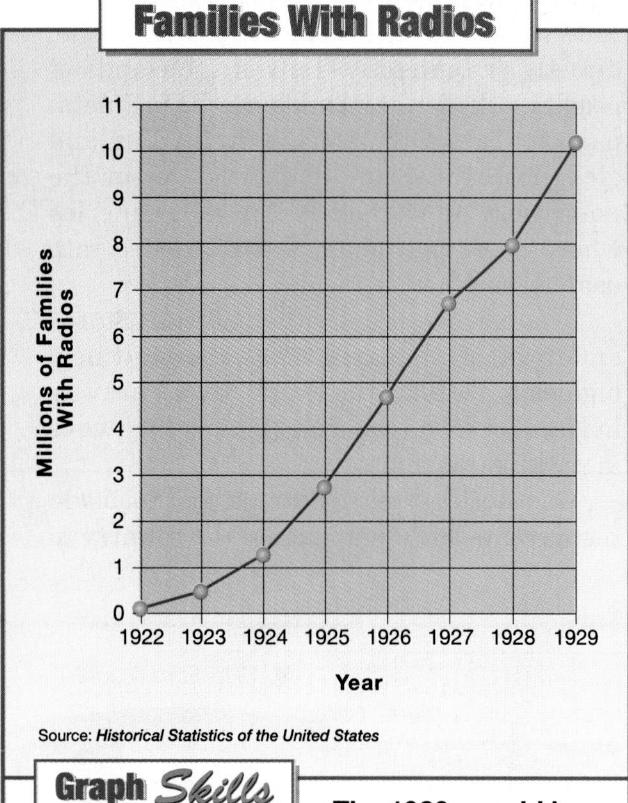

Graph Skills **The 1920s could be called the age of radio. Millions of American families bought radios and listened to popular programs.**

1. **Comprehension** About how many families owned radios in 1924? In 1929?
2. **Critical Thinking** Do you think radio is as important today as it was in the 1920s? Why or why not?

Radio of the 1920s

serve the millions who traveled by car. In 1920, there were only about 1,500 filling stations in the entire United States. By 1929, there were more than 120,000.

Social effects

Cars shaped life in the city and in the country. Many city dwellers wanted to escape crowded conditions. They moved to nearby towns in the country, which soon grew into suburbs. A **suburb** is a community located outside a city. With cars, suburban families could drive to the city even though it was many miles away. They could also drive to stores, schools, or work. No longer did people have to live where they could walk or take a trolley to work.

Another major shift came when suburban housewives refused to be confined to the passenger seat. Instead, they took their place behind the wheels of their own automobiles. As they did, they broke down still another barrier that separated the worlds of men and women.

In the country, cars brought people closer to towns, shops, and the movies. Such trips had taken several hours by horse and buggy. One farm woman bought a car before she got indoor plumbing. "You can't go to town in a bathtub," she explained.

Creating a Mass Culture

By making travel easier, cars helped Americans from different parts of the country learn more about one another. They thus played a role in creating a new, national culture that crossed state lines.

New forms of entertainment also contributed to the rise of a mass culture. In the 1920s, rising wages and labor-saving appliances gave families more money to spend—and more leisure time in which to spend it.

Radio

Radio became very popular in the 1920s. The country's first radio station, KDKA, started broadcasting in Pittsburgh in 1920. By 1929, more than 10 million American families owned radios.

A new lifestyle emerged. Each night after dinner, families gathered around the radio to tune in to shows such as "Roxy and His Gang" or "Jack Frost's Melody Moments." Radio listeners enjoyed comedies and westerns, classical music and jazz, news reports and play-by-play sports broadcasts.

The movies

In the late 1800s, Thomas Edison and George Eastman had helped to develop the first moving picture cameras. In the 1920s, the movie industry came of age. Southern California's warm, sunny climate allowed filming all year round. Soon, Hollywood became the movie capital of the world.

Why Study History?

Because Movies Have a Powerful Effect on Us

Historical Background

He galloped across the desert on a white horse, his long Arabian robes flowing behind him. In darkened theaters from coast to coast, millions of viewers felt a thrill. In movies like *The Sheik* (1921), Rudolph Valentino became the most popular romantic star of his day.

Then, in 1926, came the shocking news. Valentino was dead! More than 100,000 weeping fans mobbed the funeral home to say goodbye to their favorite star.

The reaction to Valentino's death showed the enormous popularity of movies and movie stars. At the same time, it raised concerns about the unhealthy effects of movies, especially on young people. Critics warned that movie stars were being worshipped like gods.

Connections to Today

Today, movies continue to enjoy tremendous popularity. Large audiences watched movies ranging from cartoons like *The Lion King* to serious dramas like *Schindler's List.* In 1998, the romantic epic *Titanic* broke the all-time box office record. Every spring, hundreds of millions of television viewers around the world tune in to watch their favorite stars at the Academy Awards.

Connections to You

What role do movies play in your life? The chances are that you have seen a movie recently and that you have favorite stars. Movies entertain us, stir our imaginations, and can teach us about unfamiliar people and places. Yet today, as in the past, some critics worry about the effects of movies on young people.

One area of concern is violence. Many experts believe that watching violent movies encourages violent behavior in some younger viewers. The debate about movies will probably continue for a long time to come.

1. **Comprehension** **(a)** How did movie fans in the 1920s react to the death of Rudolph Valentino? **(b)** Why did this reaction worry some people?
2. **Critical Thinking** Do you think that viewers under a certain age should be prevented from watching violent movies? Why or why not?

Writing a Movie Review Select a movie that you think would have a positive effect on viewers. Prepare and deliver a one-minute review explaining why you recommend this film.

Moviemakers today spend millions of dollars creating films for the profitable "teen market."

In the 1920s, millions of Americans went to the movies at least once a week. They thrilled to westerns, romances, adventures, and comedies. In small towns, theaters were bare rooms with hard chairs. In cities, they were huge palaces with red velvet seats.

The first movies had no sound. Audiences followed the plot by reading "title cards" that appeared on the screen. A pianist played music that went with the action. Sometimes the audience also provided sound effects. As one movie-house musician recalled:

> " To provide sound for Western or battle scenes, the older [children] would fire cap pistols. The younger ones, identifying with the hero as he was being stalked, would blurt hysterical warnings: 'Look out! He's behind the door!' There were always children reading aloud to their immigrant parents....They supplied... translations into Italian, Yiddish, or German. "

Fans adored Hollywood movie stars. Cowboy stars like Tom Mix thrilled audiences with their heroic adventures. Clara Bow won fame playing restless, fun-seeking young women. The most popular star of all was comedian **Charlie Chaplin,** nicknamed "The Little Tramp." In his tiny derby hat and baggy pants, Chaplin presented a comical figure. His attempts to triumph over the problems of everyday life moved audiences to both laughter and tears.

Charlie Chaplin

In 1927, Hollywood caused a sensation when it produced *The Jazz Singer.* The film was a "talkie"—a movie with a sound track. Audiences were thrilled when singer Al Jolson looked down from the screen and promised, "You ain't heard nothin' yet!" Soon, all new movies were talkies.

Movies contributed to the new mass culture. When a Chaplin comedy opened, people from coast to coast rushed to see it. Immigrants and native-born Americans laughed together. Movies, said a Hollywood executive, reached "audiences speaking twenty different languages but understanding in common the universal language of pictures."

★ Section 2 Review ★

Recall

1. **Identify** **(a)** Prohibition, **(b)** League of Women Voters, **(c)** Ana Roqué de Duprey, **(d)** Equal Rights Amendment, **(e)** Henry Ford, **(f)** Charlie Chaplin.
2. **Define** **(a)** bootlegger, **(b)** speakeasy, **(c)** repeal, **(d)** suburb.

Comprehension

3. Why did a national ban on alcohol fail?
4. How did the Nineteenth Amendment change women's lives?
5. Describe one way each of the following affected American life: **(a)** the automobile, **(b)** radio, **(c)** movies.

Critical Thinking and Writing

6. **Linking Past and Present** Cars transformed American life in the 1920s. Are cars just as important in American life today? Explain.
7. **Analyzing Ideas** A mass culture began to emerge in the 1920s. **(a)** What advantages does a mass culture bring? **(b)** What disadvantages?

Activity **Writing Title Cards** You are a moviemaker producing a silent film about the Roaring Twenties. Write ten title cards for scenes that show what the decade was like.

3 The Jazz Age

As You Read

Explore These Questions

- Why were the 1920s called the Roaring Twenties and the Jazz Age?
- Why did some writers criticize American society?
- Who were the leading figures of the Harlem Renaissance?

Define

- fad
- flapper
- jazz
- expatriate

Identify

- Louis Armstrong
- Ernest Hemingway
- F. Scott Fitzgerald
- Harlem Renaissance
- Langston Hughes
- Zora Neale Hurston
- Babe Ruth
- Charles A. Lindbergh

SETTING the Scene When asked about her favorite pastime, one young woman of the 1920s promptly replied, "I adore dancing. Who doesn't?" New dance crazes such as the Charleston, the Lindy Hop, and the Shimmy forever marked the decade as the "Jazz Age" and the "Roaring Twenties."

During the 1920s, new dances, new music, new games, and other new ways to have fun swept the country. For all the serious business of the 1920s, the decade also roared with laughter. At the same time, a new generation of writers were taking a critical look at American society.

An Era of Changing Fashions

"Ev'ry morning, ev'ry evening, ain't we got fun?" went a hit song of 1921. During the "Era of Wonderful Nonsense"—yet another nickname for the 1920s—fun came in many forms.

Following the latest fads

Fads caught on, then quickly disappeared. A **fad** is an activity or a fashion that is taken up with great passion for a short time. Flagpole sitting was one fad of the 1920s. Young people would perch on top of flagpoles for hours, or even days. Another fad was the dance marathon, where couples danced for hundreds of hours at a time to see who could last the longest. Crossword puzzles and mah-jongg, a Chinese game, were other popular fads of the 1920s.

Dance crazes came and went rapidly. The most popular new dance was probably the Charleston. First performed by African Americans in southern cities like Charleston, South Carolina, the dance became a national craze after 1923. To a quick beat, dancers pivoted their feet while kicking out first one leg, then the other, backward and forward.

Dress and beads worn by a flapper

Flappers set the style

Perhaps no one pursued the latest fads more intensely than the **flappers.** These young women rebelled against traditional ways of thinking and acting. Flappers wore their hair bobbed, or cut short. They wore their dresses short, too—shorter than Americans had ever seen before. Flappers shocked their parents by wearing bright red lipstick.

To many older Americans, the way flappers behaved was even more shocking than the way they looked. Flappers smoked cigarettes in public, drank bootleg alcohol in

Biography **Louis Armstrong**

As a child, Louis "Satchmo" Armstrong liked to follow brass bands around the streets of New Orleans. After coming to Chicago in 1922, he quickly became the most popular jazz musician of his day. His recordings, such as "Potato Head Blues," brought jazz to a nationwide audience. "Satchmo" also pioneered a new form of jazz singing, called scat. ★ **What were the origins of jazz?**

speakeasies, and drove fast cars. "Is 'the old-fashioned girl,' with all that she stands for in sweetness, modesty, and innocence, in danger of becoming extinct?" wondered one magazine in 1921.

The flappers defiantly mocked such criticism. A song from a 1925 musical comedy became an informal flapper anthem:

> "Flappers are we
> Flappers and fly and free.
> Never too slow
> All on the go. . . .
> Dizzy with dangerous glee."

Only a few young women were flappers. Still, they set a style for others. Slowly, older women began to cut their hair and wear makeup and shorter skirts. For many Americans, the bold fashions pioneered by the flappers symbolized a new sense of freedom.

New Music

Another innovation of the 1920s was jazz. Born in New Orleans, **jazz** combined West African rhythms, African American work songs and spirituals, and European harmonies. Jazz also had roots in the ragtime rhythms of composers like Scott Joplin. (See page 573.)

Louis Armstrong was one of the brilliant young African American musicians who helped create jazz. Armstrong learned to play the trumpet in the New Orleans orphanage where he grew up. Too young to play in clubs, Armstrong made his debut at a picnic. One musician remembers, "Everyone in the park went wild over this boy in knee trousers who could play so great." Armstrong had the ability to take a simple melody and experiment with the notes and the rhythm. This allowed his listeners to hear many different sides of the basic tune. Other great early jazz players included "Jelly Roll" Morton and singer Bessie Smith.

Jazz quickly spread from New Orleans to Chicago, Kansas City, and the African American section of New York known as Harlem. White musicians, such as trumpeter Bix Beiderbecke, also began to adopt the new style. Before long, the popularity of jazz spread to Europe as well.

Many older Americans worried that jazz and the new dances were a bad influence on the nation's young people. Despite their complaints, jazz continued to grow more popular. Today, jazz is recognized as a uniquely American art form created by African Americans. It is considered one of the most important cultural achievements of the United States.

Connections With Arts

One unique feature of jazz was its free style. Generally, the written melody was only a framework. Musicians would improvise, playing with the tune and encouraging one another to take the mood a step farther. When a group of jazz musicians improvised together, it was known as a jam session.

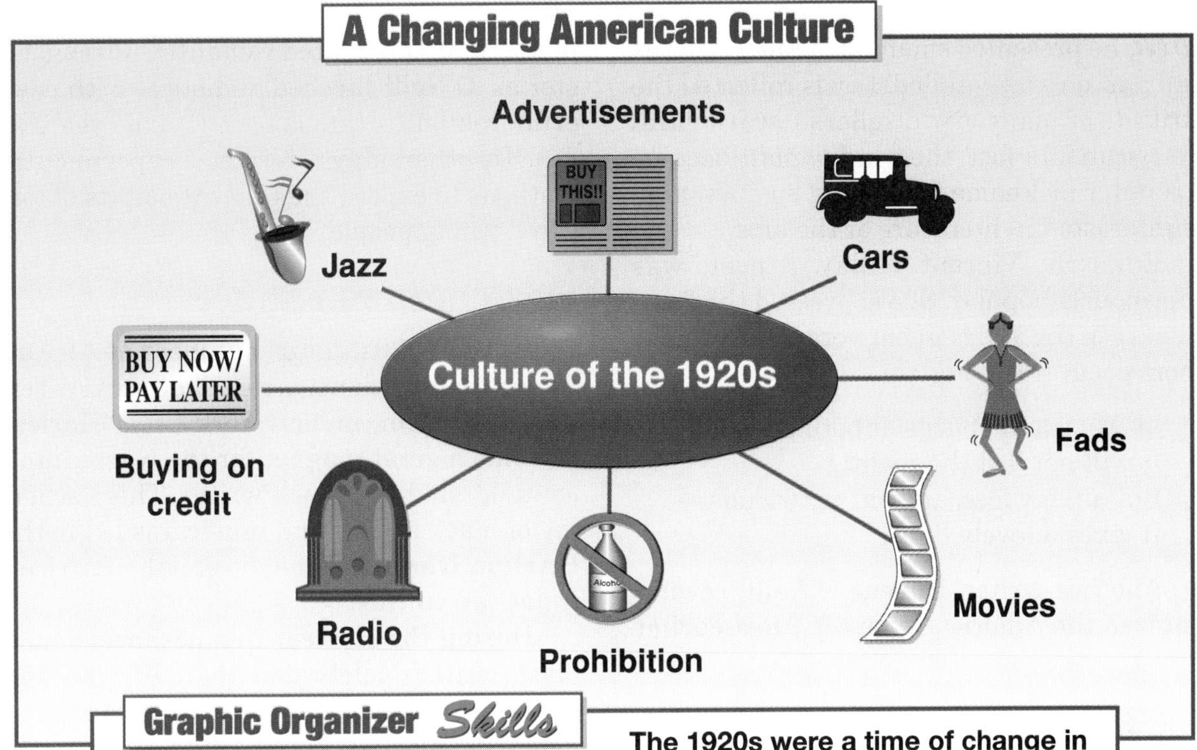

Graphic Organizer Skills The 1920s were a time of change in the United States. A number of new inventions, ideas, and practices contributed to this change.

1. **Comprehension** Identify two items on this graphic organizer that were linked to the economic boom of the 1920s.
2. **Critical Thinking** **(a)** Which items shown here affected American leisure activities? **(b)** Of these, which are still popular today?

A New Generation of Writers

A new generation of American writers earned worldwide fame in the 1920s. Many of them were horrified by their experiences in World War I. They criticized Americans for caring too much about money and fun. Some became so unhappy with life in the United States that they moved to Paris, France. There, they lived as **expatriates,** people who leave their own country to live in a foreign land.

Hemingway and Fitzgerald

Ernest Hemingway was one of the writers who lived for a time in Paris. Still a teenager at the outbreak of World War I, he traveled to Europe to drive an ambulance on the Italian front. Hemingway drew on his war experiences in *A Farewell to Arms,* a novel about a young man's growing disgust with war. In *The Sun Also Rises,* he examined the lives of American expatriates in Europe. They travel from Paris to Spain and back, searching for momentary pleasure without any plans or hopes for the future.

Hemingway became one of the most popular writers of the 1920s. His simple but powerful style influenced many other writers.

The young writer who best captured the mood of the Roaring Twenties was Hemingway's friend **F. Scott Fitzgerald.** In *The Great Gatsby* and other novels, Fitzgerald told about wealthy young people who attended endless parties but could not find happiness. His characters included flappers, bootleggers, and movie makers. Fitzgerald became a hero to college students and flappers, among others.

Other writers

Sinclair Lewis grew up in a small town in Minnesota and later moved to New York City. In novels such as *Babbitt* and *Main*

Street, he presented small-town Americans as dull and narrow-minded. Lewis reflected the attitude of many city dwellers toward rural Americans. In fact, the word *babbitt* became a popular nickname for a smug businessman uninterested in literature or the arts.

Edna St. Vincent Millay, a poet, was enormously popular. She expressed the frantic pace of the 1920s in her verse, such as her short poem "First Fig":

> ❝ My candle burns at both ends;
> It will not last the night;
> But ah, my foes, and oh, my friends—
> It gives a lovely light. ❞

Another writer, Eugene O'Neill, revolutionized the American theater. Most earlier playwrights presented romantic, unrealistic stories. O'Neill shocked audiences with powerful, realistic dramas based on his years at sea. In other plays, he used experimental methods to expose the inner thoughts of tortured young people.

Viewing HISTORY **Art of the Harlem Renaissance**

Writers and artists of the Harlem Renaissance often stressed the African heritage of black Americans. In The Ascent of Ethiopia, *painter Lois Mailou Jones links the Egyptian pharaoh (front) to the modern urban skyscraper in the background.* ★ **What point do you think Jones is making in this painting?**

Harlem Renaissance

In the 1920s, large numbers of African American musicians, artists, and writers settled in Harlem, in New York City. "Harlem was like a great magnet for the Negro intellectual," said one black writer. This gathering of black artists and musicians led to the **Harlem Renaissance,** a rebirth of African American culture.

During the Harlem Renaissance, young black writers celebrated their African and American heritage. They also protested prejudice and racism. For the first time, too, a large number of white Americans took notice of the achievements of black artists and writers.

Langston Hughes

Probably the best-known poet of the Harlem Renaissance was **Langston Hughes.** He published his first poem, "The Negro Speaks of Rivers," soon after graduating from high school. The poem connected the experiences of black Americans living along the Mississippi River with those of ancient Africans living along the Nile and Niger rivers. (See page 758.)

Like other writers of the Harlem Renaissance, Hughes encouraged African Americans to be proud of their heritage. In "My People," he wrote:

> ❝ The night is beautiful,
> So the faces of my people.
> The stars are beautiful,
> So the eyes of my people.
> Beautiful, also, is the sun.
> Beautiful, also, are the souls of
> my people. ❞

In other poems, Hughes protested racism and acts of violence against African Americans. In addition to his poems, Hughes wrote plays, short stories, and essays about the black experience.

Viewing HISTORY **Sports Heroes of the 1920s**

In the 1920s, as today, Americans loved to follow the triumphs of famous athletes. The photograph at left shows Helen Wills at age 19, when she won the second of her seven United States tennis championships. She also won the Wimbledon title eight times. The mighty hitting of Babe Ruth, right, helped the New York Yankees win seven World Series in 13 years. ★ **Why do you think sports stars attract so much admiration?**

Other writers

Other poets such as Countee Cullen and Claude McKay also wrote of the experiences of African Americans. A graduate of New York University and Harvard, Cullen taught in a Harlem high school. In the 1920s, he won prizes for his books of poetry.

McKay came to the United States from Jamaica. In his poem "If We Must Die," he condemned the lynchings and other mob violence that black Americans suffered after World War I. The poem concludes with the lines "Like men we'll face the murderous, cowardly pack, / Pressed to the wall, dying but fighting back!"

Zora Neale Hurston, who grew up in Florida, wrote novels, essays, and short stories. Hurston grew concerned that African American folklore "was disappearing without the world realizing it had ever been." In 1928, she set out alone to travel through the South in a battered car. For two years, she collected the folk tales, songs, and prayers of black southerners. She later published these in her book *Mules and Men.*

Heroes of the Roaring Twenties

Radio, movies, and newspapers created heroes and heroines known across the country. Americans followed the exploits of individuals whose achievements made them stand out from the crowd.

Athletes

Some of the best-loved heroes of the decade were athletes. Each sport had its stars. Bobby Jones won almost every golf championship. Bill Tilden and Helen Wills ruled the tennis courts. Jack Dempsey reigned as world heavyweight boxing champion for seven years. At the age of 19, Gertrude Ederle awed the world when she became the first woman to swim across the English Channel.

College football also drew huge crowds. Many Americans who had never attended college rooted for college teams. Flappers and their dates paraded in the stands wearing the latest fashion—thick, bulky raccoon

Medal honoring Charles A. Lindbergh

coats. They thrilled to the exploits of football stars like Red Grange, the "Galloping Ghost" of the University of Illinois.

Americans loved football, but baseball was their real passion. The most popular player of the 1920s was **Babe Ruth.** Ruth had grown up in an orphanage and was often in trouble as a boy. Through talent and hard work, he became the star of the New York Yankees. Fans flocked to games to see "the Sultan of Swat" hit home runs. The 60 home runs he hit in one season set a record that lasted more than 30 years. His lifetime record of 714 home runs was not broken until 1974.

Charles Lindbergh

The greatest hero of the decade, however, was not an athlete but an aviator. On a gray morning in May 1927, **Charles A. Lindbergh** took off from an airport in New York. A shy young man from Minnesota, Lindbergh planned to be the first person to fly nonstop across the Atlantic Ocean—alone.

For 33½ hours, Lindbergh piloted his tiny single-engine plane, *The Spirit of St. Louis,* over the stormy Atlantic. He carried no map, no parachute, and no radio. Lindbergh later described how he battled his worst problem, fatigue:

> "Sleeping is winning. My whole body argues dully that nothing, nothing life can attain, is quite so desirable as sleep. My mind is losing resolution and control."

Still, Lindbergh flew on. At last, he landed in Paris, France. The cheering crowd lifted him on their shoulders and carried him across the airfield. Back home, headlines announced LINDY DOES IT! "Lucky Lindy" returned to the United States as the hero of the decade.

★ Section 3 Review ★

Recall

1. **Identify** **(a)** Louis Armstrong, **(b)** Ernest Hemingway, **(c)** F. Scott Fitzgerald, **(d)** Harlem Renaissance, **(e)** Langston Hughes, **(f)** Zora Neale Hurston, **(g)** Babe Ruth, **(h)** Charles A. Lindbergh.
2. **Define** **(a)** fad, **(b)** flapper, **(c)** jazz, **(d)** expatriate.

Comprehension

3. How did flappers reflect changes in American culture?
4. What aspects of American life did writers criticize?
5. What themes did the writers of the Harlem Renaissance address in their works?

Critical Thinking and Writing

6. **Analyzing Ideas** Review Edna St. Vincent Millay's poem on page 690. How does it reflect the spirit of the 1920s?
7. **Linking Past and Present** **(a)** What new kinds of music and dancing are popular among young people today? **(b)** How do most older Americans respond to these new forms? **(c)** Is this response similar to or different from attitudes toward flappers and jazz in the 1920s? Explain.

Activity **Using Flashcards** Make a set of flashcards about the important people of the 1920s. On the front of each card, write the name of one of the heroes, writers, artists, or leaders of the times. On the back, write key facts about that person. Use the cards to review what you have learned about the 1920s.

Trouble Below the Surface

Explore These Questions
- Which Americans did not share in the prosperity of the 1920s?
- Why did many Americans want to limit immigration?
- What obstacles did African Americans face in northern cities?

Define
- company union
- sabotage
- anarchist
- deport
- nativism
- quota system

Identify
- Red Scare
- Sacco and Vanzetti trial
- Emergency Quota Act
- Jones Act
- Scopes trial
- Marcus Garvey
- Herbert Hoover
- Alfred E. Smith

Writing in the magazine *The Nation,* Oswald Garrison Villard warned Americans that the high living of the Roaring Twenties could not last. Under the surface, millions "were steadily sinking . . . worse housed and fed than any peasants in Europe."

Villard knew that no one wanted to listen. "Nobody wanted anything but to be left alone to make money," he complained. Still, he was right. Even at its height, "Coolidge prosperity" never included everyone.

Uneven Prosperity

As Villard pointed out, many Americans did not share in the boom of the 1920s. Workers in the clothing industry, for example, were hurt by changes in women's fashions. Shorter skirts meant that less cloth was needed to make dresses. Coal miners also faced hard times as oil replaced coal as the major source of energy. Railroads slashed jobs because trains were losing business to cars and trucks.

Farmers suffer

Farmers were hit the hardest. During World War I, Europeans had bought American farm products, sending prices up. Farmers borrowed money to buy more land and tractors. They planned to pay off these loans with profits from increased production.

When the war ended, however, European farmers were again able to produce for their own needs. As a result, prices for American farm products dropped sharply throughout the 1920s. Farmers were unable to pay their debts. By the end of the decade, the farmers' share of national income had shrunk by almost half.

Setbacks for labor

For labor unions, too, the 1920s were a disaster. During the war, unions had worked with the government to keep production high. Labor's cooperation contributed to victory. In return, union leaders expected the government to support labor.

During the war, wages had not kept up with prices. Now, with the war over, workers demanded higher pay. When employers refused, unions launched a wave of strikes. Management moved quickly to crush the strikes. Because the government did not step in to help them, workers felt betrayed.

The strikes turned the public against labor. One strike in particular angered Americans. In 1919, the city of Boston fired 19 police officers who had tried to join the American Federation of Labor (AFL). Boston police struck in protest. The sight of police leaving their posts shocked the country.

The later 1920s saw even more setbacks for labor. In one court case after another, judges limited the rights of unions. At the

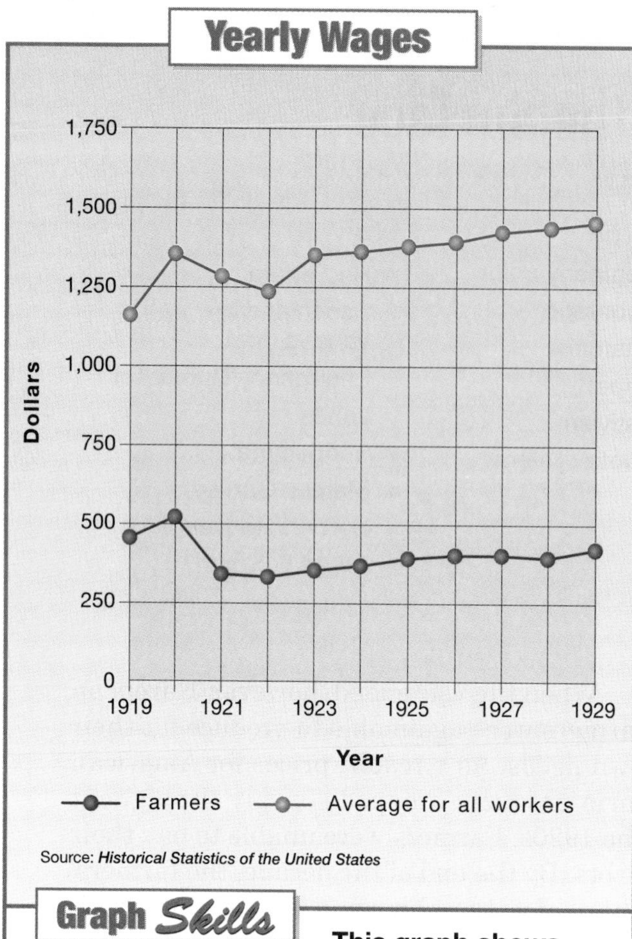

Graph Skills **This graph shows the average yearly wage for all American workers and for farmers in the 1920s. Generally, farmers earned less than most other workers.**

1. **Comprehension** **(a)** What was the average yearly wage for all American workers in 1925? **(b)** How far below the average were farmers' wages that year?
2. **Critical Thinking** Do you think farmers were able to buy many of the new goods available in the 1920s?

same time, employers created **company unions,** labor organizations that were actually controlled by management. As a result, union membership dropped from 5 million in 1920 to 3.4 million by 1929.

The Red Scare

During the war, Americans had been on the alert for enemy spies and **sabotage**—secret destruction of property or interference with work in factories. These wartime worries led to a growing fear of foreigners.

The rise of communism in the Soviet Union fanned that fear. Lenin, the communist leader, called on workers everywhere to overthrow their governments. Many Americans saw the strikes that swept the nation as the start of a communist revolution.

Rounding up radicals

The actions of **anarchists,** or people who oppose organized government, added to the sense of danger. One group of anarchists plotted to kill well-known Americans, including John D. Rockefeller, the head of Standard Oil. Because many anarchists were foreign born, their attacks led to an outcry against all foreigners.

The government took harsh actions against both communists, or "Reds," and anarchists. During the **Red Scare,** thousands of radicals were arrested and jailed. Many foreigners were **deported,** or expelled from the country.

Sacco and Vanzetti

The trial of two Italian immigrants in Massachusetts came to symbolize the antiforeign feeling of the 1920s. Nicola Sacco and Bartolomeo Vanzetti were arrested for robbery and murder in 1920. The two men admitted that they were anarchists but insisted they had committed no crime. A jury convicted them, however. Sacco and Vanzetti were then sentenced to death.

The **Sacco and Vanzetti trial** created a furor across the nation. The evidence against the two men was limited. The judge was openly prejudiced against the two immigrants. Many Americans thought that Sacco and Vanzetti were convicted, not because they were guilty, but because they were immigrants and radicals. The two men waited in jail during a six-year fight to overturn their convictions. Their appeals were turned down. In 1927, they were executed.

The issue of whether Sacco and Vanzetti received a fair trial has been debated ever since. In the meantime, many Americans felt the case proved that the United States had to keep out dangerous radicals.

Seeking Justice for Sacco and Vanzetti

Did Sacco and Vanzetti get a fair trial? Many Americans did not think so. One artist created this poster calling for a new trial. Writers such as Edna St. Vincent Millay and Countee Cullen also supported the two Italian-born anarchists. In spite of protests, Sacco and Vanzetti were executed in 1927. ★ **Why did some people question the verdict in the Sacco and Vanzetti trial?**

Limiting Immigration

In the end, the Red Scare died down. Yet anger against foreigners led to a new move to limit immigration. As you recall, this kind of antiforeign feeling is known as nativism.

The quota system

After years of war, millions of Europeans hoped to find a better life in the United States. American workers feared that a flood of newcomers would force wages down. Others worried that communists and anarchists would invade the United States.

Congress responded by passing the **Emergency Quota Act** in 1921. The act set up a quota system that allowed only a certain number of people from each country to enter the United States. "America must be kept American," said Calvin Coolidge.

The quota system favored immigrants from Northern Europe, especially Britain. In 1924, Congress passed new laws that further cut immigration, especially from Eastern Europe, which was seen as a center of anarchism and communism. In addition, Japanese were added to the list of Asians denied entry to the country.

Newcomers from Latin America

Latin Americans and Canadians were not included in the quota system. As a result, Mexican immigrants continued to move to the United States. Farms and factories in the Southwest depended on Mexican workers. By 1930, a million or more Mexicans had crossed the border. Most came to work in the vegetable fields, orchards, and factories of the Southwest. The pay was low and the housing was poor. Still, the chance to earn more money was a very powerful lure.

Puerto Ricans also moved to the mainland in large numbers. In 1917, the **Jones Act** granted American citizenship to Puerto Ricans. Poverty on the island led to a great migration to the north. In 1910, only 1,500 Puerto Ricans lived on the mainland. By 1930, there were 53,000.

The Scopes Trial

In the 1920s, cities drew thousands of people from farms and small towns. Those who stayed in rural areas often feared that new ways of life in the city were a threat to traditional values.

The clash between old and new values erupted in the small town of Dayton, Tennessee. At the center of the controversy was Charles Darwin's theory of evolution. Darwin, a British scientist, had claimed that all life had evolved, or developed, from simpler forms over a long period of time.

Some churches condemned Darwin's theory, saying it denied the teachings of the Bible. Tennessee, Mississippi, and Arkansas passed laws that banned the teaching of Darwin's theory. In 1925, John Scopes, a biology teacher in Dayton, taught evolution to his class. Scopes was arrested and tried.

Two of the nation's best-known figures opposed each other in the **Scopes trial.** William Jennings Bryan, who had run for President three times, argued the state's case against Scopes. Clarence Darrow, a Chicago lawyer who had helped unions and radicals, defended Scopes.

As the trial began, the nation's attention was riveted on Dayton. Reporters recorded every word of the battle between Darrow and Bryan. "Scopes isn't on trial," Darrow thundered at one point, "civilization is on trial." Darrow even put Bryan on the witness stand to show how little he knew about science. Bryan firmly defended his belief in the Bible.

In the end, Scopes was convicted and fined. The law against teaching evolution remained on the books, although it was rarely enforced.

The New Klan

Fear of change gave new life to an old organization. In 1915, a group of white men in Georgia declared the rebirth of the Ku Klux Klan. The original Klan had used terror to keep African Americans from voting after the Civil War. (See page 487.) The new Klan had a broader aim: to preserve the United States for white, native-born Protestants.

The new Klan waged a campaign against immigrants, especially Catholics and Jews. Klan members burned crosses outside people's homes. They used whippings and lynchings to terrorize immigrants and African Americans. The Klan strongly supported efforts to limit immigration.

Because of its large membership, the Klan gained political influence. In the mid-1920s, however, many Americans became alarmed at the Klan's growing power. At the same time, scandals surfaced that showed Klan leaders had stolen money from members. Klan membership dropped sharply.

Fighting Racism

African Americans had hoped that their service during World War I would weaken racism at home. However, returning black soldiers found that the South was still a segregated society. In the North, too, racial prejudice was widespread.

Racial tensions in the North

Many African Americans moved north during and after the war. They took factory jobs in Chicago, Detroit, New York, Philadelphia, and other large cities. The newcomers often found that only the lowest-paying jobs were open to them. Also, in many neighborhoods, whites refused to rent apartments to blacks.

Viewing HISTORY **Rebirth of the Ku Klux Klan**

This photo shows members of the Ku Klux Klan parading in front of the Capitol Building in Washington, D.C. Many Americans were alarmed by the rebirth of the Klan. Journalist William Allen White warned, "To make a case against a birthplace, a religion, or a race is wickedly un-American and cowardly." ★ **Why do you think White described the Klan as "un-American"?**

At the same time, many blacks newly arrived from the South wanted to live near one another. As a result, areas with large black populations grew in many northern cities.

Many northern white workers felt threatened by the arrival of so many African Americans. Racial tension grew. In 1919, race riots broke out in several cities. The worst took place in Chicago, leaving 38 dead.

Marcus Garvey

Shocked by the racism they found, African Americans looked for new ways to cope. **Marcus Garvey** became one of the most popular black leaders. Garvey organized the Universal Negro Improvement Association. He hoped to promote unity and pride among African Americans. "I am the equal of any white man," Garvey said.

Garvey urged African Americans to seek their roots in Africa. Although few black Americans actually went to Africa, Garvey's "Back to Africa" movement built racial pride.

Election of 1928

By 1928, Republicans had led the nation for eight years. They pointed to prosperity as their outstanding achievement. Still, when asked about the upcoming election, President Coolidge said tersely, "I do not choose to run." Instead, Secretary of Commerce **Herbert Hoover** easily won the Republican nomination. The Democrats chose as their candidate **Alfred E. Smith,** a former governor of New York.

The contrast between the candidates revealed the tensions lurking below the surface of American life. Smith, the son of Irish immigrants, was the first Catholic to run for President. City dwellers, including many immigrants and Catholics, rallied around Smith. Hoover was a self-made millionaire from the Midwest. He won votes from rural Americans and big business. Supporters of Prohibition also supported Hoover because Smith favored repeal.

In the election, Smith won the country's 12 largest cities. Rural and small-town voters, however, supported Hoover. He won by a landslide.

Americans hoped Hoover would keep the country prosperous. Less than a year after Hoover took office, however, the economy would come crashing down.

★ Section 4 Review ★

Recall

1. **Identify** **(a)** Red Scare, **(b)** Sacco and Vanzetti trial, **(c)** Emergency Quota Act, **(d)** Jones Act, **(e)** Scopes trial, **(f)** Marcus Garvey, **(g)** Herbert Hoover, **(h)** Alfred E. Smith.
2. **Define** **(a)** company union, **(b)** sabotage, **(c)** anarchist, **(d)** deport, **(e)** nativism, **(f)** quota system.

Comprehension

3. Describe the problems each of the following faced in the 1920s: **(a)** farmers, **(b)** labor unions.
4. Why did the Red Scare lead Americans to demand limits on immigration?
5. **(a)** What did African American soldiers expect when they returned home after World War I? **(b)** What conditions did they face?

Critical Thinking and Writing

6. **Linking Past and Present** **(a)** Does anti-immigration sentiment exist in the United States today? **(b)** At which groups is it directed? **(c)** What might be some reasons people give for resenting those groups?
7. **Defending a Position** "Groups such as the Ku Klux Klan have a right to exist under the Constitution." Do you agree or disagree with this statement? Defend your position.

Activity **Drawing a Political Cartoon** You are one of the great newspaper cartoonists of the 1920s. Choose one of the issues or events described in this section and draw a political cartoon expressing your own view about it.

Chapter 25 Review and Activities

★ Sum It Up ★

Section 1 Politics and Prosperity

- President Harding's administration was marred by scandals.
- The economy boomed in the 1920s as industries produced new goods and the stock market soared.
- After World War I, many Americans favored a return to prewar isolationism.

Section 2 New Ways of Life

- During Prohibition, the manufacture and sale of alcoholic beverages was banned, but many Americans ignored the law.
- After winning the vote, women enjoyed new opportunities.
- A mass culture emerged as people began to watch movies, listen to radio, and travel in cars.

Section 3 The Jazz Age

- The 1920s were a time of changing fashions, including the popularity of jazz.
- Many writers of the 1920s criticized American life.
- African American writers and artists brought about a rebirth of black arts and literature.

Section 4 Trouble Below the Surface

- Many farmers and workers did not share in the prosperity of the 1920s.
- Fearing foreign radicals, the United States acted to limit immigration.

For additional review of the major ideas of Chapter 25, see ***Guide to the Essentials of American History*** or ***Interactive Student Tutorial CD-ROM,*** which contains interactive review activities, graphic organizers, and practice tests.

Reviewing the Chapter

Define These Terms

Match each term with the correct definition.

Column 1	Column 2
1. disarmament	**a.** period of rising stock prices
2. recession	**b.** reduction of armed forces and weapons of war
3. bull market	**c.** illegal bar
4. speakeasy	**d.** person opposed to organized government
5. anarchist	**e.** economic slump

Explore the Main Ideas

1. What happened in the Teapot Dome Scandal?
2. How did the process of buying on margin work?
3. How did women's lives change during the 1920s?
4. Describe the themes explored by two American writers of the 1920s.
5. What was the Red Scare?

Graph Activity

Look at the graph below and answer the following questions. **1.** In which year were the most cars sold? **2.** About how many cars were purchased in 1923? **Critical Thinking** Do you think car sales would have increased if Ford had not introduced the assembly line? Explain.

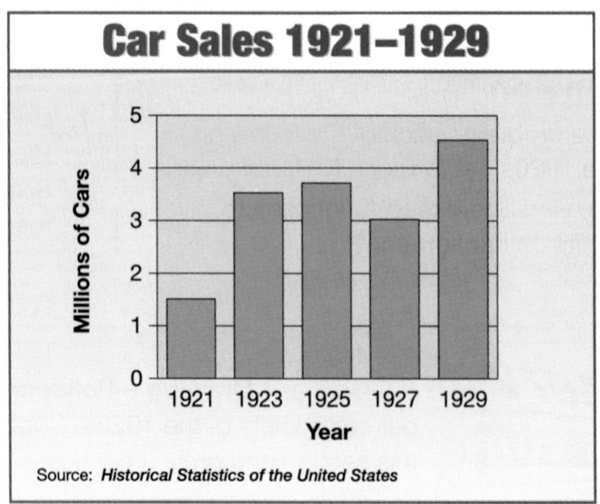

Critical Thinking and Writing

1. Exploring Unit Themes **Role of Government** What role did the United States government play in the economy during the 1920s?
2. **Predicting Consequences** During the 1920s, many Americans bought consumer goods on credit and stocks on margin. How would this make economic conditions worse after the economy began to slow down?
3. **Linking Past and Present** People sometimes compare today's war on drugs with Prohibition. **(a)** How are the two similar? **(b)** How are they different?
4. **Understanding Chronology** **(a)** Which came first, the rise of communism in Russia or the Red Scare in the United States? **(b)** How did one event follow from the other?

Using Primary Sources

Reporter Louis Stark gave this account of the final words of Bartolomeo Vanzetti just before he was executed:

> "Vanzetti spoke in English. His voice was calm throughout. There was not the slightest tremor or quaver.... He said...'I am innocent of all crime, not only of this, but all. I am an innocent man.' Then he spoke his last words: 'I wish to forgive some people for what they are doing to me.'"

Source: *The New York Times,* August 23, 1927.

Recognizing Points of View **(a)** What was Vanzetti's manner as he faced death? **(b)** What was Vanzetti's attitude toward those who were executing him? **(c)** If you had no other evidence about Vanzetti except his last words, would you think he was innocent or guilty? Explain.

Activity Bank

Interdisciplinary Activity

Exploring Economics A few experts predicted that the United States economy was headed for trouble in the 1920s. Find out what economists are predicting about today's economy. Then, write a report in which you explain the experts' predictions.

Career Skills Activity

Poets Write a poem in which you try to capture the mood of the 1920s. Remember that it was a complicated time in which some people had great wealth and fun and others struggled with poverty and racism. Try to reflect both sides of the times in your poem.

Citizenship Activity

Examining Immigration Do research in current sources to find out about the main issues surrounding immigration today. Create an illustrated poster in which you state your own view on immigration issues or explore different viewpoints.

Internet Activity

Use the Internet to find sites dealing with some aspect of jazz in the 1920s. For instance, you might focus on a famous musician or singer, a well-known jazz club, or a dance such as the Charleston. Then, do further research both on and off the Internet for a class presentation. Try to include a recording of jazz.

Eyewitness Journal

Choose one of the following important figures of the 1920s: a flapper; an African American writer; a woman moving into the world of work while also taking care of a family; a bootlegger; an Italian immigrant; or a business leader. In your Eyewitness Journal, describe the key events of the 1920s from your point of view.

Chapter 26 The Great Depression

1929–1941

What's Ahead

In October 1929, a stock market crash brought the prosperity of the Roaring Twenties to a sudden end. The period that followed, known as the Great Depression, was the worst economic disaster in United States history. Poverty, hunger, and joblessness became widespread. Believing the government should not interfere too much with the economy, President Herbert Hoover took only limited action.

Seeking bolder action, Americans elected Franklin Delano Roosevelt as President in 1932. Roosevelt started a large number of programs to restart the economy. Though Roosevelt's programs provided help for many Americans, other people criticized him for expanding the size and role of the government.

Why Study History? Few people saw the depression coming. Afterward, experts asked: What did we do wrong? By carefully studying the mistakes of the past, they hoped to prevent such a disaster from happening again. To focus on this connection, see this chapter's *Why Study History?* feature, "The Past Provides Lessons for Today."

American Events

- **1929** Stock market crash sets off Great Depression
- **1933** President Franklin Roosevelt begins New Deal
- **1935** Social Security Act sets up pensions for elderly and unemployed

1929 — 1931 — 1933 — 1935

World Events

- **1930 World Event** Effects of depression are felt worldwide
-  **1933 World Event** Economic problems lead to rise of dictator in Germany

Viewing HISTORY **Out of Work**

Millions of Americans were thrown out of work during the nation's worst economic depression. Isaac Soyer's painting Employment Agency *captures the despair felt by many Americans who lost their jobs.* ★ **How does this painting convey a mood of hopelessness?**

1935
Wagner Act gives unions right to collective bargaining

1937
President Roosevelt tries to increase number of Supreme Court justices

1941
United States enters World War II

1935 | 1937 | 1939 | 1941

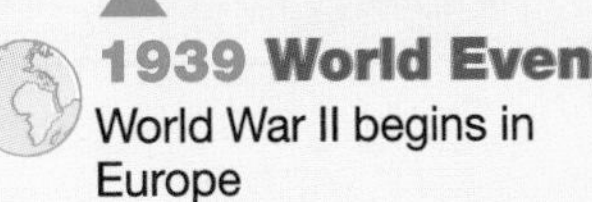

1939 World Event
World War II begins in Europe

The Economy Crashes

Explore These Questions
- Why did the stock market crash?
- How did the Great Depression affect the nation?
- How did Hoover try to end the crisis?

Define
- capital
- bankrupt
- relief program
- soup kitchen
- public works
- bonus

Identify
- Black Tuesday
- Great Depression
- Reconstruction Finance Corporation
- Bonus Army

Herbert Hoover was confident as he campaigned for election in 1928. Pointing to the booming economy, Hoover declared:

> ❝ We in America are nearer to the final triumph over poverty than ever before in the history of any land. The poorhouse is vanishing from among us. ❞

Hoover took office in March 1929. Only seven months later, a stock market crash signaled the start of the worst economic crisis in the nation's history.

An Economy in Trouble

Hoover did realize that some Americans had not shared in the prosperity of the 1920s. Farmers, especially, faced hard times. Once in office, Hoover persuaded Congress to create the Federal Farm Board. It helped farmers market their products and worked to keep prices stable. Farmers, however, did not reduce production. As a result, prices for farm products stayed low.

Low farm prices were only one sign of trouble. The economy was slowing down. The demand for new homes and office buildings fell. Consumers were buying less. Wealth was distributed unevenly, with less than 1 percent of the population controlling a third of the nation's resources. However, the government kept few detailed records, so most Americans were unaware of the problems.

Connections With Science

First Lady Lou Henry Hoover was the first American woman to earn a degree in geology. Along with her husband, she won honors for translating a 1556 textbook on mining from Latin into English. She also published many scientific articles and founded the Women's Amateur Athletic Federation.

Stock Market Crash

By August 1929, a few investors had begun selling their stocks. They felt the boom might end soon. In September, more people decided to sell. The rash of selling caused stock prices to fall. Hoover reassured investors that the "business of the country is on a sound and prosperous basis." Still, the selling continued and stock prices tumbled.

Many investors had bought stocks on margin. (See page 676.) Now, with prices falling, brokers asked investors to pay what they owed. Investors who could not pay had to sell their stock. A panic quickly set in. Between October 24 and October 29, desperate people tried to unload millions of shares. As a result, stock prices dropped even more.

On Tuesday, October 29, a stampede of selling hit the New York Stock Exchange. Prices plunged because there were no buyers. People who thought they owned valuable stocks were left with worthless paper. Millionaires lost their fortunes overnight.

Newspaper headline of October 24, 1929 ➤

BROOKLYN DAILY EAGLE

And Complete Long Island News

LATE NEWS

WALL ST. IN PANIC AS STOCKS CRASH

Attempt Made to Kill Italy's Crown Prince

Viewing HISTORY The Stock Market Crashes

After the dizzying prosperity of the Roaring Twenties, the stock market crash caught the nation by surprise. In the panic that followed, many people who had made fortunes lost them overnight. Here, a well-dressed New Yorker tries to sell the expensive car he bought when times were good. ★ **What effect did panic have on stock prices?**

After **Black Tuesday,** as it became known, business leaders tried to restore confidence in the economy. John D. Rockefeller told reporters, "My son and I have for some days been purchasing some common stocks." Replied comedian Eddie Cantor, "Sure, who else has any money left?"

Onset of the Depression

The period of economic hard times that followed the crash is known as the **Great Depression.** It lasted until 1941.

The stock market crash did not cause the Great Depression, but it did shake people's confidence in the economy. As the depression worsened, people tried to understand how the prosperity of the 1920s had vanished.

Causes

Among the chief causes of the Great Depression was overproduction. American factories and farms produced vast amounts of goods in the 1920s. Yet, because wages did not keep up with prices, workers could not afford to buy luxury goods. Farmers also had little money for cars and other items. Soon, factories and farms were producing more goods than people were buying. As orders slowed, factories closed or laid off workers.

Another cause of the depression was weakness in the banking system. During the 1920s, banks made unwise loans. For example, banks lent money to struggling farmers and people who invested in the stock market. When the stock market crashed, borrowers could not repay their loans. Without the money from the loans, the banks could not give depositors their money when they asked for it. Many banks were forced to close.

More than 5,000 banks closed between 1929 and 1932. When a bank closed, depositors lost the money they had in the bank. A family's savings could disappear overnight.

A cycle of disaster

After the stock market crash, the economy skidded downhill. One disaster triggered another. The stock market crash, for example, ruined many investors. Without **capital,** or money, from investors, businesses could no longer grow and expand. Businesses could not turn to banks for capital, since the banks were in trouble, too.

As factories cut back on production, they cut wages and laid off workers. Unemployed workers, in turn, had little money to spend, so demand for goods fell. In the end, many businesses declared that they had gone **bankrupt,** or unable to pay their debts. As bankrupt businesses closed their doors, even more people were thrown out of work.

The Great Depression led to a worldwide economic crisis. In the 1920s, the United States had loaned large sums to European

Why Study History?

Because the Past Provides Lessons for Today

Historical Background

The stock market crash of 1929 ended the prosperity and optimism of the 1920s. In the disaster that followed, everyone looked for reasons why. Economists and historians examined the evidence to find out what had gone wrong—and why no one had seen it coming.

There was more than one answer. Wild speculation, risky loans, margin buying, and in the end, panic selling all contributed to the crash. (See page 703.) Unequal distribution of wealth and income, overproduction, and widespread bank failures fueled the depression that followed.

Connections to Today

Government and business leaders took steps to prevent another depression. Today, the federal government carefully regulates banking practices to avoid a repeat of the 1929 crash. The Federal Deposit Insurance Corporation (FDIC) insures bank deposits up to $100,000. If a bank fails, depositors can still get their money. The Securities and Exchange Commission (SEC) protects investors by watching for signs of illegal activities in the stock market.

A less serious stock crash in 1987 led the government to increase the power of the SEC. Today, SEC regulators can temporarily stop trading if average prices drop too greatly and too suddenly. By doing so, regulators hope to avoid the kind of panic that contributed to the great crash.

Connections to You

Since 1929, no stock market crash has been so severe. Because we learned from the mistakes of the past, you can face a safer future.

You, too, can learn from the past—what to avoid and what to copy. As historian Gerda Lerner noted, "Human beings have always used history in order to find their direction toward the future: to repeat the past or depart from it."

1. **Comprehension** **(a)** How does the FDIC protect bank depositors today? **(b)** How does the SEC protect stock investors?
2. **Critical Thinking** Describe two things that people could have done in the 1920s to help avoid the Great Depression.

Collecting Primary Sources Put together a collection of primary sources on the Great Depression. Include the words of people who experienced hard times firsthand. You might also include copies of photographs.

The New York Stock Exchange is still an active center of American business.

nations. When American banks stopped making loans or demanded repayment of existing loans, European banks began to fail.

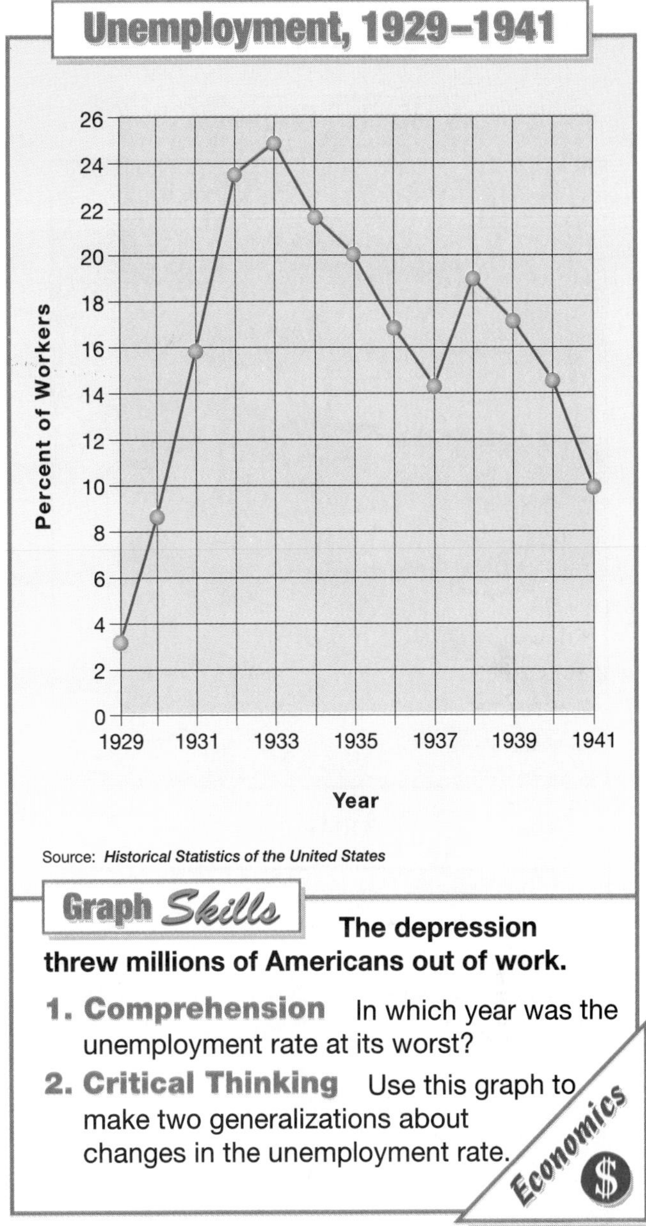

Graph *Skills* **The depression threw millions of Americans out of work.**

1. **Comprehension** In which year was the unemployment rate at its worst?
2. **Critical Thinking** Use this graph to make two generalizations about changes in the unemployment rate.

Hard Times

The United States had suffered other economic depressions. None, however, was as severe or lasted as long as the Great Depression. In earlier times, most Americans lived on farms and grew their own food. In the 1930s, millions of Americans lived in cities and worked in factories. When factories closed, the jobless had no money for food and no land on which to grow it.

Unemployment

As the depression spread, the unemployment rate soared. By the early 1930s, one in every four workers was jobless. Millions more worked shortened hours or took pay cuts. Many of the jobless lost their homes.

The chance of finding work was small. On an average day, one New York job agency had 5,000 people looking for work. Only about 300 found jobs. In another city, police had to keep order as 15,000 women pushed and shoved to apply for six jobs cleaning offices. Some of the jobless sold apples or shined shoes on street corners.

Human suffering

During the depression, families suffered. Marriage and birth rates dropped. Hungry parents and children searched through city dumps and restaurant garbage cans. In one school, a teacher ordered a thin little girl to go home to eat. "I can't," replied the girl. "This is my sister's day to eat."

The pressure of hard times led some families to split up. Fathers and even children as young as 13 or 14 years old left home to hunt for work. Their leaving meant the family had fewer people to feed.

Jobless men and women drifted from town to town looking for work. Some lived in railroad cars and hitched rides on freight trains. Louis Banks, a young black man, later described what it was like to "ride the rails":

> "Twenty-five or thirty would be out on the side of the rail, white and colored. They didn't have no mothers or sisters, they didn't have no home, they were dirty, they had overalls on, they didn't have no food, they didn't have anything."

Americans did their best to cope. Neighbors shared what little they had or exchanged services free of charge. Some families doubled up, taking in aunts, uncles, and cousins. Women began to grow vegetables and can foods instead of shopping in stores.

Still, the Great Depression shook Americans' belief in themselves. "No matter that others suffered the same fate, the inner voice whispered, 'I'm a failure,'" one unemployed man wrote.

Linking United States and the World

United States

Austria

A Worldwide Depression

The Great Depression caused misery throughout the industrialized world. From Europe to Japan, the jobless struggled desperately to survive. At top, unemployed, homeless New Yorkers camp out in rickety shacks in Central Park. At bottom, Austrians line up for hot soup on a city street. ★ **How did the depression spread from the United States to other countries?**

Hoover Responds

President Hoover expressed deep concern about the suffering of the jobless. He tried to restore confidence in the economy by predicting better times ahead. However, Hoover did not believe that government should become directly involved in helping to end the business crisis. It was up to businesses, he felt, to work together to end the downslide.

Relief programs

At first, Hoover also opposed government **relief programs**—programs to help the needy. Instead, the President urged business leaders to keep workers employed and to maintain wages.

Hoover also called on private charities to help the needy. Churches set up **soup kitchens,** places where the hungry could get a free meal. Ethnic communities organized their own relief efforts. In San Francisco's Chinatown, the Six Companies gave out food and clothing. Father Divine, an African American religious leader in New York's Harlem, fed 3,000 hungry people a day. Mexican Americans and Puerto Ricans turned to mutualistas, or aid societies. Still, the numbers of needy soon overwhelmed private charities.

Hoover realized he had to take other steps. He set up public works programs. **Public works** are projects built by the government for public use. The government hired workers to build schools, construct dams, and pave highways.

By providing jobs, government programs enabled people to earn money. Workers could then spend their wages on goods. Hoover hoped that the increased demand for goods would lead to business recovery.

Hoover also approved the **Reconstruction Finance Corporation,** or RFC. The RFC loaned money to railroads, banks, and insurance companies to help them stay in business. Saving these businesses, Hoover hoped, would also save workers' jobs.

The depression deepens

Hoover did more to reverse hard times than any previous President. Still, his efforts had little effect. In 1931, as the third winter of the depression approached, more and more people joined the ranks of the hungry and homeless.

Many people blamed the President for doing too little. They called the shacks where the homeless lived Hoovervilles. The newspapers that the homeless covered themselves with to keep warm were called "Hoover blankets." The unemployed staged hunger marches against the government.

The Bonus Army

Veterans of World War I also took action. After the war, Congress had voted to give veterans a bonus, or additional sum of money, to be paid in 1945. In 1932, more than 20,000 jobless veterans marched to Washington to demand the bonus right away.

The **Bonus Army,** as the veterans were called, traveled to the capital as cheaply as possible. One decorated soldier walked from New Jersey. "I done it all by my feet—shoe leather," he told Congress. "I come to show you people that we need our bonus." Some veterans brought their wives and children. For two months, the Bonus Army camped in a tent city along the Potomac River.

In the end, the Senate rejected a bill to pay the bonus immediately. Senators thought that the cost would destroy any hope for the country's recovery. Many of the veterans went home. Thousands of others remained, vowing to stay until 1945 if necessary.

Local police tried to force the veterans to leave. Battles with police left four people dead. Hoover then ordered General Douglas MacArthur to clear out the veterans. Using cavalry, tanks, machine guns, and tear gas, MacArthur moved into the camp and burned it to the ground. An editorial in the *Washington News* expressed the shock many Americans felt:

> "What a pitiful spectacle is that of the great American Government, mightiest in the world, chasing unarmed men, women, and children with Army tanks. . . . If the Army must be called out to make war on unarmed citizens, this is no longer America."

After the attack on the Bonus Army, the President lost what little support he still had. Convinced that the country needed a change, Americans turned to a new leader.

★ Section 1 Review ★

Recall

1. **Identify** **(a)** Black Tuesday, **(b)** Great Depression, **(c)** Reconstruction Finance Corporation, **(d)** Bonus Army.
2. **Define** **(a)** capital, **(b)** bankrupt, **(c)** relief program, **(d)** soup kitchen, **(e)** public works, **(f)** bonus.

Comprehension

3. Why did stock prices drop in October 1929?
4. What problems did Americans face during the Great Depression?
5. What steps did Hoover take to ease the economic crisis?

Critical Thinking and Writing

6. **Understanding Causes and Effects** Describe how each of the following contributed to the Great Depression: **(a)** stock market crash, **(b)** overproduction, **(c)** bank closings.
7. **Identifying Main Ideas** Review the subsection Hoover Responds on page 706. **(a)** What is the main idea of the subsection? **(b)** State two facts that support the main idea.

Activity **Formulating Questions** You're a reporter for a newspaper in 1932. It's up to you to explain President Hoover's policies to the American people. Write five questions you would like to ask Hoover during an interview.

2 The New Deal

As You Read

Explore These Questions
- Why did Americans elect Roosevelt in 1932?
- How did FDR restore faith in the banks?
- What programs made up the New Deal?

Define
- fireside chat
- surplus
- speculation

Identify
- Franklin Roosevelt
- Eleanor Roosevelt
- Frances Perkins
- Hundred Days
- New Deal
- Works Progress Administration
- Tennessee Valley Authority
- Federal Deposit Insurance Corporation

1932 campaign button

SETTING the Scene As the impact of the depression deepened, many Americans despaired. The government seemed helpless. In 1932, Democrats chose New York governor **Franklin Roosevelt** to run for President. Roosevelt seemed to respond to people's suffering. He told a friend:

> "I have looked into the faces of thousands of Americans. They have the frightened look of lost children . . . . They are saying: 'We're caught in something we don't understand; perhaps this fellow can help us out.'"

Franklin D. Roosevelt

Franklin Delano Roosevelt, known as FDR, came from a wealthy, influential family. He attended Harvard University and Columbia Law School. In 1905, he married a distant cousin, Anna Eleanor Roosevelt, a niece of former President Theodore Roosevelt. Together, Franklin and **Eleanor Roosevelt** forged a powerful partnership.

During World War I, FDR served as assistant secretary of the navy. In 1920, he was the Democratic candidate for Vice President.

Then, in the summer of 1921, Roosevelt was stricken with a severe case of polio. The disease left his legs paralyzed. With his wife's help, FDR struggled to rebuild his strength. The battle taught him patience and courage. Roosevelt once joked that, after a person had spent two years just trying to wiggle his small toe, everything else seemed easy. In the end, he was able to walk with the aid of heavy leg braces and crutches.

In time, Roosevelt returned to public life. In 1928, he was elected governor of New York. Then, in 1932, the Democrats named him their presidential candidate. The Republicans again nominated Hoover, even though they knew he had little chance of winning.

A Call to Action

Roosevelt set a new tone right from the start. He broke tradition by taking a plane to the Democratic convention to accept the nomination in person. Standing before the delegates, he declared: "I pledge myself to a new deal for the American people."

FDR did not spell out what he meant by "a new deal." Still, he sounded a hopeful note. In campaign speeches, he promised to help the jobless, poor farmers, and the elderly.

Voters responded to FDR's confident manner and personal charm. On election day, he won a landslide victory. Democrats also gained many seats in Congress. On inauguration day, the new President addressed the American people with optimism:

> "This great nation will endure as it has endured, will revive and will prosper. So, first of all, let me assert my firm belief that the only thing we have to fear is fear itself—nameless, unreasoning, unjustified terror which paralyzes needed efforts to convert retreat into advance."

FDR then issued a call to action. "The nation asks for action and action now," he said. Many Americans welcomed this energetic new President, especially since Hoover's more cautious approach had failed to end the nation's economic crisis.

The Hundred Days

During his campaign for the presidency, FDR had sought advice on how to fight the depression. He turned to a number of college professors who were experts on economic issues. These experts, nicknamed the Brain Trust, helped Roosevelt to plan bold new programs.

Once in office, President Roosevelt chose able advisers. Harold Ickes (IH keez), a Republican reformer from Chicago, became secretary of the interior. FDR named social worker **Frances Perkins** as secretary of labor. Perkins was the first woman to hold a Cabinet post.

The new President moved forward on many fronts. He urged his staff to "take a method and try it. If it fails, admit it and try another. But above all try something."

Starting with the banks

Roosevelt's first challenge was the nation's crumbling banking system. Many banks had closed. Fearful depositors had withdrawn their savings from others. People hid their money under mattresses or buried it in their yards.

FDR knew that without sound banks, the economy could not recover. On his second day in office, he declared a "bank holiday." He closed every bank in the country for eight days. He then asked Congress to pass the Emergency Banking Relief Act. Under this act, only those banks with enough funds to meet depositors' demands could reopen. Others had to stay closed.

A week after taking office, President Roosevelt spoke to Americans by radio. Under the new law, the President told the people, "it

Biography **Franklin and Eleanor Roosevelt**

Franklin and Eleanor Roosevelt belonged to a leading New York family. Both believed that the wealthy had a duty to help those less fortunate. As President, FDR put this belief into action. Eleanor used her position as First Lady to speak out on issues ranging from conditions in coal mines to justice for African Americans. She also acted as the President's "eyes and ears," traveling about the country and reporting back to him. He would often begin press conferences with the words: "My Missus says . . .". ★ **FDR told Americans that "the only thing we have to fear is fear itself." What do you think he meant?**

Skills FOR LIFE

Critical Thinking | Managing Information | **Communication** | Maps, Charts, and Graphs

Public Speaking

A middle school student gives a speech.

How Will I Use This Skill?

Knowing how to prepare and deliver a speech is a skill that you will find useful throughout your life. Some speeches are informative, such as an oral report in school or a presentation at the workplace. Other speeches may be persuasive. In a job interview, for example, you will speak about yourself and your skills to persuade an employer that you are the right person for the job.

LEARN the Skill

You can prepare and deliver a speech by following these steps:

1. Determine the topic and purpose of your speech. Some speeches are meant to be entertaining, while others may be informative or persuasive.
2. Understand the nature of your audience so that you can decide the appropriate content and style for your speech. For example, you would not speak to children the same way you would speak to adults. You would not address people who agree with you the same way you would address people with opposing ideas.
3. Prepare your speech. Do research to collect supporting information. Decide the style you will use. For example, will you be serious at all times or will you use some humor? Write your speech and practice it several times.
4. Deliver your speech. Speak clearly. If your audience is in front of you, remember to establish eye contact and use appropriate gestures. You might invite questions after the speech.

PRACTICE the Skill

Review the material about President Roosevelt's fireside chats on page 711. Then, answer the following questions:

1. (a) What was the topic of FDR's first fireside chat? (b) Why did he think it was necessary to give the speech?
2. (a) Who was Roosevelt's audience? (b) Why did his speeches need to be both informative and persuasive?
3. (a) What factual information did FDR need to support his first fireside chat? (b) What style of speaking did he use?
4. Do you think the chats might have been more effective if people could have seen the President speaking? Explain.

APPLY the Skill

Choose a topic that interests you. Then, follow the steps above to prepare and deliver a three-minute speech to the class. Afterward, invite comments from classmates as to how you might improve your presentation.

Viewing HISTORY **Recruiting for the CCC**

Posters like this one encouraged young men to join the Civilian Conservation Corps. The government provided "CCC boys" with housing, clothes, and food. This allowed them to send most of their earnings home to their families. After a hard day's work, the young men could play sports, go to dances, or attend self-improvement classes. ★ **How did the CCC benefit the country?**

is safer to keep your money in a reopened bank than under your mattress."

The radio broadcast worked. FDR explained things so clearly, said humorist Will Rogers, that even the bankers understood it. Reassured by the President, depositors returned their money to banks, and the banking system grew stronger.

FDR gave 30 radio speeches while in office. He called them **fireside chats** because he spoke from a chair near a fireplace in the White House. All across the nation, families gathered around their radios to listen. Many felt the President understood their problems.

A flood of new laws

The bank bill was the first of many bills FDR sent to Congress during his first three months in office. Between March 9 and June 16, 1933, Congress passed 15 major new laws. Even the President admitted he was "a bit shell-shocked" by the **Hundred Days,** as this period was called.

The bills covered programs from job relief to planning for economic recovery. Together, they made up Roosevelt's **New Deal.** The New Deal had three main goals: relief for the unemployed, plans for recovery, and reforms to prevent another depression.

Providing Relief

In 1933, when Roosevelt took office, 13 million Americans were out of work. The President asked Congress for a variety of programs to help the jobless.

CCC and FERA

Among the earliest New Deal programs was the Civilian Conservation Corps (CCC). The CCC hired unemployed single men between the ages of 18 and 25. For $1 a day, they planted trees, built bridges, worked on flood control projects, and developed new parks. The CCC served a double purpose. It conserved natural resources, and it gave jobs to young people.

The Federal Emergency Relief Administration (FERA) gave federal money to state and local agencies. These agencies then distributed the money to the unemployed.

WPA

In 1935, the Emergency Relief Appropriations Act set up the **Works Progress Administration** (WPA). The WPA put the jobless to work building hospitals, schools, parks, playgrounds, and airports.

The WPA also hired artists, photographers, actors, writers, and composers. Artists painted murals on public buildings. The Federal Theatre put on new plays for adults and children, as well as classics by writers such as Shakespeare.

Writers collected information about American life, folklore, and traditions. Some WPA writers interviewed African Americans who had lived under slavery. Today, scholars still use these "slave narratives" to learn firsthand about slave life.

American Heritage MAGAZINE

HISTORY HAPPENED HERE

◀ *WPA plaque on the River Walk*

San Antonio River Walk

You may ride down a highway, cross a bridge, or enter a post office—and never know you are seeing a piece of history. Hundreds of projects like these were built during the depression by the Works Progress Administration. On the San Antonio River in Texas, WPA workers constructed a network of concrete walkways, bridges, and stairs. Today, tourists from around the world enjoy the hotels, shops, and restaurants along the San Antonio River Walk, or Paseo del Rio.

★ ***To learn more about this historic site, write:*** *San Antonio Visitors Bureau, P.O. Box 2277, San Antonio, TX 78298-2277.*

Critics accused the WPA of creating make-work projects that did little to benefit the nation in the long run. "People don't eat in the long run," replied a New Dealer. "They eat every day."

Promoting Recovery

To bring about recovery, the President had to boost both industry and farming. He called for programs that greatly expanded the government's role in the economy.

Help for industry

To help industry, New Dealers drew up plans to control production, stabilize prices, and keep workers on the job. A key new law was the National Industrial Recovery Act (NIRA). Under this law, each industry wrote a code, or set of rules and standards, for production, wages, prices, and working conditions. The NIRA tried to end price cutting and worker layoffs.

To enforce the new codes, Congress set up the National Recovery Administration (NRA). Companies that followed the NRA codes stamped a blue eagle on their products. The government encouraged people to do business only with companies displaying the NRA eagle. The NRA soon ran into trouble, however. Many companies ignored the codes. Also, small businesses felt that the codes favored the biggest firms.

The NIRA also set up the Public Works Administration (PWA). It promoted recovery by hiring workers for thousands of public works projects. PWA workers built the Grand Coulee Dam in Washington, public schools in Los Angeles, and two aircraft carriers for the navy. Despite these efforts, the PWA did little to bring about recovery.

Help for farmers

On farms, overproduction remained the main problem. Surpluses kept prices and farmers' incomes low. A **surplus** occurs when farmers produce more than they can sell.

To help farmers, the President asked Congress to pass the Agricultural Adjustment Act (AAA). Under the AAA, the government paid farmers not to grow certain crops. Roosevelt hoped that with smaller harvests, prices would rise.

The government also paid farmers to plow surplus crops under the soil and to dispose of surplus cows and pigs. Many Americans were outraged that crops and livestock were being destroyed when people in the cities were going hungry. Yet the plan seemed necessary to help farmers recover.

The Rural Electrification Administration (REA) provided money to extend electric lines to rural areas. The number of farms with electricity rose from 10 percent to 25 percent. A farm woman recalled, "I just turned on the light and kept looking at Paw. It was the first time I'd ever seen him after dark." Electricity helped save many farms from ruin. For example, refrigeration meant that dairy farmers did not have to worry about milk going sour before it could be sent to market.

TVA

Perhaps the boldest program of the Hundred Days was the **Tennessee Valley Authority** (TVA). It set out to remake the Tennessee River valley. This vast region often suffered terrible floods. Because the farmland was so poor, more than half the region's families were on relief.

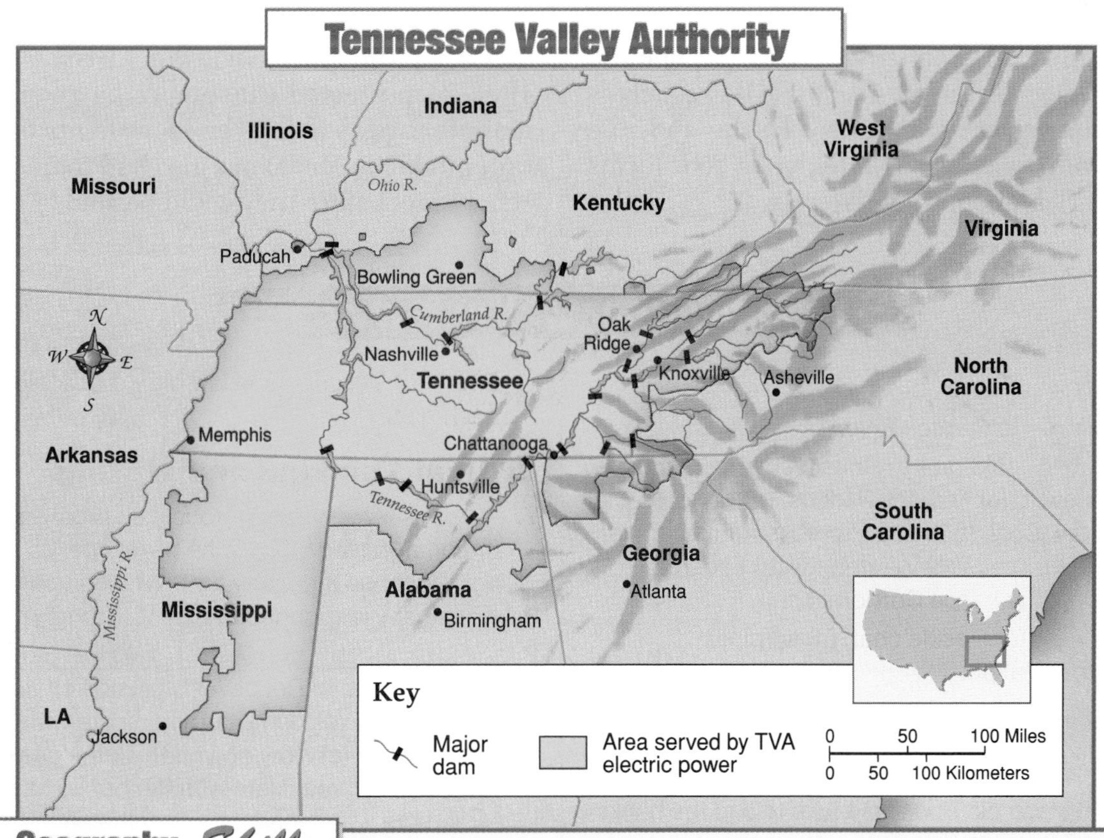

Geography Skills **The Tennessee Valley Authority directed projects that helped millions of people in the South.**

1. **Location** On the map, locate: **(a)** Tennessee River, **(b)** Cumberland River, **(c)** Nashville, **(d)** Knoxville.
2. **Interaction** What did the Tennessee Valley Authority do to control flooding of the Tennessee and Cumberland rivers?
3. **Critical Thinking** Based on this map, why was the Tennessee River valley a good area in which to develop hydroelectric power?

The TVA was a daring experiment in regional planning. To control flooding, TVA engineers built 40 dams in seven states. (See the map on page 713.) The dams also produced cheap electric power. In addition to building dams, the TVA deepened river channels for shipping. It planted new forests to conserve soil and developed new fertilizers to improve farmland. The agency also set up schools and health centers.

The TVA sparked a furious debate. Critics argued that the government had no right to interfere in the economy of the region. Power companies in the Tennessee River valley were especially outraged. They pointed out that the government could supply electrical power more cheaply than a private company could. Having to compete with the government, they said, might force them out of business.

Supporters replied that the TVA showed how the government could use its resources to help private enterprise. In the end, the program transformed a region of poor farms into a rich and productive area.

Long-Term Reforms

The third New Deal goal was to prevent another depression. During the Hundred Days, Congress passed laws regulating the stock market and the banking system. The Truth-in-Securities Act was designed to end wild **speculation**—risky buying and selling of stocks in the hope of making a quick profit. Experts agreed that uncontrolled speculation was a leading cause of the 1929 crash.

The **Federal Deposit Insurance Corporation** (FDIC) insured savings accounts in banks approved by the government. If a bank insured by the FDIC failed, the government would make sure depositors received their money.

Later New Deal laws strengthened government regulations. Laws regulated gas and electric companies. In 1938, a new law extended the Pure Food and Drug Act of 1906. It protected consumers by requiring manufacturers to list the ingredients of certain products. Medicines also had to undergo strict tests before they could be sold.

★ Section 2 Review ★

Recall

1. **Locate** Tennessee River.
2. **Identify** **(a)** Franklin Roosevelt, **(b)** Eleanor Roosevelt, **(c)** Frances Perkins, **(d)** Hundred Days, **(e)** New Deal, **(f)** Works Progress Administration, **(g)** Tennessee Valley Authority, **(h)** Federal Deposit Insurance Corporation.
3. **Define** **(a)** fireside chat, **(b)** surplus, **(c)** speculation.

Comprehension

4. Why did Americans elect Roosevelt in 1932?
5. What steps did Roosevelt take to end the banking crisis?
6. **(a)** What were the three main goals of the New Deal? **(b)** Describe one law aimed at achieving each goal.

Critical Thinking and Writing

7. **Making Inferences** Roosevelt promised the nation a "new deal," but he never spelled out exactly what he meant by that. Why do you think Americans responded to him so strongly?
8. **Linking Past and Present** **(a)** How did Americans respond to Roosevelt's fireside chats? **(b)** How do Presidents communicate with Americans today? **(c)** How do you think the use of mass media to communicate with the public has affected the way Americans view their Presidents?

Activity **Writing Persuasively** Do you have the "gift of gab"? You are a speechwriter for FDR. Write a radio speech in which you explain to ordinary Americans one of the programs of the New Deal. Remember, your goal is to be both reassuring and informative.

3 Reaction to the New Deal

As You Read

Explore These Questions

- Why did some Americans object to the New Deal?
- How did New Deal programs help workers and the elderly?
- Why was the New Deal a turning point in American history?

Define

- pension
- collective bargaining
- sitdown strike
- unemployment insurance
- laissez faire
- deficit spending
- national debt

Identify

- Huey Long
- Francis Townsend
- Charles Coughlin
- Liberty League
- Wagner Act
- John L. Lewis
- Social Security Act

SETTING the Scene The first hundred days of the New Deal encouraged a sense of hope among Americans. As noted political columnist Walter Lippmann commented:

> "At the end of February, we were a [group] of disorderly panic-stricken mobs and factions. In the hundred days from March to June, we became again an organized nation confident of our power to provide for our own security and control our own destiny."

Still, the New Deal failed to end the depression. As hard times lingered, critics of FDR and his policies grew louder.

Huey Long

Critics of the New Deal

From the beginning, a number of Americans had opposed the New Deal. Many of these critics wanted the government to do more. Others wanted it to do less.

Senator **Huey Long** of Louisiana had supported Roosevelt in 1932. However, Long soon turned on the President. The Kingfish, as Long was nicknamed, believed that FDR had not gone far enough to help the poor. Adopting the motto "Share Our Wealth," Long called for heavy taxes on the rich. He promised to use the tax money to provide every family with a house, a car, and a decent annual income. Millions of people, especially the poor, cheered Long's idea. They overlooked the fact that he had used bribery and threats to win political power.

A California doctor, **Francis Townsend,** also had a plan. The government, he said, had turned its back on older citizens. Townsend wanted everyone over age 60 to get a pension of $200 a month. A **pension** is a sum of money paid to people on a regular basis after they retire. People receiving the pension would have to retire, thus freeing a job for someone else. They would also agree to spend the pension money at once to boost the economy.

Like Long and Townsend, **Charles Coughlin** (KAWG lihn), a Roman Catholic priest, felt the New Deal did not go far enough. Father Coughlin spoke over the radio each week to almost 10 million listeners. The popular "radio priest" criticized Roosevelt for not taking strong action against bankers and rich investors.

On the other hand, many conservative political and business leaders felt the New Deal went too far. They formed the **Liberty League** to combat FDR's actions. The League complained that the New Deal interfered too

Viewing History: Trying to "Pack" the Supreme Court

Even supporters of FDR protested when the President asked Congress to increase the number of justices on the Supreme Court. This 1937 cartoon comments on the reaction of the Congress to FDR's plan. ★ **What does the donkey represent? Why do you think the cartoonist included it?**

much with business and with people's lives. The government, they warned, was taking away basic American freedoms.

FDR and the Supreme Court

In 1935, the Supreme Court entered the debate. Roosevelt and his advisers defended the New Deal by comparing the depression to a national emergency. The government had to increase its powers, they said, just as it had during World War I. The Supreme Court disagreed.

In 1935, the Supreme Court ruled that the National Industrial Recovery Act was unconstitutional. The NIRA, said the Court, gave too much power to the President and to the federal government. A year later, the Court struck down the Agricultural Adjustment Act. Then it overturned nine other New Deal laws. To Roosevelt, the Supreme Court rulings threatened not only the New Deal but his ability to lead the nation.

A plan to expand the Court

Roosevelt waited until after the 1936 election to take action. He easily beat his Republican opponent. FDR thought the election results showed that Americans favored his programs.

Soon after his inauguration in January 1937, Roosevelt put forward a plan to reshape the federal courts. He called for raising the number of Justices on the Supreme Court from 9 to 15. The change would make it possible for him to appoint six new Justices who supported his programs.

A defeat and a victory

The President's move raised a loud outcry. Both supporters and critics of the New Deal accused him of trying to "pack" the Court with Justices who supported his views. They saw his move as a threat to the separation of powers set up by the Constitution.

For six months, the President fought for his plan. Even his allies in Congress deserted him. Finally, he withdrew his proposal.

Still, in the end, Roosevelt got the Supreme Court majority he wanted without a battle. One Justice who had voted against many New Deal laws changed his views. Another retired. FDR filled his place with a new Justice who was favorable to his programs. During his years in office, FDR had the chance to appoint nine new Justices—more than any President since Washington.

Labor Reforms

During the New Deal, FDR supported programs to help workers. In 1935, Congress passed the National Labor Relations Act, or **Wagner Act.** Senator Robert Wagner, the act's sponsor, was a strong supporter of labor.

Unions grow stronger

The Wagner Act protected American workers from unfair management practices, such as firing a worker for joining a union. It also guaranteed workers the right to collec-

New Deal Programs

Program	Initials	Begun	Purpose
Civilian Conservation Corps	CCC	1933	Provided jobs for young men to plant trees, build bridges and parks, and set up flood control projects
Tennessee Valley Authority	TVA	1933	Built dams to provide cheap electric power to seven southern states; set up schools and health centers
Federal Emergency Relief Administration	FERA	1933	Gave relief to unemployed and needy
Agricultural Adjustment Administration	AAA	1933	Paid farmers not to grow certain crops
National Recovery Administration	NRA	1933	Enforced codes that regulated wages, prices, and working conditions
Public Works Administration	PWA	1933	Built ports, schools, and aircraft carriers
Federal Deposit Insurance Corporation	FDIC	1933	Insured savings accounts in banks approved by the government
Rural Electrification Administration	REA	1935	Loaned money to extend electricity to rural areas
Works Progress Administration	WPA	1935	Employed men and women to build hospitals, schools, parks, and airports; employed artists, writers, and musicians
Social Security Act	SSA	1935	Set up a system of pensions for the elderly, unemployed, and people with disabilities

Graph Skills **Congress passed dozens of new laws as part of FDR's New Deal. This chart describes 10 major New Deal programs.**

1. **Comprehension** **(a)** Which programs provided work for the unemployed? **(b)** Which provided financial aid?
2. **Critical Thinking** Which of the New Deal programs do you consider to be most important today? Explain.

Economics $

tive bargaining. **Collective bargaining** is the process in which a union representing a group of workers negotiates with management for a contract. Workers had fought for this right since the late 1800s.

The Wagner Act helped union membership grow from 3 million to 9 million during the 1930s. Union membership got a further boost when **John L. Lewis** set up the Congress of Industrial Organizations (CIO). The CIO represented workers in whole industries, such as steel, automobiles, and textiles.

With more members, unions increased their bargaining power. They also became a powerful force in politics.

Struggles and victories

Despite the Wagner Act, employers tried to stop workers from joining unions. Violent confrontations often resulted.

Workers then tried a new strategy. At the Goodyear Tire Factory in Akron, Ohio, workers staged a **sitdown strike.** They stopped all machines and refused to leave the factory until Goodyear recognized their union. The sitdown strike worked. Workers at other factories made use of this method until the Supreme Court outlawed it in 1939.

Roosevelt persuaded Congress to help nonunion workers, too. The Fair Labor Standards Act of 1938 set a minimum wage of 40

Launching the Social Security System

Posters like these encouraged workers to sign up for the new Social Security system. Today, Social Security continues to provide income for retired or disabled Americans.

★ **How does the government get the money to pay Social Security benefits?**

cents an hour. The act also set maximum hours—44 a week—for workers in a number of industries. At the same time, it banned children under the age of 16 from working in these industries.

Social Security

On another front, the President sought to help the elderly. In the 1930s, the United States was the only major industrial nation that did not have a formal pension program. FDR and Secretary of Labor Perkins pushed to enact an old-age pension program.

In September 1935, Congress passed the **Social Security Act.** The new law had three parts. First, it set up a system of pensions for older people. Payments from employers and employees supported this system.

Second, the new act set up the nation's first system of **unemployment insurance.** People who lost their jobs received small payments until they found work again. Third, the act gave states money to support dependent children and people with disabilities.

Critics condemned Social Security. Some argued that it did too little for the elderly and unemployed. Others pointed out that it did not include farm workers, domestic servants, or the self-employed—many of whom were women or members of minority groups. Conservatives, on the other hand, saw Social Security as another way for the government to meddle in people's lives.

Despite these attacks, the Social Security system survived. It has been expanded over the years. Today, it provides medical benefits to older Americans as well as pensions and unemployment insurance.

The New Deal: Good or Bad?

The New Deal changed American government forever. Ever since, Americans have debated whether the change was good or bad for the country.

Arguments against the New Deal

Before the 1930s, most Americans had little contact with the federal government. New Deal programs, however, touched almost every citizen. The federal government grew in size and power. It took on new jobs—from helping the needy to ensuring that the economy prospered.

Many people worried about the increased power of government. They complained that the government was intruding into people's lives, threatening both individual freedoms and private property. These critics called for a return to the traditional policy of **laissez faire**—a policy based on the idea that government should play as small a role as possible in the economy. Former President Hoover warned:

> ❝ Either we shall have a society based upon ordered liberty and the initiative of the individual, or we shall have a planned society that means dictation no matter what you

call it or who does it. There is no half-way ground. ”

Critics also expressed alarm because the government was spending more than it took in. This practice of **deficit spending** was creating a huge increase in the **national debt,** or the total sum of money the government owes.

Finally, despite its vast spending, the New Deal had not achieved its major goal—ending the depression. In fact, full economic recovery did not come until 1941. By then, the United States was producing goods for nations fighting in World War II.

Arguments for the New Deal

Supporters of the New Deal noted that FDR had steered the nation through the worst days of the depression. New Deal legislation had ended the banking crisis, protected farmers, and found work for millions of unemployed.

Supporters also argued that the government had a responsibility to use its power to help all its citizens, not just business and the wealthy. Programs like Social Security, New Dealers said, were necessary for national survival.

Most important of all, supporters argued, the New Deal had saved the nation's democratic system. Elsewhere in the world, people were turning to dictators to lead them out of hard times. President Roosevelt, on the other hand, worked to use the powers of the federal government to restore the nation to economic health while preserving its liberties. Roosevelt declared:

> “I believe in my heart that... here in America we are waging a great and successful war. It is not alone a war against want and destitution and economic demoralization.... It is a war for the survival of democracy. ”

Over the years, Americans have continued to debate the expanded role of government that began during the New Deal. The question of whether government management of the economy will harm the free enterprise system remains a lively one today.

★ Section 3 Review ★

Recall

1. **Identify** **(a)** Huey Long, **(b)** Francis Townsend, **(c)** Charles Coughlin, **(d)** Liberty League, **(e)** Wagner Act, **(f)** John L. Lewis, **(g)** Social Security Act.
2. **Define** **(a)** pension, **(b)** collective bargaining, **(c)** sitdown strike, **(d)** unemployment insurance, **(e)** laissez faire, **(f)** deficit spending, **(g)** national debt.

Comprehension

3. Describe why each of the following criticized the New Deal: **(a)** Huey Long, **(b)** Francis Townsend, **(c)** the Liberty League.
4. How did the Wagner Act help workers?
5. **(a)** How did the New Deal change the role of the government? **(b)** State one argument for and one argument against the New Deal.

Critical Thinking and Writing

6. **Defending a Position** **(a)** Why did many Americans oppose Roosevelt's plan to increase the size of the Supreme Court? **(b)** Do you agree or disagree with these critics? Explain.
7. **Linking Past and Present** **(a)** Describe three ways in which the federal government directly affects your life today. **(b)** Do you think you are better off or worse off as a result? Explain.

Activity **Writing an Editorial** Which side are you on? Write an editorial in which you agree or disagree with one of the critics of the New Deal—Huey Long, Francis Townsend, Charles Coughlin, or the Liberty League. Give reasons for the position you take.

4 Surviving Hard Times

As You Read

Explore These Questions
- What was the Dust Bowl?
- How did the Great Depression affect women and minorities?
- How did Americans find escape from the hardships of the depression?

Define
- migrant worker
- civil rights
- repatriate

Identify
- Dust Bowl
- Black Cabinet
- Mary McLeod Bethune
- Indian New Deal
- John Steinbeck
- Richard Wright
- Dorothea Lange

A cotton picker in Texas sat by the road as others worked in nearby fields. "I picked all week and made 85 cents," the man said in a hopeless voice. "I can starve sitting down a lot easier than I can picking cotton."

Across the country, Americans struggled to survive. New Deal programs helped some. Others made ends meet as best they could.

The Dust Bowl

During much of the 1930s, states from Texas to the Dakotas suffered a severe drought. One region—including parts of Oklahoma, Kansas, Colorado, New Mexico, and Texas—was especially hard hit. The topsoil dried out. High winds carried the soil away in blinding dust storms. As a result, this area of the Great Plains became known as the **Dust Bowl.**

Black blizzards

Dust storms, called black blizzards, buried farmhouses, fences, and even trees. People put shutters over doors and windows, but the dust blew in anyway. Even food crunched when it was chewed.

Dust storms were widespread. One storm blew dust from Oklahoma to Albany, New York, and out into the Atlantic Ocean. When the dry winds came, a third of the Great Plains just blew away. A Kansas farmer sadly reported that he sat by his window counting the farms going by.

What caused the disaster? Years of overgrazing by cattle and plowing by farmers destroyed the grasses that once held the soil in place. The drought of the 1930s and high winds did the rest.

Migrant workers

Hardest hit by the drought and dust storms were poor farmers in Oklahoma and Arkansas. Hundreds of these "Okies" and "Arkies" packed their belongings into cars and trucks and headed west. They became **migrant workers**—people who move from one region to another in search of work. They hoped to find jobs in the orchards and farms of California, Oregon, or Washington.

Once they reached the West Coast, the migrants faced a new disaster—they were not wanted. Local citizens feared that the newcomers would take away jobs from people already living in the West. Sometimes, angry crowds blocked the highways and sent the migrants away. Those who did find work were paid little. They lived in tents and cardboard shacks without any water or electricity.

Working Women

Working women faced special problems during the depression. If jobs were available, employers hired men before they would hire women. Even the federal government refused to hire a woman if her husband had a job. Some New Deal programs, such as the CCC, were not open to women at all.

Geography Skills **In the 1930s, drought and wind erosion ruined farmlands across much of the Great Plains. The hardest hit area became known as the Dust Bowl.**

1. **Location** On the map, locate: **(a)** Kansas, **(b)** Oklahoma, **(c)** Texas, **(d)** Nebraska, **(e)** South Dakota.
2. **Region** According to the map, which three states were most affected by severe drought and erosion?
3. **Critical Thinking** Why did many farmers migrate from the Great Plains to California in the 1930s?

Women in the workplace

Despite such obstacles, millions of women earned wages in order to support themselves and their families. During the 1930s, the number of married women in the workforce increased by 52 percent. Educated women took jobs as secretaries, school teachers, and social workers. Other women earned a living as maids, factory workers, and seamstresses.

Some women workers struck for better pay. In San Antonio, Texas, at least 80 percent of the pecan shellers were Mexican American women. When employers lowered their pay, a young worker, Emma Tenayuca, organized the shellers and led them off the job. Tenayuca said later, "I had a basic faith in the American idea of freedom and fairness. I felt something had to be done."

Biography **Marian Anderson**

In 1939, Marian Anderson was already a world-famous singer. Yet she was refused permission to sing at a private hall in Washington. Outraged, Eleanor Roosevelt arranged for Anderson to give a concert at the Lincoln Memorial. On Easter, some 75,000 people gathered to hear Anderson. Anderson later became the first African American to sing at the Metropolitan Opera in New York. ★ **Why was the Lincoln Memorial a fitting place for Anderson's concert?**

An active First Lady

Eleanor Roosevelt created a new role for herself as First Lady. Acting as the "eyes and ears" of the President, she toured the nation—traveling 40,000 miles in one year alone. She visited farms and Indian reservations and even traveled deep down into a coal mine. She talked to homemakers, observing the condition of their clothing on the washline. Back in Washington, she told the President what she had seen and heard.

The First Lady did more than just aid the President. She used her position to speak out for women's rights, as well as other issues. She gave press conferences for women reporters only. In her newspaper column, "My Day," she called on Americans to live up to the goal of equal justice for all. By speaking out on social issues, Eleanor Roosevelt angered some people. However, many other Americans admired her strong stands.

African Americans

When the Great Depression hit, African American workers were often the first to lose their jobs. Many times, they were denied public works jobs. At relief centers, young African American men were threatened or beaten when they signed up for work. Some charities even refused to serve blacks at centers giving out food to the needy.

Eleanor Roosevelt and others close to the President urged him to improve the situation of African Americans. Thousands of young black men learned a trade through the CCC, for example.

FDR reached out to African Americans. In doing so, he won their support for the Democratic party. The President invited black leaders to the White House to advise him. These unofficial advisers became known as the **Black Cabinet.** They included Robert C. Weaver, a Harvard-educated economist, and **Mary McLeod Bethune,** a well-known Florida educator. FDR appointed Bethune to head the National Youth Administration's Division of Negro Affairs. She was the first African American to head a government agency.

Often, Roosevelt followed the advice of the Black Cabinet. However, when African American leaders pressed the President to support an antilynching law, he refused. He feared that by doing so he would lose the support of southerners in Congress for his New Deal programs.

Connections With Civics

Arthur W. Mitchell of Chicago was the first black Democrat elected to Congress. In 1937, a railroad conductor ejected Representative Mitchell from a Pullman car because Arkansas state law prohibited blacks from riding in the same car as whites. Mitchell took his case to the Supreme Court and won.

Many black leaders called on African Americans to unite to achieve **civil rights**—the rights due to all citizens. They used their votes, won higher-level government jobs, and kept up pressure for equal treatment. Slowly, they made a few gains. However, the struggle for civil rights would take many more years.

Mexican Americans

By the 1930s, Mexican Americans worked in cities around the country. A large number, however, were farm workers in the West and Southwest. There, they faced discrimination in education, jobs, and at the polls.

In good times, employers had encouraged Mexicans to move north and take jobs. When hard times struck, however, many Americans wanted Mexicans to be **repatriated,** that is, sent back to their original country. More than 400,000 people were rounded up and sent to Mexico. Some of them were citizens who had been born in the United States.

Asian Americans

Asian Americans also faced discrimination. They were often refused service at barber shops, restaurants, and other public places. White Americans resented Chinese, Japanese, and Filipino workers who competed with them for scarce jobs. Sometimes violence against Asians erupted.

Responding to pressure, the government sought to reduce the number of Asians in the United States. In 1935, FDR signed the Repatriation Act. This law provided free transportation for Filipinos who agreed to return to the Philippines and not come back. Many took advantage of this offer.

Native Americans

In 1924, Congress had granted all Native Americans citizenship. Still, most Native Americans lived in terrible poverty. President Roosevelt encouraged new policies toward Native Americans.

In the 1930s, Congress passed a series of laws that have been called the **Indian New Deal.** The laws gave Native American nations greater control over their own affairs.

Cause and Effect

Causes

- Great Depression deepens
- Banking system nears collapse
- Millions of people are jobless
- Many businesses are bankrupt
- FDR becomes President

The New Deal

Effects

- Role of government in the economy increases
- Social Security gives pensions to retired people
- People who lose their jobs can receive money from unemployment insurance
- Savings accounts in banks are insured by government
- Government pays for building projects, such as highways, schools, and dams

Effects Today

- Increased government spending contributes to national debt
- Congress debates how to reform Social Security system
- People disagree about proper size of government

Graphic Organizer *Skills*

The New Deal eased the impact of the depression. Its effects are still felt today.

1. **Comprehension** What problems did the New Deal try to solve?
2. **Critical Thinking** Do you think the New Deal led to lower or higher taxes? Explain.

Economics $

Viewing HISTORY **Portraits of the Rural Poor**

Photographer Dorothea Lange gained fame for pictures like this one that showed the despair of rural Americans during the depression. Commenting on her work, Lange said, "We don't see what's right before us. We don't see it until someone tells us." ★ **Why do you think the government hired photographers like Dorothea Lange?**

The President chose John Collier, a longtime defender of Indian rights, to head the Bureau of Indian Affairs. He ended the government policy of breaking up Indian land holdings. In 1934, Congress passed the Indian Reorganization Act (IRA). It protected and even expanded land holdings of Native American reservations.

The government also ended its efforts to wipe out Native American religions. Rather, it supported the right of Native Americans to live according to their own traditions. It also strengthened Native American governments by letting reservations organize corporations and develop their own economic projects.

To provide jobs during the depression, the government set up the Indian Emergency Conservation Work Group. It employed Native Americans in programs of soil-erosion control, irrigation, and land development. In 1935, Congress launched the Indian Arts and Craft Board. It promoted the creation and sale of Native American art.

Arts of the Depression

Creative artists recorded images of depression life. Many writers depicted the hard times Americans faced across the country. In *The Grapes of Wrath,* **John Steinbeck** told the heartbreaking story of the Okies:

> "Carloads, caravans, homeless and hungry. . . . They streamed over the mountains, hungry and restless—restless as ants, scurrying to find work to do . . . anything, any burden to bear, for food."

Black writers of the Harlem Renaissance continued to create new works. In *Uncle Tom's Children,* **Richard Wright** described racial violence against black southerners.

Many painters turned to familiar themes. The huge murals of Thomas Hart Benton brought the history of the frontier to life. In *American Gothic*, Grant Wood painted an Iowa farmer and his daughter who look determined enough to survive any hardship.

The government sent out photographers to create a lasting record of American life during the Great Depression. The vivid photographs of **Dorothea Lange** showed the suffering of Dust Bowl farm families. Margaret Bourke-White photographed poor tenant farmers in the South.

Escaping Hard Times

Americans found ways to escape the hard times of the 1930s. Among their favorite pastimes were listening to the radio and going to the movies.

Radio

Every night, millions of Americans tuned in to their favorite radio programs. Comedians such as George Burns and Gracie Allen made people forget their troubles for a time. Classical music broadcasts let Americans enjoy music that they could not have heard otherwise.

With so many people out of work, daytime radio shows became popular. People listened to dramas like "Ma Perkins" that told a story over weeks or months. Because many of these serials were sponsored by soap companies, they became known as soap operas.

Perhaps the most famous broadcast took place in 1938. On Halloween night, actor Orson Welles presented a newscast based on a science fiction novel, *The War of the Worlds.* Welles grimly reported the landing of invaders from the planet Mars. People who tuned in late mistook the program for a real newscast. Thousands of terrified people ran into the streets, seeking ways to escape the Martian invasion.

Movies

In the 1930s, moviemakers tried to restore people's faith in the United States. Movies told optimistic stories about happy families or people finding love and success. Shirley Temple became a hugely popular star at the age of five. When Temple sang "On the Good Ship Lollipop" or danced with popular black entertainer Bill "Bojangles" Robinson, her upbeat spirit cheered up audiences.

One of the most popular movies was Walt Disney's *Snow White and the Seven Dwarfs.*

1937 movie poster

It was the first full-length animated film. In 1939, Judy Garland won American hearts in *The Wizard of Oz.* The movie told of a young girl's escape from a bleak life in depression-era Kansas to the magical land of Oz.

The most expensive and most popular movie of the 1930s was *Gone With the Wind.* It showed the Civil War in a romantic light. For more than three hours, many Americans forgot their worries as they watched the story of love and loss in the old South. The movie also encouraged many Americans. They had survived hard times before. They would do so again.

★ Section 4 Review ★

Recall

1. **Identify** **(a)** Dust Bowl, **(b)** Black Cabinet, **(c)** Mary McLeod Bethune, **(d)** Indian New Deal, **(e)** John Steinbeck, **(f)** Richard Wright, **(g)** Dorothea Lange.
2. **Define** **(a)** migrant worker, **(b)** civil rights, **(c)** repatriate.

Comprehension

3. **(a)** Give two causes of the dust storms of the 1930s. **(b)** What problems did farmers in the Dust Bowl region face?
4. Explain how each of these people tried to improve life for others during the depression: **(a)** Eleanor Roosevelt, **(b)** Emma Tenayuca, **(c)** Robert C. Weaver, **(d)** John Collier.
5. Why were movies and radio important to Americans during the depression?

Critical Thinking and Writing

6. **Understanding Causes and Effects** Why do you think minorities suffered greater discrimination during the depression than during good times?
7. **Making Inferences** Why do you think movies that told stories about good times were popular during the depression?

Activity **Writing a Diary** You are one of the people shown in the Dorothea Lange photograph on page 724. Write a diary entry about what was happening in your life at the time the photograph was taken.

Chapter 26 Review and Activities

★ Sum It Up ★

Section 1 The Economy Crashes

- The stock market crashed in 1929, partly because of unhealthy investment practices.
- The stock crash triggered a slide into a severe economic depression, made worse by overproduction and a weak banking system.
- President Hoover eventually began relief and public works programs.

Section 2 The New Deal

- Hoping for a bold new approach to the depression, Americans elected Franklin Roosevelt as President in 1932.
- The goals of Roosevelt's New Deal were to help the unemployed, promote recovery, and prevent another depression.

Section 3 Reaction to the New Deal

- Some critics argued that the New Deal did not do enough to help the poor, while others argued that it went too far.
- Roosevelt met with strong criticism when he tried to "pack" the Supreme Court.
- Later New Deal measures strengthened labor unions and set up Social Security to help the elderly and disabled.

Section 4 Surviving Hard Times

- Dust storms destroyed many farms in the Great Plains region.
- Women and members of minority groups faced particular problems during the Great Depression.
- Americans frequently turned to radio and movies to escape from their troubles.

For additional review of the major ideas of Chapter 26, see ***Guide to the Essentials of American History*** or ***Interactive Student Tutorial CD-ROM,*** which contains interactive review activities, graphic organizers, and practice tests.

Reviewing the Chapter

Define These Terms

Match each term with the correct definition.

Column 1	Column 2
1. public works	**a.** amount owed by the government
2. speculation	**b.** rights due to citizens
3. national debt	**c.** sum paid to people after they retire
4. pension	**d.** government-funded projects for public use
5. civil rights	**e.** risky buying and selling

Explore the Main Ideas

1. Why did Hoover start public works programs?
2. Describe one way the New Deal helped each of the following groups: **(a)** the unemployed, **(b)** farmers, **(c)** factory workers.
3. Why was the TVA controversial?
4. Why did the Supreme Court rule that the NIRA was unconstitutional?
5. How did FDR reach out to African Americans and Native Americans?

Geography Activity

Match the letters on the map with the following locations: **1.** Tennessee Valley Authority, **2.** Dust Bowl, **3.** Oklahoma, **4.** Arkansas, **5.** California, **6.** Washington, D.C. **Interaction** How did the TVA solve the problem of flooding in the Tennessee River valley?

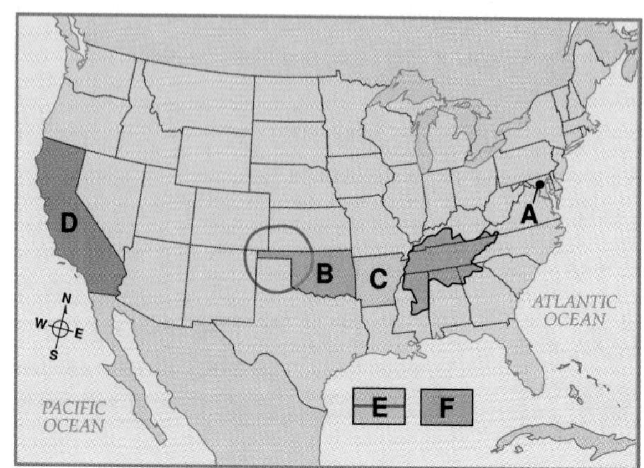

Critical Thinking and Writing

1. **Thinking Creatively** If you were President and a Great Depression struck today, what would you do?
2. **Understanding Chronology** **(a)** What problem did FDR tackle first? **(b)** Why did he target this problem?
3. **Linking Past and Present** **(a)** Identify a major ecological problem in the world today. **(b)** How is it similar to, and how is it different from, the Dust Bowl problem of the 1930s?
4. Exploring Unit Themes **Role of Government** Many Americans during the Great Depression feared that, under the New Deal, the government was gaining too much power. Do you think this fear was justified? Explain your answer.

Using Primary Sources

Evalyn Walsh McLean, a wealthy Washingtonian, helped feed the starving men of the Bonus Army. She later wrote:

> “Nothing I had seen before in my whole life touched me as deeply as what I had seen in the faces of those men. . . . Their way of righting things was wrong—oh, yes; but it is not the only wrong. . . . I was out in California when the United States army was used to drive them out of Washington. In a moving-picture show I saw in a news reel the tanks, the cavalry, and the gas-bomb throwers running those wretched Americans out of our capital. I was so raging mad I could have torn the theater down. They could not be allowed to stay, of course; but even so I felt myself one of them.”

Source: *Father Struck It Rich,* Evalyn Walsh McLean, 1936.

Recognizing Points of View **(a)** Describe McLean's opinion of the Bonus Army. **(b)** Why was she outraged by the government's actions?

Activity Bank

Interdisciplinary Activity

Exploring Economics Find out more about the steps taken by FDR to resolve the banking crisis. Prepare a presentation for a class of younger students, such as third graders, that explains the banking crisis and how FDR's actions ended it. Use charts and graphs to illustrate your presentation.

Career Skills Activity

Musicians In songs such as “Roll On, Columbia,” folksinger Woody Guthrie celebrated some of the programs of the New Deal. Find out more about Guthrie's songs. Then, write a song of your own either celebrating or criticizing a New Deal action.

Citizenship Activity

Understanding the Role of Charities The question of who should take care of needy Americans is still controversial. Working with a classmate, locate an organization in your community that helps people in need. Interview the leaders of the organization about what they do and where they get funds. Report what you have learned to the class.

Internet Activity

Use the Internet to find sites dealing with the Tennessee Valley Authority. Do research in the sites to create a data sheet of fascinating facts about the TVA. If possible, include images.

You are an investor in the stock market, a member of FDR's Brain Trust, a worker employed by the CCC or WPA, a farmer, or a business leader who opposes the New Deal. In your EYEWITNESS JOURNAL, describe your reaction to one of the key events of the Great Depression.

Chapter 27

World War II

1935–1945

What's Ahead

Section 1
Dictatorship and Aggression

Section 2
The War Begins

Section 3
The Home Front

Section 4
The Allies Advance

Section 5
Final Victory

After World War I, most Americans wanted to avoid involvement in international conflicts. However, during the 1930s, Germany, Italy, and Japan increased their military power and invaded other nations. The United States responded by gradually abandoning its policy of neutrality. After the Japanese attacked Pearl Harbor in 1941, the United States entered World War II.

Millions of Americans joined with troops from Britain and other allies to fight for victory. At home, civilians worked hard to support the soldiers. First, Italy was defeated, and then Germany. Finally, in 1945, the United States defeated Japan by using a new weapon—the atomic bomb.

Why Study History? During World War II, millions of innocent men, women, and children were executed. Today we know this tragic event as the Holocaust. To learn more about the Holocaust and why it is important to study, see this chapter's *Why Study History?* feature, "We Must Never Forget."

American Events

1935 Congress passes first of three Neutrality Acts

1936 Roosevelt visits Argentina as part of Good Neighbor Policy

1940 United States establishes its first peacetime draft

1934 | 1936 | 1938 | 1940

World Events

1937 World Event Japan launches full-scale war against China

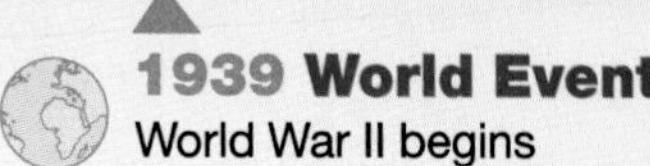

1939 World Event World War II begins

Viewing HISTORY — Battle of the Coral Sea

World War II was fought all over the world—on land, at sea, and in the air. In the Battle of the Coral Sea, shown above in a dramatic painting by Robert Benney, American ships and planes forced a large Japanese fleet to turn away. The battle was one of the first American victories in the war. ★ **How do you think new technology affected the way World War II was fought?**

1941 Attack on Pearl Harbor brings United States into World War II

1944 Allied troops invade Europe on D-Day

1945 World War II ends

1940 | 1942 | 1944 | 1946

1940 World Event
France surrenders to Axis powers

1943 World Event
Soviet armies defeat Germans at Stalingrad and Leningrad

Dictatorship and Aggression

As You Read

Explore These Questions

- How did dictators take away people's freedoms?
- How did dictators threaten world peace in the 1930s?
- How did the United States respond to the rise of dictators?

Define

- dictator
- totalitarian state
- collective farm
- nationalism
- aggression
- concentration camp

Identify

- Joseph Stalin
- Benito Mussolini
- Fascist party
- Haile Selassie
- Adolf Hitler
- Nazis
- Final Solution
- Neutrality Acts
- Good Neighbor Policy

After World War I, many Americans believed that the nation should never again become involved in a war. As one writer noted:

> "Humanity is not helpless. This is God's world! We can outlaw this war system just as we outlawed slavery and the saloon."

"Bread through work," says this Soviet poster

In the 1930s, however, war clouds again gathered. In Europe and Asia, ambitious rulers gained power and set out to conquer neighboring lands. When other nations did not act to stop their expansion, the rulers became bolder.

A Dictator in the Soviet Union

In the Soviet Union, as you recall, communists under V. I. Lenin had staged a revolution in Russia in 1917. Later, they set up the Soviet Union.

After Lenin's death in 1924, **Joseph Stalin** came to power and soon ruled as a dictator. A **dictator** is a ruler who has complete power over a country. Stalin used all the weapons of the totalitarian state. In a **totalitarian state,** a single party controls the government and every aspect of people's lives. Citizens must obey the government without question. Criticism of the government is severely punished.

To strengthen the Soviet economy, Stalin launched a series of five-year plans. His goal was to modernize Soviet industry and farming. In the 1930s, the government ordered peasants to hand over their land and farm animals and to join **collective farms**—farms run by the government. When farmers resisted, millions were executed or sent to labor camps.

Under Stalin's harsh rule, Soviet industry expanded. Steel and oil production rose. Stalin knew that these materials were important for building a modern military force.

Fascists in Italy

Meanwhile, in Western Europe, dictators came to power in both Italy and Germany. These dictators won support by exploiting people's fears about the economy and feelings of extreme nationalism. **Nationalism,** as you recall, is a feeling of patriotic pride and devotion to one's country.

Mussolini becomes dictator

In 1922, **Benito Mussolini** seized power in Italy. He played on Italian anger about the Versailles Treaty ending World War I. Many

Italians felt cheated by the treaty because it did not grant Italy the territory it wanted. Mussolini also used economic unrest and fears of a communist revolution to win support for himself and his **Fascist party.**

Once in power, Mussolini outlawed all political parties except his own. He controlled the press and banned criticism of the government. In schools, children recited the motto "Mussolini is always right." They learned total obedience to "Il Duce" (ihl DOO chay)—the leader—as Mussolini was called.

Invading Ethiopia

In the 1930s, Mussolini used foreign conquest to distract Italians from economic problems at home. Remembering the glories of ancient Rome, he promised to restore Italy to greatness. Under Mussolini's leadership, Italy committed several acts of aggression. **Aggression** is any warlike act by one country against another without just cause.

As a first step to building a new Roman empire, Mussolini invaded Ethiopia, in North Africa, in 1935. The Ethiopians fought bravely. However, their cavalry and outdated rifles were no match for the tanks and airplanes of Mussolini's modern army.

Emperor **Haile Selassie** (HI lee suh LAS ee) of Ethiopia called on the League of Nations for help. The League responded weakly. The democratic powers Britain and France were concentrating on their own economic problems. Also, grim memories of World War I made the British and French unwilling to risk another war. Unable to secure help, Ethiopia fell to the invaders.

Rise of Nazi Germany

Like Mussolini, Germany's **Adolf Hitler** took advantage of anger about the Versailles Treaty. Germans bitterly resented the treaty because it blamed their country for World War I and saddled them with heavy war costs. Hitler organized a political party—the National Socialist German Workers' Party, or **Nazis**—to help him win power.

Hitler becomes dictator

Germany had not lost the war, he said. Rather, Jews and other traitors had "stabbed Germany in the back" in 1918. The argument was false, but in troubled times, people welcomed a scapegoat on which to blame their problems.

Hitler was a powerful speaker and skillful leader. By the late 1920s, a growing number of Germans had accepted his ideas. When the depression struck, many Germans turned to Hitler as a strong leader with answers to their problems.

In 1933, Hitler became chancellor, or head, of the German government. Within two years, he ended democratic government. In Hitler's Nazi Germany, the government controlled the press, schools, and religion. Hitler crushed all rivals and created a militaristic totalitarian state.

American reporter William Shirer visited Nazi Germany in 1934. At Nuremberg, he watched a week-long rally organized by

Viewing HISTORY **Two Dictators**

In full military uniform, Italian dictator Benito Mussolini (left) and German dictator Adolf Hitler stand together to view parading soldiers. The swastika on Hitler's armband was a symbol of the Nazi party. ★ **Why do you think many Italians and Germans supported these dictators?**

Viewing History: Nuremberg Rally

In the 1930s, in Nuremberg, thousands of Germans attended massive Nazi rallies. The crowds viewed Germany's military might and listened to Hitler's hypnotic speeches. They also chanted slogans, such as "We want one leader! Nothing for us! Everything for Germany! Heil Hitler!*"*

★ **How do you think people in nearby countries felt about the rallies?**

Hitler. The rally was an unforgettable display. Germans marched in endless parades and chanted slogans praising Hitler and the Nazi party. One day, the army staged a mock battle. Shirer noted in his diary:

> “It is difficult to exaggerate the frenzy of the three hundred thousand German spectators when they saw their soldiers go into action, heard the thunder of the guns, and smelt the powder.”

Attacks on Jews

Hitler and the Nazis preached a message of racial and religious hatred. Hitler claimed that Germans belonged to a superior "Aryan" race. He blamed Jews, Gypsies, communists, and others for Germany's troubles.

The Nazi government singled out the Jews for special persecution. It passed many laws against Jews. Jews were deprived of their citizenship, forbidden to use public facilities, and driven out of almost every type of work.

As Nazi power grew, attacks on Jews increased. The government rounded up thousands of Jews and sent them to concentration camps. A **concentration camp** is a prison camp for civilians who are considered enemies of the state. In time, Hitler would unleash a plan to kill all the Jews in Europe. He called the plan the **Final Solution.** (See pages 754–755).

German military buildup

Under Hitler, Germany built up its armed forces in violation of the Versailles Treaty. Hitler also claimed that Germany had the right to expand to the east.

In response, the League of Nations condemned Hitler's actions. Still, Hitler moved ahead with his plans. The rest of Europe will "never act," he boasted. "They'll just protest. And they will always be too late."

In the meantime, Hitler pressed ahead with plans for conquest. In 1936, he moved troops into the Rhineland, near the border of France and Belgium. His action violated the terms of the Versailles Treaty. France and Britain protested, but they took no action.

Military Rule in Japan

Japan's economy suffered severely in the Great Depression. Trade slowed, and businesses failed. As the economic crisis worsened, many Japanese grew impatient with their democratic government.

In the early 1930s, military leaders took power. The new leaders believed that Japan, like Britain and France, had the right to win an overseas empire. They set out to expand into Asia.

In 1931, Japanese forces seized Manchuria in northeastern China. The Japanese wanted Manchuria because it was rich in coal and iron. As a small island nation, Japan lacked adequate supplies of these important resources. Japan set up a state in Manchuria, and called it Manchukuo.

China called on the League of Nations for assistance. The League condemned Japanese aggression but did little else. Similarly, the United States refused to recognize the state of Manchukuo, but took no other action against Japan.

American Foreign Policy

During the depression, Americans had too many economic worries to care much about events overseas. A strong isolationist mood gripped the country. As threats of war in Europe and Asia grew, Americans were determined to keep the United States from becoming involved.

Isolationists in Congress pressed for a series of **Neutrality Acts.** These laws banned arms sales or loans to countries at war. They also warned Americans not to travel on ships of countries at war. By limiting economic ties with warring nations, the United States hoped to stay out of any foreign conflict.

Closer to home, the United States tried to improve relations with Latin American nations. In 1930, President Hoover rejected the Roosevelt Corollary. (See page 634.) The United States, he declared, no longer claimed the right to intervene in the affairs of Latin American nations.

When Franklin Roosevelt took office, he announced a **Good Neighbor Policy** of establishing friendlier relations with Latin American countries. He withdrew American troops from Nicaragua and from Haiti. He also canceled the Platt Amendment, which had limited the independence of Cuba. (See page 628.)

As tensions increased in other parts of the world, the need to build friendly relations with the nations of the Western Hemisphere became more pressing. On a visit to Argentina in 1936, President Roosevelt said,

> "[Nations seeking] to commit acts of aggression against us will find a hemisphere wholly prepared to consult together for our mutual safety and our mutual good."

★ Section 1 Review ★

Recall

1. **Identify** **(a)** Joseph Stalin, **(b)** Benito Mussolini, **(c)** Fascist party, **(d)** Haile Selassie, **(e)** Adolf Hitler, **(f)** Nazis, **(g)** Final Solution, **(h)** Neutrality Acts, **(i)** Good Neighbor Policy.
2. **Define** **(a)** dictator, **(b)** totalitarian state, **(c)** collective farm, **(d)** nationalism, **(e)** aggression, **(f)** concentration camp.

Comprehension

3. Describe the totalitarian state that Adolf Hitler established in Germany.
4. Describe one way that each of the following nations threatened world peace in the 1930s: **(a)** Italy, **(b)** Germany, **(c)** Japan.
5. Why did the United States Congress pass a series of Neutrality Acts?

Critical Thinking and Writing

6. **Making Generalizations** **(a)** Make a generalization about how democratic nations responded to aggression in the 1930s. **(b)** Give two examples to support your generalization.
7. **Predicting Consequences** Do you think United States isolationism encouraged or discouraged future acts of aggression by dictators? Explain.

Activity **Identifying Alternatives** You are a foreign policy adviser to the President of the United States. Japan has just seized Manchuria. The President wants you to identify and describe the various ways in which the United States might respond. The President also wants you to explain the benefits and drawbacks of each possible response.

The War Begins

As You Read

Explore These Questions

- How did World War II begin?
- How did the United States respond to the outbreak of World War II?
- Why did the United States enter the war?

Define

- annex
- appeasement
- blitzkrieg

Identify

- Munich Conference
- Nazi-Soviet Pact
- Axis
- Allies
- Winston Churchill
- Battle of Britain
- Edward R. Murrow
- Lend-Lease Act
- Atlantic Charter

"I hate war," FDR had told an audience as he campaigned for the presidency in 1936.

> "I have passed unnumbered hours, I shall pass unnumbered hours, thinking and planning how war may be kept from this nation."

During the late 1930s, Italy, Japan, and Germany continued their policies of aggression. The United States and the European democracies did little in response. Americans and Europeans hoped to avoid another bloody conflict like the world war that had ended only 20 years before.

War in Asia

In 1937, Japan began an all-out war against China. Japanese planes bombed China's major cities. Thousands of civilians were killed. Japanese troops defeated Chinese armies and occupied northern and central China.

The Japanese advance into China alarmed American leaders. They felt it undermined the Open Door Policy, which promised equal access to trade in China. It also threatened the Philippines, which the United States controlled. Nevertheless, isolationist feelings remained strong among the American people and kept the United States from taking a firm stand against the Japanese.

War in Europe

In Europe, Hitler continued his plans for German expansion. In 1938, just two years after occupying the Rhineland, Hitler **annexed,** or took over, Austria. By this action, he once again violated the Treaty of Versailles.

Later that year, Hitler claimed the Sudetenland, the western part of Czechoslovakia. He justified his demand by claiming that the Sudetenland contained many people of German heritage.

The Munich Conference

Britain and France had signed treaties to protect Czechoslovakia, but were reluctant to go to war. The two nations sought a peaceful solution to the crisis. In September 1938, the leaders of Britain, France, Italy, and Germany met in Munich, Germany.

At the **Munich Conference,** Hitler promised that Germany would seek no further territory once it acquired the Sudetenland. To preserve peace, Britain and France gave in. They agreed that Germany should have the Sudetenland. This practice of giving in to aggression in order to avoid war is known as **appeasement.**

The policy of appeasement failed. Nazi Germany seized the rest of Czechoslovakia the very next year. Only then did Britain and France realize that they had to take action to stop further Nazi aggression.

Invasion of Poland

Hitler's next target was Poland. To achieve his goal, he made an alliance with the Soviet Union. In August 1939, Hitler and Stalin signed the **Nazi-Soviet Pact.** The two agreed not to attack each other. Secretly, they also agreed to divide Poland and other parts of Eastern Europe between them.

In September 1939, Hitler launched Germany's military might in a swift attack against Poland. The Germans used planes and tanks, while the Poles used cavalry and old rifles. Unable to withstand the German **blitzkrieg,** or lightning war, the Poles soon surrendered.

Meanwhile, the Soviet Union seized eastern Poland. Stalin's forces also invaded Finland and later annexed Estonia, Lithuania, and Latvia. Stalin claimed that these steps were needed to build Soviet defenses.

Geography Skills In the late 1930s, Germany and Italy seized territory from other countries and threatened the peace of Europe.

1. **Location** On the map, locate: **(a)** Rhineland, **(b)** Austria, **(c)** Sudetenland, **(d)** Czechoslovakia, **(e)** Albania.
2. **Movement** To what African country did Italy send an invasion force in 1935?
3. **Critical Thinking** Why did Poland have much to fear from an alliance between Nazi Germany and the Soviet Union?

Viewing HISTORY **Battle of Britain**

In the Battle of Britain, German planes bombed London and other English cities such as Dover, shown here. During World War II, both the Axis and Allies bombed major population centers. ★ **Do you think German bombings weakened or strengthened the morale of the English people? Explain.**

A Global Conflict

Britain and France declared war on Germany two days after the invasion of Poland. In time, Italy, Japan, and six other nations would join Germany to form the **Axis** powers. Opposing the Axis powers were the **Allies.** Before World War II was over, the Allies would include Britain, France, the Soviet Union, the United States, China, and 45 other countries.

World War II was a global conflict. Military forces fought all over the world. Many millions of people were killed. When it finally ended, cities across Europe and Asia lay in ruins.

France surrenders

In the spring of 1940, Hitler's armies marched north and west. In April, they smashed through Denmark and Norway. In May, they overran Holland and Belgium and pushed into France. Hitler's ally, Italy, also attacked France. Britain sent troops to help France resist the assault.

The British and French, however, were quickly overpowered. By May, the Germans had forced them to retreat to Dunkirk, a French port on the English Channel. There, they were trapped.

In a bold action, the British sent every available merchant ship, fishing boat, and pleasure craft across the channel to rescue the trapped soldiers. They carried 338,000 soldiers to safety in England.

Unhindered, German armies marched on to Paris, the French capital. On June 22, 1940, France surrendered.

Battle of Britain

Britain then stood alone. Even so, the new prime minister, **Winston Churchill,** was confident. He informed the world that the British people would stand firm:

> "We shall defend our island, whatever the cost may be, we shall fight on the beaches, we shall fight on the landing grounds, we shall fight in the fields and in the streets . . . we shall never surrender."

Connections With Science

Britain used the new invention of radar to detect incoming German planes. Radar works because radio waves bounce off things. When radio waves bounce off an airplane in the sky, a blip appears on a screen.

German planes dropped bombs on London and other British cities during the **Battle of Britain.** British fighter pilots fought back, gunning down nearly 2,000 German planes. By late 1940, after months of bombing, Hitler gave up his planned invasion of Britain.

In the United States, people listened to the radio reports of **Edward R. Murrow** and other war correspondents who saw the fighting firsthand. As they listened, Americans wondered how much longer the United States could stay out of the war.

FDR and American Policy

After the invasion of Poland, President Roosevelt announced that the United States would remain neutral. He realized that most Americans sympathized with the Allies but did not want to enter the war.

Helping the Allies

Roosevelt sought ways to help the Allies. He asked Congress to repeal the neutrality law that banned the sale of arms to warring nations. Isolationists blocked the move, but FDR won a compromise. The United States could sell arms to the Allies under a "cash-and-carry" plan. The Allies had to pay cash for the goods and carry them away in their own ships.

By 1940, German submarines had sunk many British ships. Churchill asked the United States for ships. Roosevelt agreed to give Britain 50 old American destroyers. In exchange, Britain gave the United States 99-year leases on military bases in Newfoundland and the Caribbean.

Preparing for war

The United States also took several steps to prepare for war. Congress approved greater spending for the army and navy. In September 1940, it passed a law that set up the first peacetime draft in American history.

Isolationists opposed these moves, especially aid for Britain. Many other Americans, however, felt that the United States had no choice. If Britain fell, Hitler might control the Atlantic Ocean.

FDR wins a third term

The threat of war persuaded FDR to run for a third term in 1940. His decision broke the precedent set by George Washington of serving only two terms as President.

Republicans nominated Wendell Willkie. Willkie and Roosevelt agreed on many issues. Like Roosevelt, Willkie favored sending aid to Britain. Both candidates also pledged not to send Americans into any foreign wars.

Republicans—and some Democrats—criticized Roosevelt for breaking the two-term tradition. Still, the voters gave FDR a clear victory. They seemed to agree with a slogan used by Roosevelt in his campaign: "Don't change horses in mid-stream."

Biography **Edward R. Murrow**

After attending Washington State College, Murrow traveled abroad and served as assistant director of the Institute of International Education. As director of the European bureau of CBS, he personally described the Nazi takeover of Austria for radio audiences. His broadcasts from London during German bombing raids made him famous. After the war, Murrow hosted influential news programs for both radio and TV. ★ **How did Murrow's experience prepare him for a journalism career?**

AmericanHeritage
M A G A Z I N E

HISTORY HAPPENED HERE

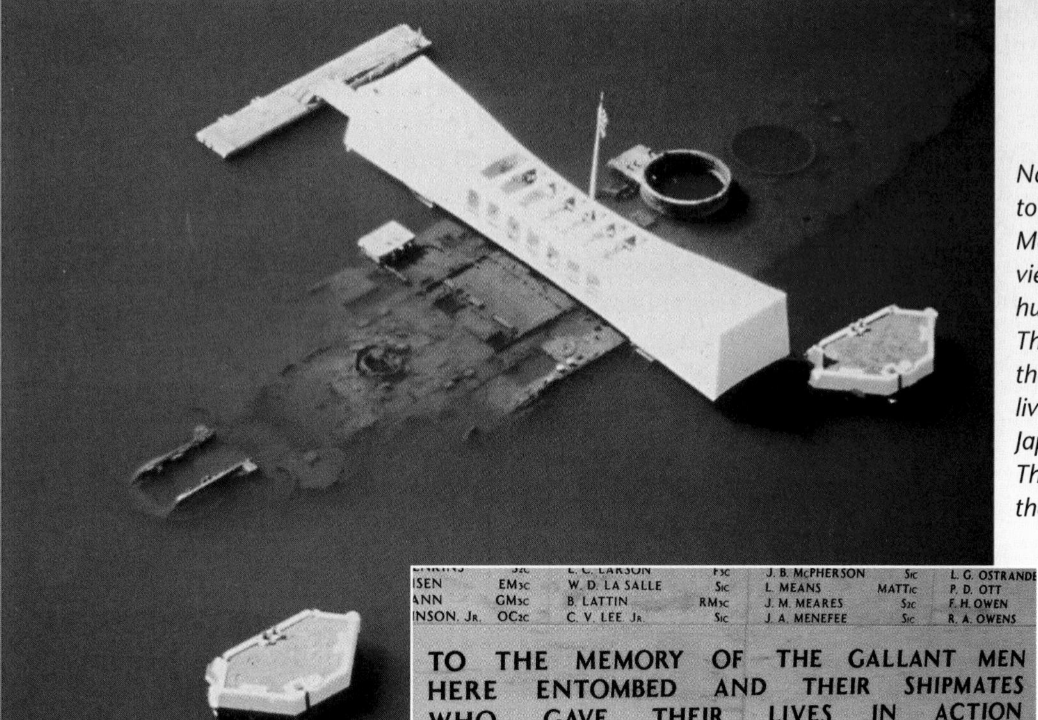

▲ *The "remembrance exhibit" names all who died in the attack on Pearl Harbor.*

USS *Arizona* Memorial

Navy shuttle crafts take visitors to and from the USS Arizona *Memorial. There, visitors can view beneath them the sunken hull of the battleship* Arizona. *The Memorial commemorates those Americans who lost their lives in the December 7, 1941, Japanese attack on Pearl Harbor. The USS* Arizona *was sunk in that attack with 1,102 sailors trapped inside.*

★ ***To learn more about this historic site, write:*** *USS* Arizona *Memorial, 1 Arizona Memorial Place, Honolulu, HI 96818.*

"Arsenal of democracy"

By late 1940, Britain was running out of cash to buy arms. Roosevelt boldly suggested lending supplies to Britain. Isolationists were outraged.

Roosevelt proclaimed that Britain was defending democracy against totalitarian forces. The United States, he declared, "must be the great arsenal of democracy." He urged Americans to defend "Four Freedoms"—freedom of speech, freedom of worship, freedom from want, and freedom from fear.

In March 1941, Congress passed the **Lend-Lease Act.** It allowed sales or loans of war materials to "any country whose defense the President deems vital to the defense of the United States." Under Lend-Lease, the United States sent airplanes, tanks, guns, and ammunition to Britain. British merchant ships transported the goods, with escorts of American warships providing protection as far as Iceland.

In June 1941, Hitler launched a surprise invasion of the Soviet Union. The Soviets were now fighting on the Allied side. Although Roosevelt condemned Stalin's totalitarian rule, he extended Lend-Lease aid to the Soviet Union.

The Atlantic Charter

In August 1941, Roosevelt and Churchill issued the **Atlantic Charter,** which set goals for the postwar world. The two leaders agreed to seek no territorial gain from the war. They pledged to support "the right of all peoples to choose the form of government under which they will live." The charter also called for a "permanent system of general security," such as an organization like the League of Nations.

The United States Enters the War

To Roosevelt, Japanese aggressions in Asia were as alarming as Germany's advance through Europe. The Japanese had seized much of China. After Germany defeated France in 1940, Japan took control of French colonies in Southeast Asia. (See the map on page 752.) In September 1940, the Japanese signed an alliance with Germany and Italy.

Opposing Japanese aggression

The United States tried to stop Japanese aggression by refusing to sell oil and scrap metal to Japan. This move angered the Japanese because they badly needed these resources. "Sparks will fly before long," predicted an American diplomat.

Japanese and American officials held talks in November 1941. Japan asked the United States to lift the embargo on oil and scrap metal. The United States called on Japan to withdraw its armies from China and Southeast Asia. Neither side would compromise. As the talks limped along, Japan completed plans for a secret attack on the United States.

Japan attacks

On Sunday, December 7, 1941, Japanese planes swept through the skies in a surprise attack on Pearl Harbor, Hawaii. There, the American Pacific fleet rode peacefully at anchor. In less than two hours, the Japanese sank or seriously damaged 19 American ships, destroyed almost 200 American planes, and killed about 2,400 people.

Americans were stunned by the attack. The next day, President Roosevelt asked Congress to declare war on Japan.

> "Yesterday, December 7, 1941—a date which will live in infamy—the United States of America was suddenly and deliberately attacked by naval and air forces of the Empire of Japan.... No matter how long it may take us to overcome this premeditated invasion, the American people, in their righteous might, will win through to absolute victory."

Congress declared war on Japan. In response, Germany and Italy declared war on the United States. Americans were now united in the cause of freedom. Even isolationists backed the war effort.

★ Section 2 Review ★

Recall

1. **Locate** **(a)** Czechoslovakia, **(b)** Poland, **(c)** France, **(d)** Britain, **(e)** Pearl Harbor.
2. **Identify** **(a)** Munich Conference, **(b)** Nazi-Soviet Pact, **(c)** Axis, **(d)** Allies, **(e)** Winston Churchill, **(f)** Battle of Britain, **(g)** Edward R. Murrow, **(h)** Lend-Lease Act, **(i)** Atlantic Charter.
3. **Define** **(a)** annex, **(b)** appeasement, **(c)** blitzkrieg.

Comprehension

4. What nations did Hitler conquer in 1939 and 1940?
5. What did Roosevelt mean when he called the United States the "arsenal of democracy"?
6. **(a)** Why did Japan attack Pearl Harbor? **(b)** How did Americans respond to the attack?

Critical Thinking and Writing

7. **Analyzing Ideas** At the start of World War II, the official policy of the United States was neutrality. Do you think the United States was truly neutral in its actions toward the Axis and Allies? Explain.
8. **Recognizing Points of View** Why did Roosevelt urge Americans to support the Lend-Lease Act?

Activity **Drawing a Cartoon** You are a political cartoonist for an American newspaper during the 1930s. Your assignment is to draw a cartoon criticizing German aggression and British and French appeasement. The title of your cartoon is "Hitler Is a Spoiled Child!"

3 The Home Front

As You Read

Explore These Questions

- How did Americans mobilize for war?
- How did American women and minorities contribute to the war effort?
- How were some Americans treated unjustly during the war?

Define

- ration
- segregation

Identify

- victory garden
- A. Philip Randolph
- Tuskegee airmen
- bracero program
- Navajo code-talkers

SETTING the Scene The Japanese attack on Pearl Harbor plunged the United States into World War II. Isolationism died almost overnight as the nation mobilized all its resources to fight the enemy. As one woman recalled:

> "There was a great coming together of people, working as a team, being proud of what you were doing because you knew it was contributing something to the war effort. Everybody did their share, from the oldest gentleman on the street . . . to little children who saved things that were crucial at that time—paper, tin cans, scrap, anything that could be reused for the war."

Mobilizing for Victory

During World War II, more than 15 million American men and women served in the military. Many millions more spent the war years at home, far from the battlefields. Winning the war depended on military victories and on mobilizing the home front to support and supply the armed forces.

Training for combat

In 1941, the military's first task was to train forces for combat. Army, navy, and air bases were built all over the country. Recruits were trained to fight in the jungles of the Pacific, the deserts of North Africa, and the towns and farmlands of Europe.

Poster showing a strong and confident factory worker

Women joined all the armed services. Women pilots logged 60 million air miles ferrying bombers from base to base, towing targets, and teaching men to fly. Although women were not allowed in combat, many served close to the front lines.

Organizing the economy

Even more than in World War I, the government controlled the economy during World War II. Government agencies set the prices of goods and negotiated with labor unions. They also decided what products should be produced.

The War Production Board helped factories shift from making consumer goods to making guns, ships, aircraft, and other materials needed to win the war. Auto makers, for example, switched from turning out cars to producing tanks and trucks. A Nazi leader once scoffed that "Americans can't build planes, only electric iceboxes and razor blades." He was wrong. Americans performed a miracle of production. In 1942 alone, American workers produced more than 60,000 planes and shipped more than 8 million tons of goods.

As production of war materials grew, consumer goods became scarcer. The government **rationed,** or limited, the amount of certain goods that Americans could buy. Americans used ration coupons issued by the government to purchase all sorts of goods, including coffee, sugar, meat, shoes, gasoline, and tires. When people ran out of coupons, they could not buy the rationed items until new coupons were issued.

To combat food shortages, many Americans planted **victory gardens.** At the height of the war, there were more than 20 million victory gardens in the country. They produced 40 percent of all vegetables grown in the country during World War II.

To pay for the war, the government raised taxes. It also borrowed huge amounts of money by selling war bonds to millions of American citizens. Movie stars and other celebrities took part in drives to sell bonds and boost patriotic spirit.

The war quickly ended the Great Depression. Unemployment fell as millions of jobs opened up in factories. Minority workers found jobs where they had been rejected in the past.

Jobs for Women

"If you can drive a car," the government told American women, "you can run a machine." Newspapers and magazines echoed this call to American women to work for victory. "Why do we need women workers?" asked a radio announcer. The answer: "You can't build ships, planes, and guns without them."

During World War II, women responded to the urgent demand for their labor. Almost 5 million women entered the work force. They replaced men who joined the armed services. Many women worked in offices. Millions more kept the nation's factories operating around

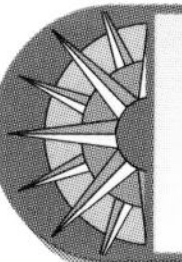

Linking Past and Present

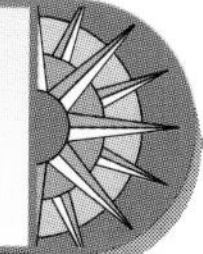

Past

Present

National Defense

During World War II, American workers achieved a miracle of production by turning out all the equipment needed to win the war. Today, American workers continue to build the military hardware needed for national defense. The photos above show a B-29 bomber of World War II and a modern stealth bomber. ★ **Why does the United States spend massive amounts of money on military equipment even during peacetime?**

Skills FOR LIFE

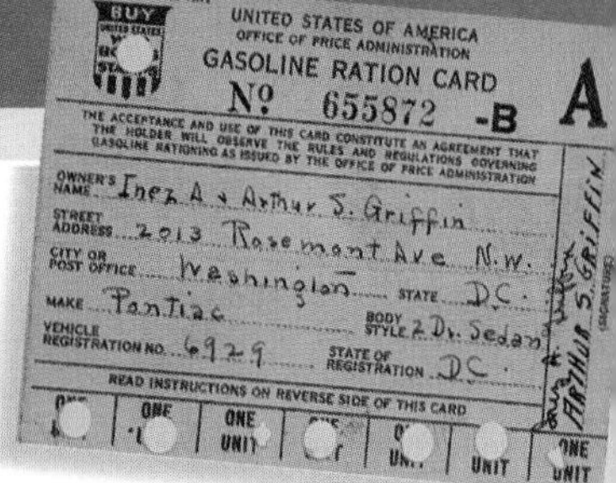

Critical Thinking | **Managing Information** | Communication | Maps, Charts, and Graphs

Managing Resources

During World War II, Americans used ration cards and coupons.

How Will I Use This Skill?

A common economic problem is providing what is needed or desired with a limited amount of resources. As a family member, you may have to balance the family's income and expenses. In business, you may have to figure out how to get the job done with a limited budget and number of workers. Whatever the situation, knowing how to manage resources will help you get the most out of what you have.

LEARN the Skill

To manage resources, use the following plan:

1. List the goods and services that are needed or wanted.
2. Rank the items on the list according to importance. Remember that basic needs are most important and cannot be disregarded. Luxuries make life more enjoyable, but you can live without them.
3. List your available resources. These include things like materials, time, money, and people.
4. Figure out what goods and services you can afford. Be sure to take care of basic needs first and luxuries last.
5. Try to increase your resources and save some resources for later needs.

PRACTICE the Skill

Review pages 740 and 741. Then, answer the following questions.

1. Before the United States entered World War II, what two different types of goods did American factories produce?
2. After the United States entered World War II, which type of goods did the government consider more important than any other? Why?
3. Why were there shortages of workers and food?
4. What did the government do to make sure that there were enough goods for the soldiers overseas?
5. How did the government try to raise money to pay for the war?

APPLY the Skill

Make a monthly budget for yourself. Start by estimating your total income from all sources, such as work, allowances, and gifts. List what you must pay for or buy and what you would like to buy. Complete your budget, or resource management plan, by continuing to follow the steps that you learned above.

the clock. Some welded, ran huge cranes, and tended blast furnaces. Others became bus drivers, police officers, and gas station attendants.

Because women were badly needed in industry, they were able to win better pay and working conditions. The government agreed that women and men should get the same pay for the same job. Many employers, however, found ways to avoid equal pay.

The war changed fashions for women. Instead of wearing skirts on the job, many women dressed in trousers. They wore overalls and tied scarves around their hair.

More important, war work gave many women a new opinion of themselves. One woman noted how her confidence increased:

> "I never could handle the simplest can openers, or drive a nail without getting hurt, and now I put in half my nights armed with hammers and wrenches handling the insides of giant machines."

African Americans

When the war began, African Americans rallied to their nation's cause. The war helped end some of the worst discrimination against African Americans. Still, the struggle for equality was not easy.

Discrimination at home

As industry geared up for war, factories replaced "No Help Wanted" signs with "Help Wanted, White" signs. Such discrimination angered African Americans.

In 1941, **A. Philip Randolph,** head of the Brotherhood of Sleeping Car Porters, called for a protest march on Washington. The government, he said, "will never give the Negro justice until they see masses—ten, twenty, fifty thousand Negroes on the White House lawn."

Government officials worried that such a march would feed Hitler's propaganda machine. "What will Berlin say?" they asked. After meeting with Randolph, FDR ordered employers doing business with the government to end discrimination in hiring. As a result, the employment of skilled black craftsworkers doubled during the war.

However, as black employment increased, so did racial tension. Thousands of Americans—blacks and whites—moved to cities to work in industry. Competition for scarce housing led to angry incidents and even violence. In 1943, race riots broke out in Detroit, New York, and other American cities.

Heroism in the military

While FDR acted against discrimination in hiring, he refused to end **segregation,** or separation, of the races in the military. Nearly a million African Americans enlisted or were drafted. They had to serve in all-black units commanded by white officers.

Despite such treatment, blacks served heroically. The **Tuskegee airmen** were African American fighter pilots who trained

Viewing History **Tuskegee Airmen**

After training at Tuskegee, African American combat pilots compiled an enviable combat record in action over North Africa and Europe. None of the bombers they escorted was shot down. Here, Colonel Benjamin O. Davis gives advice to Lieutenant Charles Dryden. ★ **How did prejudice affect African Americans in the military?**

Viewing HISTORY **Tragedy for Japanese Americans**

By order of the United States government, troops moved Japanese American families from their homes to relocation camps. "Herd 'em up, pack 'em off," was the recommendation of one newspaper columnist.
★ **What reason did the government give for this relocation policy?**

at Tuskegee, Alabama. By the end of the war, the Tuskegee airmen had destroyed or damaged about 400 enemy aircraft.

African Americans served heroically in all branches of the armed forces. In the army, African American combat units included artillery and tank units. African Americans in the navy served as gunner's mates and helped build bases in the Pacific. African American marines helped defend American posts against Japanese attacks.

One of the earliest heroes of World War II was Dorie Miller, an African American sailor serving on the battleship *West Virginia* during the attack on Pearl Harbor. As the battle raged. Miller dragged his wounded captain to safety. Then, though he had no training as a gunner, Miller manned a machine gun and shot down four enemy planes. For heroism in action, Miller was awarded the Navy Cross.

Tragedy for Japanese Americans

The war brought suffering to many Japanese Americans. Most Japanese Americans lived on the West Coast or in Hawaii. Many of those on the West Coast were successful farmers and business people. For years, they had faced prejudice, in part because of their success.

Following the attack on Pearl Harbor, many people on the West Coast questioned the loyalty of Japanese Americans. Japanese Americans, they said, might act as spies and help Japan invade the United States. No evidence of disloyalty existed. Yet the President agreed to move Japanese Americans from their homes to "relocation" camps.

About 110,000 Japanese Americans were forced to sell their homes and businesses at great loss. In the relocation camps, Japanese Americans lived in crowded barracks behind barbed wire. They could not understand why they were singled out for such treatment.

Even though they and their families were treated unfairly, thousands of Japanese

Connections With Civics

Italian immigrants also suffered during the war. Hundreds were held in government camps for up to two years. Thousands more were forbidden to travel more than 5 miles from home and were forced to turn in cameras and shortwave radios.

American men served in the armed forces. Most were put in segregated units and sent to fight in Europe. There, they won many honors for bravery. The 442nd Nisei Regimental Combat Team became the most highly decorated military unit in United States history.

Years later, in 1988, Congress apologized to Japanese Americans who had been driven from their homes in World War II. They also approved a payment of $20,000 to every survivor of the camps.

Latinos

Many Puerto Rican Americans and Mexican Americans served in the military during World War II. In fact, Latinos—people of Latin American origin or descent—won many awards for bravery, including 17 Congressional Medals of Honor. Guy Gabaldon, a Marine Corps private, received a Silver Star for capturing 1,000 Japanese.

Because of the need for workers during the war, the United States signed a treaty with Mexico in 1942. The agreement allowed the recruitment of Mexican laborers to work in the United States. The program was called the **bracero program.** During the war, many Mexicans arrived in the United States to work on farms and railroads.

Despite their contribution to the war effort, Latinos still faced prejudice. In June 1943, for example, white sailors on leave from their ships savagely attacked a group of young Mexican Americans, beating and clubbing them on the streets. The incident sparked several days of rioting in Los Angeles.

Newspapers blamed the violence on the Mexican Americans. Eleanor Roosevelt disagreed. In her newspaper column, she noted that the riots were the result of "longstanding discrimination against the Mexicans in the Southwest."

Native Americans

Native Americans supplied the highest proportion of servicemen of any ethnic group. More than one out of three able-bodied Native American men were in uniform.

Navajo soldiers in the Pacific made an unusual contribution. They used their own language as a code for sending vital messages. Although the Japanese intercepted the messages, they could not understand these **Navajo code-talkers.**

★ Section 3 Review ★

Recall

1. **Identify** **(a)** victory garden, **(b)** A. Philip Randolph, **(c)** Tuskegee airmen, **(d)** bracero program, **(e)** Navajo code-talkers.
2. **Define** **(a)** ration, **(b)** segregation.

Comprehension

3. Describe two economic policies that helped the United States produce the military equipment needed to win the war.
4. Why did job opportunities for women expand during the war?
5. Describe one way the war affected each of these groups: **(a)** African Americans, **(b)** Japanese Americans, **(c)** Latinos, **(d)** Native Americans.

Critical Thinking and Writing

6. **Analyzing Ideas** How did prejudice affect the organization of units in the United States army?
7. **Making Inferences** Why do you think Japanese Americans were the only group forced to live in relocation camps?

Activity **Researching** What role did your community play in the effort to win World War II? In the local library, consult news articles that appeared in your town's newspaper during the war years. You might also interview people who lived in your community during the war.

The Allies Advance

As You Read

Explore These Questions

- Why was 1942 a difficult year for the Allies?
- What victories turned the war in favor of the Allies?
- How did the Allies force Germany to surrender?

Identify

- Douglas MacArthur
- Battle of Midway
- Dwight D. Eisenhower
- Operation Overlord
- D-Day
- Battle of the Bulge
- Harry S Truman

When British Prime Minister Winston Churchill heard about the attack on Pearl Harbor, he rejoiced. "We have won the war," he remarked. Churchill felt sure that the United States would lead the Allies to victory.

Despite Churchill's optimism, Allied prospects seemed grim in December 1941. Hitler's armies occupied most of Europe and much of North Africa. Japan was advancing across Asia and the Pacific. As 1942 began, the Allies faced the bleakest days of the war.

A Time of Peril

In early 1942, the Germans seemed unbeatable. German submarines were sinking ships faster than the Allies could replace them. Most of Europe was in German hands. German armies were closing in on Moscow, Leningrad, and Stalingrad in the Soviet Union.

The Soviets resisted heroically. They burned crops and destroyed farm equipment so that the Germans could not use them. In Leningrad and elsewhere, people suffered terrible hardships. More than one million Russian men, women, and children died during the 900-day siege of Leningrad.

Meanwhile, Japanese forces were on the move in the Pacific. After Pearl Harbor, they seized Guam, Wake Island, Hong Kong, and Singapore. (See the map on page 752.)

General **Douglas MacArthur,** commander of United States forces in the Pacific, faced a difficult task. With few troops, he had to defend a huge area. MacArthur directed American and Filipino troops in the defense of the Philippines. They fought bravely against enormous odds. In the end, however, MacArthur was forced to withdraw. "I shall return," he vowed. A Filipino described the defeat in these words:

> "Besieged on land and blockaded by sea,
> We have done all that human endurance can bear....
> Our defeat is our victory."

The Japanese pressed on. They captured Malaya, Burma, and the Dutch East Indies. They threatened India to the west and Australia and New Zealand to the south.

Turning the Tide

The Allied leaders had to agree on a strategy if they were to succeed against the Axis powers. Even before Pearl Harbor, American and British planners had decided that the Allies must defeat Germany and Italy first. Then, they would send their combined forces to fight Japan.

Victories in the Pacific

The adoption of the "beat Hitler first" strategy did not mean abandoning the war in the Pacific. Luckily, the United States's aircraft carriers in the Pacific had survived the attack on Pearl Harbor. Relying on the carriers, a naval task force engaged a Japanese fleet in the Coral Sea near Java in May 1942. After a three-day battle, the Japanese fleet turned back.

One month later, the United States Navy won a stunning victory at the **Battle of Midway.** American planes sank four Japanese aircraft carriers. The battle severely hampered the Japanese offensive. It also kept Japan from attacking Hawaii again.

Success in North Africa

British and American forces began to push back the Germans in North Africa. In October 1942, the British won an important victory at El Alamein in Egypt. German

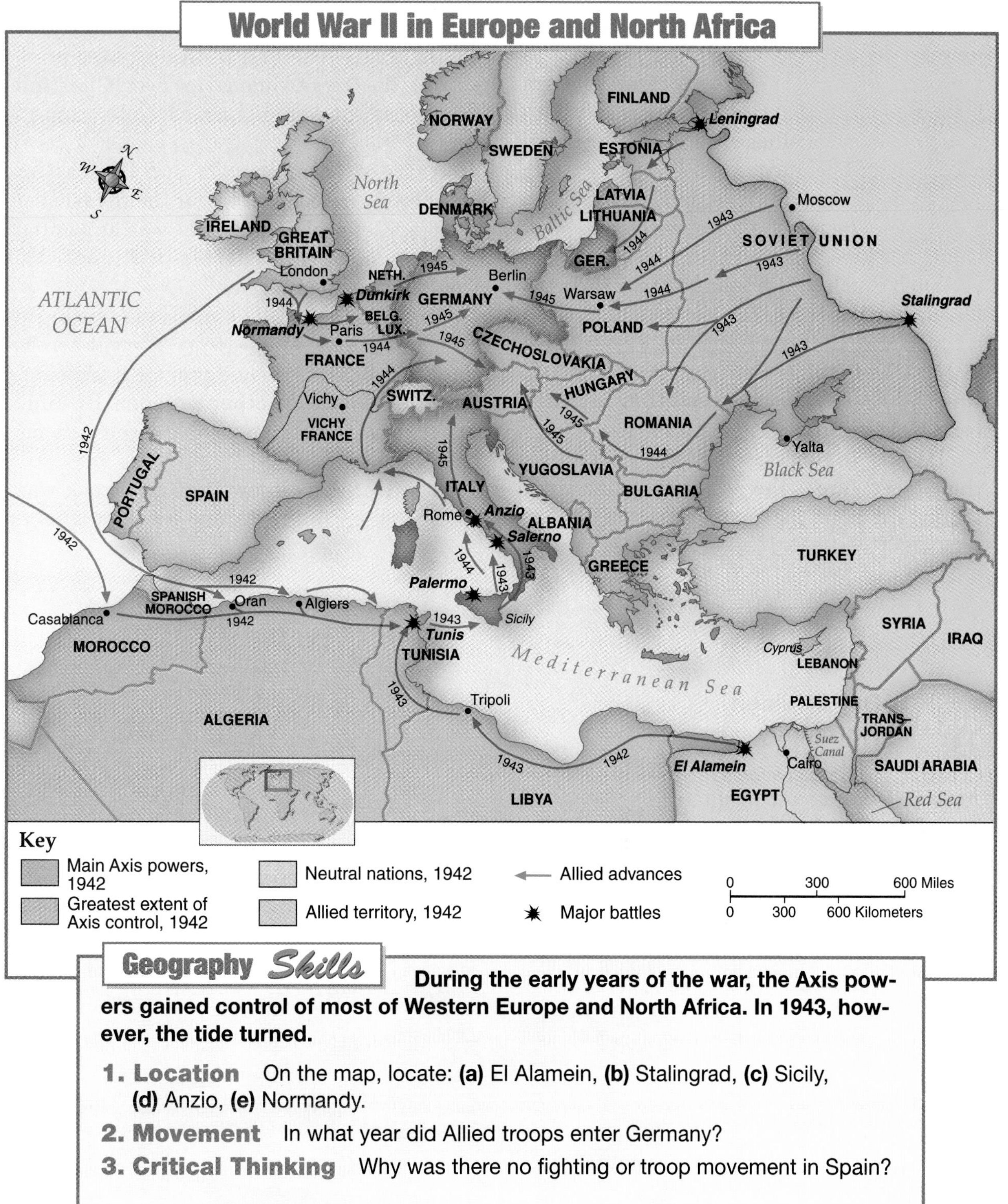

Geography Skills **During the early years of the war, the Axis powers gained control of most of Western Europe and North Africa. In 1943, however, the tide turned.**

1. **Location** On the map, locate: **(a)** El Alamein, **(b)** Stalingrad, **(c)** Sicily, **(d)** Anzio, **(e)** Normandy.
2. **Movement** In what year did Allied troops enter Germany?
3. **Critical Thinking** Why was there no fighting or troop movement in Spain?

forces under General Erwin Rommel were driven west into Tunisia.

Meanwhile, American troops landed in North Africa. Under the command of General **Dwight D. Eisenhower,** they occupied Morocco and Algeria. The Allied armies trapped Rommel's forces in Tunisia. In May 1943, his army had to surrender.

Allied advances in Europe

From bases in North Africa, the Allies organized the invasion of Italy. They used paratroopers, or airborne troops, and soldiers brought by sea to capture Sicily. In early September 1943, the Allies crossed from Sicily to the mainland of Italy.

By then, the Italians had overthrown Mussolini. The new Italian government sided with the Allies. The Germans, however, still occupied much of the country. In a series of bloody battles, the Allies slowly fought their way up the Italian peninsula. On June 4, 1944, Allied troops marched into Rome. It was the first European capital to be freed from Nazi control.

Despite the massive German assault on the Soviet front, the Russians held their ground. In 1943, the Soviet army pushed the Germans back from Leningrad. At Stalingrad, after months of fierce house-to-house fighting, Soviet soldiers forced the German army to surrender. Slowly, the Soviet army pushed the Germans westward through Eastern Europe.

D-Day Invasion at Normandy

Soon after Hitler invaded the Soviet Union in 1941, Stalin had urged Britain and the United States to send armies across the English Channel into France. Such an attack would create a second front and ease pressure on the Soviet Union. However, Churchill and Roosevelt were not prepared to attempt it until 1944.

Years of planning went into **Operation Overlord,** the code name for the invasion of Europe. General Eisenhower was appointed commander of Allied forces in Europe. He would direct the invasion.

Eisenhower faced an enormous task. He had to organize a huge army, ferry it across the English Channel, and provide it with ammunition, food, and other supplies. By June 1944, almost 3 million troops were ready for the invasion.

The Germans knew that an attack was coming. They did not know when or where.

D-Day Invasion at Normandy

American, British, and Canadian forces opened the long-awaited second front against Germany on June 6, 1944, known as D-Day. Tens of thousands of troops landed on the beaches of Normandy in France. ★ **Why had Stalin urged such an invasion?**

They had built a strong "Atlantic wall" against an Allied invasion. They had mined beaches and strung barbed wire. Machine guns and concrete antitank walls stood ready to stop an advance.

On June 6, 1944—**D-Day,** as it was known—a fleet of 4,000 Allied ships carried the invasion force to France. Allied troops scrambled ashore at Normandy. Despite intense German gunfire and heavy losses, they pushed on. Every day, more soldiers landed to reinforce the advance.

On August 25, 1944, the Allies entered Paris. After four years under Nazi rule, the Parisians greeted their liberators with joy. Within a month, all of France was free.

Advancing on Germany

By September, the Allies were moving east toward Germany. However, a shortage of truck fuel hindered their efforts to supply the troops. The advance slowed.

On December 16, 1944, German forces began a fierce counterattack. They pushed the Allies back, creating a bulge in the front lines. The **Battle of the Bulge,** as it was later called, slowed the Allies but did not stop them.

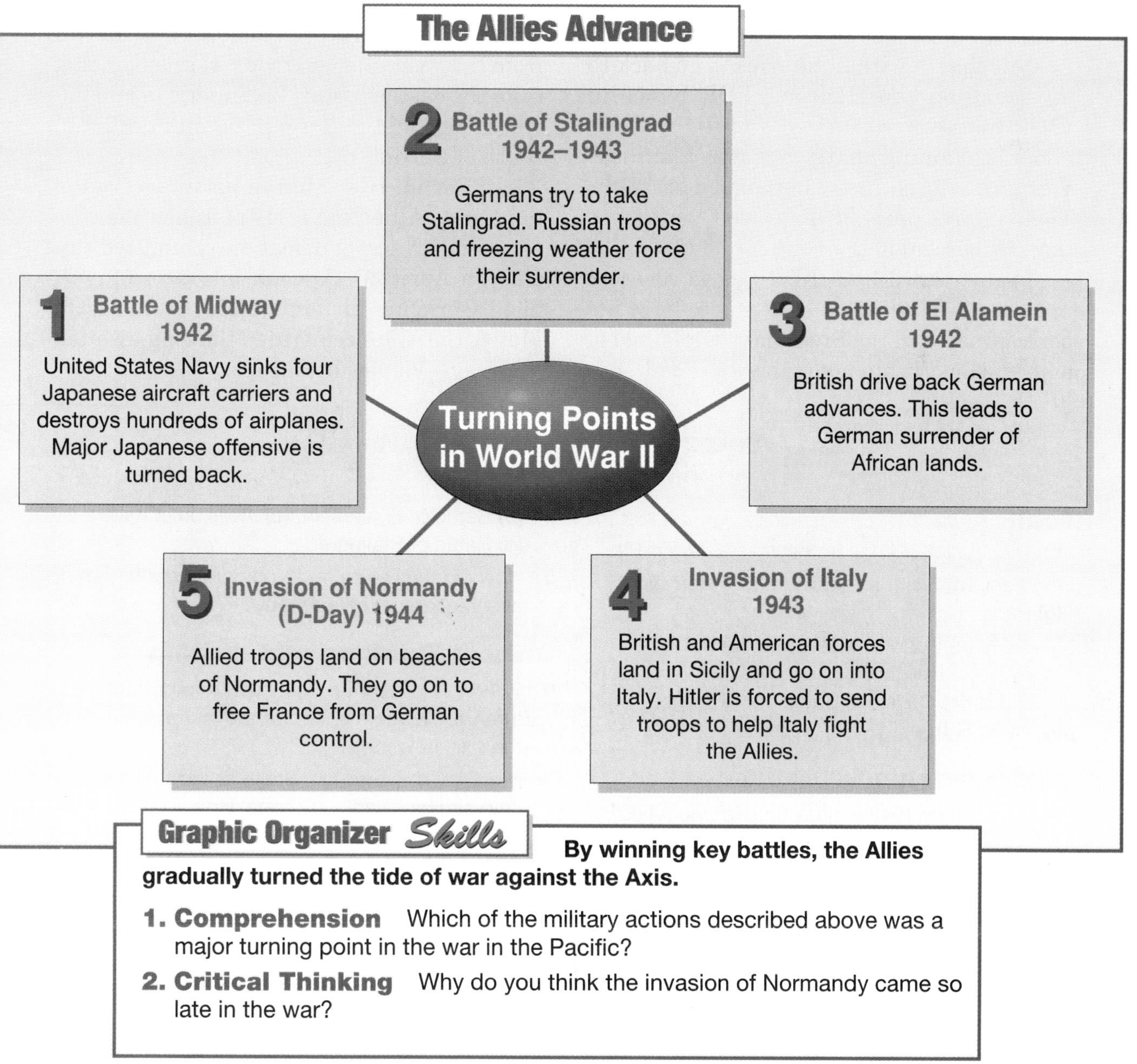

Graphic Organizer *Skills* **By winning key battles, the Allies gradually turned the tide of war against the Axis.**

1. **Comprehension** Which of the military actions described above was a major turning point in the war in the Pacific?
2. **Critical Thinking** Why do you think the invasion of Normandy came so late in the war?

While Allied armies advanced on the ground, Allied planes bombed Germany. At night, British airmen dropped tons of bombs on German cities. By day, the Americans bombed factories and oil refineries. The bombing caused severe fuel shortages in Germany and reduced the nation's ability to produce war goods.

A New President

By mid-1944, the Allied advance shared headlines in American newspapers with the upcoming election. Breaking all tradition, President Roosevelt ran for a fourth term. His opponent was Governor Thomas E. Dewey of New York, who was nominated by the Republican Party.

"All that is within me cries to go back to my home on the Hudson," FDR wrote in 1944. Roosevelt was tired and ill. Still, he and his running mate, Senator **Harry S Truman** of Missouri, campaigned strongly. Their efforts paid off. Roosevelt won more than 54 percent of the vote.

In early April 1945, FDR was on vacation in Georgia. While he was sitting to have his portrait painted, the President complained of a headache. Within hours, he was dead.

Franklin D. Roosevelt was mourned by people all over the world. His death especially shocked Americans. Roosevelt had been President for 12 years. Many Americans could hardly remember anyone else as their leader.

Vice President Harry S Truman had to take over a country in the midst of war. Truman described his reaction:

> "I felt like the moon, the stars, and all the planets had fallen on me. I've got the most terribly responsible job a man ever had."

Victory in Europe

By April 1945, Germany was collapsing. American troops were closing in on Berlin from the west. Soviet troops were advancing from the east. On April 25, American and Soviet troops met at Torgau, 60 miles (96 km) south of Berlin.

In Berlin, Hitler hid in his underground bunker as Allied air raids pounded the city. Unwilling to accept defeat, he committed suicide on April 30. A week later, on May 7, 1945, Germany surrendered to the Allies. On May 8, the Allies celebrated the long-awaited V-E Day—Victory in Europe.

★ Section 4 Review ★

Recall

1. **Locate** **(a)** Leningrad, **(b)** Philippines, **(c)** El Alamein, **(d)** Sicily, **(e)** Stalingrad, **(f)** Normandy, **(g)** Paris.
2. **Identify** **(a)** Douglas MacArthur, **(b)** Battle of Midway, **(c)** Dwight D. Eisenhower, **(d)** Operation Overlord, **(e)** D-Day, **(f)** Battle of the Bulge, **(g)** Harry S Truman.

Comprehension

3. Why was early 1942 a bleak time for the Allies?
4. How did each of the following help the Allies to turn the tide of war? **(a)** Battle of Midway, **(b)** Battle of El Alamein, **(c)** invasion of Italy, **(d)** Battle of Stalingrad
5. How did the D-Day invasion contribute to the eventual defeat of Germany?

Critical Thinking and Writing

6. **Solving Problems** Why was it important for the Allied leaders to cooperate in the defeat of the Axis powers?
7. **Making Inferences** Stalin asked the Allies to help him by invading Europe. How would a second front in Europe help ease pressure on the Soviet Union?

Activity **Writing a News Report** You are a reporter with the Allied troops landing at Normandy. Write a radio news report summarizing the sights you see and the sounds you hear. Try to describe the emotions the soldiers feel as they wait for the invasion and as they land on the beaches.

5 Final Victory

As You Read

Explore These Questions

- What strategy did the United States follow in the Pacific war?
- Why did the United States use the atomic bomb on Japan?
- Why was World War II the deadliest war in history?

Define

- island hopping
- kamikaze
- atomic bomb

Identify

- Potsdam Declaration
- Bataan Death March
- Holocaust
- Nuremberg Trials

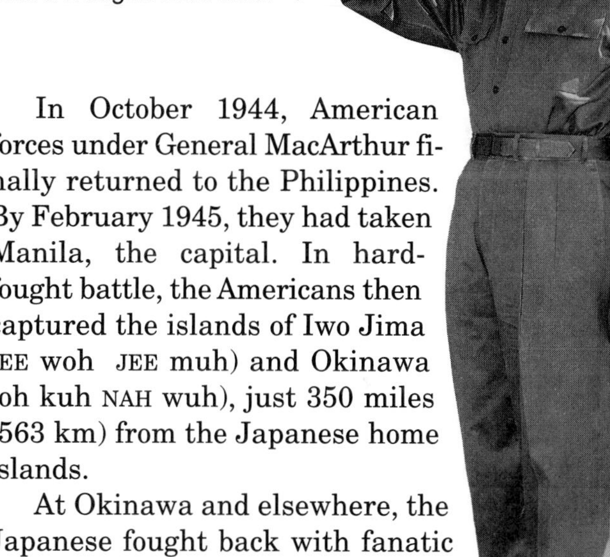

General Douglas MacArthur ➤

SETTING the Scene Soon after FDR's death, a reporter addressed Harry Truman. "Mr. President..." he began. "I wish you didn't have to call me that," Truman interrupted.

As Vice President, Truman had met with Roosevelt fewer than 10 times. He knew little about the plans that had been made for ending the war and keeping the postwar peace. As President, Truman had to learn quickly. Just weeks after he took office, Germany surrendered. The Allies then turned their full attention to defeating Japan.

Campaign in the Pacific

Even while the war raged in Europe, the Allies kept up pressure on Japan. By mid-1942, the United States had two main goals in the Pacific war: to regain the Philippines and to invade Japan.

For its plan to work, the United States had to control the Pacific Ocean. American forces conducted an **island hopping** campaign, capturing some Japanese-held islands and going around others. The Americans used the islands they won as stepping stones toward Japan.

The strategy of island hopping became a deadly routine. First, American ships shelled a Japanese-held island. Next, troops waded ashore under heavy gunfire. Then, in hand-to-hand fighting, Americans overcame fierce Japanese resistance.

In October 1944, American forces under General MacArthur finally returned to the Philippines. By February 1945, they had taken Manila, the capital. In hard-fought battle, the Americans then captured the islands of Iwo Jima (EE woh JEE muh) and Okinawa (oh kuh NAH wuh), just 350 miles (563 km) from the Japanese home islands.

At Okinawa and elsewhere, the Japanese fought back with fanatic zeal. Japanese **kamikaze** (kah muh KAH zee) pilots carried out suicide missions. They loaded old planes with bombs and then deliberately crashed them into Allied ships.

By April 1945, United States forces were close enough to launch repeated attacks against the Japanese home islands. American bombers pounded Japanese factories and cities. American warships bombarded the coast and sank ships. The Japanese people were suffering terribly. Still, their leaders talked about winning a glorious victory over the Allies.

United States military leaders made plans to invade Japan in the autumn. They warned that the invasion might cost between 150,000 and 250,000 American casualties.

World War II in the Pacific

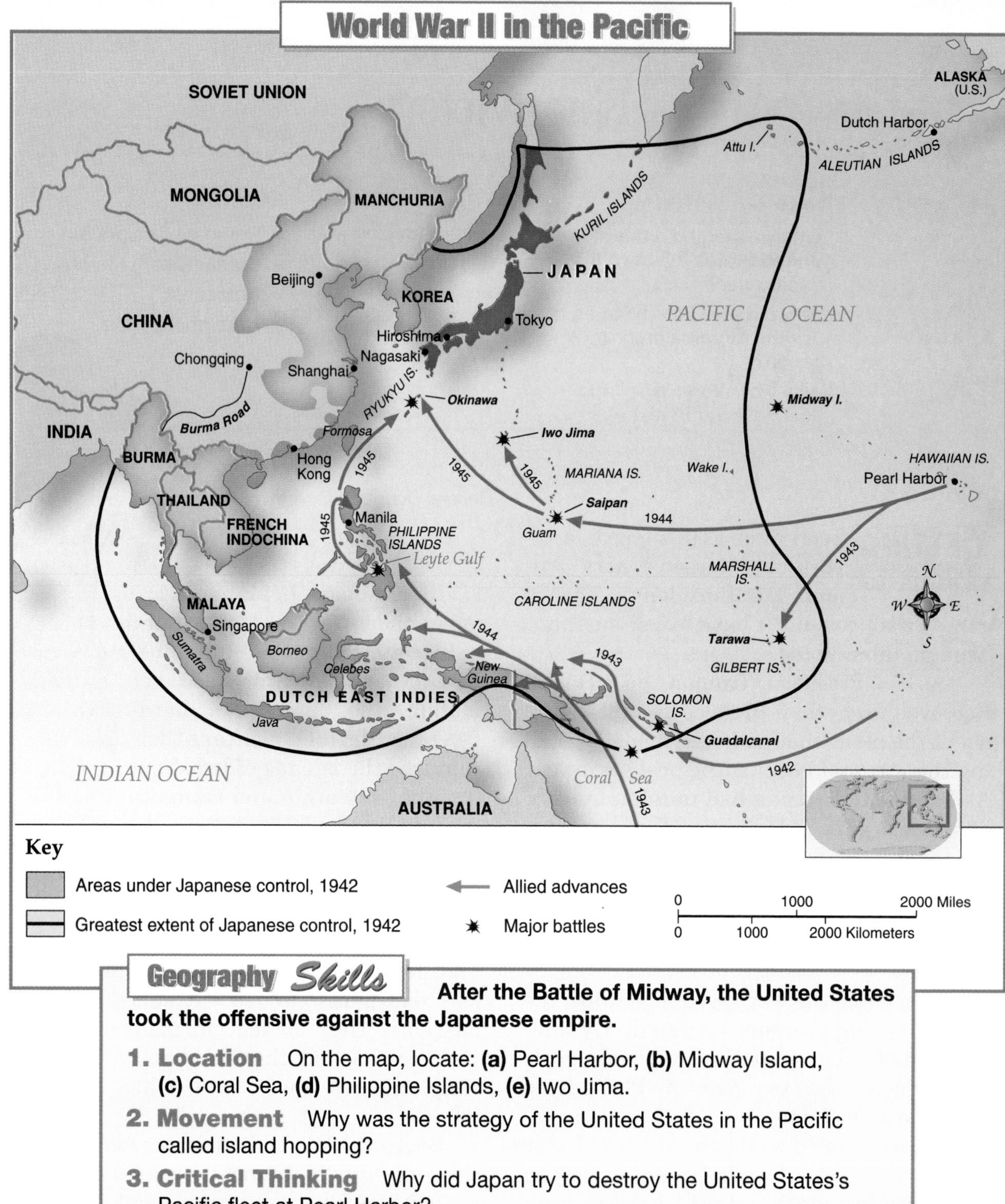

Geography Skills **After the Battle of Midway, the United States took the offensive against the Japanese empire.**

1. **Location** On the map, locate: **(a)** Pearl Harbor, **(b)** Midway Island, **(c)** Coral Sea, **(d)** Philippine Islands, **(e)** Iwo Jima.
2. **Movement** Why was the strategy of the United States in the Pacific called island hopping?
3. **Critical Thinking** Why did Japan try to destroy the United States's Pacific fleet at Pearl Harbor?

Defeat of Japan

In late July 1945, the Allied leaders—Truman, Churchill, and Stalin—met at Potsdam, Germany. While there, Truman received startling news from home. American scientists had successfully tested a secret new weapon—the **atomic bomb.** The new weapon was so powerful that a single bomb could destroy an entire city. Some scientists believed that it was too dangerous to use.

From Potsdam, the Allied leaders sent a message warning Japan to surrender or face "prompt and utter destruction." Japanese leaders did not know about the atomic bomb. They ignored the **Potsdam Declaration.**

On August 6, 1945, the *Enola Gay,* an American bomber, dropped an atomic bomb on Hiroshima, Japan. The blast killed at least 70,000 people and injured an equal number. It destroyed most of the city.

On August 9, the United States dropped a second atomic bomb—this time on Nagasaki. About 40,000 residents died instantly. Later, many more people in both Nagasaki and Hiroshima died from the effects of atomic radiation—deadly particles released by the bombs.

After a furious debate in the Japanese cabinet, the emperor of Japan announced that his nation would surrender on August 14, 1945. The formal surrender took place on September 2 aboard the USS *Missouri* in Tokyo Bay. The warship flew the same American flag that had waved over Washington, D.C., on the day Japan bombed Pearl Harbor.

News of Japan's surrender sparked wild celebrations across the United States. People honked their car horns. Soldiers and sailors danced in victory parades. Workers in tall office buildings showered confetti on people in the streets below.

Costs of the War

After the celebrations, people began to count the costs of the war—the deadliest in human history. The exact number of casualties will probably never be known. However, historians estimate that somewhere between 30 million and 60 million people were killed in battle or behind the lines. (See the chart on page 756.)

World War II was different from World War I, which had been fought mainly in trenches. During World War II, aircraft bombed cities and towns and destroyed houses, factories, and farms. By 1945, millions were homeless and had no way to earn a living.

During the war, stories trickled out about the mistreatment of prisoners. Afterward, Americans learned horrifying details about brutal events such as the **Bataan Death March.** After the Japanese captured the Philippines in 1942, they forced about 75,000

Viewing HISTORY **Bombing of Hiroshima**

"We had seen the city when we went in," said the pilot of the Enola Gay. *"There was nothing to see when we came back." In the photo, below, two Japanese passersby view the blasted landscape.* ★ **Why do you think President Truman decided to use atomic bombs?**

Atomic mushroom cloud over Hiroshima

Why Study History?

Because We Must Never Forget

Historical Background

More than one million children—Jews and non-Jews—were victims of Hitler's "Final Solution." Those who were not sent to concentration camps were left to suffer malnutrition and disease in Jewish ghettoes. Age was no protection from the horrors of the Holocaust.

Connections to Today

Today, young people are encouraged to learn about the Holocaust. It is hoped that by understanding the causes of the Holocaust we can ensure it never happens again. Many cities have museums that commemorate the victims and their suffering. These museums serve as a reminder that we must guard against history repeating itself.

Connections to You

Could a state like Nazi Germany ever exist again? Could people once again follow a leader like Adolf Hitler? Some years ago, with questions like these in mind, a social studies teacher taught his class a special lesson.

The California teacher re-created elements of Nazism in his high school classroom. He selected "gifted students" to join a special youth group. Other students were left out because they were "not gifted." The teacher set up a strict system where obedience was rewarded. The system depended on the cooperation of student informers.

To the teacher's surprise, students eagerly participated. In fact, many liked the system and earned higher grades. Most alarming was that "gifted students" were willing to follow instructions and turn in fellow students.

The teacher ended the lesson with a film about the Holocaust. The students grew silent as they understood. They had given up freedoms and followed a leader. They had turned on others. They had embraced ideas that had led to the Holocaust.

1. **Comprehension** Why is it important for students to learn about the Holocaust?
2. **Critical Thinking** Why do you think some people have been willing to follow the orders of a dictator?

Using the Internet On the Internet, visit one of the many Holocaust museums that exist in the United States. Gather information and write a report about one young person who was a victim of the Holocaust.

Starving prisoners in a Nazi concentration camp

American and Filipino prisoners to march 65 miles (105 km) with little food or water. About 10,000 of the prisoners died or were killed during the march.

The Holocaust

In the last months of the European war, the Allied forces uncovered other horrors. The Allies had heard about Nazi death camps. As they advanced into Germany and Eastern Europe, they discovered the full extent of the **Holocaust**—the slaughter of Europe's Jews by the Nazis.

During the war, the Nazis imprisoned Jews from Germany and the nations they conquered. In prison camps, they tortured and murdered more than 6 million Jews. When Allied troops reached the death camps, they saw the gas chambers the Nazis had used to murder hundreds of thousands. The battle-hardened veterans wept at the sight of the dead and dying human beings.

Photographer Margaret Bourke-White made a record of the horrors. She worked "with a veil over my mind.... I hardly knew what I had taken until I saw prints of my own photographs." After touring one death camp, General Omar Bradley wrote:

> "The smell of death overwhelmed us even before we passed through the stockade.... More than 3,200 naked, emaciated bodies had been flung into shallow graves."

The Nazis murdered other groups as well as Jews. Nearly 6 million Poles, Slavs, and Gypsies were also victims of the death camps. Nazis killed prisoners of war and people they considered unfit because of physical or mental disabilities.

As the full horror of the Holocaust was revealed, the Allies decided to put Nazi leaders on trial. In 1945 and 1946, they conducted war crimes trials in Nuremberg, Germany. As a result of the **Nuremberg Trials,** 12 Nazi leaders were sentenced to death. Thousands of other Nazis were found guilty of war crimes and imprisoned. The Allies also tried and executed Japanese leaders accused of war crimes.

★ Section 5 Review ★

Recall

1. **Locate** **(a)** Philippines, **(b)** Iwo Jima, **(c)** Okinawa, **(d)** Hiroshima, **(e)** Nagasaki.
2. **Identify** **(a)** Potsdam Declaration, **(b)** Bataan Death March, **(c)** Holocaust, **(d)** Nuremberg Trials.
3. **Define** **(a)** island hopping, **(b)** kamikaze, **(c)** atomic bomb.

Comprehension

4. **(a)** What two goals did the United States set for the war in the Pacific? **(b)** What strategy did it adopt to achieve these goals?
5. How did the United States force Japan to surrender?
6. Why was World War II more deadly than World War I?

Critical Thinking and Writing

7. **Analyzing Ideas** The Allies did not try enemy leaders as war criminals after World War I. **(a)** Why do you think they conducted war crimes trials after World War II? **(b)** Do you think they were right to do so?
8. **Defending a Position** After the war, President Truman said he had agreed to the use of the atomic bomb "to shorten the agony of war [and] save the lives of thousands of young Americans." Do you think he made the right decision? Defend your position.

Activity **Linking Past and Present** Write a brief essay on how World War II affects your life today. Consider in your essay the following points: **(a)** the defeat of the Axis dictatorships, **(b)** the threat of nuclear weapons, **(c)** the Holocaust.

Chapter 27 Review and Activities

★ Sum It Up ★

Section 1 Dictatorship and Aggression

- Rulers in the Soviet Union, Germany, Italy, and Japan established dictatorships and threatened world peace.
- The League of Nations and the leading democracies did little to stop international aggression.

Section 2 The War Begins

- As World War II began, the Axis powers overran much of China and Europe.
- Although officially neutral, the United States offered aid to the Allies.
- After the Japanese attack on Pearl Harbor, the United States entered the war.

Section 3 The Home Front

- The United States mobilized its military and economic strength.
- Women and minorities made important contributions to the war effort.
- Prejudice and segregation affected many Americans.

Section 4 The Allies Advance

- The Allies won key victories in the Pacific, in North Africa, and in Italy.
- After the D-Day Invasion, Allied troops advanced into Germany and forced its surrender.

Section 5 Final Victory

- The United States used atomic bombs to defeat Japan.
- World War II was the deadliest war in history.
- Millions of Jews died in the Holocaust.

For additional review of the major ideas of Chapter 27, see ***Guide to the Essentials of American History*** or ***Interactive Student Tutorial CD-ROM,*** which contains interactive review activities, graphic organizers, and practice tests.

Reviewing the Chapter

Define These Terms

Match each term with the correct definition.

Column 1	Column 2
1. dictator	**a.** a suicide soldier or pilot
2. blitzkrieg	**b.** limit the availability of goods
3. ration	**c.** take over a land
4. annex	**d.** lightning war
5. kamikaze	**e.** one who has total power over a country

Explore the Main Ideas

1. What policies did dictators and military rulers follow in the 1930s?
2. What were the effects of isolationism and appeasement?
3. **(a)** How did American civilians contribute to the war effort? **(b)** How did some American civilians suffer unjustly during the war?
4. Identify and describe some of the major turning points of World War II.
5. Describe the terrible costs of World War. II

Chart Activity

Use the table below to answer the following questions: **1.** Which country suffered the most deaths? **2.** Which Axis state had the most civilian deaths? **Critical Thinking** Why did the United States have very few civilian deaths?

World War II Deaths

	Military Dead	Civilian Dead
Britain	389,000	65,000
France	211,000	108,000
Soviet Union	7,500,000	15,000,000
United States	292,000	*
Germany	2,850,000	5,000,000
Italy	77,500	100,000
Japan	1,576,000	300,000

* Very small number
All figures are estimates

Source: Henri Michel, *The Second World War*

Critical Thinking and Writing

1. **Linking Past and Present** **(a)** Why do you think George Washington chose to retire after two terms? **(b)** Why do you think FDR broke this precedent?
2. **Drawing Conclusions** Why do you think Japanese Americans volunteered to serve in the army even though the government was treating Japanese Americans unjustly?
3. **Understanding Chronology** Create a time line illustrating the major events in Europe leading to the start of war in 1939.
4. **Exploring Unit Themes** **Role of Government** **(a)** How did the government control the United States economy during the war? **(b)** Do you think many people complained about the government's economic laws? Explain.

Using Primary Sources

A reporter filed this report after flying with the team of planes that dropped the second atomic bomb on Japan:

> "Observers in the tail of our ship saw a giant ball of fire rise as though from the bowels of the earth, belching forth enormous white smoke rings. Next they saw a giant pillar of purple fire, ten thousand feet high, shooting skyward with enormous speed.... Awe-struck, we watched it... become ever more alive as it climbed skyward through the white clouds. It was no longer smoke, or dust, or even a cloud of fire. It was a living thing, a new species of being, born right before our incredulous eyes."

Source: William L. Laurence, *The New York Times,* September 9, 1945.

Recognizing Points of View **(a)** What emotions do you sense in the reporter's words? **(b)** Does the reporter seem to liken the aftermath of the atomic bomb explosion to some terrible monster? Explain.

Activity Bank

Interdisciplinary Activity

Exploring Geography Find out more about one land or sea battle in World War II. Then, prepare a map showing the locations and movements of the opposing forces in the battle.

Career Skills Activity

Statistician Study the casualty statistics that appear in the table on page 756. Use the statistics to create a bar graph or pie graph showing the same information.

Citizenship Activity

Creating a Poster Create a poster that urges American citizens to support the war effort in some way. Your poster could illustrate the idea of joining the military, working in a factory, buying war bonds, planting a victory garden, rationing, or some other idea.

Internet Activity

Use the Internet to find sites that contain images of World War II, such as art, photographs, and posters. Select a topic having to do with the war. Then, print out images pertaining to the topic. Write a brief caption to go with each image. Display your work in a folder or on a bulletin board.

Eyewitness Journal

Choose one of the following: a soldier in France on D-Day; a woman factory worker; a Tuskegee airman; a Navajo code-talker; a Mexican American in California; a Japanese American on the West Coast. In your EYEWITNESS JOURNAL, describe how the person contributed to World War II or was affected by it.

Poems of the Harlem Renaissance

Various authors

Introduction

Injustice, pride in African heritage, hope for the future—these were some of the major themes of the Harlem Renaissance. In the 1920s, New York City's Harlem was the center of a great flowering of African American art, music, and literature. The many poets who added their voices to the Harlem Renaissance included Langston Hughes, Countee Cullen, and Georgia Douglas Johnson.

Vocabulary

Before you read the selection, find the meaning of these words in a dictionary: **tableau, sable, indignant, oblivious, discerning.**

The Negro Speaks of Rivers

Langston Hughes

I've known rivers:
I've known rivers ancient as the world and
older than the flow of human blood in
human veins.

I bathed in the Euphrates when dawns
were young.
I built my hut near the Congo and it lulled
me to sleep.
I looked upon the Nile and raised the
pyramids above it.*
I heard the singing of the Mississippi when
Abe Lincoln went down to New Orleans,
and I've seen its muddy bosom turn all
golden in the sunset.

I've known rivers:
Ancient dusky rivers.

My soul has grown deep like the rivers.

Mother to Son

Langston Hughes

Well, son, I'll tell you:
Life for me ain't been no crystal stair.
It's had tacks in it,
And splinters,
And boards torn up,
And places with no carpet on the floor—
Bare.
But all the time
I'se been a-climbin' on,
And reachin' landin's.
And turnin' corners,
And sometimes going in the dark
Where there ain't been no light.
So boy, don't you turn back.
Don't you set down on the steps
'Cause you finds it's kinder hard.
Don't you fall now—
For I'se still goin', honey,
I'se still climbin',
And life for me ain't been no crystal stair.

* The Euphrates is a river in the Middle East. The Nile and Congo are rivers in Africa.

Tableau

Countee Cullen

Locked arm in arm they cross the
  way,
 The black boy and the white,
The golden splendor of the day,
 The sable pride of night.

From lowered blinds the dark folk
  stare,
 And here the fair folk talk,
Indignant that these two should dare
 In unison to walk.

Oblivious to look and word
 They pass, and see no wonder
That lightning brilliant as a sword
 Should blaze the path of thunder.

A Painter of the Harlem Renaissance

Aaron Douglas was one of the many black artists who came to New York during the Harlem Renaissance. In works like his 1936 painting Aspiration *(above), he celebrated the African American experience. Douglas also illustrated books of poetry by Langston Hughes and Countee Cullen.* ★ **Summarize the theme of this painting.**

Common Dust

Georgia Douglas Johnson

And who shall separate the dust
Which later we shall be:
Whose keen discerning eye will scan
And solve the mystery?

The high, the low, the rich, the poor,
The black, the white, the red,
And all the chromatique* between,
Of whom shall it be said:

Here lies the dust of Africa;
Here are the sons of Rome;
Here lies one unlabeled
The world at large his home!

Can one then separate the dust,
Will mankind lie apart,
When life has settled back again
The same as from the start?

* Chromatique refers to the range of colors from darkest to lightest.

Analyzing Literature

1. **(a)** In "Mother to Son," what kind of life has the mother had? **(b)** What advice does she give her son?
2. **(a)** In "Tableau," what sight upsets both the blacks and the whites in the neighborhood? **(b)** How do the two children react?
3. **Critical Thinking Summarizing** Summarize what you think are the main points of: **(a)** "The Negro Speaks of Rivers"; **(b)** "Common Dust."

Unit 9 The Nation Today and Tomorrow

What's Ahead

Viewing UNIT THEMES

A Leader in a Changing World

In Modern Business World, *Boris Lyubner shows the United States at the center of a busy global economy. Technology and free enterprise have contributed to American economic leadership. Since World War II, the United States has also become the world's leading military power.* ★ **Identify three examples of advanced technology in this picture. Which do you think is most important to the economy?**

Unit Theme World Leadership

As World War II ended, the United States entered a long rivalry with its former ally, the Soviet Union. Conflict between these two "superpowers" influenced events all over the world. Then, in 1991, the Soviet Union broke up. The United States stood alone as the leading military, political, and economic power in the world.

Still, Americans often disagreed on how to use that power. Should the United States stay out of the affairs of other nations? Or should we take the lead in keeping peace around the world?

How did Americans of the time feel about their role in the world? They can tell you in their own words.

Viewpoints on World Leadership

"The free peoples of the world look to us for support in maintaining their freedom. If we falter in our leadership, we may endanger the peace of the world."

President Harry S Truman (1947)

"Leadership does come with a price tag, and there is an eagerness to let someone else pick up the tab. But it is a price worth paying."

Senator Robert Dole of Kansas (1995)

"The United States is still acting as the world's policeman, rushing armed forces to any place on the globe where conflict erupts.... Why not help ourselves first?"

A North Carolina high school student (1996)

Activity **Writing to Learn** War has broken out between two small countries thousands of miles away. Hundreds of people are being killed, including children. The United States could send in troops to keep the peace, but it would cost money and some American soldiers might lose their lives. Write a letter to the President expressing what you think the United States should do.

Chapter 28

The Cold War Era

1945–1991

What's Ahead

Section 1
The Nation Faces a Cold War

Section 2
The Cold War Heats Up

Section 3
Cold War Battlegrounds

Section 4
The Vietnam War

Section 5
The End of the Cold War

Soon after World War II, a new kind of struggle developed. As the Soviet Union sought to expand its influence around the world, the United States tried to protect non-communist governments. Both superpowers built many atomic weapons. Tensions during the Cold War, as the conflict became known, led to several crises and military conflicts. However, Soviet and American forces never faced each other directly in battle.

For more than 40 years, the Cold War divided the world into opposing camps. This state of tensions continued until the 1990s, when the breakup of the Soviet Union brought an end to the Cold War.

Why Study *History?*

During the Cold War, both sides armed themselves with powerful atomic weapons. However, American and Soviet leaders were able to avoid a full-scale nuclear war. The lesson of how to resolve dangerous conflict can also be applied to everyday life. To examine this connection, see the *Why Study History?* feature, "We Can Learn to Ease Conflict."

American Events

1950 Korean War begins

1962 Cuban missile crisis almost begins a nuclear war

1964 Gulf of Tonkin Resolution increases United States role in Vietnam War

1945 | **1951** | **1957** | **1963** | **1969**

World Events

1949 World Event Chinese Communists set up People's Republic of China

1957 World Event Soviet Union launches first artificial satellite into space

Viewing HISTORY **Military and Industrial Power**

This painting, Preparedness, *by artist Roy Lichtenstein reflects the growing power of the United States during the Cold War years. For over four decades, the Soviet Union and United States competed in many ways. Each tried to have greater political, economic, and military strength than the other.* ★ **Identify two images that Lichtenstein uses to symbolize American might.**

1972 President Nixon visits China and the Soviet Union

1973 United States withdraws troops from Vietnam

1987 President Reagan signs arms reduction treaty with Soviet Union

1969 **1975** **1981** **1987** **1993**

1975 World Event North Vietnam defeats South Vietnam

1985 World Event Mikhail Gorbachev becomes leader of Soviet Union

1 The Nation Faces a Cold War

As You Read

Explore These Questions

- How did the United States and the Soviet Union become rivals?
- What steps did the United States take to prevent the spread of communism in Europe?
- Why did Berlin become a focus of Cold War tension?

Define

- satellite nation
- containment

Identify

- Cold War
- Truman Doctrine
- George Marshall
- Marshall Plan
- Berlin Wall
- Chiang Kai-shek
- Mao Zedong
- United Nations
- North Atlantic Treaty Organization
- Warsaw Pact

SETTING the Scene On March 5, 1946, Winston Churchill gave a speech in Fulton, Missouri. In the audience was President Harry Truman. He nodded as Churchill warned of the growing power of the Soviet Union in Europe:

> “From Stettin in the Baltic to Trieste in the Adriatic, an iron curtain has descended across the Continent. . . . Warsaw, Berlin, Prague, Vienna, Budapest, Belgrade, Bucharest, and Sofia, all these famous cities and populations around them lie in what I must call the Soviet sphere and all are subject to a very high and, in many cases, increasing measure of control from Moscow.”

To Churchill, the Iron Curtain was a barrier cutting off Eastern Europe from the rest of the world. Behind that barrier, the Soviet Union was setting up harsh governments. Churchill urged Americans to stand firm against the Soviet dictator Joseph Stalin.

The United States heeded that plea. For the next half century, it remained locked in a new kind of war with the Soviet Union. The two powers competed for influence around the world, but did not face each other directly in battle. This long, bitter rivalry became known as the **Cold War.**

Roots of the Conflict

During World War II, the Allies had worked together. Yet, even before the war ended, divisions developed. On one side were the United States and Britain; on the other, the Soviet Union.

Growing distrust

The United States and Britain had long distrusted the Soviet Union and its communist government. Communists openly rejected religion and the idea of private property. Soviet leaders boasted that they would spread their revolutionary ideas throughout the world.

For their part, the Soviets distrusted the western powers.* In both world wars, Germany had invaded Russia. For many Russians, invasion from the West remained a deadly threat. The Soviets also accused the United States of trying to gain control over the economies of Europe after World War II.

Soviet expansion

By the end of the war, the Soviets had driven German forces out of the Soviet Union and back to Germany. As a result, Soviet troops occupied much of Eastern Europe.

* The Cold War pitted the West (the United States and its allies) against the East (the Soviet Union and its allies).

American Heritage MAGAZINE

Harry S Truman National Historic Site

President Truman's home in Independence, Missouri, was far removed from Cold War tensions. At his "Missouri White House," Truman could think quietly about crucial decisions. Today, you can visit the house and the nearby Truman Library. It contains papers, photographs, and even a sign he kept on his desk. Its message—"The Buck Stops Here"—suggested that United States Presidents cannot pass their responsibilities to others.

★ ***To learn more about this historic site, write:*** *Harry S Truman National Historic Site, 223 North Main Street, Independence, MO 64050.*

◄ Truman's desk sign

▲ Harry Truman

Stalin promised the other Allies that he would hold "free elections as soon as possible" in the Eastern European nations.

After the war, however, Stalin went back on his promise. "A freely elected government in any of the Eastern European countries would be anti-Soviet," he said, "and that we cannot allow." By 1948, the government of every Eastern European country was under communist control.

Except for Yugoslavia, all of these communist nations remained satellites of the Soviet Union. A **satellite nation** is one that is dominated politically and economically by a more powerful nation. In each satellite nation, the Soviets supported harsh governments. Citizens who protested were imprisoned or killed.

Communist parties supported by the Soviets enjoyed success in other nations. After the war, the Italian Communist party won 104 out of 556 seats in the Italian parliament. In Greece, communist rebels fought a civil war to overthrow the king. Neighboring Turkey felt Soviet pressure, too, when Stalin canceled a treaty of friendship between the two nations.

American Response

Truman decided that a show of strength was needed to stop Soviet expansion. Like Churchill, he saw danger in letting communist governments take power in other countries. He was determined to keep Soviet influence contained within existing boundaries. This Cold War policy was known as **containment.**

The Truman Doctrine

In March 1947, President Truman asked Congress for $400 million in military and economic assistance for Greece and Turkey.

With American aid, both countries were able to put down communist revolts.

The President's program of helping nations threatened by communist expansion became known as the **Truman Doctrine.** Truman explained why the policy was needed:

> ❝ The free peoples of the world look to us for support in maintaining their freedoms. If we falter in our leadership, we may endanger the peace of the world—and we shall surely endanger the welfare of our own nation. ❞

The Marshall Plan

Other European nations needed aid, too. The war had left homes, roads, and factories in ruins. When Secretary of State **George Marshall** toured Europe, he saw thousands of refugees without homes or struggling to find food.

Marshall feared that hungry, homeless people might support communist revolutions. As a result, in June 1947, he proposed a large-scale plan to help Europe rebuild its economy. The President and Congress accepted the **Marshall Plan.**

Stalin angrily rejected the Marshall Plan. He saw it as a plot to weaken Soviet influence. Under pressure from the Soviet Union, Eastern European nations refused to accept American aid.

Between 1948 and 1952, the Marshall Plan provided more than $12 billion in aid to Western European countries. By helping these nations recover, the Marshall Plan lessened the chance of communist revolutions in Western Europe.

Viewing HISTORY **Stalin and the Marshall Plan**

Under the Marshall Plan, the United States spent billions of dollars to help Europe recover from World War II. This 1947 cartoon shows Soviet dictator Joseph Stalin attempting to block the plan. On the back of his uniform are the hammer and sickle, symbols of the Soviet Union. ★ **Why did Stalin oppose the Marshall Plan?**

Focus on Berlin

In 1948, a crisis developed over Berlin, the former capital of Germany. After the war, the Allies had divided Germany into four zones. American, British, French, and Soviet troops each occupied a zone. Berlin was also divided among the Allies, even though it lay deep inside the Soviet zone.

By 1948, the United States, Britain, and France were ready to allow Germans to reunite into a single nation. Stalin, on the other hand, opposed a unified Germany. He feared that if Germany became too strong, it might again threaten the Soviet Union. Also, he wanted to preserve Soviet influence in the eastern part of Germany.

In June 1948, the United States, Britain, and France announced that they would join their zones into the German Federal Republic, or West Germany. In response, Stalin closed all the roads, railway lines, and river routes connecting Berlin with West Germany. The blockade cut off West Berlin from the rest of the world.

Berlin airlift

President Truman did not want to let West Berlin fall into Soviet hands. At the same time, he feared ordering American troops to open a path to West Berlin through the Soviet-occupied zone. Such an action might lead to a new war.

In the end, Truman decided to set up a huge airlift. Day after day, planes flew in food, fuel, and other supplies to 2 million

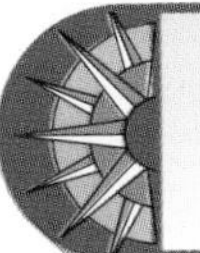

Linking Past and Present

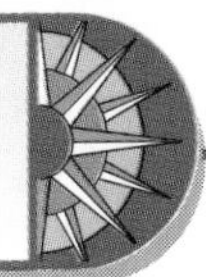

Past

Present

Americans to the Rescue

During the Berlin Airlift, the United States sent tons of food to the people of West Berlin. On the left, Berliners watch eagerly as an American cargo plane brings needed supplies. Today, Americans continue to respond generously to needy people around the world, such as these refugees from the war-torn African nation of Rwanda (right). ★ **Why do you think many Americans are willing to help people in faraway lands?**

West Berliners. At the height of the Berlin Airlift, hundreds of planes carried more than 5,000 tons of supplies into West Berlin each day.

For nearly a year, the airlift continued. Stalin became convinced that the western powers were determined to keep Berlin open. In May 1949, he lifted the blockade.

Berlin Wall

Both Germany and Berlin remained divided, however. With aid from the United States, West Germany rebuilt its economy. The Soviet zone became the German Democratic Republic, or East Germany.

Over the next 12 years, 3 million East Germans, discontented with life under communism, fled to West Berlin. They then continued on to West Germany. The flight of so many people embarrassed East Germany and the Soviet Union.

Suddenly, in August 1961, East German soldiers began building a wall of concrete and barbed wire all across Berlin. Within days, the wall sealed off East Berlin from West Berlin—and from the rest of the noncommunist world. East Berliners who tried to escape to the West risked being shot by border guards. The **Berlin Wall** became a symbol of the Cold War that divided Europe.

The Shocks of 1949

Until 1949, many Americans felt confident that they could restrain the Soviet Union. After all, only the United States had the powerful atomic bomb.

Then, on September 3, 1949, an American B-29 aircraft brought back startling news. On patrol in the North Pacific, it had detected radioactivity high in the atmosphere. This could mean only that the Soviet Union had exploded its own atomic bomb. Suddenly, the threat of communism loomed larger. "This is now a different world," warned Senator Arthur Vandenberg of Michigan.

Cold War in Europe

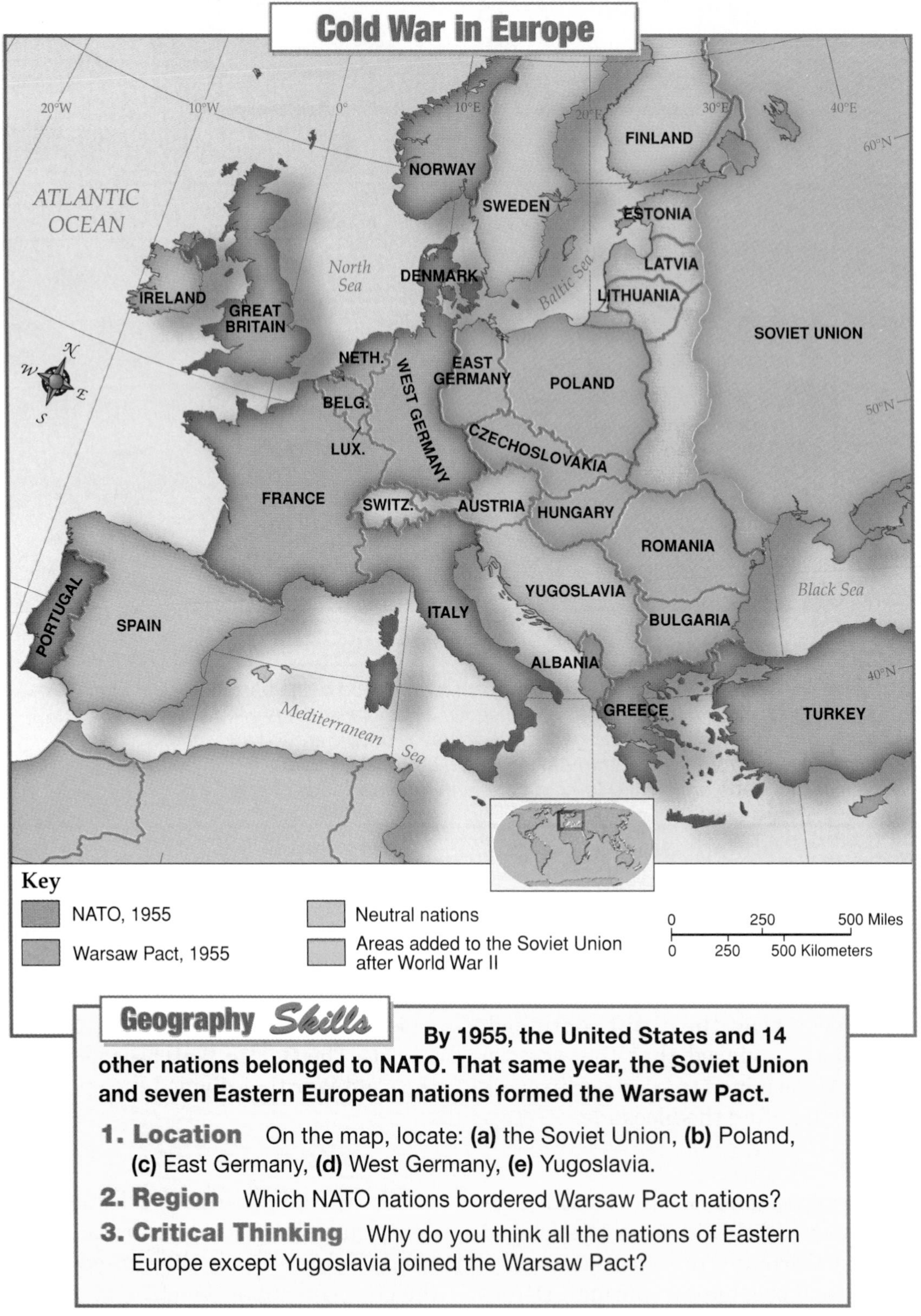

Geography Skills **By 1955, the United States and 14 other nations belonged to NATO. That same year, the Soviet Union and seven Eastern European nations formed the Warsaw Pact.**

1. **Location** On the map, locate: **(a)** the Soviet Union, **(b)** Poland, **(c)** East Germany, **(d)** West Germany, **(e)** Yugoslavia.
2. **Region** Which NATO nations bordered Warsaw Pact nations?
3. **Critical Thinking** Why do you think all the nations of Eastern Europe except Yugoslavia joined the Warsaw Pact?

Soon after, Americans received a second shock when communists took over the government in China. For years, **Chiang Kai-shek** (chang ki SHEHK) had ruled China. Chiang's government was corrupt, however, and over the years, he lost most of his support. Beginning in the 1930s, communist forces led by **Mao Zedong** (mow dzuh DOONG) fought to overthrow Chiang. In October 1949, Mao set up the People's Republic of China. By December, the communists had driven all of Chiang's forces from the Chinese mainland.

Mao Zedong's victory meant that the largest nation in Asia had become communist. The Chinese communists often disagreed with the Soviet Union. Yet, between them, these two communist nations controlled almost one quarter of the Earth's surface. Many Americans worried that communist forces might take over all of Asia.

Striving for Peace

Many of the disputes in the Cold War were debated in a new international peacekeeping organization, known as the **United Nations** (UN). The UN came into being in October 1945, when 51 original members ratified its charter.

The United Nations

Under the United Nations charter, member nations agreed to bring disputes before the UN for peaceful settlement. Every member had a seat in the General Assembly, where problems could be discussed. A smaller Security Council conferred on conflicts that threatened the peace.

Over the years, the UN's greatest successes have been in fighting hunger and disease and improving education. United Nations health officers have vaccinated millions of children. UN relief programs have provided tons of food, clothing, and medicine to victims of disasters.

Preventing wars has proved more difficult. Sometimes, nations have refused to go along with United Nations decisions. In other cases, UN negotiators or troops have kept crises from becoming full-scale wars. As you will read, the UN played an active part in the Korean War.

Competing alliances

As another way of keeping international peace, the United States created alliances with friendly nations. In 1949, it joined with many Western European countries to form the **North Atlantic Treaty Organization,** or NATO. By joining NATO, the United States made it clear that it would help to defend the nations of Western Europe against any Soviet aggression.

In 1955, the Soviet Union formed its own military alliance, called the **Warsaw Pact.** The Soviet Union demanded complete loyalty from its Warsaw Pact neighbors. The Iron Curtain that Winston Churchill had warned about was now firmly in place.

★ Section 1 Review ★

Recall

1. **Locate** **(a)** Greece, **(b)** Turkey, **(c)** Berlin, **(d)** China.
2. **Identify** **(a)** Cold War, **(b)** Truman Doctrine, **(c)** George Marshall, **(d)** Marshall Plan, **(e)** Berlin Wall, **(f)** Chiang Kai-shek, **(g)** Mao Zedong, **(h)** United Nations, **(i)** North Atlantic Treaty Organization, **(j)** Warsaw Pact.
3. **Define** **(a)** satellite nation, **(b)** containment.

Comprehension

4. Why did tensions develop among the Allied powers?
5. How did the Marshall Plan help prevent the spread of communism?
6. **(a)** Describe the events leading up to the Berlin Airlift. **(b)** What were the results of the airlift?

Critical Thinking and Writing

7. **Identifying Alternatives** **(a)** What alternatives did President Truman consider for dealing with the Soviet blockade of Berlin? **(b)** Which alternative did he adopt? **(c)** Do you think he made a wise choice? Why or why not?
8. **Making Inferences** After World War I, the United States refused to join the League of Nations. Why do you think Americans were willing to join the United Nations after World War II?

Activity **Writing a Letter** You are a teenager in East or West Berlin. Write a letter to your cousin in the United States telling her about the building of the Berlin Wall. Describe how you feel about the wall.

The Cold War Heats Up

As You Read

Explore These Questions

- Why did the United States become involved in the Korean War?
- How did Cold War tensions feed fears of communism at home?
- How did the United States react to the rise of communism in Cuba?

Define

- censure
- superpower
- exile

Identify

- Joseph McCarthy
- Nikita Khrushchev
- National Aeronautics and Space Administration
- Fidel Castro
- John F. Kennedy
- Bay of Pigs
- Cuban missile crisis

SETTING the Scene "For me, it was a typical Sunday night in Japan," recalled Sergeant Bill Menninger. In June 1950, Menninger was one of the American troops stationed in Japan after World War II.

> "My wife was giving the kids a bath prior to putting them to bed, and I was reading a book . . . when the call came for me to report at once to headquarters! The wife wanted to know what the call was about. 'Something must be wrong with next week's training schedule,' I answered. 'I'll be back as soon as I can.'"

Dogtags of an American soldier in Korea

As it turned out, Menninger did not return for 11 months. When he got to headquarters, he learned that communist North Korea had invaded South Korea. The Cold War was turning hot.

War in Korea

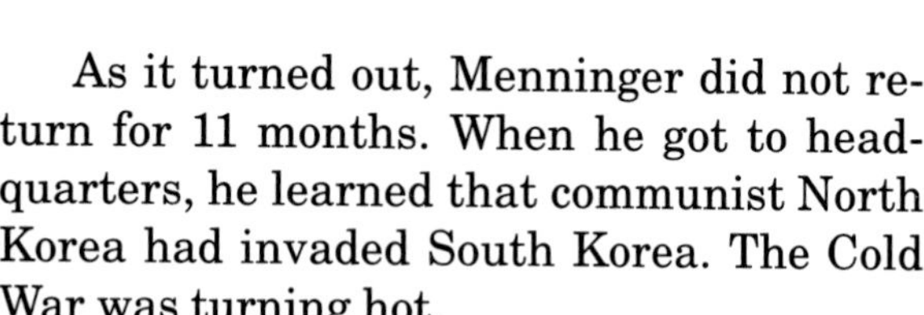

The Korean peninsula borders Russia and China in northeastern Asia. From 1910 to 1945, Korea had been a Japanese colony. After World War II, it was divided at the 38th parallel of latitude. North Korea was governed by communists supported by the Soviet Union. The United States backed a noncommunist government in South Korea.

In June 1950, North Korean soldiers swept across the 38th parallel into South Korea. President Truman acted quickly. He asked the United Nations to send armed forces to Korea to stop the invasion. The Security Council agreed to set up a force, under the command of a general chosen by Truman. The President named Douglas MacArthur. About 80 percent of the UN force was American.

Advances and retreats

At first, UN forces were outnumbered and poorly supplied. Armed with new Soviet tanks, the North Koreans pushed steadily southward. By August 1950, communist troops controlled almost all of South Korea.

MacArthur launched a daring counterattack. He landed by sea at Inchon, behind North Korean lines. Caught by surprise, the North Koreans were forced to retreat back across the 38th parallel. (See the map on page 771.)

MacArthur's original orders called for him to drive the North Koreans out of South Korea. Truman and his advisers, however, wanted to punish North Korea for its aggression. They also wanted to unite Korea. With these goals in mind, they won UN approval for MacArthur to cross into North Korea.

As MacArthur advanced, the Chinese warned that they would not "sit back with folded hands" if the United States invaded North Korea. When UN forces neared the Chinese border, thousands of Chinese troops rushed across the Yalu River into North Korea. Once again, MacArthur was forced to retreat deep into South Korea.

Truman versus MacArthur

By March 1951, UN troops had regained control of the south. MacArthur argued that, to win, the UN had to attack China. Truman, though, feared that an attack on China might start a new world war. He preferred to limit the war and restore the boundary between North and South Korea.

MacArthur complained publicly that politicians in Washington were holding him back. "There is no substitute for victory," he insisted. Angry that MacArthur was defying orders, Truman fired the general.

Many Americans were furious. They gave MacArthur a hero's welcome when he returned home. Truman, however, successfully defended his action. Under the Constitution, he pointed out, the President is commander in chief, responsible for key decisions about war and peace. MacArthur's statements, said Truman, undermined attempts to reach a peace settlement.

Declaring a cease-fire

Peace talks began in July 1951. At first, there was little progress. Then, in 1952, the popular World War II General Dwight D. Eisenhower was elected President. To fulfill a campaign promise, he journeyed to Korea to get the stalled peace talks moving.

In July 1953, the two sides finally signed a cease-fire agreement. It set the border between North and South Korea near the 38th parallel, where it had been before. In this sense, the Korean War changed nothing. Still, the UN had pushed back North Korea's invasion. The United States and its allies showed that they were ready to go to war to prevent communist expansion.

The human cost of the Korean War was high. About 54,000 Americans, as well as 2 million Koreans and Chinese, lost their lives.

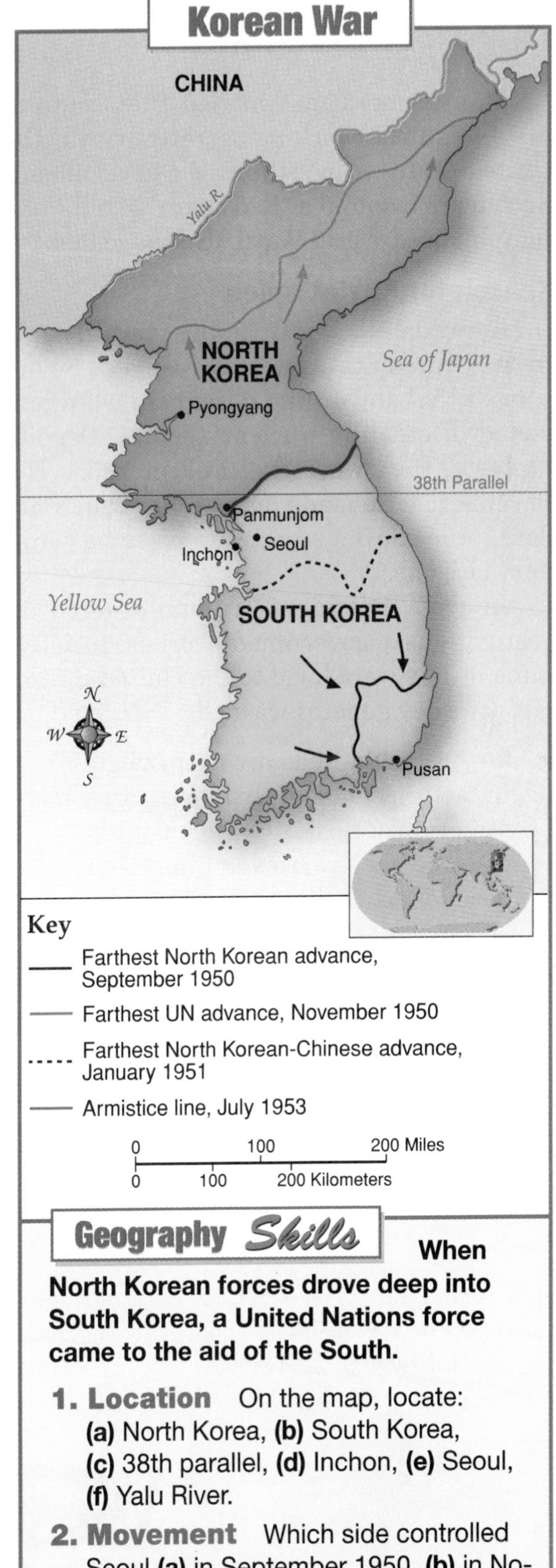

Geography Skills When North Korean forces drove deep into South Korea, a United Nations force came to the aid of the South.

1. **Location** On the map, locate: **(a)** North Korea, **(b)** South Korea, **(c)** 38th parallel, **(d)** Inchon, **(e)** Seoul, **(f)** Yalu River.
2. **Movement** Which side controlled Seoul **(a)** in September 1950, **(b)** in November 1950, **(c)** at the end of the war?
3. **Critical Thinking** Based on this map, do you think communist forces would have won control of all of Korea if the UN had not sent troops?

Hunting Communists at Home

Many Americans worried that communists might be working secretly within the United States to overthrow the government. Such fears inspired a "Red Scare" like the one that followed World War I. (See page 694.)

Search for Soviet spies

Between 1946 and 1950, several people in the United States were arrested as Soviet spies. Ethel and Julius Rosenberg were convicted of stealing nuclear secrets. Despite protests, they were executed in 1953. The Rosenberg case made many Americans wonder if other Soviet spies were posing as ordinary citizens.

In 1947, President Truman ordered investigations of government workers to determine if they were loyal to the United States. His attorney general warned:

> "American Reds are everywhere—in factories, offices, butcher stores, on street corners, in private businesses—and each carries in himself the germ of death for society."

Thousands of government employees underwent questioning. Nearly 3,000 people were forced to resign, even though little evidence of communist activity was found.

McCarthy's campaign

In 1950, Senator **Joseph McCarthy** of Wisconsin announced that he had a list of 57 State Department employees who were Communist party members. McCarthy was never able to prove his claims. Yet his dramatic charges won him national attention.

During the next four years, McCarthy's campaign spread fear and suspicion across the nation. Businesses and colleges questioned employees. Many people were fired. Others, afraid of losing their own jobs, refused to defend accused co-workers.

In 1954, the Senate held televised hearings to investigate McCarthy's charges that there were communists in the United States Army. Under the glare of the television lights, McCarthy came across to the public as a bully, not a hero. His popularity plunged.

In December 1954, the Senate passed a resolution to **censure,** or officially condemn, McCarthy for "conduct unbecoming a member." As a result, McCarthy lost power. By the time he died, three years later, the worst of the Red Scare was over.

The Arms Race

Meanwhile, the United States and the Soviet Union embarked on an arms race. Each side built up its supply of missiles and atomic weapons. Each wanted to have enough weapons to withstand an attack by the other. By 1953, both nations had tested powerful new hydrogen bombs.

In 1957, a Soviet rocket launched *Sputnik,* the world's first artificial satellite. **Nikita Khrushchev** (KROO shawf), who had become Soviet leader after Stalin's death in

Red Channels
The Report of
COMMUNIST INFLUENCE IN RADIO AND TELEVISION
Published By
COUNTERATTACK
THE NEWSLETTER OF FACTS TO COMBAT COMMUNISM
55 West 42 Street, New York 18, N. Y.
$1.00 per copy

Viewing History **Hunting Communists in Entertainment**

In 1947, the House Committee on Un-American Activities held hearings to see if movie makers were affected by communist infiltration. As a result, studios denied work to many writers, directors, and actors. The publication Red Channels, *at left, listed suspected communists in radio and television.* ★ **Why do you think some Americans feared communist influence in movies, radio, and television?**

Viewing HISTORY **Responding to the Arms Race**

During the 1950s, Americans responded in many ways to the threat of nuclear war. Some families and communities built "fallout shelters" (left). These underground hideaways were designed to protect against the radiation of an atomic blast. At right, school children learn to "duck and cover" in case of an atomic missile attack.

★ **Do schools conduct air raid drills today? Why or why not?**

1953, boasted that Soviet factories were turning out new rockets "like sausages." Americans were stunned. If the Soviets could launch a satellite, their atomic missiles could reach the United States as well.

Many Americans worried that the United States faced a "missile gap." In fact, the United States remained well ahead of the Soviet Union in the arms race. Between 1958 and 1960, the number of atomic weapons stockpiled by the United States tripled—from 6,000 to 18,000. Both sides spent billions of dollars on weapons and missiles.

In response to the launching of *Sputnik,* the government also created the **National Aeronautics and Space Administration** (NASA) in 1958. The goal of this agency was to establish an American space program to compete with that of the Soviets. The United States quickly moved ahead in the "space race."

Connections With Science

The arms race stimulated a uranium mining rush in the West. Uranium was needed to produce atomic weapons. In the early 1950s, prospectors with Geiger counters swarmed through the mountains and canyons of Colorado and Utah in search of uranium.

Conflicts in Cuba

By the 1960s, the United States and the Soviet Union were **superpowers**—nations with enough military, political, and economic strength to influence events in many areas around the globe. One place where the superpowers clashed was Cuba.

In 1959, **Fidel Castro** led a revolution that set up a socialist state in Cuba. Castro's government took over private companies, including many owned by American businesses. Thousands of Cubans, especially those from the middle and upper classes, fled to the United States.

Bay of Pigs invasion

Castro's actions worried American leaders. Cuba was located just 90 miles (145 km) off the coast of Florida. The Soviet Union had begun supplying the new socialist state with large amounts of economic aid. In response, President Eisenhower approved a secret plan to train an army of Cuban exiles to invade Cuba. **Exiles** are people who have been forced to leave their own country.

Why Study History?

Because We Can Learn to Ease Conflict

Historical Background

The Cuban missile crisis of 1962 sticks in the memory of everyone who lived through it. (See page 775.) One American recalled, "I went to bed that night thinking that if there would ever be a World War III, it would probably be now."

Despite such fears, war was avoided. As the conflict eased, the United States and the Soviet Union set up a direct telephone link so their leaders could communicate instantly. The famous "hot line" symbolized the willingness of two enemies to resolve any conflicts that might lead to nuclear war.

Connections to Today

The Cold War ended in 1991 with the breakup of the Soviet Union. Today, schoolchildren no longer have to interrupt classes to take part in air raid drills. Families do not build underground nuclear fallout shelters in the backyard.

Still, dangerous conflicts continue to exist throughout the world. As in the Cold War, communication can be the key to easing tensions. Often, the United States plays the role of mediator, bringing enemies together to find solutions. American negotiators have helped hammer out peace agreements in the Middle East, Yugoslavia, Northern Ireland, and other trouble spots.

Connections to You

Today, few young Americans dread the outbreak of nuclear war. Yet you may face other kinds of fears and tensions. For some, school violence is a major concern. We have all heard of cases where simple arguments have had tragic outcomes.

For many schools, "peer mediation" programs are part of the solution to violence. Volunteers train to act as negotiators between other students. The mediator listens to both sides and tries to get them to reach an agreement. Both parties then sign a copy of the agreement. In schools, as in the world, communication can be the key to easing tension and reducing violence.

1. **Comprehension** **(a)** What was the purpose of the "hot line" between the United States and the Soviet Union? **(b)** What is the goal of peer mediation programs today?
2. **Critical Thinking** Some people think dress codes are one way to curb gang violence. Why might such a solution be effective?

★*Activity* **Writing a Speech** You are running for office on the platform of ending school violence. Write a speech explaining how you would solve the problem. Include a catchy slogan that could be used on posters or buttons.

These students are learning to become "peer mediators" to resolve conflicts in their schools.

In 1961, **John F. Kennedy** became President. A few months later, on April 17, about 1,200 Cuban exiles landed at the **Bay of Pigs** on the southern coast of Cuba. They hoped other Cubans who opposed Castro would join them. The landing, however, was badly planned. Also, Kennedy canceled air support for the attack. Castro's forces quickly rounded up the invaders. In the end, the Bay of Pigs incident strengthened Castro in Cuba and embarrassed the United States.

Cuban missile crisis

After the Bay of Pigs invasion, the Soviet Union decided to give Cuba more weapons. In October 1962, President Kennedy learned that the Soviets were secretly building missile bases on the island. If the bases were completed, atomic missiles could reach American cities within minutes.

For a week, Kennedy and his advisers debated in secret. Then, in a dramatic television statement, the President told Americans about the missile sites. He announced that the navy would begin a "strict quarantine" of Cuba. American warships would turn back any Soviet ship carrying missiles.

A tense week followed as Soviet ships steamed toward Cuba. Attorney General Robert Kennedy, the President's brother, recalled one grim moment at the White House during the crisis:

> “Was the world on the brink of a holocaust?... [The President's] hand went up to his face and covered his mouth. He opened and closed his fist. His face seemed drawn, his eyes pained, almost gray. We stared at each other across the table.”

At the last minute, the Soviet ships turned back. "We're eyeball to eyeball," said Secretary of State Dean Rusk, "and I think the other fellow just blinked."

Kennedy's strong stand led the Soviets to compromise. Khrushchev agreed to take the missiles out of Cuba. In turn, the United States agreed not to invade the island. Kennedy also promised to dismantle American missiles in Turkey.

The **Cuban missile crisis** had shaken both American and Soviet officials. In all the years of the Cold War, the world never came closer to a full-scale nuclear war.

★ Section 2 Review ★

Recall

1. **Locate** **(a)** North Korea, **(b)** South Korea, **(c)** Cuba.
2. **Identify** **(a)** Joseph McCarthy, **(b)** Nikita Khrushchev, **(c)** National Aeronautics and Space Administration, **(d)** Fidel Castro, **(e)** John F. Kennedy, **(f)** Bay of Pigs, **(g)** Cuban missile crisis.
3. **Define** **(a)** censure, **(b)** superpower, **(c)** exile.

Comprehension

4. **(a)** What action led to the Korean War? **(b)** Why did the Chinese join the fighting? **(c)** How did the war end?
5. **(a)** What steps did President Truman take to fight communism at home? **(b)** How did Senator Joseph McCarthy come to national attention?
6. Why did Castro's revolution in Cuba worry the United States?

Critical Thinking and Writing

7. **Analyzing Ideas** Why do you think the Constitution made the President commander in chief of the military?
8. **Linking Past and Present** Television played a major role in the downfall of Senator Joseph McCarthy. Does television influence public opinion today? Give an example to support your answer.

Activity **Understanding Psychology** You are a psychologist who views history in terms of people's feelings. Give three examples of how fear affected American history between 1950 and 1962. (Remember, fear is not always a weakness. Sometimes, it can even save your life!)

Cold War Battlegrounds

Explore These Questions

- Why did many new nations emerge after World War II?
- Why did the Cold War spread to Asia and Africa?
- What policies did the United States follow in Latin America?

Identify

- Alliance for Progress
- Peace Corps
- Organization of American States
- Ronald Reagan
- Iran-Contra deal

In September 1959, Soviet premier Nikita Khrushchev arrived in New York. He had come to address the United Nations. At first, Khrushchev spoke calmly, expressing hopes that the Cold War between the United States and the Soviet Union would end. Soon, however, Khrushchev's manner changed. Twice, he became so angry that he took off his shoe and pounded it on the table.

Khrushchev's visit symbolized the calms and storms of the continuing Cold War. As the two superpowers confronted each other, the nations of Africa, Asia, and Latin America became battlegrounds in the struggle.

Emerging Nations

After World War II, people in Asia and Africa began to demand independence. For years, they had been governed as colonies of European and other foreign powers. In the postwar years, many new nations emerged.

In the colonies, communist rebels often campaigned to overthrow foreign control. Khrushchev promised support for what he called "wars of national liberation." Both openly and secretly, the Soviets gave economic and military aid to rebel forces.

The West tried to prevent the Soviets from expanding their influence. In doing so, American leaders faced difficult choices. Should the United States provide aid to a nation even if that meant helping a military dictator? Should Americans use secret aid to counter the Soviets? Should they send troops into other nations to influence their internal affairs? In the end, the United States used all these tactics at one time or another to contain communism and win the Cold War.

The Philippines

The United States also had to address the issue of its own colonies. On July 4, 1946, it granted independence to the Philippines. Crowds in Manila braved heavy rains to attend the independence ceremony. They cheered as the American flag was lowered and the Filipino flag hoisted high.

Still, the transition to independence was not easy. A few wealthy Filipinos owned most of the land. Many Filipinos wanted to divide the land more equally among the peasant farmers. When the government did not act quickly to make changes, fighting broke out. Some of the rebels were communists. By 1954, the government defeated the rebels. It also made some land reforms.

In 1965, Ferdinand Marcos became president of the Philippines. Under Marcos, the government became less democratic. In the years that followed, both noncommunists and communists pushed for reforms.

India and Southeast Asia

In 1947, the people of India won independence from Britain. The land was divided into two nations—India and Pakistan. Both the United States and the Soviet Union tried to win the support of these giant new nations. Feeling threatened by the Soviet Union to its north, Pakistan became an ally of the United States. India accepted both American and Soviet economic aid, but remained neutral in the Cold War. India also led other neutral nations in calling on the superpowers to stop their arms race.

In Southeast Asia, Burma, Malaysia, and Singapore became independent from Britain. Indonesia won freedom from the Netherlands. In Indochina, nationalists fought for independence from France.* The war in Indochina lasted for almost 30 years and eventually involved the United States, as you will read in Section 4.

African Nations

During the 1950s and 1960s, Africans worked to win independence from European colonial rule. By 1970, more than 30 independent states had been formed. Most political divisions within emerging African nations were based on tribal loyalties.

As part of the Cold War, both the United States and Soviet Union sought allies among Africa's new states. To achieve this goal, the superpowers offered economic and military aid to nations or tribal groups within nations.

The Cold War fueled international conflicts and civil wars in Africa. In East Africa, the superpowers were involved in a long war between Somalia and Ethiopia. The United States backed Somalia, while the Soviet Union backed Ethiopia. In southern Africa, the Cold War intensified a civil war in Angola. Angola's communist government was aided by Soviet finances and by more than 50,000 Cuban troops. The United States, meanwhile, supported anticommunist rebel groups.

* Indochina included the present-day countries of Laos, Cambodia, and Vietnam.

Latin America and the Cold War

Closer to home, American leaders focused on Latin America. In the early 1900s, the United States had frequently intervened in the internal affairs of Latin American nations. Now, Cold War tensions led the United States to resume its active role. As you have read, American efforts to keep Soviet missiles out of Cuba nearly resulted in nuclear war. As the Cold War continued, American leaders worked to contain communism in other Latin American nations as well.

Economic issues

Latin America had long faced severe social and economic problems. As populations grew, governments found it impossible to provide enough jobs, schools, and hospitals. Poor people migrated to cities, seeking work. There, they often lived in tin or cardboard shacks, without heat, light, or water.

Many poor Latin Americans saw communism as a solution to their problems. Communists pointed out that a small number of wealthy citizens owned most of the land in Latin America. They called for land to be divided more equally. Some noncommunists also supported this view.

The economies of many Latin American nations depended on American corporations.

Fear of World Communism

This panel appeared in an American anticommunist comic book during the 1950s. The man standing is Soviet premier Nikita Khrushchev. He is shown plotting to spread the communist ideas of Marx and Lenin throughout the world. ★ **Why do you think foes of communism published this comic book?**

Viewing History: Protests in Latin America

Vice President Richard Nixon got a stormy welcome when he visited Venezuela in 1958. Here, an angry mob throws rocks and eggs at Nixon's limousine. At one point, Nixon faced protesters directly and challenged them to a debate.

★ **Why did some people in Latin America distrust the United States?**

◄ Vice President Richard Nixon

These businesses made large profits from their Latin American investments, yet they paid workers very low wages. Reformers called for stronger regulation of foreign corporations. Communists demanded that such companies be taken over by the state.

American aid

Many American leaders agreed with the need for reform. They hoped that American aid would help make Latin American nations more democratic, ease the lives of the people, and lessen communist influence.

President Kennedy worked to strengthen ties to Latin America. In 1961, he set up a program called the **Alliance for Progress.** The Alliance tried to help the people of Latin America build schools and hospitals, improve farming, and win economic and social reform.

Kennedy also formed the **Peace Corps.** Under this program, thousands of American volunteers went to Latin America or other developing areas. Volunteers lived with the local people for two years, teaching or giving technical advice. One volunteer later said:

> ❝ Just imagine a person thinking he can actually do something about world hunger, poverty, illiteracy, or disease. Those are not 'just' problems, but problems the size of mountains, yet the average Peace Corps volunteer believes he can do his part by chipping away at those mountains . . . one person at a time. ❞

The United States also backed the **Organization of American States,** or OAS. Through the OAS, it encouraged economic progress in Latin America by investing in transportation and industry.

Military intervention

At other times, the United States sent troops or military aid to Latin American countries. In doing so, it often supported military dictators because they were strongly anticommunist. Between 1950 and 1990, American forces were sent to Guatemala, the Dominican Republic, Panama, and Grenada.

Many Latin Americans complained that the United States had begun using its "big stick" again in foreign policy. When Vice President Richard Nixon toured eight Latin American nations in 1958, angry mobs pelted his car with eggs and stones.

Through the years, American Presidents defended their actions. The United States would intervene in Latin America, said President Lyndon Johnson, whenever "the object [of rebels] is the establishment of a Communist dictatorship."

Nicaragua

American actions in Latin America increased during the 1980s. President **Ronald Reagan** took office in 1981. As a strong anticommunist, he provided aid to friendly forces in both Nicaragua and El Salvador.

In Nicaragua, a revolutionary group called the Sandinistas had taken power in 1979 and set up a socialist government. The Sandinistas later won an election in 1984. Their opponents were known as Contras, from the Spanish word meaning "against." President Reagan supported the efforts of Contra rebels to overthrow the Sandinistas.

Many members of Congress disagreed with President Reagan's policy in Nicaragua. They passed laws banning military aid to the Contras. Even so, some people on the President's staff provided military aid secretly. To finance their program, the officials used profits from illegal weapons sales to Iran, a country in the Middle East.

In 1986, news reporters discovered the details of the secret **Iran-Contra deal.** The news stirred a great deal of debate because officials working for the President had lied to Congress about their actions. After an investigation, several members of the President's staff were put on trial. The President, however, said he did not know his staff had done anything to break the law.

In 1987, the president of Costa Rica helped arrange a peace plan for Nicaragua. In elections in 1990, Nicaraguans rejected the Sandinistas and voted in new leaders.

El Salvador

In El Salvador, Reagan sent arms and military advisers to help the government in a civil war that raged there. The United States supported the government even though it was often brutal and oppressive. Fighting between rebels and the government lasted 12 years and cost more than 50,000 lives.

Finally, through the efforts of the United Nations, a cease-fire agreement was reached in early 1992. "This is a new country," said one former rebel leader. Two years later, El Salvador held democratic elections. Many hoped the elections would lead to greater democracy and stability in the country.

★ Section 3 Review ★

Recall

1. **Locate** **(a)** the Philippines, **(b)** India, **(c)** Pakistan, **(d)** Nicaragua, **(e)** El Salvador.
2. **Identify** **(a)** Alliance for Progress, **(b)** Peace Corps, **(c)** Organization of American States, **(d)** Ronald Reagan, **(e)** Iran-Contra deal.

Comprehension

3. What major changes took place in Asia and Africa after World War II?
4. How did the Soviet Union try to win support from emerging nations?
5. Describe two ways that the United States tried to influence Latin America during the Cold War.

Critical Thinking and Writing

6. **Understanding Causes and Effects** Why might the competition between the United States and the Soviet Union have hindered development in the new nations of Asia and Africa?
7. **Recognizing Points of View** Why do you think that relations between the United States and Latin America were often strained?

Activity **Writing a Position Statement** You are an adviser to an American President during the Cold War. The President is trying to decide whether the United States should or should not support an anticommunist dictator in an African nation. Write a brief statement in which you explain your position.

4 The Vietnam War

As You Read

Explore These Questions
- Why did the United States send troops to Vietnam?
- Why did many Americans oppose United States involvement in the Vietnam War?
- What were the results of the war?

Define
- guerrilla
- domino theory
- escalate

Identify
- Ho Chi Minh
- Vietcong
- Lyndon Johnson
- Gulf of Tonkin Resolution
- Vietnam War
- Tet Offensive
- Richard Nixon
- Khmer Rouge

SETTING the Scene In 1961, journalist Stanley Karnow stopped by the White House to talk with Attorney General Robert Kennedy. Karnow had been reporting from Southeast Asia for several years. He wanted to warn Kennedy that the nation of Vietnam was becoming a serious trouble spot.

Kennedy was not convinced. "We've got 20 Vietnams a day to handle," he said. Karnow turned out to be right, though. During the 1960s, a small conflict in Asia grew steadily into the longest war in American history.

The Two Vietnams

Vietnam is a narrow country that stretches 1,000 miles (1600 km) along the South China Sea. Since the late 1800s, it had been ruled by France as a colony.

After World War II, a Vietnamese communist named **Ho Chi Minh** (HOH CHEE MIHN) led a war for independence. Ho's army finally defeated the French in 1954. An international peace conference divided Vietnam into two nations. North Vietnam, led by Ho Chi Minh, received aid from the Soviet Union. South Vietnam, under Ngo Dinh Diem (NOH DIN dee EHM), was backed by the United States.

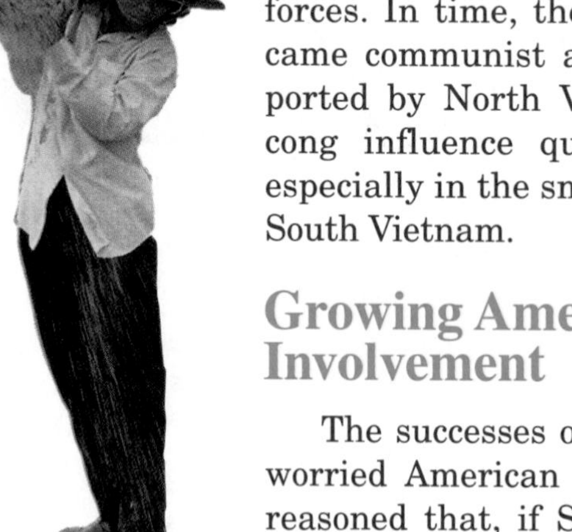

Vietnamese peasant

By the time President John Kennedy took office in 1961, many South Vietnamese had come to distrust Diem. They felt that he favored the nation's few wealthy landowners and ignored the problems of its peasants.

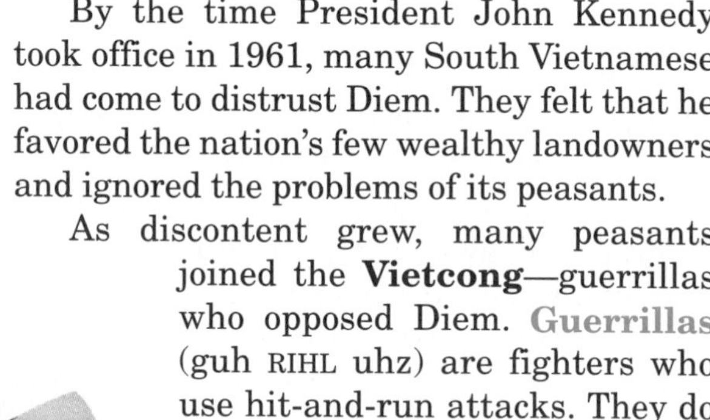

As discontent grew, many peasants joined the **Vietcong**—guerrillas who opposed Diem. **Guerrillas** (guh RIHL uhz) are fighters who use hit-and-run attacks. They do not wear uniforms or fight in large forces. In time, the Vietcong became communist and were supported by North Vietnam. Vietcong influence quickly spread, especially in the small villages of South Vietnam.

Growing American Involvement

The successes of the Vietcong worried American leaders. They reasoned that, if South Vietnam fell to the communists, neighboring countries in Southeast Asia would follow—like a row of falling dominoes. This idea became known as the **domino theory.** The goal of the United States was to prevent the first domino from falling.

President Kennedy strongly believed in the domino theory. In 1961, he sent military advisers to help Diem fight the Vietcong.

These advisers were not to take part in combat. Their mission was to help organize and train the South Vietnamese army. Meanwhile, Diem continued to lose support. In November 1963, he was assassinated.

In 1963, **Lyndon Johnson** became President. Like Kennedy, Johnson believed that the United States could not allow the Vietcong to take over South Vietnam. Johnson increased aid to South Vietnam. Still, the Vietcong continued to gain influence.

Americans in combat

Then, in August 1964, North Vietnamese torpedo boats attacked an American ship patrolling in the Gulf of Tonkin. A second attack was reported but never confirmed. North Vietnam claimed that the American ships were spying in North Vietnamese waters.

At Johnson's urging, Congress passed the **Gulf of Tonkin Resolution.** It allowed the President "to take all necessary measures to repel any armed attack or to prevent further aggression." Johnson used the resolution to order the bombing of North Vietnam, as well as some targets in South Vietnam.

As a result of the Gulf of Tonkin Resolution, the role of Americans in Vietnam changed from military advisers to active fighters. Across South Vietnam, American troops battled against North Vietnamese and Vietcong communist forces. By 1968, President Johnson had sent more than 500,000 troops to fight in the **Vietnam War.**

Fighting a jungle war

As the war **escalated,** or expanded, Johnson used the draft to raise troops. The draft affected American youths unequally. Many young men from wealthy or middle-class families found legal ways to avoid being drafted. As a result, a high percentage of the troops in Vietnam were poor, including many African Americans and Latinos.

American soldiers quickly discovered that the Vietnam War was different from other wars. Rather than trying to gain ground, Americans were sent on "search and destroy" missions. The goal was to search for Vietcong strongholds and destroy them. Then, the Americans moved on.

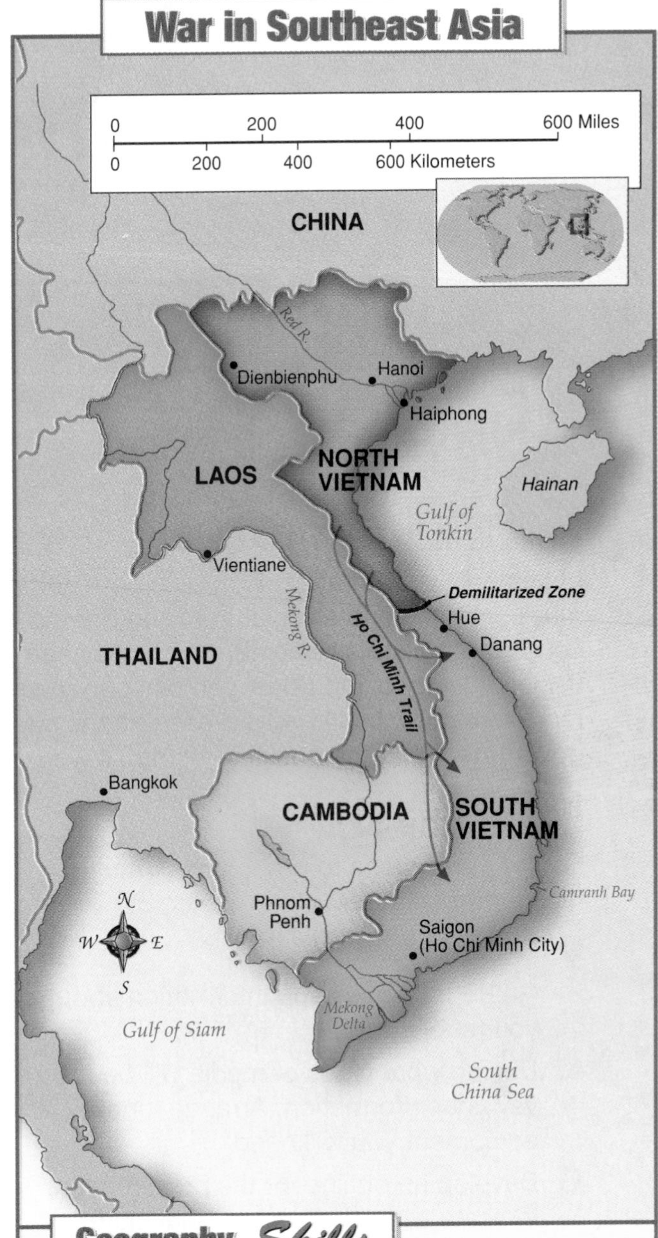

Geography *Skills* **During the Vietnam War, North Vietnam supplied arms to communist guerrillas in the South. The system of supply routes from the North was known as the Ho Chi Minh Trail.**

1. **Location** On the map, locate: **(a)** North Vietnam, **(b)** South Vietnam, **(c)** Gulf of Tonkin, **(d)** Saigon, **(e)** Cambodia.
2. **Movement** Through which countries did the Ho Chi Minh Trail run?
3. **Critical Thinking** According to the domino theory, what nations would be threatened if the communists won control of South Vietnam?

Skills FOR LIFE

Critical Thinking | Managing Information | **Communication** | Maps, Charts, and Graphs

Planning a Multimedia Presentation

How Will I Use This Skill?

Multimedia presentations combine both audio and visual formats, including music, moving and still pictures, and printed material. They are effective because most people remember what they see better than what they hear. By using a variety of methods, you can communicate your ideas clearly and more forcefully. Multimedia presentations are used not only in class but in government and the business world as well.

LEARN the Skill

Follow these steps to prepare your multimedia presentation:

1. Choose your topic.
2. Gather materials and information about your subject.
3. Decide what types of media will best convey your information. Arrange for any equipment you will need.
4. Develop an outline for the presentation. Indicate what audio and visual materials you will use, and when.
5. Practice and give your multimedia presentation.

You can use tools like these to create a multimedia presentation.

PRACTICE the Skill

1. Focus your presentation on this topic: What was life like in the United States during the Vietnam War era?
2. Research the topic. What books or videos are available on this topic? What kinds of music can you use for background? Are there any Internet sites related to the Vietnam War? What people might you interview in your family or community?
3. List answers to these questions: Will visuals include videotapes, overheads, interactive computer displays? Will audio include taped interviews, music, CD-ROMs? What equipment will you need?
4. Complete your outline, indicating where and how you will use audio and visual materials.
5. Make your presentation.

APPLY the Skill

Use the steps you have learned to create a multimedia presentation about your family history or cultural background. Consider using photos, taped interviews, family mementos, or antiques.

Vietcong forces were hard to pin down, however. When Americans took an area, the Vietcong retreated into dense jungle forests. After the Americans moved on, the Vietcong returned and reclaimed the territory. As a result, Americans found themselves going back again and again to fight in the same areas with the same uncertain results.

American soldiers faced an even more frustrating problem in Vietnam. Often, they could not tell which villagers were Vietcong. The enemy might be the old woman cooking rice outside her hut or the man walking down the village path to the market. As one American soldier explained:

> “The farmer you waved to from your jeep in the day... would be the guy with the gun out looking for you at night.”

In such an uncertain situation, it was difficult to win clear victories.

Divisions at Home

When Congress approved the Gulf of Tonkin Resolution, President Johnson received overwhelming support. However, as casualties mounted, more and more people began to question American involvement in the war.

Television reports increased this growing sense of doubt. For the first time, Americans could sit in their own living rooms and witness the sights and sounds of warfare. They watched villages burn and saw wounded soldiers, children, and old people.

Hawks and doves

The country soon divided into two camps. Those who supported the war became known as hawks. Hawks argued that North Vietnamese aggression had forced Americans into war. Therefore, the United States should do whatever was necessary to win.

Doves—those who opposed the war—saw the conflict in Vietnam as a civil war. They believed that the United States had no right to interfere in it. Further, doves noted that the billions spent on the war could have been better spent on social programs at home.

Protesting the war

Many doves took part in antiwar protests. Protests were especially strong on college campuses. Students staged marches and sit-ins. Young men burned their draft cards and counseled others to avoid the draft. At some universities, militant protesters took over buildings and destroyed property.

The protesters charged that American lives and money were being wasted on an unjust war. The government of South Vietnam, they said, was no better than the Vietcong or the North Vietnamese.

Antiwar protests fed a widespread spirit of rebellion. Some young people of the 1960s

The Vietnam War, at Home and Overseas

At left, two American soldiers on patrol wade through muddy waters in the jungles of South Vietnam. While some young Americans fought, others protested. At right, college students march to demonstrate their opposition to the war.

★ **How did television affect public support for the war effort?**

Antiwar medallion ➤

Biography Maya Lin

In the late 1970s, architecture student Maya Lin won a competition to design a Vietnam War memorial to be built in Washington, D.C. Lin's plan called for two black granite walls inscribed with the names of more than 58,000 Americans killed in Vietnam. Since 1982, millions of Americans have visited the memorial. "It does not glorify the war or make an antiwar statement," Lin said. "It is a place for private reckoning."

★ **Why do you think many Americans have visited this memorial?**

and early 1970s rejected traditional American values and culture. They experimented with clothing, music, and ways of life that shocked their parents. Unfortunately, many young rebels also experimented with illegal drugs. Drug abuse became a growing social problem in the United States.

A Turning Point

In January 1968, the Vietcong launched surprise attacks on cities throughout South Vietnam. Vietcong guerrillas even stormed the walls of the American embassy in Saigon, the capital of South Vietnam. The attack became known as the **Tet Offensive** because it took place during Tet, the Vietnamese New Year's holiday.

In the end, American and South Vietnamese forces pushed back the enemy. Still, the Vietcong had won a major political victory. The Tet Offensive showed that even with half a million American troops, no part of Vietnam was safe from Vietcong attack.

Hoping to bring calm to the nation, a weary President Johnson announced that he would not seek reelection in 1968. That year, Republican **Richard Nixon** was elected President in a close race. During the campaign, he had pledged to end the war.

The War Winds Down

At first, President Nixon escalated the war. Protests grew, especially after Nixon ordered the bombing of Cambodia, Vietnam's neighbor to the west.

Bombing of Cambodia

Throughout the war, North Vietnamese soldiers carried supplies and arms into South Vietnam along trails in Cambodia. They also used Cambodia as a place where they could escape from American and South Vietnamese forces.

In 1969, Nixon secretly ordered the bombing of communist bases in Cambodia. American and South Vietnamese forces also made ground attacks on the bases in 1970. As Cambodians took sides in the struggle, their nation was plunged into a civil war.

End of the war

Meanwhile, the President gradually began to bring troops home from Vietnam. At the same time, peace talks were held in Paris. In January 1973, Henry Kissinger, Nixon's national security adviser, reached a cease-fire agreement. The following year, the last American troops left Vietnam.

The United States continued to send billions of dollars in aid to South Vietnam. Even so, the South Vietnamese were unable to stop the North Vietnamese advance. In April 1975, communist forces captured Saigon and renamed it Ho Chi Minh City. Soon after, Vietnam was reunited.

Tragedy in Cambodia

That year, the civil war in Cambodia was won by the communist **Khmer Rouge** (kuh MER ROOJ). For the next few years, Cambodians suffered under a brutal reign of terror. The Khmer Rouge forced millions of people to work in the fields from dawn to dark. More than a million Cambodians were killed or starved to death.

In 1979, Vietnam invaded Cambodia and set up a new communist government. It was less harsh than the Khmer Rouge, but it could not end the fighting.

Vietnam Balance Sheet

For all concerned, the Vietnam War was a costly conflict. Between 1961 and 1973, more than 58,000 American soldiers lost their lives. For the Vietnamese, the statistics were even more grim. More than a million Vietnamese soldiers and perhaps half a million civilians died. The destruction caused by the war shattered the Vietnamese economy.

After 1975, hundreds of thousands of people fled Vietnam and Cambodia. Refugees from Vietnam escaped in small boats. Many of these "boat people" drowned or died of hunger and thirst. The United States took in many refugees.

The Vietnam War era was one of the most painful periods in American history. The government spent vast amounts of money on the war. Beyond that, the war had divided the nation in an often-bitter debate. In the Cold War, it was not easy to decide how far Americans should go to fight communism.

★ Section 4 Review ★

Recall

1. **Locate** **(a)** Vietnam, **(b)** Cambodia.
2. **Identify** **(a)** Ho Chi Minh, **(b)** Vietcong, **(c)** Lyndon Johnson, **(d)** Gulf of Tonkin Resolution, **(e)** Vietnam War, **(f)** Tet Offensive, **(g)** Richard Nixon, **(h)** Khmer Rouge.
3. **Define** **(a)** guerrilla, **(b)** domino theory, **(c)** escalate.

Comprehension

4. **(a)** Why did President Kennedy send advisers to Vietnam? **(b)** How did President Johnson increase American involvement in Vietnam?
5. What arguments did protesters use against the Vietnam War?
6. **(a)** Why did civil war break out in Cambodia? **(b)** What were the results of the war?

Critical Thinking and Writing

7. **Synthesizing Information** How did the Cold War affect American policy in Vietnam?
8. **Comparing** **(a)** Compare American attitudes about fighting in World War II with those about the Vietnam War. **(b)** How might you explain the difference?

Activity **Summarizing** Write a series of newspaper headlines that summarize the history of the Vietnam War. Include headlines that describe events in Vietnam, Southeast Asia as a whole, and the United States. Be sure to write headlines that would have caught your attention if you had been an American teenager at that time!

The End of the Cold War

Explore These Questions

- How did President Nixon ease tensions with the communist world?
- What events led to the breakup of the Soviet Union?
- What steps did Americans take to help the people of the former Soviet Union?

Define

- détente
- martial law
- glasnost
- summit meeting
- free market

Identify

- SALT Agreement
- Gerald Ford
- Jimmy Carter
- Star Wars
- Solidarity
- Mikhail Gorbachev
- INF Treaty
- Boris Yeltsin

It was November 1989, and the world was witnessing one of the strangest celebrations it had ever seen. In Berlin, far into the night, cheering people wielded pickaxes and sledgehammers against barbed wire and concrete. After nearly 30 years, the wall between East and West was coming down.

As you read, communist East German troops had put up the wall dividing East and West Berlin in 1961. Those who tried to escape to the West were often shot on sight by East German border guards. The Berlin Wall stood as a symbol of tensions between the communist and noncommunist worlds.

By the late 1980s, however, the Cold War was coming to an end. One East German woman described her visit to West Berlin:

> ❝ One day last week, I took my bike and—just went over. I had to stop and laugh! I felt so strange. For 40 years we couldn't do something so simple. I just had to stop and laugh! ❞

Berlin was only one of many places where citizens celebrated their release from communist oppression.

A Temporary Thaw

The first hopes that the Cold War might end came in 1971. In that year, American troops were still fighting communists in Vietnam. Even so, President Richard Nixon looked for ways to ease world tension. His first move was to seek improved relations with the People's Republic of China.

Recognizing China

Since 1949, the United States had refused to recognize Mao Zedong's communist government in China. Richard Nixon had been one of the most outspoken opponents of recognizing communist China. As President, however, in 1971, Nixon began secret talks to consider closer ties with China. To show its good will, China invited the American ping-pong team to a competition in Beijing.

To the surprise of many Americans, President Nixon himself visited the People's Republic of China in February 1972. Television cameras captured the President walking along the Great Wall of China and attending state dinners with Chinese leaders.

The visit was a triumph for Nixon and the start of a new era in relations with China. As tensions continued to ease, the United States established formal diplomatic relations with China in 1979.

A policy of détente

President Nixon followed his visit to China with another historic trip. In May 1972, he became the first American President to visit the Soviet Union since the Cold

War began. The trip was part of Nixon's effort to reduce tensions between the superpowers. This policy was known as **détente** (day TAHNT).

Détente eased the Cold War by allowing more trade and other contacts between the United States and the Soviet Union. More important, the two nations signed a treaty agreeing to limit the number of nuclear warheads and missiles that they built. This treaty was known as the **SALT Agreement.** (SALT stands for Strategic Arms Limitation Talks.)

Détente continued under the next two Presidents—**Gerald Ford,** who served from 1974 to 1977, and **Jimmy Carter,** who served from 1977 to 1981. Trade between the United States and the Soviet Union increased. The Soviets bought tons of American wheat. In 1975, Soviet and American astronauts conducted a joint space mission. In June 1979, President Carter met with Soviet leader Leonid Brezhnev (BREHZH nehf). They worked out the details of a SALT II Treaty.

Biography Henry Kissinger

At the age of 15, Henry Kissinger fled Germany to escape Nazi persecution of Jews. A brilliant student of history, he became a college professor. In the 1970s, Dr. Kissinger was President Nixon's closest adviser on foreign policy, working tirelessly to bring about détente. Kissinger was also known for "shuttle diplomacy"—traveling back and forth between nations in an attempt to ease conflicts.

★ **How did Kissinger and Nixon change American policy toward China?**

New Tensions

Before the Senate could ratify the new SALT treaty, hopes for détente faded. In 1979, the world entered another decade of Cold War tensions.

Soviet invasion of Afghanistan

In December 1979, Soviet troops invaded Afghanistan, a mountainous nation along the Soviet Union's southern border. Soviet forces seized major cities and gave military support to a pro-Soviet government that had seized power there.

"The Soviet Union must pay a price for its aggression," President Carter declared. He withdrew the SALT II Treaty from the Senate. He also announced that American athletes would not compete in the 1980 summer Olympic Games in Moscow.

Despite the tough American response, Soviet troops remained in Afghanistan for eight years. They suffered heavy losses as Afghan rebels, supplied by the United States, battled the communist government. The war in Afghanistan became so costly for the Soviets in the long run that it eventually contributed to the downfall of the Soviet Union. For the time being, however, the invasion marked the end of détente.

Aleksandr Solzhenitsyn, a major Russian writer of the twentieth century, won the Nobel Prize for literature in 1970. His novels present vivid accounts of the struggle for freedom against Soviet repression. After the Soviet government exiled him in 1974, Solzhenitsyn and his family moved to a town in Vermont.

Reagan's strong stand

When Ronald Reagan took office in 1981, he firmly believed that the Soviet Union was "the focus of evil in the modern world." He called on Americans to "oppose it with all our might." As you read, Reagan strongly supported anticommunist forces in Latin America.

Reagan wanted to deal with the Soviets from a position of strength. He told the American people that "we must find peace through strength." He persuaded Congress to increase military spending by more than $100 billion during his first five years in office. His defense program included research on weapons that he hoped could shoot down Soviet missiles from space. The system was nicknamed **Star Wars.**

Throughout Reagan's first term, the two superpowers viewed each other with deep mistrust. During Reagan's first year in office, an event in Eastern Europe set the tone for new tensions.

In December 1981, Poland's communist government cracked down on **Solidarity,** an independent labor union. The Polish government, with the backing of the Soviet Union, declared **martial law,** or emergency military rule.

President Reagan quickly condemned what he called the police-state tactics of Poland's communist government. He urged the Soviets to permit the restoration of basic human rights in Poland. He also put economic pressure on Poland to end martial law.

Reforms and Cooperation

Cracks in the Soviet empire began to appear in the mid-1980s. Growing economic problems plagued the Soviet Union as it continued to spend large sums of money on military production. One major problem was that consumer products were in short supply. Soviet citizens spent hours waiting in lines for poorly made goods. The time was ripe for reform.

Reforms in the Soviet Union

In 1985, a new Soviet leader, **Mikhail Gorbachev** (mee kah EEL GOR buh chawf),

Cause and Effect

Causes

- Soviet Union takes control of Eastern European nations
- Communism gains influence in Western Europe, the Middle East, and Asia
- Western powers fear Soviet expansion

The Cold War

Effects

- Arms race between United States and Soviet Union results in heavy military spending
- Western powers and Soviet Union create separate military alliances
- Armed conflicts erupt in Korea and Vietnam
- United States and Soviet Union compete for influence in developing nations

Effects Today

- United States is world's greatest military power
- Eastern European countries are struggling to create democratic governments
- Southeast Asian countries are still recovering from war

Graphic Organizer *Skills*

For 45 years, the Cold War pitted the United States against the Soviet Union.

1. **Comprehension** **(a)** What event in Europe helped spark the Cold War? **(b)** Which effects of the Cold War involved Americans in actual fighting?
2. **Critical Thinking** How did the Cold War help the United States become the world's greatest military power?

came to power. Only 54 years old, Gorbachev was younger and more energetic than the leaders who had come before him. He believed that he had to take bold steps to improve the failing Soviet economy.

Gorbachev called for **glasnost,** a policy of speaking out honestly and openly. Earlier leaders had cracked down on anyone who criticized their policies or exposed problems in Soviet life. Now, under Gorbachev, Soviet newspapers could write about poor harvests, crime, and corruption. Gorbachev hoped that allowing public discussion of problems would help the nation find solutions.

Reagan and Gorbachev cooperate

Gorbachev also decided that he had to cut military spending sharply in order to solve the Soviet Union's economic problems. To achieve this goal, he tried to improve relations with the United States.

President Reagan agreed to meet with Gorbachev in several summit meetings. A **summit meeting** is a conference between the highest-ranking officials of different nations. Reagan's own staff members were stunned by his willingness to meet with Gorbachev. The President, however, explained that Gorbachev was unlike earlier Soviet leaders and that glasnost was very different from the bad old days of the "evil empire."

In 1987, Reagan and Gorbachev signed an arms control pact called the **Intermediate Nuclear Force (INF) Treaty.** In the treaty, the United States and Soviet Union agreed to get rid of short-range and medium-range missiles. President Reagan signed the agreement despite strong objections from officials in the Defense Department.

In 1989, Gorbachev withdrew Soviet troops from Afghanistan. This action removed another barrier to cooperation between the superpowers.

Communist governments fall in Eastern Europe

For nearly 50 years, the communist governments of Eastern Europe had crushed independent political parties or open debate. Sometimes, the Soviet Union intervened militarily in its satellite nations. In 1956, Soviet tanks had helped crush a revolt in Hungary. In 1968, Soviet tanks had again rolled when a new leader tried to reform the communist government of Czechoslovakia.

Now, Eastern Europeans greeted news of Gorbachev's reforms with demands of their own. To everyone's surprise, Gorbachev viewed the Eastern European protests as signs of needed change. Encouraged by this response, reformers pressed their demands. With opposition so widespread, most Eastern European governments did not dare use military force to block change.

Viewing HISTORY **The Berlin Wall**

For nearly 30 years, the grim concrete and barbed wire barrier of the Berlin Wall divided the city. Then, in 1989, the wall was opened. At left, joyful Berliners climb over and through the wall before tearing it down completely. ★ **How did the fall of the Berlin Wall mark a turning point in the Cold War?**

Viewing HISTORY **The End of the Soviet Union**

As the Soviet Union toppled, so did statues of former communist leaders. Here, two Russian girls and their dog sit peacefully atop a statue of Joseph Stalin in a Moscow park. ★ **Why do you think many Russians were happy to see the end of communist rule?**

In 1989, Poland's communist government held the nation's first free elections in 50 years. Rejecting communism, the Poles voted into office all the candidates put up by Solidarity, the trade union. Solidarity leader Lech Walesa, who had been thrown in jail eight years earlier, became head of the new Polish government.

In Romania, demonstrators overthrew and executed a brutal dictator. Communist governments also fell in Hungary, Czechoslovakia, Bulgaria, and Albania.

In 1989, peaceful protests swept major cities in East Germany. The communist government was forced out and replaced with reformers who promised democratic changes. East and West Berliners demolished the wall that had divided their city since 1961. Within a year, Germany was reunited under a democratic government.

Breakup of the Soviet Union

The Soviet Union itself was made up of 15 republics held together by a strong central government. The republics enjoyed few freedoms. By 1990, unrest led to a flare-up of ancient rivalries among some of the nation's 120 ethnic groups. Some groups, including Lithuanians, Latvians, and Estonians, boldly demanded self-rule.

Democratic reforms

Amid the turmoil, Gorbachev announced new moves toward democracy. For nearly 70 years, the Soviet Union had been a one-party state. Under Gorbachev's reforms, new political parties were allowed to form. For the first time, groups could openly oppose the communists.

In August 1991, some desperate communist officials tried to overturn the new reforms. Holding Gorbachev captive, they sent military forces to surround the parliament building in Moscow.

To the surprise of the plotters, thousands of Russians turned out to block the soldiers. Led by a politician named **Boris Yeltsin,** the reformers turned the tide. Standing on top of a tank that the crowd had surrounded, Yeltsin shouted his defiance to the plotters and his belief in democracy:

> “By their criminal actions, they have confronted the country with the danger of terror, and have placed themselves outside the law.... Aggression will not go forward! Only democracy will win!”

In the months that followed, republic after republic declared its independence from the Union of Soviet Socialist Republics. In December 1991, Gorbachev resigned and the Soviet Union ceased to exist.

Economic reforms and American aid

Eventually, the Soviet Union broke up into 15 separate nations. Of these, Russia was the largest and most powerful. With

Yeltsin as its president, Russia began the difficult task of rebuilding its economy and introducing a free-market system. In a **free market,** individuals decide what to produce and sell. Under communism, the government had made such economic decisions.

Most Americans agreed that it was important for the new republics to succeed with their reforms. Along with Western European nations, the United States provided economic aid to Russia. American experts advised business leaders in the former republics and in Eastern Europe about the shift to a free-market system. The United States hoped that the former communist states would in time become profitable trading partners.

Half a Century of Cold War

For nearly half a century, the shadow of the Cold War touched every corner of American life. Students in the 1950s practiced hiding in fallout shelters in case an atomic war broke out. Millions of young Americans went off to fight in Korea and Vietnam. From 1946 to 1990, the United States spent over 6 trillion dollars on national defense.

Most Americans were happy to claim victory in the Cold War. President Truman's policy of containment had been followed by eight other American Presidents, both Republicans and Democrats. The United States had slowed down or stopped communist expansion in Asia and Africa as well as in Europe and the Americas. Free elections had come to many nations for the first time in decades.

Victory did not come without its price. During the 1950s, exaggerated fears of communists led many loyal Americans to lose their jobs. The threat of nuclear war demanded caution from both American and Soviet leaders. Even one mistake could plunge the world into an atomic war that might destroy civilization.

Americans also debated how to contain communism effectively. Some criticized military aid to anticommunist dictators. Hundreds of thousands of citizens protested against the war in Vietnam.

No matter what their individual opinions, Americans viewed their freedom to debate as a precious heritage. Though many argued over how the Cold War was fought, they could agree that freedom was worth fighting for.

★ Section 5 Review ★

Recall

1. **Locate** **(a)** China, **(b)** the Soviet Union, **(c)** Afghanistan, **(d)** Poland, **(e)** Russia.
2. **Identify** **(a)** SALT Agreement, **(b)** Gerald Ford, **(c)** Jimmy Carter, **(d)** Star Wars, **(e)** Solidarity, **(f)** Mikhail Gorbachev, **(g)** INF Treaty, **(h)** Boris Yeltsin.
3. **Define** **(a)** détente, **(b)** martial law, **(c)** glasnost, **(d)** summit meeting, **(e)** free market.

Comprehension

4. **(a)** How did United States relations with China and the Soviet Union change in the 1970s? **(b)** Why did détente end?
5. **(a)** Why did the Soviet Union cease to exist? **(b)** How did the Soviet collapse affect the nations of Eastern Europe?
6. How did the United States respond to the breakup of the Soviet Union?

Critical Thinking and Writing

7. **Thinking Creatively** **(a)** Describe one way the United States could help the former communist nations make the shift to democracy and a free-market economy. **(b)** Do you think that the United States should provide that help? Why?
8. **Linking Past and Present** List two ways that the end of the Cold War has affected your life.

Activity **Writing a News Dispatch** You are a foreign correspondent for a major American newspaper. Write three reports to send to your paper, dated in 1985, 1989, and 1991. In each report, describe the events leading to the collapse of the Soviet Union.

Chapter 28 Review and Activities

★ Sum It Up ★

Section 1 The Nation Faces a Cold War

- After World War II, Soviet expansion and growing distrust between the United States and the Soviet Union led to the Cold War.
- The United States followed a policy of containing communism to the countries where it already existed.

Section 2 The Cold War Heats Up

- The United States reacted forcefully to communist expansion in Korea and Cuba.
- Fear of communism at home led to a Red Scare that cost thousands of Americans their jobs.

Section 3 Cold War Battlegrounds

- The Soviet Union sought to gain influence in newly independent nations.
- The United States supported anticommunist governments and rebels in Asia and Latin America.

Section 4 The Vietnam War

- The United States sent troops to Southeast Asia to prevent a communist takeover of South Vietnam.
- Many people in the United States protested American involvement in Vietnam.

Section 5 The End of the Cold War

- In the 1970s, efforts to ease tensions with the Soviet Union ended with the Soviet invasion of Afghanistan.
- Economic problems and growing demands for democracy contributed to the breakup of the Soviet Union.

For additional review of the major ideas of Chapter 28, see ***Guide to the Essentials of American History*** or ***Interactive Student Tutorial CD-ROM,*** which contains interactive review activities, graphic organizers, and practice tests.

Reviewing the Chapter

Define These Terms

Match each term with the correct definition.

Column 1	Column 2
1. exile	a. emergency military rule
2. guerrilla	b. person who has been forced to leave his or her country
3. glasnost	c. policy of reducing tension
4. détente	d. fighter who uses hit-and-run tactics
5. martial law	e. policy of allowing open and honest public speech

Explore the Main Ideas

1. What was the Iron Curtain?
2. How did the Cuban missile crisis end?
3. What was the goal of the Peace Corps?
4. Describe three results of the Vietnam War.
5. What efforts at détente were made in the 1970s?

Geography Activity

Match the letters on the map with the following places: **1.** Soviet Union, **2.** Cuba, **3.** China, **4.** South Korea, **5.** Vietnam, **6.** West Germany. **Movement** Why do you think many Cubans fled to the United States in the 1960s?

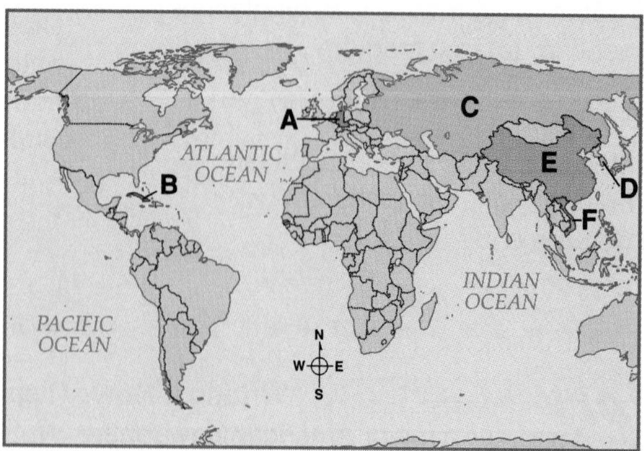

Critical Thinking and Writing

1. **Linking Past and Present** Do you think people feel the same way about nuclear war today as they did during the Cold War? Explain.
2. **Comparing** Compare and contrast the Korean War with the Vietnam War in terms of **(a)** American goals and **(b)** results.
3. **Understanding Chronology** **(a)** Which began first, glasnost or the breakup of the Soviet Union? **(b)** Explain why these two events occurred in the order in which they did rather than the other way around.
4. **Exploring Unit Themes** **World Leadership** With the breakup of the Soviet Union, the United States became the only superpower. Explain whether you think this will increase or decrease tensions in the world.

Using Primary Sources

In October 1962, President John F. Kennedy appeared on television to tell the American people that the Soviets were shipping missiles to Cuba:

> "I have directed the Armed Forces to prepare for any eventualities. ... We will not prematurely or unnecessarily risk the costs of worldwide nuclear war in which even the fruits of victory would be ashes in our mouths, but neither will we shrink from that risk at any time it must be faced."

Source: Television address, October 22, 1962.

Recognizing Points of View **(a)** According to Kennedy, would he be willing to risk the possibility of nuclear war? **(b)** How do you think American viewers responded to Kennedy's message? **(c)** How do you think Nikita Khrushchev responded?

Activity Bank

Interdisciplinary Activity

Exploring Economics Research the economies of the United States and the Soviet Union during the 1980s. Create a display of graphs to show how both the communist system and the free-market system provided goods and services for people. Present your graphs to the class, explaining their meaning.

Career Skills Activity

Travel Agent You are planning a trip for a client who wants to see sights that were important during the Cold War. Gather material on tourist travel in Russia, Eastern Europe, China, Korea, and Vietnam today. Plan a tour, using the information you have gathered. Include an explanation of why you have included each site on the trip.

Citizenship Activity

Debating National Security Issues Do further research on the search for communists in the United States government during the 1940s and 1950s. Then, organize a mock debate between those who are in favor of investigating the political beliefs of citizens and those who oppose it.

Internet Activity

Use the Internet to find sites dealing with the Vietnam War. Drawing on the information you find, write an essay on the personal impact of the war on Americans, both during the war and in the present.

Eyewitness Journal

You are an American teenager growing up in either the 1950s, the 1960s, the 1970s, or the 1980s. In your Eyewitness Journal, describe three Cold War events that have had the most impact on your life.

Chapter 29

Prosperity and Reform

1945–1980

What's Ahead

Section 1
The Booming Postwar World

Section 2
The Civil Rights Movement Begins

Section 3
Years of Crisis and Change

Section 4
The Civil Rights Movement Expands

In the 1950s, as the United States struggled with the Cold War, the nation entered an era of remarkable economic growth. Prosperity made many Americans feel secure and comfortable. As a result, many wanted to follow a course of political conservatism. Most Americans opposed any form of radical change.

In the 1960s and 1970s, however, American politics went through upheaval. One President was assassinated and another resigned. Citizens disagreed over the war in Vietnam. Women and minorities struggled for justice and equality with protests and demonstrations. By the 1980s, they had won increased recognition for their rights.

Why Study History? Dr. Martin Luther King, Jr., was a leading figure in the struggle for justice and equality. Today, King's birthday is a federal holiday. Some Americans celebrate the day by participating in community service. To learn more about this, see this chapter's *Why Study History?* feature, "You Can Learn About Helping Others."

American Events

1950s Baby boom increases United States population

1954 Supreme Court rules that school segregation is unconstitutional

1963 Civil rights supporters march on Washington, D.C., to end discrimination

1945 | 1951 | 1957 | 1963

World Events

1950 World Event Korean War begins

1960s World Event Nations gain independence across Africa

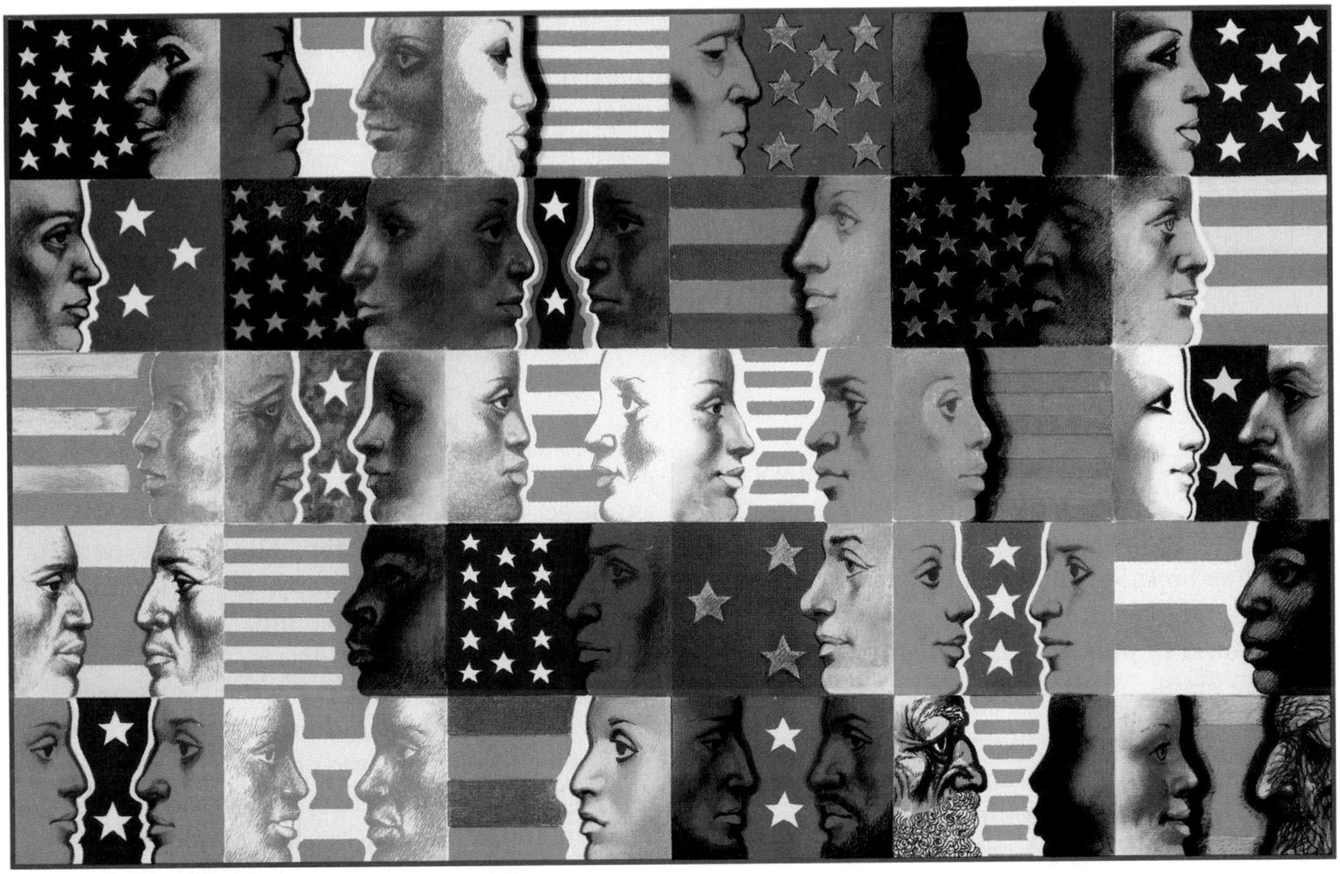

Viewing HISTORY **Many People, One Nation**

Colleen Browning celebrated the diversity of the United States in her lithograph Union Mixer. *It shows a wide mix of Americans—male and female, young and old, of many races and nationalities. Behind them are the stars and stripes of the flag that unites them all into a single people.* ★ **How can diversity be a source of both strength and conflict?**

1966
National Organization for Women (NOW) is formed

1974
Watergate Scandal leads to resignation of President Nixon

1963 **1969** **1975** **1981**

1960s World Event
United States involvement in the Vietnam War grows

1975 World Event
Helsinki Agreement defines basic human rights

The Booming Postwar World

As You Read

Explore These Questions

- What domestic policies did Presidents Truman and Eisenhower follow?
- What factors contributed to the economic prosperity of the 1950s?
- How did American lifestyles change in the 1950s?

Define

- inflation
- birth rate
- baby boom
- productivity
- standard of living
- affluence
- suburb

Identify

- GI Bill of Rights
- Fair Deal
- Dwight D. Eisenhower
- Levittown
- Sunbelt
- Interstate Highway Act
- Elvis Presley
- beatnik

Setting the Scene After World War II, Americans resumed their lives. Veterans went back to peacetime jobs. Many hoped to buy a home and start a family. Now that rationing was over, Americans wanted to purchase a host of new products. *Life* magazine made an exciting boast:

> ❝ The year 1946 finds the U.S. on the threshold of marvels, ranging from runless stockings and shineless serge suits to jet-propelled airplanes that will flash across the country in just a little less than the speed of sound. ❞

Life magazine had made an accurate prediction. For the United States, the Cold War era after World War II was a time of strong economic growth. Many Americans enjoyed the period of prosperity.

The Truman Years

Following World War II, President Harry Truman tried to help the society and the economy return to peacetime conditions.

Economic difficulties

Even before the war ended and Truman was President, Congress aided returning soldiers by passing what became known as the **GI Bill of Rights.*** Under this law, the government spent billions of dollars to help veterans set up farms and businesses. Many GIs received loans to pay for college or a new home. The GI Bill's many aid programs helped the economy to expand.

Inflation, or rising prices, was a major postwar problem. After the war, the government removed wage and price controls. The cost of food, clothing, and other goods soared.

To help pay these increased prices, workers demanded more pay. When employers refused, labor unions called strikes. Steelworkers, meatpackers, auto workers, coal miners, and railroad workers all walked off the job.

Truman agreed that workers deserved higher wages, but he feared such increases would add to inflation. Truman pressured strikers to return to work. He even threatened to draft some striking workers into the army.

Election of 1948

In 1948, the prospects for President Truman and his Democratic party were poor. Labor strikes and soaring prices had helped Republicans win a majority in both the House and the Senate for the first time since the 1920s. The Republicans confidently nominated Governor Thomas Dewey of New York as their candidate for President.

Truman fought back, crisscrossing the country by train. At every stop, he made hard-hitting speeches warning that Republicans were "all set to do a hatchet job on the New Deal." Crowds warmed to his scrappy

*GI stands for "government issue." During World War II, GI came to mean any member of the United States armed forces.

style and encouraged him with cries of "Give 'em hell, Harry." When all the votes were counted, Truman won a stunning surprise victory over Dewey.

The Fair Deal

During his presidency, Truman introduced a 21-point program of proposed reforms known as the **Fair Deal.** The goal was to extend New Deal policies. Truman, however, faced heavy opposition from a coalition of conservative Democrats and Republicans in Congress.

Only a few of the proposed reforms were passed by Congress. Congress raised the minimum wage, expanded Social Security benefits, and provided loans for people to buy low-cost houses. Among the ideas rejected by Congress was a plan to provide health insurance financed by the government.

The Eisenhower Years

Truman did not run for reelection in 1952. The Democratic presidential candidate was Adlai Stevenson of Illinois. Republicans chose General **Dwight D. Eisenhower.** They thought that "Ike" could win the conflict in Korea and lead Americans through the Cold War. The voters liked Eisenhower's military experience and foreign policy skills. They gave Ike a landslide victory.

President Eisenhower said his political course was "that straight road down the middle." He considered himself "conservative when it comes to money and liberal when it comes to human beings." Like most Republicans, Eisenhower believed that the federal government should limit its spending and its involvement in the economy. Still, he agreed to expand the benefits of Social Security and some other New Deal programs.

Most Americans supported Eisenhower's middle-of-the-road approach. In the 1956 presidential election, American voters reelected Ike to a second term of office.

The Baby Boom

In the late 1940s and 1950s, the **birth rate**—or number of children being born relative to the total population—soared. Population experts called the phenomenon a **baby boom.** In the 1950s, the population of the United States grew by 29 million, compared with 19 million in the 1940s and only 9 million in the 1930s.

In part, American families were growing in order to make up for lost time. During the hard years of the Great Depression, it was

"I Like Ike" campaign button

Viewing HISTORY **We Like Ike**

In 1952, women from the Republican National Committee were eager to show support for presidential candidate Dwight D. Eisenhower. Americans liked "Ike" well enough to elect him to two terms as President. ★ **How do you think Eisenhower's role in World War II affected the election results?**

Viewing HISTORY **Economic Prosperity**

For the growing number of people who made up the American middle class, the 1950s was a time of economic prosperity. Middle-class families had more money and leisure time than ever before. In this photograph, a suburban family packs the car in preparation for a vacation trip. ★ **How does this photograph show the affluence of the 1950s?**

difficult to support a large family. Also, many couples who married during World War II did not have children until after the war.

Improvements in health care also contributed to the baby boom. Better care for pregnant women and newborn infants meant that more babies survived. Fewer children died from childhood diseases than in the past.

Economic Prosperity

In addition to a baby boom, there was an economic boom. In the mid-1950s, the United States accounted for about 35 percent of total world production. Corporate profits rose, as did average wages for workers.

The baby boom was in fact a major reason for the economic boom. Newspaper columnist Sylvia Porter was amazed by the census figures that reported more than 3,548,000 babies born in 1950. Porter predicted the baby boom would lead to economic expansion:

> "Just imagine how much these extra people . . . will absorb—in food, in clothing, in gadgets, in housing, in services. Our factories must expand just to keep pace."

Federal projects also increased output from factories. The government provided money to build new roads, houses, and schools. Government spending on Cold War military production spurred the economy, too.

New technology was another factor that contributed to economic growth. Improved methods of production led to steady rises in **productivity,** or the average output per worker. Corporations began using computers to perform calculations and keep records. In 1957, Navy captain Hyman G. Rickover oversaw the development of the first commercial nuclear plant in Shippingport, Pennsylvania.

The economic boom raised Americans' **standard of living,** an index based on the amount of goods, services, and leisure time people have. Many people celebrated their **affluence,** or wealth, by going on a spending spree. Americans bought large numbers of washing machines, vacuum cleaners, televisions, and automobiles.

Life in the 1950s

With the changes in the economy came changes in lifestyle. Americans were eager to enjoy the fruits of their economic success.

The suburbs

As families and economic opportunities grew, so did the demand for new housing. Many people moved to the **suburbs**—communities outside the cities. During the 1950s,

Critical Thinking | Managing Information | Communication | **Maps, Charts, and Graphs**

Using a Special-Purpose Map

How Will I Use This Skill?

Special-purpose maps communicate information on a particular topic or theme. Some examples are a road map, a map of your school, and a map showing the layout of a shopping mall. Whatever kind of work you do in the future, you will probably use special-purpose maps.

LEARN the Skill

The following steps will help you read special-purpose maps.

1. Read the map title and key to identify the topic and region that the map deals with.
2. Analyze the map key. Make sure you understand the meaning of all terms. Determine the purpose of colors and symbols.
3. Locate and study each symbol and color on the map itself.
4. Use the map and your critical thinking skills to draw conclusions.

PRACTICE the Skill

Study the special-purpose map on this page. It shows the Syracuse area of New York. Use the steps you have learned to answer the following questions.

1. (a) What is the topic of the map? (b) On what region does the map focus?
2. (a) Define the terms *residential* and *industrial.* (b) What different types of land use are indicated by color? (c) What do the two symbols represent?
3. Identify one region of the Syracuse area that was occupied mostly by (a) businesses, (b) homes, (c) fields and woods.
4. How do you think the economic boom of the 1950s affected the development of Syracuse and nearby towns?

APPLY the Skill

Construct a special-purpose map to communicate information about one of the following: (a) land use in your neighborhood or town, (b) the location of books on various subjects in your school or local library, (c) the location of different types of shops in a nearby mall.

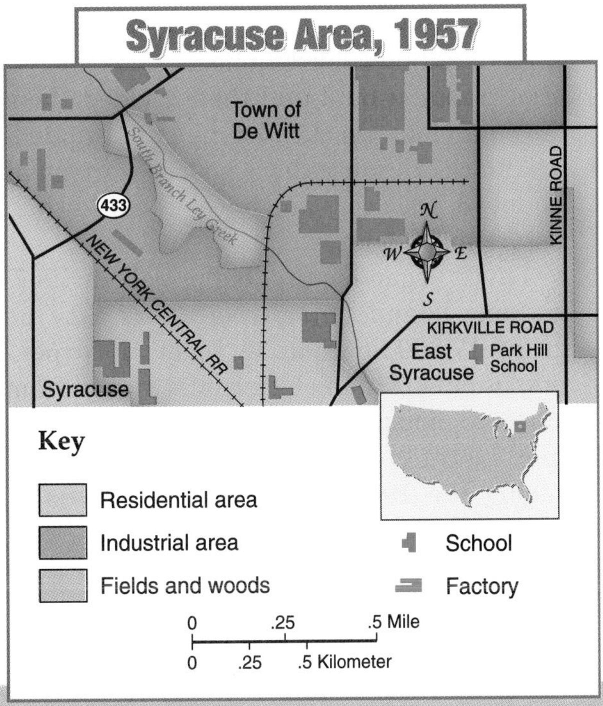

Syracuse Area, 1957

Town of De Witt
South Branch Ley Creek
433
NEW YORK CENTRAL RR
KINNE ROAD
N
W
E
S
KIRKVILLE ROAD
East Syracuse
Park Hill School
Syracuse

Key
Residential area
Industrial area
Fields and woods
School
Factory
0 .25 .5 Mile
0 .25 .5 Kilometer

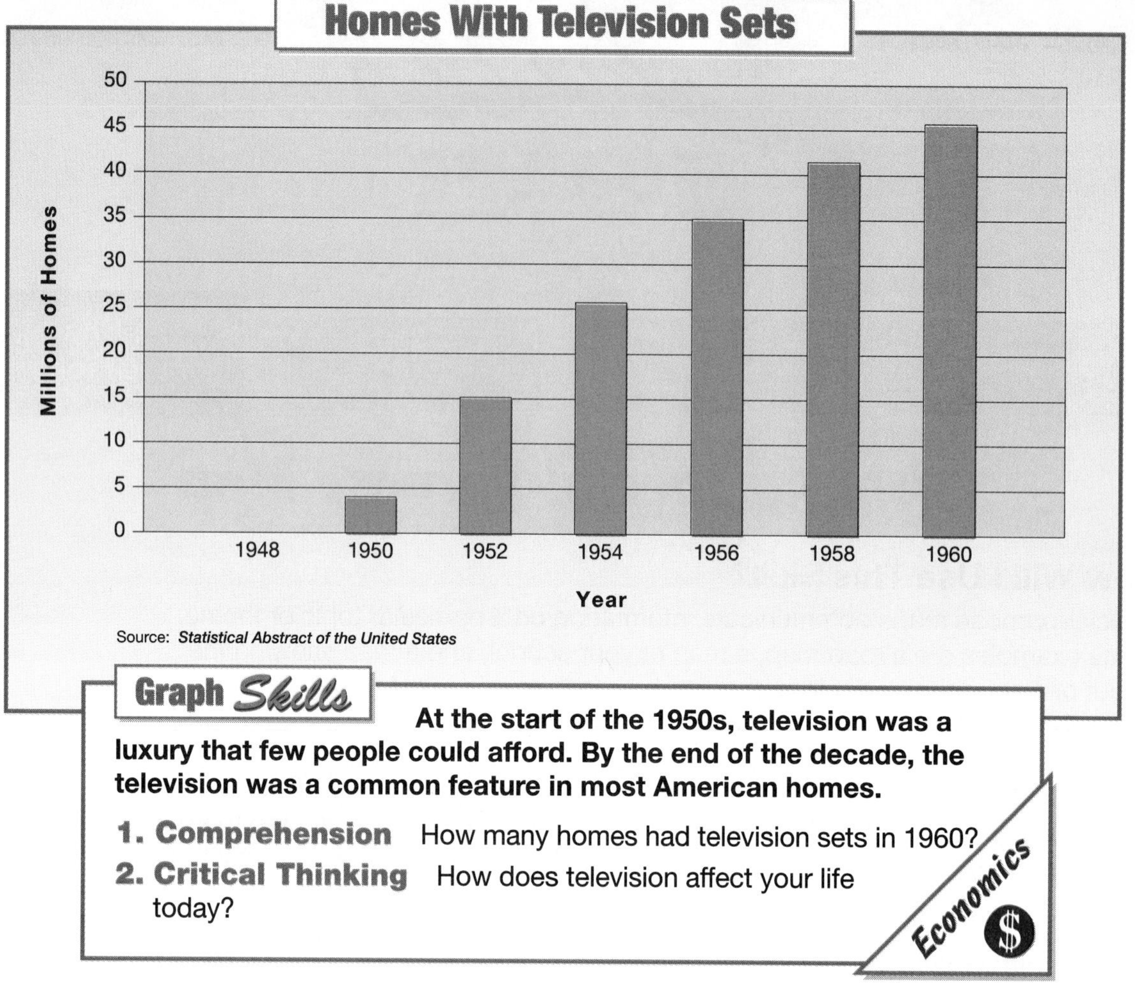

suburbs grew 40 times faster than cities. The GI Bill encouraged home building in the suburbs by offering low-interest loans to veterans.

Builder William Levitt pioneered a new way of building suburban houses. He bought large tracts of land and then divided them into small lots. On each lot, he built an identical house. Because these houses were mass produced, they cost much less to build than custom-made houses.

Levitt began his first big project in 1947. On Long Island, outside New York City, he put up 17,000 new homes. Teams of carpenters, plumbers, and electricians moved from house to house, finishing them in record time. Levitt called the project **Levittown.** During the 1950s, he built Levittowns in New Jersey and Pennsylvania as well.

Soon, shopping centers sprang up near the suburban housing developments. In the 1950s, these shopping centers with their modern department stores were an exciting novelty.

The Sunbelt

While millions of people were moving to the suburbs, millions more were moving into the South and West. The populations of California, Texas, and Florida grew rapidly. In time, the region to which so many people were moving came to be known as the

$ Connections With Economics

American teenagers shared in the affluence that the nation was enjoying. In 1959, *Life* magazine summarized the buying power of teens: "Counting only what is spent to satisfy their special teenage demands, the youngsters and their parents will shell out about $10 billion this year, a billion more than the total sales of General Motors."

Sunbelt. The Sunbelt stretches across the southern part of the nation from Florida to California.

There were several reasons for migrating to the Sunbelt. Some people liked the warm climate that could be found through much of the region. Others were looking for better jobs. They were attracted by the Sunbelt's prosperous economy, based on agriculture, oil, electronics, and national defense industries.

Businesses also moved to the region. They liked the low taxes commonly found in Sunbelt states. Companies were also attracted by the Sunbelt's growing workforce. The workforce included many recent immigrants from Latin America and Asia.

The automobile

Unlike people in the older cities of the East, suburbanites and residents of the Sunbelt often needed a car to commute to work or drive to a store. During the 1950s, cars became more important to daily life. By 1960, 9 out of 10 families living in the suburbs owned a car.

The federal government encouraged the growing dependence on automobiles by building thousands of miles of highways. In 1956, Congress passed the **Interstate Highway Act.** It called for a network of high-speed roads linking the nation. The project would cost more than $250 billion.

The interstate highway system was partly a result of Cold War fears. It was designed so that troops and military equipment could move quickly across the country. The new roads would also enable people to leave major cities rapidly in case of a Soviet attack.

Television

Television was another product that had a great effect on American life. In 1946, only about 17,000 television sets existed in the entire country. In the 1950s, nearly 7 million sets were sold each year.

Television offered something for everyone. Children enjoyed a puppet show called *Howdy Doody.* Parents watched variety specials, quiz shows, dramas, and westerns. The husband-and-wife team of Desi Arnaz and Lucille Ball starred in a zany comedy series, *I Love Lucy.* Millions of Americans also tuned in to nightly news programs.

Television affected American culture in several ways. It brought news and entertainment into people's homes. Its commercials encouraged spending and buying. Television also helped to make the 1950s a time when people wanted to look and act the same. Many programs presented a single view of the ideal middle-class family. However, not all families were like the ones that appeared on television.

Rock 'n' roll

A new music style burst onto the scene in the mid-1950s. Rock 'n' roll combined the sounds of rhythm, blues, country, and gospel.

Biography Elvis Presley

Elvis Presley did not invent rock 'n' roll, but he probably did more than anyone to popularize it. From the mid-1950s, the "King's" attitude, vocal mannerisms, sideburns, and gyrating movements made him an international star of the young. The U.S. Postal Service honored Presley in 1993 by releasing a stamp with his image. ★ **Why do you think many older Americans disliked Presley's style?**

It provided an opportunity for younger Americans to show their independence. Many teenagers embraced rock 'n' roll, rejecting the sweetly tuneful "pop" music of their parents' generation. African American singers Chuck Berry and Little Richard gained national fame. Out of the south came Buddy Holly and Elvis Presley. Latino singer Richie Valens also picked up the beat.

Of all the rock 'n' roll stars of the era, **Elvis Presley** gained the greatest fame—a fame that has endured even years after his death. In 1956, millions of young Americans across the country would wait eagerly for one of his television appearances. Teenagers dressed like him, bought his records, and nicknamed him "the King." Many parents, however, disapproved of Presley's long hair, sideburns, music, and dance style.

Hints of Change

Not everyone was swept up in the optimism of the 1950s. As the expanding economy encouraged increased spending, some Americans opposed what they saw as the growing materialism of American society. To them, people seemed more interested in material goods than in spiritual values.

Some writers and artists criticized American society for its devotion to business and its lack of individuality. A popular novel of the day, *The Man in the Gray Flannel Suit,* painted a bleak picture of business people working for large, faceless corporations. Novelist Jack Kerouac coined the term *Beat,* meaning "weariness with all forms of the modern industrial state." Middle-class observers called Kerouac and others like him **beatniks.** Kerouac's best-selling novel *On the Road* influenced many young Americans.

Challenges to the mainstream, however, were not very common in the 1950s. Millions of Americans enjoyed the comforts and prosperity of the period after World War II. They hoped that the "good life" would continue.

Still, in some corners, a growing outcry could be heard. It came from the Americans who were denied an equal share in the American dream. More and more, these Americans would struggle for change.

★ Section 1 Review ★

Recall

1. **Identify** (a) GI Bill of Rights, (b) Fair Deal, (c) Dwight D. Eisenhower, (d) Levittown, (e) Sunbelt, (f) Interstate Highway Act, (g) Elvis Presley, (h) beatnik
2. **Define** (a) inflation, (b) birth rate, (c) baby boom, (d) productivity, (e) standard of living, (f) affluence, (g) suburb.

Comprehension

3. (a) What reforms did Congress pass as part of Truman's Fair Deal? (b) How did Eisenhower follow a middle-of-the-road policy?
4. Describe two factors that helped the economy to expand after World War II.
5. Describe one way in which each of the following changed the way some Americans lived: (a) growth of suburbs, (b) Interstate Highway Act, (c) television, (d) rock 'n' roll.

Critical Thinking and Writing

6. **Recognizing Points of View** Why did some people dislike the cultural changes that were occurring in the 1950s?
7. **Linking Past and Present** Today, some people are concerned about the type of programming on television. Others fear that young Americans watch too much television. Do you agree or disagree with these concerns? Explain the reasons for your opinion.

Activity **Formulating Questions** You are a news reporter writing an article on how the United States changed during the 1950s. Write five questions you would ask someone who lived during those years. Each question should be based on one of the headings in this section.

The Civil Rights Movement Begins

As You Read

Explore These Questions

- What kinds of discrimination did minorities face?
- What advances were made in the fight for equality?
- What methods did Martin Luther King, Jr., use to fight for equal rights?

Define

- segregation
- integration
- boycott
- civil disobedience

Identify

- NAACP
- Thurgood Marshall
- civil rights movement
- *Brown* v. *Board of Education of Topeka*
- *Hernández* v. *Texas*
- Martin Luther King, Jr.
- Mohandas Gandhi
- Southern Christian Leadership Conference
- Ralph Abernathy

SETTING the Scene In 1957, William Myers, Jr., went looking for a house. He and his wife were expecting a baby, and they needed more living space. Myers, a World War II veteran, liked the look of Levittown, Pennsylvania, a new suburban community of about 60,000 people.

Myers and his family were African Americans. When they moved into their Levittown home, a hostile white resident threw a rock through their window. Others made threatening telephone calls. It took a judge's court order to restore calm.

Throughout the United States, African Americans and other minority groups faced discrimination in jobs, housing, and education. After World War II, their struggle for equality and civil rights intensified.

Patterns of Discrimination

Discrimination existed throughout the nation. In the North, many qualified African Americans could not get decent jobs. In the South, Jim Crow laws enforced strict separation, or **segregation,** of the races in schools, theaters, restaurants, and other public places. Signs even identified restrooms and drinking fountains for "colored" users only.

Mexican Americans and other Latinos also faced discrimination. Although they were not subject to Jim Crow laws, other laws—as well as traditions—worked against them.

Mexican Americans were prevented from attending neighborhood schools. Instead, they had to attend poorly equipped "Mexican schools." Custom kept them from living in certain neighborhoods or using some hotels or restaurants. Often, better-paying jobs were not open to them.

Early Successes

Those opposed to segregation applauded two historic "firsts" in the 1940s. In 1947, Jackie Robinson became the first African American to play on a major league baseball team. Playing for the Brooklyn Dodgers, he was honored with the rookie-of-the-year award. The following year, President Truman ordered **integration,** or the mixing of different ethnic groups, in the armed forces.

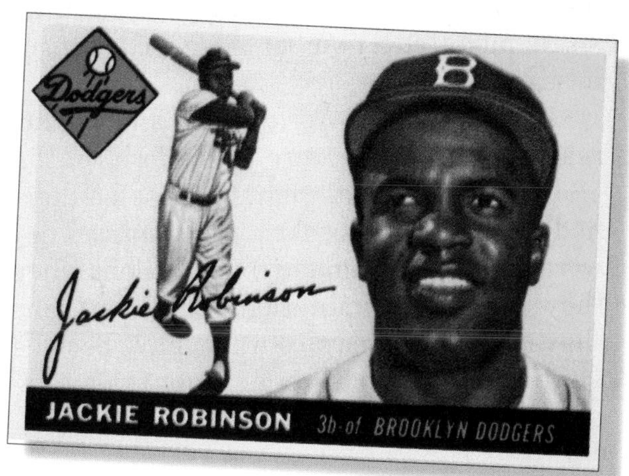

Jackie Robinson baseball card

Biography **Thurgood Marshall**

After earning a law degree from Howard University in 1933, and graduating first in his class, Thurgood Marshall became chief of the legal-defense section of the NAACP. Seeking equality under the law for African Americans, Marshall brought 32 cases before the Supreme Court. He won 29 of them. Marshall later became the first African American Supreme Court Justice. ★ **How did Marshall help African Americans gain equality in education?**

During the Korean War, black and white soldiers fought together in the same units.

During World War II, membership in the **NAACP** (National Association for the Advancement of Colored People) jumped from about 50,000 to 500,000. The NAACP conducted voter registration drives and fought against discrimination in housing and employment. Its Legal Defense and Education Fund, led by the attorney **Thurgood Marshall,** mounted a number of legal challenges to segregation.

After serving in World War II and the Korean War, veterans were in the forefront in efforts to win equal rights. These soldiers had risked their lives for their country. They were no longer willing to remain silent when they faced discrimination. Such veterans "have acquired a new courage, have become more vocal in protesting inequalities," reported one observer.

Struggle for Equality

During the 1950s, African Americans, Latinos, and others stepped up the struggle for equality. Their efforts became known as the **civil rights movement.**

In the schools

In 1896, the U.S. Supreme Court had decided in *Plessy* v. *Ferguson* that "separate but equal" facilities for blacks and whites were constitutional. (See page 495.) The NAACP had challenged this idea with some success in the 1940s. Yet in the early 1950s, laws in 21 states and the District of Columbia still allowed segregated public schools.

Oliver Brown of Topeka, Kansas, decided to challenge the Kansas law. He asked the local school board to let his daughter, Linda, attend the all-white school near their home rather than the distant, segregated school where she had been assigned. The school board refused.

With the help of the NAACP, Brown filed a suit against the school board. The case of ***Brown* v. *Board of Education of Topeka*** reached the Supreme Court.

Brown's lawyer, Thurgood Marshall, argued that "separate" could never be "equal." Segregated schools, he said, could never provide equal education. By their very nature, said Marshall, segregated schools violated the Fourteenth Amendment, which gave "equal protection" to all citizens.

The Supreme Court ruled in Brown's favor in 1954. In writing the decision, Chief Justice Earl Warren noted that segregation affected the "hearts and minds" of black students "in a way unlikely ever to be undone." A year later, the Court ordered the schools to

Connections With Arts

In 1959, Lorraine Hansberry wrote a play about an African American family in Chicago that buys a house in an all-white suburban neighborhood. The play, *A Raisin in the Sun,* became the first play by a black woman to be produced on Broadway.

be desegregated "with all deliberate speed." In a few places, schools were integrated fairly smoothly. In many others, officials resisted.

In Little Rock, Arkansas, Governor Orval Faubus opposed integration. In 1957, he called out the National Guard to keep African American students from attending Central High School. President Eisenhower stepped in because the Arkansas governor was defying a federal law. Eisenhower sent troops to Little Rock. Under their protection, black students entered Central High.

Eisenhower was the first President since the days of Reconstruction to use armed federal troops in support of African American rights. The action showed that the federal government could make significant efforts in the protection of people's civil rights.

In the courts

In the same year as *Brown* v. *Board of Education,* the Supreme Court decided another case, ***Hernández* v. *Texas.*** That case had been brought by Mexican Americans seeking their own civil rights.

James DeAnda, a Mexican American, was one of the lawyers who helped bring the Hernández case before the Supreme Court. DeAnda had previously worked to desegregate areas of Corpus Christi, Texas, where Mexican Americans were not allowed to buy houses.

In the case of *Hernández* v. *Texas,* DeAnda and other lawyers argued that Mexican Americans in Texas were denied equal protection under the law in that they were prevented from serving on juries. The Supreme Court agreed and ended the exclusion of Mexican Americans from Texas jury lists. In future years, other minority groups would use this decision to help them claim their civil rights.

Montgomery Bus Boycott

In December 1955, Rosa Parks was riding home from work on a crowded bus in Montgomery, Alabama. The driver ordered her to give up her seat so that a white man could sit down, as Alabama's Jim Crow laws required. Parks, a well-known activist and secretary of the local chapter of the NAACP, refused to leave her seat. She was arrested, fingerprinted, and sent to jail.

Organized protest

In response, a number of women from the NAACP composed a letter asking all African Americans to **boycott,** or refuse to use, the buses. The women hoped that the boycott would financially hurt the city and force it to end segregation on the buses. The women made thousands of copies of the letter and distributed them to the African American people of Montgomery.

To support the protest, Montgomery's black leaders formed a new organization, the Montgomery Improvement Association (MIA). They chose Dr. **Martin Luther King, Jr.,** a Baptist minister, to head the organization.

Viewing History **Ending Segregated Schools**

In 1957, the governor and many citizens of Arkansas opposed a federal court order to integrate Central High School in Little Rock. In the end, President Eisenhower had to send soldiers to protect students going to and from school. ★ **How do you think the students in this photograph felt as they went to school each day?**

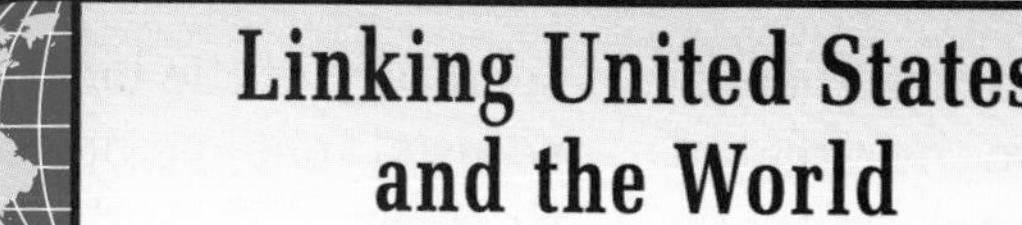

Linking United States and the World

India

United States

Peaceful Protest

Martin Luther King, Jr., shown above right in a 1965 protest march, believed that African Americans should use civil disobedience and other peaceful protest methods to gain justice and equality. King admired Mohandas Gandhi (above left), who used peaceful protest methods to help India gain independence from Great Britain in the 1940s. ★ **How do you think religious beliefs affected King's strategy for gaining civil rights?**

Dr. King spoke at a meeting in the Holt Street Baptist Church. Hundreds were in the church, and thousands more stood outside. Upon his arrival, it took King 15 minutes to work his way through the crowd.

"We are here this evening—for serious business," King began. "Yes, yes!" the crowd shouted. As the crowd cheered him on, King continued:

> ❝ You know, my friends, there comes a time when people get tired of being trampled over by the iron feet of oppression. . . . [W]e are determined here in Montgomery—to work and fight until justice runs down like water, and righteousness like a mighty stream! ❞

The boycott succeeds

The boycott went on for just over a year. The MIA organized a system of car pools to get African Americans to and from their workplaces. Each day, as many as 20,000 rides were provided. Many people simply walked. One elderly woman made a remark that became a common response of boycotters: "My feets is tired, but my soul is rested."

Some members of the white community fought back. Police harassed boycotters by giving them numerous traffic tickets. King and others were arrested. King's house was bombed. Still, Montgomery's blacks persisted.

King insisted that his followers limit their actions to **civil disobedience,** or nonviolent protests against unjust laws. He said, "We must use the weapon of love. We must have compassion and understanding for those who hate us."

Throughout the bus boycott struggle, African Americans held mass meetings in local churches. These church meetings helped keep morale high. The boycotters sang together, prayed together, and listened to individual stories of sacrifice. By coming together in this way, they gave courage and inspiration to one another.

To end bus segregation in Montgomery, the MIA filed a lawsuit in federal court. In 1956, almost a year after the boycott started, the Supreme Court ruled that segregation of riders on Alabama buses was unconstitutional. The Montgomery bus company agreed to integrate the buses and to hire black bus drivers.

National significance

The Montgomery bus boycott had several lasting effects. The boycott gained national attention for the civil rights movement. It also introduced nonviolent protest as an important method in the struggle for social equality. The boycott made clear that a new generation of African American leaders was emerging. One of the most prominent of these new national figures was Martin Luther King, Jr.

Martin Luther King, Jr.

Martin Luther King, Jr., was an educated and religious man. He was the son of a prominent Baptist minister. King graduated from Morehouse College, a prestigious all-black school. He later earned a Ph.D. in theology from Boston University.

King's education had introduced him to a wide range of philosophers and political thinkers. He studied the philosophy of ancient Greece and the European Enlightenment. Above all, King came to admire **Mohandas Gandhi,** a lawyer and spiritual man who had led a successful nonviolent movement against British rule in India.

Following the Montgomery victory, King and other African American leaders founded the **Southern Christian Leadership Conference** (SCLC) to carry on the struggle for equal rights. The group, consisting of nearly 100 black ministers, elected King president and the Reverend **Ralph Abernathy** treasurer. The SCLC urged African Americans to fight injustice by using civil disobedience:

> "Understand that nonviolence is not a symbol of weakness or cowardice, but as Jesus demonstrated, nonviolent resistance transforms weakness into strength and breeds courage in the face of danger."

Still, segregation remained widespread. The protests of the 1950s would soon grow into much larger protests in cities and towns all across the United States.

★ Section 2 Review ★

Recall

1. **Identify** **(a)** NAACP, **(b)** Thurgood Marshall, **(c)** civil rights movement, **(d)** *Brown* v. *Board of Education of Topeka,* **(e)** *Hernández* v. *Texas,* **(f)** Martin Luther King, Jr., **(g)** Mohandas Gandhi, **(h)** Southern Christian Leadership Conference, **(i)** Ralph Abernathy.
2. **Define** **(a)** segregation, **(b)** integration, **(c)** boycott, **(d)** civil disobedience.

Comprehension

3. Describe three forms of discrimination faced by minorities.
4. Describe three victories made by the civil rights movement in the 1950s.
5. What methods did Martin Luther King, Jr., support in the struggle for equality?

Critical Thinking and Writing

6. **Making Decisions** If you were an African American in Montgomery in the 1950s, would you have decided to participate in the bus boycott? Explain the reasons for your decision.
7. **Solving Problems** Do you think that civil disobedience is an effective method of protest? Explain.

Activity **Writing an Editorial** It is the 1950s and you are a newspaper editor in the American Southwest. You are upset about discrimination against Mexican Americans. Write an editorial protesting the treatment of Mexican Americans in the 1950s.

3 Years of Crisis and Change

Explore These Questions
- What goals did Presidents Kennedy and Johnson set for the nation?
- What problems did President Nixon face?
- What principles guided President Carter?

Define
- counterculture
- "silent majority"
- stagflation
- deficit

Identify
- Warren Commission
- Great Society
- Medicare
- Medicaid
- Neil Armstrong
- Watergate Affair
- Gerald R. Ford
- Jimmy Carter
- Helsinki Agreement

At age 43, John F. Kennedy was the youngest man ever elected President of the United States. During his campaign, he had inspired Americans with his youthful ideals and high hopes for the future. In his inaugural address, on January 20, 1961, Kennedy captured the imagination of many with these words:

> "Now the trumpet summons us again . . . to bear the burden of a long twilight struggle . . . against the common enemies of man: tyranny, poverty, disease, and war itself."

As it turned out, Kennedy and the Presidents who followed him faced very difficult challenges. For American Presidents—and for the nation as a whole—the 1960s and 1970s were years of uncertainty and turmoil.

The Kennedy Years

In 1960, the Republicans chose Vice President Richard Nixon to run for President. The Democrats chose Senator John F. Kennedy of Massachusetts. Kennedy was Irish American and Roman Catholic. After serving heroically in World War II, he had been elected to the House and the Senate.

Nixon led through much of the campaign. One reason was that no Catholic had ever been President. Many Americans feared that Kennedy's first loyalty might be to the Roman Catholic Church rather than the country. Kennedy responded by stressing his belief in separation of church and state.

The first televised debates ever held in a presidential campaign constituted a turning point in the campaign. Kennedy appeared youthful and confident. Nixon, recovering from a recent illness, looked tired and nervous. In the election that soon followed, Kennedy won by a narrow margin.

Economic and social policies

As President, Kennedy urged Congress to pass laws to help the millions of Americans living in poverty. In his travels as a candidate, he had been shocked to find hungry families in the United States. Visiting a poor area in West Virginia, Kennedy exclaimed, "Just imagine, kids who never drink milk!"

Congress did not support the President's poverty programs. It did, however, approve funds to explore the "new frontier" of space. It also funded the Peace Corps—as you recall, volunteers sent to teach or provide technical help in developing nations of the world.

Kennedy proposed many other programs. Before these could be enacted, however, a tragic event shattered the nation.

Kennedy assassinated

On November 22, 1963, Kennedy was in Dallas, Texas, on a political tour. As he rode in an open car past cheering crowds, shots rang out. The President slumped back in his seat. The car raced to a nearby hospital, but it was too late. President Kennedy was dead. That afternoon, Vice President Lyndon Johnson was sworn in as President.

Dallas police arrested Lee Harvey Oswald for the murder. Two days later, as police escorted Oswald to a more secure jail, Jack Ruby shot and killed him.

There were many questions. Did Oswald act alone? How was Ruby able to get near him? Chief Justice Earl Warren led an investigation. The **Warren Commission** concluded that Oswald had acted alone. Today, most historians agree with the Warren Commission's conclusion.

Johnson and the Great Society

President Johnson continued many of Kennedy's programs. In November 1964, voters chose to keep him in the White House. Johnson defeated Republican senator Barry Goldwater of Arizona in a landslide victory.

Johnson developed a plan he called the **Great Society.** Its ambitious goal was to improve the standard of living of every American. To achieve his Great Society, Johnson asked the nation to join him in a "war on poverty."

Congress had been unwilling to support such a plan under Kennedy. Johnson, however, used his strong persuasive powers to make Congress act. One senator recalled the "Johnson treatment" as being like "a great overpowering thunderstorm that consumed you as it closed in around you." During his first two years in office, Johnson persuaded Congress to pass more than 50 new laws.

One important Great Society program was **Medicare.** Under this plan, the government helped pay the hospital bills of citizens over age 65. Another program, **Medicaid,** gave states money to help poor people of all ages with their medical bills.

At Johnson's urging, Congress passed the Economic Opportunity Act in 1964. The act set up job-training programs for the poor. It

Viewing History **Kennedy Assassinated**

Millions of stunned Americans watched President Kennedy's funeral procession on television. Later, a Life *magazine cover showed a mournful Jacqueline Kennedy and her children during the funeral.* ★ **How do you think the assassination affected the mood of the nation?**

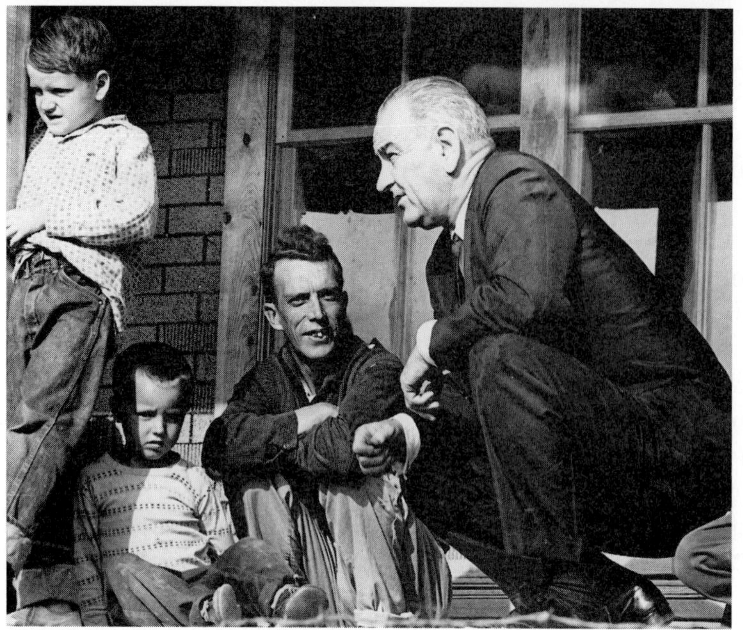

Viewing HISTORY **War on Poverty**

Lyndon Johnson had grown up on a farm in central Texas and lived through the hard times of the 1920s and 1930s. As President, he battled against poverty in both rural and urban America. Here, he learns about the problems of one American family. ★ **How was Johnson's Great Society plan similar to the New Deal?**

also gave loans to poor farmers and to businesses in poor sections of cities.

The government also set up programs to build housing for low-income and middle-income families. To carry out these programs, Congress created the Department of Housing and Urban Development, or HUD. Robert Weaver was named to head the department. He became the first African American to serve in a Cabinet post.

An Era of Protest

Despite these social reforms, the 1960s was an era of protest. The civil rights movement was gaining strength. More and more people opposed the Vietnam War. Many young Americans questioned the way of life they had grown up with.

The counterculture

Many young Americans became involved in the **counterculture** movement. Like the Beat Generation of the 1950s, members of the counterculture rejected traditional customs and ideas.

Young people protested against the lifestyle of their parents by trying to be different. They developed their own lifestyle. They liked to wear torn, faded jeans and simple work clothes. Women wore miniskirts. Men often wore beards and let their hair grow long. Many listened to new forms of rock music. Some experimented with illegal drugs.

Members of the counterculture adopted new attitudes and values. They criticized competition and the drive for personal success. They questioned some aspects of traditional family life. Inspired by the civil rights movement, protesters called for peace, justice, and social equality.

The antiwar movement

During the Johnson presidency, many youthful protesters focused their attention on the Vietnam War. Antiwar protesters staged rallies, burned draft cards, and refused to serve in the military. Many of the largest demonstrations took place on college campuses.

By 1968, the antiwar movement was in full swing. As a result, President Johnson's popularity rapidly declined. To avoid being confronted by angry crowds of protesters, Johnson stayed in the White House more and more. He decided not to seek reelection.

The election of 1968

Several Democrats sought their party's nomination in 1968. One was New York senator Robert Kennedy, brother of the late President. While campaigning in Los Angeles, Kennedy was shot and killed by a Palestinian who opposed the senator's support for the nation of Israel. (See page 838.)

In Chicago, the Democrats selected Vice President Hubert Humphrey as their candidate. Humphrey's chances for success were

American Heritage MAGAZINE

HISTORY HAPPENED HERE

At the Space Center, an entry sign advises visitors about the next shuttle launch.

Kennedy Space Center

The history of United States space exploration is on display at the Kennedy Space Center in Florida. Visitors can view IMAX movies, walk among actual rockets, explore a simulated space station, and climb aboard a full-sized replica of a space shuttle. Exhibits honor the past achievements of American astronauts and highlight goals for the future. On some days, visitors might even view a space-shuttle launch.

★ ***To learn more about this historic site, write:*** *NASA Visitor Services, Kennedy Space Center, FL 32899.*

hurt, however, by antiwar demonstrations outside the convention hall.

The Republicans again nominated former Vice President Richard Nixon to run for President. He promised to win "peace with honor" in Vietnam and restore "law and order" at home. Alabama governor George Wallace entered the race as a third-party candidate. Helped by this and by divisions in the Democratic party, Nixon won the election.

The Nixon Era

During his years as President, Nixon took steps to fulfill his campaign promises. He also wanted to reduce the involvement of the federal government in people's lives.

Helping the "silent majority"

The new President considered himself to be the leader of a group of Americans that he called the **"silent majority."** These were people who were disturbed by the unrest of the 1960s. Nixon defined these people as the "great majority of Americans, the non-shouters, the nondemonstraters."

As part of a "law-and-order" program, he used federal funds to help local police departments. He also named four Justices to the Supreme Court. The new Justices were more conservative than those who had retired.

Success in space

One of the greatest successes of the Nixon years occurred in the space program that Nixon inherited from Kennedy and Johnson. (See page 773.) In 1969, astronauts **Neil Armstrong** and Buzz Aldrin piloted a small craft onto the moon's surface. With millions of television viewers around the world watching, Armstrong became the first person to step onto the moon. "That's one small step for

Viewing HISTORY **Nixon's Farewell**

After resigning as President, Richard Nixon bid a final farewell as he left Washington, D.C., in August 1974. Nixon was so entangled in the Watergate scandal that his impeachment seemed certain. ★ **Who succeeded Nixon as President?**

man, one giant leap for mankind," he radioed back to Earth. American astronauts visited the moon five more times.

Economic policies

Nixon opposed some programs of the Great Society. He thought that they were too costly and that they contributed to inflation. As a result, Nixon backed off from many of the reforms of the Johnson years. He cut federal funds for education and low-income housing.

During the Nixon era, the economy was afflicted by what some called **stagflation,** a combination of rising prices, high unemployment, and slow economic growth. Nixon tried several remedies. To battle inflation, he established a temporary freeze on wages and prices. To stimulate the economy, he increased federal spending.

Despite Nixon's efforts, economic problems remained. Increased federal spending caused federal budget **deficits,** in which the government spent more than it received in revenues. Early in Nixon's second term, an oil embargo put added pressure on the economy. (See page 838.) Higher energy prices caused the price of goods to rise even more.

Scandal and resignation

During his second term of office, Nixon faced a scandal arising out of a burglary in Washington, D.C. On June 17, 1972, while Nixon was campaigning for reelection, police caught five men breaking into Democratic party headquarters in the Watergate apartment building. Evidence suggested that the burglars were linked to Nixon's reelection committee. The President assured the public that no one in the White House was involved in the **Watergate Affair.**

New evidence, however, soon linked the burglars to the White House. In May 1973, a Senate committee began public hearings. The hearings revealed that Nixon had made secret tape recordings of conversations in his office. These tapes showed that the President and several close advisers had tried to cover up the truth about the Watergate break-in.

In the midst of the Watergate Affair, another scandal erupted. Vice President Spiro Agnew was accused of taking bribes and was forced to resign. Under the Twenty-fifth Amendment, the President had to choose a new Vice President. Nixon selected Representative **Gerald R. Ford** of Michigan, who had served in Congress for 25 years. Congress approved the appointment.

The Watergate crisis came to a head in July 1974. A House of Representatives committee passed articles of impeachment against the President. One charge was obstructing, or blocking, justice. Even the President's strongest defenders found the evidence to be convincing.

The scandal completely overshadowed Nixon's foreign policy successes. The President who had brought the troops home from Vietnam, established relations with communist China, and achieved détente with the Soviet Union, was finished. (See pages 784, 786.) In August 1974, before an impeachment trial could begin, Richard Nixon became the first President to resign from office.

Ford Takes Office

Gerald Ford, the new President, added to the controversy. Soon after taking office, Ford granted Nixon a "full, free, and absolute pardon." Some felt that Nixon should have been brought to trial. Ford, however, wanted to save the country from a long and bitter debate over Watergate.

The Carter White House

In 1976, Ford won the Republican nomination for President. To run against him, the Democrats chose **Jimmy Carter,** a former governor of Georgia.

Carter used the fact that he had no experience in Washington to his advantage. He admitted to being a Washington outsider, but claimed that "the vast majority of Americans ... are also outsiders." Carter promised a change from Washington politics and scandals. In the 1976 election, he defeated Ford by a narrow margin.

Carter's term began with hope for a fresh approach. During his first year in office, the new President sent Congress almost a dozen major bills. They included reforms in the Social Security system and in the tax code. Carter, however, could not win congressional support for his legislation.

Another problem the President faced was inflation rates of 10 percent or higher. The government tried to slow inflation, yet prices kept rising. Many families had a hard time paying for food, clothing, and rent.

Carter took a firm stand on human rights. In 1975, the United States had signed the **Helsinki Agreement.** In it, 35 nations pledged to respect basic rights such as religious freedom and freedom of thought. Carter took this pledge seriously. The United States, he said, should not aid countries that violated human rights.

★ Section 3 Review ★

Recall

1. **Identify** **(a)** Warren Commission, **(b)** Great Society, **(c)** Medicare, **(d)** Medicaid, **(e)** Neil Armstrong, **(f)** Watergate Affair, **(g)** Gerald R. Ford, **(h)** Jimmy Carter, **(i)** Helsinki Agreement.
2. **Define** **(a)** counterculture, **(b)** "silent majority," **(c)** stagflation, **(d)** deficit.

Comprehension

3. **(a)** What did President Kennedy think should be the role of the government in the economy? **(b)** Describe two Great Society programs that became law.
4. Explain how Nixon tried to deal with each of the following: **(a)** stagflation, **(b)** Watergate Affair.
5. **(a)** What were the goals of Carter's domestic program? **(b)** Did he achieve them? Why or why not?

Critical Thinking and Writing

6. **Analyzing Ideas** Referring to the Watergate Affair, President Ford said, "The Constitution works." What do you think he meant?
7. **Comparing** **(a)** Compare the ability of the following four Presidents in getting Congress to pass their domestic programs: Kennedy, Johnson, Nixon, Carter. **(b)** How might you explain the success or failure of each?

Activity **Interviewing** To learn more about the difficult times you have read about, interview several older friends and relatives who lived through the turbulent times of the 1960s and 1970s. Prepare a list of questions. Keep a written or audio record of the interviews. What similarities and differences do you find in the responses?

4 The Civil Rights Movement Expands

As You Read

Explore These Questions

- What were the major goals of the civil rights movement?
- How did civil rights groups bring about change?
- What civil rights laws were passed in the 1960s and 1970s?

Define

- sit-in
- affirmative action
- migrant worker
- bilingual

Identify

- Freedom Rider
- Civil Rights Act of 1964
- Voting Rights Act
- Black Panthers
- Malcolm X
- National Organization for Women
- César Chávez
- Voting Rights Act of 1975
- Asian American Political Alliance
- American Indian Movement

One day in 1960, four college students sat talking in their dorm room. The students, all African Americans, went to college in Greensboro, North Carolina. Downtown, the "whites only" lunch counters refused to serve blacks. The students were angry at the unjust laws that limited the rights of black Americans.

The more they talked, the more the students felt that they ought to do something to change things. They went to a local department store and sat down at a segregated lunch counter. When the waitress would not serve them, they refused to leave.

News of the **sit-in**, a form of protest in which people sit and refuse to leave, spread rapidly. In the months ahead, thousands of blacks and whites conducted sit-ins at public places across the South. The protests signaled a new determination to bring about equality for all Americans.

African Americans Seek Change

Segregated lunch counters were only one example of racial discrimination in the South in 1960. As you read in Section 2 of this chapter, segregation laws also restricted blacks to separate facilities in bus stations, restrooms, and other public places. The Greensboro sit-ins inspired African American leaders to press harder for change.

Peaceful protests

Several civil rights organizations led the struggle. The NAACP brought cases of discrimination before the courts. The Southern Christian Leadership Conference, led by Martin Luther King, Jr., taught African Americans about various methods of peaceful protest. The Congress of Racial Equality (CORE) organized "Freedom Rides." **Freedom Riders** rode buses from town to town throughout the South, trying to integrate bus terminals.

These early civil rights groups held firmly to the tactics of peaceful civil disobedience. They used sit-ins, boycotts, marches, and other peaceful methods to achieve their goals.

It took courage to participate in acts of civil disobedience and other methods of peaceful protest. Police sometimes used attack dogs or water hoses against protesters. More than once, mobs bombed the houses and churches of black leaders. Many civil rights workers, black and white, were injured or killed.

In 1963, more than 200,000 Americans marched on Washington, D.C. They wanted Congress to pass laws to end discrimination and help the poor. Among the speakers that day was Martin Luther King, Jr. In a now-famous speech, he proclaimed:

> "When we let freedom ring... we will be able to speed up that day when all of God's children, black men and white men, Jews and Gentiles, Protestants and Catholics, will be able to join hands and sing in the words of the old Negro spiritual, 'Free at last! Free at last! Thank God Almighty, we are free at last!'"

Civil rights laws

The demonstrations spurred Presidents Kennedy and Johnson to push for strong civil rights laws. The **Civil Rights Act of 1964** protected the right of all citizens to vote. It outlawed discrimination in hiring and ended segregation in public places.

Other laws soon followed. In 1964, the Twenty-fourth Amendment was ratified. It banned poll taxes, which prevented African Americans from voting. In 1965, the **Voting Rights Act** ended literacy tests. It also allowed federal officials to register voters in states where local officials practiced discrimination. Thanks to these laws, tens of thousands of African Americans voted for the first time.

Despite new civil rights laws, discrimination remained a problem. Northern states had no formal system of segregation. Informally, though, housing in certain neighborhoods and employment in many companies remained closed to African Americans. Millions of blacks lived in rundown areas of cities. Many were unemployed or could get only low-paying jobs.

New voices and views

Some African Americans thought nonviolent protest was not working. Radical groups such as the **Black Panthers** urged African Americans to arm themselves. The Panthers argued that blacks must be prepared to fight for their rights if necessary.

Black Muslims, such as **Malcolm X,** argued that African Americans could succeed only if they separated from white society. Malcolm X later modified his views. Before he was assassinated in 1965, he called for "a society in which there could exist honest white-black brotherhood."

Both moderates and radicals talked about "black power." They urged African Americans to achieve economic independence by starting their own businesses and shopping in black-owned stores. Leaders also called for "black pride," encouraging African Americans to learn more about their heritage.

Violent protests

In crowded city neighborhoods, many blacks were angry about discrimination, the

Viewing HISTORY **Freedom Riders**

In 1961, black and white protesters rode together on buses through the South. They were protesting segregation on buses and in bus terminals. Some freedom riders were assaulted, while others were arrested. ★ **Why did it take a special kind of courage to engage in nonviolent protest?**

Viewing HISTORY **Violent Protests**

In the 1960s, riots became all too common in American cities. Here, National Guard troops help put out the fires after the 1965 riot in the Watts section of Los Angeles.
★ **What were the causes of the urban riots of the 1960s?**

lack of jobs, and poverty. In several cities, their anger exploded into violence. One of the most violent riots took place in Watts, a black neighborhood in Los Angeles. During six days in August 1965, rioters set fire to buildings and looted stores. Some 4,000 people were arrested, 34 were killed, and 1,000 were injured.

In the summers of 1966 and 1967, much more violence occurred. More than 40 cities experienced rioting in 1966. In July 1967, days of rioting in Newark, New Jersey, resulted in the deaths of 23 people and millions of dollars in damaged property. Just one week later, rioting broke out in Detroit. Before order was restored, 43 people died and blocks of buildings were burned.

King assassinated

During the years of riots, Martin Luther King, Jr., remained committed to nonviolence. In April 1968, he went to Memphis, Tennessee, to support black sanitation workers who were on strike. When he stepped outside his motel room, a white gunman shot and killed him.

King was buried in Atlanta, Georgia. His life has continued to inspire Americans to work for peaceful change. In 1986, his birthday was made a national holiday.

Progress is made

During the 1970s, the civil rights movement began to show results. African Americans won public offices in small towns and large cities. Atlanta, Cleveland, Detroit, New Orleans, and Los Angeles all had black mayors by 1979. African Americans made gains in the federal government as well. In 1967, Edward Brooke of Massachusetts became the first black senator since Reconstruction. A year later, President Johnson appointed Thurgood Marshall to the Supreme Court.

Businesses and universities provided more opportunities for African Americans. **Affirmative action** programs were set up to hire and promote minorities, women, and others who had faced discrimination. By the 1970s, more African Americans were entering professions such as medicine and law. Still, many blacks faced discrimination in receiving promotions and advancement in their jobs.

Rights for Women

Like African Americans, women struggled to win equal rights. Since the 1960s, women's struggle for equality has been known as the women's rights movement.

Women faced discrimination in many areas. Many employers refused to hire women for certain jobs even though the women were qualified. When women were hired, they were not treated the same as men. A female steelworker complained:

> "One woman . . . worked in the masonry department. She could carry two buckets when most of the men carried only one. She got fired because she was too short and they said it was unsafe for her."

Why Study History?

Because You Can Learn About Helping Others

Historical Background

In 1986, Martin Luther King, Jr.'s, birthday was declared a federal holiday. Since then, many schools and businesses have observed the day just as they observe other federal holidays. They close and give their students and employees a day off.

Some people, however, thought that this was not the best way to honor Martin Luther King, Jr. As a civil rights leader, King had stressed the importance of helping people. He once said, "Life's most persistent and urgent question is, What are you doing for others?" Inspired by words such as these, Congress passed the Martin Luther King Day of Service Act. Its purpose was to urge Americans to turn a day away from school or work into a day of community service.

These middle school students are packing donated clothes to help those in need.

Connections to Today

Philadelphia was one of the first communities to embrace the spirit of the new law. Each year, the city celebrates King's birthday through a program of community service. Thousands of Philadelphians of all ages work together to help others. They volunteer their time and energy in more than 100 projects. These include cleaning up parks, visiting senior citizens, renovating people's homes, tutoring children, and much more.

Connections to You

What can you do to celebrate the birthday of Martin Luther King, Jr.? As in Philadelphia, students in every city and community can create their own tradition of helping others. To get started, just look around your community and see what needs to be done.

According to Coretta Scott King, serving others is an ideal way to honor her husband. As she put it, "Our goal is to change the way Americans think about the holiday, from seeing it as a day off to a day on."

1. **Comprehension** Why did Congress create the Martin Luther King Day of Service Act?
2. **Critical Thinking** How can service projects make a community a better place to live and work?

Make a list of service projects that could help people in your community. Choose one and develop an action plan for carrying out the project. Your plan should outline the materials needed, the number of people needed, the amount of time the project will take, and the benefits of the project.

Viewing History **Marching for Women's Rights**

In the 1960s and 1970s, American women became more politically active. Here, women marchers seek support for the Equal Rights Amendment. The ERA died in 1982 when the ratification time limit expired. ★ **How many states are needed to ratify a constitutional amendment?**

◀ *National Organization for Women button*

When men and women held the same job, women were often paid less. Also, women were seldom promoted as fast as men. Many law schools and medical schools gave preference to male applicants.

In 1966, Betty Friedan helped to set up the **National Organization for Women** (NOW). It worked for equal rights for women in jobs, pay, and education. The NOW helped women bring discrimination cases to court. It campaigned for maternity leave and child care centers and urged women to become more politically active.

Women made some gains through new laws. The Equal Pay Act of 1963 required equal pay for equal work. The Civil Rights Act of 1964 outlawed discrimination in hiring based on gender as well as on race.

In the 1970s, the women's movement suffered a major defeat. In 1972, Congress passed a proposal for the Equal Rights Amendment (ERA) to the Constitution. The amendment would ban discrimination based on gender. However, Phyllis Schlafly and other conservative women led a successful campaign against the amendment.

Schlafly and other opponents of the ERA argued that the amendment would lead to undesired changes. One of these, they said, would be the drafting of women into the armed forces. They also charged that the ERA would cause the decline of the traditional family. In the end, the amendment failed to be ratified in enough states.

Despite this defeat, the decades of reform brought women more power and equality. The leaders of the women's movement promised that they would continue the fight for equal opportunity.

Latinos

By the end of the 1970s, more than 10 million Latinos lived in the United States. Like African Americans, women, and other groups, they joined in the struggle for equality and civil rights.

Mexican Americans

Mexican Americans are the largest group of Latinos. Large numbers of Mexicans were living in the Southwest when the United States annexed the region after the Mexican War. Since then, Mexicans have continued to immigrate to the United States. From 1960 to 1980, the largest number of immigrants to the United States came from Mexico.

Many Mexican Americans lived and worked in urban areas. Many others were **migrant workers** who traveled from farm to farm looking for work.

In both the cities and rural areas, life was difficult for Mexican Americans. They received low wages and their working conditions were poor. Few schools offered programs for children whose first language was Spanish. Migrants had little chance to get an education because families moved often, and it was hard for children to attend school.

Puerto Rican Americans

Many Latinos in the eastern United States trace their origins to Puerto Rico. Since 1898, Puerto Rico has been governed by the United States. As you recall, Puerto Ricans became American citizens in 1917. In 1952, the island became a self-governing commonwealth. This gave the people more say over their own affairs. Many Puerto Ricans have been happy to remain a commonwealth. Others have called for independence.

In the 1950s, thousands of people left Puerto Rico and headed to the mainland United States in search of work. Many took jobs in the factories of New York City, New Jersey, Connecticut, and Pennsylvania. Others settled in cities such as Boston, Chicago, and San Francisco. Many Puerto Ricans faced discrimination in housing and jobs.

Cuban Americans

Another major Latino group came from Cuba. After Fidel Castro set up a communist government in Cuba in 1959, more than 200,000 Cubans fled to the United States. (See page 773.) Most settled in southern Florida. Many of the immigrants were well educated and they adapted quickly to their new home.

In 1980, a new wave of Cubans arrived when Castro allowed thousands of people to leave the country. Most of the new refugees were unskilled workers who found it difficult to make a living.

As their numbers grew, Cuban Americans became an important force in southern Florida. Miami took on a new look. Shop windows displayed signs in Spanish. Cuban restaurants and shops opened. Cubans published Spanish-language newspapers and operated radio and television stations.

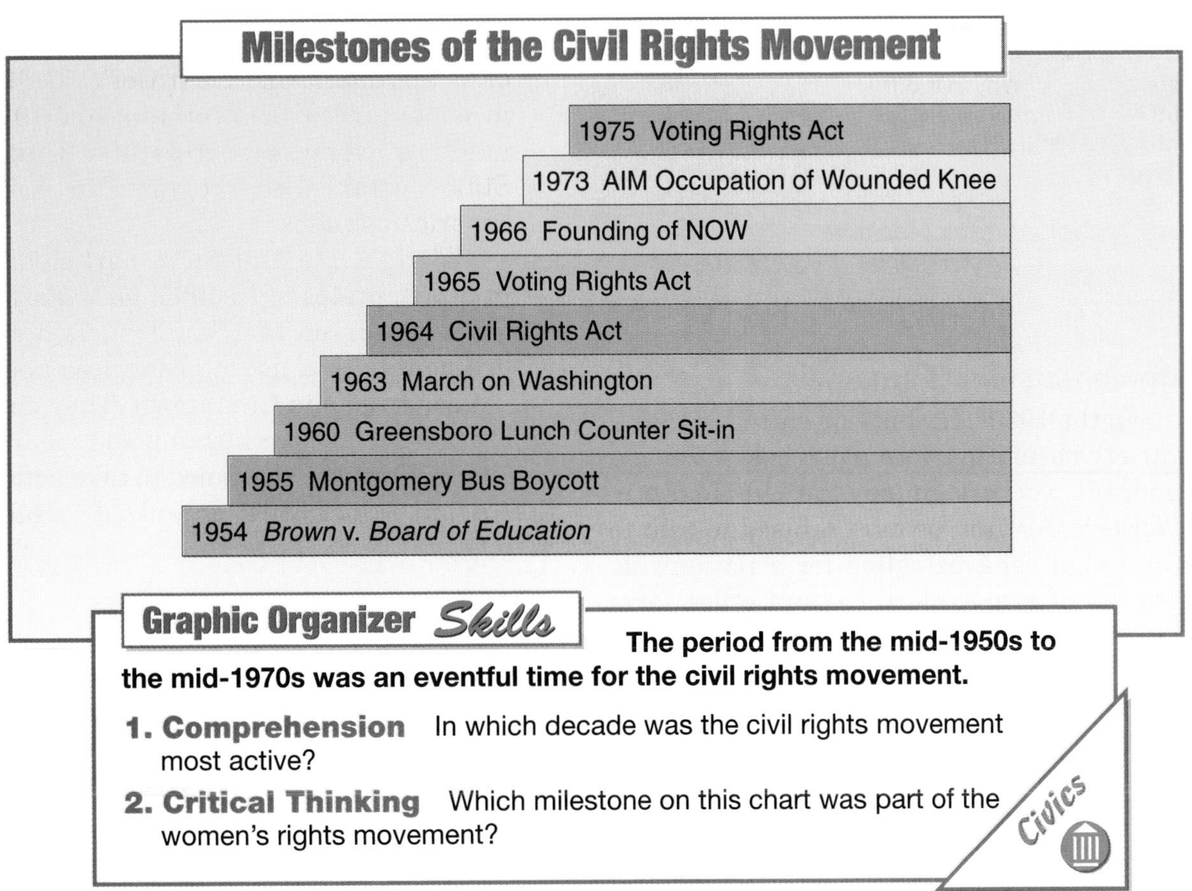

Graphic Organizer Skills **The period from the mid-1950s to the mid-1970s was an eventful time for the civil rights movement.**

1. **Comprehension** In which decade was the civil rights movement most active?
2. **Critical Thinking** Which milestone on this chart was part of the women's rights movement?

Biography César Chávez

The son of a migrant farm worker, César Chávez attended more than 30 elementary schools. In 1965, he organized the United Farm Workers among California farm workers. He used nationwide boycotts of grapes, wine, and lettuce to pressure California growers into raising wages and improving working conditions. ★ **Why is it difficult for migrant workers to get a good education?**

Symbol urging people to boycott grapes ➤

Organizing for reform

In the 1960s, Latinos organized to seek a variety of reforms. **César Chávez** formed a migrant workers' union, the United Farm Workers. At first, owners refused to talk to the union. Chávez called for a nationwide boycott of grapes, lettuce, and other farm products. In the end, farm owners recognized the union, and workers won higher wages.

By the mid-1960s, Latinos began to take increased pride in their history and culture. Mexican Americans expressed this pride by calling themselves Chicanos, a name that comes from the Spanish word *Mexicano.* Latino groups registered voters and made sure that voting laws were enforced. As a result, voters elected more Latino officials to represent their interests.

One result of these efforts was the **Voting Rights Act of 1975.** This law required areas with large numbers of non-English-speaking citizens to hold bilingual elections. **Bilingual** means in two languages. In a bilingual election, information is provided in more than one language. With a ballot that was written in Spanish, it was easier for Latinos to vote.

Other important laws were the Bilingual Education Acts of 1968 and 1973. These laws promoted bilingual programs in public schools with Spanish-speaking and Asian students.

Asian Americans

Asian Americans also took part in the civil rights movement of the 1960s and 1970s. In 1968, students at the University of California at Berkeley founded the **Asian American Political Alliance** (AAPA). Students of Chinese, Japanese, Filipino, and other Asian descent worked together to promote the rights and cultural heritage of Asian Americans. Their work resulted in some success. Between 1968 and 1973, major universities across the United States established programs in Asian American studies.

Young Asian Americans participated in public protests. In 1968, for example, activists presented the San Francisco city government with a list of grievances about unjust conditions in Chinatown. They cited problems such as poor housing and medical facilities. When the city failed to take action, the Asian Americans organized protest marches.

Native Americans

Native Americans also worked to achieve full rights under the law. In their case, they claimed rights not only as individuals but as members of tribal groups. Over the years, the federal government had recognized tribal governments by signing treaties with them.

During the late 1940s and the 1950s, the federal government sought to break up tribal governments. They also encouraged Indians to leave their reservations. By the late 1960s, more than half of all Native Americans lived off the reservations, mainly in urban areas. Gradually, city life weakened traditional tribal ties and customs.

Native Americans organized to counter the government's policies. The National Congress of American Indians regularly sent delegations to Washington to defend Indian rights.

Another organization, the Native American Rights Fund, stressed legal action. Its members worked to regain title to lands or to mineral and fishing rights that had been given to them in earlier treaties. In some cases, courts awarded Native Americans money for lands that had been taken illegally in the past.

The **American Indian Movement** (AIM) actively protested the treatment of Indians. In 1973, AIM members occupied Wounded Knee, South Dakota, for several weeks. As you may recall, the United States Army had killed nearly 300 Indians at Wounded Knee in 1890. (See page 520.) AIM wanted to remind people of the government's failure to deal fairly with Native Americans.

Protests and court cases have won sympathy for Indian causes. They have also won more rights for Native Americans. Today, Native Americans continue to speak out forcefully to achieve their goals.

Indian rights poster

★ Section 4 Review ★

Recall

1. **Identify** **(a)** Freedom Rider, **(b)** Civil Rights Act of 1964, **(c)** Voting Rights Act, **(d)** Black Panthers, **(e)** Malcolm X, **(f)** National Organization for Women, **(g)** César Chávez, **(h)** Voting Rights Act of 1975, **(i)** Asian American Political Alliance, **(j)** American Indian Movement.
2. **Define** **(a)** sit-in, **(b)** affirmative action, **(c)** migrant worker, **(d)** bilingual.

Comprehension

3. Describe three forms of injustice that some Americans experienced in the 1960s.
4. **(a)** Describe three peaceful methods used in the struggle for civil rights. **(b)** Give two examples of the violence that afflicted American society in the 1960s and 1970s.
5. Describe any three laws or developments that established more justice and equal rights in the United States.

Critical Thinking and Writing

6. **Linking Past and Present** Many schools and businesses began affirmative action programs in the 1960s. Today, some Americans charge that affirmative action gives minorities an unfair advantage. What is your opinion? Explain.
7. **Understanding Causes and Effects** How did the civil rights movement begun by African Americans in the 1950s help other groups in their struggle for equality?

Activity **Writing a Speech** You are a leader of one of the civil rights movements described in this section. Write a speech to inspire other Americans to support your cause.

Chapter 29 Review and Activities

★ Sum It Up ★

Section 1 The Booming Postwar World

- Growing numbers of people moved to the suburbs and the Sunbelt.
- The automobile and television helped shape American life.

Section 2 The Civil Rights Movement Begins

- African Americans and other minorities faced discrimination and inequality.
- Martin Luther King, Jr., urged African Americans to use nonviolent methods in their struggle for equality.

Section 3 Years of Crisis and Change

- Kennedy and Johnson supported government programs to help Americans living in poverty.
- Political and economic troubles weakened the effectiveness of several Presidents in the late 1960s and 1970s.

Section 4 The Civil Rights Movement Expands

- By using a variety of methods, African Americans won greater equality.
- Women sought equal opportunities in government and in the workplace.
- In the 1960s and 1970s, American minorities of many different backgrounds worked to end social, political, and economic injustices.

For additional review of the major ideas of Chapter 29, see ***Guide to the Essentials of American History*** or ***Interactive Student Tutorial CD-ROM,*** which contains interactive review activities, graphic organizers, and practice tests.

Reviewing the Chapter

Define These Terms

Match each term with the correct definition.

Column 1	Column 2
1. baby boom	**a.** nonviolent protests against unjust laws
2. civil disobedience	**b.** inflation and slow economic growth
3. stagflation	**c.** expenditures are greater than revenues
4. segregation	**d.** large increase in the birth rate
5. deficit	**e.** separation of people of different backgrounds

Explore the Main Ideas

1. Describe three characteristics of American life in the 1950s.
2. How did Martin Luther King, Jr., rise to national prominence?
3. What domestic problems did Richard Nixon face as President?
4. What gains did African Americans make in the 1960s and 1970s?
5. Describe one way in which each of the following groups fought against injustice: **(a)** women, **(b)** Latino Americans, **(c)** Asian Americans, **(d)** Native Americans.

Graph Activity

Use the graph below to answer the following questions: **1.** About how much money did the federal government spend on highways in 1950? **2.** In which two-year period did spending increase the most? **Critical Thinking** How do you think the building of highways affected where Americans lived? Explain.

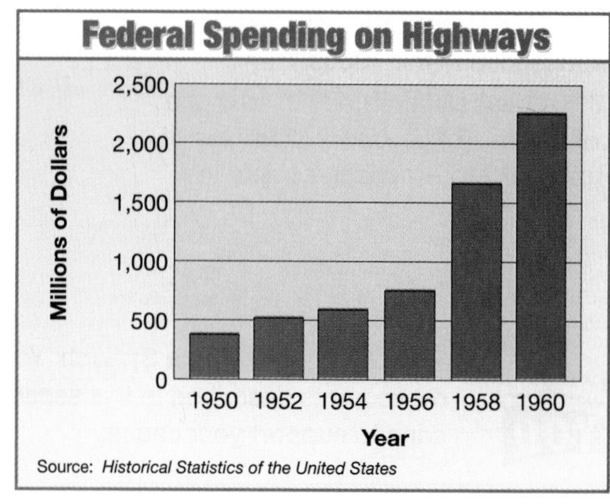

Source: *Historical Statistics of the United States*

Critical Thinking and Writing

1. **Comparing** Compare the Great Society programs of the 1960s with the New Deal programs of the 1930s. **(a)** How were they similar? **(b)** How were they different?
2. **Linking Past and Present** One of the reforms of the civil rights era was the establishment of bilingual education. Today, some people question the benefits of that program. What is your opinion? Explain.
3. **Understanding Chronology** Why did the baby boom occur after World War II rather than before or during the war?
4. **Exploring Unit Themes** **World Leadership** How do you think events in the United States during the 1960s and 1970s affected the way nations around the world viewed the United States?

Using Primary Sources

In 1957, during the troubles over school desegregation in Little Rock, Arkansas, one of the students commented:

> "I think [that opposition to African Americans entering the white high school] is downright un-American. I think it's the most terrible thing ever seen in America. I mean, I guess I'm sounding too patriotic or something, but I always thought all men were created equal."

Source: *Eyes on the Prize: America's Civil Rights Years, 1954–1965* by Juan Williams.

Recognizing Points of View **(a)** What did the student believe about opposition to African Americans entering the high school in Little Rock? **(b)** Do you agree with the student? Explain your thinking.

Activity Bank

Interdisciplinary Activity

Exploring the Arts Learn some songs that were used in the civil rights movement. Perform these songs for the class. Then, hold a discussion with other class members to explore why the songs were so important for the movement.

Career Skills Activity

Historians Research one of the Presidents you have read about in this chapter. Explore in depth the President's policy goals and how well he achieved them. Then, present a report to the class.

Citizenship Activity

Creating an Action Plan Every citizen in a democracy can have an influence on current issues. Choose a problem or issue in your community and create a plan showing ways that you would go about having an influence on that issue.

Internet Activity

On the Internet, find sites dealing with any one of the interesting personalities discussed in this chapter. Use the information to write a brief biography of the person.

You are a foreign correspondent from Britain covering the news in the United States. What do you think are the two most important events or developments in the United States in the 1950s? Explain the reasons for your choices in your EYEWITNESS JOURNAL. Do the same for the 1960s and the 1970s.

Chapter 30

New Directions

1980–Present

What's Ahead

Section 1
A Conservative Tide

Section 2
The Post–Cold War World

Section 3
War and Peace in the Middle East

Section 4
The Environment and the World Economy

Section 5
A Diverse Nation

In the 1980s, the nation entered a new political era. President Ronald Reagan, a conservative Republican, vowed to cut taxes and reduce the size of government. The nation entered a period of economic growth. After a brief recession, growth continued in the 1990s under Democratic President Bill Clinton. Clinton also worked with a Republican Congress to bring government spending under control.

With the Cold War over, Americans debated the role of the United States in the world. The environment, foreign competition, and greater diversity brought their own challenges. Still, Americans faced a new century with hopes for a bright future.

Why Study *History?* You have learned a lot about American history this year. Studying history can help you become an informed, responsible citizen. Did you know that a background in history also prepares you for many jobs? To focus on this connection, see the *Why Study History?* feature, "Knowing History May Help Your Career," in this chapter.

American Events

1981 Ronald Reagan becomes President

1986 Immigration Reform and Control Act reduces illegal immigration

1990 Americans With Disabilities Act outlaws discrimination against disabled people

1980 — **1985** — **1990**

World Events

1979 World Event Revolution in Iran overthrows the shah

1989 World Event China crushes pro-democracy demonstration

Viewing History: Celebrating Liberty

As they entered a new century, Americans sometimes disagreed on the best ways to protect their precious rights. Yet the nation still worked to preserve liberty at home and support democracy in other lands. In his painting Liberty States, *Taiwanese-born artist Tsing-fang Chen used familiar images to stress the continuing value of liberty.* ★ **What do you think are the two greatest challenges facing the United States in the future?**

1991
United Nations allies defeat Iraq in Persian Gulf War

1996
Welfare reform limits federal aid to the poor

1990 **1995** **Present**

1994 World Event
South Africa holds first multiracial elections

1998 World Events
India and Pakistan conduct nuclear tests; peace accord in Northern Ireland

A Conservative Tide

As You Read

Explore These Questions

- What goals did conservatives have in the 1980s and 1990s?
- What domestic policies did Presidents Reagan and Bush pursue?
- What successes and failures did President Clinton have?

Define

- deregulation
- balanced budget
- downsizing
- recession

Identify

- Barry Goldwater
- Moral Majority
- Reaganomics
- George Bush
- Sandra Day O'Connor
- Bill Clinton
- Hillary Rodham Clinton
- Newt Gingrich

"Government is not the solution to our problem, government is the problem." Ronald Reagan spoke those words in 1981 after being sworn in as President of the United States. The new President called for a conservative revolution that would change the direction of the federal government.

Conservative Goals

Ronald Reagan swept into office on a rising conservative tide. A growing number of Americans were beginning to view conservative ideas and values as the answer to the nation's problems. These ideas contrasted sharply with the political thinking that had prevailed in the 1960s and 1970s.

Limiting the role of government

Since the time of President Franklin Roosevelt's New Deal, the size of the federal government had grown steadily. (See Chapter 26.) Later Presidents followed FDR's lead. John F. Kennedy and Lyndon Johnson believed that the federal government should take an active role in managing the economy and providing for the welfare of its citizens. Such a position came to be known as liberal.* Kennedy and Johnson sponsored federal programs to erase poverty, build low-income housing, or provide medical care to those who could not afford it.

Kennedy and Johnson were both Democrats. Many Republicans, however, also expanded the role of the federal government. President Richard Nixon created agencies to set safety standards for workers and to protect the environment.

Against this liberal trend, a new conservative movement began to take shape in the 1960s. Its leading voice was Arizona senator **Barry Goldwater.** Early on, Goldwater warned against growing federal power:

> "None of us here in Washington knows all or even half of the answers. You people out there in the 50 states had better understand that. . . . If you cherish your freedom, don't leave it all up to big government."

Goldwater lost the presidential election to Johnson in 1964. Still, his ideas influenced a new generation of conservatives, including Ronald Reagan.

By the 1980s, these conservative critics of "big government" dominated the Republican party. Reagan and others argued that federal social programs had become too costly, driving taxes up. Another concern was that government regulations kept businesses from growing. State and local governments, conservatives said, should decide what regulations were needed.

* Generally, the term *liberal* refers to people who favor change, while the term *conservative* refers to people who want to preserve or return to established traditions. However, both terms have taken on different political meanings at different times in history.

Religion and values

Many conservatives also called for a return to traditional values after decades of social change. These conservatives praised family life, religion, and patriotism.

Growing church membership reflected the renewed emphasis on traditional values. During the 1970s and 1980s, evangelical Christian churches grew rapidly. Evangelicals stress a personal conversion experience. Leading evangelical ministers used television to reach a wider audience.

Not all conservatives were evangelicals, and not all evangelicals supported the new conservative movement. Still, many evangelicals took an active role in conservative political causes. In 1979, the Reverend Jerry Falwell founded the **Moral Majority.** The group aided political candidates who favored conservative religious goals, such as a constitutional amendment allowing prayer in the public schools. With other conservative religious organizations, the Moral Majority strongly supported Reagan in 1980.

The Reagan Years

Ruggedly handsome, Ronald Reagan had been a popular movie star. After entering politics, he was elected governor of California. His skill at presenting ideas in terms ordinary people could understand won him the nickname the Great Communicator.

In 1980, Reagan defeated Jimmy Carter for President. After the protests of the 1960s and the high inflation of the 1970s, voters responded to Reagan's reassuring promise to "Make America Great Again." Reagan was reelected in 1984 by an even greater margin.

Economic policies

Once in office, Reagan began to put his economic program—often called **Reaganomics**—into effect. He persuaded Congress to cut taxes in an effort to stimulate the economy. Reagan hoped that taxpayers would use the extra money to buy more. That would benefit businesses selling goods and services. The President also expected taxpayers to save more. Increasing the amount of money in savings accounts would allow banks to invest in new ventures.

With less tax revenue coming in, Reagan sought ways to cut government spending. He called on Congress to reduce spending on social programs such as welfare and aid to education. Critics charged that such spending cuts hurt the poor, the elderly, and children. Supporters responded that Reagan was just trimming programs that did not work.

Reagan also supported **deregulation,** or reduction of restrictions on businesses. Earlier Presidents had deregulated certain industries. For example, Jimmy Carter had reduced regulations on airlines, railroads, and truckers. Reagan increased the pace of

Viewing HISTORY **Reagan, a Popular President**

His relaxed, good-humored manner and unshakable patriotism made Ronald Reagan a popular President. His policies brought a conservative revolution to government. Here, Reagan greets young fans on a campaign stop. ★ **How did Ronald Reagan try to change the direction of the federal government?**

▲ *1980 campaign button*

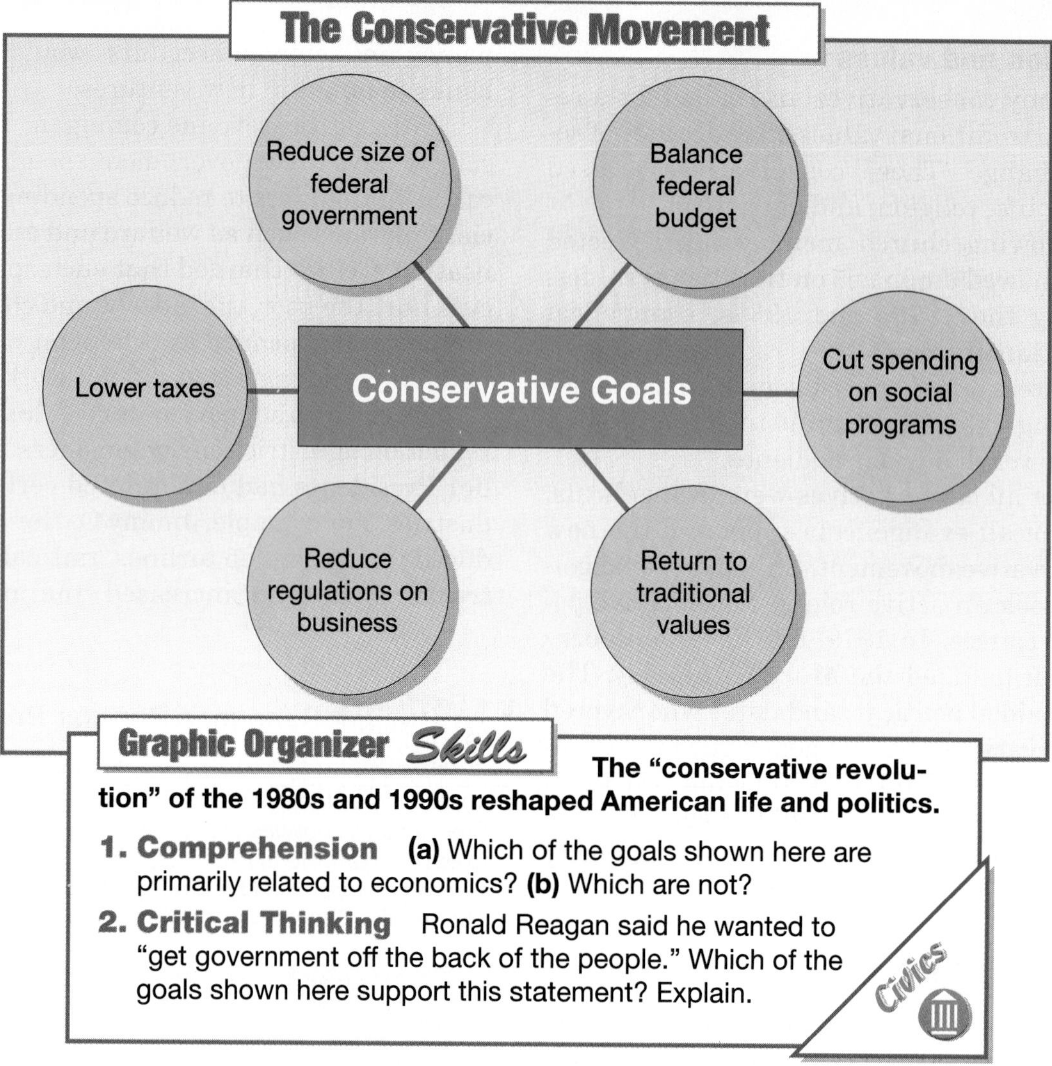

Graphic Organizer Skills The "conservative revolution" of the 1980s and 1990s reshaped American life and politics.

1. **Comprehension** **(a)** Which of the goals shown here are primarily related to economics? **(b)** Which are not?
2. **Critical Thinking** Ronald Reagan said he wanted to "get government off the back of the people." Which of the goals shown here support this statement? Explain.

Civics

deregulation. He opposed laws that required industries to install expensive antipollution devices. He also worked to give banks and corporations greater freedom in the kinds of investments they could make.

Mixed results

At first, Reagan's program slowed the economy. Many people lost their jobs. By late 1982, however, the economy was booming. Many businesses opened or grew. When Reagan left office, there were 16 million more jobs, while inflation had been kept in check.

Another Reagan goal—balancing the budget—proved more difficult to achieve. With a **balanced budget,** the government spends only as much as it takes in. Although Reagan worked to cut back social programs, he sharply increased military spending. When Reagan took office, Cold War tensions were high due to the Soviet invasion of Afghanistan. (See page 787.) To oppose the Soviet "evil empire," Reagan said, the United States needed a stronger military.

With military spending rising and taxes cut, the budget deficit soared. The deficit for 1986 was $240 billion—nearly 10 times higher than under any other President.

Still, Reagan remained highly popular, especially among young conservatives. "He moved us," noted Reagan speechwriter Peggy Noonan. "We loved him."

The Economy Under Bush

Reagan's popularity helped his Vice President, **George Bush,** win a landslide victory in 1988. Bush sought to carry on the policies of the Reagan years. In a dramatic campaign speech, he promised to cut the deficit without raising taxes. "Read my lips," he proclaimed boldly. "No new taxes."

It was a promise Bush was unable to keep. Democrats and Republicans could not agree on which government programs to cut in order to reduce the deficit. By 1990, Congress and the President were deadlocked. Finally, Bush agreed to raise taxes in order to save some popular programs. Many conservatives felt betrayed.

Even as Bush raised taxes, the nation's economy weakened. As a result of deregulation in the early 1980s, some banks had made risky loans in the hope of gaining greater profits. When these loans were not repaid, the banks lost their money. During the late 1980s, hundreds of banks failed.

As banks became more cautious about lending money, the economy slowed down. Businesses tried to cut costs by using fewer people to do the same work. This practice is known as **downsizing.** While downsizing increased business profits, it also left more people out of work.

These conditions combined to create a recession. A **recession** is an economic slump that is milder than a depression. The recession continued for more than a year.

A More Conservative Supreme Court

Both Bush and Reagan had a chance to extend the conservative revolution to the Supreme Court. Between them, they appointed five Supreme Court Justices. The new Justices were more conservative than the ones they replaced. One of Reagan's choices was **Sandra Day O'Connor,** the first woman to serve on the Supreme Court.

In several major decisions, the Court showed its more conservative bent. During the 1960s, the Court had expanded the rights of people accused of crimes. In the 1980s, the Court placed new limits on the rights of suspected criminals. It also limited the rights of prisoners to appeal their convictions.

The Court also became more conservative in the area of civil rights. Since the 1960s, many communities had tried to achieve school integration by busing black or white students to schools outside their own communities. In the 1980s, the Supreme Court cut back on busing. It also made it harder for workers to win job discrimination cases.

Clinton Takes Office

Running for reelection in 1992, President Bush faced a stiff challenge. The recession continued. Unemployment had risen to 7.8 percent—the highest level in eight years. In addition, many Americans were dissatisfied with the government. They charged that the President and Congress seemed unable to work together to solve the nation's problems.

A dissatisfied vote

The Democrats nominated **Bill Clinton,** governor of Arkansas, as their candidate for

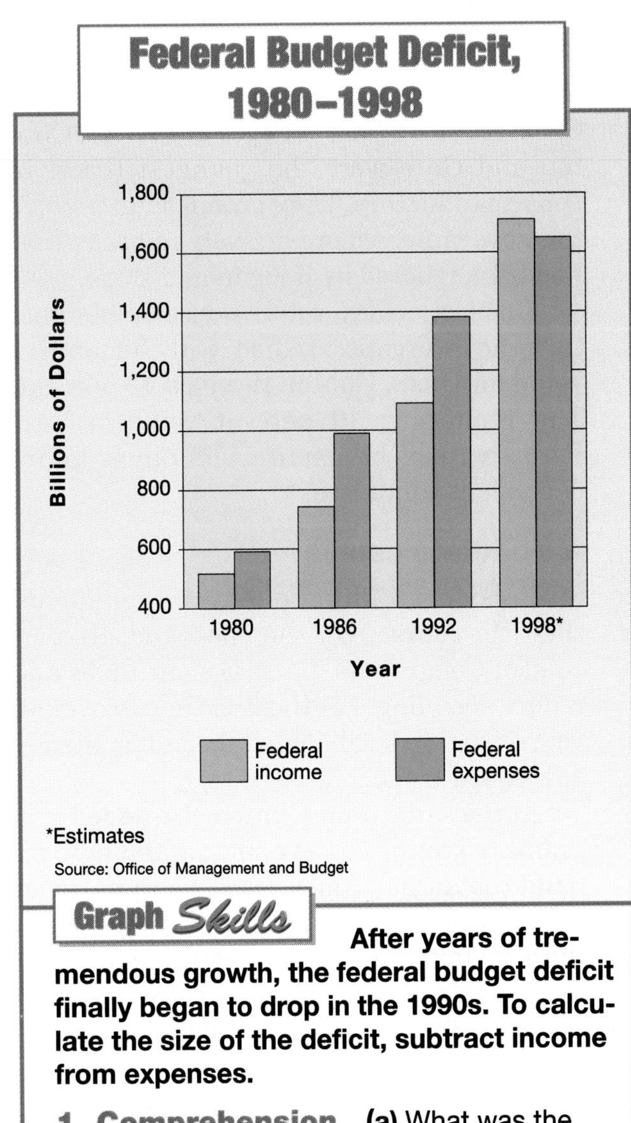

Graph Skills **After years of tremendous growth, the federal budget deficit finally began to drop in the 1990s. To calculate the size of the deficit, subtract income from expenses.**

1. **Comprehension** **(a)** What was the budget deficit in 1980? In 1992? **(b)** What happened to the deficit between 1992 and 1998?
2. **Critical Thinking** Why did the deficit increase during the 1980s?

Economics

Reforming the Welfare System

In 1996, President Bill Clinton signed a controversial welfare reform bill. It overhauled a long-standing system of cash payments to the poor. Clinton is joined by three women who had gotten off welfare and gone to work. ★ **What was the goal of welfare reform? Why did some people oppose it?**

President. His running mate was Tennessee Senator Albert Gore. At ages 46 and 44, Clinton and Gore were the youngest ticket in American history. They promised to involve the government more actively in areas that had been ignored by Reagan and Bush.

On election day, voters sent a clear signal that they were dissatisfied. Only 38 percent voted for Bush. Clinton received 43 percent. The remaining 19 percent went to Ross Perot, a Texas billionaire who ran as an independent candidate.

A moderate course

President Clinton pursued a middle-of-the-road course. On the one hand, he persuaded Congress to increase some taxes and reduce spending. For the first time in over 40 years, the federal deficit began a steady downward trend.

At the same time, Clinton also added programs to stimulate the economy and help rebuild the nation. Americorps was a national service program like the Peace Corps. More than 20,000 young Americorps volunteers worked in communities across the nation in exchange for college tuition aid.

The President pushed hardest to reform the American health care system. In 1994, some 37 million Americans had no health insurance. Even those with insurance faced sharply rising costs for medical care. Clinton appointed a team headed by his wife, **Hillary Rodham Clinton,** to draw up reforms. The First Lady had been a prominent lawyer.

The Clinton plan called for a national system guaranteeing health insurance for almost all Americans. After heated debate, however, Congress defeated the President's proposals. Many Americans worried that the plan would prove too costly and involve the government too deeply in people's lives.

Conservatives at High Tide

The health care debate fueled voter discontent. Critics of the plan charged that the Clintons were trying to return to "big government." Supporters, on the other hand, were frustrated that a Democratic President and a Democratic Congress had not been able to pass a key program.

When voters went to the polls in November 1994, they gave the Republicans a resounding victory. For the first time since the 1950s, the Republicans held a majority in both the Senate and the House of Representatives. "It was a revolution," cheered Toby Roth, a Wisconsin Republican.

The Republican program

Republican **Newt Gingrich** of Georgia became Speaker of the House. Under his leadership, the House quickly drew up legislation designed to reduce social welfare programs, such as food stamps. Other bills cut back on environmental regulations, to make it easier for businesses to expand. At the same time, Republicans proposed a $245 billion tax cut.

President Clinton attacked many of the proposals as unfair to poor and middle-class Americans. He vetoed the Republican budget. Angrily, Republicans cut off funds, forcing government agencies to close for several weeks. As time wore on and the government remained shut down, public opinion slowly turned against the new Congress.

In the end, Congress compromised with the President. It agreed on a spending plan to balance the federal budget by the year 2002. It also enacted laws to fight crime and drugs and to promote education.

Congress and Clinton also agreed on a major overhaul of the welfare system. The government limited the amount of welfare benefits available. In this way, it hoped to encourage unemployed Americans to find jobs. President Clinton noted:

> "I've been in welfare offices, I've talked to lots of folks on welfare.... Nearly everybody who is on it wants to be off. Nearly everybody who is not working is willing to work."

Critics complained that the welfare reform bill failed to guarantee aid to poor children and cut spending on food stamps. Most Americans, however, agreed that some reform was necessary. Clinton encouraged businesses to provide job training for people trying to move from welfare to work.

Clinton's second term

In 1996, Clinton easily won reelection against former Senator Robert Dole of Kansas. For the time being, it seemed that most voters wanted a smaller federal government. Yet they were not ready to accept all of Gingrich's "revolutionary" changes.

A booming economy helped keep many Americans satisfied with Clinton's middle-of-the-road course. By May 1998, unemployment had dropped to 4.3 percent, the lowest since 1970. The stock market hit record highs. By 1998, ahead of schedule, the federal government balanced its budget.

Despite good economic news, the President came under attack in several areas. A government prosecutor investigated whether the Clintons had received illegal special treatment in real estate deals made during the 1980s. In 1998, the investigation expanded into the President's personal conduct. Despite the controversy, polls showed that most Americans supported Clinton.

★Section 1 Review ★

Recall

1. **Identify** **(a)** Barry Goldwater, **(b)** Moral Majority, **(c)** Reaganomics, **(d)** George Bush, **(e)** Sandra Day O'Connor, **(f)** Bill Clinton, **(g)** Hillary Rodham Clinton, **(h)** Newt Gingrich.
2. **Define** **(a)** deregulation, **(b)** balanced budget, **(c)** downsizing, **(d)** recession.

Comprehension

3. Describe two ideas or values of the conservatives of the 1980s.
4. **(a)** Describe Reagan's economic policies. **(b)** What were the results of these policies?
5. **(a)** What economic policies did Clinton follow? **(b)** What were the results of these policies?

Critical Thinking and Writing

6. **Applying Information** **(a)** How did Reagan and Bush affect the Supreme Court? **(b)** Why is naming Supreme Court Justices one of the President's most important powers?
7. **Synthesizing Information** Why are President Reagan's years in office called a "conservative revolution"?

Activity **Composing Slogans** You want to be a campaign consultant during the next presidential election. When you apply for the job, you are asked to demonstrate your skills. Do so by writing three slogans that could have been used in the campaigns of Reagan, Bush, and Clinton.

The Post–Cold War World

As You Read

Explore These Questions

- How did the United States become involved in Bosnia?
- What attempts were made to limit nuclear arms?
- How did the end of the Cold War affect the role of the United States in the world?

Define

- sanctions
- apartheid

Identify

- Dayton Accord
- Nelson Mandela
- George Mitchell

SETTING the Scene On a wintry day in January 1998, Staff Sergeant Paul Correale patrolled the streets of Olovo. The village, in the Eastern European nation of Bosnia, was thousands of miles from Correale's home in Ohio. All around him, he saw scenes of horrifying destruction. Nearly every home and store had been damaged or destroyed by shelling.

Unlike other American military actions of the past 50 years, Correale's mission was not part of the Cold War. Instead of fighting communist guerrillas, he was helping keep the peace after a bloody civil war. In Olovo, American troops had helped to reopen the village's only hospital.

As the Cold War faded, conflicts in many areas of the globe still threatened the peace. During the 1990s, the United States worked with many nations in an effort to create a more stable, more democratic world.

Eastern Europe and the Former Soviet Union

As you read, the Soviet Union split apart in 1991. American leaders anxiously watched the former Soviet republics and the nations of Eastern Europe. How would these nations adapt to their new freedom?

Under communism, governments had owned all major businesses and industries. The transition to a free-market economy was not easy. As governments gradually sold off businesses to private enterprise, inflation and unemployment rose.

In Russia, hard times and ethnic unrest led to a revival of the Communist party. In 1995, communists won many seats in the Russian parliament. Still, the next year, Russians voted to continue moving toward a free-market economy. President Clinton supported Russian president Boris Yeltsin in his efforts to built a stable democracy.

Civil war in Bosnia

In Eastern Europe, Yugoslavia faced the most serious crisis. Yugoslavia was made up of several republics, including Croatia, Serbia, and Bosnia-Herzegovina. After the fall of communism, rivalries stirred among the nation's many ethnic groups. In 1991, Croatia and Bosnia declared their independence. However, Serbs in Croatia and Bosnia wanted to remain part of Yugoslavia. With help from Serbia, they began fighting to prevent the new governments from splitting away.

The civil war dragged on for four years. Cities were destroyed and two million people were forced to flee their homes. More than 250,000 people died. Zlata Filipovic, an 11-year-old native of Serbia, wrote in her diary:

> “Today a shell fell on the park in front of my house, the park where I used to play and sit with my girlfriends. A lot of people were hurt... AND NINA IS DEAD.... She was such a nice, sweet girl.”

Beginning in 1992, Serbs forced tens of thousands of Bosnian Muslims into detention camps. They called this practice "ethnic

Bosnian women and children at a refugee camp

Viewing HISTORY **American Troops in Bosnia**

The United States joined UN efforts to end the bloody civil war in Bosnia. One Muslim refugee said, "We hope that Americans will take us back to our homes." Above, American soldiers patrol a bombed-out town.

★ **How did the fall of communism contribute to the outbreak of civil war?**

cleansing." Other reports, however, claimed that the Serbs were carrying out mass executions. The War Crimes Tribunal, located in the Netherlands, charged more than 50 Serbs with murder, torture, and other "crimes against humanity."

Serious peace talks began only after Muslim and Croatian forces began to win back territory. In November 1995, the United States hosted peace talks at an air base in Dayton, Ohio. The **Dayton Accord** called for Bosnia to remain a single nation, but to be governed as two separate republics.

To help guarantee the peace, President Clinton sent about 20,000 American ground troops to Bosnia. There, they joined NATO and Russian forces in a peacekeeping mission. The troops helped restore order and rebuild roads and schools. In 1997, Clinton asked Congress to extend the peacekeeping mission beyond June 1998.

Changes for NATO

As the Cold War ended, Americans and Europeans debated the role of the North Atlantic Treaty Organization. NATO had been formed to protect European nations against Soviet expansion. (See page 769.)

In 1997, NATO invited Hungary, the Czech Republic, and Poland to become members. These former communist countries were making a successful transition to a free-market economy. Russia objected to the idea of expanding NATO. Its leaders worried that Russia's former allies might make NATO too powerful. Some American leaders also opposed the expansion of NATO. With the Cold War over, they argued, there was no need to supply Eastern Europe with military aid.

In 1998, the Senate approved the proposal to expand NATO. Still, only 5 of the 16 NATO members had voted for expansion. The others continued to debate the measure.

Limiting Nuclear Arms

The end of the Cold War presented other challenges. One major issue involved the thousands of missiles that the Soviet Union and the United States had stockpiled.

Linking History and Technology

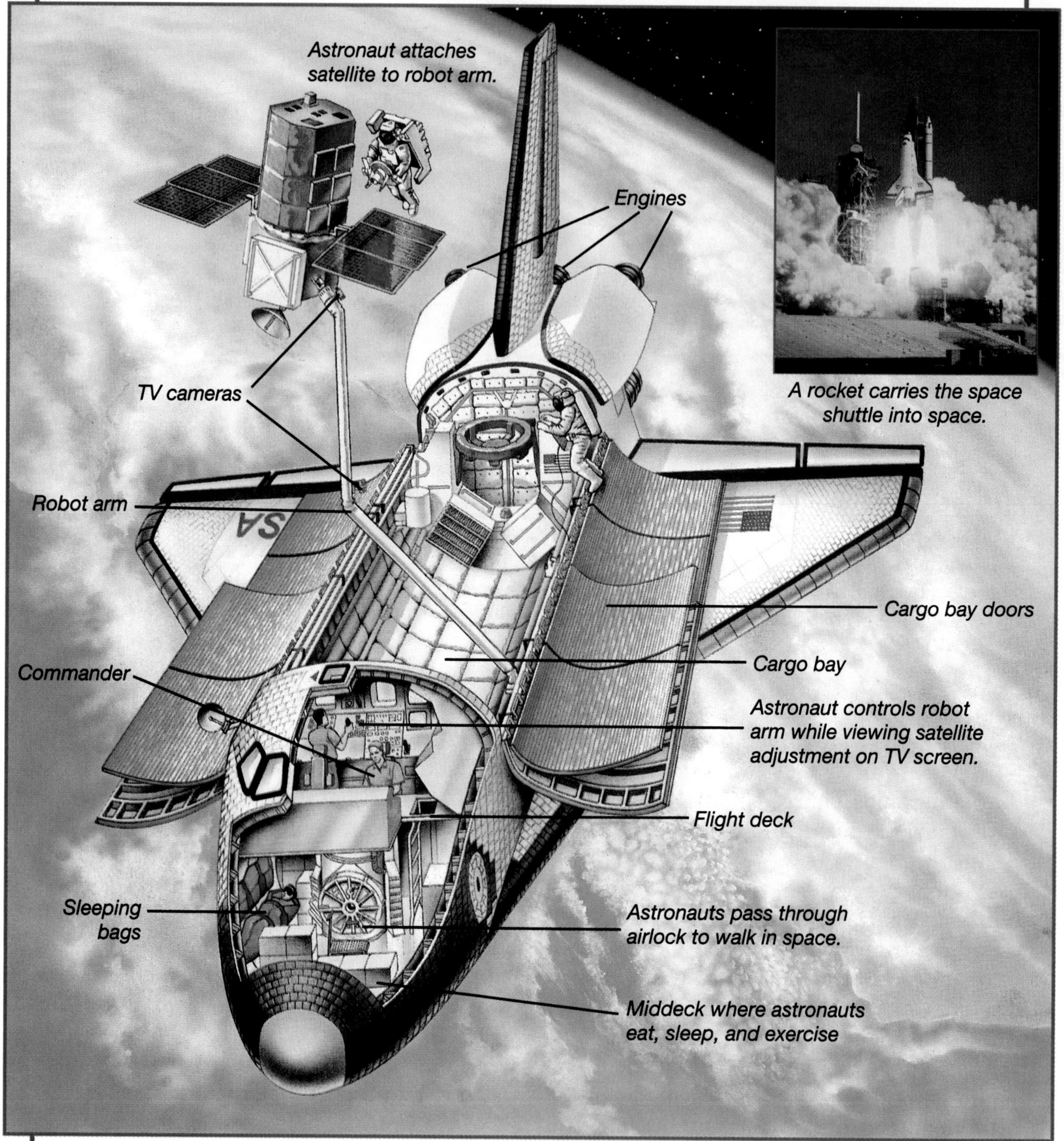

A rocket carries the space shuttle into space.

The Space Shuttle

During the Cold War, the United States developed space technology to win a "space race" with the Soviet Union. Today, American space shuttles perform a variety of peaceful tasks, from medical testing to launching communication satellites. After each mission, the shuttle returns to Earth, landing on a giant runway. ★ **Early space capsules "splashed down" in the ocean, where they were retrieved by ships. What are the advantages of a reusable spacecraft that can travel on its own power?**

Ending the arms race

Before the Soviet Union disbanded, it had already agreed to several treaties with the United States to reduce nuclear arms. The most important was the Strategic Arms Reduction Treaty, or START. The two powers signed START in 1991.

Russia later agreed to even greater reductions. The START II Treaty of 1993 cut the number of American and Russian missiles by one third. Both nations began destroying weapons, as inspection teams looked on.

The breakup of the Soviet Union complicated disarmament. For example, the former Soviet republic of Ukraine became an independent nation. Yet many nuclear missiles remained on Ukrainian territory. In 1994, Ukraine agreed to turn over its missiles to Russia to be destroyed.

New threats

Despite such progress, some other nations had begun to develop nuclear weapons. Britain, France, and China had all developed nuclear weapons during the Cold War. American intelligence agencies believed that Israel, Iran, Iraq, and North Korea also had atomic weapons programs.

In 1996, the Clinton administration helped to draft the Comprehensive Nuclear Test Ban Treaty. Its goal was to ban further testing of nuclear weapons. India and Pakistan, however, refused to sign the treaty. The two neighboring South Asian nations were long-standing enemies.

Then, in 1998, India announced that it had conducted five nuclear tests. A few weeks later, Pakistan exploded five of its own nuclear devices. "Today, we have evened the score with India," boasted Pakistan's prime minister. Other world leaders, however, condemned the tests as the beginning of a dangerous new arms race.

President Clinton called for economic sanctions against both India and Pakistan. **Sanctions** are actions taken against a country in an effort to force a change in its policy. The United States said it would block loans that had been promised to Pakistan and India.

The Spread of Freedom

During the Cold War, the United States and its allies called themselves "the free world." The name referred to political freedom. It also referred to economic freedom, where companies and individuals could compete with less interference from the state.

During the 1980s and 1990s, more nations followed the path toward greater freedom. The United States encouraged this trend.

South Africa

In 1948, the government of South Africa began enforcing a policy of **apartheid** (uh PAHR tayt), or strict separation of races. The nation's nonwhite majority was segregated and allowed no voice in the government.

In 1986, Congress approved economic sanctions against South Africa. The law forbade American companies to invest in South Africa or import South African products. The United Nations also pressured South Africa to end apartheid.

Viewing History **The Spread of Freedom**

By 1990, democratic reforms were shaking the Soviet Union and Eastern Europe. At the same time, South Africa was taking steps to end its system of racial separation. This cartoon from a Kentucky newspaper comments on these two victories for freedom. ★ **Why does the cartoonist show apartheid and communism as dinosaurs?**

Struggle for Democracy in China

In 1989, young demonstrators like these rallied to demand democratic reforms in China. An estimated one million people took to the streets of Beijing, the Chinese capital. ★ **How did the Chinese communist government respond to the prodemocracy demonstrations?**

By the 1990s, South Africa was taking steps to end apartheid. Under a new constitution, elections were held in 1994. All races were permitted to vote. **Nelson Mandela,** a black who had spent 28 years in prison for his opposition to apartheid, became the new president. Americans applauded the move toward democracy in South Africa.

Asian nations

Democracy also made headway in the Philippines. In 1986, thousands of Filipinos protested the rule of dictator Ferdinand Marcos. They accused Marcos of fraud in a recent election. Proclaiming "people power," they refused to recognize Marcos as president. When the army supported the people, Marcos fled. The United States backed Corazon Aquino, the woman who had run against him. During the 1990s, the United States continued to provide economic aid for the young Filipino democracy.

Other nations in Asia had mixed success with political reforms. During the 1970s, South Korea developed a booming economy, but its government remained undemocratic. In 1987, after fierce protests by students and other citizens, the government allowed more democratic elections.

In May 1998, violent protests shook Indonesia when that nation's economy faltered. Many Indonesians resented widespread corruption. Under pressure, Indonesia's president resigned after ruling for 30 years. His successor pledged to hold new elections.

China's struggle

During the 1980s, the communist government of China took some steps to build a free-market economy. However, Chinese leaders refused to accept political reforms.

In 1989, students and workers launched a bold campaign to bring democracy to China. Hundreds of thousands gathered at Tiananmen Square in the nation's capital, Beijing. However, the army crushed the demonstrations. Many people were killed or arrested.

President Bush disapproved of the crackdown, but he did not take strong action against the Chinese government. Instead, he hoped to influence China by keeping communication open. President Clinton followed a similar policy. On a 1998 visit to China, he pledged to strengthen ties between the two nations. At the same time, he publicly debated human rights issues with China's president.

Other communist nations

Other communist nations that refused to reform their systems faced hard times. North Korea's people faced severe famine during the 1990s. To encourage North Korea to make reforms, the United States and the UN provided famine relief.

In Cuba, Fidel Castro remained as president 40 years after coming to power. During that time, the United States had enforced a trade embargo against Cuba. With the fall of the Soviet Union, Cuba lost its main source of trade and economic aid. As the Cuban economy worsened, more than 30,000 Cubans fled by boat to the United States.

In 1994, the United States signed an agreement with Cuba to allow Cubans to emigrate more freely. The United States continued to enforce its embargo, but Americans debated whether to open up trade with Cuba.

The Last Superpower

With the Soviet Union gone, the United States became the world's remaining superpower. Some Americans hoped the country would take the opportunity to reduce its role in world affairs. "In the post–Cold War world, we will no longer require our people to carry an unfair burden for the rest of humanity," said Representative Dana Rohrabacher.

Others argued that the nation had a responsibility to use its power when needed. "The U.S. must lead, period," declared Speaker Gingrich. President Clinton said:

> "If we are going to . . . lead abroad, we have to overcome a dangerous and growing temptation in our own land to focus solely on the problems we face here in America. The new isolationists must not be allowed to pull America out of the game."

Both President Bush and President Clinton used United States influence to help bring stability to war-torn regions, such as Bosnia. In 1992, American forces led a United Nations mission to Somalia in eastern Africa. They distributed food during a famine caused by civil war. In 1994, American troops joined a UN mission to the Caribbean nation of Haiti. They forced out military dictators who had seized power. The UN then restored an elected president.

The United States also used diplomacy to bring about peace. In Northern Ireland, religious strife divided the land. Many Catholics wanted the region to be reunited with the rest of Ireland. Most Protestants wanted to remain under British rule. From 1969 to 1998, more than 3,000 people were killed by police, rival armies, and terrorist bombings. To help with peace talks, President Clinton sent former Senator **George Mitchell** of Maine to Ireland. Mitchell's negotiations helped produce a peace agreement in April 1998.

★ Section 2 Review ★

Recall

1. **Locate** **(a)** Bosnia-Herzegovina, **(b)** India, **(c)** Pakistan, **(d)** South Africa, **(e)** the Philippines, **(f)** China, **(g)** Cuba, **(h)** Northern Ireland.
2. **Identify** **(a)** Dayton Accord, **(b)** Nelson Mandela, **(c)** George Mitchell.
3. **Define** **(a)** sanctions, **(b)** apartheid.

Comprehension

4. **(a)** Why did civil war break out in Bosnia? **(b)** What role did American troops play there?
5. What agreements did the United States and Russia make regarding nuclear weapons?
6. Give two examples of how the United States used its power to promote democracy and stability.

Critical Thinking and Writing

7. **Identifying Alternatives** **(a)** How did President Bush respond when China crushed the prodemocracy movement? **(b)** What other actions might he have taken?
8. **Linking Past and Present** Review pages 664–665. How was the debate on foreign policy after World War I similar to that after the Cold War?

Activity **Writing a Letter** Write a letter to Zlata Filipovic (see page 832) to express your sympathy for her suffering. In your letter, explain what the United States might do to end the conflict in her region, and why.

3 War and Peace in the Middle East

Explore These Questions

- Why did an oil shortage occur in the United States in 1973?
- How did the United States help promote peace between Israel and Palestinian Arabs?
- Why did the United States go to war against Iraq?

Identify

- OPEC
- Camp David Accords
- Palestine Liberation Organization
- Yasir Arafat
- Saddam Hussein
- Persian Gulf War

In the fall of 1973, American motorists got a shock. Signs in front of many service stations announced, "Sorry, No Gas Today." At stations that did have gas, cars lined up for blocks.

The gas lines came about when nations in the Middle East cut back on the amount of oil they exported. Americans suddenly discovered how much events in faraway lands could affect their lives. In many different ways, conflicts in the Middle East have posed a challenge for American foreign policy.

A Vital Region

The Middle East has long been one of the "crossroads of the world," linking Africa, Asia, and Europe. The region was the birthplace of three major religions: Judaism, Christianity, and Islam. Over the centuries, tensions among various religious groups have often led to violence. The Middle East is also the focus of world attention because it has large oil reserves.

In dealing with the Middle East, the United States has had to balance conflicting interests. It has strongly supported Israel, the Jewish state created in 1948. Yet it has also tried to maintain ties with the Arab states that have opposed Israel.

Israel and Its Arab Neighbors

In the late 1800s, European Jews began to arrive in Palestine, a region along the Mediterranean coast. They hoped to create a Jewish state in the ancient home of their people. The number of Jewish settlers increased in the 1930s as European Jews fled Nazi persecution. (See page 732.)

In 1948, Jewish residents of Palestine announced the creation of the state of Israel. The United Nations recognized the new state. So did the United States and other nations.

Arab-Israeli Wars

The Arabs who lived in Palestine and the Arab nations bordering Israel refused to recognize Israel. To do so would have meant giving up Arab claims to the land. Determined to resist, they attacked the new state.

Israel won the 1948 war. It even added to its territory. After 1948, more than 500,000 Arabs fled Palestine. These Palestinians gathered in refugee camps in Jordan, Lebanon, and Syria. (See the map on page 839.)

Israel again defeated its Arab neighbors in 1967 and in 1973. As a result of these wars, Israel won control of lands from Egypt, Jordan, and Syria. Arabs referred to these lands as the "occupied territories."

The United States supported Israel with arms and supplies in the 1973 war. In response, Arab members of **OPEC,** the Organization of Petroleum Exporting Countries, cut off oil shipments to the United States. They also slowed down oil production. This caused oil shortages and higher oil prices all over the world. The oil embargo showed that the Arab states were willing to use oil as an economic weapon. The Arab nations lifted the oil embargo in 1974.

Camp David Accords

In 1977, Egyptian president Anwar el-Sadat became the first Arab head of state ever to visit Israel. His visit led to a series of peace talks between the two nations.

When talks threatened to break down, President Jimmy Carter stepped in. He invited Sadat and Israeli Prime Minister Menachem Begin (muh NAHK uhm BAY gihn) to Camp David, the President's retreat in Maryland. After nearly two weeks, Israel agreed to a timetable to return the Sinai Peninsula to Egypt. In turn, Egypt agreed to recognize the state of Israel. As a result of the **Camp David Accords,** Sadat and Begin signed a peace treaty in 1979.

The Palestinians

Palestinian Arabs continued to wage a guerrilla war against Israel. Most Palestinians lived in the occupied territories or in

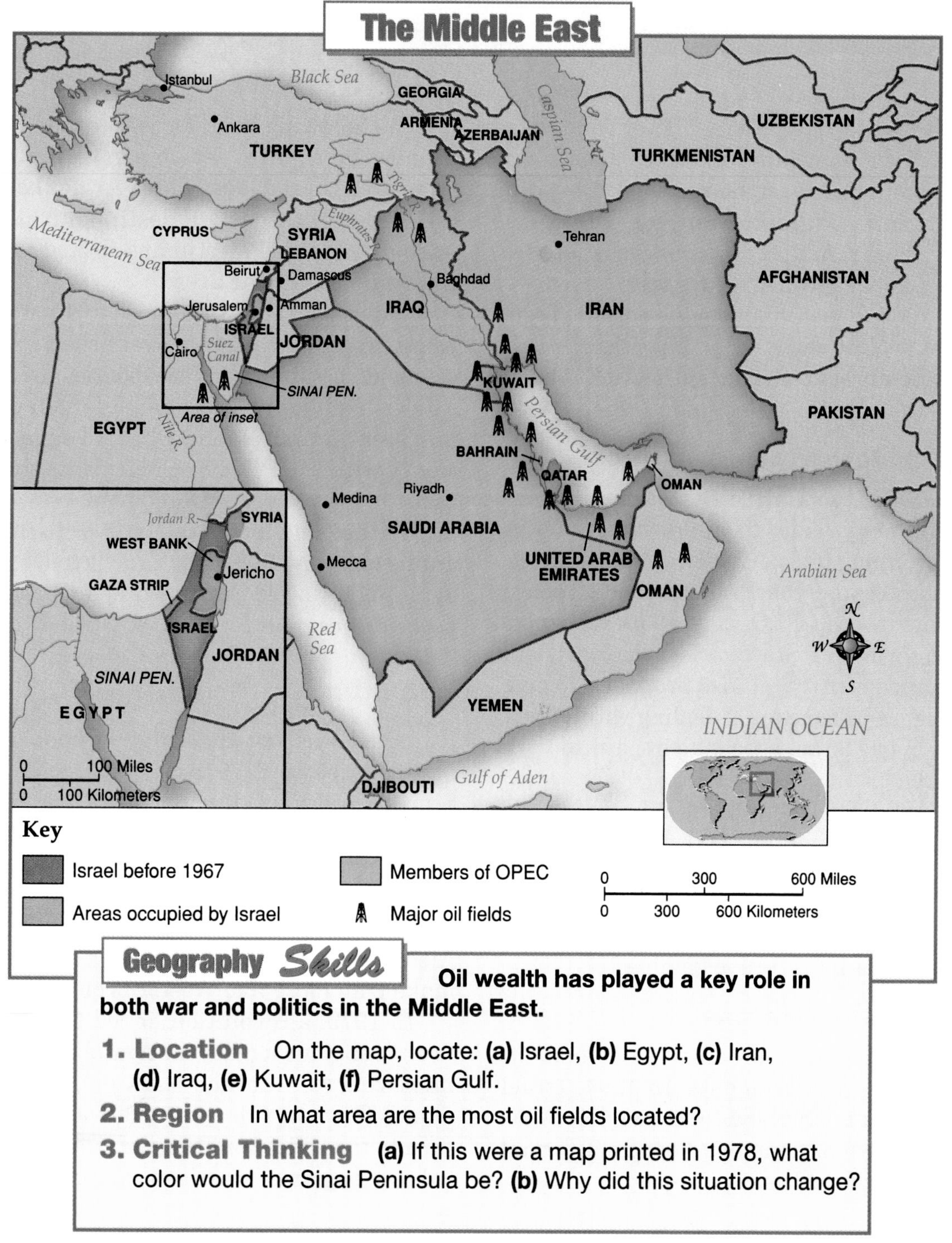

Geography Skills **Oil wealth has played a key role in both war and politics in the Middle East.**

1. **Location** On the map, locate: **(a)** Israel, **(b)** Egypt, **(c)** Iran, **(d)** Iraq, **(e)** Kuwait, **(f)** Persian Gulf.
2. **Region** In what area are the most oil fields located?
3. **Critical Thinking** **(a)** If this were a map printed in 1978, what color would the Sinai Peninsula be? **(b)** Why did this situation change?

Viewing HISTORY **Allies in the Persian Gulf War**

The United States has often been in conflict with Arab nations. During the Persian Gulf War of 1991, however, many Arab nations joined the United States in an alliance against Iraq. Here, an American cares for a wounded Saudi Arabian soldier. ★ **Why was Saudi Arabia concerned about Iraq's invasion of Kuwait?**

refugee camps outside Israel. They wanted to live in their homeland under a Palestinian government. Many supported the **Palestine Liberation Organization,** or PLO. Its leader, **Yasir Arafat,** announced that the PLO's goal was to destroy Israel.

In 1987, Palestinians in the occupied territories took to the streets to protest Israeli rule. The unrest called attention to the need for solutions to the Palestinian issue.

The road toward peace

In 1991, the United States finally persuaded the two sides to sit down together at the bargaining table. After two years of meetings, Israel and the PLO reached a peace agreement. The PLO agreed to recognize "the right of the State of Israel to exist in peace and security." It also promised to give up violence as a means of dealing with Israel. For its part, Israel agreed to negotiate with the PLO.

In 1993, President Clinton hosted a ceremony in Washington, D.C. Israel and the PLO signed a pact granting self-rule to Palestinians in the Gaza Strip and in Jericho on the West Bank. Clinton praised the two sides for making a "brave gamble."

Progress and setbacks

As the peace process continued, it brought new achievements. In 1994, Israel signed a peace treaty with its neighbor Jordan. The two nations had been in a formal state of war for 46 years.

The following year, Israel granted Palestinians the right to set up a government in some areas of the West Bank. Arafat became the leader of the new Palestinian National Authority. Eager Palestinians elected a council to administer the area.

Radicals on both sides tried to disrupt the peace process. Arab groups launched a series of suicide bombings in Israeli cities. In 1995, a Jewish student assassinated Israeli prime minister Yitzhak Rabin, who had signed the treaty with the PLO. Such incidents showed that the road to peace would not be smooth.

By the time Israel celebrated its fiftieth anniversary in 1998, negotiations had slowed again. The United States worked to keep the peace process going.

Tensions With Iran

Israel was not the only hot spot in the Middle East. In 1979, a crisis flared in Iran. Since World War II, the United States had supported Iran's ruler, Shah Muhammad Reza Pahlavi, in part because he was anticommunist. Many Iranians, however, opposed the shah's harsh, undemocratic rule. Also, devout Muslims opposed his efforts to make Iran more like Western countries.

In 1979, a revolution forced the shah to flee. A religious leader, the Ayatollah Khomeini (i yuh TOH luh koh MAYN ee), took command. The new ruler wanted Iranians to return to the strict traditions of Islam. He also led a strong anti-American campaign.

In November 1979, President Carter let the shah enter the United States for medical treatment. Iranian revolutionaries responded by seizing the American embassy in Tehran, the Iranian capital. They took 53 American hostages. The hostages were not freed until January 1981.

Conflict With Iraq

In August 1990, **Saddam Hussein,** the dictator of Iraq, sent 100,000 troops to invade neighboring Kuwait. Kuwait is one of the richest oil producers in the Middle East. Before long, Iraqi forces were in control of Kuwait and its oil wells.

Persian Gulf War

President George Bush feared that the invasion was the start of a larger plan to gain control of the Middle East's oil. To prevent further Iraqi aggression, he sent American forces to Saudi Arabia. He also persuaded the UN to impose a trade boycott on Iraq. The United States and its allies set January 15, 1991, as the deadline for Iraq to withdraw from Kuwait. Hussein ignored the demand.

One day after the deadline passed, the UN allies launched an air attack on Iraq. In an operation dubbed "Desert Storm," troops from 28 nations—including Saudi Arabia, Syria, and Egypt—joined Americans in bombing missions against the Iraqi capital of Baghdad. Within 24 hours, the Iraqi air-defense missile systems and the Iraqi air force had been rendered all but useless.

Hussein swore to fight forever. Iraq, however, could not counter the superior technology of the UN forces. By the end of February, UN troops had driven the Iraqis out of Kuwait. The **Persian Gulf War** lasted only six weeks.

Aftermath of the war

The war weakened Iraq's military strength, but Saddam Hussein maintained a firm grip on power. He also continued his defiant stand against the United States and its allies. In 1997, he broke an agreement to let UN inspectors look for illegal biological and chemical weapons in Iraq. Hussein backed down only after President Clinton sent American warships to the Persian Gulf.

In the meantime, UN economic sanctions continued, preventing Iraq from importing needed goods or selling its oil abroad. Without oil income, Iraq suffered great hardships. Still, Hussein increased his support at home by blaming the United States for Iraq's economic problems.

★ Section 3 Review ★

Recall

1. **Locate** **(a)** Israel, **(b)** Iran, **(c)** Iraq, **(d)** Kuwait.
2. **Identify** **(a)** OPEC, **(b)** Camp David Accords, **(c)** Palestine Liberation Organization, **(d)** Yasir Arafat, **(e)** Saddam Hussein, **(f)** Persian Gulf War.

Comprehension

3. **(a)** Why did Arab nations cut off oil shipments to the United States in 1973? **(b)** What were the effects of the embargo?
4. What progress has been made toward peace between Israel and the Palestinian Arabs?
5. Describe the causes of the Persian Gulf War.

Critical Thinking and Writing

6. **Understanding Causes and Effects** How do you think the Middle East's large supplies of oil affect the way the United States responds to events there?
7. **Making Generalizations** Based on what you have read, make a generalization about the role of Saddam Hussein in Middle Eastern affairs. Give two facts to support your generalization.

Activity **Creating a Time Line** Make a time line of events in the Middle East starting in 1948. Use your time line to review the events discussed in this section. Include a symbol for events that involved the United States.

The Environment and the World Economy

As You Read

Explore These Questions

- What are the goals of the environmental movement?
- How have Americans tried to save energy?
- Why has the United States had to compete in a world economy?

Define

- environmentalist
- solar energy
- renewable resource
- global warming
- trade deficit

Identify

- Rachel Carson
- Environmental Protection Agency
- Earth Summit
- North American Free Trade Agreement

SETTING the Scene One night in May 1998, Elena Marin's son woke up coughing. Marin, a doctor in Texas, recognized the symptoms of asthma, a lung disease. She also knew the cause of the attack: the heavy smoke drifting across the border from Mexico.

After two years of drought, nearly 10,000 uncontrolled forest fires blazed in Mexico. Mexican officials urged residents to stay indoors. Texas authorities declared the air quality unhealthy across the entire state.

Some scientists warned that the drought might signal a dangerous change in the Earth's climate. Said one:

> "This may be a wake-up call.... Is it some kind of isolated event? I don't think so. It seems to be part of something much, much bigger."

Whatever the cause, the sooty clouds were a sober reminder that the United States and other nations needed to pay attention to the quality of the natural environment.

The Environmental Movement

In the early 1900s, a few Americans like Theodore Roosevelt stressed the need to protect the land and conserve natural resources. (See page 600.) By the 1960s, concern for the environment was growing stronger.

Marine biologist **Rachel Carson** helped focus attention on environmental dangers. In her 1962 book, *Silent Spring,* she charged that chemical pesticides were poisoning the land and water. Carson pictured a bleak future:

> "It was a spring without voices. On the mornings that had once throbbed with the dawn chorus of robins, catbirds, doves, jays, wrens ... there was now no sound; only silence lay over the fields and woods and marsh."

Reformers known as **environmentalists** began calling attention to a wide variety of environmental dangers. Chemical wastes turned rivers into sewers. Factory smokestacks belched foul-smelling fumes. People tossed litter along roads. Massive tankers ran aground, spilling oil into the sea.

The federal government responded to environmental concerns. In 1970, the Nixon administration created the **Environmental Protection Agency** (EPA) to lead the attack on pollution. The same year, Congress passed the Clean Air Act. It required automakers to clean up car exhausts. The Clean Water Act of 1972 fought pollution in rivers and lakes. The Waste Cleanup Act of 1980 created a "superfund" to clean up chemical dumps.

Local governments also took action to clean up the environment. Many communities required residents to recycle materials such as aluminum, glass, and paper. Recycling helped the environment in two ways. It reduced the amount of garbage that had to be buried or burned. It also slowed down the rate at which resources such as aluminum and trees were used up.

Still, the environmental movement has faced opposition. In the 1980s, President Reagan sought to ease environmental laws. He argued that overregulation placed too great a financial burden on American businesses. Often, environmental concerns must be balanced against economic needs. For example, environmentalists have sought to preserve forestland in Alaska and the Pacific Northwest from logging. Loggers, however, point out that forest products are vital to the nation's economy. Also, restrictions on logging may cost many people their jobs.

Energy Use

Environmentalists also directed attention to energy use in the United States. Americans make up only 5 percent of the total population of the world, yet they consume more than one fourth of its energy supply.

▼ *An American blue jay*

Conserving energy

The 1973 Arab oil embargo made Americans realize that the United States depended heavily on foreign energy sources. When oil shipments resumed, prices skyrocketed. Within 10 years, the fuel used by homes and industries cost four times as much as before the embargo. To cover added fuel costs, businesses increased the prices they charged for goods and services.

Americans tried to use less energy. Under government pressure, carmakers made autos that burned less gasoline. Homeowners added insulation to reduce the amount of fuel needed to heat or cool their homes. Environmentalists pointed out that conserving energy did more than save money. It also cut down on pollution.

Connections With Science

In the 1990s, automobile manufacturers began producing cars that ran on fuels other than gasoline. Alternative fuels included natural gas and methanol. Other experimental automobiles were powered by solar energy.

Biography **Rachel Carson**

Rachel Carson shocked the nation with her 1962 book, Silent Spring. *Carson warned that the pesticide DDT remained in the environment, killing birds and fish, and might eventually contaminate human food supplies. The book's popularity led President Kennedy to appoint a commission to study pesticides. Shortly after Carson died, Congress passed laws that restricted the use of DDT.* ★ **Review pages 593 and 599. How was *Silent Spring* similar to *The Jungle?***

New energy sources

Since the 1970s, Americans have sought to develop other sources of energy. Many factories have switched from oil to coal. The United States has nearly one fifth of the world's coal reserves. However, compared to oil, coal is a dirty fuel. Coal-burning plants must use "scrubbers" and other devices to reduce the smoke and acids they emit into the air. That adds to the cost of using coal.

Today, nuclear plants generate about one fifth of the nation's electric power. Still, nuclear power is costly, and it produces long-lasting radioactive wastes. An accident at a nuclear power plant could release harmful radioactive gases into the air. Carried by the wind, these gases could endanger people living hundreds of miles away.

Skills FOR LIFE

Critical Thinking | Managing Information | Communication | Maps, Charts, and Graphs

Using E-Mail

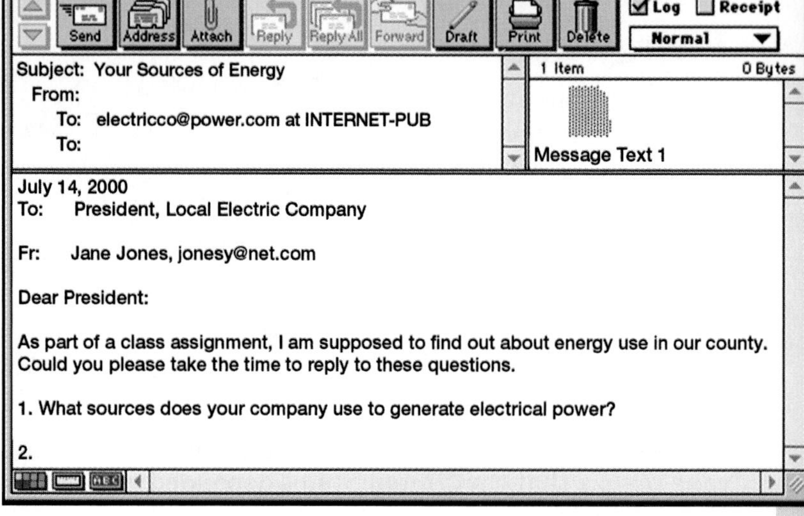

How Will I Use This Skill

The Internet allows us to have instant communication with people around the world. With its system of electronic mail, or e-mail, you can write to friends, newspapers, government officials, or even your favorite movie stars. In addition, more and more jobs today require the efficient use of e-mail.

LEARN the Skill

To send or receive messages by e-mail, use the following steps:

1. Click on the electronic mail icon. Sign on, or log in, with your password.
2. Address your message by typing in the e-mail address of the recipient. You may also give your message a title.
3. Write your message. Attach any document you may want to send. After you have written your message, read it over to make sure it says what you want it to say.
4. When you are satisfied with your message, click the Send icon. After the message is sent, you cannot change it.

PRACTICE the Skill

Use e-mail to gather information about energy use in your area.

1. Open the e-mail application on your computer and log in.
2. Type in the e-mail address of a local energy supplier, such as an electric or gas company. The address may be found on company advertisements, pamphlets, or bills. Give your message a title that describes the subject matter.
3. Ask questions about energy use. For example, you may want to find out what sources of energy the company uses, how the company sets a price for its use, or what the company is doing to safeguard the environment. Think of issues important to your household or community.
4. Make sure you check your message before it is sent. Include your e-mail address for a prompt reply.

APPLY the Skill

Use e-mail to make contact with a school in another part of the country. Form a team with two or three other students to select a school and create a list of questions about life in that state or city.

Scientists are working to harness **solar energy,** or power from the sun. Solar energy is appealing because it is renewable and clean. A **renewable resource** is one that can be quickly replaced by nature. However, for many uses solar energy remains expensive.

Wind is another renewable resource. Rows of windmills in the California hills create electricity for thousands of homes.

International Cooperation

Environmental problems do not stop at national borders. In 1992, world leaders met at the **Earth Summit** in Brazil. They focused on a number of key problems.

Global warming

In the 1980s and 1990s, a prolonged period of warmer-than-usual weather caused problems in many parts of the world. African countries suffered deadly droughts. China received unusually heavy rains.

Some scientists thought that the Earth's atmosphere was warming up. They concluded that human activities, such as driving cars and operating factories, were adding carbon dioxide to the atmosphere. Carbon dioxide holds in heat that would otherwise escape into space. The scientists predicted a slow but steady rise in the world's average temperature. **Global warming** might one day turn green fields into deserts!

Not all scientists agreed with the global warming theory. They pointed out that the Earth had gone through many cold and warm cycles in the past. Still, leaders at the Earth Summit pledged to reduce the amounts of carbon dioxide their countries released into the atmosphere. That goal, however, was hard to reach. Six years later, American carbon dioxide levels continued to rise.

Holes in the ozone layer

Miles above the Earth's surface is a layer of ozone gas. This ozone layer blocks out ultraviolet rays from the sun. Such rays can cause health problems such as skin cancer.

In the 1980s, scientists warned that gases used in homes and industries were creating holes in the ozone layer. The scientists pointed especially to gases used in aerosol cans, refrigerators, and air conditioners. Nations all over the world agreed to phase out the use of the dangerous gases.

Competing in a World Economy

The environment is only one area in which Americans have had to think beyond the borders of the United States. More than ever, American businesses sell products in a world marketplace. In 1970, foreign trade

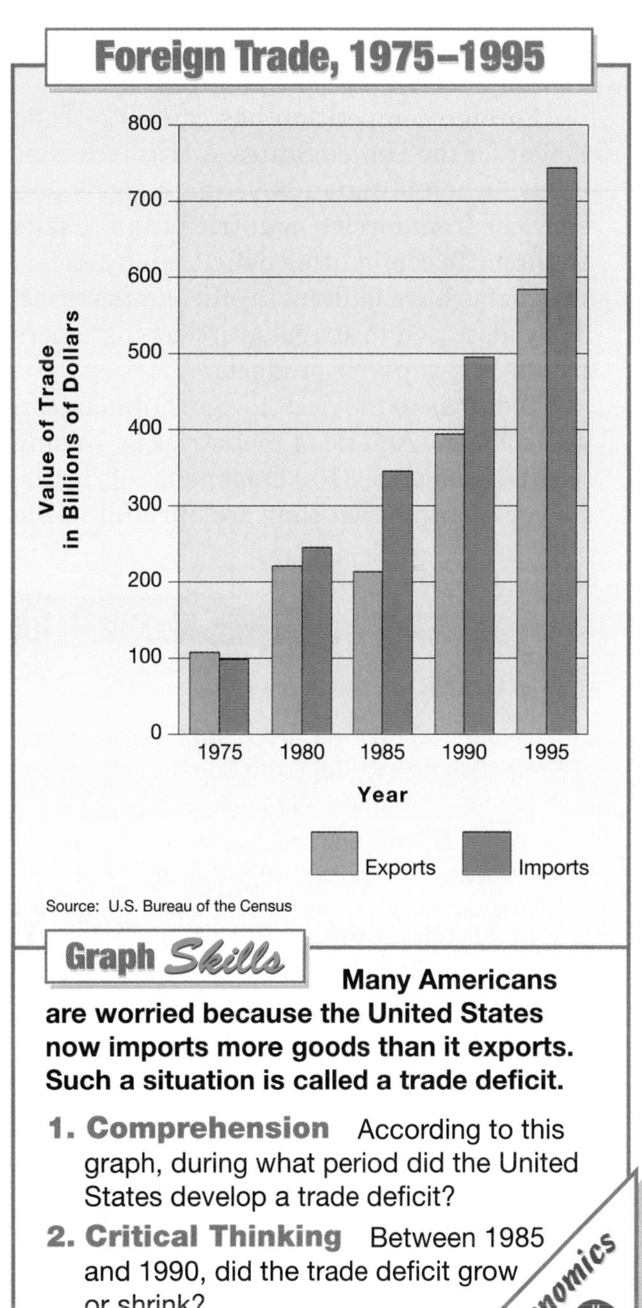

Graph Skills Many Americans are worried because the United States now imports more goods than it exports. Such a situation is called a trade deficit.

1. **Comprehension** According to this graph, during what period did the United States develop a trade deficit?
2. **Critical Thinking** Between 1985 and 1990, did the trade deficit grow or shrink?

Economics

made up only about 10 percent of the American economy. By 1997, foreign trade amounted to nearly 25 percent.

This symbol shows how NAFTA links the United States, Canada, and Mexico.

A growing trade deficit

In this growing world economy, the United States must compete with economic powers in Europe and Asia. Competition has posed some problems. For example, American companies pay their workers higher wages than companies in most other countries. As a result, many foreign products cost less than similar American products.

Foreign competition has caused a trade deficit for the United States. A **trade deficit** occurs when a nation buys more goods and services from foreign countries than it sells to them. To combat this deficit, many American firms have built more efficient factories. They also tried to attract overseas customers by offering superior products.

Today, as in the past, the government can protect some American industries by raising tariffs. (See page 310.) Opponents of tariffs, however, argue that they are harmful in the long term. Other nations respond with their own tariffs, leading to costly "trade wars."

Removing trade barriers

In 1993, after months of bitter debate, Congress ratified the **North American Free Trade Agreement** (NAFTA). The purpose of this treaty was to do away gradually with tariffs and other trade barriers among the United States and its neighbors, Canada and Mexico.

Overall, NAFTA encouraged new trade. Most economists agree that growing foreign trade created jobs and benefited the American economy.

However, critics pointed out that NAFTA hurt some industries. For example, carmakers moved many auto parts factories to Mexico, where wages were lower. Also, foreign countries did not enforce the same strict antipollution laws as the United States did.

In 1997, Congress refused to give President Clinton extra powers to negotiate more free-trade agreements. The debate over foreign trade continued into a new century.

★ Section 4 Review ★

Recall

1. **Identify** **(a)** Rachel Carson, **(b)** Environmental Protection Agency, **(c)** Earth Summit, **(d)** North American Free Trade Agreement.
2. **Define** **(a)** environmentalist, **(b)** solar energy, **(c)** renewable resource, **(d)** global warming, **(e)** trade deficit.

Comprehension

3. Describe two changes that came about as a result of the environmental movement.
4. **(a)** How did the oil embargo affect American attitudes toward energy use? **(b)** Identify two ways Americans tried to reduce dependence on foreign oil.
5. **(a)** What problems have American businesses faced in the world marketplace? **(b)** What steps have they taken to address these problems?

Critical Thinking and Writing

6. **Solving Problems** Why would many environmental problems be hard to solve without international cooperation? Give two examples.
7. **Understanding Causes and Effects** How did the United States develop a trade deficit?

Activity **Creating an Action Plan** Your community has asked you to join an environmental task force. To start off, list three actions that individual citizens like you can take to improve the environment.

A Diverse Nation

Explore These Questions

- How have Americans worked to win greater opportunities for all?
- How have immigration patterns changed in recent years?
- What challenges do Americans face as they move toward a new century?

Define

- mainstream
- refugee
- illegal alien

Identify

- American Indian Religious Freedom Act
- Colin Powell
- Jesse Jackson
- Madeleine Albright
- Americans With Disabilities Act
- Amy Tan
- Immigration Reform and Control Act

During the great wave of immigration in the early 1900s, many Americans proudly described their country as a "melting pot." They meant that people of different backgrounds blended into a single American culture.

Today, the United States is still one of the most diverse nations in the world. Civil rights leader Jesse Jackson commented:

> "America is not like a blanket—one piece of unbroken cloth, the same color, the same texture, the same size. America is more like a quilt—many patches, many pieces, many colors, many sizes, all woven and held together by a common thread."

Such diversity has brought its share of challenges. Various groups have sometimes had to struggle to protect their rights as citizens. At the same time, diversity has been a major source of pride for Americans.

Native Americans

After centuries of decline, the nation's Native American population is growing. By the year 2000, it would approach 2.5 million people. More than half live in urban areas. Another third live on reservations.

By 1970, the federal government had abandoned its policy of encouraging Indians to leave their reservations. (See page 821.) Instead, Native American tribes and organizations have won greater power to govern their own ways of life.

The Indian Education Act of 1972 focused attention on the unique educational needs of American Indians. Under the law, Indian parents became more involved in developing programs for their children in schools both on and off reservations. By taking courses on their history and traditions, said one parent, "our kids will grow up proud to be Indians."

In 1978, Congress passed the **American Indian Religious Freedom Act.** It directed federal agencies not to interfere with Native American religious practices. For example, the navy now allows Shoshone Indians to visit traditional healing springs on the China Lake Naval Weapons Center.

Connections With Arts

Many people have learned about life on Navajo reservation lands through the award-winning mystery novels of Tony Hillerman. The main characters in Hillerman's novels are Navajo tribal police officers. For his respectful portrayal of Indian life and customs, Hillerman was awarded the Navajo Tribe's Special Friend Award.

Biography **Colin Powell**

"I remember the feeling that you can't make it," Colin Powell told young people. "But you can." Powell was born in New York City's Harlem, the son of garment workers. Joining the army, he won a Purple Heart in Vietnam and eventually rose to be chairman of the Joint Chiefs of Staff. After retiring from the army, he headed a campaign to encourage Americans to volunteer for public service.

★ **A poll named Colin Powell as one of the most admired Americans among both blacks and whites. Why do you think this was so?**

Congress has also responded to Native American demands for control over artifacts from their past. A 1990 law requires museums to catalog the Indian objects in their collections. They must then give Indian groups a chance to reclaim such items as human remains and religious objects.

Indian groups have worked to develop economic independence. Many reservations set up banks, factories, and other businesses. As a result of the Tribal College Movement, a number of tribes opened their own colleges and universities.

African Americans

The civil rights movement of the 1950s and 1960s toppled many barriers. At the same time, many African Americans still work to win full equality in American society.

Success stories

In the 1980s and 1990s, African Americans made notable advances in politics and government. In 1989, Douglas Wilder of Virginia became the first black to be elected governor of a state. That same year, **Colin Powell** became chairman of the Joint Chiefs of Staff. General Powell helped plan the victory over Iraq in the Persian Gulf War.

Civil rights leader **Jesse Jackson** was a key contender for the Democratic presidential nomination in 1988. Jackson's Rainbow Coalition—made up of people of all colors working together for the good of all people—stressed the needs of the cities, nonwhites, farmers, and the unemployed.

The civil rights movement opened new jobs and educational opportunities to African Americans. As a result, by the 1990s, the black middle class was steadily growing. Some African Americans earned great success in the business world. Reginald Lewis, a Wall Street financier, became one of the nation's richest men.

Continuing issues

Despite such successes, many African Americans struggled against economic hardship. The wages of African Americans lagged behind those of whites. The unemployment rate for blacks was more than twice that for whites. At the same time, the number of African American students attending college was dropping.

Poverty and lack of education trapped many African Americans in urban slums. By the late 1990s, about 40 percent of African American children were living in poverty. Black and white leaders alike warned of a growing "underclass" of poorly educated, jobless blacks with few prospects of a better future.

Civil rights leaders such as Jesse Jackson charged that the nation's commitment to equal rights seemed to be slipping. They urged renewed attention to the problems of urban poverty and racial discrimination. In response, President Clinton appointed an advisory board in 1997 to develop a national dialogue on race. The board sponsored discussions across the nation.

Women Today

The women's rights movement has continued to press for equal treatment of women. It claims many successes.

In government

In government, women have taken increasingly prominent roles, especially on the local level. Across the nation, women became mayors or school board presidents or served on county commissions.

On the national level, more women won election to Congress. By the late 1990s, two of the nine Supreme Court Justices were women: Sandra Day O'Connor and Ruth Bader Ginsburg. In 1997, **Madeleine Albright** became the first woman to serve as secretary of state, the highest-ranking Cabinet post. Albright played a major role in shaping post–Cold War foreign policy.

In the workplace

By the 1990s, almost 60 percent of American women worked outside the home. Women held a wide range of jobs once closed to them, from police officers and firefighters to sportscasters and professional basketball players. Prodded by affirmative action programs, businesses hired and promoted many talented women. For the first time, women held large numbers of managerial and professional jobs.

Overall, women's incomes rose. The gap between women's and men's wages narrowed, but did not close. On average, women earned just 70 percent of what men earned. In many companies, women complained that a "glass ceiling" of invisible discrimination kept them out of the highest-paying positions.

At the same time, more and more households were headed by single women. Such households were likely to be poor. More than half the children in families headed by women lived below the poverty line. Working mothers also had the problem of finding affordable, adequate day care.

Americans With Disabilities

Americans with disabilities waged their own struggle for equal rights. In the past, people in wheelchairs had limited access to public transportation or buildings. Disabled rights organizations backed laws requiring reserved parking spaces, ramped curbs, and wheelchair lifts on buses.

Much of the support for disabled rights came from veterans of Vietnam or other wars. Many had lost limbs or become paralyzed serving their country. Now, they insisted on their right to make a living.

A 1975 law ensured access to public schools for children with disabilities. Some of these children have been **mainstreamed**, or placed in regular classes. Others attend small classes with specialized help.

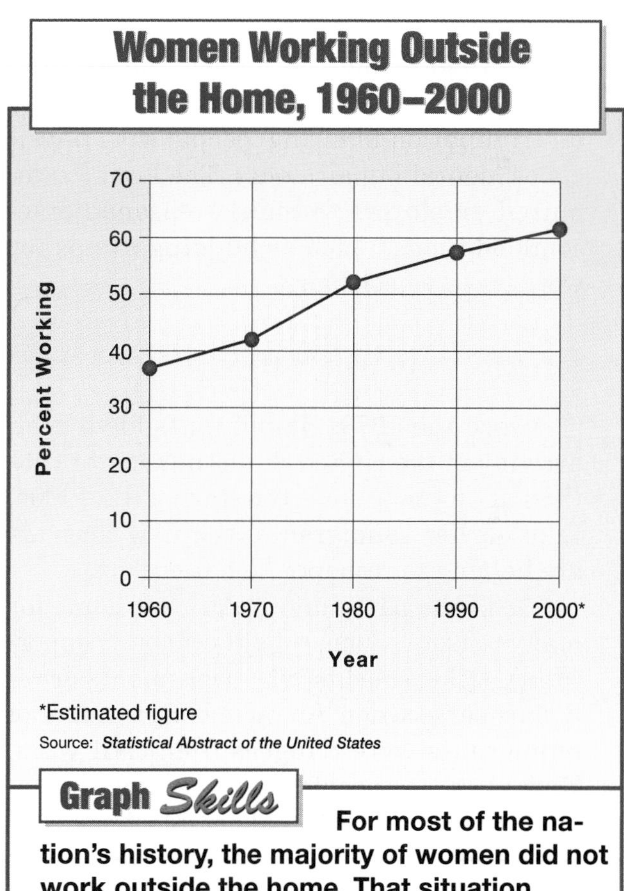

Graph Skills **For most of the nation's history, the majority of women did not work outside the home. That situation changed dramatically after the 1960s.**

1. **Comprehension** What percentage of American women worked outside the home in 1960? In 1980?
2. **Critical Thinking** During what decade did the percentage of women working outside the home increase the most?

Economics

Reserved parking sign ➤

Viewing HISTORY **Accommodating Americans With Disabilities**

Today, many laws require employers and public buildings to provide access for people with disabilities. These accommodations include reserved parking spaces and wheelchair ramps. Here, a worker in Cleveland, Ohio, goes to his office. ★ **How could ramps and parking spaces help people with disabilities achieve economic independence?**

In 1990, Congress passed the **Americans With Disabilities Act.** It outlawed discrimination in hiring people with physical or mental impairments. The law also required employers to make "reasonable accommodations," such as building ramps for workers in wheelchairs.

Immigration Continues

Since the 1970s, immigrants have been arriving in the United States at a faster rate than at any time since the start of the 1900s. Like earlier immigrants, the new arrivals are helping to reshape the nation.

As in the past, immigrants left home for many reasons. Some sought economic opportunity. Others fled harsh governments or religious persecution. An increasing number of immigrants were refugees from civil wars. **Refugees** are people who flee their homelands to seek safety elsewhere. Most refugees were women and children.

In 1965, Congress ended the quota system that began in the 1920s. (See page 695.) The old laws favored Europeans. New laws made it easier for non-Europeans to enter the country. Today, most immigrants come from Asia, Latin America, or the Caribbean.

Immigrants from Latin America

New immigrants arrived from Latin America. Some were refugees from civil wars in Nicaragua, El Salvador, and Guatemala during the 1980s. Others fled harsh governments in such places as Cuba and Chile. Still others came to escape rural poverty in Mexico, Brazil, and other nations. By the year 2000, people from Latin America and their descendants would be on their way to becoming the largest ethnic minority in the United States.

Hundreds of thousands of immigrants have also come from the islands of the Caribbean, such as Jamaica, the Dominican Republic, and Haiti. These people bring a rich mixture of African, European, Native American, and other backgrounds.

Immigrants from Asia

Wars and famines pushed many Asians to seek new homes in other parts of the world. As you read, after the Vietnam War, "boat people" from Southeast Asia sought refuge in the United States. (See page 785.) Other immigrants came from such places as the Philippines, India, and Korea. Asian Americans are now the nation's fastest-growing ethnic group.

New immigration patterns have fueled a debate over what it means to be American. Should immigrants assimilate into American society? How much should they preserve of their own cultures? Author **Amy Tan** depicted such mixed feelings in *The Joy Luck Club*. The novel looks at the lives and attitudes of Chinese-born mothers and their American-born daughters. Many are eager to adopt American ways, but do not want to abandon the traditions of their homeland.

New immigration policy

People who want to immigrate to the United States must apply for admission. Those with relatives in the United States or with valuable job skills are most likely to be accepted. Thousands of others, however, are turned down. Still others enter the nation without permission, becoming **illegal aliens.**

In 1986, Congress tried to reduce illegal immigration by passing the **Immigration Reform and Control Act.** The act allowed people who had arrived illegally before 1982 to remain and apply for citizenship. To discourage further illegal immigration, the act imposed stiff fines on employers who hire undocumented, or illegal, workers.

States with large immigrant populations found it increasingly expensive to provide education, medical care, and other services to illegal immigrants. In 1994, voters in California adopted a controversial law that banned schooling and most health services for illegal immigrants. The law faced a stiff challenge in the courts.

Two years later, Congress passed a new law that allowed local police to arrest illegal immigrants. It also nearly doubled the number of officials who patrol the borders where people try to enter illegally.

Challenges for Today and Tomorrow

Rushing toward the twenty-first century, Americans face both opportunities and challenges. They are adjusting to a changing world. At the same time, they are grappling with new challenges.

Substance abuse

One of the most serious social problems of the 1990s was the use and abuse of illegal drugs. Schools are still in the front lines in the war against drug abuse. They are trying to protect students from dangerous substances like cocaine and heroin.

Americans have been torn between two approaches to fighting illegal drugs. Some emphasize social problems that may lead to drug abuse. They favor setting up treatment centers to help drug users end their addictions. Other Americans see drug abuse as a criminal problem. They want stiffer penalties for drug dealers and users. Since 1980, the United States has spent billions of dollars pursuing drug smugglers and dealers. Yet drug abuse remains widespread.

One legal substance that has come under attack is nicotine, found in tobacco. In the 1990s, several states sued the large tobacco companies to recover money spent on treating smoking-related illnesses. The states

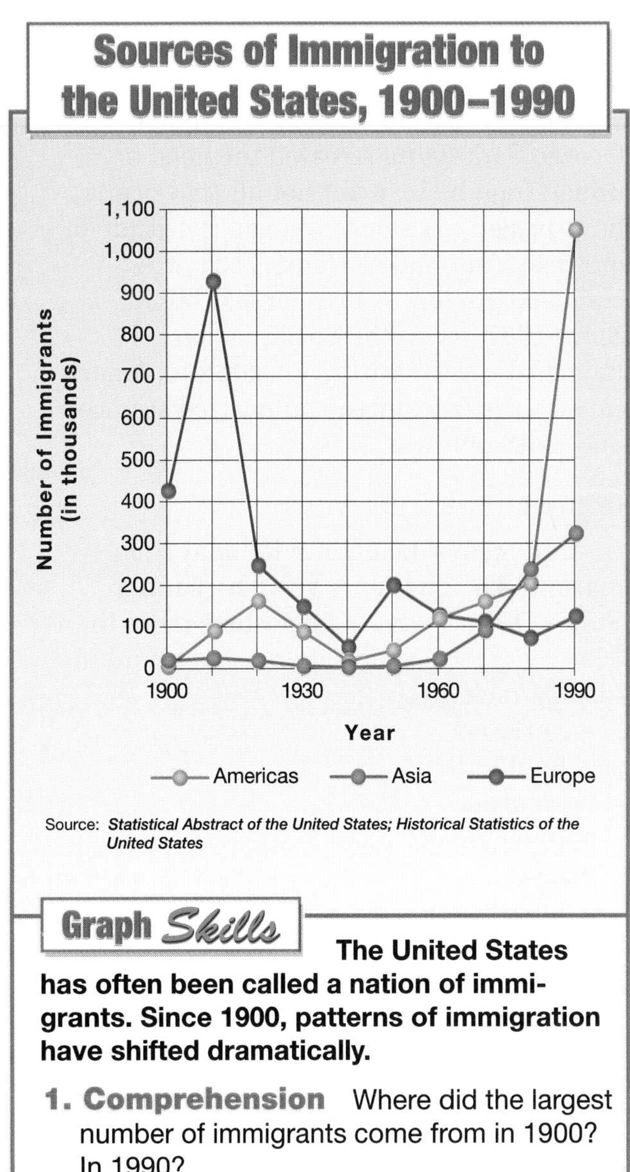

Source: *Statistical Abstract of the United States; Historical Statistics of the United States*

Graph Skills **The United States has often been called a nation of immigrants. Since 1900, patterns of immigration have shifted dramatically.**

1. **Comprehension** Where did the largest number of immigrants come from in 1900? In 1990?
2. **Critical Thinking** Why did immigration from Asia increase sharply after the 1960s?

Why Study History?

Because Knowing History May Help Your Career

To become an archaeologist, you need more than a shovel—you need a knowledge of history!

Historical Background

"Those who cannot remember the past are condemned to repeat it." With these words, Spanish American philosopher George Santayana stressed the need to understand history. Yet not all Americans have placed the same value on the study of our past. Automaker Henry Ford proclaimed, "History is more or less bunk." Since 1957, when the Soviet Union launched the first artificial satellite, American schools have often emphasized science and mathematics.

Connections to Today

Can history be helpful in today's job market? The answer is yes! The United States Department of Labor lists more than 30 careers for people with a background in history, including:

- Antiques
- Banking
- Insurance
- Journalism
- Law
- Library science
- Museum operations
- Publishing
- Research
- Teaching
- Tourism

Connections to You

Current statistics say that in the next century, people will change jobs at least five to seven times. This means that your education must prepare you for change. You will have to be adaptable, flexible, and creative. The skills you need to study history—researching, creative thinking, understanding causes and effects, recognizing other viewpoints—can be valuable no matter what career you finally choose.

1. **Comprehension** Identify two skills that the study of history can help you develop.
2. **Critical Thinking** Choose one career from the Department of Labor list above. Explain why you think knowledge of history might be helpful in that career.

Investigating Careers Do further research into one of the careers listed above. (Your school librarian can suggest resources.) Prepare a fact sheet summarizing the responsibilities of the job, the average pay range, and future opportunities in that field.

uncovered evidence that tobacco executives deliberately hid scientific studies showing that nicotine was addictive. Other evidence suggested that the companies targeted teenagers in marketing cigarettes.

In 1997, four tobacco companies agreed to a settlement that would cost them $368 billion. After much bitter debate, Congress rejected the agreement. Despite this setback, some individuals won lawsuits against tobacco companies. Health authorities continued to seek ways to discourage teen smoking.

Terrorism

Starting in the 1960s, terrorist bombings, kidnappings, and hijackings became increasingly common in Europe, the Middle East, and elsewhere. Americans were sometimes the victims of such acts. However, not until the 1990s did terrorism seem a real threat within the United States.

In 1993, a bomb rocked the World Trade Center in New York City. Two years later, a blast at a federal building in Oklahoma City killed 168 people, including 15 preschool children. A young man who resented the government was later convicted and sentenced to death for the Oklahoma City bombing.

Americans debated ways to combat terrorism. Some wanted to increase security in public places and to give the government more freedom to tap the phones of suspected terrorists. Others feared that such measures would threaten the traditional freedom of American society.

Moving toward the future

The United States faces complex issues in the future. Yet Americans have met such challenges before. In 1776, the problems were so great that many believed the new nation would not survive. Instead, it grew to become a superpower and a model for democratic nations everywhere.

From the beginning, the motto of the United States has been *E pluribus unum*—"Out of many, one." This motto reflects the nation's many regions, peoples, and cultures. This diversity is and has always been a major source of the nation's strength.

Today, the bold experiment continues. As we begin the new century, Americans continue to celebrate freedom: the freedom to be ourselves, to respect one another, and to work together, using one another's strengths to build a better nation.

★ Section 5 Review ★

Recall

1. **Identify** **(a)** American Indian Religious Freedom Act, **(b)** Colin Powell, **(c)** Jesse Jackson, **(d)** Madeleine Albright, **(e)** Americans With Disabilities Act, **(f)** Amy Tan, **(g)** Immigration Reform and Control Act.
2. **Define** **(a)** mainstream, **(b)** refugee, **(a)** illegal alien.

Comprehension

3. Describe one success each of the following groups has had: **(a)** Native Americans, **(b)** African Americans, **(c)** women, **(d)** Americans with disabilities.
4. **(a)** How have sources of immigration changed in recent years? **(b)** What is the reason for the change?
5. What two approaches have Americans taken to combat drug abuse?

Critical Thinking and Writing

6. **Making Inferences** How can individual success stories like those of Colin Powell, Reginald Lewis, or Madeline Albright inspire others?
7. **Defending a Position** Would you be willing to give up some of your personal freedom in order to protect against possible terrorism? Why or why not?

Activity **Writing a Speech** You have been selected to welcome a group of new immigrants. In your speech, describe what will be expected of them as Americans and how diversity has contributed to the nation's strength.

Chapter 30 Review and Activities

★ Sum It Up ★

Section 1 A Conservative Tide

- The conservative goals of President Ronald Reagan included reducing taxes and limiting the role of the federal government.
- President Bill Clinton generally followed middle-of-the-road policies.

Section 2 The Post–Cold War World

- After the Cold War ended, the United States reached agreements with Russia to reduce nuclear arms.
- As the last remaining superpower, the United States took a major role in promoting democracy and stability.

Section 3 War and Peace in the Middle East

- In the Middle East, the United States has supported Israel while trying to improve relations with Arab nations.
- In the Persian Gulf War, American forces helped drive Iraqi invaders out of Kuwait.

Section 4 The Environment and the World Economy

- The government and individuals have taken steps to protect the environment.
- The United States sought ways to compete in a global marketplace.

Section 5 A Diverse Nation

- Although many problems remained, groups such as Native Americans, African Americans, women, and people with disabilities have made many advances.
- Continuing challenges for the future include combating drug abuse and terrorism.

For additional review of the major ideas of Chapter 30, see ***Guide to the Essentials of American History*** or ***Interactive Student Tutorial CD-ROM,*** which contains interactive review activities, graphic organizers, and practice tests.

Reviewing the Chapter

Define These Terms

Match each term with the correct definition.

Column 1

1. apartheid
2. downsizing
3. renewable resource
4. trade deficit
5. solar energy

Column 2

a. raw material that can be readily replaced by nature
b. gap that occurs when a nation imports more than it exports
c. strict separation of races
d. power from the sun
e. using fewer people to do the same work

Explore the Main Ideas

1. How did Ronald Reagan and other conservatives view the federal government?
2. What caused the recession of the early 1990s?
3. How did the United States try to bring peace to Northern Ireland?
4. List one cause and two effects of the Arab oil embargo of 1973.
5. What changes occurred for women in the job market?

Chart Activity

Look at the table below and answer the following questions: **1.** How many tons of garbage did the United States burn or dump in 1980? **2.** What percentage of the total amount of garbage was recycled or composted in 1970? In 1990? **Critical Thinking** Why do environmentalists favor recycling?

Garbage Disposal in the United States

	1970	1980	1990	2000
Total Generated *	121	152	197	222
Recycled or Composted *	8	15	34	67
Burned or Dumped *	113	137	163	155

* In millions of tons

Source: Environmental Protection Agency

Critical Thinking and Writing

1. **Understanding Chronology** Why was the United States able to balance its budget after the Cold War ended, but not before?
2. Exploring Unit Themes **World Leadership** Reread the statements by Dana Rohrabacher and Newt Gingrich on page 837. **(a)** What do you think Rohrabacher meant by "an unfair burden"? **(b)** Has the United States continued to "lead," as Gingrich suggested? Explain.
3. **Linking Past and Present** **(a)** How was the Persian Gulf War similar to World War II? **(b)** How was it different?
4. **Ranking** What would you consider the three most important events described in this chapter? Give reasons for your choices.

Using Primary Sources

In 1996, President Bill Clinton addressed a group of American business leaders:

> "Every day all you have to do is pick up the paper or watch the evening news to see that differences among people—racial, ethnic, religious, and other differences—are tearing the heart out of societies and regions all around the world. In America we're turning all those differences to our advantage. And I think more and more we're getting comfortable with the fact that we are more than ever still a nation of immigrants."

Source: M2 PressWIRE, October 1, 1996.

Recognizing Points of View **(a)** According to Clinton, what has torn apart many societies around the world? Give three examples from this chapter that support this view. **(b)** According to Clinton, how does the United States differ from these other places?

Activity Bank

Interdisciplinary Activity

Exploring Sciences Find out more about the various energy sources available today. Make a chart showing the advantages and disadvantages of each. Accompany your chart with diagrams that show how each energy source creates power.

Career Skills Activity

Architects Find out how a public building in your area has provided access for people in wheelchairs. Create a diagram or model showing the kinds of improvements that have been made.

Citizenship Activity

Creating Posters Focus on an environmental problem in your community, such as littering or improper disposal of toxic household waste. Make educational posters to teach members of your community about the problem and possible solutions.

Internet Activity

Use the Internet to find a Web site for a national or local news agency, newspaper, or television station. Report on what kinds of news you can get from that site, and how you can use that site to keep informed about current and future issues.

You are yourself, a young student attending an American school right now. In your EYEWITNESS JOURNAL, describe three events of the past 25 years that have had the biggest impact on your life. You may write as if you had the ability to go back in time to witness these events.

History Through Literature

The Circuit

by Francisco Jiménez

Introduction

As a child, Francisco Jiménez labored in the fields of California. He later became a writer and university teacher. Many of his stories describe "the joys and disappointments of growing up in a migrant setting." In his short story "The Circuit," Jiménez describes how being constantly on the move affects Panchito, a young migrant worker.

Vocabulary

Before you read the selection, find the meaning of these words in a dictionary: **savoring, instinct, enthusiastically.**

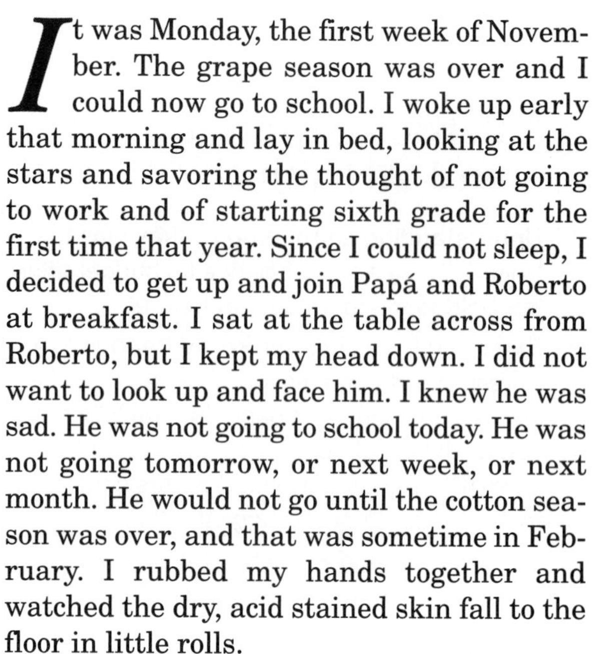

It was Monday, the first week of November. The grape season was over and I could now go to school. I woke up early that morning and lay in bed, looking at the stars and savoring the thought of not going to work and of starting sixth grade for the first time that year. Since I could not sleep, I decided to get up and join Papá and Roberto at breakfast. I sat at the table across from Roberto, but I kept my head down. I did not want to look up and face him. I knew he was sad. He was not going to school today. He was not going tomorrow, or next week, or next month. He would not go until the cotton season was over, and that was sometime in February. I rubbed my hands together and watched the dry, acid stained skin fall to the floor in little rolls.

When Papá and Roberto left for work, I felt relief. I walked to the top of a small grade next to the shack and watched the car disappear in the distance in a cloud of dust.

Two hours later, around eight o'clock, I stood by the side of the road waiting for school bus number twenty. When it arrived I climbed in. Everyone was busy either talking or yelling. I sat in an empty seat in the back.

When the bus stopped in front of the school, I felt very nervous. I looked out the bus window and saw boys and girls carrying books under their arms. I put my hands in my pant pockets and walked to the principal's office. When I entered I heard a woman's voice say: "May I help you?" I was startled. I had not heard English for months. For a few seconds I remained speechless. I looked at the lady who waited for an answer. My first instinct was to answer her in Spanish, but I held back. Finally, after struggling for English words, I managed to tell her that I wanted to enroll in the sixth grade. After answering many questions, I was led to the classroom.

Mr. Lema, the sixth grade teacher, greeted me and assigned me a desk. He then introduced me to the class. I was so nervous and scared at that moment when everyone's eyes were on me that I wished I were with Papá and Roberto picking cotton. After taking roll, Mr. Lema gave the class the assignment for

Viewing HISTORY Mexican American Art

Tony Ortega painted Los Jovenes con Bicicleta *(Young People With Bicycle) in 1991. Ortega's use of bright colors shows the influence of Mexican artistic style. Art from many different cultures has enriched American culture.* ★ **How would you describe the mood of this painting? Explain.**

the first hour. "The first thing we have to do this morning is finish reading the story we began yesterday," he said enthusiastically. He walked up to me, handed me an English book, and asked me to read. "We are on page 125," he said politely. When I heard this, I felt my blood rush to my head; I felt dizzy. "Would you like to read?" he asked hesitantly. I opened the book to page 125. My mouth was dry. My eyes began to water. I could not begin. "You can read later," Mr. Lema said understandingly.

For the rest of the reading period I kept getting angrier and angrier with myself. I should have read, I thought to myself.

During recess I went into the restroom and opened my English book to page 125. I began to read in a low voice, pretending I was in class. There were many words I did not know. I closed the book and headed back to the classroom.

Mr. Lema was sitting at his desk correcting papers. When I entered he looked up at me and smiled. I felt better. I walked up to him and asked if he could help me with the new words. "Gladly," he said.

The rest of the month I spent my lunch hours working on English with Mr. Lema, my best friend at school.

One Friday during lunch hour Mr. Lema asked me to take a walk with him to the music room. "Do you like music?" he asked me as we entered the building. "Yes, I like corridos,"* I answered. He then picked up a trumpet, blew on it and handed it to me. The sound gave me goose bumps. I knew that sound. I had heard it in many corridos. "How would you like to learn how to play it?" he asked. He must have read my face because before I could answer, he added: "I'll teach you how to play it during our lunch hours."

That day I could hardly wait to get home to tell Papá and Mamá the great news. As I got off the bus, my little brothers and sisters ran up to meet me. They were yelling and screaming. I thought they were happy to see me, but when I opened the door to our shack, I saw that everything we owned was neatly packed in cardboard boxes.

*Corridos refers to a form of dance music popular in Mexico.

Analyzing Literature

1. Why was Panchito unable to go to school before November?
2. How does Mr. Lema win Panchito's freindship?
3. **Making Inferences** **(a)** At the end of the story, what emotions do you think Panchito feels when he sees the packed boxes? **(b)** What is Jiménez suggesting about the education of young migrant workers?

Reference Section

UNIT 1 The Mayflower Compact

Introduction In 1620, the *Mayflower* anchored in what is now Provincetown Harbor off Cape Cod, Massachusetts. Before the landing, 41 male passengers on the ship signed a binding agreement that set up a basis for self-government. This document became known as the Mayflower Compact.

Vocabulary Before you read the selection, find the meaning of these words in a dictionary: **sovereign, covenant, furtherance, ordinances.**

Document in Brief

The signers of this document promise to join together to create a government for the Plymouth colony and to make laws for the good of the community.

In the name of God Amen, We whose names are underwritten, the loyal subjects of the dread sovereign Lord King James by the grace of God, of Great Britain, France, and Ireland king, defender of the faith, etc.

Having undertaken for the glory of God, and advancements of the Christian faith and honor of our King and country, a voyage to plant the first colony in the northern parts of Virginia, do by these presents solemnly and mutually in the presence of God, and one of another, covenant and combine ourselves together into a civil body politic; for our better ordering and preservation and furtherance of the ends afore said; and by virtue hereof to enact, constitute, and frame such just and equal laws, ordinances, acts, constitutions, and offices, from time to time, as shall be thought most meet and convenient for the general good of the colony: unto which we promise all due submission and obedience.

In witness whereof we have here under subscribed our names at Cape Cod the 11 of November, in the year the reign of our sovereign Lord King James of England, France, and Ireland, the eighteenth and of Scotland the fifty-fourth Anno Domini 1620

Colonial Boston in the 1660s

Analyzing Primary Sources

1. The purpose of the Mayflower Compact was to
   A. elect church members.
   B. separate from England.
   C. establish a governing body.
   D. honor the English king.
2. The signers promised to submit themselves to
   F. King James.
   G. the governor of the colony.
   H. the common good.
   J. the Church.
3. **Critical Thinking Linking Past and Present** How are the ideas in the Mayflower Compact reflected in the form of government that exists in the United States today?

UNIT 2 "Give Me Liberty or Give Me Death"

Patrick Henry

Introduction Patrick Henry gave his most famous speech in Richmond, Virginia, on March 23, 1775. Less than a month later, the battles of Lexington and Concord marked the start of the American Revolution. Portions of Henry's speech are printed below.

Vocabulary Before you read the selection, find the meaning of these words in a dictionary: **remonstrated, supplicated, prostrated, inviolate, inestimable, resounding.**

Document in Brief

In this speech, Henry argues that it is already too late for the 13 colonies to settle their differences with England.

Let us not, I beseech you, sir, deceive ourselves any longer. Sir, we have done everything that could be done to avert the storm which is now coming on. We have petitioned; we have remonstrated; we have supplicated; we have prostrated ourselves before the tyrannical hands of the ministry and parliament. Our petitions have been slighted; our remonstrances have produced additional violence and insult; our supplications have been disregarded; and we have been spurned, with contempt, from the foot of the throne. In vain, after these things, may we indulge the fond hope of peace and reconciliation. There is no longer any room for hope. If we wish to be free—if we mean to preserve inviolate those inestimable privileges for which we have been so long contending—if we mean not basely to abandon the noble struggle in which we have been so long engaged, and which we pledged ourselves never to abandon until the glorious object of our contest shall be obtained, we must fight!...

It is in vain, sir, to extenuate the matter. Gentlemen may cry peace, peace—but there is no peace. The war is actually begun! The next gale that sweeps from the North will bring to our ears the clash of resounding arms! Our brethren are already in the field! Why stand we here idle? What is it that gentlemen wish? What would they have? Is life so dear, or peace so sweet, as to be purchased at the price of chains and slavery? Forbid it, Almighty God! I know not what course others may take; but as for me, give me liberty, or give me death!

▲ *Colonial tax protest*

Analyzing Primary Sources

1. According to Henry, England has responded to the colonists' complaints by
   A. debating them in Parliament.
   B. ignoring them.
   C. calling a Congress.
   D. declaring war.
2. What is more important to Henry than life?
   F. slavery
   G. freedom
   H. democracy
   J. victory
3. **Critical Thinking Recognizing Points of View** How does Henry feel about people who want to restore peace with England?

UNIT 3 Farewell Address
George Washington

Introduction In 1796, as he neared the end of his second term, President George Washington wrote his famous Farewell Address. In it, he gave his views on the best policies for the young republic to follow. The following excerpt is from Washington's Farewell Address.

Vocabulary Before you read the selection, find the meaning of these words in a dictionary: **intimated, baneful, enfeeble, animosity, foments, insurrection, infidelity, maxim.**

Document in Brief

As he leaves office, Washington warns Americans of the dangers of forming political parties and of getting involved in the affairs of other nations.

I have already intimated to you the danger of parties in the State, with particular reference to the founding of them on geographical [bases]. Let me now take a more comprehensive view, and warn you in the most solemn manner against the baneful effects of the spirit of party, generally....

It serves always to distract the public councils and enfeeble the public administration. It agitates the community with ill-founded jealousies and false alarms, kindles the animosity of one part against another, foments occasionally riot and insurrection. It opens the door to foreign influence and corruption....

The great rule of conduct for us in regard to foreign nations is, in extending our commercial relations to have with them as little political connection as possible. So far as we have already formed engagements let them be fulfilled, with perfect good faith. Here let us stop....

It is our true policy to steer clear of permanent alliances with any portion of the foreign world, so far, I mean as we are now at liberty to do it; for let me not be understood as capable of [supporting] infidelity to existing engagements. I hold the maxim no less applicable to public than to private affairs that honesty is always the best policy. I repeat, therefore, let those engagements be observed in their genuine sense. But in my opinion it is unnecessary and would be unwise to extend them.

Taking care always to keep ourselves by suitable establishments on a respectable defensive posture, we may safely trust to temporary alliances for extraordinary emergencies.

▲ *Mug honoring President Washington*

Analyzing Primary Sources

1. What is Washington's view of political parties?
   A. They cost too much money.
   B. They cause dangerous divisions within the nation.
   C. They often lead to the rise of monarchs.
   D. They lead to war.
2. What advice about foreign policy did Washington give?
   F. Seek trade but avoid other links with Europe.
   G. Have no contact with Europe.
   H. Cancel all treaties with European countries.
   J. Build up a strong army and navy.
3. **Critical Thinking Making Inferences** Under what circumstances do you think Washington would approve of making an alliance with another country?

UNIT 4 Seneca Falls Declaration of Sentiments

Introduction In 1848, Elizabeth Cady Stanton and Lucretia Mott led a women's rights convention in Seneca Falls, New York. The convention adopted the following Declaration of Sentiments, based partly on the Declaration of Independence.

Vocabulary Before you read the selection, find the meaning of these words in a dictionary: **endowed, inalienable, allegiance, usurpations, franchise.**

Document in Brief

The leaders of the Seneca Falls women's rights convention declare that women and men should have equal rights.

We hold these truths to be self-evident that all men and women are created equal; that they are endowed by their Creator with certain inalienable rights; that among these are life, liberty, and the pursuit of happiness; that to secure these rights governments are instituted, deriving their just powers from the consent of the governed. Whenever any form of government becomes destructive of these ends, it is the right of those who suffer from it to refuse allegiance to it, and to insist upon the institution of a new government, laying its foundation on such principles, and organizing its powers in such form, as to them shall seem most likely to effect their safety and happiness. . . .

▲ *Elizabeth Cady Stanton*

The history of mankind is a history of repeated injuries and usurpations on the part of man toward woman, having in direct object the establishment of an absolute tyranny over her. To prove this, let facts be submitted to a candid world. . . .

He has compelled her to submit to laws, in the formation of which she had no voice. . . .

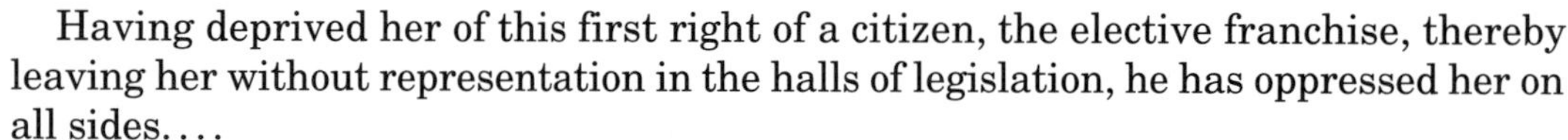

Having deprived her of this first right of a citizen, the elective franchise, thereby leaving her without representation in the halls of legislation, he has oppressed her on all sides. . . .

He has taken from her all right in property, even to the wages she earns. . . .

He has denied her the facilities for obtaining a thorough education—all colleges being closed against her.

Analyzing Primary Sources

1. What is the main point of this document?
   A. Men should have more rights than women.
   B. Women should have more rights than men.
   C. Women should have the same rights as men.
   D. Women should be paid more.
2. According to this document, women did not have the right to
   F. vote.
   G. keep their earnings.
   H. attend college.
   J. all of the above.
3. **Critical Thinking Making Inferences** Why do you think that the writers of this document echoed the wording of the Declaration of Independence?

UNIT 5 Gettysburg Address

Abraham Lincoln

Introduction At the Battle of Gettysburg in July 1863, both the North and the South suffered heavy casualties. On November 19, 1863, President Abraham Lincoln visited Gettysburg to dedicate the battlefield cemetery. The brief but stirring speech Lincoln gave on that day became known as "The Gettysburg Address."

Vocabulary Before you read the selection, find the meaning of these words in a dictionary: **score, proposition, consecrate, hallow, detract, vain, perish.**

Document in Brief

In this speech, Lincoln says the best way to honor the Union dead is to keep alive the principles of democracy for which they died.

Four score and seven years ago our fathers brought forth on this continent, a new nation, conceived in liberty, and dedicated to the proposition that all men are created equal. Now we are engaged in a great civil war, testing whether that nation, or any nation so conceived and so dedicated, can long endure. We are met on a great battlefield of that war. We have come to dedicate a portion of that field, as a final resting place for those who here gave their lives that that nation might live. It is altogether fitting and proper that we should do this. But, in a larger sense, we can not dedicate—we can not consecrate—we can not hallow—this ground. The brave men, living and dead, who struggled here, have consecrated it, far above our poor power to add or detract. The world will little note, nor long remember what we say here, but it can never forget what they did here. It is for us the living, rather, to be dedicated here to the unfinished work which they who fought here have thus far so nobly advanced. It is rather for us to be here dedicated to the great task remaining before us—that from these honored dead we take increased devotion to that cause for which they gave the last full measure of devotion—that we here highly resolve that these dead shall not have died in vain—that this nation, under God, shall have a new birth of freedom—and that government of the people, by the people, for the people, shall not perish from the earth.

▲ *Lincoln Memorial*

Analyzing Primary Sources

1. Lincoln believes the Civil War will show that
   A. slavery is wrong.
   B. the North is stronger than the South.
   C. a democratic nation can survive.
   D. Americans are brave fighters.
2. Lincoln says the world will soon forget
   F. the sacrifices of the soldiers at Gettysburg.
   G. his speech.
   H. the principles of liberty and justice.
   J. the Civil War.
3. **Critical Thinking Analyzing Ideas** Give examples of how Lincoln uses this speech to try to remind people of the ideals upon which the United States was founded.

UNIT 6 "I Will Fight No More Forever"

Chief Joseph

Introduction In 1877, the United States government tried to force the Nez Percé Indians onto a reservation. Chief Joseph led a band of Nez Percés from their home in western Oregon on a flight toward Canada. They traveled over 1,000 miles before finally surrendering. The following is Chief Joseph's surrender to the army.

Document in Brief

In this speech, Chief Joseph announces that he can no longer carry on his fight against the United States government.

Tell General Howard that I know his heart. What he told me before I have in my heart. I am tired of fighting. Our chiefs are killed. Looking Glass is dead, Tu-hul-hil-sote is dead, the old men are all dead. It is the young men who now say yes or no. He who led the young men* is dead. It is cold and we have no blankets. The little children are freezing to death. My people—some of them have run away to the hills and have no blankets and no food. No one knows where they are—perhaps freezing to death. I want to have time to look for my children and see how many of them I can find. Maybe I shall find them among the dead. Hear me, my chiefs, my heart is sick and sad. From where the sun now stands I will fight no more forever.

*Chief Joseph is referring to his own brother, Alikut.

Sioux leaders surrendering to the government

Analyzing Primary Sources

1. How would you describe Chief Joseph's mood in this speech?
   A. angry
   B. mournful
   C. hopeful
   D. proud
2. What is Chief Joseph's main concern?
   F. getting food and blankets
   G. keeping his authority over his people
   H. achieving peace
   J. restoring of Indian lands
3. **Critical Thinking Linking Past and Present** Why do you think Chief Joseph's speech is so well remembered today?

UNIT 7 The Fourteen Points
Woodrow Wilson

Introduction In January 1918, World War I was still raging in Europe. President Woodrow Wilson outlined to Congress his hopes for the peace settlement. He included a list of specific goals, which came to be known as the Fourteen Points. Six of these goals are listed below.

Vocabulary Before you read the selection, find the meaning of these words in a dictionary: **covenants, maintenance, impartial, sovereignty, equitable, integrity.**

Document in Brief

President Wilson's goals for the world after World War I include an end to secret diplomacy, arms reduction, and the formation of the League of Nations.

1. Open covenants of peace, openly arrived at, after which there shall be no private international understandings of any kind, but diplomacy shall proceed always frankly and in public view.

2. Absolute freedom of navigation upon the seas, outside territorial waters, alike in peace and in war, except as the seas may be closed in whole or in part by international action for the enforcement of international covenants.

3. The removal, so far as possible, of all economic barriers and the establishment of an equality of trade conditions among all the nations consenting to the peace and associating themselves for its maintenance.

4. Adequate guarantees given and taken that national armaments will be reduced to the lowest points consistent with domestic safety.

5. A free, open-minded and absolutely impartial adjustment of all colonial claims based upon a strict observance of the principle that in determining all such questions of sovereignty, the interests of the populations concerned must have equal weight with the equitable claims of the government whose title is to be determined....

14. A general association of nations must be formed under specific covenants for the purpose of affording mutual guarantees of political independence and territorial integrity to great and small [states] alike.

Versailles peace conference

Analyzing Primary Sources

1. In Point 1, Wilson hopes to do away with
- **A.** secret treaties.
- **B.** colonial disputes.
- **C.** open covenants.
- **D.** war.

2. Which of the Fourteen Points concerns imperialism?
- **F.** Point 2
- **G.** Point 3
- **H.** Point 4
- **J.** Point 5

3. Critical Thinking Making Inferences Point 14 was probably the most important to Wilson. **(a)** Why do you think this was so? **(b)** Why do you think he put it last on his list?

UNIT 8 First Inaugural Address
Franklin D. Roosevelt

Introduction On March 4, 1933, Franklin Delano Roosevelt took the oath of office as President. In his inaugural speech, FDR tried to build confidence while promising to do whatever was necessary to combat the Great Depression.

Vocabulary Before you read the selection, find the meaning of these words in a dictionary: **induction, candor, impels, preeminently.**

Document in Brief

President Roosevelt tells Americans that together they can combat the Great Depression.

I am certain that my fellow Americans expect that on my induction into the Presidency I will address them with a candor and a decision which the present situation of our Nation impels. This is preeminently the time to speak the truth, the whole truth, frankly and boldly. Nor need we shrink from honestly facing conditions in our country today. This great Nation will endure as it has endured, will revive and will prosper. So, first of all, let me assert my firm belief that the only thing we have to fear is fear itself—nameless, unreasoning, unjustified terror which paralyzes needed efforts to convert retreat into advance....

Our greatest primary task is to put people to work. This is no unsolvable problem if we face it wisely and courageously. It can be accomplished in part by direct recruiting by the Government itself, treating the task as we would treat the emergency of a war, but at the same time, through this employment, accomplishing greatly needed projects to stimulate and reorganize the use of our natural resources....

[I]n our progress toward a resumption of work we require... safeguards against a return of the evils of the old order: there must be a strict supervision of all banking and credits and investments; there must be an end to speculation with other people's money; and there must be provision for an adequate but sound currency.

There are the lines of attack. I shall presently urge upon a new Congress in special session detailed measures for their fulfillment, and I shall seek the immediate assistance of the several States. Through this program of action we address ourselves to putting our own national house in order and making income balance outgo....

▲ Franklin and Eleanor Roosevelt

Analyzing Primary Sources

1. What does Roosevelt say is the greatest danger facing the country?
   A. unemployment
   B. bank failures
   C. war
   D. fear
2. FDR says his top priority is to
   F. end the Depression.
   G. put people to work.
   H. stop speculation.
   J. save natural resources.
3. **Critical Thinking Applying Information** Describe how each of the following programs met one of the goals outlined in FDR's speech: **(a)** Civilian Conservation Corps; **(b)** Truth-in-Securities Act.

UNIT 9 "I Have a Dream"
Martin Luther King, Jr.

Introduction In August 1963, more than 200,000 Americans marched to Washington, D.C., in support of civil rights. Martin Luther King, Jr., gave a ringing speech in front of the Lincoln Memorial. Portions of King's "I Have a Dream" speech are printed below.

Vocabulary Before you read the selection, find the meaning of these words in a dictionary: **creed, Gentiles.**

Document in Brief

Dr. King describes a future where all Americans can live together in harmony.

I have a dream that one day, this nation will rise up and live out the true meaning of its creed: "We hold these truths to be self-evident; that all men are created equal. . . ."

I have a dream that my four little children will one day live in a nation where they will not be judged by the color of their skin but by the content of their character.

I have a dream today!

I have a dream that one day the state of Alabama . . . will be transformed into a situation where little black boys and black girls will be able to join hands with little white boys and white girls as sisters and brothers. . . .

With this faith we will be able to work together, to pray together, to struggle together, to go to jail together, to stand up for freedom together, knowing that we will be free one day. This will be the day when all of God's children will be able to sing with new meaning—"my country 'tis of thee; sweet land of liberty; of thee I sing; land where my fathers died, land of the pilgrim's pride, from every mountain side, let freedom ring"—and if America is to be a great nation, this must become true. . . .

Let freedom ring from Lookout Mountain of Tennessee.

Let freedom ring from every hill and molehill of Mississippi. From every mountainside, let freedom ring.

When we let freedom ring, when we let it ring from every village and every hamlet, from every state and every city, we will be able to speed up that day when all of God's children, black men and white men, Jews and Gentiles, Protestants and Catholics, will be able to join hands and sing in the words of the old Negro spiritual: "Free at last! free at last! thank God almighty, we are free at last!"

▲ *King leading a civil rights march*

Analyzing Primary Sources

1. King wants people to be judged by
   A. their race.
   B. their religious faith.
   C. their character.
   D. their commitment to civil rights.
2. In the selection above, King quotes from
   F. "The Star-Spangled Banner."
   G. the Declaration of Independence.
   H. "America the Beautiful."
   J. the Pledge of Allegiance.
3. **Critical Thinking** **Identifying the Main Idea** What is King's main idea?

★ The Declaration of Independence ★

On June 7, 1776, the Continental Congress approved the resolution that "these United Colonies are, and of right ought to be, free and independent States." Congress then appointed a committee to write a declaration of independence. The committee members were John Adams, Benjamin Franklin, Robert Livingston, Roger Sherman, and Thomas Jefferson.

Jefferson actually wrote the Declaration, but he got advice from the others. On July 2, Congress discussed the Declaration and made some changes. On July 4, 1776, it adopted the Declaration of Independence in its final form.

The Declaration is printed in black. The headings have been added to show the parts of the Declaration. They are not part of the original text. Annotations, or explanations, are on the tan side of the page. Page numbers in the annotations show where a subject is discussed in the text. Difficult words are defined.

dissolve: break ***powers of the earth:*** other nations ***station:*** place ***impel:*** force

The colonists feel that they must explain to the world the reasons why they are breaking away from England.

When in the course of human events it becomes necessary for one people to dissolve the political bands which have connected them with another and to assume, among the powers of the earth, the separate and equal station to which the laws of nature and of nature's God entitle them, a decent respect to the opinions of mankind requires that they should declare the causes which impel them to the separation.

The Purpose of Government Is to Protect Basic Rights

endowed: given ***unalienable rights:*** so basic that they cannot be taken away ***secure:*** protect ***instituted:*** set up ***deriving:*** getting ***alter:*** change ***effect:*** bring about

People set up governments to protect their basic rights. Governments get their power from the consent of the governed. If a government takes away the basic rights of the people, the people have the right to change the government.

prudence: wisdom ***transient:*** temporary, passing ***disposed:*** likely ***usurpations:*** taking and using powers that do not belong to a person ***invariably:*** always ***evinces a design to reduce them under absolute despotism:*** makes a clear plan to put them under complete and unjust control ***sufferance:*** endurance

We hold these truths to be self-evident, that all men are created equal; that they are endowed by their Creator with certain unalienable rights; that among these are life, liberty, and the pursuit of happiness. That, to secure these rights, governments are instituted among men, deriving their just powers from the consent of the governed; that, whenever any form of government becomes destructive of these ends, it is the right of the people to alter or to abolish it, and to institute a new government, laying its foundation on such principles and organizing its powers in such form, as to them shall seem most likely to effect their safety and happiness. Prudence, indeed, will dictate that governments long established should not be changed for light and transient causes; and, accordingly, all experience hath shown that mankind are more disposed to suffer, while evils are sufferable, than to right themselves by abolishing the forms to which they are accustomed. But when a long train of abuses and usurpations, pursuing invariably the same object, evinces a design to reduce them under absolute despotism, it is their right, it is their duty, to throw off such government and to provide new guards for their future security. Such has been the patient sufferance of these colonies, and such is now the necessity which constrains them to alter their former systems of government. The history of the present King of Great Britain is a history of repeated injuries and usurpations, all having, in direct object, the establishment of an absolute tyranny over these States. To prove this, let facts be submitted to a candid world:

constrains: forces ***absolute tyranny:*** harsh and unjust government ***candid:*** free from prejudice

People do not change governments for slight reasons. But they are forced to do so when a government becomes tyrannical. King George III has a long record of abusing his power.

Wrongs Done by the King

He has refused his assent to laws the most wholesome and necessary for the public good.

He has forbidden his governors to pass laws of immediate and pressing importance, unless suspended in their operation till his assent should be obtained; and, when so suspended, he has utterly neglected to attend to them.

He has refused to pass other laws for the accommodation of the large districts of people, unless those people would relinquish the right of representation in the legislature; a right inestimable to them and formidable to tyrants only.

assent: approval ***relinquish:*** give up ***inestimable:*** too great a value to be measured ***formidable:*** causing fear

This part of the Declaration spells out three sets of wrongs that led the colonists to break with Britain.

The first set of wrongs is the king's unjust use of power. The king refused to approve laws that are needed. He has tried to control the colonial legislatures.

He has called together legislative bodies at places unusual, uncomfortable, and distant from the depository of their public records, for the sole purpose of fatiguing them into compliance with his measures.

He has dissolved representative houses, repeatedly for opposing, with manly firmness, his invasions on the rights of the people.

He has refused, for a long time after such dissolutions, to cause others to be elected: whereby the legislative powers, incapable of annihilation, have returned to the people at large for their exercise; the state remaining, in the meantime, exposed to all the danger of invasion from without and convulsions within.

depository: storehouse ***fatiguing:*** tiring out ***compliance:*** giving in ***dissolved:*** broken up ***annihilation:*** total destruction ***convulsions:*** disturbances

The king has tried to force colonial legislatures into doing his will by wearing them out. He has dissolved legislatures (such as those of Massachusetts). (See page 90.)

He has endeavored to prevent the population of these States; for that purpose, obstructing the laws for naturalization of foreigners, refusing to pass others to encourage their migration hither, and raising the conditions of new appropriations of lands.

He has obstructed the administration of justice by refusing his assent to laws for establishing judiciary powers.

He has made judges dependent on his will alone for the tenure of their offices and the amount and payment of their salaries.

He has erected a multitude of new offices and sent hither swarms of officers to harass our people and eat out their substance.

He has kept among us, in time of peace, standing armies, without the consent of our legislatures.

He has affected to render the military independent of, and superior to, the civil power.

endeavored: tried ***obstructing:*** blocking ***naturalization:*** process of becoming a citizen ***migration:*** moving ***hither:*** here ***appropriations:*** grants ***obstructed the administration of justice:*** prevented justice from being done ***judiciary powers:*** system of law courts ***tenure:*** term (of office) ***erected:*** set up ***multitude:*** large number ***swarms:*** huge crowds ***harass:*** cause trouble ***render:*** make

Among other wrongs, he has refused to let settlers move west to take up new land. He has prevented justice from being done. Also, he has sent large numbers of customs officials to cause problems for the colonists.

He has combined with others to subject us to a jurisdiction foreign to our Constitution and unacknowledged by our laws, giving his assent to their acts of pretended legislation—

jurisdiction: authority

For quartering large bodies of armed troops among us;

quartering: housing

mock: false

The king has joined with others, meaning Parliament, to make laws for the colonies. The Declaration then lists the second set of wrongs—unjust acts of Parliament.

imposing: forcing ***depriving:*** taking away ***transporting us beyond seas:*** sending colonists to England for trial ***neighboring province:*** Quebec ***arbitrary government:*** unjust rule ***fit instrument:*** suitable tool ***invested with power:*** having the power

During the years leading up to 1776, the colonists claimed that Parliament had no right to make laws for them because they were not represented in Parliament. Here, the colonists object to recent laws of Parliament, such as the Quartering Act and the blockade of colonial ports (page 90), which cut off their trade. They also object to Parliament's claim that it had the right to tax them without their consent.

abdicated: given up ***plundered:*** robbed ***ravaged:*** attacked ***mercenaries:*** hired soldiers ***desolation:*** misery ***perfidy:*** falseness ***barbarous:*** uncivilized ***constrained:*** forced ***brethren:*** brothers ***domestic insurrections:*** internal revolts

Here, the Declaration lists the third set of wrongs—warlike acts of the king. Instead of listening to the colonists, the king has made war on them. He has hired soldiers to fight in America.

oppressions: harsh rule ***petitioned:*** asked ***redress:*** relief ***unwarrantable jurisdiction over:*** unfair authority ***magnanimity:*** generosity ***conjured:*** called upon ***common kindred:*** relatives ***disavow:*** turn away from ***consanguinity:*** blood relationships, kinship ***acquiesce:*** agree ***denounces:*** speaks out against

During this time, colonists have repeatedly asked for relief. But their requests have brought only more suffering. They have appealed to the British people but received no help. So they are forced to separate.

For protecting them by a mock trial from punishment for any murders which they should commit on the inhabitants of these States;

For cutting off our trade with all parts of the world;

For imposing taxes on us without our consent;

For depriving us, in many cases, of the benefit of trial by jury;

For transporting us beyond seas to be tried for pretended offences;

For abolishing the free system of English laws in a neighboring province, establishing therein an arbitrary government, and enlarging its boundaries, so as to render it at once an example and fit instrument for introducing the same absolute rule into these colonies;

For taking away our charters, abolishing our most valuable laws, and altering, fundamentally, the powers of our governments;

For suspending our own legislatures and declaring themselves invested with power to legislate for us in all cases whatsoever.

He has abdicated government here by declaring us out of his protection and waging war against us.

He has plundered our seas, ravaged our coasts, burnt out towns, and destroyed the lives of our people.

He is, at this time, transporting large armies of foreign mercenaries to complete the works of death, desolation, and tyranny already begun with circumstances of cruelty and perfidy scarcely paralleled in the most barbarous ages, and totally unworthy, the head of a civilized nation.

He has constrained our fellow citizens, taken captive on the high seas, to bear arms against their country, to become the executioners of their friends and brethren, or to fall themselves by their hands.

He has excited domestic insurrections amongst us and has endeavored to bring on the inhabitants of our frontiers, the merciless Indian savages, whose known rule of warfare is an undistinguished destruction of all ages, sexes, and conditions.

In every state of these oppressions, we have petitioned for redress in the most humble terms; our repeated petitions have been answered only by repeated injury. A prince whose character is thus marked by every act which may define a tyrant is unfit to be the ruler of a free people.

Nor have we been wanting in attention to our British brethren. We have warned them, from time to time, of attempts made by their legislature to extend an unwarrantable jurisdiction over us. We have reminded them of the circumstances of our emigration and settlement here. We have appealed to their native justice and magnanimity, and we have conjured them, by the ties of our common kindred, to disavow these usurpations, which would inevitably interrupt our connections and correspondence. They, too, have been deaf to the voice of justice and consanguinity. We must, therefore, acquiesce in the necessity which denounces our separation, and hold them, as we hold the rest of mankind, enemies in war, in peace, friends.

Colonies Declare Independence

We, therefore, the representatives of the United States of America, in general Congress assembled, appealing to the Supreme Judge of the world for the rectitude of our intentions, do, in the name and by the authority of the good people of these colonies, solemnly publish and declare, that these united colonies are, and of right ought to be, free and independent states: that they are absolved from all allegiance to the British Crown, and that all political connection between them and the state of Great Britain is, and ought to be, totally dissolved; and that, as free and independent states, they have full power to levy war, conclude peace, contract alliances, establish commerce, and to do all other acts and things which independent states may of right do. And, for the support of this declaration, with a firm reliance on the protection of Divine Providence, we mutually pledge to each other our lives, our fortunes, and our sacred honor.

appealing: calling on ***rectitude of our intentions:*** moral rightness of our plans ***absolved from all allegiance:*** freed from loyalty ***levy war:*** declare war ***contract alliances:*** make treaties

As the representatives of the United States, they declare that the colonies are free and independent states.

The states need no longer be loyal to the British king. They are an independent nation that can make war and sign treaties.

Relying on help from Divine Providence, the signers of the Declaration promise their lives, money, and honor to fight for independence.

★ Signers of the Declaration of Independence ★

John Hancock, President
Charles Thomson, Secretary

New Hampshire
Josiah Bartlett
William Whipple
Matthew Thornton

Massachusetts
Samuel Adams
John Adams
Robert Treat Paine
Elbridge Gerry

Rhode Island
Stephen Hopkins
William Ellery

Connecticut
Roger Sherman
Samuel Huntington
William Williams
Oliver Wolcott

Delaware
Caesar Rodney
George Read
Thomas McKean

New York
William Floyd
Philip Livingston
Francis Lewis
Lewis Morris

New Jersey
Richard Stockton
John Witherspoon
Francis Hopkinson
John Hart
Abraham Clark

Georgia
Button Gwinnett
Lyman Hall
George Walton

Maryland
Samuel Chase
William Paca
Thomas Stone
Charles Carroll

North Carolina
William Hooper
Joseph Hewes
John Penn

Virginia
George Wythe
Richard Henry Lee
Thomas Jefferson
Benjamin Harrison
Thomas Nelson, Jr.
Francis Lightfoot Lee
Carter Braxton

South Carolina
Edward Rutledge
Thomas Heyward, Jr.
Thomas Lynch, Jr.
Arthur Middleton

Pennsylvania
Robert Morris
Benjamin Rush
Benjamin Franklin
John Morton
George Clymer
James Smith
George Taylor
James Wilson
George Ross

★ The Constitution ★ of the United States of America

The Constitution is printed in black. The titles of articles, sections, and clauses are not part of the original document. They have been added to help you find information in the Constitution. Some words or lines are crossed out because they have been changed by amendments or no longer apply. Annotations, or explanations, are on the tan side of the page. Page numbers in the annotations show where a subject is discussed in the text. Difficult words are defined.

Preamble

The Preamble describes the purpose of the government set up by the Constitution. Americans expect their government to defend justice and liberty and provide peace and safety from foreign enemies.

We the people of the United States, in order to form a more perfect Union, establish justice, insure domestic tranquillity, provide for the common defense, promote the general welfare, and secure the blessings of liberty to ourselves and our posterity, do ordain and establish this Constitution for the United States of America.

Article 1. The Legislative Branch

Section 1. A Two-House Legislature

The Constitution gives Congress the power to make laws. Congress is divided into the Senate and the House of Representatives.

All legislative powers herein granted shall be vested in a Congress of the United States, which shall consist of a Senate and House of Representatives.

Section 2. House of Representatives

Clause 1 ***Electors*** refers to voters. Members of the House of Representatives are elected every two years. Any citizen allowed to vote for members of the larger house of the state legislature can also vote for members of the House.

1. Election of Members The House of Representatives shall be composed of members chosen every second year by the people of the several states, and the electors in each state shall have the qualifications requisite for electors of the most numerous branch of the state legislature.

Clause 2 A member of the House of Representatives must be at least 25 years old, an American citizen for 7 years, and a resident of the state he or she represents.

2. Qualifications No person shall be a Representative who shall not have attained to the age of twenty-five years, and been seven years a citizen of the United States, and who shall not, when elected, be an inhabitant of that state in which he shall be chosen.

Clause 3 The number of representatives each state elects is based on its population. An ***enumeration,*** or census, must be taken every 10 years to determine population. Today, the number of representatives in the House is fixed at 435.

This is the famous Three-Fifths Compromise worked out at the Constitutional Convention (page 124). ***Persons bound to service*** meant indentured servants. ***All other persons*** meant slaves. All free people in a state were counted. However, only three fifths of the slaves were included in the population count. This three-fifths clause became meaningless when slaves were freed by the Thirteenth Amendment.

3. Determining Representation Representatives ~~and direct taxes~~ shall be apportioned among the several states which may be included within this Union, according to their respective numbers ~~which shall be determined by adding to the whole number of free persons, including those bound to service for a term of years, and excluding Indians not taxed, three-fifths of all other persons.~~ The actual enumeration shall be made within three years after the first meeting of the Congress of the United States, and within every subsequent term of ten years, in such manner as they shall by law direct. The number of Representatives shall not exceed one for every 30,000, but each state shall have at least one Representative; ~~and until such enumeration shall be made, the state of New Hampshire shall~~

~~be entitled to choose three; Massachusetts, eight; Rhode Island and Providence Plantations, one; Connecticut, five; New York, six; New Jersey, four; Pennsylvania, eight; Delaware, one; Maryland, six; Virginia, ten; North Carolina, five; South Carolina, five; and Georgia, three.~~

4. Filling Vacancies When vacancies happen in the representation from any state, the executive authority thereof shall issue writs of election to fill such vacancies.

Clause 4 ***Executive authority*** means the governor of a state. If a member of the House leaves office before his or her term ends, the governor must call a special election to fill the seat.

5. Selection of Officers; Power of Impeachment The House of Representatives shall choose their Speaker and other officers; and shall have the sole power of impeachment.

Clause 5 The House elects a speaker. Today, the speaker is usually chosen by the party that has a majority in the House. Also, only the House has the power to ***impeach,*** or accuse, a federal official of wrongdoing.

Section 3. The Senate

1. Selection of Members The Senate of the United States shall be composed of two Senators from each state ~~chosen by the legislature thereof,~~ for six years, and each Senator shall have one vote.

Clause 1 Each state has two senators. Senators serve for six-year terms. The Seventeenth Amendment changed the way senators were elected.

2. Alternating Terms; Filling Vacancies Immediately after they shall be assembled in consequence of the first election, they shall be divided as equally as may be into three classes. ~~The seats of the Senators of the first class shall be vacated at the expiration of the second year, of the second class at the expiration of the fourth year, and of the third class at the expiration of the sixth year,~~ so that one-third may be chosen every second year; ~~and if vacancies happen by resignation, or otherwise, during the recess of the legislature of any state, the executive thereof may make temporary appointments until the next meeting of the legislature, which shall then fill such vacancies.~~

Clause 2 Every two years, one third of the senators run for reelection. Thus, the makeup of the Senate is never totally changed by any one election. The Seventeenth Amendment changed the way of filling ***vacancies,*** or empty seats. Today, the governor of a state must choose a senator to fill a vacancy that occurs between elections.

3. Qualifications No person shall be a Senator who shall not have attained to the age of thirty years, and been nine years a citizen of the United States, and who shall not, when elected, be an inhabitant of that state for which he shall be chosen.

Clause 3 A senator must be at least 30 years old, an American citizen for 9 years, and a resident of the state he or she represents.

4. President of the Senate The Vice-President of the United States shall be president of the Senate, but shall have no vote, unless they be equally divided.

Clause 4 The Vice President presides over Senate meetings, but he or she can vote only to break a tie.

5. Election of Senate Officers The Senate shall choose their other officers, and also a president *pro tempore,* in the absence of the Vice-President, or when he shall exercise the office of the President of the United States.

Clause 5 ***Pro tempore*** means temporary. The Senate chooses one of its members to serve as president pro tempore when the Vice President is absent.

6. Impeachment Trials The Senate shall have the sole power to try all impeachments. When sitting for that purpose, they shall be on oath or affirmation. When the President of the United States is tried, the Chief Justice shall preside; and no person shall be convicted without the concurrence of two-thirds of the members present.

Clause 6 The Senate acts as a jury if the House impeaches a federal official. The Chief Justice of the Supreme Court presides if the President is on trial. Two thirds of all senators present must vote for ***conviction,*** or finding the accused guilty. No President has ever been convicted. The House impeached President Andrew Johnson in 1868, but the Senate acquitted him of the charges (page 413). In 1974, President Richard Nixon resigned before he could be impeached.

Clause 7 If an official is found guilty by the Senate, he or she can be removed from office and barred from holding federal office in the future. These are the only punishments the Senate can impose. However, the convicted official can still be tried in a criminal court.

7. Penalties Upon Conviction Judgment in cases of impeachment shall not extend further than to removal from office, and disqualification to hold and enjoy any office of honor, trust, or profit under the United States; but the party convicted shall nevertheless be liable and subject to indictment, trial, judgment, and punishment, according to law.

Section 4. Elections and Meetings

Clause 1 Each state legislature can decide when and how congressional elections take place, but Congress can overrule these decisions. In 1842, Congress required each state to set up congressional districts with one representative elected from each district. In 1872, Congress decided that congressional elections must be held in every state on the same date in even-numbered years.

1. Election of Congress The times, places, and manner of holding elections for Senators and Representatives shall be prescribed in each state by the legislature thereof; but the Congress may at any time by law make or alter such regulations, except as to the places of choosing Senators.

Clause 2 Congress must meet at least once a year. The Twentieth Amendment moved the opening date of Congress to January 3.

2. Annual Sessions The Congress shall assemble at least once in every year, ~~and such meeting shall be on the first Monday in December, unless they shall by law appoint a different day.~~

Section 5. Rules for the Conduct of Business

Clause 1 Each house decides whether a member has the qualifications for office set by the Constitution. A ***quorum*** is the smallest number of members who must be present for business to be conducted. Each house can set its own rules about absent members.

1. Organization Each house shall be the judge of the elections, returns, and qualifications of its own members, and a majority of each shall constitute a quorum to do business; but a smaller number may adjourn from day to day, and may be authorized to compel the attendance of absent members, in such manner, and under such penalties, as each house may provide.

Clause 2 Each house can make rules for the conduct of members. It can only expel a member by a two-thirds vote.

2. Procedures Each house may determine the rules of its proceedings, punish its members for disorderly behavior, and with the concurrence of two-thirds, expel a member.

Clause 3 Each house keeps a record of its meetings. *The Congressional Record* is published every day with excerpts from speeches made in each house. It also records the votes of each member.

3. A Written Record Each house shall keep a journal of its proceedings, and from time to time publish the same, excepting such parts as may in their judgment require secrecy; and the yeas and nays of the members of either house on any question shall, at the desire of one-fifth of those present, be entered on the journal.

Clause 4 Neither house can ***adjourn,*** or stop meeting, for more than three days unless the other house approves. Both houses of Congress must meet in the same city.

4. Rules for Adjournment Neither house, during the session of Congress, shall, without the consent of the other, adjourn for more than three days, nor to any other place than that in which the two houses shall be sitting.

Section 6. Privileges and Restrictions

Clause 1 ***Compensation*** means salary. Congress decides the salary for its members. While Congress is in session, a member is free from arrest in civil cases and cannot be sued for anything he or she says on the floor of Congress. This allows for freedom of debate. However, a member can be arrested for a criminal offense.

1. Salaries and Immunities The Senators and Representatives shall receive a compensation for their services, to be ascertained by law and paid out of the Treasury of the United States. They shall in all cases, except treason, felony, and breach of the peace, be privileged from arrest during their attendance at the session of their respective houses, and in going to and returning from the same; and for any speech or debate in either house, they shall not be questioned in any other place.

2. Restrictions on Other Employment No Senator or Representative shall, during the time for which he was elected, be appointed to any civil office under the authority of the United States, which shall have been created, or the emoluments whereof shall have been increased, during such time; and no person holding any office under the United States shall be a member of either house during his continuance in office.

Clause 2 ***Emolument*** also means salary. A member of Congress cannot hold another federal office during his or her term. A former member of Congress cannot hold an office created while he or she was in Congress. An official in another branch of government cannot serve at the same time in Congress. This strengthens the separation of powers.

Section 7. Law-Making Process

1. Tax Bills All bills for raising revenue shall originate in the House of Representatives; but the Senate may propose or concur with amendments as on other bills.

Clause 1 ***Revenue*** is money raised by the government through taxes. Tax bills must be introduced in the House. The Senate, however, can make changes in tax bills. This clause protects the principle that people can be taxed only with their consent.

2. How a Bill Becomes a Law Every bill which shall have passed the House of Representatives and the Senate shall, before it become a law, be presented to the President of the United States; if he approve, he shall sign it, but if not, he shall return it, with his objections, to that house in which it shall have originated, who shall enter the objections at large on their journal, and proceed to reconsider it. If after such reconsideration two-thirds of that house shall agree to pass the bill, it shall be sent, together with the objections, to the other house, by which it shall likewise be reconsidered, and, if approved by two-thirds of that house, it shall become a law. But in all such cases the votes of both houses shall be determined by yeas and nays, and the names of the persons voting for and against the bill shall be entered on the journal of each house respectively. If any bill shall not be returned by the President within ten days (Sundays excepted) after it shall have been presented to him, the same bill shall be a law, in like manner as if he had signed it, unless the Congress by their adjournment prevent its return, in which case it shall not be a law.

Clause 2 A ***bill,*** or proposed law, that is passed by a majority of the House and Senate is sent to the President. If the President signs the bill, it becomes law.

A bill can also become law without the President's signature. The President can refuse to act on a bill. If Congress is in session at the time, the bill becomes law 10 days after the President receives it.

The President can ***veto,*** or reject, a bill by sending it back to the house where it was introduced. Or if the President refuses to act on a bill and Congress adjourns within 10 days, then the bill dies. This way of killing a bill without taking action is called the ***pocket veto.***

Congress can override the President's veto if each house of Congress passes the bill again by a two-thirds vote. This clause is an important part of the system of checks and balances (page 130).

3. Resolutions Passed by Congress Every order, resolution, or vote to which the concurrence of the Senate and House of Representatives may be necessary (except on a question of adjournment) shall be presented to the President of the United States; and before the same shall take effect, shall be approved by him, or being disapproved by him, shall be repassed by two-thirds of the Senate and House of Representatives, according to the rules and limitations prescribed in the case of a bill.

Clause 3 Congress can pass resolutions or orders that have the same force as laws. Any such resolution or order must be signed by the President (except on questions of adjournment). Thus, this clause prevents Congress from bypassing the President simply by calling a bill by another name.

Section 8. Powers Delegated to Congress

The Congress shall have the power

1. Taxes To lay and collect taxes, duties, imposts, and excises, to pay the debts and provide for the common defense and general welfare of the United States; but all duties, imposts, and excises shall be uniform throughout the United States;

Clause 1 ***Duties*** are tariffs. ***Imposts*** are taxes in general. ***Excises*** are taxes on the production or sale of certain goods. Congress has the power to tax and spend tax money. Taxes must be the same in all parts of the country.

2. Borrowing To borrow money on the credit of the United States;

Clause 2 Congress can borrow money for the United States. The government often borrows money by selling ***bonds,*** or certificates that promise to pay the holder a certain sum of money on a certain date (page 174).

Clause 3 Only Congress has the power to regulate foreign and ***interstate trade,*** or trade between states. Disagreement over interstate trade was a major problem with the Articles of Confederation (pages 117–118).

3. Commerce To regulate commerce with foreign nations, and among the several states, and with the Indian tribes;

Clause 4 ***Naturalization*** is the process whereby a foreigner becomes a citizen. ***Bankruptcy*** is the condition in which a person or business cannot pay its debts. Congress has the power to pass laws on these two issues. The laws must be the same in all parts of the country.

4. Naturalization; Bankruptcy To establish a uniform rule of naturalization, and uniform laws on the subject of bankruptcies throughout the United States;

Clause 5 Congress has the power to coin money and set its value. Congress has set up the National Bureau of Standards to regulate weights and measures.

5. Coins; Weights; Measures To coin money, regulate the value thereof, and of foreign coin, and fix the standard of weights and measures;

Clause 6 ***Counterfeiting*** is the making of imitation money. ***Securities*** are bonds. Congress can make laws to punish counterfeiters.

6. Counterfeiting To provide for the punishment of counterfeiting the securities and current coin of the United States;

Clause 7 Congress has the power to set up and control the delivery of mail.

7. Post Offices To establish post offices and post roads;

Clause 8 Congress may pass copyright and patent laws. A ***copyright*** protects an author. A patent makes an inventor the sole owner of his or her work for a limited time.

8. Copyrights; Patents To promote the progress of science and useful arts by securing for limited times to authors and inventors the exclusive right to their respective writings and discoveries;

Clause 9 Congress has the power to set up ***inferior,*** or lower, federal courts under the Supreme Court.

9. Federal Courts To constitute tribunals inferior to the Supreme Court;

Clause 10 Congress can punish ***piracy,*** or the robbing of ships at sea.

10. Piracy To define and punish piracies and felonies committed on the high seas and offenses against the law of nations;

Clause 11 Only Congress can declare war. Declarations of war are granted at the request of the President. ***Letters of marque and reprisal*** were documents issued by a government allowing merchant ships to arm themselves and attack ships of an enemy nation. They are no longer issued.

11. Declarations of War To declare war, ~~grant letters of marque and reprisal,~~ and make rules concerning captures on land and water;

Clauses 12, 13, 14 These clauses place the army and navy under the control of Congress. Congress decides on the size of the armed forces and the amount of money to spend on the army and navy. It also has the power to write rules governing the armed forces.

12. Army To raise and support armies, but no appropriation of money to that use shall be for a longer term than two years;

13. Navy To provide and maintain a navy;

14. Rules for the Military To make rules for the government and regulation of the land and naval forces;

Clauses 15, 16 The ***militia*** is a body of citizen soldiers. Congress can call up the militia to put down rebellions or fight foreign invaders. Each state has its own militia, today called the National Guard. Normally, the militia is under the command of a state's governor. However, it can be placed under the command of the President.

15. Militia To provide for calling forth the militia to execute the laws of the Union, suppress insurrections, and repel invasions;

16. Rules for the Militia To provide for organizing, arming, and disciplining the militia, and for governing such part of them as may be employed in the service of the United States, reserving to the states, respectively, the appointment of the officers, and the authority of training the militia according to the discipline prescribed by Congress;

17. National Capital To exercise exclusive legislation in all cases whatsoever, over such district (not exceeding ten miles square) as may, by cession of particular states, and the acceptance of Congress, become the seat of government of the United States, and to exercise like authority over all places purchased by the consent of the legislature of the state in which the same shall be, for the erection of forts, magazines, arsenals, dock-yards, and other needful buildings;—and

Clause 17 Congress controls the district around the national capital. In 1790, Congress made Washington, D.C., the nation's capital (page 175). In 1973, it gave residents of the District the right to elect local officials.

18. Necessary Laws To make all laws which shall be necessary and proper for carrying into execution the foregoing powers, and all other powers vested by this Constitution in the government of the United States, or in any department or officer thereof.

Clause 18 Clauses 1–17 list the powers delegated to Congress. The writers of the Constitution added Clause 18 so that Congress could deal with the changing needs of the nation. It gives Congress the power to make laws as needed to carry out the first 17 clauses. Clause 18 is sometimes called the elastic clause because it lets Congress stretch the meaning of its power.

Section 9. Powers Denied to the Federal Government

1. The Slave Trade ~~The migration or importation of such persons as any of the states now existing shall think proper to admit shall not be prohibited by the Congress prior to the year 1808; but a tax or duty may be imposed on such importation, not exceeding $10 for each person.~~

Clause 1 ***Such persons*** means slaves. This clause resulted from a compromise between the supporters and the opponents of the slave trade (page 125). In 1808, as soon as Congress was permitted to abolish the slave trade, it did so. The $10 import tax was never imposed.

2. Writ of Habeas Corpus The privilege of the writ of habeas corpus shall not be suspended, unless when in cases of rebellion or invasion the public safety may require it.

Clause 2 A ***writ of habeas corpus*** is a court order requiring government officials to bring a prisoner to court and explain why he or she is being held. A writ of habeas corpus protects people from unlawful imprisonment. The government cannot suspend this right except in times of rebellion or invasion.

3. Bills of Attainder and Ex Post Facto Laws No bill of attainder or *ex post facto* law shall be passed.

Clause 3 A ***bill of attainder*** is a law declaring that a person is guilty of a particular crime. An ***ex post facto law*** punishes an act which was not illegal when it was committed. Congress cannot pass a bill of attainder or *ex post facto* laws.

4. Apportionment of Direct Taxes ~~No capitation or other direct tax shall be laid, unless in proportion to the census or enumeration herein before directed to be taken.~~

Clause 4 A ***capitation tax*** is a tax placed directly on each person. ***Direct taxes*** are taxes on people or on land. They can be passed only if they are divided among the states according to population. The Sixteenth Amendment allowed Congress to tax income without regard to the population of the states.

5. Taxes on Exports No tax or duty shall be laid on articles exported from any state.

Clause 5 This clause forbids Congress to tax exports. In 1787, southerners insisted on this clause because their economy depended on exports.

6. Special Preference for Trade No preference shall be given any regulation of commerce or revenue to the ports of one state over those of another; nor shall vessels bound to, or from, one state, be obliged to enter, clear, or pay duties in another.

Clause 6 Congress cannot make laws that favor one state over another in trade and commerce. Also, states cannot place tariffs on interstate trade.

7. Spending No money shall be drawn from the Treasury, but in consequence of appropriations made by law; and a regular statement and account of the receipts and expenditures of all public money shall be published from time to time.

Clause 7 The federal government cannot spend money unless Congress ***appropriates*** it, or passes a law allowing it. This clause gives Congress an important check on the President by controlling the money he or she can spend. The government must publish a statement showing how it spends public funds.

Clause 8 The government cannot award titles of nobility, such as Duke or Duchess. American citizens cannot accept titles of nobility from foreign governments without the consent of Congress.

8. Creation of Titles of Nobility No title of nobility shall be granted by the United States; and no person holding any office of profit or trust under them, shall, without the consent of the Congress, accept of any present, emolument, office, or title, of any kind whatever, from any king, prince, or foreign state.

Section 10. Powers Denied to the States

Clause 1 The writers of the Constitution did not want the states to act like separate nations. So they prohibited states from making treaties or coining money. Some powers denied to the federal government are also denied to the states. For example, states cannot pass *ex post facto* laws.

1. Unconditional Prohibitions No state shall enter into any treaty, alliance, or confederation; grant letters of marque and reprisal; coin money; emit bills of credit; make anything but gold and silver coin a tender in payment of debts; pass any bill of attainder, *ex post facto* law, or law impairing the obligation of contracts, or grant any title of nobility.

Clauses 2, 3 Powers listed here are forbidden to the states, but Congress can lift these prohibitions by passing laws that give these powers to the states.

Clause 2 forbids states from taxing imports and exports without the consent of Congress. States may charge inspection fees on goods entering the states. Any profit from these fees must be turned over to the United States Treasury.

Clause 3 forbids states from keeping an army or navy without the consent of Congress. States cannot make treaties or declare war unless an enemy invades or is about to invade.

2. Powers Conditionally Denied No state shall, without the consent of the Congress, lay any imposts or duties on imports or exports, except what may be absolutely necessary for executing its inspection laws; and the net produce of all duties and imposts, laid by any state on imports or exports, shall be for the use of the Treasury of the United States; and all such laws shall be subject to the revision and control of the Congress.

3. Other Denied Powers No state shall, without the consent of Congress, lay any duty of tonnage, keep troops, or ships of war in time of peace, enter into any agreement or compact with another state, or with a foreign power, or engage in war, unless actually invaded, or in such imminent danger as will not admit of delay.

Article 2. The Executive Branch

Section 1. President and Vice-President

Clause 1 The President is responsible for ***executing,*** or carrying out, laws passed by Congress.

1. Chief Executive The executive power shall be vested in a President of the United States of America. He shall hold his office during the term of four years, and together with the Vice-President, chosen for the same term, be elected as follows:

Clauses 2, 3 Some writers of the Constitution were afraid to allow the people to elect the President directly (page 130). Therefore, the Constitutional Convention set up the electoral college. Clause 2 directs each state to choose electors, or delegates to the electoral college, to vote for President. A state's electoral vote is equal to the combined number of senators and representatives. Each state may decide how to choose its electors. Members of Congress and federal officeholders may not serve as electors. This much of the original electoral college system is still in effect.

Clause 3 called upon each elector to vote for two candidates. The candidate who received a majority of the electoral votes would become President. The runner-up would become Vice President. If no candidate won a majority, the House would choose the President. The Senate would choose the Vice President.

The election of 1800 showed a problem with the original electoral college system (page 189). Thomas Jefferson was the Republican candidate

2. Selection of Electors Each state shall appoint, in such manner as the legislature thereof may direct, a number of electors, equal to the whole number of Senators and Representatives to which the state may be entitled in the Congress; but no Senator or Representative, or person holding an office or trust or profit under the United States, shall be appointed an elector.

3. Electoral College Procedures ~~The electors shall meet in their respective states, and vote by ballot for two persons, of whom one at least shall not be an inhabitant of the same state with themselves. And they shall make a list of all the persons voted for, and of the number of votes for each; which list they shall sign and certify, and transmit sealed to the seat of the government of the United States, directed to the president of the Senate. The president of the Senate shall, in the presence of the Senate and House of Representatives, open all the certificates, and the votes shall then be counted. The person having the greatest number of votes shall be President, if such number be a majority of the whole number of electors appointed; and if~~

~~there be more than one who have such majority, and have an equal number of votes, then the House of Representatives shall immediately choose by ballot one of them for President; and if no person have a majority, then from the five highest on the list the said House shall in like manner choose the President. But in choosing the President the votes shall be taken by states, the representation from each state having one vote. A quorum for this purpose shall consist of a member or members from two-thirds of the states, and a majority of all the states shall be necessary to a choice. In every case, after the choice of the President, the person having the greatest number of votes of the electors shall be the Vice-President. But if there should remain two or more who have equal votes, the Senate shall choose from them by ballot the Vice-President.~~

for President, and Aaron Burr was the Republican candidate for Vice President. In the electoral college, the vote ended in a tie. The election was finally decided in the House, where Jefferson was chosen President. The Twelfth Amendment changed the electoral college system so that this could not happen again.

4. Time of Elections The Congress may determine the time of choosing the electors, and the day on which they shall give their votes; which day shall be the same throughout the United States.

Clause 4 By a law passed in 1792, electors are chosen on the Tuesday after the first Monday of November every four years. Electors from each state meet to vote in December.

Today, voters in each state choose ***slates,*** or groups, of electors who are pledged to a candidate for President. The candidate for President who wins the popular vote in each state wins that state's electoral vote.

5. Qualifications for President No person except a natural-born citizen ~~or a citizen of the United States, at the time of the adoption of this Constitution,~~ shall be eligible to the office of the President; neither shall any person be eligible to that office who shall not have attained to the age of thirty-five years, and been fourteen years a resident within the United States.

Clause 5 The President must be a citizen of the United States from birth, at least 35 years old, and a resident of the country for 14 years. The first seven Presidents of the United States were born under British rule, but they were allowed to hold office because they were citizens at the time the Constitution was adopted.

6. Presidential Succession In case of the removal of the President from office, or of his death, resignation, or inability to discharge the powers and duties of the said office, the same shall devolve on the Vice-President, and the Congress may by law provide for the case of removal, death, resignation, or inability, both of the President and Vice-President, declaring what officer shall then act as President, and such officer shall act accordingly, until the disability be removed, or a President shall be elected.

Clause 6 The powers of the President pass to the Vice President if the President leaves office or cannot discharge his or her duties. The wording of this clause caused confusion the first time a President died in office. When President William Henry Harrison died, it was uncertain whether Vice President John Tyler should remain Vice President and act as President or whether he should be sworn in as President. Tyler persuaded a federal judge to swear him in. So he set the precedent that the Vice President assumes the office of President when it becomes vacant. The Twenty-fifth Amendment replaced this clause.

7. Salary The President shall, at stated times, receive for his services, a compensation, which shall neither be increased nor diminished during the period for which he shall have been elected, and he shall not receive within that period any other emolument from the United States, or any of them.

Clause 7 The President is paid a salary. It cannot be raised or lowered during his or her term of office. The President is not allowed to hold any other federal or state position while in office. Today, the President's salary is $200,000 a year.

8. Oath of Office Before he enter on the execution of his office, he shall take the following oath or affirmation:—"I do solemnly swear (or affirm) that I will faithfully execute the office of President of the United States, and will to the best of my ability, preserve, protect, and defend the Constitution of the United States."

Clause 8 Before taking office, the President must promise to protect and defend the Constitution. Usually, the Chief Justice of the Supreme Court gives the oath of office to the President.

Section 2. Powers of the President

Clause 1 The President is head of the armed forces and the state militias when they are called into national service. So the military is under ***civilian,*** or nonmilitary, control.

The President can get advice from the heads of executive departments. In most cases, the President has the power to grant a reprieve or pardon. A ***reprieve*** suspends punishment ordered by law. A ***pardon*** prevents prosecution for a crime or overrides the judgment of a court.

1. Commander in Chief of the Armed Forces The President shall be Commander in Chief of the Army and Navy of the United States, and of the militia of the several states, when called into the actual service of the United States; he may require the opinion, in writing, of the principal officer in each of the executive departments, upon any subject relating to the duties of their respective offices, and he shall have power to grant reprieves and pardons for offenses against the United States, except in cases of impeachment.

Clause 2 The President has the power to make treaties with other nations. Under the system of checks and balances, all treaties must be approved by two thirds of the Senate. Today, the President also makes agreements with foreign governments. These executive agreements do not need Senate approval.

The President has the power to appoint ambassadors to foreign countries and to appoint other high officials. The Senate must ***confirm,*** or approve, these appointments.

2. Making Treaties and Nominations He shall have power, by and with the advice and consent of the Senate, to make treaties, provided two-thirds of the Senators present concur; and he shall nominate, and by and with the advice and consent of the Senate, shall appoint ambassadors, other public ministers and consuls, judges of the Supreme Court, and all other officers of the United States, whose appointments are not herein otherwise provided for, and which shall be established by law; but the Congress may by law vest the appointment of such inferior officers, as they think proper, in the President alone, in the courts of law, or in the heads of departments.

Clause 3 If the Senate is in ***recess,*** or not meeting, the President may fill vacant government posts by making temporary appointments.

3. Temporary Appointments The President shall have power to fill up all vacancies that may happen during the recess of the Senate, by granting commissions which shall expire at the end of their next session.

Section 3. Duties

The President must give Congress a report on the condition of the nation every year. This report is now called the State of the Union Address. Since 1913, the President has given this speech in person each January.

The President can call a special session of Congress and can adjourn Congress if necessary. The President has the power to receive, or recognize, foreign ambassadors.

The President must carry out the laws. Today, many government agencies oversee the execution of laws.

He shall from time to time give to the Congress information of the state of the Union, and recommend to their consideration such measures as he shall judge necessary and expedient; he may, on extraordinary occasions, convene both houses, or either of them, and in case of disagreement between them, with respect to the time of adjournment, he may adjourn them to such time as he shall think proper; he shall receive ambassadors and other public ministers; he shall take care that the laws be faithfully executed, and shall commission all the officers of the United States.

Section 4. Impeachment and Removal From Office

Civil officers include federal judges and members of the Cabinet. ***High crimes*** are major crimes. ***Misdemeanors*** are lesser crimes. The President, Vice President, and others can be forced out of office if impeached and found guilty of certain crimes.

The President, Vice-President, and all civil officers of the United States, shall be removed from office on impeachment for, and conviction of, treason, bribery, or other high crimes or misdemeanors.

Article 3. The Judicial Branch

Section 1. Federal Courts

Judicial power is the right of the courts to decide legal cases. The Constitution creates the Supreme Court but lets Congress decide the size of the Supreme Court. Congress has the power to set up inferior, or lower, courts. The Judiciary Act of 1789 (page 173) set up district and circuit courts, or courts of appeal. Today, there are 94 district courts and 13 courts of appeal. All federal judges serve for life.

The judicial power of the United States shall be vested in one Supreme Court, and in such inferior courts as the Congress may from time to time ordain and establish. The judges, both of the Supreme and inferior courts, shall hold their offices during good behavior, and shall, at stated times, receive for their services a compensation, which shall not be diminished during their continuance in office.

Section 2. Jurisdiction of Federal Courts

1. Scope of Judicial Power The judicial power shall extend to all cases, in law and equity, arising under this Constitution, the laws of the United States, and treaties made or which shall be made, under their authority; to all cases affecting ambassadors, other public ministers and consuls; to all cases of admiralty and maritime jurisdiction; to controversies to which the United States shall be a party; to controversies between two or more states; ~~between a state and citizens of another state;~~ between citizens of the same state claiming lands under grants of different states, and between a state or the citizens thereof, and foreign states, citizens, or subjects.

Clause 1 ***Jurisdiction*** refers to the right of a court to hear a case. Federal courts have jurisdiction over cases that involve the Constitution, federal laws, treaties, foreign ambassadors and diplomats, naval and maritime laws, disagreements between states or between citizens from different states, and disputes between a state or citizen and a foreign state or citizen.

In *Marbury* v. *Madison,* the Supreme Court established the right to judge whether a law is constitutional (page 197).

2. The Supreme Court In all cases affecting ambassadors, other public ministers and consuls, and those in which a state shall be a party, the Supreme Court shall have original jurisdiction. In all the other cases before mentioned, the Supreme Court shall have appellate jurisdiction, both as to law and fact, with such exceptions, and under such regulations as the Congress shall make.

Clause 2 ***Original jurisdiction*** means the power of a court to hear a case where it first arises. The Supreme Court has original jurisdiction over only a few cases, such as those involving foreign diplomats. More often, the Supreme Court acts as an appellate court. An ***appellate court*** does not decide guilt. It decides whether the lower court trial was properly conducted and reviews the lower court's decision.

3. Trial by Jury The trial of all crimes, except in cases of impeachment, shall be by jury; and such trial shall be held in the state where the said crimes shall have been committed; but when not committed within any state, the trial shall be at such place or places as the Congress may by law have directed.

Clause 3 This clause guarantees the right to a jury trial for anyone accused of a federal crime. The only exceptions are impeachment cases. The trial must be held in the state where the crime was committed.

Section 3. Treason

1. Definition Treason against the United States shall consist only in levying war against them, or in adhering to their enemies, giving them aid and comfort. No person shall be convicted of treason unless on the testimony of two witnesses to the same overt act, or on confession in open court.

Clause 1 Treason is clearly defined. An ***overt act*** is an actual action. A person cannot be convicted of treason for what he or she thinks. A person can be convicted of treason only if he or she confesses or two witnesses testify to it.

2. Punishment The Congress shall have power to declare the punishment of treason, but no attainder of treason shall work corruption of blood or forfeiture except during the life of the person attainted.

Clause 2 Congress has the power to set the punishment for traitors. Congress may not punish the children of convicted traitors by taking away their civil rights or property.

Article 4. Relations Among the States

Section 1. Official Records and Acts

Full faith and credit shall be given in each state to the public acts, records, and judicial proceedings of every other state. And the Congress may by general laws prescribe the manner in which such acts, records, and proceedings shall be proved, and the effect thereof.

Each state must recognize the official acts and records of any other state. For example, each state must recognize marriage certificates issued by another state. Congress can pass laws to ensure this.

Section 2. Privileges of Citizens

1. Privileges The citizens of each state shall be entitled to all privileges and immunities of citizens in the several states.

Clause 1 All states must treat citizens of another state in the same way it treats its own citizens. However, the courts have allowed states to give residents certain privileges, such as lower tuition rates.

Clause 2 **Extradition** means the act of returning a suspected criminal or escaped prisoner to a state where he or she is wanted. State governors must return a suspect to another state. However, the Supreme Court has ruled that a governor cannot be forced to do so if he or she feels that justice will not be done.

2. Extradition A person charged in any state with treason, felony, or other crime, who shall flee from justice, and be found in another state, shall on demand of the executive authority of the state from which he fled, be delivered up, to be removed to the state having jurisdiction of the crime.

Clause 3 ***Persons held to service or labor*** refers to slaves or indentured servants. This clause required states to return runaway slaves to their owners. The Thirteenth Amendment replaces this clause.

3. Return of Fugitive Slaves ~~No person held to service or labor in one state, under the laws thereof, escaping into another, shall in consequence of any law or regulation therein, be discharged from such service or labor, but shall be delivered up on claim of the party to whom such service or labor may be due.~~

Section 3. New States and Territories

Clause 1 Congress has the power to admit new states to the Union. Existing states cannot be split up or joined together to form new states unless both Congress and the state legislatures approve. New states are equal to all other states.

1. New States New states may be admitted by the Congress into this Union; but no new state shall be formed or erected within the jurisdiction of any other state; nor any state be formed by the junction of two of more states, or parts of states, without the consent of the legislatures of the states concerned as well as of the Congress.

Clause 2 Congress can make rules for managing and governing land owned by the United States. This includes territories not organized into states, such as Puerto Rico and Guam, and federal lands within a state.

2. Federal Lands The Congress shall have power to dispose of and make all needful rules and regulations respecting the territory or other property belonging to the United States; and nothing in this Constitution shall be so construed as to prejudice any claims of the United States, or of any particular state.

Section 4. Guarantees to the States

In a ***republic,*** voters choose representatives to govern them. The federal government must protect the states from foreign invasion and from ***domestic,*** or internal, disorder if asked to do so by a state.

The United States shall guarantee to every state in this Union a republican form of government, and shall protect each of them against invasion; and on application of the legislature, or of the executive (when the legislature cannot be convened) against domestic violence.

Article 5. Amending the Constitution

The Constitution can be ***amended,*** or changed, if necessary. An amendment can be proposed by (1) a two-thirds vote of both houses of Congress or (2) a national convention called by Congress at the request of two thirds of the state legislatures. (This second method has never been used.) An amendment must be ***ratified,*** or approved, by (1) three fourths of the state legislatures or (2) special conventions in three fourths of the states. Congress decides which method will be used.

The Congress, whenever two-thirds of both houses shall deem it necessary, shall propose amendments to this Constitution, or, on the application of the legislatures of two-thirds of the several states, shall call a convention for proposing amendments, which, in either case, shall be valid to all intents and purposes, as part of this Constitution, when ratified by the legislatures of three-fourths of the several states, or by conventions in three-fourths thereof, as the one or the other mode of ratification may be proposed by the Congress; provided that ~~no amendments which may be made prior to the year 1808 shall in any manner affect the first and fourth clauses in the Ninth Section of the First Article; and that~~ no state, without its consent, shall be deprived of its equal suffrage in the Senate.

Article 6. National Supremacy

Section 1. Prior Public Debts

The United States government promised to pay all debts and honor all agreements made under the Articles of Confederation.

All debts contracted and engagements entered into, before the adoption of this Constitution, shall be as valid against the United States under this Constitution, as under the Confederation.

Section 2. Supreme Law of the Land

This Constitution, and the laws of the United States which shall be made in pursuance thereof, and all treaties made, or which shall be made, under the authority of the United States, shall be the supreme law of the land; and the judges in every state shall be bound thereby, anything in the constitution or laws of any state to the contrary notwithstanding.

The Constitution, federal laws, and treaties that the Senate has ratified are the supreme, or highest, law of the land. Thus, they outweigh state laws. A state judge must overturn a state law that conflicts with the Constitution or with a federal law.

Section 3. Oaths of Office

The Senators and Representatives before mentioned, and the members of the several state legislatures, and all executive and judicial officers, both of the United States and of the several states, shall be bound by oath or affirmation, to support this Constitution; but no religious test shall ever be required as a qualification to any office or public trust under the United States.

State and federal officeholders take an oath, or solemn promise, to support the Constitution. However, this clause forbids the use of religious tests for officeholders. During the colonial period, every colony except Rhode Island required a religious test for officeholders.

Article 7. Ratification

The ratification of the convention of nine states shall be sufficient for the establishment of the Constitution between the states so ratifying the same.

During 1787 and 1788, states held special conventions. By October 1788, the required nine states had ratified the Constitution.

Done in convention, by the unanimous consent of the states present, the seventeenth day of September, in the year of our Lord one thousand seven hundred and eighty-seven, and of the independence of the United States of America the twelfth. In Witness *whereof, we have hereunto subscribed our names.*

Attest: William Jackson
Secretary

George Washington
President and deputy from Virginia

New Hampshire
John Langdon
Nicholas Gilman

Massachussetts
Nathaniel Gorham
Rufus King

Connecticut
William Samuel Johnson
Roger Sherman

New York
Alexander Hamilton

New Jersey
William Livingston
David Brearley
William Paterson
Jonathan Dayton

Pennsylvania
Benjamin Franklin
Thomas Mifflin
Robert Morris
George Clymer
Thomas FitzSimons
Jared Ingersoll
James Wilson
Gouverneur Morris

Delaware
George Read
Gunning Bedford, Jr.
John Dickinson
Richard Bassett
Jacob Broom

Maryland
James McHenry
Dan of St. Thomas Jennifer
Daniel Carroll

Virginia
John Blair
James Madison, Jr.

North Carolina
William Blount
Richard Dobbs Spaight
Hugh Williamson

South Carolina
John Rutledge
Charles Cotesworth Pinckney
Charles Pinckney
Pierce Butler

Georgia
William Few
Abraham Baldwin

★ Amendments to the Constitution ★

The first 10 amendments, which were added to the Constitution in 1791, are called the Bill of Rights. Originally, the Bill of Rights applied only to actions of the federal government. However, the Supreme Court has used the due process clause of the Fourteenth Amendment to extend many of the rights to protect individuals against action by the states.

Amendment 1

Freedoms of Religion, Speech, Press, Assembly, and Petition

Congress shall make no law respecting an establishment of religion, or prohibiting the free exercise thereof; or abridging the freedom of speech, or of the press; or the right of the people peaceably to assemble, and to petition the government for a redress of grievances.

Congress cannot set up an established, or official, church or religion for the nation. During the colonial period, most colonies had established churches. However, the authors of the First Amendment wanted to keep government and religion separate.

Congress may not ***abridge,*** or limit, the freedom to speak and write freely. The government may not censor, or review, books and newspapers before they are printed. This amendment also protects the right to assemble, or hold public meetings. ***Petition*** means ask. ***Redress*** means to correct. ***Grievances*** are wrongs. The people have the right to ask the government for wrongs to be corrected.

Amendment 2

Right to Bear Arms

A well-regulated militia, being necessary to the security of a free state, the right of the people to keep and bear arms shall not be infringed.

State militias, such as the National Guard, have the right to bear arms, or keep weapons. Courts have generally ruled that the government can regulate the ownership of guns by private citizens.

Amendment 3

Lodging Troops in Private Homes

No soldier shall, in time of peace, be quartered in any house, without the consent of the owner; nor in time of war, but in a manner to be prescribed by law.

During the colonial period, the British quartered, or housed, soldiers in private homes without the permission of the owners (page 90). This amendment limits the government's right to use private homes to house soldiers.

Amendment 4

Search and Seizure

The right of the people to be secure in their persons, houses, papers, and effects, against unreasonable searches and seizures, shall not be violated; and no warrants shall issue but upon probable cause, supported by oath or affirmation, and particularly describing the place to be searched, and the persons or things to be seized.

This amendment protects Americans from unreasonable searches and seizures. Search and seizure are permitted only if a judge has issued a ***warrant,*** or written court order. A warrant is issued only if there is probable cause. This means an officer must show that it is probable, or likely, that the search will produce evidence of a crime. A search warrant must name the exact place to be searched and the things to be seized. In some cases, courts have ruled that searches can take place without a warrant. For example, police may search a person who is under arrest. However, evidence found during an unlawful search cannot be used in a trial.

Amendment 5

Rights of the Accused

No person shall be held to answer for a capital, or otherwise infamous, crime, unless on a presentment or indictment of a grand jury, except in cases arising in the land or naval forces, or in the militia, when in actual service in time of war or public danger; nor shall any person be subject for the same offense to be twice put in jeopardy of life and limb; nor shall be compelled, in any criminal case, to be a witness against himself; nor be

This amendment protects the rights of the accused. ***Capital crimes*** are those that can be punished with death. ***Infamous crimes*** are those that can be punished with prison or loss of rights. The federal government must obtain an ***indictment,*** or formal accusation, from a grand jury to prosecute anyone for such crimes. A ***grand jury*** is a panel of between 12 and 23 citizens who deprived of life, liberty, or property, without due process of law; nor shall private property be taken for public use, without just compensation.

decide if the government has enough evidence to justify a trial. This procedure prevents prosecution with little or no evidence of guilt. (Soldiers and the militia in wartime are not covered by this rule.)

Double jeopardy is forbidden. This means that a person cannot be tried twice for the same crime—unless a court sets aside a conviction because of a legal error. A person on trial cannot be forced to testify, or give evidence, against himself or herself. A person accused of a crime is entitled to ***due process of law,*** or a fair hearing or trial. Finally, the government cannot seize private property for public use without paying the owner a fair price for it.

Amendment 6

Right to Speedy Trial by Jury

In all criminal prosecutions, the accused shall enjoy the right to a speedy and public trial, by an impartial jury of the state and district wherein the crime shall have been committed, which district shall have been previously ascertained by law, and to be informed of the nature and cause of the accusation; to be confronted with the witnesses against him; to have compulsory process for obtaining witnesses in his favor, and to have the assistance of counsel for his defense.

In criminal cases, the jury must be ***impartial,*** or not favor either side. The accused is guaranteed the right to a trial by jury. The trial must be speedy. If the government purposely postpones the trial so that it becomes hard for the person to get a fair hearing, the charge may be dismissed. The accused must be told the charges against him or her and be allowed to question prosecution witnesses. Witnesses who can help the accused can be ordered to appear in court.

The accused must be allowed a lawyer. Since 1942, the federal government has been required to provide a lawyer if the accused cannot afford one. In 1963, the Supreme Court decided that states must also provide lawyers for a defendant too poor to pay for one.

Amendment 7

Jury Trial in Civil Cases

In suits at common law, where the value in controversy shall exceed $20, the right of trial by jury shall be preserved, and no fact tried by a jury shall be otherwise re-examined in any court of the United States than according to the rules of the common law.

Common law refers to rules of law established by judges in past cases. This amendment guarantees the right to a jury trial in lawsuits where the sum of money at stake is more than $20. An appeals court cannot change a verdict because it disagrees with the decision of the jury. It can set aside a verdict only if legal errors made the trial unfair.

Amendment 8

Bail and Punishment

Excessive bail shall not be required, nor excessive fines imposed, nor cruel and unusual punishments inflicted.

Bail is money the accused leaves with the court as a pledge to appear for trial. If the accused does not appear for trial, the court keeps the money. ***Excessive*** means too high. This amendment forbids courts to set unreasonably high bail. The amount of bail usually depends on the seriousness of the charge and whether the accused is likely to appear for the trial. The amendment also forbids cruel and unusual punishments such as mental and physical abuse.

Amendment 9

Powers Reserved to the People

The enumeration in the Constitution, of certain rights, shall not be construed to deny or disparage others retained by the people.

People have rights not listed in the Constitution. This amendment was added because some people feared that the Bill of Rights would be used to limit rights to those actually listed.

Amendment 10

Powers Reserved to the States

The powers not delegated to the United States by the Constitution, nor prohibited by it to the states, are reserved to the states respectively, or to the people.

This amendment limits the power of the federal government. Powers that are not given to the federal government belong to the states. The powers reserved to the states are not listed in the Constitution.

Amendment 11

Suits Against States

Passed by Congress on March 4, 1794. Ratified on January 23, 1795.

The judicial power of the United States shall not be construed to extend to any suit in law or equity, commenced or prosecuted against one of the United States, by citizens of another state, or by citizens or subjects of any foreign state.

This amendment changed part of Article 3, Section 2, Clause 1. As a result, a private citizen from one state cannot sue the government of another state in federal court. However, a citizen can sue a state government in a state court.

Amendment 12

Election of President and Vice-President

Passed by Congress on December 9, 1803. Ratified on June 15, 1804.

This amendment changed the way the electoral college voted. Before the amendment was adopted, each elector simply voted for two people. The candidate with the most votes became President. The runner-up became Vice President. In the election of 1800, however, a tie vote resulted between Thomas Jefferson and Aaron Burr (page 189).

In such a case, the Constitution required the House of Representatives to elect the President. Federalists had a majority in the House. They tried to keep Jefferson out of office by voting for Burr. It took 35 ballots in the House before Jefferson was elected President.

To keep this from happening again, the Twelfth Amendment was passed and ratified in time for the election of 1804.

This amendment provides that each elector choose one candidate for President and one candidate for Vice President. If no candidate for President receives a majority of electoral votes, the House of Representatives chooses the President. If no candidate for Vice President receives a majority, the Senate elects the Vice President. The Vice President must be a person who is eligible to be President.

This system is still in use today. However, it is possible for a candidate to win the popular vote and lose in the electoral college. This happened in 1876 (pages 419–420).

The electors shall meet in their respective states, and vote by ballot for President and Vice-President, one of whom, at least, shall not be an inhabitant of the same state with themselves; they shall name in their ballots the person voted for as President, and in distinct ballots the person voted for as Vice-President, and they shall make distinct lists of all persons voted for as President, and of all persons voted for as Vice-President, and of the number of votes for each, which lists they shall sign and certify, and transmit, sealed, to the seat of government of the United States, directed to the President of the Senate; the President of the Senate shall, in the presence of the Senate and House of Representatives, open all the certificates and the votes shall then be counted; the person having the greatest number of votes for President shall be the President, if such number be a majority of the whole number of electors appointed; and if no person have such majority, then from the persons having the highest numbers not exceeding three on the list of those voted for as President, the House of Representatives shall choose immediately, by ballot, the President. But in choosing the President, the votes shall be taken by the states, the representation from each state having one vote; a quorum for this purpose shall consist of a member or members from two-thirds of the states, and a majority of all the states shall be necessary to a choice. And if the House of Representatives shall not choose a President whenever the right of choice shall devolve upon them, before the fourth day of March next following, then the Vice-President shall act as President, as in the case of the death or other constitutional disability of the President. The person having the greatest number of votes as Vice-President, shall be the Vice-President, if such number be a majority of the whole number of electors appointed, and if no person have a majority, then, from the two highest numbers on the list, the Senate shall choose the Vice-President; a quorum for the purpose shall consist of two-thirds of the whole number of Senators, and a majority of the whole number shall be necessary to a choice. But no person constitutionally ineligible to the office of President shall be eligible to that of Vice-President of the United States.

Amendment 13

Abolition of Slavery

Passed by Congress on January 31, 1865. Ratified on December 6, 1865.

The Emancipation Proclamation (1863) freed slaves only in areas controlled by the Confederacy (pages 387–388). This amendment freed all slaves. It also forbids ***involuntary servitude,*** or labor done against one's will. However, it does not prevent prison wardens from making prisoners work.

Section 2 says that Congress can pass laws to carry out this amendment.

Section 1. Neither slavery nor involuntary servitude, except as a punishment for crime whereof the party shall have been duly convicted, shall exist within the United States, or any place subject to their jurisdiction.

Section 2. Congress shall have power to enforce this article by appropriate legislation.

Amendment 14

Rights of Citizens

Passed by Congress on June 13, 1866. Ratified on July 9, 1868.

Section 1 defines citizenship for the first time in the Constitution, and it extends citizenship to

Section 1. Citizenship All persons born or naturalized in the United States and subject to the jurisdiction thereof, are citizens of the United States and of the state wherein they reside. No state shall make or enforce any law which shall abridge the privileges or immunities of citizens of the United States; nor shall any state deprive any person of life, liberty, or property, without due process of law; nor deny to any person within its jurisdiction the equal protection of the laws.

blacks. It also prohibits states from denying the rights and privileges of citizenship to any citizen. This section also forbids states to deny due process of law.

Section 1 guarantees all citizens "equal protection under the law." For a long time, however, the Fourteenth Amendment did not protect blacks from discrimination. After Reconstruction, separate facilities for blacks and whites sprang up (page 423). In 1954, the Supreme Court ruled that separate facilities for blacks and whites were by their nature unequal. This ruling, in the case of *Brown* v. *Board of Education,* made school segregation illegal.

Section 2. Apportionment of Representatives Representatives shall be apportioned among the several states according to their respective numbers, counting the whole number of persons in each state, excluding Indians not taxed. But when the right to vote at any election for the choice of electors for President and Vice-President of the United States, Representatives in Congress, the executive and judicial officers of a state, or the members of the legislature thereof, is denied to any of the male inhabitants of such state, being twenty-one years of age and citizens of the United States, or in any way abridged, except for participation in rebellion, or other crime, the basis of representation therein shall be reduced in the proportion which the number of such male citizens shall bear to the whole number of male citizens twenty-one years of age in such state.

Section 2 replaced the three-fifths clause. It provides that representation in the House of Representatives is decided on the basis of the number of people in the state. It also provides that states which deny the vote to male citizens over age 21 will be punished by losing part of their representation in the House. This provision has never been enforced.

Despite this clause, black citizens were often prevented from voting. In the 1960s, federal laws were passed to end voting discrimination.

Section 3. Former Confederate Officials No person shall be a Senator or Representative in Congress, or elector of President and Vice-President, or hold any office, civil or military, under the United States, or under any state, who, having previously taken an oath, as a member of Congress, or as an officer of the United States, or as a member of any state legislature, or as an executive or judicial officer of any state, to support the Constitution of the United States, shall have engaged in insurrection or rebellion against the same, or given aid or comfort to the enemies thereof. But Congress may, by vote of two-thirds of each house, remove such disability.

This section prohibited people who had been federal or state officials before the Civil War and who had joined the Confederate cause from serving again as government officials. In 1872, Congress restored the rights of former Confederate officials.

Section 4. Government Debt The validity of the public debt of the United States, authorized by law, including debts incurred for payment of pensions and bounties for services in suppressing insurrection or rebellion, shall not be questioned. But neither the United States nor any state shall assume or pay any debt or obligation incurred in aid of insurrection or rebellion against the United States or any claim for the loss or emancipation of any slave; but all such debts, obligations, and claims shall be held illegal and void.

This section recognized that the United States must repay its debts from the Civil War. However, it forbade the repayment of debts of the Confederacy. This meant that people who had loaned money to the Confederacy would not be repaid. Also, states were not allowed to pay former slave owners for the loss of slaves.

Section 5. Enforcement The Congress shall have power to enforce, by appropriate legislation, the provisions of this article.

Congress can pass laws to carry out this amendment.

Amendment 15

Voting Rights

Passed by Congress on February 26, 1869. Ratified on February 2, 1870.

Section 1. Extending the Right to Vote The right of citizens of the United States to vote shall not be denied or abridged by the United States or any state on account of race, color, or previous condition of servitude.

Previous condition of servitude refers to slavery. This amendment gave blacks, both former slaves and free blacks, the right to vote. In the late 1800s, southern states used grandfather clauses, literacy tests, and poll taxes to keep blacks from voting (pages 421–422).

Congress can pass laws to carry out this amendment. The Twenty-fourth Amendment barred the use of poll taxes in national elections. The Voting Rights Act of 1965 gave federal officials the power to register voters in places where there was voting discrimination.

Section 2. Enforcement The Congress shall have power to enforce this article by appropriate legislation.

Amendment 16

The Income Tax

Passed by Congress on July 12, 1909. Ratified on February 3, 1913.

Congress has the power to collect taxes on people's income. An income tax can be collected without regard to a state's population. This amendment changed Article 1, Section 9, Clause 4.

The Congress shall have power to lay and collect taxes on incomes, from whatever source derived, without apportionment among the several states, and without regard to any census or enumeration.

Amendment 17

Direct Election of Senators

Passed by Congress on May 13, 1912. Ratified on April 8, 1913.

This amendment replaced Article 1, Section 3, Clause 1. Before it was adopted, state legislatures chose senators. This amendment provides that senators are directly elected by the people of each state.

Section 1. Method of Election The Senate of the United States shall be composed of two Senators from each state, elected by the people thereof, for six years; and each Senator shall have one vote. The electors in each state shall have the qualifications requisite for electors of the most numerous branch of the state legislatures.

When a Senate seat becomes vacant, the governor of the state must order an election to fill the seat. The state legislature can give the governor power to fill the seat until an election is held.

Section 2. Vacancies When vacancies happen in the representation of any state in the Senate, the executive authority of such state shall issue writs of election to fill such vacancies: *Provided* that the legislature of any state may empower the executive thereof to make temporary appointments until the people fill the vacancies by election as the legislature may direct.

Senators who had already been elected by the state legislatures were not affected by this amendment.

Section 3. Exception ~~This amendment shall not be so construed as to affect the election or term of any Senator chosen before it becomes valid as part of the Constitution.~~

Amendment 18

Prohibition of Alcoholic Beverages

Passed by Congress on December 18, 1917. Ratified on January 16, 1919.

This amendment, known as ***Prohibition,*** banned the making, selling, or transporting of alcoholic beverages in the United States. Later, the Twenty-first Amendment ***repealed,*** or canceled, this amendment.

Section 1. Ban on Alcohol ~~After one year from the ratification of this article the manufacture, sale, or transportation of intoxicating liquors within, the importation thereof into, or the exportation thereof from, the United States and all territory subject to the jurisdiction thereof for beverage purposes is hereby prohibited.~~

Both the states and the federal government had the power to pass laws to enforce this amendment.

Section 2. Enforcement ~~The Congress and the several states shall have concurrent power to enforce this article by appropriate legislation.~~

This amendment had to be approved within seven years. The Eighteenth Amendment was the first amendment to include a time limit for ratification.

Section 3. Method of Ratification ~~This article shall be inoperative unless it shall have been ratified as an amendment to the Constitution by the legislatures of the several states, as provided in the Constitution, within seven years from the date of the submission hereof to the states by the Congress.~~

Amendment 19

Women's Suffrage

Passed by Congress on June 4, 1919. Ratified on August 18, 1920.

Neither the federal government nor state governments can deny the right to vote on account of sex. Thus, women won ***suffrage,*** or the right to vote. Before 1920, some states had allowed women to vote in state elections.

Section 1. The Right to Vote The right of citizens of the United States to vote shall not be denied or abridged by the United States or by any state on account of sex.

Congress can pass laws to carry out this amendment.

Section 2. Enforcement Congress shall have power to enforce this article by appropriate legislation.

Amendment 20

Presidential Terms; Sessions of Congress

Passed by Congress on March 2, 1932. Ratified on January 23, 1933.

Section 1. Beginning of Term The terms of the President and Vice-President shall end at noon on the 20th day of January, and the terms of Senators and Representatives at noon on the 3rd day of January, of the years in which such terms would have ended if this article had not been ratified; and the terms of their successors shall then begin.

The date for the President and Vice President to take office is January 20. Members of Congress begin their terms of office on January 3. Before this amendment was adopted, these terms of office began on March 4.

Section 2. Congressional Sessions The Congress shall assemble at least once in every year, and such meeting shall begin at noon on the 3rd day of January, unless they shall by law appoint a different day.

Congress must meet at least once a year. The new session of Congress begins on January 3. Before this amendment, members of Congress who had been defeated in November continued to hold office until the following March. Such members were known as ***lame ducks.***

Section 3. Presidential Succession If at the time fixed for the beginning of the term of the President, the President-elect shall have died, the Vice-President-elect shall become President. If a President shall not have been chosen before the time fixed for the beginning of his term, or if the President-elect shall have failed to qualify, then the Vice-President-elect shall act as President until a President shall have qualified; and the Congress may by law provide for the case wherein neither a President-elect nor a Vice-President-elect shall have qualified, declaring who shall then act as President, or the manner in which one who is to act shall be selected, and such person shall act accordingly until a President or Vice-President shall have qualified.

By Section 3, if the President-elect dies before taking office, the Vice President-elect becomes President. If no President has been chosen by January 20 or if the elected candidate fails to qualify for office, the Vice President-elect acts as President, but only until a qualified President is chosen.

Finally, Congress can choose a person to act as President if neither the President-elect nor Vice President-elect is qualified to take office.

Section 4. Elections Decided by Congress The Congress may by law provide for the case of the death of any of the persons from whom the House of Representatives may choose a President whenever the right of choice shall have devolved upon them, and for the case of the death of any of the persons from whom the Senate may choose a Vice-President whenever the right of choice shall have devolved upon them.

Congress can pass laws in cases where a presidential candidate dies while an election is being decided in the House. Congress has similar power in cases where a candidate for Vice President dies while an election is being decided in the Senate.

Section 5. Date of Effect ~~Sections 1 and 2 shall take effect on the 15th day of October following the ratification of this article.~~

Section 5 sets the date for the amendment to become effective.

Section 6. Ratification Period ~~This article shall be inoperative unless it shall have been ratified as an amendment to the Constitution by the legislatures of three-fourths of the several states within seven years from the date of its submission.~~

Section 6 sets a time limit for ratification.

Amendment 21

Repeal of Prohibition

Passed by Congress on February 20, 1933. Ratified on December 5, 1933.

Section 1. Repeal of National Prohibition The eighteenth article of amendment to the Constitution of the United States is hereby repealed.

The Eighteenth Amendment is repealed, making it legal to make and sell alcoholic beverages. Prohibition ended December 5, 1933.

Section 2. State Laws The transportation or importation into any state, territory, or possession of the United States for delivery or use therein of intoxicating liquors, in violation of the laws thereof, is hereby prohibited.

Each state was free to ban the making and selling of alcoholic drink within its borders. This section makes bringing liquor into a "dry" state a federal offense.

Section 3. Ratification Period ~~This article shall be inoperative unless it shall have been ratified as an amendment to the Constitution by conventions in the several states, as provided in the Constitution, within seven years from the date of the submission hereof to the states by the Congress.~~

Special state conventions were called to ratify this amendment. This is the only time an amendment was ratified by state conventions rather than state legislatures.

Amendment 22

Limit on Number of President's Terms

Passed by Congress on March 12, 1947. Ratified on March 1, 1951.

Before Franklin Roosevelt became President, no President served more than two terms in office. Roosevelt broke with this custom and was elected to four terms. This amendment provides that no President may serve more than two terms. A President who has already served more than half of someone else's term can serve only one more full term. However, the amendment did not apply to Harry Truman, who had become President after Franklin Roosevelt's death in 1945.

Section 1. Two-Term Limit No person shall be elected to the office of the President more than twice, and no person who has held the office of President, or acted as President, for more than two years of a term to which some other person was elected President shall be elected to the office of the President more than once. ~~But this Article shall not apply to any person holding the office of President when this Article was proposed by the Congress, and shall not prevent any person who may be holding the office of President, or acting as President, during the term within which this Article becomes operative from holding the office of President or acting as President during the remainder of such term.~~

A seven-year time limit is set for ratification.

Section 2. Ratification Period ~~This Article shall be inoperative unless it shall have been ratified as an amendment to the Constitution by the legislatures of three-fourths of the several states within seven years from the date of its submission to the states by the Congress.~~

Amendment 23

Presidential Electors for District of Columbia

Passed by Congress on June 16, 1960. Ratified on April 3, 1961.

This amendment gives residents of Washington, D.C., the right to vote in presidential elections. Until this amendment was adopted, people living in Washington, D.C., could not vote for President because the Constitution had made no provision for choosing electors from the nation's capital. Washington, D.C., has three electoral votes.

Section 1. Determining the Number of Electors The District constituting the seat of Government of the United States shall appoint in such manner as the Congress may direct: A number of electors of President and Vice-President equal to the whole number of Senators and Representatives in Congress to which the District would be entitled if it were a State, but in no event more than the least populous State; they shall be in addition to those appointed by the States, but they shall be considered, for the purposes of the election of President and Vice-President, to be electors appointed by a State; and they shall meet in the District and perform such duties as provided by the twelfth article of amendment.

Congress can pass laws to carry out this amendment.

Section 2. Enforcement The Congress shall have power to enforce this article by appropriate legislation.

Amendment 24

Abolition of Poll Tax in National Elections

Passed by Congress on August 27, 1962. Ratified on January 23, 1964.

A ***poll tax*** is a tax on voters. This amendment bans poll taxes in national elections. Some states used poll taxes to keep blacks from voting. In 1966, the Supreme Court struck down poll taxes in state elections, also.

Section 1. Poll Tax Banned The right of citizens of the United States to vote in any primary or other election for President or Vice-President, for electors for President or Vice-President, or for Senator or Representative in Congress, shall not be denied or abridged by the United States or any state by reason of failure to pay any poll tax or other tax.

Congress can pass laws to carry out this amendment.

Section 2. Enforcement The Congress shall have the power to enforce this article by appropriate legislation.

Amendment 25

Presidential Succession and Disability

Passed by Congress on July 6, 1965. Ratified on February 11, 1967.

If the President dies or resigns, the Vice President becomes President. This section clarifies Article 2, Section 1, Clause 6.

Section 1. President's Death or Resignation In case of the removal of the President from office or his death or resignation, the Vice-President shall become President.

Section 2. Vacancies in Vice-Presidency Whenever there is a vacancy in the office of the Vice-President, the President shall nominate a Vice-President who shall take the office upon confirmation by a majority vote of both houses of Congress.

When a Vice President takes over the office of President, he or she appoints a Vice President who must be approved by a majority vote of both houses of Congress. This section was first applied after Vice President Spiro Agnew resigned in 1973. President Richard Nixon appointed Gerald Ford as Vice President.

Section 3. Disability of the President Whenever the President transmits to the President pro tempore of the Senate and the Speaker of the House of Representatives his written declaration that he is unable to discharge the powers and duties of his office, and until he transmits to them a written declaration to the contrary, such powers and duties shall be discharged by the Vice-President as Acting President.

If the President declares in writing that he or she is unable to perform the duties of office, the Vice President serves as Acting President until the President recovers.

Section 4. Whenever the Vice-President and a majority of either the principal officers of the executive departments or of such other body as Congress may by law provide, transmit to the President *pro tempore* of the Senate and the Speaker of the House of Representatives their written declaration that the President is unable to discharge the powers and duties of his office, the Vice-President shall immediately assume the powers and duties of the office as Acting President.

Thereafter, when the President transmits to the President *pro tempore* of the Senate and the Speaker of the House of Representatives his written declaration that no inability exists, he shall resume the powers and duties of his office unless the Vice-President and a majority of either the principal officers of the executive department or of such other body as Congress may by law provide, transmit within four days to the President *as* of the Senate and the Speaker of the House of Representatives their written declaration that the President is unable to discharge the powers and duties of his office. Thereupon Congress shall decide the issue, assembling within 48 hours for that purpose if not in session. If the Congress, within 21 days after receipt of the latter written declaration, or, if Congress is not in session, within 21 days after Congress is required to assemble, determines by two-thirds vote of both houses that the President is unable to discharge the powers and duties of his office, the Vice-President shall continue to discharge the same as Acting President; otherwise, the President shall assume the powers and duties of his office.

Two Presidents, Woodrow Wilson and Dwight Eisenhower, have fallen gravely ill while in office. The Constitution contained no provision for this kind of emergency.

Section 3 provided that the President can inform Congress that he or she is too sick to perform the duties of office. However, if the President is unconscious or refuses to admit to a disabling illness, Section 4 provides that the Vice President and Cabinet may declare the President disabled. The Vice President becomes Acting President until the President can return to the duties of office. In case of a disagreement between the President and the Vice President and Cabinet over the President's ability to perform the duties of office, Congress must decide the issue. A two-thirds vote of both houses is needed to decide that the President is disabled or unable to fulfill the duties of office.

Amendment 26

Voting Age

Passed by Congress on March 23, 1971. Ratified on July 1, 1971.

Section 1. Lowering of Voting Age The right of citizens of the United States, who are 18 years of age or older, to vote shall not be denied or abridged by the United States or any state on account of age.

In 1970, Congress passed a law allowing 18-year-olds to vote. However, the Supreme Court decided that Congress could not set a minimum age for state elections. So this amendment was passed and ratified.

Section 2. Enforcement The Congress shall have the power to enforce this article by appropriate legislation.

Congress can pass laws to carry out this amendment.

Amendment 27

Congressional Pay Increases

Ratified on May 7, 1992.

No law varying the compensation for the services of the Senators and Representatives shall take effect, until an election of Representatives shall have intervened.

If members of Congress vote themselves a pay increase, it cannot go into effect until after the next congressional election.

★ Presidents of the United States ★

1 George Washington
(1732–1799)

Years in office: 1789–1797
Party: none
Elected from: Virginia
Vice President: John Adams

2 John Adams
(1735–1826)

Years in office: 1797–1801
Party: Federalist
Elected from: Massachusetts
Vice President: Thomas Jefferson

3 Thomas Jefferson
(1743–1826)

Years in office: 1801–1809
Party: Democratic Republican
Elected from: Virginia
Vice President: 1) Aaron Burr, 2) George Clinton

4 James Madison
(1751–1836)

Years in office: 1809–1817
Party: Democratic Republican
Elected from: Virginia
Vice President: 1) George Clinton, 2) Elbridge Gerry

5 James Monroe
(1758–1831)

Years in office: 1817–1825
Party: Democratic Republican
Elected from: Virginia
Vice President: Daniel Tompkins

6 John Quincy Adams
(1767–1848)

Years in office: 1825–1829
Party: National Republican
Elected from: Massachusetts
Vice President: John Calhoun

7 Andrew Jackson
(1767–1845)

Years in office: 1829–1837
Party: Democratic
Elected from: Tennessee
Vice President: 1) John Calhoun, 2) Martin Van Buren

8 Martin Van Buren
(1782–1862)

Years in office: 1837–1841
Party: Democratic
Elected from: New York
Vice President: Richard Johnson

9 William Henry Harrison*
(1773–1841)

Years in office: 1841
Party: Whig
Elected from: Ohio
Vice President: John Tyler

10 John Tyler
(1790–1862)

Years in office: 1841–1845
Party: Whig
Elected from: Virginia
Vice President: none

11 James K. Polk
(1795–1849)

Years in Office: 1845–1849
Party: Democratic
Elected from: Tennessee
Vice President: George Dallas

12 Zachary Taylor*
(1784–1850)

Years in office: 1849–1850
Party: Whig
Elected from: Louisiana
Vice President: Millard Fillmore

*Died in office

13 Millard Fillmore
(1800–1874)

Years in office: 1850–1853
Party: Whig
Elected from: New York
Vice President: none

14 Franklin Pierce
(1804–1869)

Years in office: 1853–1857
Party: Democratic
Elected from: New Hampshire
Vice President: William King

15 James Buchanan
(1791–1868)

Years in office: 1857–1861
Party: Democratic
Elected from: Pennsylvania
Vice President: John Breckinridge

16 Abraham Lincoln**
(1809–1865)

Years in office: 1861–1865
Party: Republican
Elected from: Illinois
Vice President: 1) Hannibal Hamlin, 2) Andrew Johnson

17 Andrew Johnson
(1808–1875)

Years in office: 1865–1869
Party: Republican
Elected from: Tennessee
Vice President: none

18 Ulysses S. Grant
(1822–1885)

Years in office: 1869–1877
Party: Republican
Elected from: Illinois
Vice President: 1) Schuyler Colfax, 2) Henry Wilson

19 Rutherford B. Hayes
(1822–1893)

Years in office: 1877–1881
Party: Republican
Elected from: Ohio
Vice President: William Wheeler

20 James A. Garfield**
(1831–1881)

Years in office: 1881
Party: Republican
Elected from: Ohio
Vice President: Chester A. Arthur

21 Chester A. Arthur
(1829–1886)

Years in office: 1881–1885
Party: Republican
Elected from: New York
Vice President: none

22 Grover Cleveland
(1837–1908)

Years in office: 1885–1889
Party: Democratic
Elected from: New York
Vice President: Thomas Hendricks

23 Benjamin Harrison
(1833–1901)

Years in office: 1889–1893
Party: Republican
Elected from: Indiana
Vice President: Levi Morton

24 Grover Cleveland
(1837–1908)

Years in office: 1893–1897
Party: Democratic
Elected from: New York
Vice President: Adlai Stevenson

****Assassinated**

25 William McKinley**
(1843–1901)

Years in office: 1897–1901
Party: Republican
Elected from: Ohio
Vice President: 1) Garret Hobart, 2) Theodore Roosevelt

26 Theodore Roosevelt
(1858–1919)

Years in office: 1901–1909
Party: Republican
Elected from: New York
Vice President: Charles Fairbanks

27 William Howard Taft
(1857–1930)

Years in office: 1909–1913
Party: Republican
Elected from: Ohio
Vice President: James Sherman

28 Woodrow Wilson
(1856–1924)

Years in office: 1913–1921
Party: Democratic
Elected from: New Jersey
Vice President: Thomas Marshall

29 Warren G. Harding*
(1865–1923)

Years in office: 1921–1923
Party: Republican
Elected from: Ohio
Vice President: Calvin Coolidge

30 Calvin Coolidge
(1872–1933)

Years in office: 1923–1929
Party: Republican
Elected from: Massachusetts
Vice President: Charles Dawes

31 Herbert C. Hoover
(1874–1964)

Years in office: 1929–1933
Party: Republican
Elected from: California
Vice President: Charles Curtis

32 Franklin D. Roosevelt*
(1882–1945)

Years in office: 1933–1945
Party: Democratic
Elected from: New York
Vice President: 1) John Garner, 2) Henry Wallace, 3) Harry S Truman

33 Harry S Truman
(1884–1972)

Years in office: 1945–1953
Party: Democratic
Elected from: Missouri
Vice President: Alben Barkley

34 Dwight D. Eisenhower
(1890–1969)

Years in office: 1953–1961
Party: Republican
Elected from: New York
Vice President: Richard M. Nixon

35 John F. Kennedy**
(1917–1963)

Years in office: 1961–1963
Party: Democratic
Elected from: Massachusetts
Vice President: Lyndon B. Johnson

36 Lyndon B. Johnson
(1908–1973)

Years in office: 1963–1969
Party: Democratic
Elected from: Texas
Vice President: Hubert Humphrey

*Died in office
**Assassinated

37 Richard M. Nixon***
(1913–1994)

Years in office:
1969–1974
Party:
Republican
Elected from:
New York
Vice President:
1) Spiro Agnew,
2) Gerald R. Ford

38 Gerald R. Ford
(1913–)

Years in office:
1974–1977
Party:
Republican
Appointed from:
Michigan
Vice President:
Nelson Rockefeller

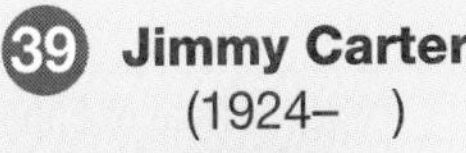

39 Jimmy Carter
(1924–)

Years in office:
1977–1981
Party:
Democratic
Elected from:
Georgia
Vice President:
Walter Mondale

40 Ronald W. Reagan
(1911–)

Years in office:
1981–1989
Party:
Republican
Elected from:
California
Vice President:
George H.W. Bush

41 George H.W. Bush
(1924–)

Years in office:
1989–1993
Party:
Republican
Elected from:
Texas
Vice President:
J. Danforth Quayle

42 William J. Clinton
(1946–)

Years in office:
1993–
Party:
Democratic
Elected from:
Arkansas
Vice President:
Albert Gore, Jr.

***Resigned

★ The Fifty States ★

State	Date of Entry to Union (Order of Entry)	Land Area in Square Miles	Population (In Thousands)	Number of Representatives in House	Capital	Largest City
Alabama	1819 (22)	50,750	4,219	7	Montgomery	Birmingham
Alaska	1959 (49)	570,374	606	1	Juneau	Anchorage
Arizona	1912 (48)	113,642	4,075	6	Phoenix	Phoenix
Arkansas	1836 (25)	52,075	2,453	4	Little Rock	Little Rock
California	1850 (31)	155,973	31,431	52	Sacramento	Los Angeles
Colorado	1876 (38)	103,730	3,656	6	Denver	Denver
Connecticut	1788 (5)	4,845	3,275	6	Hartford	Bridgeport
Delaware	1787 (1)	1,955	706	1	Dover	Wilmington
Florida	1845 (27)	53,997	13,953	23	Tallahassee	Jacksonville
Georgia	1788 (4)	57,919	7,055	11	Atlanta	Atlanta
Hawaii	1959 (50)	6,423	1,179	2	Honolulu	Honolulu
Idaho	1890 (43)	82,751	1,133	2	Boise	Boise
Illinois	1818 (21)	55,593	11,752	20	Springfield	Chicago
Indiana	1816 (19)	35,870	5,752	10	Indianapolis	Indianapolis
Iowa	1846 (29)	55,875	2,829	5	Des Moines	Des Moines
Kansas	1861 (34)	81,823	2,554	4	Topeka	Wichita
Kentucky	1792 (15)	39,732	3,827	6	Frankfort	Louisville
Louisiana	1812 (18)	43,566	4,315	7	Baton Rouge	New Orleans
Maine	1820 (23)	30,865	1,240	2	Augusta	Portland
Maryland	1788 (7)	9,775	5,006	8	Annapolis	Baltimore
Massachusetts	1788 (6)	7,838	6,041	10	Boston	Boston
Michigan	1837 (26)	56,809	9,496	16	Lansing	Detroit
Minnesota	1858 (32)	79,617	4,567	8	St. Paul	Minneapolis
Mississippi	1817 (20)	46,914	2,669	5	Jackson	Jackson
Missouri	1821 (24)	68,898	5,278	9	Jefferson City	Kansas City
Montana	1889 (41)	145,556	856	1	Helena	Billings
Nebraska	1867 (37)	76,878	1,623	3	Lincoln	Omaha
Nevada	1864 (36)	109,806	1,457	2	Carson City	Las Vegas
New Hampshire	1788 (9)	8,969	1,137	2	Concord	Manchester
New Jersey	1787 (3)	7,419	7,904	13	Trenton	Newark
New Mexico	1912 (47)	121,365	1,654	3	Santa Fe	Albuquerque
New York	1788 (11)	47,224	18,169	31	Albany	New York
North Carolina	1789 (12)	48,718	7,070	12	Raleigh	Charlotte
North Dakota	1889 (39)	68,994	638	1	Bismarck	Fargo
Ohio	1803 (17)	40,953	11,102	19	Columbus	Columbus
Oklahoma	1907 (46)	68,679	3,258	6	Oklahoma City	Oklahoma City
Oregon	1859 (33)	96,003	3,086	5	Salem	Portland
Pennsylvania	1787 (2)	44,820	12,052	21	Harrisburg	Philadelphia
Rhode Island	1790 (13)	1,045	997	2	Providence	Providence
South Carolina	1788 (8)	30,111	3,664	6	Columbia	Columbia
South Dakota	1889 (40)	75,898	721	1	Pierre	Sioux Falls
Tennessee	1796 (16)	41,220	5,175	9	Nashville	Memphis
Texas	1845 (28)	261,914	18,378	30	Austin	Houston
Utah	1896 (45)	82,168	1,908	3	Salt Lake City	Salt Lake City
Vermont	1791 (14)	9,249	580	1	Montpelier	Burlington
Virginia	1788 (10)	39,598	6,552	11	Richmond	Virginia Beach
Washington	1889 (42)	66,582	5,343	9	Olympia	Seattle
West Virginia	1863 (35)	24,087	1,822	3	Charleston	Charleston
Wisconsin	1848 (30)	54,314	5,082	9	Madison	Milwaukee
Wyoming	1890 (44)	97,105	476	1	Cheyenne	Cheyenne
District of Columbia		61	570	1 (nonvoting)		

Self-Governing Areas, Possessions, and Dependencies	Land Area in Square Miles	Population (In Thousands)	Capital
Puerto Rico	3,515	3,522	San Juan
Guam	209	133	Agana
U.S. Virgin Islands	132	102	Charlotte Amalie
American Samoa	77	52	Pago Pago

Sources: *Department of Commerce, Bureau of the Census, 1997 Information Please Almanac*

★ State Flags ★

Alabama ★ Alaska ★ Arizona ★ Arkansas ★ California

Colorado ★ Connecticut ★ Delaware ★ Florida ★ Georgia

Hawaii ★ Idaho ★ Illinois ★ Indiana ★ Iowa

Kansas ★ Kentucky ★ Louisiana ★ Maine ★ Maryland

Massachusetts ★ Michigan ★ Minnesota ★ Mississippi ★ Missouri

Montana ★ Nebraska ★ Nevada ★ New Hampshire ★ New Jersey

New Mexico ★ New York ★ North Carolina ★ North Dakota ★ Ohio

Oklahoma ★ Oregon ★ Pennsylvania ★ Rhode Island ★ South Carolina

South Dakota ★ Tennessee ★ Texas ★ Utah ★ Vermont

Virginia ★ Washington ★ West Virginia ★ Wisconsin ★ Wyoming

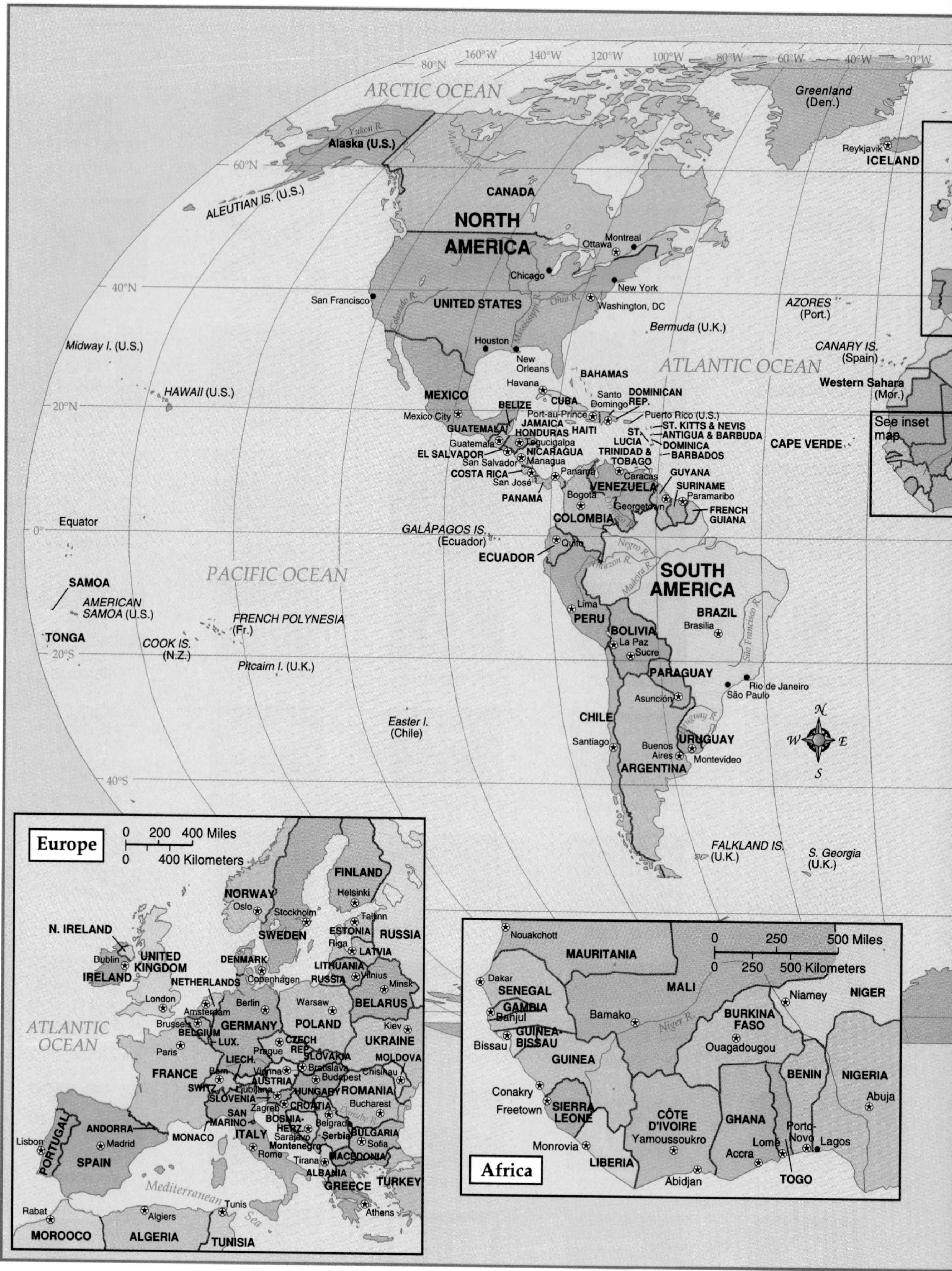

ARCTIC OCEAN
80°N
160°W
140°W
120°W
100°W
80°W
60°W
40°W
20°W
60°N
40°N
20°N
0°
20°S
40°S
Greenland (Den.)
Reykjavik
ICELAND
Yukon R.
Alaska (U.S.)
Mackenzie R.
ALEUTIAN IS. (U.S.)
CANADA
NORTH AMERICA
Montreal
Ottawa
Chicago
New York
Washington, DC
Ohio R.
San Francisco
UNITED STATES
Colorado R.
Mississippi R.
AZORES (Port.)
Bermuda (U.K.)
Midway I. (U.S.)
Houston
New Orleans
CANARY IS. (Spain)
ATLANTIC OCEAN
BAHAMAS
Havana
Western Sahara (Mor.)
HAWAII (U.S.)
MEXICO
CUBA
Santo Domingo
DOMINICAN REP.
BELIZE
Port-au-Prince
Puerto Rico (U.S.)
Mexico City
JAMAICA
HAITI
ST. KITTS & NEVIS
GUATEMALA
HONDURAS
ANTIGUA & BARBUDA
Guatemala
Tegucigalpa
ST. LUCIA
DOMINICA
EL SALVADOR
NICARAGUA
TRINIDAD & TOBAGO
BARBADOS
San Salvador
Managua
CAPE VERDE
See inset map
COSTA RICA
Panama
Caracas
GUYANA
San José
SURINAME
PANAMA
VENEZUELA
Paramaribo
Bogotá
Georgetown
FRENCH GUIANA
Equator
COLOMBIA
GALÁPAGOS IS. (Ecuador)
Quito
ECUADOR
Negro R.
Amazon R.
Madeira R.
PACIFIC OCEAN
SOUTH AMERICA
SAMOA
AMERICAN SAMOA (U.S.)
Lima
BRAZIL
FRENCH POLYNESIA (Fr.)
PERU
Brasília
São Francisco R.
TONGA
COOK IS. (N.Z.)
BOLIVIA
La Paz
Sucre
Pitcairn I. (U.K.)
PARAGUAY
Rio de Janeiro
São Paulo
Asunción
Easter I. (Chile)
CHILE
Uruguay R.
N
W
E
S
Santiago
Buenos Aires
URUGUAY
Montevideo
ARGENTINA
FALKLAND IS. (U.K.)
S. Georgia (U.K.)
Europe
0 200 400 Miles
0 400 Kilometers
FINLAND
NORWAY
Helsinki
Oslo
Stockholm
Tallinn
N. IRELAND
SWEDEN
ESTONIA
RUSSIA
Riga
LATVIA
Dublin
UNITED KINGDOM
DENMARK
LITHUANIA
IRELAND
Copenhagen
RUSSIA
Vilnius
Minsk
NETHERLANDS
London
Berlin
Warsaw
BELARUS
Amsterdam
ATLANTIC OCEAN
Brussels
BELGIUM
GERMANY
POLAND
Kiev
LUX.
CZECH REP.
UKRAINE
Paris
Prague
LIECH.
SLOVAKIA
MOLDOVA
FRANCE
Bern
Vienna
Bratislava
Budapest
Chisinau
SWITZ.
AUSTRIA
Ljubljana
HUNGARY
ROMANIA
SLOVENIA
Zagreb
CROATIA
Bucharest
SAN MARINO
BOSNIA-HERZ.
Danube R.
Belgrade
PORTUGAL
ANDORRA
Sarajevo
Serbia
BULGARIA
Lisbon
Madrid
MONACO
ITALY
Montenegro
Sofia
SPAIN
Rome
Tirana
MACEDONIA
ALBANIA
GREECE
TURKEY
Mediterranean Sea
Tunis
Rabat
Algiers
Athens
MOROOCO
ALGERIA
TUNISIA
Nouakchott
MAURITANIA
0 250 500 Miles
0 250 500 Kilometers
Dakar
SENEGAL
MALI
Niamey
NIGER
GAMBIA
Banjul
Bamako
BURKINA FASO
GUINEA-BISSAU
Niger R.
Bissau
Ouagadougou
GUINEA
BENIN
NIGERIA
Conakry
Abuja
Freetown
SIERRA LEONE
CÔTE D'IVOIRE
Yamoussoukro
GHANA
Porto-Novo
Monrovia
Lomé
Lagos
Africa
LIBERIA
Accra
Abidjan
TOGO

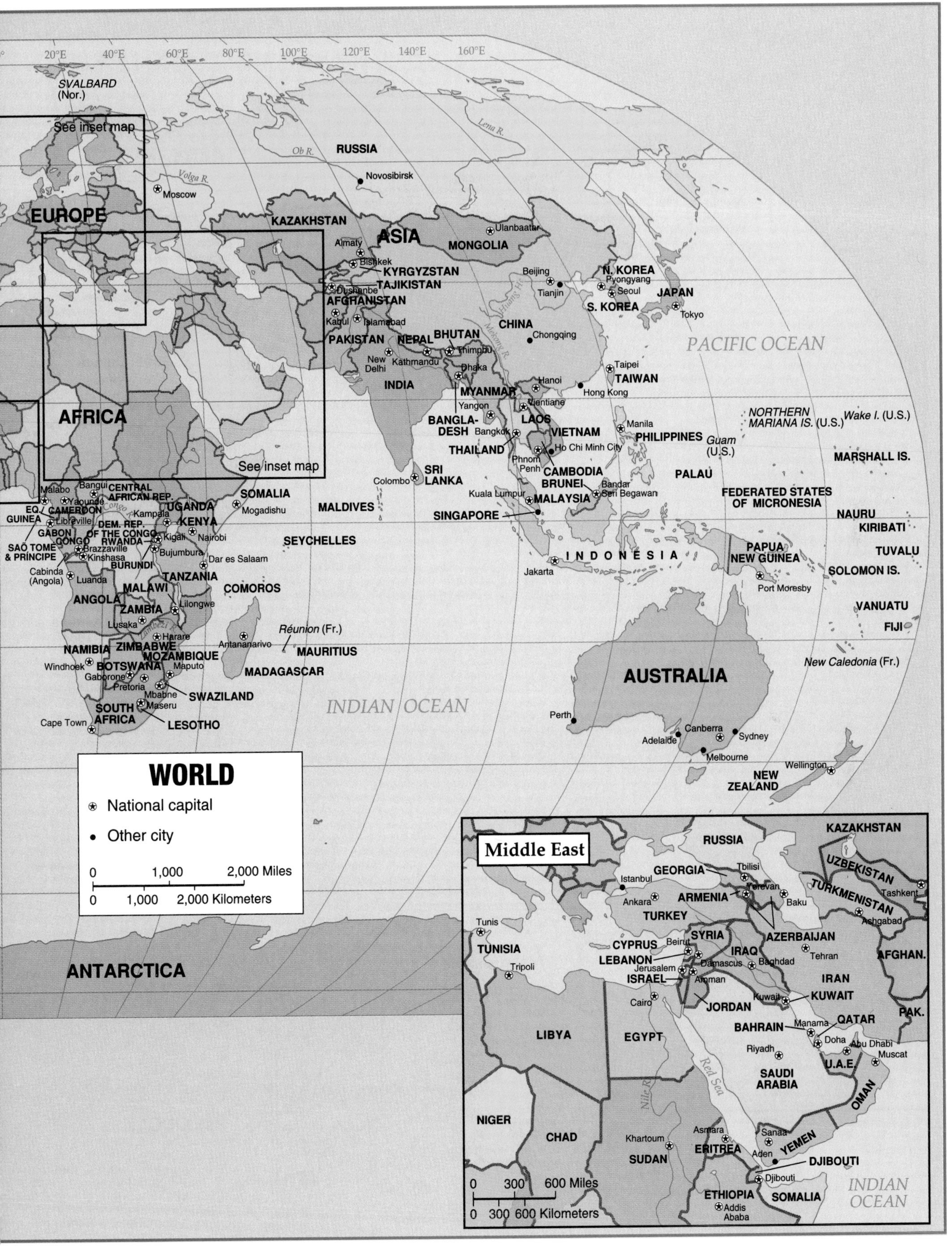

★ GEOGRAPHIC ATLAS ★

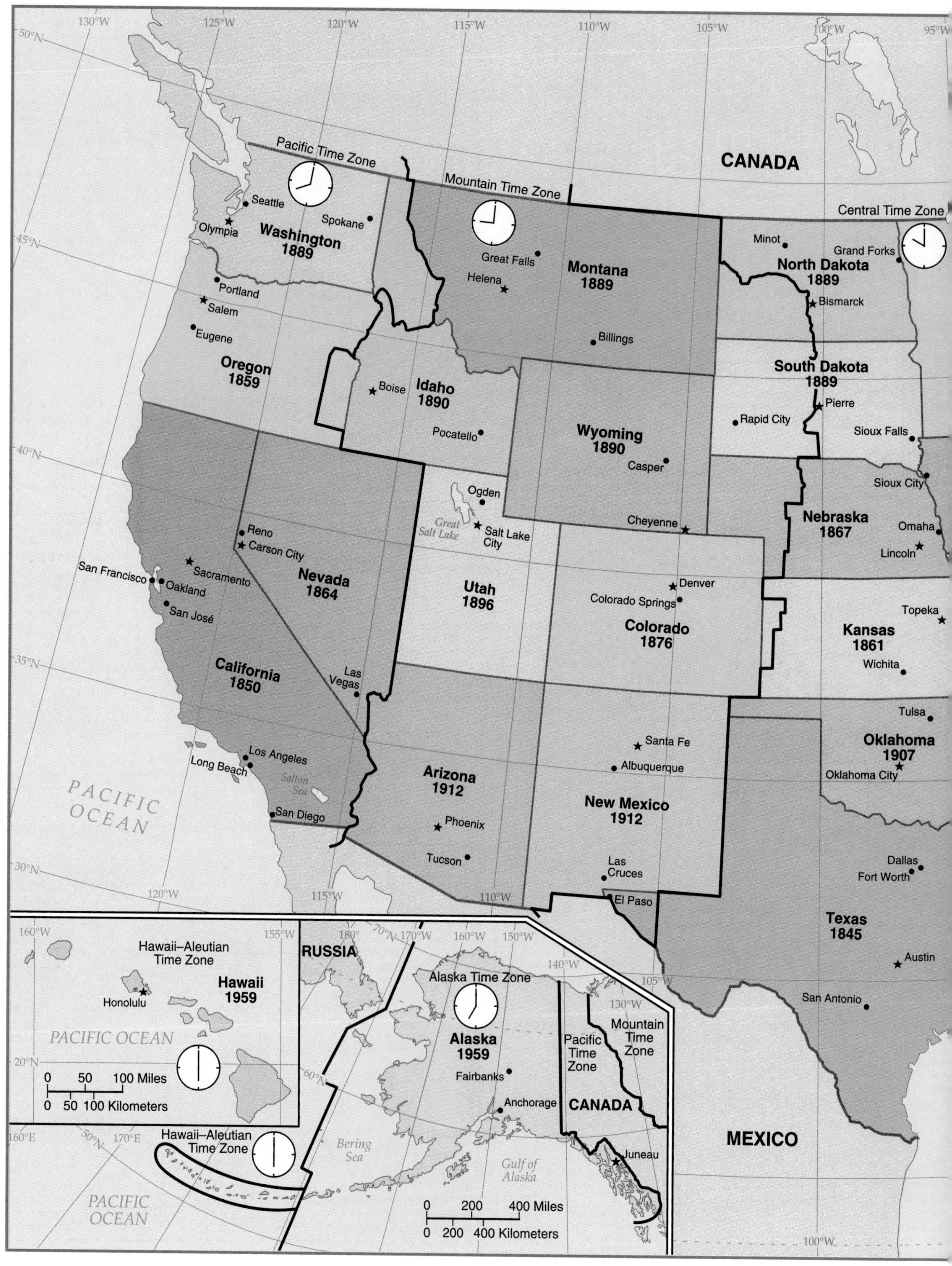

CANADA
Pacific Time Zone
Mountain Time Zone
Central Time Zone
Washington 1889
Oregon 1859
California 1850
Nevada 1864
Idaho 1890
Montana 1889
Wyoming 1890
Utah 1896
Colorado 1876
Arizona 1912
New Mexico 1912
North Dakota 1889
South Dakota 1889
Nebraska 1867
Kansas 1861
Oklahoma 1907
Texas 1845
Seattle
Olympia
Spokane
Portland
Salem
Eugene
Great Falls
Helena
Billings
Boise
Pocatello
Minot
Grand Forks
Bismarck
Pierre
Rapid City
Sioux Falls
Sioux City
Omaha
Lincoln
Casper
Cheyenne
Ogden
Great Salt Lake
Salt Lake City
Reno
Carson City
Sacramento
San Francisco
Oakland
San José
Las Vegas
Los Angeles
Long Beach
Salton Sea
San Diego
Denver
Colorado Springs
Topeka
Wichita
Tulsa
Oklahoma City
Santa Fe
Albuquerque
Phoenix
Tucson
Las Cruces
El Paso
Dallas
Fort Worth
Austin
San Antonio
PACIFIC OCEAN
MEXICO
Hawaii–Aleutian Time Zone
Hawaii 1959
Honolulu
PACIFIC OCEAN
0 50 100 Miles
0 50 100 Kilometers
RUSSIA
Alaska Time Zone
Alaska 1959
Fairbanks
Anchorage
Juneau
Bering Sea
Gulf of Alaska
Pacific Time Zone
Mountain Time Zone
CANADA
Hawaii–Aleutian Time Zone
PACIFIC OCEAN
0 200 400 Miles
0 200 400 Kilometers

★ GEOGRAPHIC ATLAS ★

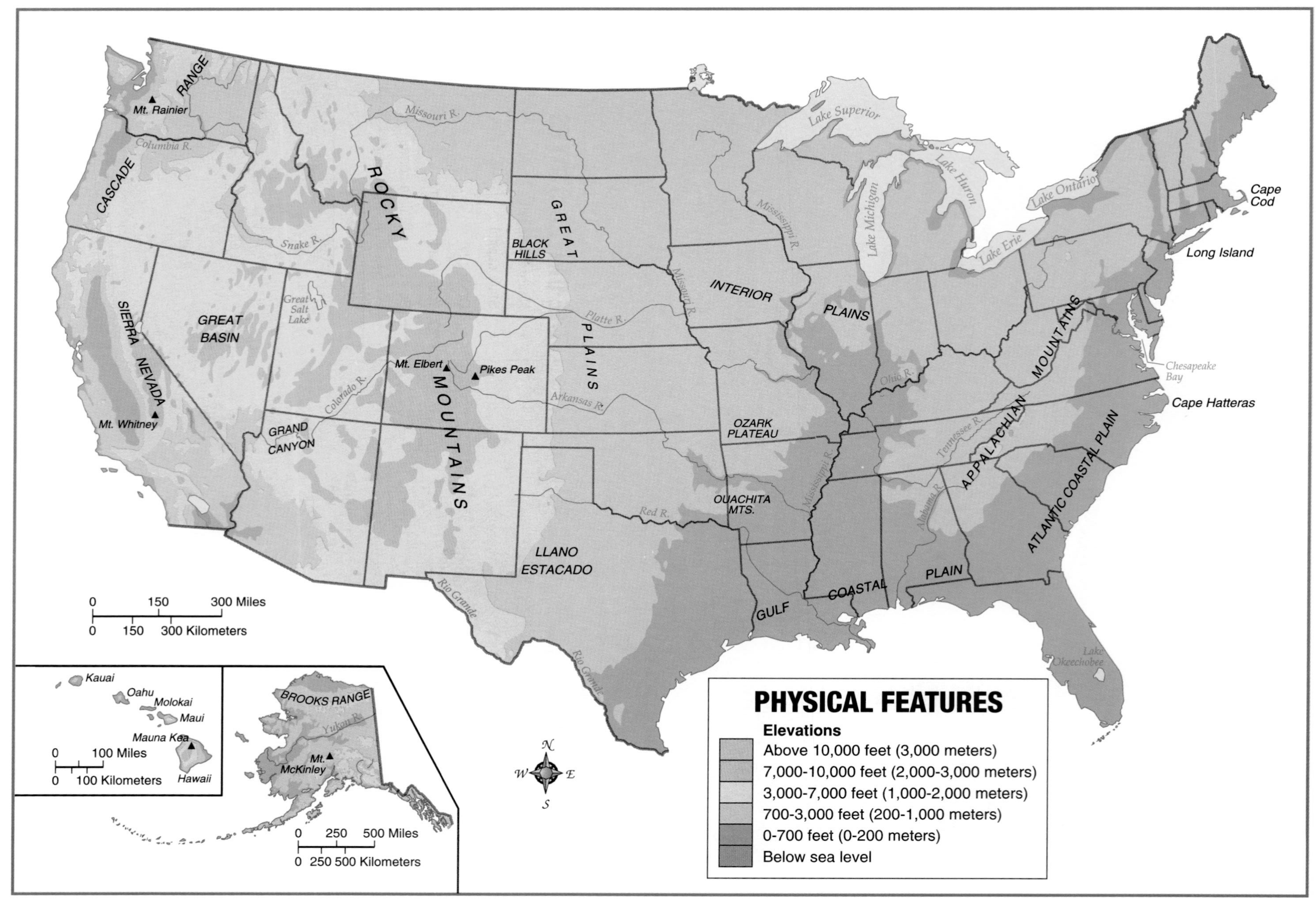
PHYSICAL FEATURES
Elevations
Above 10,000 feet (3,000 meters)
7,000-10,000 feet (2,000-3,000 meters)
3,000-7,000 feet (1,000-2,000 meters)
700-3,000 feet (200-1,000 meters)
0-700 feet (0-200 meters)
Below sea level
CASCADE RANGE
Mt. Rainier
Columbia R.
Missouri R.
Snake R.
ROCKY MOUNTAINS
GREAT PLAINS
BLACK HILLS
Lake Superior
Lake Huron
Lake Michigan
Lake Ontario
Lake Erie
Cape Cod
Long Island
Mississippi R.
INTERIOR PLAINS
Missouri R.
Platte R.
SIERRA NEVADA
GREAT BASIN
Great Salt Lake
Mt. Elbert
Pikes Peak
Arkansas R.
Colorado R.
Mt. Whitney
GRAND CANYON
OZARK PLATEAU
Ohio R.
APPALACHIAN MOUNTAINS
Chesapeake Bay
Cape Hatteras
Tennessee R.
ATLANTIC COASTAL PLAIN
OUACHITA MTS.
Red R.
Alabama R.
LLANO ESTACADO
GULF COASTAL PLAIN
Rio Grande
Lake Okeechobee
0 150 300 Miles
0 150 300 Kilometers
Kauai
Oahu
Molokai
Maui
Mauna Kea
Hawaii
0 100 Miles
0 100 Kilometers
BROOKS RANGE
Yukon R.
Mt. McKinley
0 250 500 Miles
0 250 500 Kilometers
N E S W

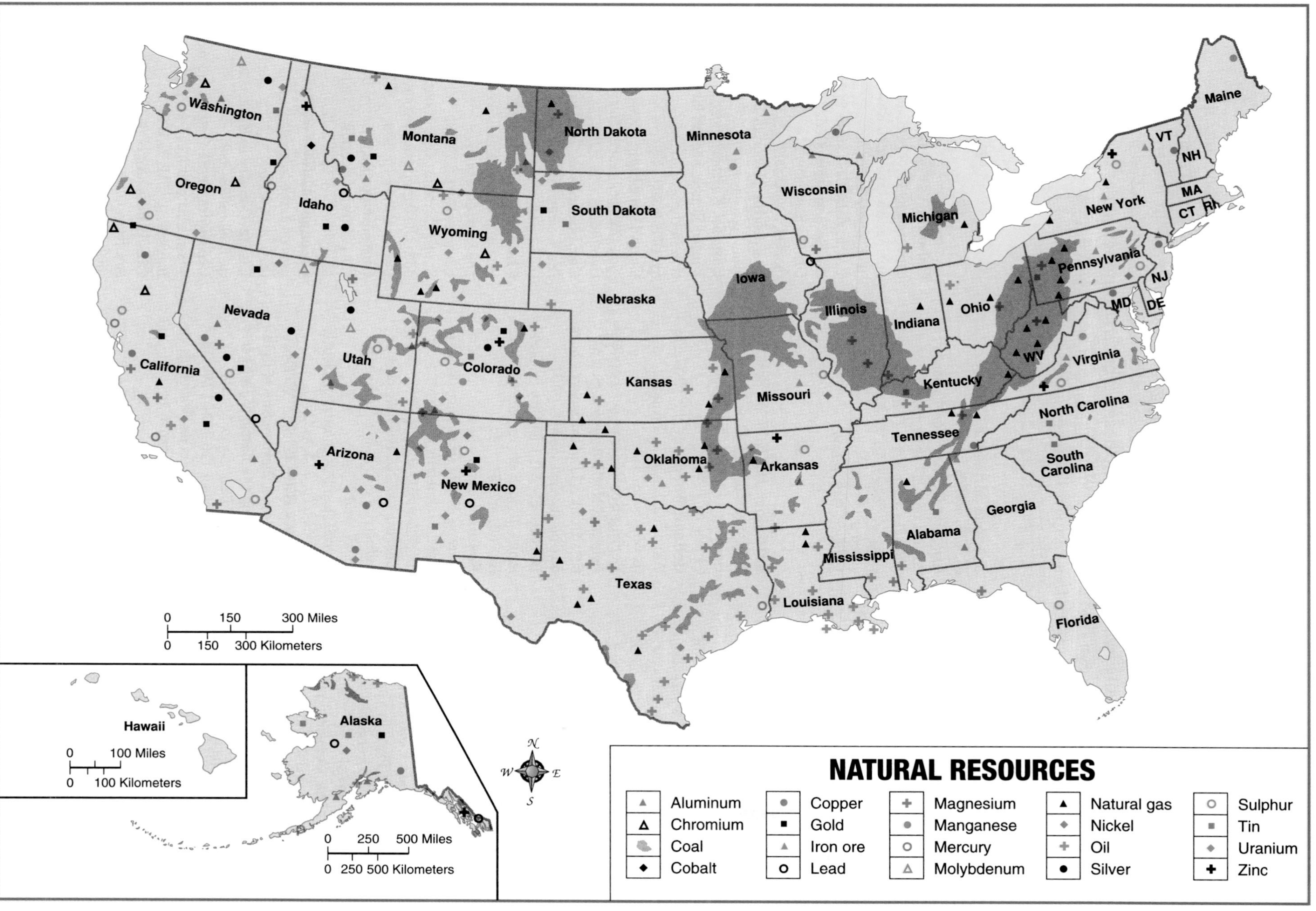
Washington
Oregon
Idaho
Montana
North Dakota
Minnesota
Wisconsin
Michigan
Maine
VT
NH
MA
CT
RI
New York
South Dakota
Wyoming
Nevada
California
Utah
Colorado
Nebraska
Iowa
Illinois
Indiana
Ohio
Pennsylvania
NJ
MD
DE
WV
Virginia
Kentucky
Kansas
Missouri
North Carolina
Tennessee
South Carolina
Arizona
New Mexico
Oklahoma
Arkansas
Georgia
Alabama
Mississippi
Texas
Louisiana
Florida
0 150 300 Miles
0 150 300 Kilometers
Hawaii
0 100 Miles
0 100 Kilometers
Alaska
0 250 500 Miles
0 250 500 Kilometers
N
W
E
S
NATURAL RESOURCES
Aluminum
Chromium
Coal
Cobalt
Copper
Gold
Iron ore
Lead
Magnesium
Manganese
Mercury
Molybdenum
Natural gas
Nickel
Oil
Silver
Sulphur
Tin
Uranium
Zinc

★ Gazetteer of American History ★

This gazetteer, or geographic dictionary, lists places that are important in American history. The approximate latitude and longitude are given for cities, towns, and other specific locations. See text page 10 for information about latitude and longitude. In the Gazetteer, after the description of each place, there are usually two numbers in parentheses. The first number refers to the text page where you can find out more about the place. The second appears in slanted, or *italic,* type and refers to a map *(m)* where the place is shown.

A

Abilene (39°N/97°W) Former cow town in Kansas at the end of the Chisholm Trail. (p. 513, *m510*)
Afghanistan Country in South Asia. Invaded by the Soviet Union in 1979. (p. 787, *m898–899*)
Africa Second largest continent in the world. (p. 12, *m10*)
Alabama 22nd state. Nicknamed the Heart of Dixie or the Cotton State. (p. 896, *m900–901*)
Alamo (29°N/99°W) Mission in San Antonio, Texas, where 255 rebels died during the Texas war for independence. (p. 352, *m352*)
Alaska 49th state. Purchased from Russia in 1867. (p. 896, *m900–901*)
Albany (43°N/74°W) Capital of New York. (p. 171, *m170*)
Andes Rugged mountain chain in South America. (p. 50, *m47*)
Appalachian Mountains Mountain chain that stretches from Georgia to Canada. (p. 16, *m19*)
Appomattox Courthouse (37°N/79°W) Town in Virginia where Lee surrendered to Grant. (p. 473, *m472*)
Argentina Country in South America. (p. 313, *m314*)
Argonne Forest (49°N/6°E) World War I battle site in France (p. 660, *m657*)
Arizona 48th state. Nicknamed the Grand Canyon State. (p. 896, *m900–901*)
Arkansas 25th state. Nicknamed the Land of Opportunity. (p. 896, *m900–901*)
Armenia Country in southwest Europe. (p. 558, *m898–899*)
Asia Largest of the world's continents. (p. 12, *m10*)
Atlanta (34°N/84°W) Capital and largest city of Georgia. Burned by Sherman during the Civil War. (p. 472, *m460*)
Atlantic Ocean World's second largest ocean. (p. 14, *m10*)
Austria-Hungary One of the Central Powers in World War I. Divided into several countries after 1918. (p. 642, *m646*)

B

Baltimore (39°N/77°W) Port city in Maryland. (p. 287, *m286*)
Beijing (40°N/116°E) Capital of China. (p. 623, *m752*)
Belleau Wood (49°N/3°E) World War I battle site in France. (p. 658, *m657*)
Bering Sea Narrow sea between Asia and North America. Scientists think a land bridge was here during the last ice age. *(m31)*
Berlin (53°N/13°E) City in Germany divided during the Cold War. (p. 766, *m767*)
Bosnia Country in southeastern Europe. Broke from Yugoslavia in 1991. Plagued by civil war. (p. 832, *m898–899*)
Boston (42°N/71°W) Seaport and industrial city in Massachusetts. (p. 17, *m96*)
Brazil Largest country in South America. (p. 313, *m314*)
Breed's Hill (42°N/71°W) Overlooks Boston harbor. Site of fighting during the Battle of Bunker Hill. (p. 162)
Buena Vista (26°N/101°W) City in Mexico. Site of an American victory in the Mexican War. (p. 362, *m361*)
Buffalo (43°N/79°W) City in New York State on Lake Erie. (p. 307, *m306*)
Bunker Hill (42°N/71°W) Overlooks Boston harbor. Site of first major battle of the Revolution. (p. 162)

C

Cahokia (39°N/90°W) British fort captured by George Rogers Clark during the American Revolution. (p. 174, *m175*)
California 31st state. Nicknamed the Golden State. Ceded to the United States by Mexico in 1848. (p. 896, *m900–901*)
Cambodia Nation in Southeast Asia. (p. 784, *m781*)
Canada Northern neighbor of the United States. Second largest nation in the world. (p. 141, *m898–899*)
Canadian Shield Lowland region that lies mostly in eastern Canada. (p. 17, *m19*)
Caribbean Sea Tropical sea in the Western Hemisphere. (p. 65, *m67*)
Chancellorsville (38°N/78°W) Site of a Confederate victory in 1863. (p. 458, *m454*)
Charleston (33°N/80°W) City in South Carolina. Site of battles in both the American Revolution and the Civil War. (p. 108, *m107*)
Chesapeake Bay Large inlet of the Atlantic Ocean in Virginia and Maryland. (p. 287, *m286*)
Chicago (42°N/88°W) City in Illinois on Lake Michigan. (p. 5, *m900–901*)
China Country in East Asia. (p. 560, *m898–899*)
Chisholm Trail Cattle trail from Texas to the railroad at Abilene, Kansas. (p. 512, *m510*)
Cincinnati (39°N/84°W) City in southern Ohio on the Ohio River. *(m900–901)*
Cleveland (41°N/82°W) City in northern Ohio on Lake Erie. (p. 520, *m303*)
Coastal Plains Region consisting of the Atlantic Plain and the Gulf

Plain along the Gulf of Mexico. (p. 17, *m19*)
Colombia Country in South America. (p. 631, *m635*)
Colorado 38th state. Nicknamed the Centennial State. (p. 896, *m900–901*)
Colorado River Begins in Rocky Mountains and flows into Gulf of California. (p. 18, *m19*)
Columbia River Chief river of the Pacific Northwest. (p. 275, *m273*)
Concord (43°N/71°W) Village in Massachusetts where battle occurred between the British and Americans at the start of the American Revolution. (p. 154, *m162*)
Connecticut One of the original 13 states. Nicknamed the Constitution State or the Nutmeg State. (p. 896, *m900–901*)
Cowpens (35°N/82°W) In South Carolina, site of an American victory in the Revolutionary War. (p. 179, *m179*)
Cuba (22°N/79°W) Island nation in the Caribbean. (p. 624, *m626*)
Cumberland Gap (37°N/84°W) Pass in the Appalachian Mountains near the border of Virginia, Kentucky, and Tennessee. (p. 143, *m303*)
Cuzco (14°S/72°W) Capital of the Incan empire. (p. 50, *m47*)
Czechoslovakia Country in Eastern Europe. Created after World War I; split into two separate countries in 1992. (p. 663, *m664*)

D

Dallas (33°N/97°W) Major city in north central Texas. (*m900–901*)
Delaware One of the original 13 states. Nicknamed the First State or the Diamond State. (p. 896, *m900–901*)
Delaware River Flows into the Atlantic Ocean through Delaware Bay. (p. 82, *m88*)
Denver (40°N/105°W) City in Colorado. (*m510*)
Detroit (42°N/83°W) Largest city in Michigan. (p. 285, *m286*)
District of Columbia Located on the Potomac River. Seat of the federal government of the United States. (p. 247, *m900–901*)
Dominican Republic Country in the Caribbean. (p. 636, *m635*)
Dunkirk (51°N/2°E) French port on the English Channel where Allied troops were trapped by the Germans during World War II. (p. 736, *m756*)
Dust Bowl During the 1930s, name for an area of the Great Plains afflicted by drought and wind erosion. (p. 720, *m721*)

E

Egypt Country in the Middle East. (p. 838, *m839*)
El Alamein (31°N/29°E) In northern Egypt, site of a British victory in World War II. (p.747, *m747*)
El Salvador Country in Central America. (p. 779, *m898–899*)
England Part of Great Britain. (p. 78, *m79*)
English Channel Narrow body of water separating Britain from the European mainland. (p. 736)
Equator Line of latitude labeled 0°. Separates the Northern and Southern hemispheres. (p. 10, *m10*)
Erie Canal Linked the Hudson and Mohawk rivers with Buffalo and Lake Erie. Built between 1817 and 1825. (p. 306, *m306*)
Europe World's second smallest continent. (p. 12, *m10*)

F

Florida 27th state. Nicknamed the Sunshine State. (p. 896, *m900–901*)
Fort Donelson (37°N/88°W) Located in Tennessee. Captured by Grant in 1862. (p. 458, *m470*)
Fort Henry (37°N/88°W) Located in Tennessee. Captured by Grant in 1862. (p. 458, *m470*)
Fort McHenry (39°N/77°W) Located in Baltimore harbor. British bombardment there in 1814 inspired Francis Scott Key to write "The Star-Spangled Banner." (p. 287)
Fort Necessity (40°N/79°W) British fort during the French and Indian War. (p. 136, *m138*)
Fort Pitt (40°N/80°W) British fort in the 1700s on the site of present-day Pittsburgh. (p. 140, *m175*)
Fort Sumter (33°N/80°W) Guarded Charleston harbor in South Carolina. First shots of the Civil War fired there in 1861. (p. 443, *m470*)
Fort Ticonderoga (44°N/74°W) Fort at the south end of Lake Champlain. Captured from the British by Ethan Allen in 1775. (p. 140, *m138*)
France Country in Western Europe. (p. 81, *m898–899*)
Fredericksburg (38°N/78°W) Located in eastern Virginia. Site of a Confederate victory in 1862. (p. 457, *m454*)

G

Gadsden Purchase Land purchased from Mexico in 1853. Now part of Arizona and New Mexico. (p. 363, *m363*)
Gaza Strip (31°N/34°E) Strip of land between Israel and the Mediterranean Sea. Palestinians were granted self-rule of the territory in 1993. (p. 840, *m839*)
Georgia One of the original 13 states. Nicknamed the Peach State or the Empire State of the South. (p. 896, *m900–901*)
Germany Country in central Europe. (p. 642, *m646*)
Gettysburg (40°N/77°W) Town in southern Pennsylvania. Site of a Union victory in 1863 and Lincoln's Gettysburg Address. (p. 469, *m454*)
Goliad (29°N//97°W) Texas town where Mexicans killed several hundred Texans during the Texas war for independence. (p. 355, *m355*)
Gonzales (29°N/97°W) City in Texas near San Antonio. Site of the first Texan victory over Mexico in 1835. (p. 352, *m355*)
Great Britain Island nation of Western Europe. Includes England, Scotland, Wales, and Northern Ireland. (p. 135, *m898–899*)
Great Lakes Chain of five lakes in central North America. Lakes Superior, Michigan, Huron, Ontario, and Erie. (p. 18, *m19*)
Great Plains Western part of the Interior Plains. (p. 16, *m19*)

Great Salt Lake (41°N/113°W) Lake in northern Utah with highly saline water. (p. 365, *m366*)
Great Wagon Road Early pioneer route across the Appalachians. (p. 105, *m102*)
Greensboro (36°N/80°W) City in North Carolina where sit-ins to protest segregation occurred in the 1960s. (p. 814, *m900–901*)
Guam (14°N/143°E) Territory of the United States. Acquired from Spain in 1898. (p. 628, *m620*)
Guatemala Country in Central America. Mayas built a civilization there about 3,000 years ago. (p. 46, *m898–899*)
Gulf of Mexico Body of water along the southern coast of the United States. (p. 17, *m19*)

H

Haiti Country in the West Indies. The nation won independence from France in the early 1800s. (p. 270, *m898–899*)
Harlem (41°N/74°W) Neighborhood in New York City known as a center of African American culture. (p. 690)
Harpers Ferry (39°N/78°W) Town in West Virginia. John Brown raided the arsenal there in 1859. (p. 438, *m454*)
Hawaii Newest of the 50 states. Nicknamed the Aloha State. (p. 896, *m900–901*)
Hawaiian Islands Region in the Pacific Ocean composed of a group of eight large islands and many small islands. (p. 17, *m19*)
Hiroshima (34°N/133°E) Japanese city. The United States dropped an atomic bomb there during World War II. (p. 753, *m752*)
Hudson River Largest river in New York State. (p. 78, *m88*)

I

Idaho 43rd state. Nicknamed the Gem State. Acquired as part of the Oregon Territory. (p. 896, *m900–901*)
Illinois 21st state. Nicknamed the Inland Empire. Settled as part of the Northwest Territory. (p. 896, *m900–901*)
India Country in south Asia. World's second most populous country. (p. 776, *m898–899*)
Indiana 19th state. Nicknamed the Hoosier State. Settled as part of the Northwest Territory. (p. 896, *m900–901*)
Interior Plains Region of the central United States that stretches from the Rockies to the Appalachians. (p. 16, *m19*)
Intermountain Region Rugged region from the Rocky Mountains to the Sierra Nevada and coastal mountains of the western United States. (p. 15, *m19*)
Iowa 29th state. Nicknamed the Hawkeye State. Acquired as part of the Louisiana Purchase. (p. 896, *m900–901*)
Iran Oil-producing country in the Middle East. Since 1979, often had tense relations with the United States. (p. 840, *m839*)
Iraq Oil-producing country in the Middle East. Fought United Nations forces in Persian Gulf War of 1991. (p. 841, *m839*)
Israel Country in the Middle East. Set up as a Jewish homeland in 1948. (p. 838, *m839*)
Isthmus of Panama Narrow strip of land in Central America joining North and South America. (p. 631, *m632*)
Italy Country in southern Europe. (p. 561, *m898–899*)

J

Jamestown (37°N/77°W) First successful English colony in North America. (p. 85, *m88*)
Japan Island nation in East Asia. (p. 616, *m620*)

K

Kansas 34th state. Nicknamed the Sunflower State. Acquired as part of the Louisiana Purchase. (p. 896, *m900–901*)
Kaskaskia (38°N/90°W) British fort on the Mississippi River captured by George Rogers Clark during the American Revolution. (p. 174, *m175*)
Kentucky 15th state. Nicknamed the Bluegrass State. (p. 896, *m900–901*)
Kilwa (8°S/39°E) East African trading state in the 1400s. (p. 73, *m75*)
King's Mountain (35°N/81°W) In South Carolina, site of an American victory in the Revolutionary War. (p. 178, *m179*)
Korea Asian nation divided in two after World War II. Site of a Cold War conflict. (p. 770, *m771*)
Kuwait Oil-producing country in the Middle East. Invaded by Iraq in 1990. (p. 841, *m839*)

L

Lancaster Turnpike Road built in the 1790s linking Philadelphia and Lancaster, Pennsylvania. (p. 302, *m303*)
Latin America Name for those parts of the Western Hemisphere where Latin languages such as Spanish, French, and Portuguese are spoken. Includes Mexico, Central and South America, and the West Indies. (p. 312, *m314*)
Lexington (42°N/71°W) Village in Massachusetts. Site of the first clash between minutemen and British troops in 1775. (p. 155, *m162*)
Liberia Country in West Africa. Set up in 1822 as a colony for free African Americans. (p. 403, *m898–899*)
Little Bighorn Site of a Lakota and Cheyenne victory over Custer in 1876. (p. 519, *m518*)
Little Rock (35°N/92°W) Capital of Arkansas. Site of 1957 school integration conflict. (p. 805, *m900–901*)
London (51°N/0°) Capital of United Kingdom. (*m898–899*)
Long Island Located in New York. Site of a British victory in the Revolution. (p. 169, *m170*)
Los Angeles (34°N/118°W) City in southern California. First settled by Spanish missionaries. (p. 15, *m67*)
Louisbourg (46°N/60°W) Fort in eastern Canada that played a major role in the French and Indian War. (p. 140, *m138*)
Louisiana 18th state. Nicknamed the Pelican State. First state created out of the Louisiana Purchase. (p. 896, *m900–901*)

Lowell (43°N/83°W) City in Massachusetts. Important site of Industrial Revolution. (p. 296)

M

Maine 23rd state. Nicknamed the Pine Tree State. Originally part of Massachusetts. (p. 896, *m900–901*)
Mali Kingdom in West Africa. Reached its peak between 1200 and 1400. (p. 73, *m75*)
Manchuria (48°N/125°E) Region of China. Seized by Japan in the 1930s. Returned to China after World War II. (p. 732, *m752*)
Maryland One of the original 13 states. Nicknamed the Old Line State or the Free State. (p. 896, *m900–901*)
Mason-Dixon Line Boundary between Pennsylvania and Maryland surveyed and marked in the 1760s. (p. 106)
Massachusetts One of the original 13 states. Nicknamed the Bay State or the Old Colony. (p. 896, *m900–901*)
Memphis (35°N/90°W) City in Tennessee on the Mississippi River. Captured by Union forces in 1862. (p. 458, *m470*)
Mexican Cession Lands acquired by the United States from Mexico under the Treaty of Guadalupe Hidalgo in 1848. (p. 363, *m363*)
Mexico Southern neighbor of the United States. Gained independence from Spain in 1821. (p. 312, *m898–899*)
Mexico City (19°N/99°W) Capital of Mexico. (p. 434, *m433*)
Michigan 26th state. Nicknamed the Great Lake State or the Wolverine State. Settled as part of the Northwest Territory. (p. 896, *m900–901*)
Middle East Region at the eastern end of the Mediterranean Sea. (p. 60, *m898–899*)
Midway Island (28°N/179°W) Pacific island. In World War II, site of a decisive American victory over Japanese forces. (p. 747, *m752*)
Minnesota 32nd state. Nicknamed the Gopher State. Most of it was acquired as part of the Louisiana Purchase from France. (p. 896, *m900–901*)
Mississippi 20th state. Nicknamed the Magnolia State. (p. 896, *m900–901*)
Mississippi River Longest river in the United States. Links the Great Lakes with the Gulf of Mexico. (p. 17, *m19*)
Missouri 24th state. Nicknamed the Show Me State. Acquired as part of the Louisiana Purchase. (p. 896, *m900–901*)
Missouri River Second longest river in the United States. Rises in the northern Rocky Mountains and joins the Mississippi River near St. Louis. (p. 17, *m19*)
Mogadishu (2°N/45°E) East African trading state in the 1400s. (p. 73, *m75*)
Montana 41st state. Nicknamed the Treasure State. Acquired in part through the Louisiana Purchase. (p. 896, *m900–901*)
Montgomery (32°N/86°W) City in Alabama. Site of bus boycott during the civil rights movement. (p. 805, *m900–901*)
Montreal (46°N/74°W) Major city in Canada. Located in the province of Quebec. (p. 141, *m138*)
Moscow (56°N/37°E) Capital of Russia and former Soviet Union. (*m898–899*)

N

Nagasaki (33°N/130°E) Japanese city. The United States dropped an atomic bomb there during World War II. (p. 753, *m752*)
National Road Early road to the West that began in Cumberland, Maryland. (p. 303, *m303*)
Nauvoo (41°N/91°W) Town founded by the Mormons in Illinois in the 1840s. (p. 365, *m366*)
Nebraska 37th state. Nicknamed the Cornhusker State. Acquired as part of the Louisiana Purchase. (p. 896, *m900–901*)
Nevada 36th state. Nicknamed the Sagebrush State or the Battle Born State. Acquired at the end of the Mexican War. (p. 896, *m900–901*)
New Amsterdam (41°N/74°W) Town established by Dutch settlers on Manhattan Island in the early 1600s. Renamed New York by the British. (p. 82)
New France Colony established by France in North America. (p. 81, *m79*)
New Hampshire One of the original 13 states. Nicknamed the Granite State. (p. 896, *m900–901*)
New Jersey One of the original 13 states. Nicknamed the Garden State. (p. 896, *m900–901*)
New Mexico 47th state. Nicknamed the Land of Enchantment. Acquired at the end of the Mexican War. (p. 896, *m900–901*)
New Netherland Dutch colony on the Hudson River. Seized by the English and renamed New York in 1664. (p. 82)
New Orleans (30°N/90°W) Port city in Louisiana near the mouth of the Mississippi River. Settled by the French in the 1600s. (p. 82, *m79*)
New Spain Area in the Americas ruled by Spain for some 300 years. Included much of present-day western United States. (p. 68, *m68*)
New York One of the original 13 states. Nicknamed the Empire State. (p. 896, *m900–901*)
New York City (41°N/74°W) Port city at the mouth of the Hudson River. (p. 101, *m102*)
Nicaragua Country in Central America. (p. 779, *m898–899*)
Normandy Region in northwest France. Allied forces landed there on D-Day in World War II. (p. 749, *m747*)
North America World's third largest continent. (p. 14, *m10*)
North Carolina One of the original 13 states. Nicknamed the Tar Heel State or the Old North State. (p. 896, *m900–901*)
North Dakota 39th state. Nicknamed the Sioux State or the Flickertail State. Acquired as part of the Louisiana Purchase. (p. 896, *m900–901*)
Northwest Territory Name for lands north of the Ohio River. Acquired by the Treaty of Paris in 1783. (p. 190, *m191*)

Nueces River Claimed by Mexico in the Mexican War as the southern border of Texas. (p. 361, *m361*)

O

Ohio 17th state. Nicknamed the Buckeye State. Settled as part of the Northwest Territory. (p. 896, *m900–901*)
Ohio River Important transportation route. Begins at Pittsburgh and flows to the Mississippi River. (p. 133, *m133*)
Oklahoma 46th State. Nicknamed the Sooner State. Acquired as part of the Louisiana Purchase. (p. 896, *m900–901*)
Oregon 33rd state. Nicknamed the Beaver State. Acquired as part of the Oregon Territory. (p. 896, *m900–901*)
Oregon Trail Overland route from Independence, Missouri, to the Columbia River valley. (p. 349, *m347*)

P

Pacific Coast Highest and most rugged region of the United States. Includes the Cascades and the Sierra Nevada. (p. 15, *m19*)
Pacific Ocean World's largest ocean. (p. 14, *m10*)
Pakistan Country in South Asia. (p. 776, *m898–899*)
Panama Country on the isthmus separating North and South America. Gained independence from Colombia in 1903. (p. 631, *m635*)
Panama Canal Canal dug through the Isthmus of Panama to link the Atlantic and Pacific oceans. (p. 632, *m632*)
Paris (49°N/2°E) Capital of France. (p. 172, *m646*)
Pearl Harbor (21°N/158°W) United States naval base in Hawaii. Site of Japanese surprise attack December 7, 1941. (p. 739, *m752*)
Pennsylvania One of the original 13 states. Nicknamed the Keystone State. (p. 896, *m900–901*)
Persian Gulf Body of water in the Middle East. Important for transportation of oil. (p. 841, *m839*)
Petersburg (37°N/78°W) City in Virginia. Union forces kept the city under siege for nine months during the Civil War. (p. 472, *m472*)
Philadelphia (40°N/75°W) Major port and chief city in Pennsylvania. (p. 247, *m102*)
Philippine Islands Group of islands in the Pacific Ocean. Acquired by the United States in 1898. Gained independence in 1946. (p. 626, *m626*)
Pikes Peak (39°N/105°W) Mountain located in the Rocky Mountains of central Colorado. (p. 275, *m273*)
Plymouth (42°N/71°W) New England colony founded in 1620 by Pilgrims. (p. 89, *m88*)
Poland Country in Eastern Europe. (p. 735, *m735*)
Portugal Country in Western Europe. (p. 61, *m75*)
Potomac River Forms part of the Maryland-Virginia border. Flows through Washington, D.C., and into Chesapeake Bay. (p. 455, *m455*)
Prime Meridian Line of longitude labeled 0°. (p. 10, *m10*)
Princeton (40°N/75°W) City in New Jersey. Site of an American victory during the Revolution. (p. 170, *m170*)
Promontory Point (42°N/112°W) Place where the Central Pacific and Union Pacific railroads were joined to form the first transcontinental railroad. (p. 511, *m520*)
Puerto Rico (18°N/67°W) Island in the Caribbean Sea. A self-governing commonwealth of the United States. (p. 624, *m626*)

Q

Quebec (47°N/71°W) City in eastern Canada. (p. 81, *m79*)

R

Rhode Island One of the original 13 states. Nicknamed Little Rhody or the Ocean State. (p. 896, *m900–901*)
Richmond (38°N/78°W) Capital of Virginia. Capital of the Confederate States of America during the Civil War. (p. 453, *m454*)
Rio Grande River that forms the border between the United States and Mexico. (p. 18, *m19*)
Roanoke Island (36°N/76°W) Island off North Carolina. Site of English "lost colony" founded in 1587. (p. 84, *m88*)
Rocky Mountains Mountains extending through the western United States and Canada. (p. 16, *m19*)
Russia Largest country in the world, spanning Europe and Asia. Part of the communist Soviet Union until 1991. (p. 558, *m898–899*)

S

Sacramento (39°N/122°W) Capital of California. Developed as a gold rush boom town. (p. 367, *m366*)
St. Augustine (30°N/81°W) City in Florida. Founded by Spain in 1565. Oldest European settlement in the United States. (p. 69, *m67*)
St. Lawrence River Waterway from the Great Lakes to the Atlantic Ocean. Forms part of the border between the United States and Canada. (p. 18, *m79*)
St. Louis (38°N/90°W) City in Missouri on the Mississippi River. Lewis and Clark began their expedition there. (p. 272, *m273*)
Salt Lake City (41°N/112°W) Largest city in Utah. Founded in 1847 by Mormons. (p. 366, *m366*)
San Antonio (29°N/99°W) City in southern Texas. Site of the Alamo. (p. 352, *m352*)
San Diego (33°N/117°W) City in southern California. Founded as the first Spanish mission in California. (p. 357, *m366*)
San Francisco (38°N/122°W) City in northern California. Boom town of the California gold rush. (p. 359, *m366*)

Santa Fe (35°N/106°W) Capital of New Mexico. First settled by the Spanish. (p.69, *m67*)
Santa Fe Trail Overland trail from Independence to Santa Fe. Opened in 1821. (p. 356, *m366*)
Saratoga (43°N/75°W) City in eastern New York. The American victory there in 1777 was a turning point in the Revolution. (p. 172, *m170*)
Savannah (32°N/81°W) Oldest city in Georgia, founded in 1733. (p. 108, *m107*)
Serbia Balkan country in southeastern Europe. Involved in the beginning of World War I. (p. 643, *m646*)
Sierra Nevada Mountain range mostly in California. (p. 15, *m19*)
Songhai West African kingdom in the 1400s. (p. 74, *m75*)
South Africa Country in southern Africa where apartheid existed. (p. 835, *m898–899*)
South America World's fourth largest continent. (p. 12, *m10*)
South Carolina One of the original 13 states. Nicknamed the Palmetto State. (p. 896, *m900–901*)
South Dakota 40th state. Nicknamed the Coyote State or the Sunshine State. Acquired as part of the Louisiana Purchase. (p. 896, *m900–901*)
Soviet Union Short name for the Union of Soviet Socialist Republics. Broke up in 1991. (p. 730, *m735*)
Spain Country in southwestern Europe. (p. 61, *m79*)
Spanish Florida Part of New Spain. Purchased by the United States in 1821. (p. 282, *m283*)
Stalingrad (49°N/45°E) During World War II, city in the Soviet Union where Russians won a decisive victory over German forces. (p. 748, *m747*)
Sudetenland Region of Czechoslovakia given to Germany by the Munich Conference in 1938. (p. 734, *m735*)

T

Tennessee 16th state. Nicknamed the Volunteer State. Gained statehood after North Carolina ceded its western lands to the United States. (p. 896, *m900–901*)
Tenochtitlán (19°N/99°W) Capital of the Aztec empire. Now part of Mexico City. (p. 48, *m47*)
Texas 28th state. Nicknamed the Lone Star State. Proclaimed independence from Mexico in 1836. Was a separate republic until 1845. (p. 896, *m900–901*)
Tikal (17°N/90°W) Ancient Mayan city. (p. 47, *m47*)
Timbuktu (17°N/3°W) City on the Niger River in Africa. (p. 74, *m75*)
Trenton (41°N/74°W) Capital of New Jersey. Site of an American victory in the Revolution. (p. 170, *m170*)

U

Utah 45th state. Nicknamed the Beehive State. Settled by Mormons. (p. 896, *m900–901*)

V

Valley Forge (40°N/76°W) Winter headquarters for the Continental Army in 1777–1778. Located near Philadelphia. (p. 173, *m170*)
Veracruz (19°N/96°W) Port city in Mexico on the Gulf of Mexico. (p. 362, *m361*)
Vermont 14th state. Nicknamed the Green Mountain State. (p. 896, *m900–901*)
Vicksburg (42°N/86°W) City in Mississippi. Site of a Union victory in 1863. (p. 468, *m470*)
Vietnam Country in Southeast Asia. Site of a war involving the United States during the Cold War. (p. 780, *m781*)
Vincennes (39°N/88°W) City in Indiana. British fort there was captured by George Rogers Clark in 1779. (p. 174, *m175*)
Virgin Islands (18°N/64°W) Territory of the United States. Purchased from Denmark in 1917. (p. 896, *m898–899*)
Virginia One of the original 13 states. Nicknamed the Old Dominion. (p. 896, *m900–901*)
Virginia City (39°N/120°W) City in Nevada. Boom town in 1800s because of Comstock Lode mines. (p. 508, *m510*)

W

Washington 42nd state. Nicknamed the Evergreen State. Acquired as part of Oregon Territory. (p. 896, *m900–901*)
Washington, D.C. (39°N/77°W) Capital of the United States since 1800. (p. 287, *m214*)
West Indies Islands in the Caribbean Sea. Explored by Columbus. (p. 62, *m68*)
West Virginia 35th state. Nicknamed the Mountain State. Separated from Virginia early in the Civil War. (p. 896, *m900–901*)
Western Hemisphere Western half of the world. Includes North and South America. (p. 12, *m10*)
Wisconsin 30th state. Nicknamed the Badger State. Settled as part of the Northwest Territory. (p. 896, *m900–901*)
Wounded Knee (43°N/102°W) Site of a massacre of Indians in 1890. Located in what is now South Dakota. (p. 520, *m518*)
Wyoming 44th state. Nicknamed the Equality State. (p. 896, *m900–901*)

Y

Yalu River River along the border between North Korea and China. (p. 771, *m771*)
Yorktown (37°N/76°W) Town in Virginia. Site of the British surrender in 1781. (p. 180, *m179*)
Yugoslavia Eastern European country created after World War I. Torn by civil war after the fall of communism in the 1990s. (p. 832, *m664*)

★ Glossary ★

This glossary defines all vocabulary words and many important historical terms and phrases. These words and terms appear in blue or boldfaced type the first time that they are used in the text. The page number(s) after each definition refers to the page(s) on which the word or phrase is defined in the text. For other references, see the index.

Pronunciation Key

When difficult names or terms first appear in the text, they are respelled to help you with pronunciation. A syllable printed in SMALL CAPITAL LETTERS receives the greatest stress. The pronunciation key below lists the letters and symbols that will help you pronounce the word. It also includes examples of words using each sound and showing how they would be pronounced.

Symbol	Example	Respelling
a	hat	(hat)
ay	pay, late	(pay), (layt)
ah	star, hot	(stahr), (haht)
ai	air, dare	(air), (dair)
aw	law, all	(law), (awl)
eh	met	(meht)
ee	bee, eat	(bee), (eet)
er	learn, sir, fur	(lern), (ser), (fer)
ih	fit	(fiht)
i	mile	(mīl)
ir	ear	(ir)
oh	no	(noh)
oi	soil, boy	(soil), (boi)
oo	root, rule	(root), (rool)
or	born, door	(born), (dor)
ow	plow, out	(plow), (owt)

Symbol	Example	Respelling
u	put, book	(put), (buk)
uh	fun	(fuhn)
yoo	few, use	(fyoo), (yooz)
ch	chill, reach	(chihl), (reech)
g	go, dig	(goh), (dihg)
j	jet, gently bridge	(jeht), (JEHNT lee), (brihj)
k	kite, cup	(kīt), (kuhp)
ks	mix	(mihks)
kw	quick	(kwihk)
ng	bring	(brihng)
s	say, cent	(say), (sehnt)
sh	she, crash	(shee), (krash)
th	three	(three)
y	yet, onion	(yeht), (UHN yuhn)
z	zip, always	(zihp), (AWL wayz)
zh	treasure	(TREH zher)

A

abdicate to give up power (p. 660)
abolitionist person who wanted to end slavery in the United States (p. 404)
absolute power total authority by a ruler over the people (p. 49)
adobe sun-dried clay brick (p. 35)
affirmative action program in areas such as employment and education to provide more opportunities for members of groups that faced discrimination in the past (p. 816)
affluence wealth (p. 798)
aggression any warlike act by one country against another without just cause (p. 731)
ally nation that works with another nation for a common purpose (p. 172)
altitude height above sea level (p. 19)
amend to change (p. 208)
amendment formal written change (p. 222)
amnesty government pardon (p. 479)
anarchist person who opposes organized government (pp. 550, 694)
annex to add on (pp. 355, 617)
apartheid South African government policy of separation of the races enforced by law (p. 835)
appeal to ask that a decision be reviewed by a higher court (p. 230)
appeasement practice of giving in to an aggressor nation's demands in order to keep peace (p. 734)
apprentice (uh PREHN tihs) person who learns a trade or craft from a master (p. 120)
appropriate to set aside money for a special purpose (p. 226)
aqueduct channel for carrying water (p. 50)
archaeology (ahr kee AHL uh jee) study of evidence left by early people in order to find out about their culture (p. 32)
armistice agreement to stop fighting (pp. 627, 660)
arsenal warehouse for guns and ammunition (p. 438)
Articles of Confederation first constitution of the United States (p. 189)
artifact (AHRT uh fakt) object made by humans and used by archaeologists to learn about past human cultures (p. 32)
artisan worker who has learned a trade, such as carpentry (p. 379)
assembly line method of production in which workers add

★ GLOSSARY ★

parts to a product as it moves along on a belt (p. 546)
assimilation process of becoming part of another culture (p. 562)
astrolabe (AS troh layb) instrument to measure the positions of stars and figure out latitude (p. 61)
atomic bomb powerful nuclear weapon that could destroy an entire city with one bomb (p. 752)

B

baby boom increased birth rate in United States during the late 1940s and 1950s (p. 797)
backcountry area of land along the eastern slopes of the Appalachian Mountains. (p. 105)
balanced budget condition that exists when the government spends only as much as it takes in (p. 828)
bankrupt unable to pay debts (p. 703)
barrio neighborhood of Spanish-speaking people (p. 610)
beatnik one who criticized American culture for its conformity and devotion to business in the 1950s (p. 802)
bilingual in two languages (p. 820)
bill proposed law (pp. 203, 221)
bill of rights list of freedoms that a government promises to protect (p. 116)
Bill of Rights first 10 amendments to the Constitution (p. 208)
birth rate number of births per year for every thousand, or other number, of a population (p. 797)
black codes laws that severely limited the rights of freedmen after the Civil War (p. 482)
blitzkrieg German word meaning lightning war; the swift attacks launched by Germany in World War II (p. 735)
blockade shutting off a port by positioning ships to keep people or supplies from moving in or out (p. 164)
bond certificate that promises to repay money loaned, plus interest, on a certain date (p. 246)
bonus additional sum of money (p. 707)
bootlegger person who smuggled liquor into the United States during Prohibition (p. 679)
Boston Massacre (1770) shooting of five colonists by British soldiers (p. 148)
Boston Tea Party (1773) protest in which colonists dressed as Indians dumped British tea into Boston harbor (p. 151)
boycott to refuse to buy certain goods or services (pp. 144, 805)
bracero program program that allowed Mexican laborers to work in the United States (p. 745)
buffer land between two other lands that reduces the possibility of conflict between the other two (p. 109)
building code laws regulating the building of new structures in order to improve the health and safety of residents (p. 566)
bull market rising stock market (p. 676)
bureaucracy system of managing government through departments run by appointed officials (p. 652)

C

Cabinet group of officials who head government departments and advise the President (pp. 224, 245)
canal artificial channel filled with water to allow boats to cross a stretch of land (p. 305)
capital money raised for a business venture (p. 703)
capitalist person who invests in a business to make a profit (p. 296)
caravel (KAR uh vehl) ship with a steering rudder and triangular sails (p. 62)
carpetbagger name for a northerner who came south after the Civil War seeking personal gain (p. 486)
cartographer person who makes maps (p. 8)
cash crop crop sold for money (p. 103)
cattle drive herding and moving of cattle, usually to railroad lines (p. 512)
caucus private meeting of political party leaders to choose a candidate (p. 327)
causeway raised road across a stretch of water (p. 48)
cavalry troops on horseback (p. 173)
cede to give up, as land (p. 363)
censure to officially condemn (p. 772)
charter legal document giving certain rights to a person or company (p. 85)
checks and balances system by which each branch of government can check, or control, the actions of the other branches (p. 202)
chinampa Aztec floating garden (p. 49)
city-state town that has its own independent government (p. 73)
civil disobedience nonviolent opposition to a government policy or law by refusing to comply with it (p. 806)
civil rights the constitutional rights due all citizens (p. 723)
civil rights movement the efforts of African Americans and others who worked for equality (p. 804)
civil service all federal jobs except elected positions and the armed forces (p. 589)
civil war war between people of the same country (p. 428)
civilian person not in the military (p. 463)
civilization advanced culture (p. 46)
clan group of related families (p. 45)
climate average weather of a place over a period of 20 to 30 years (p. 19)
clipper ship fast-sailing ship of the mid-1800s (p. 377)
Cold War after World War II, long period of conflict between the Soviet Union and the United States that never erupted into war between the two (p. 764)
collective bargaining right of unions to negotiate with management for workers as a group (pp. 551, 717)
collective farm a farm or group of farms run by the government, as in a communist state (p. 730)
colony group of people who move to a new land and are ruled by the government of their native land (p. 64)
Columbian Exchange worldwide exchange of goods and ideas that began with Columbus's voyages to the Americas (p. 53)
committee of correspondence group of colonists who wrote letters and pamphlets reporting on British actions (p. 149)
common open field where cattle grazed (p. 98)

communism economic system in which all property is owned by the community (p. 678)
company union labor organization that was controlled by the company owners (p. 694)
compensation repayment for losses (p. 815)
compromise settlement in which each side gives up some of its demands in order to reach an agreement (p. 194)
Compromise of 1850 agreement over slavery under which California joined the Union as a free state and a strict fugitive slave law was passed (p. 428)
concentration camp prison camp for persons who are considered enemies of the state (p. 732)
Confederate States of America nation formed in 1861 by the southern states that seceded from the Union (p. 442)
confederation alliance of independent states (p. 189)
conquistador (kahn KEES tuh dor) Spanish word for conqueror (p. 65)
conservation protection of natural resources (p. 600)
conservative person who wants to keep conditions as they are or return them to the way they used to be (p. 487)
consolidate to combine, such as businesses (p. 533)
constituent person who elected a representative to office (p. 228)
constitution document that sets out the laws and principles of a government (p. 188)
Constitutional Convention (1787) meeting of delegates from 12 states who wrote the United States Constitution (p. 193)
containment in the Cold War, the policy of trying to prevent the spread of Soviet or communist influence beyond where it already existed (p. 765)
Continental Army army established by the Second Continental Congress to fight the British (p. 160)
continental divide mountain ridge that separates river systems flowing toward opposite sides of a continent (p. 274)
cooperative group in which individuals pool their money to buy goods at lower prices (p. 526)
Copperheads northerners who opposed using force to keep the southern states in the Union (p. 463)
corduroy road road made of logs (p. 302)
corporation business that is owned by investors (p. 538)
corral enclosure for animals (p. 505)
cottonocracy name for the wealthy planters who made their money from cotton in the mid-1800s (p. 388)
counterculture rejection of traditional American values and culture (p. 810)
coureur de bois (koo ruhr duh BWAH) phrase meaning runner of the woods; trapper or trader in New France (p. 81)
cow town settlement that grew up at the end of a cattle trail (p. 513)
cowhand worker who tended cattle and drove herds (p. 512)
creole person born in Spain's American colonies to Spanish parents (pp. 70, 312)
Crusades wars fought by Christians in the Middle Ages to gain control of the Middle East (p. 60)
culture entire way of life developed by a people (p. 32)
culture area region in which people share a similar way of life (p. 36)
czar Russian emperor (p. 649)

D

dame school private school for girls in the New England colonies (p. 121)
debtor person who owes money (p. 108)
Declaration of Independence (1776) document stating that the colonies were a free and independent nation (p. 166)
deficit condition of spending more money than the amount received in income (p. 812)
deficit spending government practice of spending more than it takes in from taxes (p. 719)
democratic ensuring that all people have the same rights (p. 266)
deport to expel from a country (p. 694)
depression period when business slows, prices and wages fall, and unemployment rises (pp. 192, 338)
deregulation reduction of government restrictions on businesses (p. 827)
détente easing of tensions between nations (p. 787)
dictator ruler who has complete power (p.730)
dime novels in the late 1800s, low-priced paperback books offering adventure stories (p. 577)
disarmament reduction of nation's armed forces or weapons (p. 678)
discrimination policy or attitude that denies equal rights and treatment to certain groups of people (pp. 381, 461)
dissenting opinion statement explaining why a Supreme Court Justice disagrees with the opinion of the majority (p. 231)
dividend share of a corporation's profits (p. 538)
dollar diplomacy policy of building economic ties to Latin America in the early 1900s (p. 635)
domestic tranquillity peace at home (p. 215)
domino theory in the Cold War, belief that if South Vietnam became communist, other countries in Southeast Asia would become communist, too (p. 780)
downsizing practice of trying to cut costs by using fewer people to do the same work (p. 829)
draft law requiring certain people to serve in the military (pp. 464, 650)
drought long dry spell (p. 35)
due process principle that government must follow the same fair rules in all cases brought to trial (pp. 209, 232)
dumping selling of goods in another country at very low prices (p. 310)

E

electoral college group of electors from every state who meet every four years to vote for the President and Vice President of the United States (p. 202)
elevation height above sea level (p. 14)
emancipate to set free (p. 459)

Emancipation Proclamation (1863) President Lincoln's declaration freeing slaves in the Confederacy (p. 460)
embargo ban on trade with another country (p. 278)
encomienda (ehn koh mee EHN dah) right given by Spanish government to Spanish settlers to demand labor or taxes from Native Americans (p. 70)
English Bill of Rights (1689) document guaranteeing the rights of English citizens (pp. 116, 199)
Enlightenment movement in Europe in the late 1600s and 1700s that emphasized the use of reason (pp. 121, 199)
environmentalist person who works to reduce pollution and protect the natural environment (p. 842)
epidemic rapid spread of a contagious disease among large numbers of people (p. 661)
Equator imaginary line that lies at 0° latitude (p. 10)
escalate to build up, increase, or expand activity (p. 781)
ethnic group people who share a common culture (p. 561)
execute to carry out (p. 188)
executive agreement informal agreement made by the President with another head of state (p. 229)
executive branch branch of government that carries out laws (p. 194)
exile person forced to leave his or her country (p. 773)
expansionism policy of extending a nation's boundaries (p. 616)
expatriate person who leaves his or her country and lives in a foreign land (p. 689)
expedition long journey or voyage of exploration (p. 272)
export trade product sent to markets outside a country (p. 112)
extended family close-knit family group that includes grandparents, parents, children, aunts, uncles, and cousins (p. 393)

F

faction group inside a political party or other group (p. 253)
factory system method of producing goods that brought workers and machinery together in one place (p. 296)
fad style or fashion popular for a short time (p. 687)
Fair Deal program of President Truman to extend New Deal policies (p. 797)
famine severe food shortage and starvation (p. 381)
federal having to do with the national government (p. 215)
federalism division of power between the states and the national government (p. 201)
feudalism (FYOOD 'l ihz uhm) rule by lords who owe loyalty to a monarch (p. 60)
fireside chat radio speeches given by President Franklin Roosevelt (p. 711)
First Continental Congress (1774) meeting of delegates from 12 colonies in Philadelphia (p. 154)
flapper young woman in the 1920s who rebelled against traditional ways of thinking and acting (p. 687)
foreign policy actions that a nation takes in relation to other nations (p. 251)
forty-niner person who headed to California in search of gold during the Gold Rush of 1849 (p. 367)
Fourteen Points President Wilson's goals for peace after World War I (p. 662)
free enterprise system economic system in which businesses are owned by private citizens (p. 540)
free market economic system in which individuals decide for themselves what to produce and sell (p. 791)
freedmen men and women who had been slaves (p. 479)
fugitive runaway (p. 428)

G

general welfare well-being of all the people (p. 216)
gentry highest social class in the 13 English colonies (p. 117)
geography the study of people, their environments, and their resources (p. 4)
Gettysburg Address (1863) speech by President Lincoln after the Battle of Gettysburg (p. 470)
Ghost Dance religious ceremony that celebrated the time when Native Americans lived freely on the Plains (p. 519)
glacier thick sheet of ice (p. 30)
glasnost Mikhail Gorbachev's policy of speaking out openly and honestly about problems in the Soviet Union (p. 789)
global warming theory that Earth's atmosphere is warming up as a result of air pollution (p. 845)
globe sphere with a map of Earth printed on it (p. 8)
Glorious Revolution (1688) movement that brought William and Mary to the throne of England and strengthened the rights of English citizens (p. 116)
Good Neighbor policy President Franklin Roosevelt's policy intended to strengthen friendly relations with Latin America (p. 733)
graduated income tax tax on earnings that charges different rates for different income levels (p. 596)
grandfather clause law that excused a voter from a literacy test if his grandfather had been eligible to vote on January 1, 1867—protected the voting rights of southern whites but not those of southern blacks (p. 493)
Great Awakening religious movement in the English colonies in the early 1700s (p. 119)
Great Compromise plan at the Constitutional Convention that settled the differences between large and small states (p. 196)
Great Depression worst period of economic decline in United States history, beginning in 1929 and lasting until World War II (p. 703)
Great Society President Lyndon Johnson's plan to improve the standard of living of every American (p. 809)
guerrilla soldier who uses hit-and-run tactics (pp. 179, 780)

H

habeas corpus right to have charges filed or a hearing before being jailed (p. 464)
Harlem Renaissance "rebirth" of African American culture in the 1920s (p. 690)
hemisphere half of the Earth (p. 10)
hieroglyphics system of writing that uses pictures to represent words and ideas (p. 47)

hill area of raised land that is lower and more rounded than a mountain (p. 14)
history account of what has happened in the lives of different peoples (p. 4)
hogan house made of mud plaster over a framework of wooden poles (p. 41)
Holocaust murder of millions of European Jews and others by officials of Nazi Germany and its allies (p. 755)
House of Burgesses representative assembly in colonial Virginia (pp. 86, 199)
House of Representatives larger house of Congress, in which each state is represented according to its population (p. 225)
Hudson River School group of American artists who painted landscapes of New York's Hudson River region in the mid-1800s (p. 415)

I

igloo house of snow and ice, developed by the Inuits (p. 37)
illegal alien someone who enters a country without legal permission (p. 851)
illiterate unable to read or write (p. 651)
immigrant person who enters a country in order to settle there (p. 259)
impeach to bring a formal charge of wrongdoing against the President or another public official (pp. 203, 228, 484)
imperialism policy of powerful countries seeking to control the economic and political affairs of weaker countries or regions (p. 618)
import trade product brought into a country (p. 112)
impressment act of forcing someone to serve in the navy (p. 277)
inauguration ceremony at which the President officially takes the oath of office (p. 244)
income tax tax on people's earnings (p. 466)
indentured servant person who agreed to work without wages for some time in exchange for passage to the colonies (p. 117)
Industrial Revolution process by which machines replaced hand tools, and steam and other new sources of power replaced human and animal power (p. 294)
inflation rise in prices and decrease in the value of money (pp. 466, 796)
initiative process by which voters can put a bill directly before the state legislature by collecting signatures on a petition (p. 596)
injunction court order to do or not to do something (p. 553)
installment buying method of buying on credit (p. 675)
integration bringing together people of different races or ethnic groups (p. 803)
interchangeable parts identical, machine-made parts for a tool or instrument (p. 299)
intern to detain or confine, usually in a compound (p. 628)
interstate commerce trade between different states (p. 311)
intervention direct involvement in another country (p. 315)
irrigate to bring water to an area (p. 6)
island hopping strategy of Allies in World War II of capturing some Japanese-held islands and going around others (p. 751)
isolationism policy of having little to do with the political affairs of foreign nations (p. 616)
isthmus narrow strip of land (pp. 14, 631)

J

jazz music style that developed from blues, ragtime, and other earlier styles (p. 688)
jerky dried meat (p. 505)
Jim Crow laws laws that separated people of different races in public places in the South (p. 495)
joint committee congressional committee that includes both House and Senate members (p. 226)
judicial branch branch of government that decides if laws are carried out fairly (p. 194)
judicial review power of the Supreme Court to decide whether acts of a President or laws passed by Congress are constitutional (pp. 224, 269)
justice fairness (p. 215)

K

kachina masked dancer at religious ceremonies of the Southwest Indians (p. 41)
kaiser German emperor (p. 644)
kamikaze in World War II, a Japanese pilot who carried out a suicidal attack on a target (p. 751)
kayak (KI ak) small boat made of animal skins (p. 37)
kinship network close ties among family members (p. 74)
kitchen cabinet group of unofficial advisers to President Andrew Jackson (p. 331)
kiva underground chamber where Pueblo men held religious ceremonies (p. 41)

L

laissez faire (lehs ay FAYR) idea that government should play as small a role as possible in economic affairs (pp. 267, 339, 718)
latitude distance north or south from the Equator (p. 4)
lawsuit legal case brought by one person or group against another to settle a dispute (p. 434)
League of Nations association of nations formed after World War I (p. 662)
legislative branch branch of government that passes laws (p. 194)
legislature group of people who have the power to make laws (p. 114)
Lend Lease Act during World War II, law that allowed the United States to sell arms and equipment to Britain (p. 738)
libel publishing a statement that unjustly damages a person's reputation (p. 123)
liberty freedom to live as you please provided you obey the laws and respect the rights of others (p. 217)
literacy test examination to see if a person can read and write, used in the past to restrict voting rights (p. 493)
local color speech and habits of a particular region (p. 578)
locomotive engine that pulls a railroad train (p. 376)
long house Native American home built of wood poles and bark (p. 44)

longitude distance east or west from the Prime Meridian (p. 4)
Louisiana Purchase (1803) vast territory west of the Mississippi purchased from France (p. 272)
Loyalist colonist who remained loyal to Britain (p.162)
lynching illegal seizure and execution of someone by a mob (p. 495)

M

Magna Carta (1215) document that guaranteed rights to English nobles (pp. 86, 198)
magnetic compass device that shows which direction is North (p. 61)
mainstream to place children with disabilities in regular school classes (p. 849)
majority more than half (p. 324)
Manifest Destiny belief that the United States had the right and the duty to expand to the Pacific (p. 359)
manor district ruled by a lord, including the lord's castle, peasants' huts, and surrounding fields (p. 60)
map projection way of drawing the Earth on a flat surface (p. 8)
Marshall Plan American plan to help European nations rebuild their economies after World War II (p. 766)
martial law rule by the army instead of the elected government (pp. 448, 788)
martyr person who dies for his or her beliefs (p. 438)
mass production making large quantities of a product quickly and cheaply (p. 547)
Mayflower Compact (1620) agreement for ruling the Plymouth Colony, signed by Pilgrims before they landed at Plymouth (pp. 88, 199)
Medicaid government program of helping poor people pay medical bills (p. 809)
Medicare government program of helping older Americans pay medical and hospital bills (p. 809)
mercantilism (MER kuhn tihl ihz uhm) economic theory that a nation's strength came from building up its gold supplies and expanding its trade (p. 112)
mercenary soldier who fights merely for pay, often for a foreign country (p. 164)
mestizo in Spanish colonies, person of mixed Spanish and Indian background (p. 70)
Middle Ages period of time in European history from about 500 to 1350 (p. 60)
middle class in the 13 English colonies, class that included skilled craftsworkers, farmers, and some tradespeople (p. 117)
Middle Passage ocean trip from Africa to the Americas in which thousands of enslaved Africans died (p. 77)
migrant worker agricultural worker who moves with the seasons, planting or harvesting crops (pp. 720, 818)
militarism policy of building up strong armed forces to prepare for war (p. 642)
militia army of citizens who serve as soldiers in an emergency (p. 154)
minuteman colonial volunteer who trained to fight the British (p. 154)
mission religious settlement run by Catholic priests and friars (p. 69)
missionary person who tries to spread certain religious beliefs among a group of people (p. 81)
Missouri Compromise (1819) plan proposed by Henry Clay to keep the number of slave and free states equal (p. 424)
mobilize to prepare for war (p. 643)
monarch king or queen (p. 60)
monopoly company that controls all or nearly all the business of an industry (p. 540)
Monroe Doctrine (1823) President Monroe's foreign policy statement warning European nations not to interfere in Latin America (p. 315)
moral diplomacy foreign policy proposed by President Wilson to condemn imperialism, spread democracy, and promote peace (p. 636)
mountain high, steep, rugged land, usually at least 1,000 feet (372 m) above the surrounding land (p. 14)
mountain man fur trapper who lived in the western mountains in the early 1800s (p. 347)
muckraker journalist who exposed corruption and other problems of the late 1800s and early 1900s (p. 593)
mudslinging political tactic of using insults to attack an opponent's reputation (p. 341)
mutualista Mexican American mutual aid group (p. 610)

N

national debt total sum of money a government owes (pp. 245, 719)
national park natural or historic area set aside and run by the federal government for people to visit (p. 600)
nationalism pride in one's nation (pp. 282, 642, 730)
nativist person who wanted to limit immigration and preserve the United States for native-born white Protestants (pp. 381, 562)
natural rights rights that belong to all people from birth (p. 168)
network system of connected lines, as in a network of railroad lines (p. 532)
neutral not taking sides in a war (pp. 174, 282)
New Deal program of President Franklin D. Roosevelt to end the Great Depression (p. 711)
nominating convention meeting at which a political party chooses a candidate (p. 327)
North American Free Trade Agreement (NAFTA) treaty among the United States, Canada, and Mexico to gradually remove tariffs and other trade barriers (p. 846)
North Atlantic Treaty Organization (NATO) alliance formed in 1949 by the United States and Western European nations to fight Soviet aggression (p. 769)
nullification idea that a state had the right to cancel a federal law it considered unconstitutional (p. 333)
nullify to cancel (p. 260)

O

on margin practice that allowed people to buy stock with a down payment of 10 percent of the full value (p. 676)

OPEC (Organization of Petroleum Exporting Countries) league of oil-producing nations (p. 838)
Open Door Policy (1899) policy toward China that allowed a nation to trade in any other nation's sphere of influence (p. 623)
opinion a judge's official statement regarding the laws bearing on a case (p. 231)
ordinance law (p. 190)
Organization of American States association of American countries working for collective defense, cooperation, and peaceful settlement of disputes (p. 778)
override to overrule or set aside (pp. 203, 221)

P

pacifist person who opposes all wars (p. 655)
Parliament representative assembly in England (p. 86)
Patriot colonist who supported independence from British rule (p. 161)
patronage practice of giving jobs to loyal supporters (p. 589)
patroon owner of a huge estate in a Dutch colony (p. 100)
penal system system of prisons (p. 399)
peninsulare (puh nihn suh LAH ray) person from Spain who held a position of power in a Spanish colony (p. 70)
pension sum of money paid to people on a regular basis after they retire (p. 715)
pet bank state bank in which President Jackson and Secretary of the Treasury Taney deposited federal money (p. 332)
petition formal request to someone in authority, usually written and signed by a group of people (p. 144)
Pilgrims in the 1600s, English settlers who sought religious freedom in the Americas (p. 88)
plain broad area of fairly level land (p. 14)
plantation large estate farmed by many workers (pp. 72, 109)
plateau raised plain (p. 14)
pogrom in Eastern Europe, an organized attack on a Jewish community (p. 558)
poll tax tax required before a person can vote (p. 493)
pool group of companies that divided up business in an area and fixed prices (p. 535)
popular sovereignty idea that the people hold the final authority in government (p. 218), allowing each territory to decide whether to allow slavery (p. 426)
potlatch ceremonial dinner among some Native Americans of the Northwest Coast (p. 38)
preamble opening statement of a declaration, constitution, or other official document (pp. 168, 214)
precedent (PREHS uh dehnt) act or decision that sets an example for others to follow (pp. 224, 244)
precipitation (pree sihp uh TAY shuhn) water that falls as rain, sleet, hail, or snow (p. 19)
predestination belief that God decided in advance which people will gain salvation in heaven (p. 398)
presidio (prih SIHD ee oh) fort where soldiers lived in the Spanish colonies (p. 69)
primary election in which voters choose their party's candidate for the general election (p. 596)
Prime Meridian imaginary line that lies at 0° longitude (p. 10)
productivity measure of how much a given number of workers can produce in a given time (p. 798)
profiteer person who takes advantage of a crisis to make money (p. 466)
Progressives reformers who wanted to improve American life in the late 1800s and early 1900s (p. 593)
Prohibition ban on manufacture, sale, and transportation of liquor anywhere in the United States from 1920 to 1933 (p. 679)
propaganda spreading of ideas that help a cause or hurt an opposing cause (p. 646)
proprietary colony English colony in which the king gave land to proprietors in exchange for a yearly payment (p. 101)
proprietor owner of a proprietary colony (p. 101)
protective tariff tax on imported goods to protect a country's industry from foreign competition (p. 247)
protectorate nation whose independence is limited by the control of a more powerful country (p. 630)
Protestant Reformation movement to reform the Roman Catholic Church in the 1500s; led to creation of many different Christian churches (p. 79)
public interest the good of the people (p. 595)
public school school supported by taxes (p. 120)
public works projects built by the government for public use (p. 706)
pueblo adobe dwelling of the Anasazis (p. 35); town in the Spanish colonies (p. 69)
pull factor condition that attracts people to move to a new area (p. 558)
Puritans group of English Protestants who settled the Massachusetts Bay Colony (p. 94)
push factor condition that encourages people to move away from their homeland (p. 558)

Q

quota system system that limited immigration by allowing only a certain number of people from each country to immigrate to the United States (p. 695)

R

racism belief that one race is superior to another (pp. 111, 448)
radical person who wants to make drastic changes in society (p. 482)
ragtime popular music of the late 1800s that had a lively, rhythmic sound (p. 573)
ratify to approve (pp. 182, 204)
ration to limit the amount of goods people can buy (p. 741)
Reaganomics program of President Ronald Reagan to cut taxes in an effort to stimulate the economy (p. 827)
realist writer or artist who shows life as it really is (p. 578)
rebate discount on services or merchandise (p. 534)
recall process by which voters can remove an elected official from office (p. 596)
recession mild depression in which business slows and some workers lose their jobs (pp. 674, 829)

Reconstruction rebuilding of the South after the Civil War (p. 479)
referendum process by which people vote directly on a bill (p. 596)
refugee person who flees his or her homeland to seek safety elsewhere (p. 164)
relief program government program to help the needy (p. 706)
Renaissance (REHN uh sahns) French word meaning rebirth; burst of learning in Europe from the late 1300s to about 1600 (p. 61)
rendezvous (RAHN day voo) yearly meeting where mountain men traded furs (p. 348)
renewable resource natural resource that can be quickly replaced by nature (p. 845)
reparations after a war, payments from a defeated nation to a victorious nation to pay for losses suffered during the war (p. 663)
repatriate to send back to one's own country (p. 723)
repeal to cancel or undo (pp. 144, 680)
representative government government in which voters elect representatives to make laws for them (pp. 86, 218)
republic nation in which voters elect representatives to govern them (p. 198)
reservation limited area set aside for Native Americans by the government (p. 517)
revival huge meeting held to stir religious feelings (p. 398)
Roosevelt Corollary (1904) President Theodore Roosevelt's addition to the Monroe Doctrine, claiming the right of the United States to intervene in Latin America to preserve law and order (p. 634)
royal colony colony under the control of the English crown (p. 101)

S

Sabbath holy day of rest in some religions (p. 98)
sabotage secret destruction of property or interference with production in a factory or other workplace (p. 694)
sachem tribal chief of an Eastern Woodlands Native American people (p. 45)
sanction action taken against a country in an effort to force a change in its policy (p. 835)
satellite nation country that is dominated by a more powerful nation (p. 765)
scalawag white southerner who supported the Republicans during Reconstruction (p. 486)
secede to withdraw from membership in a group (pp. 335, 427)
Second Great Awakening religious movement that swept the United States in the early 1800s (p. 398)
sectionalism loyalty to a state or section rather than to the whole country (pp. 310, 425)
sedition stirring up rebellion against a government (p. 259)
segregation separation of people based on racial, ethnic, or other differences (pp. 495, 743)
self-determination right of national groups to their own territory and forms of government (p. 662)
Senate smaller house of Congress, in which each state has two senators (p. 225)
Seneca Falls Convention (1848) meeting at which leaders of the women's rights movement called for equality for women (p. 409)
separation of powers principle by which the powers of government are divided among separate branches (p. 200)
serf peasant who worked for a lord and could not leave without the lord's permission (p. 60)
settlement house community center that offers services to the poor (p. 568)
sharecropper person who farms land owned by another in exchange for a share of the crops (p. 490)
siege military blockade of an enemy town or position in order to force it to surrender (pp. 180, 354)
silent majority President Nixon's term for Americans who were disturbed by the unrest of the 1960s (p. 811)
sit-in protest in which people sit and refuse to leave (p. 814)
sitdown strike work stoppage in which workers refuse to leave a factory (p. 717)
slave code laws that controlled the lives of enslaved African Americans and denied them basic rights (pp. 111, 390)
smuggler person who violates trade laws by illegally taking goods into or out of a country (p. 278)
social reform organized attempt to improve what is unjust or imperfect in society (p. 398)
Social Security federal program begun in the 1930s to provide aid for the elderly and unemployed; the program was later expanded (p. 718)
socialist person who supports community ownership of property and the sharing of all profits (p. 655)
sod house house built of soil held together by grass roots (p. 524)
sodbuster nickname for a Plains farmer (p. 524)
solar energy power from the sun (p. 845)
soup kitchen place where food is provided to the needy at little or no charge (p. 706)
speakeasy illegal bar that served liquor during Prohibition (p. 679)
speculator person who invests in a risky venture in the hope of making a large profit (pp. 246, 338)
sphere of influence area in which a foreign nation had special trading privileges and made laws for its own citizens (p. 623)
spinning jenny machine developed in the 1760s that could spin several threads at once (p. 294)
spoils system practice of rewarding supporters with government jobs (p. 331)
Square Deal Theodore Roosevelt's promise that all groups should have an equal opportunity to succeed (p. 599)
stagflation combination of rising prices, high unemployment, and slow economic growth (p. 812)
stalemate deadlock in which neither side is strong enough to defeat the other (p. 644)
standard of living an index based on the amount of goods, services, education, and leisure time that people have (p. 798)
standard time zone one of 24 divisions of the Earth, each an hour apart (p. 12)
standing committee permanent congressional committee assigned to study a specific issue (p. 226)
states' rights idea that states have the right to limit the power of the federal government (p. 333)

steerage on a ship, the cramped quarters for passengers paying the lowest fares (p. 559)
stock share in a corporation (pp. 538, 676)
strike refusal by workers to do their jobs until their demands are met (p. 379)
strikebreaker worker hired as a replacement for a striking worker (p. 550)
subsidy financial aid or a land grant from the government (p. 509)
suburb community located within commuting distance of a city (pp. 684, 798)
suffrage right to vote (p. 326)
suffragist person who campaigned for women's right to vote (p. 604)
summit meeting conference between the highest-ranking officials of different nations (p. 789)
Sun Dance religious ceremony of the Plains Indians (p. 505)
Sunbelt name for the southern part of the United States from Florida to southern California (p. 801)
superpower nation with enough strength to influence events in many areas around the world (p. 773)
Supreme Court highest court in the United States (p. 231)
surplus an extra amount, more than is needed (pp. 50, 713)
sweatshop workplace where people labor long hours in poor conditions for low pay (p. 548)

T

tariff tax on foreign goods brought into a country (p. 247)
telegraph communication device that sends electrical signals along a wire (p. 375)
temperance movement campaign against the sale or drinking of alcohol (pp. 401, 607)
tenement small apartment in a city slum building (p. 565)
tepee (TEE pee) tent made by stretching animal skins on tall poles (pp. 42, 504)
terrace level strip of land carved into the side of a hill or mountain for farming (p. 50)
Three-Fifths Compromise agreement at the Constitutional Convention that three fifths of the slaves in any state be counted in its population (p. 196)
toleration willingness to let others practice their own customs and beliefs (p. 96)
total war all-out war that affects civilians at home as well as soldiers in combat (p. 471)
totalitarian state country where a single party controls the government and every aspect of the lives of the people (p. 730)
town meeting session in which citizens discuss and vote on local community issues (p. 98)
trade deficit when a nation buys more goods and services from foreign countries than it sells to them (p. 846)
trade union association of trade workers formed to gain higher wages and better working conditions (p. 379)
traitor person who betrays his or her country (p. 166)
transcendentalism belief that the most important truths in life go beyond human reason (p. 413)
transcontinental railroad railroad that stretches across a continent (p. 509)
travois (truh VOI) sled used by Plains people and pulled by a dog or horse (pp. 41, 504)
trench warfare type of fighting in which both sides dig trenches and attempt to overrun the enemy's trenches (p. 644)
triangular trade colonial trade route between New England, the West Indies, and Africa (p. 112)
tribe group of Native American people sharing the same customs, languages, and rituals (p. 36)
tributary stream or smaller river that flows into a bigger river (p. 17)
Truman Doctrine President Truman's policy of giving American aid to nations threatened by communism (p. 766)
trust group of corporations run by a single board of directors (p. 540)
trustbuster person who wanted to end all trusts (p. 598)
turnpike road built by a private company that charges a toll to use it (p. 302)
tutor private teacher (p. 120)

U

U-boat German submarine (p. 647)
unconstitutional not permitted by the Constitution (pp. 221, 254)
underground railroad network of abolitionists who helped runaway slaves reach freedom in the North or Canada (p. 405)
unemployment insurance program that gives payments to people who have lost their jobs until they find work again (p. 718)
United Nations international organization formed in 1945 to help solve conflicts between nations (p. 769)
urbanization movement of population from farms to cities (pp. 300, 564)

V

vaquero (vah KEHR oh) Spanish or Mexican cowhand (p. 512)
vaudeville variety show that included comedians, song-and-dance performers, and acrobats (p. 573)
vertical integration control of all phases of an industry, from raw materials to finished product (p. 537)
veto to reject (pp. 203, 221)
vigilante (vihj uh LAN tee) self-appointed law enforcer who deals out punishment without a trial (pp. 368, 508)

W

warmonger person who tries to stir up war (p. 648)
Warsaw Pact military alliance of Soviet Union and other communist states in Europe (p.769)
weather condition of the Earth's atmosphere at any given time and place (p. 19)
wholesale buying or selling of goods in large quantities at lower prices (p. 526)
women's rights movement campaign to win equality for women (p. 410)
writ of assistance legal document that let a British customs officer inspect a ship's cargo without giving any reason for the search (p. 145)

Y

yellow journalism sensational style of reporting used by some newspapers in the late 1800s (pp. 572, 625)

★ Index ★

Page numbers that are italicized refer to illustrations or quotations. An *m, p, c, g, go,* or *q* before a page number refers to a map *(m)*, picture *(p)*, chart *(c)*, graph *(g)*, graphic organizer *(go)*, or quotation *(q)* on that page.

A

★ INDEX ★

D

E

U

V

W

X

Y

Z

★ Credits ★

Acknowledgments

Art and Design: Kathryn Foot, Karen Vignola, Patty Rodriguez, Rui Camarinha, Anthony Barone, Ernest Albanese, Robert Aleman, Penny Baker, Paul Delsignore, Frances Medico, Doreen Mazur **Editorial:** Mary Aldridge, Gaynor Ellis, Marian Manners, Jeremy Naidus, Andrew Roney **Photo Research:** *PhotoSearch,* Inc., Lashonda Williams, Vickie Menanteaux, Katarina Gavilanes, Diane Alimena

Text Credits

Grateful acknowledgment is made to the following for copyrighted material:

Page 126 From *American Indian Myths and Legends,* edited by Richard Erdoes and Alfonso Ortiz (New York: Pantheon Books, a division of Random House, 1984). Copyright 1984 by Richard Erdoes and Alfonso Ortiz. **Page 238** Excerpts from "Valley Forge" by Maxwell Anderson from *America on Stage,* edited by Stanley Richards. Copyright ©1976. **Page 346** From *Nightjohn* by Gary Paulsen. Copyright ©1993 by Gary Paulsen. Used by permission of Delacorte Press, a division of Bantam Doubleday Dell Publishing Group, Inc. **Page 510** From *My Antonia* by Willa Cather, published by Houghton Mifflin Company. **Page 596** From *The Picture Bride* by Yoshiko Uchida. Copyright ©1987 by Yoshiko Uchida. Published by Northland Press, 1987. Reprinted courtesy of The Bancroft Library, University of California, Berkeley. **Page 632** From "The Circuit" by Francisco Jiménez. Copyright by Francisco Jiménez. Reprinted by permission of the author. **Page 758** "The Negro Speaks of Rivers" from *Selected Poems* by Langston Hughes. Copyright 1926 by Alfred A. Knopf, Inc. and renewed 1954 by Langston Hughes. Reprinted by permission of Alfred A. Knopf, Inc. "Mother to Son" from *Collected Poems* by Langston Hughes. Copyright ©1994 by the Estate of Langston Hughes. Reprinted by permission of Alfred A. Knopf, Inc. **Page 759** "Tableau" by Countee Cullen. Copyrights held by the Amistad Research Center, Tulane University, New Orleans, Louisiana, administered by Thompson and Thompson, New York, NY. "Common Dust" by Georgia Douglas Johnson, from *3000 Years of Black Poetry,* edited by Alan Lomax and Raoul Abdual (New York: Dodd, Mead & Co., 1970).

Note: Every effort has been made to locate the copyright owner of material used in this textbook. Omissions brought to our attention will be corrected in subsequent editions.

Illustration Credits

Cover and Title Page Wolfgang Kaehler; Day Williams/Photo Researchers, Inc. **iv** *t* Jerry Jacka Photography; *m* The Granger Collection, New York; *b The Puritan,* Augustus Saint-Gaudens, All Rights Reserved, The Metropolitan Museum of Art, Bequest of Jacob Ruppart, 1939 (39.65.53) **v** *t* Copyright © 1996 By the Metropolitan Museum of Art; *m* Gallery of the Republic; *b* Courtesy, Independence National Historical Park Collection **vi** *b* O.C. Seltzer, *Lewis and Clark with Sacajawea at the Great Falls of the Missouri,* From the Collection of Gilcrease Museum, Tulsa; *t* Rembrandt Peale, *Thomas Jefferson,* detail, Collection of The New-York Historical Society; *m* American Textile History Museum, Lowell, MA **vii** *mt* Dean Beason, *Settlers' Wagon,* National Gallery of Art, Washington; *m* National Museum of History and Technology, Smithsonian Institution, Photo no. 90-4210; *b* Museum of Art, Rhode Island School of Design, Gift of Miss Lucy T. Aldrich **viii** *m* Courtesy of the Library of Congress; *t* Photography by Larry Sherer/High Impact Photography, Time-Life Books, Inc.; *m t* Photography by Larry Sherer/High Impact Photography, Time-Life Books, Inc.; *b* Richard Norris Brooke, *Furling the Flag,* West Point Museum Collections, United States Military Academy, West Point, New York **ix** *t* Denver Art Museum; *m* © 1999 Michael Freeman; *b* The George Meany Memorial Archives **x** *t* The Granger Collection, New York; *m* The Museum of American Political Life, University of Hartford; photo by Sally Andersen-Bruce; *b* The Imperial War Museum, London, John Singer Sargent, *Gassed* **xi** *t* Culver Pictures, Inc.; *m* Brown Brothers; *b* Naval Combat Art Collection, Washington, D.C. **xii** *t* Matthew Frost/CORBIS-BETTMANN; *b* Corporation for National Service, Washington D.C., 1998 **xiii** Courtesy Erie Canal Village **xiv** *b* Myrleen Ferguson/PhotoEdit; *t* Carolyn Schaefer/Gamma Liaison **xv** Lynn Saville **xx** George Catlin, *LaSalle Claiming Louisiana for France, April 9, 1682,* 1847/1848, Paul Mellon Collection, ©1998 Board of Trustees, National Gallery of Art, Washington **3** NOAA **6** Vito Palmisano/Tony Stone Images **8** Silver Burdett Ginn **12** Map Divison, New York Public Library. Astor, Lenox and Tilden Foundation **14** Daniel J. Cox/Gamma Liaison **15** Jeff Gnass Photography **16** *r* Robert Farber/The Image Bank; *l* ©Francois Gohier/Photo Researchers, Inc. **17** *l* Siegfried Layda/Tony Stone Images; *r* ©Jeff LePore/Photo Researchers, Inc. **18** *r* UPI/Corbis-Bettmann; *l* Courtesy National Archives, photo no. NWDNS-79-AA_F09 **20** East Bay Municipal Utility District **21** *l* Duricux/SIPA; *r* Weather Graphics Courtesy of AccuWeather, Inc., 619 West College Avenue, State College, PA 16801, (814) 237-0309; Other Educational Weather Products Available © 1997 **29** Courtesy of the Wheelwright Museum of the American Indian **30** National Museum of American Art, Smithsonian Institution **33** *l* Tom Till/International Stock Photography, Ltd.; *r* Peabody Museum of Archaeology and Ethnology, Harvard University **34** *r* National Park Service; *l* ©Richard J. Green/Photo Researchers, Inc. **35** Jerry Jacka Photography **37** *r* Lee Boltin Picture Library; *l* Grove/Zuckerman/Index Stock Photography, Inc. **41** *l Kachina Doll,* The Brooklyn Museum, 05.588.7193, Museum Expedition 1905, Museum Collection Fund; *r Butterfly Maiden, Kachina,* Courtesy of the Denver Art Museum, Denver Art Museum, Denver, CO **42** National Museum of American Art, Smithsonian Institution **43** Courtesy of The New York State Museum, Albany, NY, Lewis Henry Morgan collection **44** Neg./Trans. no. K 10302. Courtesy Department of Library Services, American Museum of Natural History **46** The Granger Collection, New York **48** Laurie Platt Winfrey, Inc. **50** Museo Nacional de Arqueologia, Antropologia E Historia del Peru **51** Loren Mcintyre/Woodfin Camp & Associates **52** ©University Museum of National Antiquities, Oslo, Norway. Photo: Eirik Irgens Johnsen **53** The Granger Collection, New York **54** ©Index Stock Photography, Inc. **59** New York Public Library, Rare Book Division; Astor, Lenox and Tilden Foundations **61** Erich Lessing/Art Resource, NY **62** *l Christopher Columbus,* Sebastiano del Piombo, All rights reserved, The Metropolitan Museum of Art; The Metropolitan Museum of Art, The Edward C. Moore Collection, Bequest of Edward C. Moore, 1891, Copyright ©The Metropolitan Museum of Art **63** Colin Fisher for Prentice Hall **65** Victoria & Albert Museum, London/The Bridgeman Art Library, London **66** *t* The Granger Collection, New York; *b* The Metropolitan Museum of Art, Bashford Dean Memorial Collection, Purchase, 1929.(29.158.142) **69** *t* Luis Castañeda/The Image Bank; *b* ©Brent Winebrenner/International Stock Photography, Ltd. **70** Ampliaciones y Reproducciones MAS (Arxiu Mas) **73** All rights reserved, The Metropolitan Museum of Art, Louis V. Bell and Rogers Funds, 1972 (1972.63ab) **74** *r* Merrit Vincent/PhotoEdit; *l* The Granger Collection, New York **76** *l* Photo Bibliothèque Nationale, Paris; *r Sugar Harvest in Louisiana & Texas,* 1856–1860, #65.39.120, Collection: Glenbow Museum, Calgary, Alberta **81** *t* North Wind Picture Archives; *b* Minnesota Historical Society **82** New York Public Library, Rare Book Division; Astor, Lenox and Tilden Foundations **85** detail, National Portrait Gallery, Smithsonian Institution/Art Resource, NY **86** State Capitol, Commonwealth of Virginia. Courtesy The Library of Virginia

89 Courtesy of the Pilgrim Society, Plymouth, Massachusetts **93** Stephen & Carol Huber **95** *l* Eliot Elisofon/LIFE Magazine©TIME Inc.; *r The Puritan,* Augustus Saint-Gaudens, All Rights Reserved, The Metropolitan Museum of Art, Bequest of Jacob Ruppart, 1939 (39.65.53) **97** Courtesy of the Library of Congress **98** *r* Courtesy of the Peabody Essex Museum, Salem, MA. Photo by Mark Sexton; *l* North Wind Picture Archives **100** Museum of the City of New York, Museum purchase, Mrs. Elon Huntington Hooker Fund **101** Collection of The New-York Historical Society **103** *l* Courtesy of the Library of Congress; *r* Kelly Mooney/Corbis **105** New York State Historical Association, Cooperstown **108** The Granger Collection, New York **109** *l* North Wind Picture Archives; *r* The Granger Collection, New York **110** *l* Courtesy, American Antiquarian Society; *r* Gibbes Museum of Art, Carolina Art Association **115** John Lei/Omni-Photo Communications, Inc. for Prentice Hall **117** John Lewis Stage **118** *l Mrs. Elizabeth Freake and Baby Mary,* unknown artist, Worcester Art Museum, Worcester, Massachusetts, Gift of Mr. and Mrs. Albert W. Rice; *r* Breton Littlehales ©National Geographic Society **120** *George Whitefield,* 1742, John Wollaston, By Courtesy of the National Portrait Gallery, London **121** *l* Yale University Art Gallery; *r* New York Public Library, Rare Book Division; Astor, Lenox and Tilden Foundations **122** *r* Richard T. Nowitz/Corbis **127** Courtesy of W. E. Channing & Co., Santa Fe, NM **128** From the collections of Henry Ford Museum & Greenfield Village, MI/#63.41 **131** detail, The Granger Collection, New York **134** National Gallery of Canada, Ottawa **136** The West Point Museum, United States Military Academy, West Point, New York, Photo by Paul Warchol **137** *l* The Historical Society of Pennsylvania; *r* Giraudon/Art Resource, NY **143** The Granger Collection, New York **145** *l* Courtesy of the Library of Congress; Colorized by Marilynn Hawkridge; *br* Colonial Williamsburg Foundation; *tr* Courtesy of the Library of Congress **146** *t* Chuck Nacke/Woodfin Camp & Associates; *b* Corel Professional Photos CD-ROM™ **147** Bequest of Winslow Warren, Courtesy, Museum of Fine Arts, Boston **148** Courtesy American Antiquarian Society **149** *Samuel Adams,* detail, John Singleton Copley. Deposited by the City of Boston. Courtesy Museum of Fine Arts, Boston **151** *l* Courtesy of the Library of Congress; *r* Courtesy of The Bostonian Society Old State House **152** National Museum of American History, Smithsonian Institution, Photo No. 86-4091 **154** *r* Ivan Massar/Black Star; *l* Kevin Fleming/Corbis **159** *Surrender of Lord Cornwallis at Yorktown,* John Trumbull, Yale University Art Gallery **161** Fort Ticonderoga Museum **163** *t Attack on Bunker's Hill, with the Burning of Charles Town,* Gift of Edgar William and Bernice Chrysler Garbisch, ©Board of Trustees, National Gallery of Art, Washington; *b* Courtesy of The Bostonian Society Old State House **165** Boston Athenaeum **166** United States Capitol Historical Society **167** ©Darryl Heikes/Stock South,1992/PNI **169** West Point Museum Collections, United States Military Academy, West Point, New York **171** The Historical Society of Pennsylvania **176** *l* Fraunces Tavern Museum, New York City; *r* ©Les Stone/Sygma **178** Copyright ©1996 By the Metropolitan Museum of Art **180** Collections of The Virginia State Historical Society, Richmond, VA **183** Gallery of the Republic **187** Architect of the Capitol **188** *The National Archives of the United States* by Herman Viola. Publisher, Harry N. Abrams, Inc. Photograph by Jonathan Wallen **190** *l* The Granger Collection, New York; *b* The Granger Collection, New York **193** Leif Skoogfors/Woodfin Camp & Associates **194** Yale University Art Gallery, gift of Roger Sherman White, B. A. 1859, M.A. **195** Courtesy, Independence National Historical Park Collection **196** *l* Leif Skoogfors/Corbis; *r* Michael Bryant/Woodfin Camp & Associates **199** Bulloz/Art Resource, NY **205** Courtesy of the Library of Congress **206** The Granger Collection, New York **207** *l* John Ficara/Woodfin Camp & Associates; *r* Pat & Tom Leeson/Photo Researchers, Inc. **208** *l* Virginia Historical Society, Richmond, VA; *r* Alan Klehr/Tony Stone Images **213** Mark Hess/The Image Bank **214** Joseph Sohm/ChromoSohm, Inc./Corbis **216** Food and Drug Administration **218** ©Copyright 1997 PhotoDisc, Inc. **219** George Hall/Woodfin Camp & Associates **225** U.S. House of Representatives **228** *t* C.L. Chryslin/The Image Bank; *b* Corel Professional Photos CD-ROM™ **229** *r* Wally McNamee/Woodfin Camp & Associates; *l* Dirck Halstead/Gamma Liaison **230** Collection, The Supreme Court of the United States, courtesy The Supreme Court Historical Society. Photo by Richard Strauss, Smithsonian Institution **232** Corbis **233** *m* ©Alon Reininger/Contact/Stock Market; *l* Jack Bender/Waterloo Courier/Rothco; *r* ©Alon Reininger/Contact/The Stock Market **234** PEOPLE weekly ©1997 Andrew Kaufman **239** Courtesy of The Valley Forge Historical Society **240** John Lewis Krimmel, *Election Day in Philadelphia,* 1815, Courtesy, The Henry Francis du Pont Winterthur Museum **243** Courtesy, The Henry Francis du Pont Winterthur Museum **245** *t* Private Collection; *b* The Museum of American Political Life, University of Hartford; photo by Sally Anderson-Bruce **246** Courtesy of the Art Commission of the City of New York **248** David Young Wolff/Tony Stone Images **251** *t* Giraudon/Art Resource, NY; *b* Roger Viollet **252** Courtesy of The Mount Vernon Ladies' Association **254** *l* Unknown, American, Pennsylvania, *He That Tilleth His Land Shall be Satisfied,* detail, Philadelphia Museum of Art: The Edgar William and Bernice Chrysler Garbisch Collection; *r* John Neagle, *Pat Lyon at the Forge,* Henry M. and Zoë Oliver Sherman Fund, Courtesy, Museum of Fine Arts, Boston **255** Corel Professional Photos CD-ROM™ **259** *r* The Granger Collection, New York; *l* The Huntington Library, San Marino, California **260** *r John Adams,* c. 1800, James Sharples, The Museum of Fine Arts, Houston; The Bayou Bend Collection, gift of Miss Ima Hogg; *m* Gilbert Stuart, *Abigail Smith Adams (Mrs. John Adams),* detail, Gift of Mrs. Robert Homans, ©1997 Board of Trustees, National Gallery of Art, Washington, Photo by: Richard Carafelli; *l* National Park Service, Adams National Historic Site **265** *Lewis and Clark on the Lower Columbia,* Charles M. Russell, 1905, 1961.195, gouache, watercolor and graphite on paper, Amon Carter Museum, Forth Worth **267** *r* Rembrandt Peale, *Thomas Jefferson,* detail, Collection of The New York Historical Society; *l* Robert Llewellyn Photography **268** *t* Silver Burdett Ginn; *b* ©Junebug Clark/Photo Researchers, Inc. **270** Missouri Historical Society, St. Louis **271** Chicago Historical Society **274** *l* John Woodhouse Audubon, *Antelope Americana,* detail, Neg./Trans. no._3267 (2) (Photo by: P. Hollembeak/ Bauer) Courtesy Department of Library Services, American Museum of Natural History; *r* O.C. Seltzer, *Lewis and Clark with Sacajawea at the Great Falls of the Missouri,* From the Collection of Gilcrease Museum, Tulsa **276** The Granger Collection, New York **279** Ohio State Historical Society, Jim Roese, photographer, courtesy Historic Waynesborough **280** Collection of Cranbrook Institute of Science, #CIS 2207. ©Robert Hensleigh, Photographer **281** *r* Courtesy of the Library of Congress; *l* The Field Museum, Neg.# A93851.1c, Chicago **283** Courtesy Scott Baker, Ohio Society War of 1812 **285** U.S. Navy Photos **287** *l* From the collection of Mac G. and Janelle C. Morris; *r* Ted Baker/The Image Bank **288** Courtesy of the Library of Congress **293** Leon Pomarede, *View of St. Louis,* 1835, The Saint Louis Art Museum, Private collection of Dorothy Ziern Hanon & Joseph B. Hanon **295** *r* James Higgins; Use courtesy of Lowell National Historical Park **297** American Textile History Museum, Lowell, MA **298** Reprinted with permission of the News-Press of Fort Myers **301** Dean Beason, *Settlers' Wagon,* National Gallery of Art, Washington **302** Pavel Petrovich Svinin, *Travel by Stagecoach near Trenton, New Jersey,* All rights reserved, The Metropolitan Museum of Art, Rogers Fund, 1942. (42.95.11) **304** Silver Burdett Ginn and Colonial Williamsburg Foundation **305** Courtesy Erie Canal Village **309** *l* Architect of the Capitol; *m* Francis Alexander, Daniel Webster, 1835, Hood Museum of Art, Dartmouth College, Hanover, New Hampshire; gift of Dr. George C. Shattuck, Class of 1803; *r* Charles Bird King, John Caldwell Calhoun, National Portrait Gallery, Smithsonian Institution, Transfer from the National Gallery of Art; Gift of Andrew W. Mellon, 1942 **313** *t* Anne S.K. Brown Military Collection; *b* Coleccion Museo Nacional de Colombia, Bogotá **319** John Quidor, *Return of Rip Van Winkle,* 1829, Andrew W. Mellon Collection, ©1998 Board of Trustees, National Gallery of Art, Washington **320** Scotts Bluff National Monument **323** George Caleb Bingham, *The County Election,* 1851–52, oil on canvas, The Saint Louis Art Museum **326** Eunice Pinney, *Two Women,* c. 1815, New York State Historical Association, Cooperstown **327** *l* Courtesy of the Library of Congress; *r* D.

Walker/Gamma Liaison **329** Anna Claypoole Peale, *Andrew Jackson,* Yale University Art Gallery **331** The Granger Collection, New York **333** Courtesy of Salem Maritime NHS **334** Lynn Saville **335** Courtesy of the Library of Congress **339** Becker Collection, Division of Political History, National Museum of American History, Smithsonian Institution, #564-97 **340** ©Robert E. Daemmrich/Tony Stone Images **345** Courtesy of Bexar County and The Witte Museum, San Antonio, Texas **348** Alfred Jacob Miller, *Fort Laramie,* 1837, Walters Art Gallery, Baltimore **349** *t* Handtinting by Ladleton Studio/Culver Pictures, Inc.; *b* Courtesy of the Lane County Historical Museum **351** Courtesy Local History Programs **353** Corel Professional Photos CD-ROM™ **354** *l* Courtesy of the Texas Memorial Museum; *r* Archives Division, Texas State Library **357** *r* Courtesy of The Oakland Museum History Department; *l* Jim Zuckerman/West Light **360** Bill Pogue/The Stockhouse, Inc. **361** Courtesy of the Costume Department, Chicago Historical Society, 1920.38 **364** *Nuestra Señora del Rosario / Our Lady of the Rosary*, by Santo Nino Santero, New Mexico, 1830–60. Gesso, cloth, tin, wood, and water soluble paint. H: 40 1/2 inches. Courtesy Museum of New Mexico Collections at the Museum of International Folk Art, Santa Fe. Photo by Blair Clark. **368** *l* North Wind Picture Archives; *r* California State Library **373** *b* The Warner Collection of Gulf States Paper Corporation, Tuscaloosa, Alabama; *t* American Steel Foundries **374** National Museum of History and Technology, Smithsonian Institution, Photo no. 90-4210. **379** *l* State Historical Society of Wisconsin; *r* American Textile History Museum, Lowell, MA **380** Michael Newman/PhotoEdit **382** Aaron E. Darling, *John Jones,* 1865, Chicago Historical Society, #1904.0018 **383** National Museum of American History, Smithsonian Institution, Photo No. 73-11287 **384** ©Robert Finken/Photo Researchers, Inc. **387** The Old Print Shop **389** *t* D. Donne Bryant Stock Photography; *b* Courtesy Rosedown Plantation and Historic Garden **391** *t* Maynard Frank Wolfe/Globe Photos; *b* Bob Daemmrich/Stock, Boston/PNI **392** John Antrobus, *Plantation Burial,* 1860, The Historic New Orleans Collection, Museum/Research Center, Acc. No. 1960.46 **397** Museum of Art, Rhode Island School of Design, Gift of Miss Lucy T. Aldrich **399** Courtesy of the Library of Congress **400** Tony Freeman/PhotoEdit **401** *r* Winslow Homer, *Homework,* 1874, watercolor, Canajoharie Library and Art Gallery, Canajoharie, New York; *b* Victor R. Boswell, Jr./National Geographic Society; *m* Richard Nowitz *l* Richard T. Nowitz 1991 **403** The Trustees of the Wedgwood Museum, Barlaston, Staffordshire, England **404** *t* Southworth and Hawes, *William Lloyd Garrison,* All Rights Reserved, The Metropolitan Museum of Art, Gift of I.N. Phelps Stokes, Edward S. Hawes, Alice Mary Hawes, Marion Augusta Hawes, 1937. (37.14.37); *b* Courtesy of the Massachusetts Historical Society **405** Sophia Smith Collection, Smith College **406** C.T. Webber, *The Underground Railroad,* Cincinnati Art Museum, Subscription Fund Purchase **409** *l* Library of Congress/Corbis; *r* Sophia Smith Collection, Smith College **411** Photograph courtesy of the American Medical Women's Association, photograph by Silver Burdett Ginn **413** *l* Culver Pictures, Inc.; *r* The Kobal Collection **414** The Warner Collection of Gulf States Paper Corporation, Tuscaloosa, Alabama **419** Illustration from the cover of the book NIGHTJOHN copyright © 1993 by Jerry Pinkney. Written by Gary Paulsen. Published by Delacorte Press. All rights reserved. Used with permission. **420** Winslow Homer, *Prisoners from the Front,* 1866, All rights reserved, The Metropolitan Museum of Art, Gift of Mrs Frank B. Porter, 1922 (22.207) **423** Theodor Kaufmann, *On to Liberty,* 1867, All rights reserved, The Metropolitan Museum of Art, Gift of Erving and Joyce Wolf, 1982/95 (1982.443.3) **425** *l* Edwin Taylor, *American Slave Market,* 1852, Chicago Historical Society, 1954.15; *r* Sovfoto/Eastfoto **428** *r* North Wind Pictures; *l* State Historical Society of Wisconsin **432** *r* Anne S.K. Brown Military Collection; *l* Kansas State Historical Society **433** Missouri Historical Society (S-126 E) **435** Ontario County Historical Society **436** Courtesy of the Illinois State Historical Library **437** Carolyn Schaefer/Gamma Liaison **439** Corbis-Bettmann **442** *t* Emory Kristoff/National Geographic Society; *b* Fort Sumter National Monument **447** Winslow Homer, *A Rainy Day in Camp,* All Rights Reserved, The Metropolitan Museum of Art, Gift of Mrs. William F. Milton, 1923. (23.77.1) **448** North Carolina Museum of History **453** Chicago Historical Society **455** E.B.D Julio, *The Last Meeting of Lee and Jackson,* detail, The Museum of the Confederacy, Richmond, Virginia, Photography by Katherine Wetzel **457** Courtesy of the Library of Congress **459** Chicago Historical Society **460** Courtesy of the Library of Congress **461** *Attack at Battery Wagner* ©1993 Tom Lovell ©1993 The Greenwich Workshop, Inc. Courtesy of The Greenwich Workshop, Inc., Shelton, CT **463** Photography by Larry Sherer/High Impact Photography, Time-Life Books, Inc. **464** Cook Collection Valentine Museum, Richmond, Virginia **465** *t* Courtesy National Archives; *b* Courtesy of the American Red Cross. All Rights Reserved in all Countries. Photo by Silver Burdett Ginn **466** Architect of the Capitol **469** *l* ©The Stock Market/Lance Nelson; *r* John Elk III/Stock, Boston **473** Appomattox Court House NHP, National Park Service, USDI **477** Dennis Malone Carter, *Lincoln's Drive Through Richmond,* Chicago Historical Society, Gift of Mr. Philip K. Wrigley, 1955.398 **479** *l* Courtesy of the Library of Congress; *r* Richard T. Nowitz /Virginia Division of Tourism **480** Moorland-Spingarn Research Center, Howard University **481** Culver Pictures, Inc. **483** Courtesy of the Library of Congress **486** The Children's Museum of Indianapolis **487** detail, Chicago Historical Society, P&S-1904.0018 **488** *t* The Granger Collection, New York; *b* Old Court House Museum, Vicksburg, Photo by Bob Pickett **489** New York Public Library, Print Collection. Miriam and Ira D. Wallach Division of Art, Prints and Photographs; Astor, Lenox and Tilden Foundations **490** Brown Brothers **493** The Granger Collection, New York **494** Courtesy of Jim Osborn **499** West Point Museum Collections, United States Military Academy, West Point, New York **500** Collection of The New-York Historical Society **503** SuperStock **505** *r* Collection of the Flint Institute of Arts. FIA 85.27. Photograph © Dirk Bakker; *l* Charles M. Russell, *Following the Buffalo Run,* c. 1894, oil on canvas, 1961.134, Amon Carter Museum, Forth Worth **506** Denver Art Museum **509** Sandra Baker/Gamma Liaison **511** Special Collections Division, University of Washington Libraries **512** Seaver Center for Western History Research, Museum of Natural History, Photo by Henry Groskinsky **513** James Walker, *California Vaqueros,* The Anshutz Collection **514** J. Pat Carter/Gamma Liaison **517** *l* Smithsonian Institution, 3689; *r* G.R. Roberts **520** Culver Pictures, Inc. **521** Courtesy of The National Museum of the American Indian/Smithsonian Institution, (neg #2/1133) **523** Courtesy of the Library of Congress **524** Nebraska State Historical Society **525** Bob Daemmrich/Stock, Boston **526** Kansas State Historical Society **531** ©C.C.I. 1998 **533** *b* Brown Brothers; *t* Courtesy of the Library of Congress **534** Courtesy of the Library of Congress **537** *Andrew Carnegie,* The National Portrait Gallery, Smithsonian Institution, Gift of Mrs. Margaret Carnegie Miller/Art Resource, NY **539** *m* Larry Lee/Westlight; *t* Silver Burdett Ginn; *b* Corel Professional Photos CD-ROM™ **540** *l* Brown Brothers; *r* Jonathan Kirn/Gamma Liaison **542** ©1999 Michael Freeman **543** *m* National Park Service, U.S. Dept. of Interior, Edison National Historic Site; *l* ©1999 Michael Freeman; *r* Breton Littlehales/National Geographic Society **546** From the collections of Henry Ford Museum & Greenfield Village **548** The George Meany Memorial Archives **549** Courtesy of the Library of Congress **551** Corbis-Bettmann **557** The Saint Louis Art Museum, Bequest of Marie Setz Hertslet **560** *m* Bob Krist/Corbis; *r* Photo by John Lei/Omni Photo Communications; *l* Photo by John Lei/Omni Photo Communications **562** *l* Bancroft Library, University of California; *r* ©C.C.I. 1998 **564** Collection of Picture Research Consultants, Inc. Photo © Rob Huntley/Lightstream **566** *l* Eastman Johnson, *The Brown Family,* 1869, The Fine Arts Museum of San Francisco; *r* Cooper-Hewitt Museum, Smithsonian Institution/Art Resource, NY **567** Brown Brothers **568** *l* National Portrait Gallery, Smithsonian Institution/Art Resource, NY; *r* International Museum of Photography At George Eastman House **571** Chicago Historical Society, ICHI1066 **572** North Wind Picture Archives **573** *r* New York Public Library at Lincoln Center; *l* ©Frank Driggs/Archive Photos **574** Rebus Inc. **576** *b* Spencer Grant/Stock, Boston; *t* image ©Copyright 1997 PhotoDisc, Inc. **577** *l* Culver Pictures, Inc.; *r* Brown Brothers **578**

Los Angeles County Museum of Art, *Mother About to Wash Her Sleepy Child,* Mary Cassatt, Mrs. Fred Hathaway Bixby Bequest **583** Sallie Cover, *Homestead of Ellsworth L. Ball,* 1880–1890, Nebraska State Historical Society; photographed by R. Bruhn **584** Chicago Historical Society, ICHI–25185 **587** Collection of The New-York Historical Society **588** From the collection of Roger Lathbury; photo by SBG **589** Courtesy of the Library of Congress **590** Collection of The New-York Historical Society **593** *t* The Jacob A. Riis Collection 157, Museum of the City of New York; *b* Courtesy George Eastman House **594** *t* Bob Daemmrich/Stock, Boston; *b* Terry Vine/Tony Stone Images **597** The Museum of American Political Life, University of Hartford; photo by Sally Anderson-Bruce **598** *l* Courtesy of the Library of Congress; *r* National Museum of American History, Smithsonian Institution **599** *t* Culver Pictures, Inc.; *b* Silver Burdett Ginn **601** *t* ©The Stock Market/John M. Roberts; *b* Guido Alberto Rossi /The Image Bank **602** Collection of The New-York Historical Society **603** The Granger Collection, New York **604** The Granger Collection, New York **605** *l* Corbis-Bettmann; *r* Sally Andersen-Bruce **609** *t* Courtesy of the NAACP National Headquarters; *b* Schomburg Center for Research in Black Culture, Prints and Photographs Division, The New York Public Library, Astor, Lenox and Tilden Foundations **610** Courtesy Museum of New Mexico **611** ©The Burns Archive **615** Courtesy United States Naval Academy Museum **617** *t* Courtesy United States Naval Academy Museum; *b* Courtesy of the Library of Congress Manuscript Division **618** ©Jeff Greenberg/Photo Researchers, Inc. **619** Courtesy of The Oakland Museum History Department **621** *t* Bishop Museum; *b* Seth Joel/Bishop Museum **622** Culver Pictures, Inc. **624** Theodore Roosevelt Birthplace **625** New York Journal and Advertiser **627** Courtesy of the Library of Congress **628** *t* Courtesy National Archives, photo no. 111-RB-2939; *b* Theodore Roosevelt Birthplace **629** ©Klaus Reisinger, 1992/Black Star/PNI **631** National Postal Museum, Smithsonian Institution, Washington, D.C. **633** Lynn Saville **634** *l* UPI/CORBIS-BETTMANN; *r* Archives Center, National Museum of American History, Smithsonian Institution, no. 95-5305 **641** Smithsonian Institution, photo No. 57043 **643** ©John McCutchson/The Chicago Tribune, 1914. Photo: Ken Karp **645** Culver Pictures, Inc. **647** The Granger Collection, New York **648** The Museum of American Political Life, University of Hartford; photo by Sally-Anderson Bruce **650** *r* UPI/CORBIS-BETTMANN; *l* Courtesy of the Library of Congress **651** Culver Pictures, Inc. **653** *l* Courtesy National Archives, photo no. 86-G-11F-7; *r* Culver Pictures, Inc. **654** Courtesy of the Library of Congress **656** Collection of Colonel Stuart S. Corning, Jr. Photo ©Rob Huntley/Lightstream **658** *t* The Imperial War Museum, London, John Singer Sargent, *Gassed;* *b* Musee de Verdun/Luc Joubert/Tallandier **659** Jack Kurtz/Impact Visuals **661** Corbis-Bettmann **662** *Woodrow Wilson,* 1919, John Christen Johansen, The National Portrait Gallery, Smithsonian Institution, Art Resource, NY **663** Imperial War Museum, London **669** Museum of Fine Arts, Boston/Laurie Platt Winfrey, Inc. **670** Tennessee Valley Authority **673** Culver Pictures, Inc. **674** Corbis-Bettmann **675** Culver Pictures, Inc. **676** Historical Pictures/Stock Montage, Inc. **677** UPI/Corbis-Bettmann **679** Stanley King/Museum of Political Life **680** Culver Pictures, Inc. **681** Brown Brothers **683** Library of Congress/Corbis **684** Courtesy John Gilman **685** *b* David Young-Wolff/PhotoEdit; *t* Copyright SBG ©1998 **686** Everett Collection **687** National Museum of American History, Smithsonian Institution **688** Corbis-Bettmann **690** Courtesy of the Artist **691** *l* Culver Pictures, Inc.; *r* ©Archive Photos/PNI **692** National Museum of American History, Smithsonian Institution **695** Collection of David J. and Janice L. Frent **696** Culver Pictures, Inc. **701** Whitney Museum of American Art **703** *l* UPI/CORBIS-BETTMANN; *r* Icon Communications Ltd. **704** Corel Professional Photos CD-ROM™ **706** *b* AP/Wide World Photos; *t* Grant Smith/Corbis **708** Franklin Delano Roosevelt Library, Hyde Park, NY **709** UPI/CORBIS-BETTMANN **710** Richard Hutchings/PhotoEdit **711** Courtesy of the Library of Congress **712** *r* ©Bob Daemmrich Photos; *l* Sandy Felsenthal/Corbis **715** AP/Wide World Photos **716** The Granger Collection, New York **718** Courtesy of the Library of Congress **722** Corbis-Bettmann **724** Courtesy of the Library of Congress **725** Disney. Courtesy Kobal **729** Naval Combat Art Collection, Washington, D.C. **730** Christel Gerstenberg/Corbis **731** UPI/CORBIS-BETTMANN **732** Culver Pictures, Inc. **736** Culver Pictures, Inc. **737** UPI/CORBIS-BETTMANN **738** *t* H.K. Owen/Black Star; *b* Ken Sakamoto/Black Star **740** Smithsonian Institution **741** *l* UPI/CORBIS-BETTMANN; *r* ©Copyright 1997 PhotoDisc, Inc. **742** National Museum of American History, Smithsonian Institution, Washington, D.C. **743** UPI/CORBIS-BETTMANN **744** Courtesy of the Library of Congress **748** Hulton Deutsch Collection **751** Brown Brothers **753** Courtesy, National Archives **754** *t* Pete Souza/Gamma Liaison; *b* Franklin Delano Roosevelt Library, Hyde Park, NY **759** Evans-Tibbs Collection, Washington, D.C. **760** ©Boris Lyubner/Stock Illustration Source, Inc. **763** Roy Lichtenstein, *Preparedness;* Collection, Solomon R. Guggenheim Museum, New York, 1969, Photograph by David Heald **765** *t* Harry S Truman Library; *br* Harry S Truman Library; *bl* U.S. Army Courtesy Harry S Truman Library **766** Library of Congress/Corbis **767** *l* Walter Sanders; *r* AP/Wide World Photos **770** Matthew Frost/CORBIS-BETTMANN **772** Past Perfect **773** UPI/CORBIS-BETTMANN **774** ©Carolina Kroon/Impact Visuals **777** Michael Barson/Past Perfect **778** *l* AP/Wide World Photos; *r* UPI/CORBIS-BETTMANN **780** Agence France Presse/Corbis-Bettmann **783** *l* UPI/CORBIS-BETTMANN; *r* Ted Streshinsky/Corbis **784** *r* Richard Howard/Black Star; *l* Paul Miller/Black Star **787** AP/Wide World Photos **789** Lionel Cironneau/AP/Wide World Photos **790** Charles Steiner/The Image Works **795** Brooklyn Museum of Art, Gift of Lorillard **797** *l* UPI/CORBIS-BETTMANN; *r* Dwight D. Eisenhower Library **798** ©1993, Willinger/FPG International Corp. **801** UPI/CORBIS-BETTMANN **803** The Granger Collection, New York **804** UPI/CORBIS-BETTMANN **805** Ed Clark, Life Magazine ©Time Inc. **806** *l* Porterfield/Chickering/Photo Researchers, Inc.; *r* UPI/CORBIS-BETTMANN **809** *r* Fred Ward/Black Star; *l* UPI/CORBIS-BETTMANN **810** UPI/CORBIS-BETTMANN **811** *t* NASA/John F. Kennedy Space Center; *b* NASA **812** UPI/CORBIS-BETTMANN **815** Steve Schapiro/Black Star **816** UPI/CORBIS-BETTMANN **817** *r* Myrleen Ferguson/PhotoEdit; *l* Corporation for National Service, Washington D.C., 1998 **818** *r* National Organization for Women, Copyright 1992; *l* Frank Johnston/Black Star/PNI **820** ©Bill Nation/Sygma **821** ©1977 Paul Davis **825** Tsing-fang Chen, *Liberty States,* Chen Foundation/Lucia Gallery **827** *l* National Museum of American History, Political History Collection, Smithsonian Institution; *r* UPI/CORBIS-BETTMANN **830** Stephen Jaffe/Gamma Liaison **833** *r* Laurent Van Der Stockt/Gamma Liaison; *l* AP/Wide World Photos **834** NASA **835** Rothco Cartoons **836** Reuters/CORBIS-BETTMANN **840** ©David Turnley/Black Star/PNI **843** *r* AP/Wide World Photos; *l* Stephen J. Krasemann/DRK Photo **846** Lisa Knouse Braiman/Business Week **848** AP/Wide World Photos **850** *r* Corel Professional Photos CD-ROM™; *l* Piet van Lier/Impact Visuals **852** University of North Carolina at Wilmington **857** Los Jovenes con Bicicleta, 1993, Tony Ortega, Courtesy of Tony Ortega **858** *t* Pat & Tom Leeson/Photo Researchers, Inc.; *r* Courtesy of Bexar County and The Witte Museum, San Antonio, Texas; *l* Joseph Sohm/ChromoSohm, Inc./Corbis **859** North Wind Picture Archives **860** Courtesy of the Library of Congress; Colorized by Marilynn Hawkridge **861** The Museum of American Political Life, University of Hartford; photo by Sally Anderson-Bruce **862** Library of Congress/Corbis **863** Carolyn Schaefer/Gamma Liaison **864** Smithsonian Institution, 3689 **865** Imperial War Museum, London **866** UPI/CORBIS-BETTMANN **867** UPI/CORBIS-BETTMANN **892–895** Portrait nos. 1, 2, 4, 5, 6, 9, 10, 12, 14, 15, 18, 20,2 1, 25, 26, 27, 35, National Portrait Gallery, Smithsonian Institution/Art Resource, NY; Portrait nos. 3, 7, 8, 11, 13, 16, 17, 19, 22–24, 28–34, 36–42, White House Collection, Copyright White House Historical Association **895** *b* John Ficara/Woodfin Camp and Associates **940** David Young Wolff/Tony Stone Images

Stop the Presses

Not so long ago, publishers had to stop the presses to get late-breaking information into their books. Today, Prentice Hall can use the Internet to update you quickly and easily on the most recent developments in Social Studies.

Visit Prentice Hall on the Internet at

http://www.phschool.com

for the Prentice Hall Social Studies Update.

There you will find periodic updates in the following areas:

- ★ **United States History**
- ★ **World Studies**
- ★ **American Government**

Each update topic provides you with background information as well as carefully selected links to guide you to related content on the Internet.